P9-DYZ-920

SUPPLEMENT XI
Toni Cade Bambara to Richard Yates

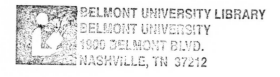
BELMONT UNIVERSITY LIBRARY
BELMONT UNIVERSITY
1900 BELMONT BLVD.
NASHVILLE, TN 37212

American Writers
A Collection of Literary Biographies

JAY PARINI
Editor in Chief

SUPPLEMENT XI
Toni Cade Bambara to Richard Yates

Charles Scribner's Sons
an imprint of the Gale Group
New York • Detroit • San Francisco • London • Boston • Woodbridge, CT

© 2002 by Charles Scribner's Sons, an imprint of The Gale Group

Charles Scribner's Sons
300 Park Avenue South, 9th Floor
New York, New York 10010

All rights reserved. No part of this book may be reproduced or transmitted in any form or by any means, electronic or mechanical, including photocopying, recording, or by an information storage or retrieval system, without permission in writing from the publisher.

1 3 5 7 9 11 13 15 17 19 20 18 16 14 12 10 8 6 4 2

Library of Congress Cataloging-in-Publication Data

American writers : a collection of literary biographies

Leonard Unger, editor in chief. p. cm.

The 4-vol. main set consists of 97 of the pamphlets originally published
as the University of Minnesota pamphlets on American writers; some have been
rev. and updated. The supplements cover writers not included in the original series.
Supplement 2, has editor in chief, A. Walton Litz; Retrospective suppl. 1, c1998, was edited by A. Walton Litz & Molly Weigel; Suppl.
5–7 have as editor-in-chief, Jay Parini. Includes bibliographies and index.
Contents: v. 1. Henry Adams to T. S. Eliot — v. 2. Ralph Waldo Emerson to Carson McCullers — v. 3. Archibald MacLeish to George
Santayana — v. 4. Isaac Bashevis Singer to Richard Wright — Supplement: 1, pt. 1. Jane Addams to Sidney Lanier. 1, pt. 2. Vachel
Lindsay to Elinor Wylie. 2, pt. 1. W.H. Auden to O. Henry. 2, pt. 2. Robinson Jeffers to Yvor Winters. — 4, pt. 1. Maya Angelou to
Linda Hogan. 4, pt. 2. Susan Howe to Gore Vidal — Suppl. 5. Russell Banks to Charles Wright — Suppl. 6. Don DeLillo to W.D.
Snodgrass — Suppl. 7. Julia Alvarez to Tobias Wolff.
ISBN 0-684-19785-5 (set) — ISBN 0-684-13662-7
1. American literature—History and criticism. 2. American literature—Bio-bibliography. 3. Authors, American—Biography. I. Unger,
Leonard. II. Litz, A. Walton. III. Weigel, Molly. IV. Parini, Jay. V. University of Minnesota pamphlets on American writers.

PS129 .A55 810'.9 73-001759

ISBN 0-684-31231-X

BELMONT UNIVERSITY LIBRARY

Ref
PS
129
. A55
sup. 11

12149

Editorial and Production Staff

Project Editor
ALJA KOOISTRA COLLAR

Copyeditors
JANET L. BADGLEY
BARBARA BIGELOW
MELISSA A. DOBSON
GRETCHEN GORDON
NANCY GRATTON
ROBERT E. JONES
MARCIA MERRYMAN MEANS

Proofreader
CAROL HOLMES

Indexer
KATHARYN DUNHAM

Permissions
UMA KUKATHAS
SHALICE SHAH-CALDWELL
SARAH TOMASEK

Production Manager
EVI SEOUD

Compositor
GARY LEACH

Manufacturing Buyer
STACY MELSON

Publisher
FRANK MENCHACA

Acknowledgments

Acknowledgment is gratefully made to those publishers and individuals who have permitted the use of the following material in copyright. Every effort has been made to secure permission to reprint copyrighted material.

TONI CADE BAMBARA Excerpts from *Deep Sightings and Rescue Missions: Fiction, Essays, and Conversations*, by Toni Cade Bambara. Pantheon Books, 1996. Copyright © 1996 by The Estate of Toni Cade Bambara. All rights reserved. Used by permission of Pantheon Books, a division on Random House, Inc. Excerpts from *Gorilla, My Love,* by Toni Cade Bambara. Random House, 1972. Copyright © 1972 by Toni Cade Bambara. All rights reserved. Used by permission of Random House, Inc. In the UK by permission of Women's Press, Ltd. Excerpts from *The Sea Birds Are Still Alive: Collected Stories,* by Toni Cade Bambara. Random House, 1977. Copyright © 1974, 1977 by Toni Cade Bambara. All rights reserved.

FREDERICK BARTHELME Excerpts from *Bob the Gambler,* by Frederick Barthelme. Houghton Mifflin Company, 1997. Copyright © 1997 by Frederick Barthelme. All rights reserved. Reproduced by permission of Houghton Mifflin Company. In the UK by permission of The Wylie Agency. Excerpts from "'Just Like Old Times': Frederick Barthelme and the Aesthetics of Postmodernism," by Grant Pheloung. *Critique,* vol. 40, winter 1999. Copyright © 1999 Helen Dwight Reid Educational Foundation. Reproduced with permission of the Helen Dwight Reid Educational Foundation, published by Heldref Publications, 1319 18th Street, NW, Washington, D.C. 20036-1802. Excerpts from *Double Down: Reflections on Gambling and Loss,* by Frederick Barthelme. Houghton Mifflin Company, 1999. Copyright © 1999 by Frederick and Steven Barthelme. All rights reserved. Reproduced by permission. In the UK by permission of The Wylie Agency. Excerpts from "Suburban Culture, Imaginative Wonder: The Fiction of Frederick Barthelme," by Robert H. Brinkmeyer Jr. *Studies in the Literary Imagination,* vol. 27, fall 1994. Copyright 1994 Department of English, Georgia State University. Reproduced by permission. Excerpts from "Brand-Name Blues," by James Kauffmann. *Washington Book World,* July 28, 1985.

STEPHEN VINCENT BENÉT Excerpts from "By the Waters of Babylon," "The Devil and Daniel Webster," "The Die-Hard," "Freedom's a Hard-Bought Thing," "The Three Fates," in *The Devil and Daniel Webster,* by Stephen Vincent Benét. Farrar & Rinehart, Inc., 1939. Reprinted by permission of Henry Holt and Company, LLC. Excerpts from *John Brown's Body,* by Stephen Vincent Benét. Doubleday, Doran and Company, 1928. Reproduced by permission. Excerpts from "Listen to the People," in *Listen to the People: Independence Day,* by Stephen Vincent Benét. New York City: Council for Democracy, 1941. Copyright, 1941, by Stephen Vincent Benét. Reproduced by permission.

Excerpts from "Tuesday, November 5th, 1940," by Stephen Vincent Benét. *The New York Post,* 1940. Copyright, 1940, by N. Y. Post. Reproduced by permission. Excerpts from "My Most Unforgettable Character," by Stephen Vincent Benét. *Reader's Digest,* October, 1940. Reproduced by permission. Excerpts from "The Mountain Whippoorwill," by Stephen Vincent Benét. *The Saturday Evening Post,* 1940. © Copyright 1940 Saturday Evening Post Society. Reproduced by permission. Excerpts from "All Around the Town" and "Jacob and the Indians," in *Selected Works of Stephen Vincent Benét: Volume One, Poetry.* Holt, Rinehart and Winston, 1969. Copyright, 1936, 1938 by Stephen Vincent Benét, copyright renewed © 1964, 1966 by Thomas C. Benét, Stephanie Mahin and Rachel B. Lewis. All rights reserved. Reprinted by permission of Henry Holt and Company, LLC. Excerpts from "The Last of the Legions" and "The Story about the Anteater," in *Tales before Midnight,* by Stephen Vincent Benét. Farrar & Rinehart, Inc., 1939. Copyright, 1939, by Farrar & Rinehart, Inc. All rights reserved. Reproduced by permission of Henry Holt and Company, LLC. Excerpts from "A Creed for Americans," by Stephen Vincent Benét. *The Democratic Tradition in America.* Edited by Clayton E. Wheat. Council for Democracy, 1942. Copyright 1942 by Stephen Vincent Benét. Reproduced by permission. Excerpts from "Daniel Webster," by Stephen Vincent Benét. *There Were Giants in the Land: Twenty-Eight Historic Americans as Seen by Twenty-Eight Contemporary Americans.* Farrar & Rinehart, Inc., 1942. Copyright, 1942, by Farrar & Rinehart, Inc. All rights reserved. Reprinted by permission of Henry Holt and Company, LLC. Excerpts from "A Death in the Country" and "The King of the Cats," in *Twenty-Five Short Stories,* by Stephen Vincent Benét. The Sun Dial Press, 1943. Copyright © 1943 Stephen Vincent Benét. All rights reserved. Reproduced by permission.

WANDA COLEMAN Excerpts from "Sweet Mama Wanda Tells Fortunes: An Interview with Wanda Coleman," by Tony Magistrale and Patricia Ferreira. *Black American Literature Forum,* vol. 24, autumn 1990. Copyright © 1990 by the authors. Reproduced by permission of the authors. Excerpts from "I Died with the First Blow and Was Reborn Wrong," in *Bathwater Wine,* by Wanda Coleman. Black Sparrow Press, 1998. Copyright © 1998 by Wanda Coleman. All rights reserved. Reproduced by permission of Black Sparrow Press. Excerpts from "Rape," in *Imagoes,* by Wanda Coleman. Black Sparrow Press, 1983. Excerpts from "Doing Battle with the Wolf," "Drone," "Women of My Color," in *Mad Dog Black Lady,* by Wanda Coleman. Black Sparrow Press, 1979. Copyright © 1979 by Wanda Coleman. All rights reserved. Reproduced by permission of Black Sparrow Press.

MARK DOTY Excerpts from "'How to Live. What to Do.': The Poetics and Politics of AIDS," by Deborah Landau. *American Literature,* vol. 68, March 1996. Copyright © 1996 by Duke University Press, Durham, N.C. Reproduced by permission.

publishers and individuals who have permitted the use of the following material in copyright. Excerpts from "Atlantis," "Aubade: Opal and Silver," "Crêpe de Chine," "A Green Crab's Shell," "Grosse Fuge," "Homo Will Not Inherit," "Long Point Light," in *Atlantis*, by Mark Doty. HarperCollins Publishers, 1995. Copyright © 1995 by Mark Doty. All rights reserved. Reproduced by permission. Excerpts from "Paradise," in *Bethlehem in Broad Daylight*, by Mark Doty. David R. Godine, Publisher, Inc., 1991. Copyright © 1991 by Mark Doty. All rights reserved. Reproduced by permission. Excerpts from "A Reader's Tale," by Mark Doty. *Contemporary Authors, Volume 183*. Edited by Scot Peacock. Gale Group, 1998. Copyright © 2000 by Gale Group, Inc. All rights reserved. Reproduced by permission. Excerpts from "An Island Sheaf," in *Island Sheaf*, by Mark Doty. Dim Gray Bar Press, 1998. Excerpts from "Becoming a Meadow," "Brilliance," "Foreword," "Lament-Heaven," "Night Ferry," "The Wings," in *My Alexandria*, by Mark Doty. University of Illinois Press, 1993. © 1993 by Mark Doty. Reproduced by permission. Excerpts from "About Mark Doty: A Profile," by Mark Wunderlich. *Ploughshares*, vol. 25, spring 1999. © 1999 by Emerson College. Reproduced by permission of the author. Excerpts from "Essay: The Love of Old Houses," "Letter to Walt Whitman," "Manhattan Luminism," "Source," in *Source*, by Mark Doty. HarperCollins Publishers, 2001. Copyright © by Mark Doty. All rights reserved. Reproduced by permission. Excerpts from "Concerning Some Recent Criticism of His Work," "Fog Suite," "Mercy on Broadway," "Shelter," "Thirty Delft Tiles," in *Sweet Machine*, by Mark Doty. HarperCollins Publishers, 2001. Copyright © 1998 by Mark Doty. All rights reserved. Reproduced by permission. Excerpts from "A Reader's Tale" and "Turtle, Swan," in *Turtle Swan*, by Mark Doty. David R. Godine, Publisher, Inc., 1987. Copyright © 1987 by Mark Doty. All rights reserved. Reproduced by permission.

STEPHEN DUNN Excerpts from "Between Angels," "Kindness," "On the Way to Work," "Tenderness," in *Between Angels*, by Stephen Dunn. W. W. Norton & Company, 1989. Copyright © 1989 by Stephen Dunn. All rights reserved. Used by permission of W. W. Norton & Company, Inc. Excerpts from "Midnight," in *A Circus of Needs*, by Stephen Dunn. Carnegie-Mellon University Press, 1978. Copyright © 1978 by Stephen Dunn. All rights reserved. Reproduced by permission. Excerpts from "Stephen (Elliott) Dunn," by Robert Miltner. *Contemporary Authors: New Revision Series, Volume 53*. Edited by Jeff Chapman, Pamela S. Dear, and John D. Jorgenson. Gale Research, 1997. Copyright © 1997 Gale Research. All rights reserved. Reproduced by permission. Excerpts from "Interview with Stephen Dunn," by Philip Dacey. *The Cortland Review*, March 2000. © 2002 The Cortland Review. Reproduced by permission of Stephen Dunn. Excerpts from "The Last Hours," "A Postmortem Guide," "The Sexual Revolution," in *Different Hours*, by Stephen Dunn. W. W. Norton & Company, 2000. Copyright © 2000 by Stephen Dunn. All rights reserved. Used by permission of W. W. Norton, Inc. Excerpts from "Beneath the Sidewalk," "The Big Winner Rises Late," "California, This Is Minnesota Speaking," "Prairie Life: A Citizen Speaks," "A Private Man Confronts His Vulgarities at Dawn," "Truck Stop," "The Visitant," in *Full of Lust and Good Usage*, by Stephen Dunn. Carnegie-Mellon University Press, 1976. Copyright © 1976 by Stephen Dunn. All rights reserved. Reproduced by permission. Excerpts from "Blues for Another

Time," by Stephen Dunn. *Kansas Quarterly*. Reproduced by permission. Excerpts from "After the Resolution," "Smiles," "Update," "What They Wanted," in *Landscape at the End of the Century*, by Stephen Dunn. W. W. Norton & Company, 1991. Copyright © 1991 by Stephen Dunn. All rights reserved. Used by permission of W. W. Norton & Company, Inc. Excerpts from "After the Argument," "Halves," "He/She," "Round Trip," in *Local Time*, by Stephen Dunn. William Morrow & Co., 1986. Excerpts from "After Making Love," "Ars Poetica," "Because You Mentioned the Spiritual Life," "Diminuendo," "The Living," "Loosestrife," "Solving the Puzzle," "Tucson," "The Voice," in *Loosestrife*, by Stephen Dunn. W. W. Norton & Company, 1996. Copyright © 1996 by Stephen Dunn. All rights reserved. Used by permission of W. W. Norton & Company, Inc. Excerpts from "Degrees of Fidelity," by Stephen Dunn. *Mid-American Review*, vol. 21, fall 2000. Excerpts from "The Snowmass Cycle," in *New and Selected Poems 1974–1994*, by Stephen Dunn. Carnegie-Mellon University Press, 1976. Copyright © 1976 by Stephen Dunn. All rights reserved. Used by permission of W. W. Norton & Company, Inc. Excerpts from "On Hearing the Airlines Will Use a Psychological Profile to Catch Potential Skyjackers," by Stephen Dunn. *The New Republic*, 1972. © 1972 Harrison-Blaine of New Jersey, Inc. Reproduced by permission of The New Republic. Excerpts from "At Every Gas Station There Are Mechanics," by Stephen Dunn. *New Voices in American Poetry*. Winthrop Publishers, Inc., 1973. Copyright © 1973 by Stephen Dunn. Reproduced by permission. Excerpts from "Poets and Pulitzers, Such Is the State's Fate," by Robert Strauss. *The New York Times*, May 27, 2001. Copyright © 2001 by The New York Times Company. Reproduced by permission. Excerpts from "What," by Stephen Dunn. *The New York Quarterly*. © 1971 by The New York Quarterly. Excerpts from "Legacy," in *Not Dancing*, by Stephen Dunn. Carnegie-Mellon University Press, 1984. Copyright © 1984 by Stephen Dunn. All rights reserved. Reproduced by permission. Excerpts from "The Routine Things around the House," by Stephen Dunn. *The Ohio Review*. Copyright © 1984 by Stephen Dunn. Used by permission of W. W. Norton & Company, Inc. Excerpts from "Corners," by Stephen Dunn. *Poetry*. © Modern Poetry Association. Reproduced by permission of the Editor of Poetry and the author. Excerpts from "Biography in the First Person," by Stephen Dunn. *Poetry Northwest*, 1971. Copyright © 1971 Poetry Northwest. Reproduced by permission. Excerpts from "My Brother's Work" and "Poem for People Who Are Understandably Too Busy to Read Poetry," in *Work and Love*, by Stephen Dunn. Carnegie-Mellon University Press, 1981. Copyright © 1981 by Stephen Dunn. All rights reserved. Used by permission of W. W. Norton & Company, Inc.

CRISTINA GARCÍA Excerpts from *The Agüero Sisters*, by Cristina García. Alfred A. Knopf, 1997. Copyright © 1997 by Cristina García. All rights reserved. Used by permission of Alfred A. Knopf, a division of Random House. In the UK by permission of Ellen Levine Literary Agency on behalf of the author. Excerpts from "A Conversation with Cristina García" from www.randomhouse.com. Copyright © 2000 by Random House, Inc. Used by permission of Random House, Inc. Excerpts from *Dreaming in Cuban*, by Cristina García. Alfred A. Knopf, 1992. Copyright © 1992 by Cristina García. All rights reserved. Used by Alfred A. Knopf, a division of Random House. In the UK by permission of Ellen Levine Literary Agency on behalf of the author. Excerpts from "At Home on the Page: An Interview with Cristina García," by Bridget Kevane and Juanita Heredia. *Latina Self-Portraits: Interviews with Contemporary Women Writers.* University of New Mexico Press, 2000. © 2000 by the University of New Mexico Press. All rights reserved. Reproduced by permission. Excerpts from "A Cuban Odyssey: It Took a Trip to Havana to Piece Cristina García's History and Literary Quest," by Cynthia Adina Kirckwood. *Los Angeles Times,* August 30, 1992. Copyright, 1992, *Los Angeles Times.* Reproduced by permission. Excerpts from "'And There Is Only My Imagination Where Our History Should Be': An Interview with Cristina García," by Iraida H. López. *Michigan Quarterly Review,* vol. xxxiii, summer 1994. Copyright © The University of Michigan, 1994. All rights reserved. Reproduced by permission of the author. Excerpts from "The Dreams and Yearnings of a Family of Exiles," by Michiko Kakutani. *The New York Times,* February 25, 1992. Copyright © 1992 by The New York Times Company. Reproduced by permission. Excerpts from "Exile Among Exiles: Cristina García," by Joseph M. Viera. *Poets & Writers,* vol. 26, September/October 1998. Reproduced by permission. Excerpts from "Star-Spangled," by Cristina García. *Washington Post Magazine,* July 18, 1999.

CHARLOTTE PERKINS GILMAN Excerpts from *The Living of Charlotte Perkins Gilman: An Autobiography,* by Charlotte Perkins Gilman. D. Appleton-Century Company, 1935. Reproduced by permission of D. Appleton-Century Company, a division of Penguin Putnam Inc.

JAMES JONES Excerpts from "The Wars of James Jones," by Pearl K. Bell. *Commentary,* vol. 65, April 1978. Copyright © 1978 by the American Jewish Committee. All rights reserved. Reproduced by permission. Excerpts from "The Writer Speaks: A Conversation between James Jones and Leslie Hanscom," in *James Jones: A Checklist.* Edited by John R. Hopkins. Gale Research Company, 1974. Copyright © 1974 by Matthew J. Bruccoli and C. E. Frazer Clark, Jr. Reproduced by permission. Excerpts from *James Jones: Reveille to Taps: 1985–86.* Edited by J. Michael Lennon and Jeffrey Van Davis. Reproduced by permission of the University of Illinois, Springfield.

MARY KARR Excerpts from "The Choice," by Mary Karr. *The New Yorker,* November 26, 2001. © 2001 by the author. All rights reserved. Reproduced by permission of the author. Excerpts from "Beauty and the Shoe Sluts" and "Viper Rum," in *Viper Rum,* by Mary Karr. New Directions, 1998. Copyright © 1994, 1995, 1996, 1997, 1998 by Mary Karr. All rights reserved. Reproduced by permission of New Directions Publishing Corp.

LARRY LEVIS Excerpts from "The Double," "Linnets: #12," "The Morning after My Death," "Rhododendrons," in *The Afterlife,* by Larry Levis. The University of Iowa Press, 1977. Copyright © 1977 Larry Levis. Reproduced by permission of the author. Excerpts from "A Divinity in Its Fraying Fact," in *Black Freckles,* by Larry Levis. Peregrine Smith Books, 1992. Excerpts from "For a Ghost Who Once Placed Bets in the Park," "García Lorca: A Photograph of the Granada Cemetery, 1966," "Some Ashes Drifting above Piedra, California," "The Spirit Says, Your Are Nothing:," "To My Ghost Reflected in the Auxvasse River," in *The Dollmaker's Ghost,* by Larry Levis. E. P. Dutton, 1981. Copyright © 1981 by Larry Levis. All rights reserved.

Reproduced by permission of E. P. Dutton, a division of Penguin Putnam Inc. In the UK by permission of the Literary Estate of Larry Levis. Excerpts from "Elegy Ending in the Sound of a Skipping Rope," "Elegy with a Thimbleful of Water in the Cage," "Photograph: Migrant Worker, Parlier, California, 1967," in *Elegy,* by Larry Levis. Edited by Philip Levine. University of Pittsburgh Press, 1997. Copyright © 1997, University of Pittsburgh Press. All rights reserved. Reproduced by permission. Excerpts from "Eden and My Generation," by Larry Levis. *Field: Contemporary Poetry and Poetics,* spring 1982. Copyright © 1982 by Oberlin College. Reproduced by permission. Excerpts from "Some Notes on the Gazer Within," by Larry Levis. *A Field Guide to Contemporary Poetry and Poetics.* Edited by Stuart Friebert and David Young. Longman, 1980. Copyright © 1980 by Longman Inc. All rights reserved. Reproduced by permission of Addison Wesley Longman, Inc. Excerpts from "Philip Levine," by Larry Levis. *Pacific Review,* winter 1990. Excerpts from "A Conversation with Philip Levine," by Christopher Buckley. *Quarterly West,* vol. 43, 1996–1997. Excerpts from "At the Grave of My Guardian Angel: St. Louis Cemetery, New Orleans," "Caravaggio: Swirl & Vortex," "Slow Child with a Book of Birds," in *The Widening Spell of the Leaves,* by Larry Levis. University of Pittsburgh Press, 1991. Copyright © 1991, Larry Levis. All rights reserved. Reproduced by permission. Excerpts from "Oklahoma," "South," "Those Graves in Rome," "Winter Stars," in *Winter Stars,* by Larry Levis. University of Pittsburgh Press, 1985. Copyright © 1985, Larry Levis. All rights reserved. Reproduced by permission. Excerpts from "Fish" and "The Poem You Asked For," in *Wrecking Crew,* by Larry Levis. University of Pittsburgh Press, 1972. Copyright © 1972, Larry Levis. All rights reserved. Reproduced by permission.

PAULE MARSHALL Excerpts from "'Talk as a Form of Action':An Interview with Paule Marshall, September 1982," by Sabine Bröck. *History and Tradition in Afro-American Culture.* Edited by Gunter H. Lenz. Campus Verlag, 1984. Copyright © 1984 Campus Verlag GmbH, Frankfurt/Main. Reproduced by permission. Excerpts from "Recreating Ourselves All Over the World: Interview with Paule Marshall," by Omolara Ogundipe-Leslie. *Matatu: Journal for African Culture and Society,* vol. 3, 1989. Reproduced by permission. Excerpts from "To Be in the World: An Interview with Paule Marshall," by Angela Elam. *New Letters,* vol. 62, 1996. Copyright © 1996. It is included here with the permission of New Letters and Curators of the University of Missouri at Kansas City. Excerpt from "Sailing to Byzantium," in *The Tower,* by W. B. Yeats. Macmillan, 1928.

TERRY SOUTHERN Excerpts from "Terry Southern," by Jerry McAninch. *Dictionary of Literary Biography, Volume Two: American Novelists Since World War II.* Edited by Jeffrey Helterman and Richard Layman. Gale Research Company, 1978. Copyright © 1978 Gale Research Company. Reproduced by permission. Excerpts from "'...now dig this..': The Terry Southern Interview," by Mike Golden. *SmokeSignals,* www.carminestreet.com/smoke_signals.html.

WILLIAM STAFFORD Excerpts from "With Kit, Age 7, at the beach," in *Allegiances,* by William Stafford. Harper & Row, Publishers, 1970. Copyright © 1970 by William Stafford. Reproduced by permission of HarperCollins Publishers. Excerpts from "William Stafford: 1941–" by William Stafford. *Contemporary Authors, Volume 3: Autobiography Series.* Edited by Adele Sarkissian. Gale Research Company, 1986. Copyright © 1986 by Gale Research Company. Reproduced by permission. Excerpts from "If I Could Be Like Wallace Stevens" and "Tuned in Late One Night," in *A Glass Face in the Rain: New Poems,* by William Stafford. Harper & Row, Publishers, 1982. Copyright © 1982 by William Stafford. Reproduced by permission of HarperCollins Publishers. Excerpts from "The Poet as Religious Moralist." *Literature and Belief,* vol. 2, 1982. Reproduced by permission. Excerpts from "A Poet Responds," by Charles Digregorio. *Oregon Historical Quarterly,* vol. 81, summer 1980. Reproduced by permission. Excerpts from "First Grade," "1940," "Thinking about Being Called Simple by a Critic," in *An Oregon Message,* by William Stafford. Harper & Row, Publishers, 1987. Copyright © 1987 by William Stafford. Reproduced by permission of HarperCollins Publishers. Excerpts from "Life Work" and "Vita," in *Passwords,* by William Stafford. HarperPerennial, 1991. Copyright © 1991 by William Stafford. Reproduced by permission of HarperCollins Publishers. Excerpts from "Doubt on the Great Divide," "The Epitaph Ending in And," "The Rescued Year," in *The Rescued Year,* by William Stafford. Harper & Row, Publishers, 1966. Copyright © 1966 by William E. Stafford. Reproduced by permission of HarperCollins Publishers. Excerpts from "Taking Note: From Poets Notebooks," by William Stafford. *Seneca Review,* vol. XXI, 1991. Copyright © 1991 by Hobart and William Smith Colleges. Reproduced by permission. Excerpts from "An Introduction to Some Poems" and "Report to Crazy Horse," in *Someday, Maybe,* by William Stafford. Harper & Row, Publishers, 1973. Copyright © 1973 by William Stafford. Reproduced by permission of HarperCollins Publishers. Excerpts from "Ask Me" and "A Story That Could Be True," in *Stories That Could Be True: New and Collected Poems,* by William Stafford. Harper & Row, Publishers, 1977. Copyright © 1977 by William Stafford. Reproduced by permission of HarperCollins Publishers. Excerpts from "Thinking for Berky" and "Traveling through the Dar," in *Traveling through the Dark,* by William Stafford. Harper & Row, Publishers, 1962. Copyright © 1962 by William Stafford. Reproduced by permission of HarperCollins Publishers. Excerpts from "Are You Mr. Stafford?" in *The Way It Is: New & Selected Poems,* by William Stafford. Graywolf Press, 1998. Copyright © 1998 by William Stafford and the Estate of William Stafford. Reproduced by permission. Excerpts from "At the Bomb Testing Site," "Bi-Focal," "Midwest," in *West of Your City,* by William Stafford. Talisman Press, 1960. Copyright © 1960. Reproduced by permission.

RICHARD YATES Excerpts from "A Sure Narrative Voice," by James Atlas. *Atlantic Monthly,* vol. 248, November 1981. Reproduced by permission of the author. Excerpts from "A Harrowing Mirror of Loneliness," by Stephen Amidon. *Atlantic Monthly,* vol. 288, July/August 2001. Excerpts from "A Salute to Mister Yates," by Andre Dubus. *Black Warrior Review,* vol. 15, spring 1989. Excerpts from "The Lost World of Richard Yates: How the Great Writer of the Age of Anxiety Disappeared from Print," by Stewart O'Nan. *Boston Review,* vol. 24, October/November 1999. Excerpts from "The Wages of Maturity," by Theodore Solotaroff. *Commentary,* vol. 32, July 1961. Copyright 1961 by the American Jewish Committee. Renewed 1989. All rights reserved. Reproduced by permission of the publisher and author. Excerpts from "Richard Yates: 1926–" by Jean W. Ross. *Contemporary Authors, Volume 10: New Revision Series.* Edited by Ann Evory and Linda Metzger. Gale Research Company, 1983. Copyright © 1983 by Gale Research Company. Reproduced by permission. Excerpts from "Builders" and "Dr. Jack-o'-Lantern," in *Eleven Kinds of Loneliness,* by Richard Yates. Atlantic—Little, Brown, 1962. Excerpts from "The Books That Made Writers," by Richard Yates. *The New York Times Book Review,* November 25, 1979. Copyright © 1979 by The New York Times Company. Reproduced by permission. Excerpts from "An Interview with Richard Yates," by DeWitt Henry and Geoffrey Clark. *Ploughshares,* vol. 1, winter 1972. Excerpts from "Requiem for Richard Yates," by Seymour Lawrence. *Poets & Writers Magazine,* vol. 21, September/October 1993.

List of Subjects

Introduction

A Victorian critic, Stopford Brooke, once observed, "Writing is not literature unless it gives to the reader a pleasure which arises not only from the things said, but from the way in which they are said." It seems the special province of criticism to notice the way things are said, how the language of a particular text operates to embody and enhance meaning. The essays in this supplement of *American Writers* are focused with considerable intensity on the language of some our best writers, some contemporary and some from the past. The essays are written to increase the reader's pleasure, and understanding, in the work of each writer.

This supplement brings together a range of articles on American writers, most of them contemporary, although a few of them reach back to neglected, but important, writers from earlier decades. Readers will find the eighteen essays included here both lively and intelligent, designed to interest readers unfamiliar with the work of a given author and to assist those who know the work quite well by providing a sense of the biographical and critical context.

American Writers had its origin in a series of monographs that appeared between 1959 and 1972. The Minnesota Pamphlets on American Writers were incisively written and informative, treating ninety-seven American writers in a format and style that attracted a devoted following of readers. The series proved invaluable to a generation of students and teachers, who could depend on these reliable and interesting critiques of major figures. The idea of reprinting these essays occurred to Charles Scribner Jr. (1921–1995). The series appeared in four volumes entitled *American Writers: A Collection of Literary Biographies* (1974).

Since then, numerous supplements have appeared, treating well over two hundred American writers: poets, novelists, playwrights, essayists, and autobiographers. The idea has been consistent with the original series: to provide clear, informative essays aimed at the general reader. These essays often rise to a high level of craft and critical vision, but they are meant to introduce a writer of some importance in the history of American literature, and to provide a sense of the scope and nature of the career under review. In each case, the critics are asked to avoid using jargon and to write clearly. I think they have succeeded especially well in this regard.

The authors of these critical articles are mostly teachers, scholars, and writers. Most have published books and articles in their field, and several are well-known writers of poetry or fiction as well as critics. As anyone glancing through this volume will see, they are held to the highest standards of good writing and sound scholarship. The essays each conclude with a select bibliography intended to direct the reading of those who want to pursue the subject further.

This supplement focuses on contemporary writers, many of whom have received little sustained attention from critics. For example, Harry Crews, Terry Southern, Frederick Barthelme, Cristina García, Michael Chabon, Paule Marshall, Richard Yates, and Toni Cade Bambara have been written about in the review pages of newspapers and magazines, and their writing has acquired a substantial following, but their work has yet to attract significant scholarship. That will certainly follow, but the essays included here constitute a beginning.

Some of important writers from the past—such as Stephen Vincent Benét, Charlotte Perkins Gilman, John Fante, and James Jones—have already attracted a good deal of sustained attention, and their work—especially that of Gilman—is often taught in college courses, but for various reasons their careers have not yet been discussed in *American Writers*. It is time they were added to the series.

The poets included here—from Mary Karr (also a well-known memoirist) and Wanda Coleman to William Stafford, Mark Doty, Stephen Dunn, and Larry Levis—are well known in the poetry world, and their work has in each case been honored with major literary prizes. These poets have been widely anthologized as well. Nevertheless, the real work of assimilation, of discovering the true place of each poet in the larger traditions of American poetry, has only begun. In each case, these poets are written about by critics who are themselves poets, and the depth and eloquence of their essays should be obvious even to casual readers.

The critics who contributed to this collection represent a wide range of backgrounds and critical approaches, although the baseline for inclusion was that each essay should be accessible to the non-specialist reader or beginning student. The creation of culture involves the continuous reassessment of major texts produced by its writers, and my belief is that this supplement performs a useful service here, providing substantial introductions to American writers who matter, and it will assist readers in the difficult but rewarding work of close reading.

——JAY PARINI

Contributors

Bert Almon. Professor of English at the University of Alberta. Author of a book on William Humphrey and a study of autobiography, *This Stubborn Self: Texas Autobiographies 1925–2001,* as well as eight collections of poetry. Born in Port Arthur, Texas. MARY KARR

Charles R. Baker. Poet, short story writer and essayist. Published works include "What Miss Johnson Taught," "Christmas Frost," "A Peacock in a Pecan Tree," and "A Fireman's Christmas." Curator of "Mark Twain: Father of Modern American Literature" at Bridwell Library, Southern Methodist University. RICHARD YATES

Kim Bridgford. Professor of English at Fairfield University, where she directs the writing program and is poetry editor of *Dogwood.* Her poetry has appeared in *North American Review, Christian Science Monitor,* and *Iowa Review.* Her fiction has been published in the *Georgia Review, Massachusetts Review,* and *Witness.* Named Connecticut Professor of the Year by the Carnegie Foundation for the Advancement of Teaching and has received an NEA fellowship. MARK DOTY

Christopher Buckley. Teacher in the creative writing program at the University of California, Riverside. Author of eleven books of poetry, most recently, *Star Apocrypha.* Editor of *On The Poetry of Philip Levine: Stranger to Nothing.* LARRY LEVIS

Laurie Champion. Associate Professor of English at San Diego State University. Specializes in contemporary American literature, with an emphasis on minority writers and on the American short story genre. Editor of several anthologies, including *American Women Writers, 1900–1945: A Bio-Bibliographical Sourcebook.* Recent publications have appeared in *Southern Quarterly, Studies in Short Fiction, Journal of the Short Story in English,* and *Midwest Quarterly.* FREDERICK BARTHELME

Stephen Cooper. Professor of English at California State University, Long Beach. Author of *Full of Life: A Biography of John Fante* and the editor of Fante's posthumous *The Big Hunger: Stories 1932–1959* as well as *The John Fante Reader.* JOHN FANTE

Joseph Dewey. Associate Professor of American Literature for the University of Pittsburgh. Author of *In a Dark Time: The Apocalyptic Temper of the American Novel in the Nuclear Age; Novels from Reagan's America: A New Realism;* and *Understanding Richard Powers.* MICHAEL CHABON, HARRY CREWS

Deborah Kay Ferrell. Assistant Professor of English at SUNY, Finger Lakes Community College, where she teaches courses in writing and literature. She is also a creative writer and was awarded the Florida Arts Council Grant in 1996 for her short fiction. Currently working on a novel, titled *Gringa.* CRISTINA GARCÍA

Paul Johnston. Chair of the English Department at the State University of New York at Plattsburgh, where he teaches American literature. He has published articles on James Fenimore Cooper, Nathaniel Hawthorne, and attitudes toward nature in American literature. STEPHEN VINCENT BENÉT

Brian Kent. Lecturer at the University of Vermont, where he teaches writing and American literature. Author of articles about Stephen King and Tom Robbins and a forthcoming book about Gore Vidal. JAMES JONES

Alexander Long. Graduate of the Writing Seminars at the Johns Hopkins University, who lives and teaches in West Chester, Pennsylvania. Coeditor of *A Condition of the Spirit: The Work and Life of Larry Levis.* Author of a forthcoming chapbook, *Elegy for the Dark Anniversaries,* and pieces published in *Quarterly West, Solo, Connecticut Review, 5 AM,* and elsewhere. WILLIAM STAFFORD

Tony Magistrale. Professor of English at the University of Vermont. Author of*The Student Companion to Edgar Allan Poe.* Currently writing *Hollywood's Stephen King,* the first book-length analysis of the films that have been made from Stephen King's fiction. WANDA COLEMAN

Robert Niemi. Associate Professor of English, St. Michael's College. Author of books on Russell Banks and Weldon Kees and numerous articles on literature and popular culture. TERRY SOUTHERN

Sylvia Bailey Shurbutt. Professor of English, Shepherd College. Author *Reading Writing Relationships;* articles in *Essays in Literature, Women's Studies, Southern Humanities Review, Southern Literary Journal, Women and Language, Victorian Poetry;* and chapters and essays on Zelda Fitzgerald, Caroline Norton, Kate Chopin, Matthew Arnold, John Stuart Mill, and Emily Dickinson. CHARLOTTE PERKINS GILMAN

Barbara C. Solaro. Associate Professor in the Department of Language, Literature, and Communication at Elizabeth City State University, a constituent university of the University of North Carolina system. TONI CADE BAMBARA

Victoria D. Sullivan. Professor in the English Department at Saint Peter's College. Has published on Zelda Fitzgerald, Saul Bellow, Caryl Churchill, Samuel Beckett and others. As playwright, has had five Equity Showcase productions of her work in Manhattan, as well as numerous staged readings. As poet, has read her poetry on radio and television and been published widely, including in the journals *Artist and Influence, Poetry in Performance,* and *Northeast Corridor.* Coauthor of the poetry collection *The Divided Bed* and coeditor of *Plays by and about Women.* STEPHEN DUNN

Joseph M. Viera. Assistant Professor of English at Nazareth College, where he teaches American and U.S. Latino/a literatures. Author of published articles on Cristina García and the Cuban-American novelist Oscar Hijuelos. Currently working on a book-length study of Oscar Hijuelos. CRISTINA GARCÍA

Dana Cairns Watson. Teacher of writing and literature at the University of California, Los Angeles. PAULE MARSHALL

SUPPLEMENT XI
Toni Cade Bambara to Richard Yates

Toni Cade Bambara

1939–1995

*B*ORN MILTONA MIRKIN Cade in New York City on March 25, 1939, Toni Cade Bambara was the daughter of Walter Cade II and Helen Brent Henderson Cade. She grew up in New York, in Harlem, Bedford-Stuyvesant, and Queens, and in Jersey City, New Jersey, the urban settings of much of her fiction. As a child Bambara was influenced by the writings of Gwendolyn Brooks and Langston Hughes and instructed by the movies she saw while living in Harlem.

Bambara attended Queens College (now Queens College of the City University of New York), where she received a B.A. degree in 1959. She traveled to Europe in 1961, studying at the University of Florence and at the Commedia dell'Arte in Milan, Italy, and taking classes in mime at Ecole de Mime Etienne Decroux in Paris. Returning to the United States, she received an M.A. from City College of the City University of New York in 1964. She did further study in linguistics at New York University and the New School for Social Research. She also attended the Katherine Dunham Dance Studio, the Syvilla Fort School of Dance, the Clark Center of Performing Arts (1958–1969), and the Studio Museum of Harlem Film Institute (1970).

A freelance writer and editor, lecturer, educator, civil rights activist, and documentary filmmaker, Bambara held a variety of jobs over the course of her career. She was a social investigator for the New York State Department of Welfare from 1959 to 1961; director of recreation in the psychiatry department of Metropolitan Hospital, New York City, from 1961 to 1962; program director for Colony House Community Center, New York City, from 1962 to 1965; an English instructor for the Seek Program, City College of the City University of New York, from 1965 to 1969, and for the New Careers Program of Newark, New Jersey, in 1969. She was assistant professor of English at Livingston College, Rutgers University, from 1969 to 1974. She was visiting professor of African American studies at Stephens College, Columbia, Missouri, in 1975, and at Atlanta University in 1977. Bambara served as production-artist-in-residence at Stephens College (1976) and Spelman College (1978–1979). She was a production consultant for WHYY-TV in Philadelphia and conducted numerous workshops on writing, self-publishing, and community organizing for various schools and institutions. From 1986 until 1995, she taught scriptwriting at Scribe Video Center in Philadelphia. Bambara lectured widely and conducted literary readings at the Library of Congress and the Smithsonian Institution, among other places.

Known for her masterful use of black dialect and for exploring issues of personal responsibility and communal accountability in the wake of the civil rights and Black Power movements, Bambara wrote three novels: *The Salt Eaters* (1980), *If Blessing Comes* (1987), and *Those Bones Are Not My Child* (1999). She is perhaps best known for her short stories, collected in *Gorilla, My Love* (1972) and *The Sea Birds Are Still Alive* (1977). Bambara also published a collection of short fiction and nonfiction titled *Deep Sightings and Rescue Missions: Fiction, Essays, and Conversations* (1996). In addition, she edited the anthologies *The Black Woman* (1970) and *Tales and Stories for Black Folks*

(1971). Bambara wrote a number of screenplays and had contributed to television productions.

Bambara, who adopted her surname in 1970, died of colon cancer in Philadelphia on December 9, 1995. She had one daughter, Karma Bene Bambara.

GORILLA, MY LOVE

Bambara introduced the stories in her 1972 collection *Gorilla, My Love* with "A Sort of Preface," a playful characterization of her fiction. "It does no good to write autobiographical fiction," she asserts, because even if the facts are disguised, the friends and family members whom the characters are based upon will consider themselves "stab[bed] in the back with a pen." Instead, Bambara "deal[s] in straight-up fiction . . . mostly cause I lie a lot anyway."

In this collection the cheeky young girls and audacious young women, mothers, and Other Mothers threading their way through black urban neighborhoods reflect Bambara's own girlhood in New York and New Jersey. The stories in *Gorilla, My Love* are about surviving and evolving among a community of black brothers and sisters. Many of the stories are realistic depictions of the development of young women; Rena Korb sees an affinity between Bambara's streetwise young narrators, particularly Hazel in the title story "Gorilla, My Love," and J. D. Salinger's Holden Caulfield. As in much of Bambara's fiction, the prose employed in these stories, in the words of Margaret Mazurkiewicz, "swings from colloquial narrative to precarious metaphorical heights and over to street talk, at which Bambara is unbeatable."

The narrator of "My Man Bovanne," the first story in the collection, is Hazel, a mother whose grown children chastise her for having too good a time at a political benefit. Hazel concludes that the Black Power movement encourages young people to be disrespectful toward their mothers. Her children are embarrassed that she

has been dancing, according to her daughter Elo, "like a bitch in heat" with the elderly blind gentleman Bovanne, whom Hazel defends as a community mainstay, a man who "fixed skates and skooters for all these folks when they was just kids." Like Hazel, in old age Bovanne has been largely discarded by the community, especially its young people. Hazel declares that the Black Power movement has "mess[ed] em around till they can't be civil to ole folks."

Clearly embarrassed by Hazel's manner of dress and behavior, her children want her to get in touch with her African heritage. Apparently, she concludes, she "can't get Black enough to suit em." Even though Hazel has done more than her share to help bring about change for the new generation, her daughter Elo calls her "apolitical"; still, the young people are quick to enlist the support of the senior members of the community "on account," says Hazel, "of we grass roots." Her children want Hazel to help form a "Council of the Elders" to act as an advisory group to the movement, but their interests are hypocritical. Intent on rectifying the injustices of the prejudices they themselves face, the new generation remains, ironically, intolerant, blind to their own prejudices against, for example, the blind and the elderly. In their minds, they do not need the wisdom and experience of the old folks; they speak of black pride but are ashamed of people like Bovanne. Defiantly, Hazel rebels, asserting that "the older folks" need to "know they still needed" and that, indeed, "old folks is the nation." She takes Bovanne home to her bed, having decided to remain "the hussy my daughter always say I was."

Another defiant elderly figure whose wisdom is discounted is the title character of "Maggie of the Green Bottles." Maggie pins her hopes on her great-granddaughter, Peaches, to rescue the family and, it is understood, the race from subjugation and degradation, from "taking in laundry, buckling at the knees, putting their faith in Jesus . . . too squeamish to band together and take the world by storm, make history." Maggie has no patience with complacency in the midst of oppression; in one scene, she slaps the underfed family dog for licking her hand after she has offered it a scrap from the cooking pot: "too dumb to even know you're supposed to bite the hand that feeds you," she comments. Maggie is the only one in the family to stand up to her son-in-law, Mr. Tyler, a domineering, intolerant "runabout" who even his daughter Peaches refers to as a "gross Neanderthal." To Mr. Tyler, Maggie is a freeloading drunk, a crazy voodoo woman; to Peaches, she is a gutsy heroine who teaches her legends and folktales and assures Peaches of her "capacity for wings," convincing her that she is an extraordinary girl "destined for greatness."

After Maggie dies, Peaches is given Maggie's colored herb and emollient bottles, although what she really wanted was her great-grandmother's "enchantment," her magic green bottles. The family makes Peaches feel small, ordinary, not at all extraordinary, the way Maggie made her feel. She remains silent on the issue, however. Unless Peaches retains Maggie's defiant spirit—and readers are led to suspect she will—she is in danger of having her wings clipped.

In "Blues Ain't No Mockin Bird," predatory white filmmakers invade a black homestead, recording images for a documentary on the food stamps program. The young narrator of this story watches as the men trample her grandmother's garden and disrespectfully ignore the elderly woman's wishes that they leave. Her Granny is no pushover, however; a shrewd, proud woman, Granny has always had a low tolerance of "triflers." It is not surprising, then, that Granny objects to the voyeuristic camera that invades her privacy and exploits her and her surroundings, turning them into commercialized objects. Because she is elderly and because she is a woman, and a black woman, the filmmakers ignore her, but they are caught off guard by the kingly bearing of Granddaddy, who seizes their camera in his huge hands and destroys it and the film, reminding the men, "This is our own place." As a filmmaker herself, Bambara understands the camera's potential for a depersonalizing, intrusive way of seeing. Also evident is her objection to what she describes in *Deep Sightings and Rescue Missions* as colonizing images of African Americans.

The collection's title story, "Gorilla, My Love," has been the subject of a great deal of critical response. The story's young narrator, Hazel—whom the family affectionately calls Peaches, Badbird, Scout, Precious, and Miss Muffin—is a much-loved child whose family believes in her whole-heartedly. Hazel's mother supports her by showing up at Hazel's school and making the teacher "come undone" for telling young Hazel her questions are "out of order." Hazel's own sense of personal power stems, it is suggested, from her mother's self-confidence; the teachers are intimidated by Hazel's mother because she "got pull with the Board and bad by her own self anyhow."

Exacting in her standards, Hazel is incensed when a movie she and her friends pay to see turns out to be religious in subject matter. "And I am ready to kill," she explains, "not cause I got anything gainst Jesus. Just that when you fixed to watch a gorilla picture you don't wanna get messed around with Sunday School." Her daddy grants Hazel her point that the theater manager failed to keep his word by showing the "churchy" movie when he had advertised "Gorilla, My Love." Hazel's family has taught her that "when you got something on your mind, speak up and let the chips fall where they may." Because of this, she is not afraid to scrutinize her elders, to demand of the theater manager that he refund her money, even to question "simple ass" religious orthodoxy; Hazel is convinced that "just about anybody in my family is better than this god they always talkin about."

Continuing in her exactness, Hazel accuses Hunca Bubba, her young uncle and idol, of betraying her trust by falling in love with someone instead of waiting for her. In his mind, he had just been teasing her because she was a little girl; in her mind, he is just another grown-up who believes he can treat her "just anyhow." Children, Bambara argues, are people too, and when strong families give them the courage to do so, they are watching and judging the actions of adults.

But where Hazel in "Gorilla, My Love" enjoys solid familial reinforcement, Ollie Larkins, in "Happy Birthday," is on her own. The neighborhood's indifference to the plight of the orphaned Ollie bears uncanny resemblance to the indifference of the community to the suffering of Petula in Toni Morrison's *The Bluest Eye* (1970). On a summer day, her birthday, Ollie aimlessly wanders the streets alone; her caregiver, Granddaddy Larkins, has drunk himself into a stupor and will be "asleep for days." The omniscient narrator casts a telescopic lens around the ghetto neighborhood: Wilma, the child next door in the tenement, will be "holed up somewhere stuffing herself with potato chips" the entire day; the owner of the Chicken Shack Restaurant does not want Ollie loitering in front of the establishment, "ruining the business"; the men pitching pennies outside the shoe store prevent her from playing handball; no one is home at Mrs. Robinson's house, so she cannot offer to walk the woman's dog; the teenage boys she knows are drowsing on a rooftop after, apparently, smoking dope; Chalky, the building superintendent, is inconstant in his attention due to addiction or mental illness. "Everyone was either at camp or at work or was sleeping like the boys on the roof or dead or just plain gone off." Even Reverend Hall, the pastor of the local church, has no time for her. He seems to make it his life's work to chase off pigeons, dogs, drunks, and children. So much for the communal support for one unloved, lonely, vulnerable child of the inner-city projects.

The grimness of Ollie's situation is underscored by the fact that the story takes place on her birthday. This is a community unable to care for, let alone celebrate, this neglected child. The only solace offered her comes from Miss Hazel, a neighbor, who tells Ollie that when she gets old, she will no longer care about birthdays. As Ollie stands in the middle of the street howling in rage and despair, Miss Hazel responds by shutting the window so she can hear the TV. The neighborhood is either too busy trying to earn a living or too preoccupied to care about Ollie. As Jason remarks in Bambara's later collection, *The Sea Birds Are Still Alive,* the adults of the black community have shirked their responsibility to their children.

Another neglected child of the urban slums is Manny, the subject of "The Hammer Man." Manny carries a hammer in the loop of his pants, presumably in case he needs it to defend himself or bash someone's head in. This child is a walking time bomb, ready to explode from the pressures of the conditions in which he lives. The children play on a dangerous, crumbling tenement roof; Manny's mother and a neighbor woman go at each other in the alley with bicycle chains and knives; Manny's home is a disaster area with a "tumbled-down kitchen of dirty clothes and bundles and bundles of rags and children." When Manny accidentally falls off the roof, the threat he poses to the narrator and the rest of the community is diminished.

When next we see him, Manny's anger has evidently been defused. The narrator comes across him at night, doing lay-ups on a basketball court at a local park. She watches, captivated, as he relives over and over again the end of a school tournament in which he "muffed the goddamn shot." "Hypnotized" by Manny's obsessive need to recapture the moment and make it right, the narrator is compelled to defend her old enemy when two white police officers pull up in a squad car and begin harassing him. Antagonized perhaps by his talent, his grace and ease in shooting the ball, as the narrator says, "damn near like he was some kind of very beautiful bird," the police officers provoke him into fighting back, then arrest him. The last we hear of Manny he is in a psychiatric institution. And the narrator too seems to undergo a diminution, from willful defiance to complacency, preoccupied with a "very boss" fashion show staged by the neighborhood youth center, the same center that had typed her family and neighborhood as "deviant."

In "Basement," the young narrator comes under the influence of the female relatives of her friend Patsy. Norma and Fay—known to the narrator as Patsy Mother and Patsy Aunt—are presumably prostitutes; her mother disapproves of them and has forbidden her daughter from spending time in their house. These women drink highballs and talk all day, either recovering from the night before or preparing for work that evening. The narrator is attracted to their direct conversation and their soft, flamboyant clothes. They invite the girls into their world by speaking openly about sex, although they both, and especially Patsy Mother, are fiercely protective of them and intent on shielding them from the predatory ways of men. Young Patsy plays on her relatives' fears, seemingly for attention; "You always telling tales on people," the narrator chides; the narrator's mother warns her daughter to "stay out of Patsy way cause she sex crazy and always talkin nasty." Patsy Mother ultimately resorts to violence when Patsy tells her that the building superintendent exposed himself to her and her friends. The narrator rightly suspects that this story is a lie, and the reader is left uncertain that these girls can develop a healthy sexual identity.

Unlike that of Norma and Fay, Miss Moore's interest in the neighborhood children in "The Lesson" is as a mentor. A black educated woman, she takes it upon herself to try to inspire them to achieve beyond their own limited world, planning excursions in an attempt to teach them the relationship between what they study in their schoolbooks and what she feels they must know in real life in order to escape the ravages of the slums. But because she is so different from them, and so intent on opening their eyes to the poverty and degradation of their lives, Miss Moore is disliked and ridiculed by the children, especially by the narrator, Sylvia. Their mothers outwardly show respect for her, but they "talked behind her back like a dog." Everyone seems to resent "her goddamn college degree." The children are impatient with the abstract thinking Miss Moore tries to introduce. They would much rather spend their Saturday afternoons in the cool theaters "terroriz[ing] the West Indian kids."

A trip to the Fifth Avenue toy store FAO Schwarz organized by Miss Moore only serves to make the children aware for the first time that they are "poor" and that their mothers and fathers could never afford to buy them the things they see in the shop window. Sylvia's reaction is to become angry at the idea that she should be ashamed to browse in a shop like that, and then her shame is replaced by anger over Miss Moore's assumption that she and the other kids know nothing about the value of money. It is "crazy" white folks who apparently fail to realize that the same thirty-five dollars they spend on a toy in the window "could buy new bunk beds" for a family or "pay for the rent and the piano bill too." Most of all, she is angry about the evident difference between her and those who could afford to shop at FAO Schwarz: "What kinda work they do and how they live and how come we ain't in on it?" Clearly, the unequal distribution of wealth in America is the lesson Miss Moore intended, but the trip has the more immediate outcome, intentional or not on the part of Miss Moore, of devaluing the children and their lives. Sylvia especially takes Miss Moore's lesson as a personal attack, keeping the change from the taxi money the woman had given her for the trip to Midtown. Thus, what Sylvia gains from Miss Moore's lesson is the dark determination that "nobody," presumably including Miss Moore, is "gonna beat me at nuthin."

Miss Ruby in "Playin with Punjab" is a different kind of outsider from Miss Moore, because she is white and, as she tells the narrator, Violet, does not "speak Negro too tough." The efforts of "this gray lady," a social worker, to help better the lot of the people in the neighborhood are misunderstood and inevitably unappreciated. Because she is not one of them, they cannot conceive of her as a neighborhood leader but opt instead for a ruthless loan shark who cares nothing for the people. According to Violet, Miss Ruby "came all the way out here to Brooklyn to straighten us folks out and get the rats taken care of and get us jobs and stuff like that." Miss Ruby counts on Punjab, the neighborhood extortionist whom everybody knows "don't play"—who is only out for his own gain—to put up bail for the people she is trying to help. Miss Ruby somehow "worked her thing" on Punjab and was able to "[open] his nose" to finance the building of a clinic for the local junkies. This is the same Punjab who had "iced" a local man the day the man was discharged from the army, to which he had fled in order to avoid repaying Punjab.

Since "a whole lotta long bread" was coming into the area, thanks to Miss Ruby's organizational efforts and Punjab's cooperation, the neighborhood suspected that "Punjab was going to get his cut" in the form of a community leadership position, "him being the only kind of leader we could even think of." But in the election organized by Miss Ruby, only a handful of people bother to vote, while the rest of the community "act[s] up" when the votes are legally counted and Punjab is not among the victors.

Opposed to being represented by the newly elected leaders, the community turns against Miss Ruby. According to one woman, they do not like "this 'grass roots' and 'poor folks' . . . coming out of no white mouth." Blood money, apparently, is better than accepting help from a white woman and better than taking responsibility for themselves through participation in a democratic process. When Miss Ruby remains unmoved by their objections, "Punjab [comes] to collect"; her office is trashed and Miss Ruby disappears, presumably run out of town. Punjab, it seems, "don't play." Convinced of their own powerlessness and used to the way things are, no matter how bad, out of fear of this vicious extortionist the neighborhood digs itself right back into the hole it was in before. The general feeling is that Miss Ruby "was full of shit with all her foolishness about power and equality and responsibility and sacrifice, and then cop right out when the chips were down."

The refusal to take responsibility is also at issue in "Talkin Bout Sonny." Sonny, who just "iced his wife," offers the excuse that "something came over me." The community's toleration of male violence is apparent in the remarks of Delauney, one Sonny's friends, who describes Sonny's crime as simply "one of them things." He says, "Fifty-some-odd days of pure shit jammed into one mad moment and boom—you plant a razor in your wife's throat." This story is eerily reminiscent of Ann Petry's "The Winding Street," in which a factory worker comes home from a day of unappreciated toil and abuse and kills his devoted wife. Even though Sonny's friends witnessed his medical problems prior to the murder, they discounted them: Sonny is "just tired." When his girlfriend Betty, the story's narrator, expressed concern that perhaps Sonny was suffering from seizures, Delauney had derided her for spewing "nursery-school-marm shit." After the murder, he warns her not to "pull one of those I-told-you-so things on me." Delauney, like Sonny, does not want to take or to assign responsibility for what happened. "It is nobody's fault—nobody's," he insists. "These things happen." In fact, maybe "killing the bitch" was "the most beautiful thing Sonny has ever done in his whole life," Delauney speculates. He waits for Betty, a social worker, to agree. It is not at all clear that Betty will; however, in the neighborhood it is assumed that a woman will let her man think for her and never question the men's misogynist views. If she does, she might, as Sonny's wife presumably did, catch him on a bad day.

The last story of the collection, "The Johnson Girls," is a superb rendering of inner-city black dialect, as well as a fine example of Bambara's uncanny knack for creating scene and dialogue. Perhaps Bambara's most engaging story, "The Johnson Girls" is a dramatization of black sisterhood and black women's difficulties with black men; the story asserts that black women yearn for "a grown man," for what they refer to as "the blue-plate special."

The narrator of the story is a beginning writer, in college as a result of the intervention of her cousin Inez, an educated, professional woman who owns a brownstone in New York City, where the narrator gathers with Sugar, Marcy, and Gail, single women in their thirties. Inez's live-in boyfriend, Roy, a jazz musician, has moved to Knoxville while Inez was out of town because she "refus[ed] to marry him." As Inez prepares to fly to Knoxville herself to confront Roy, the women gather in her bedroom, offering their advice. The reader is treated to a brilliant scene of rich visual and auditory impressions. It is clear that Roy and Inez's relationship has been a model for the other women, who are concerned that Inez is too independent and strong-minded to make a commitment to Roy: her motto is "I got a right to be exactly who I am." The narrator explains that Inez "offers a tax-free relationship—no demands, no pressure, no games, no jumpin up and down with ultimatums." But Roy is the kind of man that the oth

ers would not let slip away. "A rare bird," Gail calls him, and Marcy affirms that he "is somethin special."

Any man, according to Marcy, "can always get some good woman . . . to go for his shit," no matter how bad a "basket case" he might be; but "if her shit ain't together, [a woman] can forget it." On the other hand,

> If she got her johnson together, is fine in her do, superbad in her work, and terrible, terrible extra plus with her woman thing . . . she'll just bop along the waves forever with nobody to catch her up, cause her thing is so tough, and it's so crystal clear she ain't goin for bullshit, that can't no man pump up his boyish heart good enough to come deal with her one on one.

Because they can take care of themselves, and enjoy the nurturing support of one another, these women are able to state with confidence what they want out of a relationship. But because of the quantity of "little boys" masquerading as men in their lives, the only choice these women may have is to go it alone in the end. Although as Sugar says, Roy and Inez "kept my faith in the blue-plate special"—if Roy and Inez can make it, perhaps there is hope for all of them.

The collective wisdom of women bonding together, a recurrent theme of Bambara's work, seems to nudge Inez toward a greater level of understanding and maturity, enabling the narrator to reveal her awe at the power of "Love love love love love."

THE SEA BIRDS ARE STILL ALIVE

Published in 1977, *The Sea Birds Are Still Alive* is a collection of ten stories, each with a revolutionary tenor influenced by Bambara's international travels, about the experiences of people of color in the United States and elsewhere. Lois F. Lyles notes the relevance in these stories of the expression "revolution in my lifetime," which she cites as the "rallying cry of some radical black organizations of the sixties."

In the title story, "The Sea Birds Are Still Alive," a group of locals, presumably in Southeast Asia, find themselves thrown together on a ferryboat, in what amounts to a societal microcosm. Some are ordinary villagers and hill people; some are refugees, displaced by the Vietnam War. One, a wealthy native landlord, has compromised himself to Western ideals, promising improvements to the people in his district but evicting the farmers who cannot pay the tithes he demands. The others are resentful of the rich foreigners who pick over native goods at the bazaars or, like a French woman and her child, throw perfectly good bread to the greedy seagulls. While the impoverished people of the countryside starve, the impervious foreigners flaunt the money they have amassed working for unscrupulous governments eager to exploit the land and the people. These new colonial forces are represented by insensitive American tourists and government officials hoping for a soft job back in Washington, D.C. They are no different from the previous colonizers, the Spanish, the French, and the Japanese.

In Bambara's view, these neocolonials make bigoted assumptions about people whom they make no effort to understand. They plant mines along the beaches, suppress rebellions, displace and contaminate, and then issue halfhearted warnings about toxic fallout. They ruthlessly, or by more subtle means, wrest from hungry mouths taxes of one sort or another and then threaten eviction or worse. And then, having come to power through bribery or other illegal and covert operations, they announce through "official" sources that everything is under control. Yet we know the sea birds have not all been destroyed. There is hope when a daughter defies her father's fascination with what the West can do for his career and regains her heritage and when a young mother, survivor of unspeakable torture, refuses to betray her collaborators and bequeaths to her young daughter the conviction that "We cannot be defeated."

Lyles observes that these revolutionaries display, in their desire to create a new world order, "the fervor of the devout"; however, Bambara suggests that what motivates them is the fervor of the deeply committed, as in the collection's opening story, "The Organizer's Wife." This story is about a grassroots organizer and his young wife, Virginia, who comes into her own when she realizes the urgent needs of the downtrodden southern black farmers and the importance of the work her husband, Graham, has begun on their behalf. Virginia had fallen into the exhaustion of defeat after Graham's arrest for attempting to unionize the farmers. Intent as she had been on plotting her own escape from the impoverished rural South, Virginia felt trapped by the poverty of the inhospitable farmland. Although she admired him for it, she had never fully understood Graham's decision to return to his roots to fight for the people. In her yearning for freedom beyond the imprisonment of the hot, dusty roads and worn-out farms, Virginia had yearned for opportunity, education, escape from living at the bottom of what she had come to think of as "a stream of garbage." But Graham knows that "discipline, consciousness, and unity," as well as education, can defeat the "greed, technological superiority, and legal lawlessness" that keeps rural black children languishing in inferior, unheated schoolrooms and their parents in despair. Graham has dedicated his life to thwarting the buyout by unscrupulous parties of whole towns and good farmland. Sensing Virginia's vulnerability, the local white authorities had summoned her to the prison to persuade her husband to abandon the fight; but the farmers' loyalty to Graham brings her to the realization that Graham can never belong just to her, that the struggle is not just about her. Most of all, Virginia now knows that land is power and that the "slashed trees" are only "oozing out money into the white man's pails." The only legacy the ruthless white authorities leave behind is "an open grave." As in "The Sea Birds Are Still Alive," the story ends with affirmation: "We ain't nowhere's licked yet though, huhn?"

"The Long Night" focuses on another grass-roots organizer, a young urban female dissident, presumably of the period of the American civil rights movement of the 1960s, who is reduced to cowering in terror in her own bathtub as a riot takes place in the streets below her apartment window. Dispensing with the need for search warrants, the police raid local apartments, firing indiscriminately and making arbitrary arrests. As she tries to avoid thinking about the very real possibility of dying that night, and how she will resist revealing the names of her friends while her head is being bashed against a faucet, she remembers what the struggle is about: workers who toil for $1.10 an hour "for the privilege of eating," drafty schools, cruel caretakers, the Vietnam War draft. And again, there is affirmation: she knows that after the long night, survivors will emerge into the light, joining together to "generate new food out of the old staple wisdoms."

In "Medley," Sweet Pea, another of Bambara's survivors, assisted by her cousin Sinbad, opens beauty shop after beauty shop in increasingly better neighborhoods, in an effort to keep moving up and eventually provide a decent life for herself and her young daughter. She has two ex-husbands, and it looks as if she might have to leave her boyfriend, Larry, behind too. Larry is an aspiring bass player with no talent but lots of style. It is uncertain as to whether Larry, who works as a bartender, will ever get a job with a band, but at least he is not a bootlegging womanizer like his brother, "evil, hell-raising Bam," who was "cut down" by a police officer and mourned by no one.

Everyone else in the neighborhood, it seems, is trying not only to stay alive but to be the best they can be, whatever their talents. The narrator takes people as they are: she appreciates the fact that Hector, Larry's buddy, turns window

washing into an art; that "the good-looking gambler" Moody is the best card shark, gambler, and hustler she has ever seen, and she says she has seen plenty (but then, she is the best manicurist he will probably ever have, and he knows it). She plays Moody shrewdly but straight, and for his part, Moody keeps his hands off her, appreciates her work, and pays her well, especially when he takes her with him on the dangerous gambling circuit. They both play each other but, unlike Larry, make it "clear whose weight is whose." As she says, "I'll go when the wagon comes, but I ain't going out behind somebody else's shit."

"A Tender Man" pivots around Cliff's response to Aisha's question, "What did you want to be when you grow up?" Aisha, a nurse, has recently begun dating Cliff, a man who abandoned both his wife and child. Cliff replies that he wants to be "a tender man," which is heartening because up to that point Cliff had managed to avoid thinking of himself as responsible for his child and had cared less about her mother's precarious mental health. Cliff's excuse had been that he associates his child with her white mother, whom he had married and then left, it seems, as a discarded trophy. His other excuse had been that because he was involved in what later came to be known as the Bay of Pigs invasion of Cuba, he could have been killed, therefore it was better not to get involved with his baby anyway. And besides, he had thought, black women are responsible for the black man's troubles. He had heard it a thousand times: men are low-down; just remember how your father left you and your mother in the lurch and "that no-good nigger . . . done Cousin Dorcas dirty."

Cliff had convinced himself that the insecurity of the mother of his child—which he had helped cause—had prevented him from properly dedicating himself to his work. Aisha angrily responds that changing diapers is work, "revolutionary work," and, furthermore, one can never say one's relationship with a former wife is "over"—not if there is a child involved. Under attack by Aisha's straightforward persistence, Cliff's impatience with "people who saw and heard but would not move on what they knew" begins to assume a certain irony. Cliff is both angry and fascinated by this independent-minded Aisha and begins to understand that a man's "work"—in Cliff's case, his teaching and his activist participation—can never be separate from a man's family.

"Broken Field Running" is another of Bambara's powerful depictions of children growing up in the ghetto while trying to avoid the "wrong-looking characters," who establish squatter's rights and lurk about. Yet the neighborhood children are aided by the love and encouragement of Mommy Barbara, an elderly resident in the projects, and Lacey and Jason, young and dedicated adults who bring the youngsters home on a cold, windy night from an excursion to the city museum, where they introduce the children to an exhibit of African art. Lacey despairs over having to return the children to the violence and degradation of the ghetto, where, she says, "We blind [them] . . . to their potential. . . . [and] cripple them, dispirit them," turning them into "good clients, wards, beggars, victims." Jason cautions Lacey not to be consumed by her anger. "Gotta side-step some of the shit," he says, "Gotta keep stepping." In a very real sense they are running against the bitter wind of defeat and despair.

Jason and Lacey seem to be the only two adults in the neighborhood who are aware of the urgent need to prepare the children for "a whole new era [that] is borning." The community elders, who might instill discipline in the children and work together for better living conditions, are instead focused on cars, eight-track cassette decks, and other consumerist trappings of what Bambara calls "the gold rush stampede." The estrangement bred by the ghetto's poverty has put a hard edge on every-

thing, turning the schools into prisons and the fenced-in, treeless cement grounds into "places for plotting." The adult members of the community "can't afford no trouble" and therefore "can't afford to make a human response." Before "all families turn [in]to cargo cults" and "all restraints gone," the children must be taught to keep "the vision vibrant" so that they, who someday will inherit the earth, will have a better future. To young Malaika, keenly observant of the conversation between Lacey and Jason, this means "everybody'll have warm clothes and we'll all trust each other and can stop at anybody's house for hot chocolate cause won't nobody be scared or selfish." A dispirited Lacey doubts whether such a future is possible, but bolstered by Jason's vision and the innocence of the children, she allows herself to hope.

The love and support of committed adults is also at issue in "A Girl's Story." The story's protagonist, Rae Ann, is torn between the guardianship of Dada Bibi—who leads African heritage workshops at the community center and relays the legends of the African queens who fought against slavery—and her grandmother M'Dear. M'Dear agrees with her friend Miz Gladys, who asserts, "I ain't nobody's African"; she is pleased to be "one hundred percent American and proud of it." Unaware of or unimpressed by young Rae Ann's admiration for the achievements of Harriet Tubman and other African American leaders, and without a clue as to the child's growing doubts about whether or not she should be proud to be American, M'Dear thoughtlessly disposes of the flyers Rae Ann brings home from the center.

Rae Ann is terrified at the onset of her first menses, which brings back memories of her mother, "The smell of death . . . her mother's sickroom years ago." Dada Bibi had recognized the child's blossoming into womanhood and had offered her love and support. But Rae Ann is too unaccustomed to love and affection to take advantage of the opportunity to talk to Dada

Bibi about the event—even though, too late, she wants to. The only discussion about sexual awakening Rae Ann had with M'Dear was her insensitive, crude injunction not to let boys "feel on your tits." It is not surprising, therefore, that M'Dear reacts to Rae Ann's reluctant confession that she is bleeding by assuming that her granddaughter had undergone a botched abortion. M'Dear threatens the child with, "Who's the boy? Tell me his name quick. And you better not lie," and, the most cruel of all, "You going be your mama all over again." Even when M'Dear finally correctly surmises that Rae Ann's menses have begun, she explains nothing, subverting the superficial solicitude of "Girl, why didn't you say so?" M'Dear goes out and later returns to thoughtlessly pitch "the bag [of sanitary belt and pads] onto the bed," following with the perfunctory remark, "Dinner be on in a minute."

As M'Dear beats a hasty retreat from the bedroom, Rae Ann is left with the bewildering conviction that she is being punished for something. Her heartbreaking "What's wrong with me . . . What have I done?" leaves the reader with the certainty that unless there are Other Mothers out there like Dada Bibi, or Lacey and Jason from "Broken Field Running," this rare and precious young life will remain at risk. As in "Broken Field Running," the older members of the community have failed their children, leaving them no inner resources with which to build a better vision of themselves and their future.

In "Witchbird" Honey, who is one of the witchbirds in the story, envisions herself as "a singer . . . an actress," but she feels "locked up inside, hostage," the feeling that she gets when she hears "that damn bird . . . caterwauling . . . in the woods, tearing up the bushes, splitting twigs with the high notes." Inspired by the songs of "ole Bessie . . . Ma Rainey, Trixie Smith, early Lena," she wants to write new songs about women waiting to be free from the friends "who trap you in their scenarios" and forget that "you ain't some bronze Barbie doll" or a "big fro murder-mouth" or the object of somebody's "mammy fantasies." Witchbird wants to sing their songs, songs about a woman standing "in an empty road . . . and the train not stopping," about women in the lock-ups and about mothers whose children grow up either too fast to escape the lynch mob and the posse or too slow "to take hold." These are the songs and the stories that "got to be sung, hummed, shouted, chanted, swung." Even though witchbird is not sure who is her audience or who to bring to life with these new songs, she says she is "here to transform what I can."

Honey's aspirations, however, are constantly thwarted by the demands others make on her as well as her own need to "absorb" and "transform" others' sorrow. Heywood, her "sometime piano player—sometime manager—mosttime friend," depends on her to take care of his discarded women, including Laney and Gayle. Heywood, Honey says, "mammyfies" her by counting on her to "wet-nurse his girls." All three women are Heywood's castoffs, whom he uses, entraps, and finally discards with his endless song and dance. With the support of a community of black sisters, Honey is able to see that Heywood "got me bagged somehow. Put me in a bag when I wasn't looking." In choosing to free herself from the witchbird that is Heywood, the reader is assured that Honey will go on to write and sing her new songs.

The last story in this collection, "Christmas Eve at Johnson's Drugs N Goods," is about a young black woman, the narrator Candy, who works at a black-owned drugstore. Working at the store on Christmas Eve, she keeps an anxious lookout for her estranged father, even while she knows that "his new family would be expecting him to spend the holidays with them." At first she admires the hip style of a couple of holiday shoppers, the cynical Ethel and a woman the narrator dubs "Fur Coat," who call attention to themselves and charm the clerks, fingering the merchandise and "having fun and all." They play to their audience, shrilly demanding to know "what kind of crooked shell game is you running here in this joint?" Candy observes that "they got plenty of style" and decides, "I wouldn't mind being like that when I am full-grown." But when Fur Coat makes a request of a fellow employee Candy respects, the young "dude in Drugs," to show them "the latest in rubberized fashions for men," her game suddenly does not sit well with the young woman, who can tell that "It's real, rather than play snooty." Fur Coat, with Ethel's encouragement, baits the young clerk with her crude sexual innuendos; but the young man gets the better of her and refuses to play the "chump." Candy changes her mind about Fur Coat, believing that "she's not discriminating with her stuff." Her Uncle Henry had told her that there were "different kinds of folks . . . when you boil it right down there's just nice and not nice." Fur Coat, the girl decides, although "dazzling," is not nice.

Christmas this year, the girl ultimately realizes, will involve just her and her sister and Uncle Henry and Aunt Harriet; her mother, a performer who "got her life to lead," was on the road again. She could maybe expect a phone call, with her mother asking if she's been "a good girl, it's been that long since she's taken a good look at me." Her father, too, "got a life to lead," and evidently not with her. Her father had told her once, "Got to make up your mind now what kind of woman you're going to be." But Candy, it seems, is on her own to decide this.

Although some critics have seen in this collection an excess of political ideology and verbal energy, Bambara effectively suggests in *The Sea Birds Are Still Alive* that the future lies in the present. It demands a new man, a new woman, whose good will and self-discipline will resist the worm of despair that, as in "The Organizer's Wife," menaces the garden of hope.

THE SALT EATERS

Published in 1980, Bambara's first novel, *The Salt Eaters,* is a rather daunting, at times difficult book, jammed with characters and details but nonetheless a powerful tale of the black inhabitants of Claybourne, Georgia. They endure the indignities and heartaches of small-town southern life while continuing to dedicate themselves to the ideals of the civil rights movement. Like the graceful deer who come to the salt lick for its healing properties, the characters, as well as the readers of this novel, which can be seen as a salt lick of another kind, seek healing from bitter suffering and painfully gained renewal. These folks are also the salt of the earth, Bambara suggests, the common, everyday people who bear the burden of the struggle to bring about change, usher in a new era. They struggle to survive the wounds aggravated by salty tears rubbed into the deep gashes in their souls. Besides, they say, "you never really know a person until you've eaten salt together."

Among the novel's myriad characters is Velma, the "elusive . . . the swift," the dedicated civil rights worker who runs the office; handles the payroll; keeps the books; supervises the office staff; writes proposals for seminars, conferences, trips; raises funds; and, in short, does the work of the eight people needed to replace her after she tries to commit suicide. *The Salt Eaters* is also Obie's story. Obie, Velma's husband, works in support of the movement and the people and their plans, works "to develop, to de-mystify, to build, to consolidate and escalate." He knows that Velma and, to some extent, he have allowed the cause to overwhelm both their vision and their marriage.

Another character is Sophie Heywood, a faith healer who knows but is about to further discover what it costs to "hang onto old pains" and that intimacy and love mean taking a chance. We also learn about Fred Holt, a bus driver who is being pressured into early retirement and who wonders what he has to show for forty years of hard work, and about Porter, who muses that "some asshole expert releases radioactive fumes in the air" just as "you're minding your business . . . paying your bills and trying to make a go of your marriage." Yet another character, Campbell, a local news reporter, struggles against the bigotry of the big-time news agencies. His "ability to discuss fission in terms of billiards and . . . couch principles of thermonuclear dynamics in the language of down-home Bible-quoting folks" has led him to uncover stories about a labor-management dispute at a local chemical plant, and about the environmental crisis posed by the plant's release into the air of fluorocarbons, as well as the existence of a vigilante group poised to exploit the crisis. He also knows the power plant's practices of hiking its rates to cover expenses and shutting off the water, gas, and electricity of residents who protest. No one knows better than Campbell about Claybourne's gradual transformation into "the back wards of the asylum."

John Leonard described *The Salt Eaters* as almost "incantation"; as a "poem-drunk, myth happy, mud-caked, jazz-ridden" text, it adeptly switches, in nonlinear narrative fashion, from folk legend to political statement. Throughout the novel's rambling, stream-of-consciousness narrative, in which point of view constantly shifts from character to character, some who appear only briefly, and in which the past drifts into the present, Velma seems to be the central focus, although at times she recedes into the background as a sort of everywoman of the Black Power movement. Velma, who has been "a borderguard all her life," is no longer able to live by the "relentless logic" that has heretofore sustained her. She has found herself in the hospital ward, desperately trying to become inviolate but rapidly turning into salt, instead of eating salt as an antidote for the snakebites that come to her in the form of women raped and children terrorized, or in the form of dissension, egotism, and exploitation of the women in the movement. Especially hurtful to Velma are the snakebites in the form of the hopeless despair of the slums.

All this, and its effects on the children, who are "burned, beaten, stabbed, stomped, starved, dropped, flung, dumped in boiling water," have left Velma with the desire to retreat. Minnie Ransom tries to pass on to Velma her mother's wisdom: "Doan letcha mouf gitcha in what ya backbone caint stand." She urges Velma to "forgive everyone" and in so doing, to free herself. But even Minnie falls into momentary despair, wondering "what is happening to the daughters of the yams?" The women of the community shoulder the work of the reform movement and the men "lollygag." Overwhelmed, the women "stick their head in the oven" and wind up in hospital wards. The movement and the black community is "at the crossroads."

While everyone wants to "feel good all the time," "you deal with what you're dealt"; "we're *supposed*" to grieve and to mourn; it is the human condition, Minnie reminds Velma. Even Sophie Heywood, who had known Velma as a child, "turning a warm eye on the child's triumphs, a glass eye on everything else, which was a lot," experiences a crisis of faith and turns her back on her at the moment Velma "has made her bed hard." "Real healing" will take more than a single revival meeting or the women circling the wagons without their men to help. The health that is everyone's right, Bambara argues, will take everyone working together to keep "the dream real" by eschewing black-on-black violence, avoiding negative and defeatest thinking, being "a player instead of a mooching miscreant." But, as everyone knows, "The most confounding labyrinth of all is a straight line."

As each character tries to "maintain an equilibrium" between "longing for clarity and the dread of finding too severe a challenge," the building shakes and the flood overflows the curbs. The ancestors are watching, for there is still work to be done. Each of these characters must "try and pull more closely together the two camps of adepts still wary of the other's way." Fearing for herself as well as for Velma, Sophie Heywood knows she had backed off from Velma out of her own fear, knowing that what had driven Velma to despair was the prospect of the effort that awaits her. Yet, under the steadying touch of Sophie's hands, Velma now is able to bear the thunder approaching in the distance and to rise "on steady legs" once again, like a phoenix from the ashes. Bambara's novel is a complex, at times convoluted, but always moving celebration of the indomitable spirit of American blacks. In a *Times Literary Supplement* review, Carol Rumens called *The Salt Eaters* "a hymn to individual courage."

DEEP SIGHTINGS AND RESCUE MISSIONS

Published posthumously in 1996, *Deep Sightings and Rescue Missions: Fiction, Essays, and Conversations* was edited by Toni Morrison. In the book's preface, Morrison writes of Bambara's craft as "woven, aware of its music," as an "implacable trajectory" of narrative, as a "heart cling," as "wisdom's clarity." She reminds us that Bambara would have answered her critics' objections that her fiction is overly political with "tears of laughter," perceiving no difference between "aesthetic obligation and the aesthetics of obligation." Morrison concludes that Bambara had "flawless pitch" and that her writing is "integrity embedded in the bone."

The first selection of *Deep Sightings and Rescue Missions,* "Going Critical," is a poignant fictionalized depiction of a mother and daughter struggling with illness and death. Clara is dying of cancer, the result of having been exposed to radiation as a media observer during a nuclear testing exercise in Utah. Briefings had assured the observers that there was no danger, "providing, so long as, on the condition that, and if." Any mention of the future gives both Clara and her daughter, Honey, pain. Yet Clara wants to talk with Honey of last things, about "not . . . abus[ing] [her] gifts," about budgeting for the future while the army drags out Clara's lawsuit, and about Clara's body "yearning to return to the earth—disoriented, detached and unobliged."

But Honey wants no talk of death, "deliberately allowing . . . cyclists, skaters to come between them" as they walk along the boardwalk on their outing to the seashore. Clara wants to tell her child to "try to push at least one life in the direction of resurrection," but Honey is angry, as Clara rightly suspects, that her mother is leaving her. While she suffers for her daughter's grief, Clara feels her child is "a magnet, drawing her back." As the dying woman takes leave of life and her beloved daughter, she realizes that she can no longer protect her child and "depend on tomorrow for what went undone today." But that is "the way of things," Bambara makes clear: that the elders precede their children in death.

"Madame Bai and the Taking of Stone Mountain" is a precursor to Bambara's later work, what Morrison calls "her magnum opus," *Those Bones Are Not My Child.* The story told here, central to Bambara's postcolonial theme, describes Atlanta during a time in the early 1980s when black children were victims of a serial killer, as "hunched up . . . shivery and intense." Mustafa and Tram, like the black community in Atlanta, are fugitives from the terror of the colonizers. Mustafa is a young Jordanian poet who was tortured by Israeli soldiers; Tram is Vietnamese and was tortured by Diem's secret police. Now they, like Atlanta's inner-city blacks, face white skinheads, cops, FBI investigators who make the parents of the victims suspects in the crimes, and white supremacist publications that superimpose faces of minorities on bodies of apes. "The sagelike wonder" Madame Bai, a Korean, arrives in Atlanta to teach her self-defense system, designed especially for women, in a series of workshops. The narrator of the story, Tram and Mustafa's friend and English tutor, attends the workshop with her two students. During this time, one man is charged with two counts of murder in the serial killing case and "headlines around the country announce the monster's been nabbed." The community wants to forget about Atlanta's troubles: "amnesia drifts in like fog to blanket the city." In this context, Madame Bai, who teaches her disciples to "be still" and "silence the relentless chatter inside in favor of that small-voiced guide," poses a question to the narrator: "Stone Mountain . . . What is it for?" The narrator struggles with the question, a riddle that she finally answers with the words "Stone Mountain is for taking," having come to the knowledge that race hatred, symbolized by the mountain, a monument to the Confederacy, serves the purpose of presenting a challenge to overcome. To overcome it, one must defend oneself, as well as aggressively charge the mountain, as Mustafa and Tram use their martial arts training to defeat the street gangs who would molest them. By introducing into the community of black Atlanta these Asian survivors of discrimination and brutality, Bambara suggests that American race discrimination, as perpetuated by the Atlanta and federal authorities, is just another form of colonial oppression. The struggle to overcome is international and, once again, can be accomplished through the cooperation of brothers and sisters worldwide.

"Baby's Breath" features a conversation between a grown man, Louis, and his mother, and as such seems to point out the importance of a "straight-up" mother in a black man's life, a mother who will tell it like it is. Louis laments the fact that he has been unlucky in love, that his women keep "killing his babies." At the moment of the conception of his and his now ex-girlfriend Norma's baby, he felt that "something opened up to him and he was new all through and knew what he wanted to do, to be." Louis has been looking for something "to give some value to how he spent his life," perhaps counting on a child of his own to motivate him, but it is clear that he has not the wherewithal to become self-motivated.

Louis's mother had in the past "always assured him he was special," protected him from the "bumps and jolts of the world," favoring him over his brother Bobby, who had been "unwanted." But her opinion of him is changing, Louis realizes, and he must ask himself, "Had he missed a beat somewhere?" His mother bluntly reminds Louis that he has "no degree, no place of [his] own, no bank account, no prospects even of a good job." At twenty-four, he is "too damn old to be a child prodigy." His mother suggests that the sacrifices she made on Louis's behalf have not been worth it, that he squandered the opportunities she provided for him by working "like a slave." While Louis is clearly shocked by his mother's words, it is not clear that they will have the effect of moving him beyond his feelings of victimization, his passivity and dependence. Bambara's story is an admonition both to black males to take responsibility for their own lives and to mothers to stop coddling their children and allow their sons to become men.

"The War of the Wall" describes the undeclared war between an inner-city community and a lone reformer, impassioned by her mission but not, apparently, by the people her mission serves. When the reformer, an artist, begins to paint a mural on the outside wall of the community barbershop, the narrator and her cousin, Lou, are outraged. These children are aware of the wall as a symbol, and they object to anyone, especially an outsider, interfering with that symbol: "It was our wall," the narrator asserts.

The wall has served the neighborhood as a monument to the community's struggle during integration. It has been a place where the children played handball and pop fly, and it has served as a witness to police brutality and racial profiling. It is also a makeshift Vietnam War memorial, where Lou chiseled the name of a local boy who did not come home from the war. Oblivious to everything but her inspiration, "the painter lady" takes no notice of the people or their stories as recorded by the wall. As the child narrator sees it, she has destroyed the "evidence" of the community's suffering at the hands of its oppressors by painting over the wall, and has spurned the community's hospitality, first by refusing a meal cooked by one of the local women, and then by questioning the narrator's mother about the food served in her restaurant.

But when the mural is completed, the locals gather to view, in a festive atmosphere, the "painter lady's" work. By the end of the story the people appear to have relinquished their wall as a monument to their pain and now welcome it, and the creation that now adorns it, as a celebration of themselves. The old wall, evidence of a community's suffering, has been transformed into a new monument to pride, tolerance, and understanding.

The children of "Ice" hold the neighborhood elders responsible when a litter of stray puppies freezes to death during an ice storm while the children are at school. Due to a variety of circumstances, including hard economic times, most adults are at home when the storm hits and the puppies are left to die. What the children do not seem to fully appreciate is that their elders are on the verge of freezing to death too; for they are reduced to burning in the fireplace "anything that . . . will give heat," including, eventually, the narrator's dollhouse. Preoccupied with their attempts to keep their own families warm, the adults fail to notice the neighborhood dog and her puppies shivering in the cold.

Ironically, the children are attuned to the suffering of young, cute, and cuddly animals but lack compassion for Mrs. Blue, "the crazy old lady calling us from her house on the hill at the corner." Because she is old and impoverished, they fear Mrs. Blue, who stands in the window "looking like some Halloween thing." Only one of the children, Marcy, makes the connection between the puppies and the old woman: "She could starve to death or freeze right there in the window and nobody would go and see about her." But because of her fear, the narrator refuses to accompany Marcy to check on the old woman. Later, while reflecting on the fate of the puppies in the context of the struggle of her ancestors and of the black community, in "putting together the story of the storm" that she hopes to one day tell her own children, the young narrator must acknowledge that "there's a hole in my story . . . a hole I will fall right through in the telling." In considering her future children's possible response to her tale, she says to herself, "Suppose they ask, 'But, Mommy, didn't you go and see about the old lady?'" She does not want her children to wonder why she didn't do anything to help someone in need, as she herself was forced to confront her elders on why no one came to the aid of the helpless puppies. Bambara's story is a poignant description of a child's developing moral consciousness; it is also a plea for community support and solidarity so that no one is left out in the cold.

The title character in "Luther on Sweet Auburn" is an irresponsible, needy charmer who does not seem to understand that the 1960s are over and that he is now in his late thirties and is still expecting handouts from those who "look after their own." Neither is he aware that the narrator of the story, "Miz Nap," no longer does social work; in other words, like Louis's mother in "Baby's Breath," she is no longer interested in responding to his pleas for help and protests of victimization. Like "Baby's Breath," this story is a statement on Bambara's part that black males must mature from boys to men.

The second half of *Deep Sightings and Rescue Missions* features "essays and conversations," the first of which, in Morrison's arrangement, is "Reading the Signs, Empowering the Eye." In this essay Bambara examines the black independent film movement, focusing primarily on Julie Dash's 1991 film *Daughters of the Dust,* and its challenge to both the "imperialism as entertainment" approach of Hollywood in such films as *The African Queen,* and the images of American blacks propagated by the moneymaking "Blaxpo" films of the 1970s, including Melvin Van Peebles' *Sweet Sweetback's Baadasss Song* and Gordon Parks Sr.'s *Shaft.* In the latter films, according to Bambara, cultural revolution is equated with criminality, and "militants sell dope and women." According to this approach, the "system" is invincible, and "the only triumph possible is in a throw-down" with minor Mafia figures and crooked cops. In these films, black neighborhoods are portrayed as occupied territory, black families are subject to liberation by whites, and women's sexuality is yoked to capitalistic exploitation. It is a discourse that "dichotomizes culture and politics" and defines resistance as male led.

Rather than depicting blacks from a black perspective, the approach to Africa taken by the classic Hollywood film impressed in the minds of millions, according to Bambara, the image of "the European as schoolmarm-adventuress-mercenary-disguised-as-missionary," who "helps sell the conquest of Africa as a heroic adventure." Bambara objects to the stereotypical portrayals of such actresses as Katharine Hepburn, "the White star venturing into Tarzan's heart of darkness" wearing "Banana Republic colonial-nostalgia clothing." She further objects to the predatory, voyeuristic camera, in which space is "dominated by the hero" and the spectator's eye is made to view anyone else in the hierarchy of race, class, gender, or caste as "background."

In films of the dominating cinema, Bambara argues, social injustice and supremacist doctrines and policies are minimized as personal conflicts resolved not by cultural revolution but by shootouts, savvy cops, and fistfights. This subverts the potential of cinema, which becomes "industrialized," tamed. The humanist is thus estranged, and such qualities as blackness, dark skin, and femaleness become dreadful, sinful, evil.

Dash's *Daughters of the Dust* epitomizes the independent black filmmaker's accountability and commitment to the community rather than to a film industry that exploits, makes trivial, and renders black people invisible. Here, the community rather than the classroom is seen as the appropriate training ground for filmmakers who seek to reconstruct cultural memory rather than imitate white models. Such films make world cultures accessible to cinema audiences. Dash, as well as others Bambara identifies, reconsiders conventional film techniques and themes to develop a "film language" that focuses on cultural particularity and black ideas. In an effort to challenge an "imperialist" system that promotes a consumerist ethic, these films promote women and black history and folklore.

According to Bambara, Dash's work highlights the impact of sexist representations on women's efforts to be self-validating. Dash's films offer an alternative to the connection between sexism and racism. In her work, space is shared, rather than dominated; the spiritual and the religious community, fostered by a sense of family, combats the threat of lynch-mob violence. In this ethos of cultural resistance, family members are not victims accountable to their employers but powerful sources of social change, whose responsibility it is to acknowledge the legacy of their ancestors. Communalism as embodied by the past, the present, and the future resists the cultural amnesia of assimilation, resists the seduction of technique as practiced by conventional films, and promotes the autonomy of the individual. Independent black cinema is seen as a source of emancipation, which is fostered by African American female mentors and artists.

In "Language and the Writer," Bambara continues her discussion of film and poses the question, "What role can, should, or must the film practitioner . . . play in producing a desirable vision of the future?" The challenge lies in the fact that, according to Bambara, the "tools of the trade" and the global screen have been "colonized," and "the audience—readers and viewers—is in bondage to an industry." In Bambara's view, film conventions of editing, narrative structure, genre development, spatial use, and acting styles are based on "a history of imperialism and violence." A writer's worth is determined by how powerful his or her country of origin is. However, a new alternative cinema composed of African Americans, Native Americans, American Latinos, American Asians, and the peoples of the Pacific Rim explores the potential of cinema for social transformation. These independent screenwriters resist conventional film's appropriation of cultural memory, music, language, style and posture, and space. Bambara argues that in Hollywood, film space is "hidden": it utilizes tight space and the reaction shot; the land becomes turf, real estate. It is appropriated by the elite or the outsider.

The essay from which the book's title is drawn, "Deep Sight and Rescue Missions," is about cultural assimilation. Here Bambara writes that she is "sure of only four things." The first is that race relations continue to be marked by ambivalence, that is, the tension between integrationists and nationalists still prevails. Second, there is still a lack of respect for cultural and racial differences in the United States. Whites are still seen as "major" and people of color as "minorities." Third, the pressure to assimilate, to forget one's cultural heritage, is still great. Lastly, it is still necessary to counter propaganda and programming that results in a widening of the gap between the black working and middle classes.

Taking Philadelphia as an example, Bambara remonstrates against economic practices that result in delayed paychecks for municipal workers and protests what she sees as the "hijacking" of neighborhoods by developers. She condemns FBI harassment of black and Latino task forces that uncover corruption at financial institutions. Bambara denounces social services cutbacks and protests black flight to the suburbs, which she refers to as "bleached-out respectability." She hails Paule Marshall's 1983 novel *Praisesong for the Widow* as promoting "a refamiliarization with blackness" and compares it to Dash's *Daughters of the Dust,* which urges the protagonist to "resist amnesia," even as the viewer is liberated from imperialism.

"Invisibility" of the kind Ralph Ellison wrote about in *Invisible Man* is not easy for young blacks to understand, Bambara argues, because blacks are active participants in the entertainment and sports industries, which prevent the young black generation from perceiving what she defines as three types of alienation: from the African past, from U.S. economic and political power, and from oneself as a participant in history. Bambara calls for "a repositioning" of people of color "closer to the center of the national narrative." This must involve a reexamination of such ideas as "identity, belonging, community." She wants a reassessment of traditional dualisms (such as black/white), which she sees as essentially a bribe that keeps Asians, "Amero-Africans," Native Americans, and Chicanos invisible as "indigenous" or "former slaves." This "Two-Worlds obsession," she asserts, characterizes the critical approach to the work of Maxine Hong Kingston, Leslie Marmon Silko, and other women writers of color, "reducing complex narrative dramas . . .

to a formula that keeps White World as a prominent/given/eternal factor in the discussion."

Bambara finds disturbing the fact that the dominant media are controlled by white corporations and thus are in no position to challenge what she sees as the following destructive binaries: "We are ordained/You are damned"; "We make history/You make dinner"; "We speak/You listen"; "We are rational/You are superstitious, childlike (as in minor)"; "We are truly human/You are grotesques . . . dolls, vixens, gorillas, chicks, kittens, utensils."

The rest of the essay assesses what Bambara sees as "the complex of longing, irony, and insistence" that describes blacks' "angular" relationship to America. Some blacks, she says, feel that "the less the children know, the easier it'll be for them to fit in and make their way." Other blacks want the children to learn about black history. During the McCarthy era, blacks were seen as subversive; according to the Smith Act trials, independent thought threatened "national security." After the 1948 presidential election, African Americans were urged to "play ward politics for local spoils" and forget larger issues of conscience, or they were urged to bloc vote with the National Association for the Advancement of Colored People (NAACP), which was backing Henry Wallace rather than working to establish an independent black national party. This, she maintains, "keeps us locked into other peoples' tournaments."

Gradually, black debate came down to the question of creating a new society, either in the United States or elsewhere, or investing time, energy, money, and genius in trying to become first-class citizens in a "barbarous" country in which blacks were urged to prove their loyalty by fighting in World War II. Yet, in "the gravest forms of White sight," Bambara argues, the State Department kept secret black participation in the war. In conclusion, Bambara sees four basic responses to blacks' position in the United States: accommodation ("please-White-folks-include-us-in works . . . I speak good English and stay off the streets"); opportunism ("capitaliz[ing] on the miserable and gullible"); denial ("I-have-never-experienced-prejudice-in-the-all-White-school-and-church-I-attend") and flight ("what the hell, the point was to beat Whitey at his own game"); and resistance in the form of reading black books that challenge a white version of reality, activism, involvement, scholarship and creative enterprises.

"School Daze," Bambara's discussion of Spike Lee's film of that title, describes the work as a "seriocomic look at caste, class, and gender contradictions" on a southern black college campus. She finds impressive the film's opening soundtrack, which evokes the Middle Passage, the course of the Atlantic slave trade, and "presents a chronicle of a diasporized people's effort to make a home in the 'new world.'" The history of the fictitious Mission College reminds the viewer of the black struggle to achieve literacy and autonomy. She acknowledges that the film, which she calls a pageant, or a spectacle of theatrically staged moments, is intended as "a wake-up call . . . for African folk asleep in the West." Yet, in Bambara's view, because it is a musical it fails to critically examine the "colorist, elitist, sexist, and heterosexist behaviors" that characterize the film. She regards the participation of Spike Lee's character Half Pint in a gang-rape fraternity-initiation ritual as a form of what she calls "gender coercion," as well as a deplorable expression of misogyny. She decries the film's gay-hating sensibility and sees as divisive the black characters' own "colorphobia." She points to alternatives, Marlon Riggs's 1989 film *Tongues Untied*, which challenges the attempt by blacks to exclude gays from their own radical history, and Isaac Julien's *Looking for Langston*, which speaks of gay artists in Britain during the period of the Harlem Renaissance. She also refers her readers to Ayoka Chenzira's short film *Hairpiece: A Film for*

Nappy-Headed People, Julie Dash's *Illusions,* Shu Lea Cheang's *Color Schemes,* and Sharon Alile Larkin's *A Different Drummer.* She concedes that the three films, *School Daze, Tongues Untied,* and *Looking for Langston,* perform an important service in depicting identity as negotiable. Moreover, she attributes Lee's commercial success with helping create a receptive climate for black filmmakers in Hollywood.

Nonetheless, Bambara is disappointed in *School Daze*'s use of the musical genre, which she argues co-ops conventional cinema's appeal to "voyeurism, fetishism, spectacle, mystifying notions of social relations." The pro-racist "pathology" of color is left unexplored, as is Half Pint's willingness to abandon his working-class origins and submit to humiliation and corruption in realizing his middle-class ambitions. The film makes no effort to reexamine male "power, prestige, and prerogative" and internalizes what Bambara refers to as "the Euro-American standard of height, weight, and aggression" in the film's socialization of the male to exploit and degrade women, who are seen as narcissistic, masochistic, and hysterical.

In "How She Came By Her Name: An Interview with Louis Massiah," Bambara emphasizes the importance of naming oneself, for in so doing one constructs for oneself a self. She refers us to Maya Angelou and Toni Morrison, both of whom changed their names, and to Audre Lorde, who changed the spelling of her first and last names. Also in this interview, Bambara speaks of childhood influences, her social and political activism, her writings and creative life, her international travels, motherhood, and illness.

The last entry in *Deep Sightings and Rescue Missions,* "The Education of a Storyteller," recalls her wise grandmother ("who was in fact no kin to me, but we liked each other") and her mother, both of whom encouraged her to "fly." She recounts her grandmother's telling question, when, as a young girl, Bambara would

pretend she was unintelligent: "What are you pretending not to know today, Sweetheart?"

THOSE BONES ARE NOT MY CHILD

Bambara spent the last twelve years of her life researching and writing *Those Bones Are Not My Child* (1999), a fact-based novel about a serial murder case in which forty children, mostly black boys younger than age fifteen, were abducted and murdered in Atlanta. Incomplete at the time of her death, the manuscript was edited for publication by Toni Morrison. The novel evokes the cultural climate of the United States from the late 1970s through the late 1980s, when the case finally made headlines coast to coast. The novel is based on a wealth of investigative material, including journal entries, newspaper clippings, bulletins, leaflets, rally flyers, and memorial programs. It is set against the background of the Iranian hostage crisis and makes reference to the murders of Dr. Martin Luther King Jr. and Vernon Jordan, the National Urban League head who was shot to death in Fort Wayne, Indiana, in 1980; the 1983 U.S. invasion of Grenada; CIA involvement in Jamaica and South America; the activities of the Ku Klux Klan; the 1963 Birmingham, Alabama, church bombing; and the Vietnam War; as well as, among other sources, a March 17, 1978, memorandum issued by the National Security Council, identifying ways to "keep African people of the Americas separated from African people on the continent." Toni Morrison is quoted on the book's flap copy as pointing out that the novel reveals the inner politics and conflicts of a major city of the New South.

Bambara's fictional device is the Spencer family, whose twelve-year-old son, Sonny, is missing. His mother, Marzala ("Zala"), and her estranged husband, Spence, a veteran of the Vietnam War, join STOP, the Committee to Stop Children's Murders, which was organized by Atlanta parents dissatisfied with the efforts of city and federal authorities to solve the child murders case. Suspecting a coverup, Bambara, through Zala, Spence, and a host of other characters, begins to identify a pattern tying together city corruption, Klan connections, clandestine federal activities, and a child pornography ring. Atlanta blacks feel that the Atlanta Metropolitan Emergency Task Force, formed in 1980 to investigate the cases involving missing and murdered children, dismisses eyewitness accounts, lets suspects go, refuses to examine two-thirds of the cases, ignores parents' opinions, and rejects links noted by STOP members and investigators. Bambara charges the task force with making arrests without sufficient evidence. STOP accuses the task force of dragging its heels on the case and practicing race and class discrimination in an effort to protect Atlanta's image as a progressive city, host to the upcoming Atlanta Trade Convention.

Independent community investigators identify several patterns of murders: Klan hate killings, cult/ritual murders, child-porn thrill killings, drug-vengeance killings, and commando/mercenary training killings. In addition to Klan and skinhead thugs, possible killers are racist white cops who patrol black neighborhoods, cultists, whites avenging the murder of Dewey Baugus, beaten to death in the spring of 1979, allegedly by black youth. Also suspected are plantation kidnappers of slave labor and white mercenaries training death squads for future overseas and domestic wars, strengthened due to the Reagan administration's support of covert right-wing insurgents. Also suspected are those involved in drug traffic wars. STOP accuses the FBI of illegal break-ins, surveillance, and wire taps.

Bambara further accuses the Atlanta authorities and media of sandwiching stories of child killings between back-page ads; she points out that the Missing Persons emergency phone number was unstaffed on weekends and that the police department offered no support staff for relatives of the missing children. Indeed, the police assumed that the missing children were runaways or runners for drug lords. The police even question whether the children are illegitimate and assume that the black working mother needs a social worker to help straighten out her life. The newly elected black mayor, Maynard Jackson, is under pressure not to replace Atlanta police chief John Inman, who instituted what Bambara calls a "reign of terror" against blacks.

Bambara wishes to remind the reader that Atlanta, the "Black Mecca of the South," was "not built from slavery, convict labor, red-light districts, or legerdemain with the public coffers, but from hard work and clean living." "A family of five," she tells her readers, may have four jobs between them, "with two jobs apiece, but look out if one library book was overdue." Of Atlanta, where Bambara was living while she researched this novel, there is the "White Atlanta of the promotional brochures" and the poorer black Atlanta. Creating the sense of Atlanta as occupied territory, Bambara describes the unidentified officials who flood into the city as citizen groups speculate what government agency they issue from. As the media institutes a whiteout of stories involving cross burnings, firebombings, snipings, racist graffiti, police riots, and ambushes of biracial couples, Bambara wonders whether a race war has been declared. Black residents are largely kept in the dark about the investigation. Municipal authorities seem to fear that news of the serial murders will panic the public and embarrass the police. A local judge notes the cooperation between the intelligence community and the attorney general and admits to Spence, "We'll always be . . . losing this country, because we do not wish to know." Indeed, a tragedy of such magnitude as the Atlanta missing and murdered children gives the lie to the American dream of "invulnerability, progress, health, and superiority."

In the mind of FBI director William Webster, the killings of black children might indicate a "preference for," rather than a prejudice against, blacks; and a representative of Freedom Focus proposes to "help" blacks by studying black teen pregnancies. Bambara seeks to expose common stereotypes of blacks as "emotional people" who "don't respond to facts, research statistics." She objects to the focus on Mayor Maynard Jackson, rather than Atlanta's children, as the victim of this tragedy.

Bambara sees Wayne Williams, the man charged with several of the child murders, as a scapegoat who happened to be in the wrong place at the wrong time. Even though no guilt was established, safety precautions in the community and the investigation itself were curtailed as a result of Williams' arrest. However, in the summer of 1986, the Williams family attorney, aided by a legal team including William Kunstler, Alan Dershowitz, and Bobby Lee Cook, demanded that Williams's conviction be overturned on the grounds that the authorities had withheld evidence. By the fall of 1986, *Spin* magazine began publishing a series that reviewed the case in the light of this new evidence. Bambara asks whether Williams would have been arrested at all if the evidence had not been suppressed.

Spence, who often speaks as the voice of Bambara, criticizes both black and white radicals as doing little more than reacting to the authorities' agenda. Instead, they appealed to the same fear and hatred as the "enemy" practiced against them, by provoking the authorities and thus keeping their own leadership in a bad light, and then appointing themselves as saviors of the people. The same parents who planned to sue the local, state, and federal authorities for obstruction of justice also wanted to petition the feds to reexamine the case. "Gossip was some people's idea of citizens in action," and polls were supposed to be as good as public debate. Black parents and citizens, Bambara writes, have allowed themselves to be manipulated by labels like "para-noids" and "agitators." They do not demand answers from those they pay to run the city. Yet, the truth "leaks out, because . . . we by nature want to be up front."

Selected Bibliography

WORKS OF TONI CADE BAMBARA

BOOKS
Gorilla, My Love. New York: Random House, 1972.
The Sea Birds Are Still Alive: Stories. New York: Random House, 1977.
The Salt Eaters. New York: Random House, 1980.
If Blessing Comes. New York: Random House, 1987.
Deep Sightings and Rescue Missions: Fiction, Essays, and Conversations. Edited and with a preface by Toni Morrison. New York: Pantheon, 1996.
Those Bones Are Not My Child. Edited by Toni Morrison. New York: Pantheon, 1999.

EDITED WORKS
The Black Woman: An Anthology. New York: New American Library, 1970.
Tales and Stories for Black Folks. Garden City, N.Y.: Zenith Books, 1971.
Southern Black Utterances Today. With Leah Wise. Durham, N.C.: Institute for Southern Studies, 1975.

SCREENPLAYS
Zora. Produced by WGBH-TV, Boston, 1971.
The Johnson Girls. Produced by National Educational Television, 1972.
Transactions. Produced by School of Social Work, Atlanta University, 1979.
The Long Night. Produced by American Broadcasting Co., 1981.
Epitaph for Willie. Produced by K. Heran Productions, 1982.
Tar Baby. Produced by Sanger-Brooks Film Productions, 1984.

Raymond's Run. Produced by Public Broadcasting System, 1985.

The Bombing of Osage Avenue. Produced by WHYY-TV, Philadelphia, Pa., 1986.

Cecil. B. Moore: Master Tactician of Direct Action. Produced by WHYY-TV, Philadelphia, Pa., 1987.

W. E. B. Du Bois: A Biography in Four Voices. Produced by Public Broadcasting System, 1997.

CONTRIBUTIONS

"Black Theater." In *Black Expression: Essays by and about Black Americans in the Creative Arts.* Edited by Addison Gayle Jr. New York: Weybright and Talley, 1969. Pp. 134–143.

"Written After Hearing Ellington in Concert, July 1961." In *Black and White in American Culture: An Anthology from the Massachusetts Review.* Edited by Jules Chametsky and Sidney Kaplan. Amherst: University of Massachusetts Press, 1970.

"What It Is I Think I'm Doing Anyhow." In *The Writer on Her Work.* Edited by Janet Sternburg. New York: Norton, 1980.

"Beauty Is Just Care . . . Like Ugly Is Carelessness" and "Thinking About My Mother." In *On Essays: A Reader for Writers.* Edited by Paul H. Connolly. New York: Harper, 1981.

"Medicine Man." In *Women Working: An Anthology of Stories and Poems.* Edited by Nancy Hoffman and Florence Howe. Old Wesbury, N.Y.: Feminist Press, 1982.

"Salvation Is the Issue." In *Black Women Writers (1950–1980): A Critical Evaluation.* Edited by Mari Evans. Garden City, N.Y.: Anchor Press/Doubleday, 1984. Pp. 41–71.

CRITICAL AND BIOGRAPHICAL STUDIES

Guy-Sheftall, Beverly. "Commitment: Toni Cade Bambara Speaks." In *Sturdy Black Bridges: Visions of Black Women in Literature.* Edited by Roseann P. Bell, Bettye J. Parker, and Beverly Guy-Sheftall. Garden City, N.Y.: Anchor Press/Doubleday, 1979.

Hargrove. Nancy D. "Youth in Toni Cade Bambara's *Gorilla, My Love.*" In *Women Writers of the Contemporary South.* Edited by Peggy Whitman Prenshaw. Jackson: University Press of Mississippi, 1984.

Korb, Rena. "Dialect and Story-Telling in 'Blues Ain't No Mockin Bird.'" *Short Stories for Students: Presenting Analysis, Context, and Criticism on Commonly Studied Short Stories.* Edited by Kathleen Wilson. Detroit: Gale, 1997.

Leonard, John. Review of *The Salt Eaters. New York Times,* April 4, 1980, p. C23.

Lyles, Lois F. "Time, Motion, Sound, and Fury in *The Sea Birds Are Still Alive.*" *CLA Journal* 36, no. 2:134–144 (December 1992).

Mazurkiewicz, Margaret. "Toni Cade Bambara: Overview." In *Reference Guide to American Literature,* 3d ed. Edited by Jim Kamp. Detroit: St. James Press, 1994.

Rumens, Carol. Review of *The Salt Eaters. Times Literary Supplement,* June 18, 1982, p. 676.

Vertreace, Martha M. "The Dance of Character and Community." In *American Women Writing Fiction: Memory, Identity, Family, Space.* Edited by Mickey Pearlman. Lexington, Ky.: University of Kentucky, 1989.

Ya Salaam, Kalamu. "Searching for the Mother Tongue: An Interview." *First World* 2, no. 4: 48–52 (1980).

INTERVIEW

Tate, Claudia. "A Conversation with Toni Cade Bambara." In her *Black Women Writers at Work.* Washington, D.C.: Howard University Press, 1984; New York: Continuum, 1989.

—BARBARA C. SOLARO

Frederick Barthelme

1943–

ONE ANSWER TO the question "What's the story, exactly?" in Frederick Barthelme's prose is Del's response to his girlfriend, Jen, in Barthelme's novel *The Brothers* (1993). "There isn't any story," Del states. "It's not the story. . . . It's just this breathtaking world, that's the point. It's like the story's not important—what's important is the way the world looks. That's what makes you feel the stuff. That's what puts you there." The "breathtaking world" that Barthelme creates consists of strip malls, ATM machines, and Tostitos, a world in which characters read *TV Weekly* and dream of Choco-Mints before heading for a drive along a familiar path that leads nowhere in particular. The dream vacation of a Barthelme character might consist of a week spent waking up to a Kool cigarette and a half-eaten box of Hostess donuts, followed by an excursion to the mall, where the Levi's jacket is a size too small. Then it is off to Kmart, where an ex, or soon-to-be ex, appears. The afternoon begins with a quick order at the KFC drive-through and ends in the always vacant motel, where the vacationer falls asleep watching an infomercial after a sexual encounter, only to awaken to discover that he is alone and the sock drawer has been rearranged.

Although Frederick Barthelme has many artistic interests, he is best known as a fiction writer. He has found success as a novelist and as a short-story writer. Barthelme was born on October 10, 1943, in Houston, Texas, the fourth of five children of Donald Barthelme, a successful architect and professor, and Helen Barthelme (née Bechtold), a teacher. His siblings include a sister, Joan, and three brothers, Donald, Steven, and Peter. The oldest of the children, Donald, became a well-known writer before his death in 1989; Peter and Steven are also writers. Barthelme attended Tulane University from 1961 to 1962 and the University of Houston from 1962 to 1967. During 1965–1966, he was a student at the Museum of Fine Arts in Houston, where he studied to be a painter. After completing his undergraduate degree, he performed various artistic jobs, such as drafting architectural plans, installing exhibits, and assisting the director of the Kornblee Gallery in New York City and writing at several advertising firms in Houston.

In the late 1960s and early 1970s, Barthelme's artwork was presented at many galleries across the nation, including the Louisiana Gallery in Houston, the Museum of Normal Art and the Museum of Modern Art in New York City, and the Seattle Art Museum in Washington State. In the early 1970s Barthelme shifted his attention from the visual arts and began to pursue a writing career. His brother Donald, a well-known writer, was commissioned to write a book in which literary and visual art appeared together. Donald turned down the commission and asked Frederick if he would be interested in working on the project. The result was Frederick's first book, *Rangoon* (1970), a collection of anecdotes, stories, and illustrations. Soon after, he produced *War and War* (1971), which is similar in format to the cut-and-paste style of *Rangoon*. Barthelme has said that these first two projects say more than anything else about him and that time in his life. When "Pool Lights," his first publication in *The New Yorker*, appeared in 1981, *War and War* and *Rangoon* faded to the background of Barthelme's career. Soon after

"Pool Lights," Barthelme wrote and published "Shopgirls." It was during this time that he found his own voice, separating his work from the style of his brother by focusing not on the extraordinary but on the ordinary objects and daily routines of our lives. In 1977 he received a master's degree from Johns Hopkins University and began teaching at the University of Southern Mississippi.

MINIMALISM

Many writers who emerged at the time Barthelme began to publish his works are considered minimalist writers. Some of the key figures of this style of writing include Raymond Carver, Ann Beattie, Bobbie Ann Mason, Mary Robison, and Tobias Wolff. Minimalism is a writing technique defined by a sparse, terse style, in which much of the action occurs beneath the surface of the plot. The fiction is character or image driven, with plots that defy summary and narratives that are open-ended. These works frequently are written in the present tense, from the first-person and sometimes from the second-person points of view. Often, the subject matter consists of ordinary incidents, described using realistic details. Sometimes, the actions of the characters become hyperreal, magnifying mundane incidents or actions. "Less is more" is the credo of minimalist artists. The opening sentences of Barthelme's short stories define them as minimalist. Examples include "So I pass this woman in the hall" ("Restraint," *Chroma,* 1987); "Harry Lang's company Chevrolet breaks down on the highway fifteen miles outside of Dallas" ("Trip," *Moon Deluxe,* 1983); "Sally meets me in the driveway" ("Fish," *Moon Deluxe*); "My sister's husband Byron called and asked how I would like it if he stayed a couple days at our place" ("Sis," *Chroma*); and "Each summer I teach a course in BASIC at the junior college" ("Pupil," *Chroma*).

Representative of the minimalist technique, many of Barthelme's stories are told from the second-person point of view as open-ended narratives. In second-person narrative the author uses "you" as the point of view. Although the "you" is internal to the story, this point of view gives the reader the sense that the implied author is talking directly to him or her. Barthelme uses the second person in such stories as "Shopgirls," "Moon Deluxe," "Pool Lights," and "Safeway" (*Moon Deluxe*); "Trick Scenery" and "Aluminum House" (*Chroma*); and "Harmonic" (*The Law of Averages,* 2000).

Many of Barthelme's second-person stories involve some sort of voyeurism, an act that almost parallels the narrative technique itself. In these stories, readers seem to watch the "you" in action, almost participating in the action with the protagonist/narrator. "Shopgirls" concerns a man's obsession with stalking young female salesclerks. One of the young women confronts him, and she and two other women from the department store take him to lunch. He goes to one of their apartments, only to have idle conversation. At the end of the story, he buys a spatula from a young girl at another department store, suggesting that he is either breaking his habit or returning to it. Similarly, in "Moon Deluxe," after the protagonist stares at a woman while stuck in traffic, he glares at another woman in a drugstore but is unable to act on his impulse to talk to her. The protagonist walks his neighbor's friend home and discovers that she is a lesbian. Her lover is the woman he saw in traffic at the beginning of the story. The protagonist concludes, "You wonder what it would be like . . . to be part of their routine." Like the main character of "Shopgirls," however, he is unable to take any action except gazing at the women; his means of engaging with women is to live vicariously by gazing at them.

"Pool Lights" describes a man who, from the window of his apartment, watches his fellow tenants at the pool. He becomes acquainted with

Dolores, one of the women he has been observing, but, similarly to the men in "Shopgirls" and "Moon Deluxe," he does not succeed in developing a meaningful relationship with her. Rather than becoming better acquainted with Dolores, he returns to his voyeuristic habit. "Safeway" continues this pattern: a man follows a woman in a grocery store, she approaches him in the parking lot, and they walk to a coffeehouse. Although she says that she will drive to his apartment, he gives her a made-up apartment number. The open-ended narrative invites readers to consider that the narrator fears that she may come over and for this reason gives her a fictitious address. Another feasible interpretation is that the narrator knows that she has no intention of coming over, so he gives her the wrong apartment number to maintain his dignity. In either case, the main character has chosen the "safe way" out of a potential relationship by ensuring that the woman will not come to his house.

In some of these voyeuristic stories written from the second-person point of view, subtle references are made to looking and watching. In "Shopgirls" one of the young women the man watches in the department store tells him that the saleswomen must "learn how to look," explaining that the management requires them to dress and groom professionally. Similarly, in "Moon Deluxe," when the main character and the woman he has been watching leave the store, she asks, "Who's watching the store?" In both instances, the characters' comments also symbolically refer to the voyeurism in the stories.

In *Double Down* (2000), the memoir Barthelme wrote with his brother Steven, the second person is used frequently, especially when the authors try to explain the psychology of gambling addiction. Other sections of *Double Down* employ second-person narration in a manner known as "recipe fiction." In this form the narrator gives a set of instructions, usually concerning ironic subjects, such as how to have an affair or how to become an insecure person—subjects that, when read beneath the surface of the plot, instruct readers to take action opposite that of the protagonist. In *Double Down* the Barthelme brothers literally instruct readers how to derive the feeling that gambling offers. After explaining that whether you win or lose is not the point of gambling, the authors say,

> If you're skeptical about winning and losing being so similar, take this test. Go to your nearest casino with a thousand dollars and buy ten black chips. Put the thousand in the betting circle at a blackjack table. . . . Await your fate. . . . If you win, leave the chips there, stacked in the betting circle, and await the next round of cards. Repeat this until you lose. When you lose everything, move away from the table and dwell on what has happened. Don't be content with telling yourself how stupid you are. Don't be satisfied with calling yourself names. Don't simply conclude that you were insane to follow these instructions, to take this test. Instead, dwell on how it *felt*. Go over it and over it in your head, recalling every detail. . . . Remember . . . how your heartbreak rested on the fall of a card. Think of the chips you had on the table, think about what else you could have done with that money. . . . Try to figure how you let yourself be so foolish, how you took leave of your senses, how you got into this thing. And most of all, once it's done, gently close your eyes, fade back, and feel it.

CONSUMERISM PERSONIFIED

Throughout his fiction Barthelme creates a suburban landscape, an environment in which his characters become ultimate consumers. Barthelme mentions specific establishments by name and refers by brand name to items the characters consume. His characters dine at Baskin-Robbins, Taco Bell, Popeyes, KFC, and McDonald's; they eat Edward's pie, Sarah Lee bagels, and Pillsbury pancakes and drink Grapette, Jitney Juice, and Diet Cokes. They call

Bekins and U-Haul when they move and shop at Safeway, Wal-Mart, Goodwill, Kmart, and K & B Drugstore. They rent rooms at Motel 6 and Ramada Inn, check out videos at Blockbuster, and send Hallmark greetings. They wear Depends and wipe their noses with Kleenex; they eat from Chinet plates and use Saran Wrap to cover the leftovers. They empty their trash in Hefty lawn bags. They drive Vespa scooters, hail Yellow Cabs, and cruise in Hondas and Ford Explorers. They finance much of their goods with MasterCard or Visa.

The actions of Barthelme's characters often are framed in terms of the pop culture that surrounds them. They idolize Cary Grant, Ray Charles, Hillary Clinton, Marilyn Monroe, and John Laroquette. They are enthralled with the media: they watch MTV, listen to Geraldo Rivera and Jay Leno, and read *Cosmopolitan, Time,* and *Rolling Stone*; episodes of *Cheers, Night Court,* and *ER* are the highlight of their week. Against the background of media-driven society and contemporary consumerism, Barthelme creates characters who need fulfillment and enrichment in their lives. Often they long for the intangible, a sensation or feeling they cannot define for themselves and are unable to articulate to others.

This undefined need for fulfillment presents itself in several themes that run through Barthelme's fiction, including those found in the subject of temptation versus the lack of change and the compartmentalization of emotion. To present such themes, Barthelme portrays characters with value systems so construed that they cannot communicate the difference between a person and a plastic spoon. The geometric patterns of his writing echo in the character's action or inaction. Similar to Dorothy Parker's description of the Bloomsbury writers, who "lived in squares and loved in triangles," Barthelme's characters move in circles and love in triangles. Through a combination of character and circumstance, Barthelme reminds us that

our society inevitably is marked by the golden arches of McDonald's rather than the triumphant arches of the Roman aqueducts.

Barthelme's characters struggle with change—the desire for change, the inability to accept change, or the motivation to follow through on plans for change. As a result, these characters often refuse to commit to people, projects, or ideas. One strong example of a character unable to define or reach goals is Peter, the narrator of *Natural Selection* (1990). Peter, who is experiencing a premature midlife crisis, tells his wife, Lily, "Everything was some kind of low-grade wrongness—things not quite fitting, feeling empty, feeling useless, without direction. I felt like I was stuck in the job, in the life, marking time until I don't know what, until I got older, I guess." Peter has lost his ambition and feels so disinterested in his middle-class lifestyle that he often wishes for anything at all to occur—he would welcome tragedy or bliss equally. He longs for any reason to express emotion and complains because he has nothing to be angry about, no sickness, death, poverty, nothing he would term as being "driven by the elemental." Peter concludes that it is "a hard life for the non-poor." He takes the lack of motivation and the inability to set goals to the extreme by hoping for catastrophe along with, and often instead of, success.

In *Painted Desert* (1995), Jen summarizes Peter's dilemma when, after viewing footage of the Los Angeles riots of 1992, she tells her boyfriend, Del (the two characters met in a previous novel, *The Brothers*), "We need to do something. We can't sit here and watch it on television anymore. I can't take that. . . . There's something about being there physically. Like occupying the physical space." After this comment, Del and Jen depart with her father, Mike, on a journey across America, destined for California, where the O. J. Simpson scandal is raging. After their travels, Jen and Del retreat, deciding that living the life of those they have met at the Painted Desert is more rewarding. Jen explains herself to Del when he asks what the truth is:

> The truth is that we saw this horrible thing on television which seemed more horrible than the usual stuff we see on television, and we decided to do something, only we couldn't think of what to do, so we thought we'd go to the West Coast and either see Damian Williams or see where it all happened, in the hopes that some idea of what to do would come to us then. Is that right? We also decided that even if we didn't do anything about Damian Williams, we would do something else, something less ordinary than our regular lives, so that we could have an impact on the world around us, so we wouldn't just sit there and watch the stuff on TV and complain, so we wouldn't just say the people on TV were assholes, we'd do something about it.

Jen explains in a letter that after visiting the Painted Desert, "almost every idea seems small and you can't imagine why we spend our time the way we do. Why we sit in our little houses complaining about people doing things wrong, sit there having our little precious thoughts, clinging to our ideas and opinions, arguing for our 'beliefs.'" She says that her perception of the world no longer seems valid and that although she and Del think that contributing to society is what they should do, she has come to believe that one or two people cannot make a difference. So Del and Jen forgo their dream to try to contribute to society and decide instead to get married—the only resolution in the novel. Readers are informed that Jen and Del will go on to be "regular married. Just like everybody." Beyond that, the couple no longer will concern themselves with becoming informed spectators of daily events. They not only lose the dream to participate in the world, but they also lose interest in keeping abreast of it. Their there's-nothing-we-can-do attitude becomes, by the end of the novel, an I-don't-want-to-know-about-the-things-that-there's-nothing-I-can-do-about

way of life. Here we see that in addition to refusing to fulfill their dreams, they refuse to dream.

Frequently potential opportunities are lost not because of circumstance but because of the failure of a character to follow through on something that he or she may or may not want. For example, in *The Brothers,* Del has come to Biloxi to move into a condo that his former father-in-law has given him; however, the space is not yet vacant, so Del decides to stay with his brother, Bud, in the interim. When he arrives, Del's sister-in-law, Margaret, tells Del that Bud has left for California spontaneously to pursue a film career. Bud calls and tells Del that he knows that "California [is] the perfect place for a guy like him, and he [isn't] even there yet." Del responds by asking Bud about his plan and telling him that he expected Bud to be in Biloxi and does not know what do without him. Obviously, neither man has a clearly defined goal. When Del asks Bud why he left, Bud responds, "I can't really explain it, can't make it clear. It's not even clear to me. I'm going on empty here. Instinct. It's just one of those things. You know it when it hits you. Need." Bud says that he does not know how long he will be gone, but he returns in a month, explaining to Del that things "didn't go the way they were supposed to." Bud leaves Biloxi and returns on impulse, whereas Del comes to Biloxi only because of his new condo. The brothers seem to be flailing from place to place, with no real intention, no logic, and no dream to support their journeys. At the end of *The Brothers,* Bud wraps his head in towels, blinding himself even from a glow of light, and bobs around "like an enormous Q-Tip" on the balcony. Bud parades blindly as both brothers have done throughout the novel. The brothers take actions simply because, as Del asks, "What else is there to do?"

Throughout Barthelme's writing, there are continual reminders of the loss of ambition and motivation in his characters. Characters frequently almost take action, regret taking it, or state what they should but do not do. In *The Brothers,* for instance, Del tells Jen (of Margaret) that he "didn't screw her. I almost screwed her. . . . I'm feeling lucky that I didn't fuck up all the way. There's some grace in that." Whether the question at hand concerns saving one's marriage or eating a hot dog, the response most often is expressed as "maybe": "maybe" I'll move, "maybe" I'll stay, "maybe" we'll have sex, "maybe" we'll get a divorce, "maybe" we'll have a baby, or "maybe" we'll order a pizza. Barthelme's fiction also is full of dialogue in which characters say, "that's not what I meant," "I meant something else," or "you know what I mean." A good example is in "Perfect Things," from *Chroma.* Jerry continually doubts his expression. His wife, Ellen, has informed him that she is having an affair with Toby, a younger man. When Jerry refers to their affair as "hanky-panky," he is separating himself from Ellen and from such behavior—making the behavior so foreign to him that he cannot even give it an appropriate or timely name, thus cutting Ellen off from their life together:

> "Hanky-panky" had just come out. He hadn't thought about it, and it didn't describe what he saw in his head when he thought about Ellen and her lover, and it gave the impression, he thought, of a man hopelessly out of touch. . . . He was so self-conscious about this unfortunate choice of words that he could not even look up from the tabletop. . . . "Or whatever you people call it now."

Jerry attempts to rephrase his statement in order to redeem what he feels will be Ellen's perception of it. In response to why she cannot have the affair, Jerry states, "We don't do that because that's the definition of rabbits." He regrets this statement; as soon as he makes it, he "immediately wished he hadn't. There were so many things wrong with it. It was clumsy, didn't quite fit as an answer." Jerry thinks that he should have said "hot monkey" instead of

rabbits and wonders if he could still use the phrase "hot monkey" in the conversation. Later, he exclaims that he hates Toby's guts, only to change his mind immediately: "He didn't feel this, he felt nothing like it; in fact, he didn't have much feeling about Toby one way or the other." During one of his intense conversations with Ellen, Jerry signals a "minimal nod." Not only does Jerry question his word choice, he also is unable fully to commit even to a nod. Jerry is a primary example of Barthelme's characters—always regretting, always changing, never content with what is being said or done.

In addition to having issues related to personal relationships, most of Barthelme's characters demonstrate the level of their lack of commitment on a widespread scale. They arrive in rent-a-trucks, live in motels or apartments, eat fast food, and even travel arbitrarily. They do not love people; they like them. They either are unemployed or have jobs that are in transition or are undefined. They do not despise things or the world in which they live, but they dislike them. Perhaps this lack of commitment results from fear of defeat. Many have found success economically, as they do not lack material goods; their lifestyles, however, epitomize the consequences of contemporary consumerism, for they remain emotionally and spiritually empty. Their condition is summed up in an insight Bob has in *Bob the Gambler* (1997): "You could spend your whole life wanting something and never even come close." Throughout his fiction, Barthelme demonstrates that the fast-paced suburban lifestyle often creates an environment in which people have difficulty expressing emotions or experiencing personal growth.

CIRCULAR PATTERNS

Because the characters in Barthelme's fiction lack clearly defined ambitions, they often go in circles, a pattern that the narrative designs often parallel. As exemplified in the title story of *Chroma,* these characters have "no particular destination but a strict timetable, a schedule for [their] return." A good example of this pattern is found in *Bob the Gambler,* in which the predicament of Ray and Jewel, the main characters, is signified both literally and symbolically throughout the novel. Circular actions are most evident in Ray's and Jewel's gambling addictions, manifested in their money. They repeatedly lose and win money at the casino. As Ray says, "Slots giveth and slots taketh away." Jewel explains that she once hit five thousand on a slot machine but gambled it all away on another. She says, "It was their money, anyway. . . . I'll get it back. Don't worry." After Jewel and Ray admit that they both have gambling addictions, Jewel says, "That's the way it works—money takes a trip, money comes home."

Eventually, Ray and Jewel's bankrupt financial situation compels them to consider economic options. Jewel's solution is "to lose everything. . . . Just get rid of it," and Ray asks, "Start over?" At the end of the novel, Jewel urges Ray to spend their last six thousand dollars at the casino. She says, "A couple hits and we're in business, we're right back where we started." Ray responds, "Oh gee, thanks. That's just where I want to be." Adopting the pattern of their money ebb and flow, Ray and Jewel plan to begin where they started in terms of material accumulations.

In addition to making explicit comments about the circular patterns of their wins and losses and the course of Ray and Jewel's lives, Barthelme describes these patterns symbolically. Representative of the merry-go-round pattern of their money, their "Chase" credit card is denied because it is over the limit. When Ray visits his mother early in the novel, she entices her dog to "go around in circles" and shortly afterward rearranges three issues of *Family Circle,* symbolically foreshadowing Ray's move in with his mother, which will create an extended family. Then, following a discussion of how seriously they should take the situation of their potential bankruptcy, Ray leaves the house and drives "one of the Explorers in circles." After the couple moves in with Ray's mother, Jewel's daughter suggests that the family move to a trailer park at Lake Forgetful: "We could buy two or three. Put 'em in a circle. It'd be so great to be out here all the time."

Even the death of Ray's father is not a linear experience for Ray and his mother. On the way home from the trip to Texas to make funeral arrangements and to sort out the estate, Ray's mother says,

> Nothing changes. A point on your compass goes dark. In a few months it won't matter. It'll be like he never existed. That wallet is the only thing. He used it, needed it to carry out his life. Now he doesn't need it, but it's still ready to carry out a life. We'll put it in a nice drawer somewhere.

Ray's mother acknowledges that after a while her life will return to what it was before her husband died. Moreover, the wallet, symbolic of Ray's father's life, is stashed in a drawer, taking him from death, to life, and back to death again. Regretting that she and Ray's father were separated when he died, Ray's mother explains that his father was talking about moving to Mississippi to live with her. As she talks, she "swivels" the wallet. Ray's mother literally and symbolically moves the representation of Ray's father in circles.

The circular pattern of behavior also is revealed in ways that the characters react to each other. For example, in *Tracer* (1985), Martin has come to Fort Myers to visit his possibly-soon-to-be-ex-wife's sister, Dominica. During the same visit to Fort Myers, he sleeps with his soon-to-be-ex, Alex. As Martin returns to the airport, he asks Dominica if she plans to leave as well. "I think so," she replies. "There really isn't much to do, and I want to see what it's like there. I mean, I may come back in a week." Martin responds, "Maybe I should hang around." Here we see Martin and Dominica acting on impulses and moving back and forth both physically and emotionally. Even though, at the end of the novel, Martin is boarding a plane, it is apparent that he will continue to move in a circular pattern; moreover, his indecisiveness motivates others to become indecisive. As he leaves, he is more confused than when he arrived. This type of open-ended narrative invites readers to consider possibilities for Martin's future.

Martin's experience is similar to Bud's, in *The Brothers*—neither character achieves anything throughout his journey. At one point Del asks Bud, "What is the point of this trip, really? You're going to hang out a week and then you're back here like nothing ever happened? I don't get it." Del's question to Bud is ironic to the reader of *Painted Desert,* in which Del and Jen's entire plight comes full circle. They go from having no knowledge about issues to not caring about what they know to wanting to care and trying to do something and back to having no knowledge. The circle manifests itself materially in *Second Marriage* (1984). Henry is married to Theo when his first wife, Clare, visits him. Clare and Theo form a relationship and ask Henry to leave the house. He moves into an apartment complex and waits for Theo to return. When they reunite at the end of the novel, Theo tells Henry that their daughter, Rachel, said that he was circling the block before he parked in the driveway. As in *Bob the Gambler,* in which the literal actions of the characters symbolize the circular patterns of their lives, Rachel's description of Henry represents the course his life takes. He spends this period of his life in a holding pattern, waiting for the moment to return to what he knows. This nonlinear pattern also is found in *Two against One* (1988): Elise visits her possibly-soon-to-be-ex-husband, Edward, and tells him that "this place is just

like it was," speaking of their house before she left. She continues, "Nothing's changed. Usually when a person leaves, the other person changes everything, but you haven't changed a thing—it's all exactly the way it was when I left." Frequently, Barthelme's characters prefer to re-enter their past lives in precisely the same states as when they left. They have the desire to change but also fear to do so; therefore, they maintain the status quo and hope their lives will adjust accordingly.

Throughout Barthelme's fiction, indecisive and noncommittal attitudes are manifested most strongly through the portrayals of romantic relationships. Couples rarely dedicate themselves to remaining in or getting out of their current relationships. In *Two against One,* Edward and Elise experience a trial separation. Rather than divorcing or deciding to separate, the characters want to leave romantic involvement open-ended and remain in a neutral status for as long as possible. Their affections for each other fluctuate, as seen in Edward's capricious feelings for Elise: "It was typical of his life with Elise, when he'd had a life with Elise, that he would like her one minute and dislike her the next, that he would find her heartbreaking and lovable and then turn around moments later and find her repellent." This back-and-forth commitment frequently is linked to the loss of the ability to aspire as a couple. Similarly to Edward and Elise, who express capricious feelings for each other, Peter and Lily, the main characters in *Natural Selection,* briefly separate from each other, but Peter moves only a few miles away and visits often. Eventually, they reunite. Likewise, in the span of three sentences, Martin, of *Tracer,* states that he is "getting away from [his] divorce," that he is going to see his "wife's sister," and that the divorce is not "final." Martin moves from being divorced to being married to being not quite divorced. This attitude is represented symbolically in *The Brothers,* when Jen asks Del to buy her a dog because she believes it to be a symbol of his commitment to her. She tells him, "Until you buy me a dog you're nothing. You're dirt under my nails, like all the other chumps I've hung it up with." Del responds later by agreeing to get a hamster or "anything in a box," suggesting that he is looking for temporary, movable objects in his life.

The characters' reluctance to change permanently the status of their personal relationships, because they fear the consequent life alterations, often results in triangular relationships. This reluctance frequently produces frustrated lovers who attempt to add to the equation rather than solve the problem. For example, in *Two against One,* Roscoe, Elise's on-again, off-again lover, accompanies her to Edward's when she visits. She suggests that the three of them live together. Similarly, when Del visits Bud in *The Brothers,* Margaret and Del exchange gestures and innuendoes that extend beyond innocent flirting, causing friction among the three. Other examples of the triangular relationships that abound in Barthelme's fiction include the love triangle of Martin, Dominica, and Alex in *Tracer*; the twofold triangular relationship (the one with Theo and Henry, in which Clare is the third party, and the one between Clare and Theo, in which Henry is the third party) in *Second Marriage*; the romantic triangle represented by Ellen's affair with Toby in "Perfect Things"; and the possible relationship between the narrator of "Moon Deluxe" and Lily and Antonia, if the narrator's desire "to be part of their routine" is fulfilled.

DEPICTION OF DETAILS, OBJECTS, AND LISTS

Throughout Barthelme's fiction, he portrays characters who focus on small physical details or seemingly insignificant material objects rather than assessing a particular situation or evaluating a person from broad points of view. Frequently, this narrowly defined hyperreal perspective manifests in men noting the flaws of women. For example, in *Two against One,* Edward criticizes Elise's voice, her skin, and the way her bra sometimes shows. In *Chroma's* "Perfect Things," Jerry notices similar flaws about his wife, Ellen: "He wondered why things seemed to accumulate around her wherever she lit for more than a moment. . . . He hadn't, heretofore, been bothered by it the way he was this morning." Similarly, in *Natural Selection,* Peter states,

> Usually I find the reasons not to be attracted to women pretty quick. I see flaws the way other people find things to hope for. . . . I see faults in eyeliner, clinging hunks of mascara, errant lipstick, badly chosen colors, stinky hair, splotched skin, hanging fat, bad arms.

Sometimes men concentrate on what they perceive as flaws in women to avoid coping with intense, usually painful or confrontational situations. For example, in "Shopgirls," Andrea tells the narrator in detail that her father shot himself; after hearing the story, he says, "I'm sorry." But the narrator's internalized response is that he notices that one of her

> eyebrows is plucked too much, and that the brows are not symmetrical with respect to the bridge of her nose. . . . Once you have seen this tiny imbalance, you cannot stop seeing it. . . . You stare at it. Her face looks wrong suddenly, almost deformed. You try to think of something to say about her father, but you can't think of anything.

More frequently than focusing on someone's physical flaws to avoid confronting emotionally uncomfortable situations, Barthelme's characters concentrate on a specific object or task and exhibit obsessive-compulsive traits. Many characters in the short-story collection *Chroma* respond to intense situations by carrying out or refusing to carry out mundane tasks. In "Perfect Things," when Jerry discovers that Ellen is having an affair, he refuses to take out the garbage; her response is to take out the garbage herself, performing the task in an overly dramatic way. When Ellen tells Jerry that she does not enjoy living alone, readers expect her to elaborate on emotional and psychological disadvantages; instead, she explains that she hates grinding the coffee in the morning. Jerry agrees with her, saying that he does not like having to go outside to get the newspaper while wearing his old robe. Continuing to focus on mundane details instead of the more important issue at hand, their estranged relationship, Ellen attempts to comfort him by promising him a new robe, but Jerry only responds with "I don't want a robe. That's the point."

The couple continues this trivial conversation by discussing how each of them likes the blinds positioned. Ellen tells Jerry that she prefers to put plywood up instead of windows, explaining, "It's what I feel." She summarizes the discussion of the windows in emotional, not rational, language. It is almost as if she makes a slip of the tongue and refers unconsciously to the relationship between them. In "Parents," from *Chroma,* Heinz tells Agnes that he wants to have a baby. She responds soon after with "I want an electric mixer." Then he tells her that he thinks that his father is sick; Agnes answers again, "I want the mixer." Barthelme puts the decision in physical terms when he links Agnes's decision to her diaphragm case. First, Agnes slides it to Heinz, telling him that it is up to him. Later she tosses it into the bushes. Both Agnes and the story are unable to discuss the prospect of parenting in communicative terms; physical objects suffice for both.

Throughout *Bob the Gambler,* Ray and Jewel repeatedly focus on unimportant details, usually an object of some sort or a product of their consumerism, instead of coping with their financial problem. While Jewel is at the casino trying to recover some of her gambling losses, Ray concentrates on the Edward's brand key lime pie he is eating. Ironically, he says that it does not taste like key lime pie and admits it

represents "a new obsession. [He] couldn't get enough." Obviously, his addiction to the pie parallels his and Jewel's gambling addiction. The pieces of his pie come in "individual wedge-shaped boxes." Like other objects of consumerism, Ray's key lime pie, a symbol for his gambling addiction, is compartmentalized. Later, Ray and Jewel begin to discuss their gambling addiction, and although they consciously think that they are not taking the situation seriously enough, they turn their attention from their gambling addiction to Ray's gesture of feeding the family dog Mongolian beef. Jewel scolds Ray for feeding the dog table scraps, so Ray tells the dog to go watch TV, the very activity Ray and Jewel use as a means to evade their problems. When Ray resigns from his position as stock boy/clerk, he accuses Clo, the store's manager, of abusing his managerial authority. The conversation is quite intense, as Clo defends himself against Ray's charges. Immediately after this discussion, Ray is described as standing near "the packaged meats, idly straightening some rib-eye steaks and some filets, some strip steaks, some boneless cuts."

Seemingly insignificant details often are exaggerated when characters make specified lists. The habit of making lists occurs most vividly in *Bob the Gambler* and *Double Down.* In *Bob the Gambler,* after Ray and Jewel have lost everything, Ray wonders one evening if they are not taking their financial ruin seriously enough. He gets up in the middle of the night and goes for a drive, stopping at the twenty-four-hour Wal-Mart to get doughnuts. Once he is back driving on the highway, he shouts obscenities and tosses a doughnut out the window, followed by "all the other shit I could find in the car—two magazines, a Coke can, the first aid kit, some receipts, a paperback book, a half-eaten candy bar, an old dog collar, a yellow towel, all the crap Jewel had jammed into the ashtray." When Jewel tells Ray they need to sell everything, he asks her to define "everything," so she specifies: "House, cars, furniture, equipment, appliances, dishes, clothes, books, lamps, stereos, files, anything we can get a dime for at a garage sale. Everything." Later, Ray takes inventory of what they have sold: "In a little more than a week we managed to sell the cars, get the house on the market, sell the TVs, stereos, kitchen appliances, washer and dryer, beds, and the best of the furniture."

In both *Bob the Gambler* and in *Double Down,* lists are used in ways that express the characters' grief after their fathers die. In *Bob the Gambler,* after the death of his father, Ray travels to Houston from Biloxi with his mother, who was separated from his father at the time of his death. The task becomes more difficult when they begin to sort though his father's belongings. Ray comments that his mother decides to classify items so that she will know what to keep. He helps her sort his father's "papers, . . . the china, the books, the family records, photographs, and the rest of it." Ray and his mother spend time "sorting, boxing, wrapping, reducing [his] father's life to its simplest parts." He notes that his father had "kept files for bills, insurance, Social Security, investments, medical expenses, and so on" and that the only business that appears to need examining is his father's wallet, "stuffed with cards and bits of paper, cash, a flat key, . . . a fingernail-size chip of mica, an old Saint Christopher medal." After Ray returns to Biloxi, he arranges the boxes of items in a storage unit, and when he shuts and locks the storage door, he feels as if he is "finally burying [his] father."

Similarly to Ray, in his descriptions of the actions he and his mother take after his father's death, Frederick and Steven, in *Double Down,* take listed inventory of their own father's estate.

> We spent a week cleaning up the place, tearing down things Father had built there: drafting tables, an elaborate stereo system, special cabinetry. We emptied the closets, tossing everything we could bear to toss. We threw away beds, pots and pans, half-filled bottles of liquor, paper, pens, and pencils. We threw away soap, salt, houseplants, toothpaste, towels, Windex, zinc ointment.

The sons also list items of their mother's that they

> packed up in boxes: slippers, dresses she wore often, some jewelry, a coffee cup. We did the same for Father though we picked different things. Not his clothes or shoes or leather jacket, though we did save his hat, the comical gray leather cap he once wore on his walks, cocked back on his head. The other things we picked for him were architectural design books—Corbu and Mies, Gropius, Neutra, Wright, Aalto—and objects that were special to him or seemed especially like him.

The warmth the characters feel for their father is expressed much more explicitly in *Double Down,* perhaps because the memoir genre lends itself more to psychological explanations from authors and narrators than does fiction. Upon arriving at their father's house after he has died, Frederick and Steven sort through their material goods. They say they want to feel the sense of family and connectedness "in all the *stuff* in that apartment, touch it, remember it, steep in it." Frequently, when they makes lists of their parents' belongings, they add a memory or personal feeling to the description of the listed items. For example, they say, "We buried [our parents] in boxes of photographs and slides and cameras, boxes of letters, boxes of books, boxes of stereo equipment, boxes of architectural drawings, boxes of special clothes and knick-knacks and old magazines with Father's 'fame' in them."

OBSESSIVE-COMPULSIVE BEHAVIORS

Barthelme's characters engage in a mild form of obsessive-compulsive behavior that manifests in making lists and compartmentalizing objects:

storing possessions inside boxes, which are packed inside of crates, which are stored inside of sheds. Moreover, they frequently rearrange and reorganize the stacks of boxes and the items inside the boxes. In *Two against One,* for instance, Edward obsesses for two pages about assembling his vacuum cleaner. Instead of discussing his troubled relationship with his estranged wife, he asks, "Do you want me to show you the new vacuum. . . . I really love it." Barthelme embellishes the mechanics of Edward's actions. The narrator explains that Edward reads the instructions in both English and Spanish, checks the diagram, looks at and dusts the parts, and begins the assembly, while noting small differences between his model and others. After assembling the vacuum cleaner, he wishes that there were more parts for him to put together and turns the task into a more tedious chore by taking apart larger sections and reassembling them one at a time. Afterward, he checks the brushes, winds the cord meticulously, and pushes the vacuum so that it aligns with the coffee table. When his task is completed, he rereads the operations manual and the consumer information from cover to cover. Later in the story, Edward is touched because Elise has rearranged his closet, "forgetting that she was in his house, that it wasn't hers, forgetting that the arrangement of his closet was no longer her territory." Obviously, arranging items and organizing physical objects is an obsession for Edward: when he is not engaging in the activity himself, he is analyzing the meaning of someone else's engagement in it.

The protagonist of the short story "Safeway" exhibits similar obsessive-compulsive traits. While the woman he sits with in a coffee shop is in the restroom, he situates the containers of coffee cream in the design of a football play and pretends to play football. He explains why he no longer feels compelled to arrange the coffee creamers: "But because you have too few cartons, and because you must move the cartons in sequence, one after another, and because you have no defensive team at all, the play isn't much fun." After deciding not to rearrange the cream containers, he thinks about the frozen waffles in his grocery sack, which he has carried into the coffee shop with him. He immediately begins to obsess over whether the waffles are defrosting. The protagonist of "Shopgirls" also is obsessive-compulsive. While sitting in an apartment with a woman, he goes into the kitchen and methodically and meticulously rinses a plate and washes his hands, the classic form of obsessive-compulsive behavior:

> You carry your plate into the small kitchen and drop the bones into the garbage sack under the sink. Then you rinse the plate and turn it upside down on the flecked Formica counter, then you wash your hands with her Ivory soap. As you run the water over your hands, you splash a little first on your lips, then over your entire face. You pull two paper towels off the roll alongside the sink and dry your face and hands. You throw the crumpled towels at the garbage sack, miss it by a full yard.

Similarly, in "Moon Deluxe" the protagonist is compelled to count the number of blue cars that pass by while he is stuck in traffic. In "Pool Lights" the protagonist's particular obsession involves a collection of unread magazines he has kept after moving twice, once across the country. His summer project consists of organizing all the magazines by title, stripping the covers off, and clipping together with Acco fasteners all the magazines with the same title. He then clips ads or articles from some of the magazines and organizes them for future reading.

The most destructive compulsive behavior Barthelme illustrates is in *Bob the Gambler* and *Double Down.* In both works, characters cannot stop betting at the casinos, even though they lose huge amounts of money. In *Bob the Gambler,* the action is presented almost straightfor-wardly, with little philosophizing from the first-person narrator; in *Double Down,* however, the authors, Steven and Frederick Barthelme, repeatedly explain various facets of their addiction. Although they understand the dynamics of their addiction quite well and even offer profound psychological motives for their gambling addiction, they remain addicts. The closest insight about gambling that Ray makes is when Jewel holds up a copy of *The Gambler,* by Fyodor Dostoyevsky. Ray looks at the novel to see whether there are any hard-core gambling tips. He reads some speeches Dostoyevsky wrote but decides the author would have been better off gambling than illustrating society.

Unlike Ray and Jewel, Frederick and Steven repeatedly philosophize about their gambling addictions. As university professors, they have a higher understanding of their gambling habit than do Ray and Jewel. They say that a psychiatrist "would have a field day with us—guilt, depression, loss, loneliness, destroying the inheritance." They also understand that gambling is not the desire to get rich quickly or an attempt to win a game:

> It is as good to lose as to win. There is only a shadow of difference between them, and that shadow is insignificant. Winning is better than losing but neither one is the goal of gambling, which is *playing.* Losing never feels like the worst part of gambling. Quitting often does.

All the philosophizing and understanding of their compulsion does not help them break the habit. They remain as addicted as Ray and Jewel, who do not seem to understand the psychology of gambling.

During discussions of compulsiveness and addiction, Frederick and Steven, like Barthelme's fictional characters, make lists, a mild compulsion in itself—within their explanations of addiction and compulsion, they are revealing these very traits. For example, they say

> An addict is someone who "surrenders" to something, the dictionary will tell you, "habitually or

obsessively." Most people are at least a little addicted to something—work, food, exercise, sex, watching sports on television, cooking, reading the stock market. Some people are addicted to washing their hands. Some people trim their hedges from dawn to dusk. Some people play too much golf. Almost anything can be the object of addiction.

On another occasion, when they explain how money is devalued for those gambling in casinos, they say, "A hundred dollars is a lot of money. Think of it outside the casino and it translates into lots of things, lots of goods and services—shirts, dinners, hamburgers, movie tickets, tire repairs, shots for the dogs or cats, computer software, sets of bed sheets." Later, they define the impulse to gamble as "beating *logic*":

> It's about chance confirming everything you knew but could make no place for in your life. Gambling is of course a very expensive way to beat reason. You can get pretty much the same thing by staying awake for a night and a day, or however long it takes you to get a little psychologically unhinged, destabilized, detached from whatever you believed the day before, and then staring at the cat, the dog, the stapler, the back of your hand, water. Most anything'll do it, once you've shed your silly confidence.

Although the Barthelme brothers lose hundreds of thousands of dollars gambling, are indicted for cheating in a casino, and have heavy legal charges brought against them, the memoir is often upbeat and told with a humorous tone. During one of the discussions concerning how gambling is not really about money, they write, "At home, you might drive across town to save a buck on a box of Tide, but at the table you tip a cocktail waitress five dollars for bringing a free coke. You do both these things on the same day."

In some aspects, *Double Down* is a tribute to the Barthelme family, a story about two brothers trying to preserve their family's history. They discuss their talks during the trips they take together from their homes in Hattiesburg to the casinos in Biloxi, the feeling of connectedness that gambling together provides them, and the warmth they gain from the sense of a larger community of other gamblers at the casino. From this perspective, gambling provides the framework for a narrative about how two brothers cope with the death of their parents and their older brother. Despite all the money they lose, they conclude: "Even when we were losing, we knew our conversations were something of value, a feature of the addiction, and that in any system of values this one could clearly be marked as priceless."

CRITICAL RECEPTION

In general, Frederick Barthelme's work has been received positively. Most critics regard him as a minimalist writer who uses the contemporary American consumerism landscape to define his characters as well as his writing. Frequently, critics point out ways in which the environment that surrounds the characters influences them, and they note Barthelme's ability to create a glamorous commonplace, turning a Motel 6 into the Ritz or a McDonald's into a seasoned restaurant. In "Suburban Culture, Imaginative Wonder: The Fiction of Frederick Barthelme," Robert H. Brinkmeyer Jr. states, "At first glance, Barthelme's suburban world of apartment complexes, shopping malls, and consumer culture appears far from wondrous. A drab sameness seems to color everything . . . yet, for all its shoddiness, Barthelme's suburban world always verges on opening into wonder and mystery." Brinkmeyer adds that "while Barthelme's work typically focuses on the commonplace, it all the while suggests that the ordinary can be the site of transfiguration."

For Barthelme, there are no glorious scenes of realization; he creates an environment in which, as Bill Gifford puts it, "epiphanies occur in parking lots." Reviewers agree that Barthelme's fiction is filled with examples of crowded emptiness. While they cite ways in which he reveals consumerism in his writing, they also note the void it leaves in the lives of those that inhabit this environment. In "One Part Humor, 2 Parts Whining," Michiko Kakutani states, "Whether the setting is Texas, Florida or some unnamed town in the new South, his characters live in anonymous developments, devoid of history, tradition, and a sense of place."

Critics also describe the way in which Barthelme's characters respond to a society that focuses on material goods. D. D. Guttenplan characterizes it as "an America of freeways and shopping malls, of chain stores and fake ethnic restaurants and apartment complexes . . . a nation whose deepest emotions have been turned into slogans, where even the language of dreams is cluttered with commercial interruptions." In her review of *Chroma,* Kakutani argues that this landscape causes the characters to "uniformly suffer from boredom and other forms of spiritual ennui." They fill the void by "inventing tiny distractions—like trying to tell the difference between three brands of chrome tape or cutting the heads off people in photographs."

Most critics agree that Barthelme has skillfully woven place and character to provide a strong sense of the emptiness that surrounds every decision made by the men and women in his fiction. Other critics point out similarities between the male characters Barthelme portrays: he is usually a middle-aged man who suffers from lack of ambition and emotion and is experiencing a quasi-separation from his wife. Ann Hulbert notes that the men, who "rarely resemble grown up men," in Barthelme's fiction typically do not have a defined career, and their primary action consists of awkward meetings with women. She argues that the compulsion of many of the men is linked to the nervousness caused by the women in their lives. This refusal of self-definition is regarded as an inability of Barthelme's characters to place emotional value properly onto people and events. Roz Kaveney states that "quasi-incest and cabalistic signs in the motel car-park are ultimately not seen as more important to the characters than another motel resident's lectures about pancake-making." Most critics however, regard this characterization not as a fault, but rather as a strength, in Barthelme's writing.

Similarly, while the carbon-copy pattern of men in Barthelme's novels is frequently criticized, many praise the reality that it exhibits. In "'80s Pastoral: Frederick Barthelme's *Moon Deluxe* Ten Years On," Timothy Peters argues that "there is something heroic about Barthelme's refusal—and the refusal of his characters—to look back, to be nostalgic, or even to scheme for a more aesthetically or materially rewarding future." Most critics agree that the lack of desire in Barthelme's characters correlates directly with the environment in which they have been placed. Grant Pheloung states, "Obviously consumer capitalism has deeply infiltrated the world of Barthelme's characters and given them a . . . transformation of reality into the hyper-real." Like others, Peters argues that the soul-deadened response of the men in Barthelme's fiction to their environment is the only available choice. Because the characters feel ambivalent toward most of their circumstances, some critics, such as Tom De Haven, complain that the events in Barthelme's writing "don't follow human intention."

Just as the environment causes Barthelme's characters to adjust, it also influences their relationships with others. As Pheloung puts it, "There seems to be indifference in the face of relations between the sexes and an abandonment of emotional and sexual commitment. . . . Sexuality has now become part of the language of advertising or the desire for consumer products." The love triangle motif that Barthelme frequently uses illustrates the indifference his characters feel and, as James Kaufmann points out in "Brand-Name Blues," is "a vehicle for Barthelme. . . . He's not particularly interested in plot or story, but in scenes, in snapshots which illustrate such fashionable problems as fear of intimacy, loneliness, hostility, and other subclinical manifestations of the modern malaise." Critics also equate the characters' failure to commit to relationships to the environment in which they have been placed.

Critics of Barthelme's work have noted his ability to capture a new American landscape and frequently remark on the connections between character, environment, and action within his fiction. Barthelme's characters show readers the drab world that Barthelme describes, and they know that they must accept it. As Kaufmann states, "Yes, this is emotionally freeze-dried and shrink-wrapped fiction which puts on exhibit a world where life has little meaning and there is no exit. This empty world needs a witness, though, and Barthelme is it."

CONCLUSIONS

As these critics point out, Barthelme portrays a landscape of suburban America in which characters who are constantly influenced by media and pop culture become the ultimate consumers. Barthelme's work provides visual, image-driven symbolic portraits of human emotion. His characters often need fulfillment and enrichment and are unable to articulate specifically their wants and desires. Frequently, when they are able to recognize their goals, they are unable to commit to achieving them. Indeed, Barthelme offers a vivid portrayal of contemporary American society. He neither criticizes this society nor supports it; rather, in his minimalist style of writing, he invites readers to derive their own conclusion.

Selected Bibliography

WORKS OF FREDERICK BARTHELME

NOVELS

War and War. Garden City, N.Y.: Doubleday, 1971.

Second Marriage. New York: Simon & Schuster, 1984.

Tracer. New York: Simon & Schuster, 1985.

Two against One. New York: Weidenfeld & Nicolson, 1988.

Natural Selection. New York: Viking, 1990.

The Brothers. New York: Viking, 1993.

Painted Desert. New York: Viking, 1995.

Bob the Gambler. Boston: Houghton Mifflin, 1997.

SHORT STORIES

Rangoon. New York: Winter House, 1970.

Moon Deluxe. New York: Simon & Schuster, 1983.

Chroma. New York: Simon & Schuster, 1987.

The Law of Averages: New and Selected Stories. Washington, D.C.: Counterpoint, 2000.

MEMOIR

Double Down: Reflections on Gambling and Loss. With Steven Barthelme. Boston: Houghton Mifflin, 2000.

CRITICAL AND BIOGRAPHICAL STUDIES

Brinkmeyer, Robert H., Jr. "Suburban Culture, Imaginative Wonder: The Fiction of Frederick Barthelme." *Studies in the Literary Imagination* 27:105–114 (fall 1994).

———. "Regeneration through Nonviolence: Frederick Barthelme and the West." In *The World Is Our Home: Society and Culture in Contemporary Southern Writing.* Edited by Jeffrey J. Folks and Nancy Summers Folks. Lexington: University Press of Kentucky, 2000. Pp. 176–185.

Hughes, John. "Sex Wars in *Moon Deluxe*: Frederick Barthelme and the Postmodern Prufrock." *Studies in Short Fiction* 33:401–410 (summer 1996).

Mooney, Louise. "Barthelme, Frederick 1943–." In *Contemporary Authors,* vol. 122. Detroit: Gale, 1988. Pp. 46–51.

Peters, Timothy. "'80s Pastoral: Frederick Barthelme's *Moon Deluxe* Ten Years On." *Studies in Short Fiction* 31:175–185 (spring 1994).

Pheloung, Grant. "'Just Like Old Times': Frederick Barthelme and the Aesthetics of Postmodernism." *Critique* 40:172–180 (winter 1999).

BOOK REVIEWS

Atwood, Margaret. "Male and Lonely." *New York Times Book Review,* July 31, 1983, pp. 1, 22. (Review of *Moon Deluxe.*)

De Haven, Tom. "Drive, She Said." *New York Times Book Review,* September 24, 1995, p. 11. (Review of *Painted Desert.*)

Gifford, Bill. "Barthelme Writes Lovingly of Ordinary People." *Washington Times,* August 27, 1990, sec. F, p. 2. (Review of *Natural Selection.*)

Guttenplan, D. D. "Huck Finn Adrift in Suburbia." *Newsday,* August 12, 1990, p. 20. (Review of *Natural Selection.*)

Hempel, Amy. "A Hard Life for the Non-Poor." *New York Times Book Review,* August 19, 1990, p. 13. (Review of *Natural Selection.*)

Hulbert, Ann. "Welcome the Wimps." *New Republic,* October 31, 1983, pp. 35–38. (Review of *Moon Deluxe.*)

Kakutani, Michiko. *"Chroma." New York Times,* April 15, 1987, sec. C, p. 23.

———. "One Part Humor, 2 Parts Whining." *New York Times,* August 17, 1990, sec. C, p. 26. (Review of *Natural Selection.*)

Kaufmann, James. "Brand-Name Blues." *Washington Post Book World,* July 28, 1985, p. 11. (Review of *Tracer.*)

Kaveney, Roz. "A Model Muddle." *Times Literary Supplement,* March 21, 1986, p. 307. (Review of *Tracer.*)

Loewinsohn, Ron. "Looking for Love after Marriage." *New York Times Book Review,* September 30, 1984, pp. 1, 43. (Review of *Second Marriage.*)

Prado, Holly. "Tracer." *Los Angeles Times Book Review,* October 6, 1985, p. 14.

Prose, Francine. "Each Man Hates the Woman He Loves." *New York Times Book Review,* November 13, 1988, p. 9. (Review of *Two against One.*)

Yardley, Jonathan. "Marriage-Go-Round." *Washington Post,* September 19, 1984, sec. B, pp. 1, 15. (Review of *Second Marriage.*)

—LAURIE CHAMPION

Stephen Vincent Benét

1898–1943

AT THE TIME of his death in 1943, Stephen Vincent Benét, who was born in Bethlehem, Pennsylvania, on July 22, 1898, maintained two homes, a house he and his family rented in New York City and a summer home they owned in Stonington, Connecticut. Benét's death of a heart attack in New York early on the morning of March 13 was national news, as the radio dramas that he wrote on behalf of the American war effort were enormously popular. But first his death was news among those who knew him, including friends and acquaintances in Stonington. Something of the impact of Benét's death, and of the high regard in which he was held, is suggested by the anecdote that concludes Charles Fenton's account of Benét's life:

> Someone else telephoned a friend in Stonington to tell him Steve was dead. "Oh, no!" the small-town operator interrupted, her voice formal and shocked as she broke in on the conversation. "Is Mr. Benét dead? That will be a great loss to all of us."

In one sense the distressed operator was speaking for the people of Stonington, who felt pride and affection for the famous writer who was part of their community. In a larger sense, though, she was speaking for the people of the entire United States, who found in Benét a writer whose work expressed the essence of American life and called Americans, particularly in the midst of a world war, to rise to the best that their spirit could attain.

Benét's devotion to his country and to its participation in World War II were in part a manifestation of his family history. His grandfather and namesake, Stephen Vincent Benét (1827–1895), was a general and the chief of

ordnance for the United States Army. His father, James Walker Benét (1857–1928), was also a career army officer, a colonel, in ordnance. A family photograph shows Benét as a child of four sitting in the breech of a large cannon maintained under his father's supervision at the arsenal in Watervliet, New York, one of four military bases where his father was stationed during Benét's childhood.

Benét himself left Yale University in 1918, after his junior year, in order to enlist in the army as American forces began taking part in World War I. His stint in the army lasted three days. He had memorized the eye chart to pass his physical exam, but his poor vision quickly became evident. Unable to serve in the military, Benét worked a time for the State Department before returning to Yale to finish his degree in June of 1919.

While he was at Yale, another family trait—an interest in poetry—also was manifest. Like his older brother William Rose Benét (1886–1950), Stephen was prominent in the undergraduate literary culture at Yale. He began as a freshman to publish poems in the *Yale Literary Magazine* and eventually became the chairman of its editorial board. Even before he entered college, he had completed the six dramatic monologues that became *Five Men and Pompey* (1915), his first book of poetry, published in his freshman year when he was seventeen years old. In his junior year in 1917 his poem "The Drug Shop, or Endymion in Edmonstoun," written in homage to John Keats, won a prize for the best unpublished poem by a Yale student and was subsequently published by the Brick Row Book Shop. Among the three judges was Robert Frost.

William by this time too was a published poet and an assistant editor of *Century Magazine*. He would eventually publish twelve volumes of poetry, win the Pulitzer Prize in 1942, become a poetry critic for *The Saturday Review of Literature,* write a standard reference work, *The Reader's Encyclopedia: An Encyclopedia of World Literature and the Arts* (1948), and marry the poet Elinor Wylie. William and Stephen's older sister, Laura (1884–1979), was also a poet and the author of numerous books on literary subjects. Benét, in his contribution to the *Reader's Digest*'s "Most Unforgettable Character" series, remembered his father as the source of his family's interest in poetry:

> He taught me most of what I know about the technique of English verse. He could do it because he knew it—from Chaucer to Mary Anne O'Byrne, the washerwoman poet of Watervliet, N.Y. He could write any fixed form of it with deftness and tang. And if you came to him with a limping meter, an inchoate idea, he could show you, with the precision of a surgeon, what was wrong.

Benét wrote and published his second volume of verse, *Young Adventure* (1918), before completing his senior year at Yale. His third volume, *Heavens and Earth* (1920), was submitted as his graduate thesis for his master's degree. While a graduate student he also began work on his first novel, *The Beginning of Wisdom* (1921), a semiautobiographical tale whose young protagonist, like Benét, attends military school unhappily as a child before becoming a gifted but erratic student at Yale. Benét completed the novel while living in Paris on a fellowship from Yale following the completion of his M.A. There he met Rosemary Carr (1900–1962), also a young American writer, to whom he became engaged. They returned to the United States and were married in 1921. Benét soon completed his second novel, *Young People's Pride* (1922), set in the publishing world of New York.

By the time he was twenty-four, then, Benét was not only a young married man getting a start in New York City, he was also the author of two novels and three books of poetry. Despite this, little that he had written up to this point would be remembered by future generations if not for his later, more significant successes. In his early verse Benét often strove to be both traditional and modern without fully succeeding at either. Written on conventional themes— homages to Keats and Shelley, meditations on Helen of Troy, evocations of sensitive temperament and worldly wisdom set in the modern world—much of what he wrote after the dramatic monologues of *Five Men and Pompey* hardly suggested the particular genius that would make him the most widely read American poet of his generation. And though he would publish three more novels, the novel would not prove to be among his strengths.

Among his early poems, however, is "The Hemp," subtitled "A Virginia Legend," a pirate narrative written in ballad meter. Though itself a minor effort, it points the direction Benét's later more successful writing would go, combining an easy folksy manner with a strong narrative and an ironic sensibility. In the four years following his marriage he published, among other poems and a third novel (*Jean Huguenot,* 1923), three poems in ballad form—"The Ballad of William Sycamore," "The Mountain Whippoorwill," and "King David"—that won him a wide readership and the beginnings of his permanent place in American literature. Two of these poems consciously developed American themes whereas the third presented the familiar Old Testament figure in both a full-blooded and an ironic vein without conventional piety. The fiddling contest of "The Mountain Whippoorwill" has entered American lore, with its young boy of the Georgia hills giving it his all after the performances of the legendary fiddlers Big Tom Sargent, Little Jimmy Weezer, and Old Dan Wheeling:

An' hell broke loose,
Hell broke loose,
Fire on the mountains—snakes in the grass.
Satan's here a-bilin'—oh, Lordy, let him pass!
Go down Moses, set my people free,
Pop goes the weasel thu' the old Red Sea!
Jonah sittin' on a hickory-bough,
Up jumps a whale—an' where's yore prophet
    now?
Rabbit in the pea-patch, possum in the pot,
Try an' stop my fiddle, now my fiddle's gettin'
    hot!

The three ballads were collected with other poems in *Tiger Joy,* Benét's fourth poetry volume, in 1925. The following year he published his fourth novel, *Spanish Bayonet,* and more importantly he received a Guggenheim Fellowship, allowing him to move with his wife and infant daughter Stephanie to Paris to work on a long poem. In France he would be able to live inexpensively and concentrate on his poetry without feeling the necessity to earn money. The long poem Benét was working on took the better part of two years, during which time his son Thomas was born.

Few readers now would think that so American a poem as *John Brown's Body,* published in 1928, was actually written in Paris. This verse "cyclorama" (a term Benét preferred to epic) of the American Civil War, consisting of an invocation, a prelude, and eight books totaling 11,835 lines, drew both on the skill at characterization that Benét had developed in his early dramatic monologues and on the interest in American language and themes evidenced in his ballads. It also drew on his interest in American military history, fostered by his heritage, and on his appreciation for the variety of American backgrounds that he experienced as an army child moving from base to base, from New York to Illinois to California to Georgia. He tried as much as possible not to take a side in the poem, though his moral opposition to slavery is clear in the prelude set aboard a slave ship. The poem

was painstakingly researched and carefully written. It was also a phenomenal success.

Benét returned to New York in 1929 as a celebrity, the winner of a Pulitzer Prize. *John Brown's Body* was both a popular and a critical success. For the first time he was financially secure. This good fortune did not last long, however, as Benét invested much of his windfall in stocks, only to see his investments wiped out in the stock market crash in 1929. Yet even as the nation descended into the Great Depression, money still flowed plentifully in Hollywood as motion pictures continued to thrive after the advent of talking pictures in the late 1920s. Leaving his young family behind, Benét went to Hollywood shortly after the crash to work for the director D. W. Griffith on a screenplay about the life of Abraham Lincoln. Despite his admiration for Griffith, Benét found the life of a Hollywood screenwriter intolerable. In a letter of January 23, 1930, to his agent, Carl Brandt, he complained of the "waste, stupidity and conceit" of the motion picture business:

> Since arriving, I have written 4 versions of *Abraham Lincoln,* including a good one, playable in their required time. That, of course, is out. Seven people, including myself, are now working in conferences on the 5th one which promises hopefully to be the worst yet. If I don't get out of here soon I am going crazy. Perhaps I am crazy now. I wouldn't be surprised.

Benét returned to New York after three months in California. His difficult financial circumstances were compounded by poor health, and he entered into one of his least productive periods. In the years prior to *John Brown's Body* Benét had earned a living by writing what he often considered to be vapid short stories for the magazine market, and as his health improved he turned again to this expedient. Ironically, however, he found with the publication of "The Devil and Daniel Webster" in the *Saturday Evening Post* in 1936 that his earnings from short fiction would rise considerably when he stopped writing the stories he thought he had to write and instead wrote the stories he wanted to write. Like *John Brown's Body* and "The Mountain Whippoorwill," "The Devil and Daniel Webster" combined American themes with an easy style and a compelling narrative. Benét's strong sense of irony tempered his equally strong patriotic feeling to produce a story enjoyable for its many small touches as much as for its overall embrace of American character. Though two additional stories featuring Daniel Webster were less successful, Benét for the first time began to think of himself not simply as a poet who wrote stories for money but as a writer of short stories. Two collections of short stories appeared toward the end of the decade, *Thirteen O'Clock* (1937) and *Tales before Midnight* (1939), bringing together the best of his new work and a handful of his earlier stories. Not all were historical fiction. Some were studies of contemporary American life, some reflected Benét's concerns about developments in Europe, and some were set in the more imaginative worlds of fantasy and fable. The best of them had in common, though, a sure craftsmanship and a benevolent imagination.

Benét's poetry during this time became more politically aware and also less optimistic. He saw earlier than many the trend toward totalitarianism and fascism in Europe as well as the increasing materialism and mechanization of American life. *Burning City* (1936), his fifth collection of poems (not counting *A Book of Americans* [1933], a volume of children's poems written in collaboration with his wife), is notable for the prominence of these concerns in such poems as "Notes to Be Left in a Cornerstone," "Litany for Dictatorships," "Ode to the Austrian Socialists," and the three "Nightmare" poems that had originally appeared in *The New Yorker*. Though socially Benét enjoyed the company of wealthy conservatives, his own politics became more liberal and democratic. He defended Franklin Roosevelt against detrac-

tors from both the Left and the Right, presenting him in "Tuesday, November 5th, 1940" (in *The Last Circle*) as

> A country squire from Hyde Park with a Harvard accent,
> Who never once failed the people
> And whom the people won't fail.

Throughout this period Benét planned and worked on a long poem on the spirit of America expressed in the continual movement west of the American people, beginning in the crossing of the Atlantic and continuing to the completion of the transcontinental railroad and beyond. *Western Star* (1943) was to be grander even than *John Brown's Body*. When World War II arrived, however, Benét had to put it aside to do the work that gave him perhaps his largest contemporary audience, the series of radio plays and public statements that he regarded as frankly propagandistic but that he thought were the obligation of any artist able to use his talents in this way. His mastery of the radio drama was evident in the scripts he provided, often on short notice, for broadcasts such as "Dear Adolph," a series of monologues by "typical" Americans—a farmer, a businessman, a working man, a housewife, a soldier, an immigrant—and "A Child Is Born" (1942), a dramatization of the Christmas story emphasizing the necessity to stand for human values in a time of great stress. "We Stand United" (1940) and "They Burned the Books" (1942) championed the American spirit while challenging the totalitarian mind-set with which Benét felt America to be at war. At the request of the Office of War Information, he wrote a short history, *America* (1944), which as a consequence of its wide distribution after the war helped to shape the understanding that people everywhere had of the United States.

This work, for which he refused to accept payment, took a physical toll. While working on *America* in February 1943, he suffered a heart attack. He appeared to recover, and he finished *America*. He also began work on a follow-up to "A Child Is Born"; it was to be an Easter drama entitled "The Watchers by the Stone." Early in the morning of March 13, 1943, however, he suffered a second heart attack and died. *Western Star* was still unfinished, but the publication of the completed Book One later that year brought him his second Pulitzer Prize.

THE SPIRIT OF AMERICA

"I tried to put America in it—at least some of the America I knew. If I did so, some of it should stand till a better man comes along." So Benét wrote of *John Brown's Body* to his publisher, John Farrar in late 1927. Though he at times resisted, the identification of Benét with American themes—in *John Brown's Body*; in "The Mountain Whippoorwill," "The Ballad of William Sycamore," and "American Names"; in "The Sobbin' Women" (in *Thirteen O'Clock*), "The Devil and Daniel Webster," and "Freedom's a Hard-Bought Thing"; in *A Summons to the Free* (1941), *America,* and *A Book of Americans*—is inescapable. Its strongest theoretical statement comes in the Invocation to *John Brown's Body,* which calls upon the

> American muse, whose strong and diverse heart
> So many men have tried to understand
> But only made it smaller with their art,
> Because you are as various as your land.

Here Benét emphasizes what he saw as the great strength of the political entity that became the United States of America: not its supposed ancestry stepping ashore at Plymouth Rock, but its great geographic and cultural diversity.

Benét's desire to do justice to this diversity is evident in the construction of *John Brown's Body.* Not only does he give us Jack Ellyat, son of Yankee New England, and Clay Wingate, son of the cavalier South, he gives us as well the Pennsylvania farmer Jake Diefer and the hill-billy Luke Breckinridge, Sally Dupré, the

daughter of a French dancing master, and Meloras Villas, the nomadic child of no fixed place. There are slaves: Spade escaping to the north, old Cudjo helping his mistress bury the silver at the approach of Sherman's army, and fat Aunt Bess. All are American—Jefferson Davis as much as Abraham Lincoln, deserters and spies as well as prisoners and generals, Judah P. Benjamin, the Jew among the Confederate leadership, as much as the fanatical Puritan John Brown, Wingate Hall and the slave's cabin, Richmond and Washington, Andersonville and Petersburg.

Acknowledgment of American diversity was the goal of much of Benét's fiction was well. If "The Devil and Daniel Webster" ironically celebrates New England stubbornness and shrewdness, "The Mountain Whippoorwill" celebrates the vivacity to be found among the poor of the Georgia hills. *Spanish Bayonet,* set in colonial America on the eve of the Revolutionary War, takes place not in Boston or Philadelphia but in Florida. (The title refers not to a weapon but to a plant characteristic of Florida.) Of the novel's four main characters, two are English and two are Spanish, poor émigrés from the island of Minorca, as were Benét's own ancestors. "O'Halloran's Luck" (in *Tales before Midnight*), written at a time when anti-Irish prejudice was common, opens with the statement: "They were strong men built the Big Road, in the early days of America, and it was the Irish did it." "Jacob and the Indians" (also in *Tale before Midnight*) follows a young Jewish peddler as he seeks his fortune among the native people beyond the limits of Philadelphia. "Do you know why I came to this country?" a successful Jew asks young Jacob rhetorically. "My house has lent money to kings. A little fish, a few furs—what are they to my house? No, it was for the promise—the promise of Penn—that this land should be an habitation and a refuge, not only for the Gentiles." Later, when Jacob has traveled deep into the great eastern forest, he feels the affinity between America and his Jewish heritage. "He was eating deer's meat in a forest and sleeping beside embers in the open night. It was so that Israel must have slept in the wilderness. He had not thought of it as so, but it was so."

American racial and ethnic diversity is only a part, though, of the diversity Benét observes. America consists too of city and country, rich and poor and the range between, small town characters and those who have left the small towns for the fortune and sophistication of the cities, industrialists and bankers and working people in working-class neighborhoods. *James Shore's Daughter* (1934), Benét's last novel, follows the fortunes of the daughter of a wealthy financier who earned his first fortune from the mines of the West not as a prospector but as a speculator and owner. "All Around the Town" (in *Selected Works of Stephen Vincent Benét*), on the other hand, looks literally beneath the prosperity of America to appreciate the work that built it. The narrator, one of the invisible men who built the New York subway, says:

> If it wasn't for the thousands of men whose names you've never heard of, all living their lives underground, it wouldn't be a city, or the same city. I'd think of it, now and again, on the night shift, when things got quiet above. They'd have gone to sleep by then—yes, even the rich and proud,—but we'd be working. It's hard to put to you so you'll understand it. You see the place in the street where it's planked over, and the taxi has to slow up, and you start to swear. But, underneath, there's the work gangs, and the lights.

Benét also recognized, however, that the promise of Penn—the promise that America would be a place of refuge for all—had not always been kept. "Freedom's a Hard-Bought Thing," published in the *Saturday Evening Post* in 1940 as the world was heading again toward war, reminded its readers of the American commitment to liberty and freedom, but did so not in a story of our war for independence from England, but through the story of Cue, a slave who makes his way to freedom in Canada. "A long time ago, in times gone by, in slavery times, there was a man named Cue," the story's narrator begins. "I want you to think about him. I've got a reason." The reason is two-fold: to rededicate Benét's readers to the cause of freedom and to remind them of their own country's shortcomings. At the story's conclusion, having arrived safely in Canada via the Underground Railroad, Cue reflects on his fortune:

> He say to himself in his mind, *I'm free. My name's Cue—John H. Cue. I got a strong back and strong arms. I got freedom in my heart. I got a first name and a last name and a middle name. I never had them all before.*
>
> He say to himself, *My name's Cue—John H. Cue. I got a name and a tale to tell. I got a hammer to swing. I got a tale to tell my people. I got recollection. I call my first son "John Freedom Cue." I call my first daughter "Come-Out-of-the-Lion's-Mouth."*

Nor was Benét uncritical of American society, though he believed resolutely in its foundation in justice and liberty. His criticism was more muted than his celebration and was perhaps more effective for its understatement. Benét recognized, for instance, the tendency to conformity and to shallow Protestant optimism that characterized American sensibility both before and after the Great Depression. In "The Three Fates," among Benét's last stories, and reprinted in *The Devil and Daniel Webster and Other Writings* (1999), a young boy comes to recognize the limitations of his typically American middle-class family. The Tenterdens are on the surface a model family:

> It was the sort of family that believes in fresh air and cold baths and family jests and councils— they were all rather good at games and practical jokes, and a stranger in their midst was instantly made at home. That is to say, if he or she were "their sort"—if not, the Tenterdens agreed in

private that the stranger was a stick or a queer duck, but redoubled their attentions, politely, nevertheless.

John Tenterden is sixteen, the middle child of five, and a little different even before he suffers the misfortune of being fallen in love with by a sickly Catholic girl only fourteen years old. John's eyes are darker than his parents' and siblings', and his skin is slightly olive, suggesting "some distant Latin ancestor." He collects moths, not recognizing his own attraction to the beautiful in a family little interested in beauty. "The Tenterdens were not very fond of art— they were well-informed and doughty at pencil-and-paper games, but art itself, art unaccredited by teachers and public opinion, they considered, quite sensibly, a little queer."

When Mona Gregg becomes not only infatuated with him but seriously ill as well, John is brought to feelings beyond the Tenterden range. Though "privacy and thought" are alike missing from the Tenterden household, John becomes thoughtful and secretive. Fearful that he himself, in rejecting Mona Gregg's attentions, is somehow responsible for her illness, he ventures out of his wholesome, optimistic home to visit a Catholic church in the poorer part of town. The church is different from the upbeat Protestant church his family sometimes attends without any real belief. He finds there "something foreign, mysterious, and powerful in its dimness and strangeness. He could not approve of it, but it was obviously strong magic." He lights candles and says prayers to the saints. On the way home the crowded streets and shops of this foreign part of town "seemed no longer alien and disreputable but normal and friendly." The cost to John, though, is alienation from his "typical" American family. He too becomes strange, thoughtful. "There was a whole world beyond the Tenterden cosmos"—the cosmos of conventional America—"a world where people died and fell in love."

The shallow, relatively emotion-free, determinedly nonethnic world of mainstream Protestant America appears as well in "The King of the Cats" (in *Thirteen O'Clock*). Tommy Brooks is "just one of those pleasant, normal young men who seem created to carry on the bond business by reading the newspapers in the University Club during most of the day." Tommy Brooks's fate, however, is not to be fallen in love with, but to fall in love, in this case with the Princess Vivrakanarda. Unlike Tommy or the Tenterdens, the princess is of mixed heritage. Though writing in a culture still very much race conscious, Benét does not present this as an indication of inferiority to her would-be suitor, but rather just the opposite.

> The mingling of races in her had produced an exotic beauty as distinguished as it was strange. She moved with a feline, effortless grace, and her skin was as it had been gently powdered with tiny grains of the purest gold—yet the blueness of her eyes, set just a trifle slantingly, was as pure and startling as the sea on the rocks of Maine.

Competing with Tommy Brooks for the princess's attention is a figure equally exotic— Monsieur Tibault, a conductor who is all the rage of Europe not just for his musical flair but for his strange appendage, a tail like the tail of a cat, which he wields instead of a baton in front of his orchestra.

Like the Tenterdens, Tommy Brooks, though pleasant and successful for his age, has his limitations. Monsieur Tibault leads the orchestra at Carnegie Hall with great success through Gluck's overture to "Iphigenie in Aulis" and Beethoven's Eighth Symphony. The music, however, is lost on one such as Tommy Brooks. "To a man whose simple Princetonian nature found in 'Just a Little Love, a Little Kiss,' the quintessence of musical art, the average symphony was a positive torture." Tommy instead focuses jealously on the rapt response of the princess, for, though Tommy's "infatuated daydreams were beginning to be beset by smart solitaires and imaginary apartments on Park Avenue," he can not compete with the strange Monsieur Tibault for the attention of the exotic Princess Vivrakanarda.

Monsieur Tibault, true to the folktale Benét has adapted to modern New York, turns out quite literally to be "a black cat," just as Princess Vivrakanarda turns out to be "a Siamese kitten." In the Manhattan of the 1920s, however—the Manhattan of Harlem and the Cotton Club as much as the Manhattan of the University Club and Park Avenue—this folktale takes on a deeper resonance, as Tommy Brooks is finally left out while the two lovers come to "reign together now, King and Queen of all the mysterious Kingdom of Cats." Just as in "The Three Fates" there is a depth of existence in "the district beyond the tracks" that is unknown to the all-American Tenterdens, there is a vivacity, genius, and élan that is beyond the scope of the white, Protestant, well-educated, successful Tommy Brooks.

Benét's mixed feelings about America—both loving and critical—are nowhere more successfully interwoven than in "The Devil and Daniel Webster." Daniel Webster embodies for Benét the strengths that have made the United States of America a great nation. A half-dozen years after the success of "The Devil and Daniel Webster," in the midst of World War II, the Treasury Department asked Benét to contribute an essay on Webster to a patriotic book entitled *There Were Giants in the Land* (1942). "He did one central thing," Benét wrote of Daniel Webster.

> He set up and affirmed in men's minds the idea of the United States, not just as a haphazard, temporary league or a partnership between states to be dissolved at their convenience, but as an entity, a deep reality, a living thing that deserved and must have the deepest devotion of every American.

Webster's reputation in his native New England was tarnished, however, by his speech in support of the Compromise of 1850, which tempo-

rarily held the Union together by extending the possibility of slavery into the territories newly acquired from Mexico and by strengthening fugitive slave laws in the north. Northern abolitionists condemned Daniel Webster, most enduringly in the poem "Ichabod" by John Greenleaf Whittier. In his essay for *There Were Giants in the Land* Benét rejects such criticism, declaring that "they thought he was trying to compromise with slavery when what he was trying to do was seek for a peaceful solution of the differences between North and South."

"The Devil and Daniel Webster," however, is less straightforward. Its very title links Daniel Webster with the devil, though ostensibly the story presents them as antagonists. The action of the story takes place before the 1850 speech, when Webster is in his prime, and an admiring, even mythic tone is immediately established. At the same time, however, the narrative places this mythic tone not just in the past, but in a past that will perhaps come to be doubted.

> You see, for a while, he was the biggest man in the country. He never got to be President, but he was the biggest man. There were thousands that trusted in him right next to God Almighty, and they told stories about him that were like the stories of patriarchs and such. They said, when he stood up to speak, stars and stripes came right out of the sky. . . . A man with a mouth like a mastiff, a brow like a mountain and eyes like burning anthracite—that was Dan'l Webster in his prime.

Daniel Webster and the devil (or Scratch, as local tradition would have it) share their prominence in the story with an ordinary New Englander, Jabez Stone, who "wasn't a bad man to start with, but . . . an unlucky man." His luck changes, however, when he sells his soul to the devil in a fit of frustration. He becomes a prosperous farmer, a good citizen with political aspirations. Nothing in the story suggests that he engages in anything evil or even dishonest. He is, rather, a sympathetic, if also humorous, figure, a stubborn New Hampshireman who has gotten himself into a fix. Looked at another way, though, the humor carries a sharper irony: when at last Jabez Stone wishes to back out of his deal with the devil, he declares that he has some doubts about the deal they have made, "this being the U.S.A. and me always having been a religious man." Yet this quintessential American citizen has prospered not by his own hard work and character but by a pact with the devil.

Benét's association between American success and the devil is subtly reinforced throughout the story, much in the way it is in Nathaniel Hawthorne's darker "Young Goodman Brown." When Daniel Webster attempts to void Stone's pact with the devil by declaring that "Mr. Stone is an American citizen" and, as was established by the War of 1812, "no American citizen may be forced into the service of a foreign prince," the devil replies that he is no foreigner. When Webster says that he has never heard of the devil claiming American citizenship, the devil answers him.

"And who with better right?" said the stranger, with one of his terrible smiles. "When the first wrong was done to the first Indian, I was there. When the first slaver put out for the Congo, I stood on her deck. Am I not in your books and stories and beliefs, from the first settlements on? Am I not spoken of, still, in every church in New England? 'Tis true the North claims me for a Southerner and the South for a Northerner, but I am neither. I am merely an honest American like yourself—and of the best descent—for, to tell the truth, Mr. Webster, though I don't like to boast of it, my name is older in this country than yours."

The jury that the devil convenes to hear the case continues this critical look at America. The majority of those named—King Philip, Walter Butler, Simon Girty, Blackbeard the pirate, John Smeet—are either criminals or men opposed to the development of America, yet they too, the narrative affirms, "had all played a part in America." The judge, on the other hand, has been neither outlaw nor traitor. Justice Hathorne, an ancestor of Nathaniel Hawthorne, was among the judges at the Salem witch trials and thus represents, as he did for Hawthorne, a spirit of persecution embedded in the American psyche.

In his summation Daniel Webster retells the story of America. He speaks of the evil of slavery in a land dedicated to freedom. He acknowledges "all the wrong that had ever been done," but not to denounce America. Rather, "he showed how, out of the wrong and the right, the suffering and the starvations, something new had come." He also acknowledges that Jabez Stone, the representative American, is just a man, with faults and shortcomings as well as strengths. But for this should he, should the America he represents, be punished for all eternity?

The jury finds no, and in this we have both Benét's affirmation of American character and his irony. The jury that affirms him is after all a jury of ne'er-do-wells. And Benét affirms Webster as well, allowing him to declare that he will not care what others will say of him in response to his speech in support of the Compromise of 1850 if he speaks honestly and the Union stands. The good in America finally matters more than its failings and shortcomings.

Benét would feel this even more strongly as he watched the rise of fascism in Europe with the threat to freedom and democracy it presented. Putting aside his other projects, Benét turned his abilities to what he himself frankly acknowledged to be propaganda, a weapon of war in a war justly waged on behalf of liberty. There is little that is critical or ironic in either the radio dramas or the speeches, essays, and history written in the context of the war with Germany, Italy, and Japan. The book of juvenile verse he wrote with his wife, Rosemary, in 1933, *A Book of Americans,* had more irony and more criticism than the history *America* written for the War Department ten years later. In "Listen to the People," a radio drama broadcast on July 4, 1941, five months before the United States entered the war, Benét defended the

American ideal not only against challenges from European totalitarianism but from those, both conservative and radical, who challenged it from within American society. "Forget everything but the class-struggle," a radical voice urges. "Forget democracy." At the same time a conservative voice counsels, "Hate and distrust your own government. Whisper, hate and never look forward." Opposed to these are other voices that speak out of the American commitment to liberty: a housewife, a workingman, a man on relief, an old man, everyday Americans.

> Our voice is not one voice but many voices,
> Not one man's, not the greatest, but the people's.
> The blue sky and the forty-eight States of the
>   people.
> Many in easy times but one in the pinch
> And that's what some folks forget.
> Our voice is all the objectors and dissenters
> And they sink and are lost in the groundswell of
>   the people,
> Once the people rouse, once the people wake and
>   listen.
> People, you people, growing everywhere,
> What have you got to say?
> There's a smart boy here with a question and he
>   wants answers.
> What have you got to say?

And the people reply. They speak of the four freedoms put forward by Franklin Delano Roosevelt in his State of the Union Address six months earlier, on January 6, 1941: "Freedom to speak and pray / Freedom from want and fear." They speak of America as "a refuge and a fortress and a hope." They speak of "a new world rising," a world of liberty, justice, law, and hope, not for a few or for a master race but for all.

Benét's patriotism was a liberal patriotism, expressed in his poem affirming the reelection of Roosevelt, "Tuesday, November 5th, 1940," and in his "Ode to Walt Whitman." It is most direct and perhaps most eloquent in "A Creed for Americans," written for the Council for Democracy shortly before his death:

We are unalterably opposed to class hatred, race hatred, religious hatred, however manifested, by whomever instilled. . . . We believe that political freedom implies and acknowledges economic responsibility. We do not believe that any state is an admirable state that lets its people go hungry when they might be fed, ragged when they might be clothed, sick when they might be well, workless when they might have work. We believe that it is the duty of all of us, the whole people, working through our democratic system, to see that such conditions are remedied, whenever and wherever they exist in our country.

By declaring these goals Benét implicitly acknowledges the existence of racism, prejudice, intolerance, and poverty in his America. He also affirms, however, that American ideals and institutions are the best hope in the world for their remedy.

LIFE'S JOURNEY

In his summation in "The Devil and Daniel Webster," Daniel Webster speaks not only "about the things that make a country a country" but also about the things that make "a man a man." Benét too was not simply, or even primarily, interested in what makes America what it is. He was also interested in human beings—their lives, their hopes, their successes and failures. He was interested in the difficulties the young face in coming of age, in courtship and marriage, in parenthood and particularly in fatherhood, in civic duty, in the foibles and pleasures of everyday life. As with America, he finds in life more to affirm than to protest or lament. In "Blossom and Fruit" (in *Thirteen O'Clock*), among the earliest stories Benét chose to reprint, two old men—friends throughout their long lives though now too frail to meet more than once or twice a year—go to the cellar of a country farmhouse to drink a cup or two of hard cider. They try to puzzle out the meaning of life and love, the impulses that bring life into being even in the relentless presence of death, with no success. But they don't really mind. "Adorable life," one of them later calls it. Nothing more needs to be said.

Benét knew as well the difficulties and unhappiness of life, as shown in stories collected in *Tales before Midnight:* in "Too Early Spring" the lives of the young protagonists are blighted by the narrow-mindedness and gossip of a small town; in "A Life at Angelo's" and "Among Those Present" the failed marriages and shallow lives of Manhattan society are revealed all too effectively by voices, one male and one female, confidently unaware of their superficiality. The narrator of "Everybody Was Very Nice" (in *Thirteen O'Clock*) a partner in a conservative brokerage firm who is unhappy in his second marriage, is shocked by his sixteen-year-old daughter's future plans, which include marrying once for the experience and maybe a second time for something more lasting, though the mother of a friend of hers has just married for the fourth time. He asks her if she might think about marriage differently if he and her mother had stayed married. "'But you didn't, did you?' she said, and her voice wasn't hurt or anything, just natural. 'I mean, almost nobody does any more. Don't worry, daddy. Bud and I understand all about it—good gracious, we're grown up!'"

Benét also understands how marriages can work out, sometimes in the most unlikely ways. "The Story about the Anteater" (in *Tales before Midnight*) revolves around a story the husband repeatedly tells, a mildly racist tale that the wife finds offensive the first time he tells it, before their marriage.

> It was just the kind of story she'd always hated—cruel and—yes—vulgar. Not even healthily vulgar—vulgar with no redeeming adjective. He ought to have known she hated that kind of story. He ought to have known!
>
> If love meant anything, according to the books, it meant understanding the other person, didn't it? And, if you didn't understand them, in such a little thing, why, what was life going to be afterwards?

Yet they marry anyway, and he continues to tell the story at parties and to dinner guests, and then often at the most awkward moments, moments when she cannot imagine how their marriage can continue. But it does, and eventually the story about the anteater ceases to be unbearable. No harm is meant and none is done. It is simply absorbed into their larger life together, a life that has become comfortable and familiar, a life that on balance is more good than bad. Though she would never tell it herself—she has her own story about Joan and the watering pot—it is hers as much as his. Like their house, like their children, like their life together, it is theirs.

A more complex and deeply felt story on marriage, "A Death in the Country" (in *Thirteen O'Clock*) follows a husband away from his wife as he travels from the city back to the small town where he'd grown up to attend the funeral of an aunt. The first two-thirds of the story shows Benét's technique at its most subtle, as the reader comes, through the thoughts of Tom Carroll, to recognize not just his shallowness but, more painfully, the shallowness of Claire, his wife, not least in her refusal to accompany him home, though he goes himself primarily as a formality. The dichotomy of small town and big city—New York City—is also familiar and well developed. The reader observes that Tom's "escape" from Waynesville and Hessian Street has been an escape into emptiness and meaninglessness, however unsophisticated and tiresome his cousins and aunts and uncles may be. Claire's belief, read in a book, that "the family was the jungle that you grow up in and, if you did not, somehow, break through to light and air of your own when you were young, you died," rings hollow, indicative of the superficiality of modern progressive thought, just as her resistance to buying a house can be recognized by the reader simply as a refusal to grow up. When Tom thinks that "naturally, then, it was only right for him to come to this death in his own country alone . . . any other course would have been a monstrous selfishness," the reader is ahead of him, recognizing that it is Claire who is monstrous and selfish.

At the funeral, though, a subtle shift sets in. Rather than watching Tom gradually discover his wife's immaturity and selfishness, the reader begins to see that Tom does not understand the world very well, not the world he grew up in nor the woman to whom he is married. Another level of understanding must be reached, in which the easy dichotomies of small town and big city, selfish immaturity and mature selfless-ness, need to be reexamined. Claire's mind and experience, Tom Carroll comes to realize, have been unknown to him. The reader, then, cannot have come to any clear understanding of her shortcomings or her strengths through Tom's limited thoughts. He returns to her at story's end with a new appreciation for who she might be and what pain she might suffer. He comes to this awareness in a conversation with his surviv-ing aunt. And though earlier in the story he thought he had grown by unlearning what she'd taught him as a child, now he sees that he hasn't learned enough. Claire would need his help in life, he realizes, but he doesn't know that he can give her any. "I don't know how," he admits. "Well, you're fond of her," his aunt reassures him. "They say that helps."

Benét's own marriage was successful, and so it is no surprise that he wrote stories suggesting how marriages do work out. Similarly it is not surprising that some of his best stories positively portray the role of fathers, reflecting the beneficial influence his own father had in his life. The father in "The Die-Hard" (in *Tales before Midnight*) is a doctor—fittingly he restores health to the world of the story when he discovers his son Jimmy with the pistol given him by the delusional Colonel Cappalow. The plot that the colonel has drawn Jimmy Williams into—to restore the Confederacy nearly thirty years after Lee's surrender to Grant at Appo-

mottax—is the supreme expression of the colonel's delusion, but Jimmy, thirteen years old, is duped by it. This does not discredit Jimmy's intelligence, however. "He was a bright boy," we are told, "maybe a little to bright for his age. He'd think about a thing till it seemed real to him—and that's a dangerous gift." Instead it reflects his immaturity, his lack of experience. Colonel Cappalow teaches Jimmy history, and his long-nursed resentment of the world seems admirable to the inexperienced boy.

> "Yes," he said, "there are many traitors. Men I held in the greatest esteem have betrayed their class and their system. They have accepted ruin and domination in the name of advancement. But we will not speak of them now." He took the frosted silver cup from the tray and motioned to Jimmy Williams that the small fluted glass was for him. "I shall ask you to rise, Mr. Williams," he said. "We shall drink a toast." He paused for a moment, standing straight. "To the Confederate States of America and damnation to all her enemies!" he said.
>
> Jimmy Williams drank. He'd never drunk any wine before, except blackberry cordial, and this wine seemed to him powerfully thin and sour. But he felt grown up as he drank it, and that was a fine feeling. . . .
>
> When Jimmy Williams went out into the sun again, he felt changed. and excited too. For he knew about Old Man Cappalow now, and he was just about the grandest person in the world.

Colonel Cappalow's plan to start a rebellion against the federal government by capturing the post office and the railway station, even at the cost of shooting the postmaster and the station agent, is scary yet at the same time exciting to Jimmy's adolescent imagination. When Benét wrote "The Die-Hard" in 1938, he no doubt intended it as a metaphor for the ways in which young boys left to their own thoughts can be drawn to destruction, but he could not have anticipated the degree to which, by the end of the twentieth century, the story would seem not metaphorical but prophetic, as adolescents take guns to school and delusional young men plot violent schemes to overthrow the federal government. Jimmy's drift toward destruction, however, is stopped by the intervention of his father, when Doctor Williams comes upon him getting ready in the family woodshed.

> Well, naturally, Jimmy dropped the pistol and jumped. The pistol didn't explode, for he'd forgotten it needed a cap. But with that moment something seemed to break inside Jimmy Williams. For it was the first time he'd really been afraid and ashamed in front of his father, and now he was ashamed and afraid. And then it was like waking up out of an illness, for his father saw his white face and said, "What's the matter, son?" and the words began to come out of his mouth.

Doctor Williams is himself a Confederate veteran, but his rejection of Colonel Cappalow and his ideas is absolute. The doctor had fought until the surrender, but that was the past. With Jimmy waiting in the buggy the doctor confronts the old colonel: "We've got something better to do than fill up a boy with a lot of magnolious notions and aim to shoot up a postmaster because there's a Republican President. . . . Hate stinks when its kept too long in the barrel, no matter how you dress it up and talk fine about it." The Colonel's long-rumored treasure, a million dollars kept hidden in the house, turns out to be worthless Confederate money, and it is up to the father to teach his son true values, to bring him out of the dangerous world and back to the world of health.

"Doc Mellhorn and the Pearly Gates" (in *Tales before Midnight*), also published in 1938, presents a fatherly figure in a lighthearted rather than a serious vein. When the small-town doctor arrives at the pearly gates with his black bag in hand, he realizes that there will be no work for him there, and so he gets back in his car and drives to the other place, where there is much for him to do, though the authorities there don't much like his doing it. Benét's pleasure in

irony for its own sake is given full play, with little social commentary, though there are glimpses here and there, as when the doctor reflects on the afflictions he attends: "It was mostly sprains, fractures, bruises and dislocations, of course, with occasional burns and scalds—and, on the whole, it reminded Doc Mellhorn a good deal of his practice in Steeltown, especially when it came to foreign bodies in the eye."

As with many of Benét's admirable characters, Doc Mellhorn is happiest doing something useful for others, a trait lacking in the unhappy figures of Benét's stories of modern failure masquerading as success. Sometimes, as in "Schooner Fairchild's Class" (another story from 1938), doing something useful for others means merely sharing with them a genuine enthusiasm for life. More often civic duty combines with a relish for life, as it does with Doc Mellhorn and with Daniel Webster. Webster's fishing rod, the enormous country breakfasts he serves to guests, the jug he shares with Jabez Stone the night of the visit from the devil—these are as important to Webster's character as his prowess with words and his commitment to the Union. Benét's anti-Puritanism is evident: freedom and equality are necessary so that life—"This Bright Dream," as another of his best stories is titled—might be enjoyed.

HUMANITY'S JOURNEY

When Daniel Webster pleads Jabez Stone's case, more is at stake than the soul of one New Hampshire farmer who in a fit of frustration has sold his soul to the devil. "He wasn't pleading for any one person any more, though his voice rang like an organ. He was telling the story and the failures and the endless journey of mankind." Similarly Benét himself is not interested only in Americans and life in America. Like Thomas Paine, Benét believed that the cause of

America is the cause of all humanity.

Many of Benét's stories do not have American settings. "The Last of the Legions" (in *Tales before Midnight*) is set in Britain at the time of the withdrawal of the Roman legions. "The Bishop's Beggar" (in *The Last Circle*) is set in Renaissance Italy. "The Blood of the Martyrs" (in *Thirteen O'Clock*) and "Into Egypt" (in *Selected Works of Stephen Vincent Benét*) take place in twentieth-century Europe. Some, like "The Land Where There Is No Death" and "As It Was in the Beginning" (both in *The Last Circle*), take place in purely imaginary places. "By the Waters of Babylon" (in *Thirteen O'Clock*) takes place in America, but an America transformed by catastrophe into a prehistoric world. Benét's interests remain the same however: the adjustments human beings make to the challenges of love and death, our human responsibilities, the progress and the failures of the human journey.

John Brown's Body, though written by the son of a military family, is not a celebration of military might devoted to a good cause. Rather it shows the interweaving of success and failure that is characteristic of Benét's thought. In the stories of its individual characters, both historical and imaginary, failure is more common than victory. The imaginary characters in particular are rarely heroic. Some go into battle with heroic aspirations and some remain true to those aspirations, but the exigencies of war generally go otherwise. Confusion, capture, sickness, injury, futility, death, desertion, and execution—these are the experiences of war that *John Brown's Body* gives its readers. Victory often amounts to little more than surviving the brutality and suffering of the prison camps or not bleeding to death on the battlefield. The execution of a spy is less an act of justice or even military necessity than it is an act of petty cruelty.

The historic characters are no less figures of failure and tragedy. The two most admirable of them—Lincoln and Lee—exemplify Benét's complex view, as one leads his side to victory only to be claimed by the bitterness and fury of the defeated, while the other in defeat points the way forward by his insistence that there be no bitterness once the cause is lost. John Brown's cause is just, yet he was "a man of iron tears / With a bullet for a heart." The first man killed in the raid on Harpers Ferry is Shepherd Heyward, "Free negro, baggage-master of the small station, / Well-known in the town, hardworking, thrifty and fated," shot by Brown's men as they attempt to take over the train station:

> A rifle cracked.
> He fell by the station-platform, gripping his belly,
> And lay for twelve hours of torment, asking for water
> Until he was able to die.

The parallel between John Brown's raid on Harpers Ferry and the attack planned by Colonel Cappalow in "The Die-Hard" is unmistakable. Both John Brown and Colonel Cappalow envision that a universal uprising will follow their assaults on small targets, assaults that will take the lives of victims who have no other guilt than to be at the places targeted for capture—the armory, the train station, the post office. And just as Colonel Cappalow is delusional, so is John Brown, however right his cause:

> So the night wore away, indecisive and strange.
> The raiders stuck by the arsenal, waiting perhaps
> For a great bell of jubilation to toll in the sky,
> And the slaves to rush from the hills with pikes in their hands,
> A host redeemed, black rescue-armies of God.
> It did not happen.

Yet there is courage too on both sides. When one of Brown's men, carrying a white flag of truce, is shot down, one of Brown's prisoners goes out among the flying bullets and carries him to the town's hotel where he can be attended by a doctor, then returns to the armory to take his place again among the prisoners.

Among the most memorable of Benét's brief portraits is that of General Burnside of the Union army, chosen by Lincoln to replace McClellan when it became clear that McClellan was not up to the task of leadership. Burnside's subsequent failure exemplifies the tragedy that pervades much of the poem.

> Burnside succeeds him—
> and the grimly
> bewildered
> Army of the Potomac has a new rider,
> Affable, portly, whiskered and self-distrusting,
> Who did not wish the command and tried to
> decline it,
> Took it at last and almost wept when he did.
> A worried man who passes like a sad ghost
> Across November, looking for confidence,
> And beats his army at last against stone walls
> At Fredericksburg in the expected defeat
> With frightful slaughter.
> The news of the thing
> comes back.
> There are tears in his eyes. He never wanted
> command.
> "Those men over there," he groans. "Those men
> over there"
> —They are piled like cordwood in front of the
> stone wall—
> He wants to lead a last desperate charge himself,
> But he is restrained.
> The sullen army draws back,
> Licking its wounds. The night falls. The
> newspapers rave.
> There are sixty-three hundred dead in that doomed
> attack
> That never should have been made.
> His shoulders
> are bowed.
> He tries a vain march in the mud and resigns at
> last
> The weapon he could not wield.
> Joe Hooker
> succeeds him.

Yet for all its failure and tragedy, the Civil War is finally part of the human journey forward, represented in *John Brown's Body* by the

two marriages foreshadowed in its final book. The epic poem that was to be Benét's next large project, *Western Star,* would give wider scope to the story of human progress, following the expansion of the American spirit westward from Europe to the American west. But Benét's belief in the triumph of progress over failure was strained as the optimism of the 1920s gave way in the 1930s first to the Great Depression and then to the rise of fascism and totalitarianism in Europe.

His short story "The Last of the Legions," set in Britain at the time of the withdrawal of the Roman military under Constantine III in A.D. 407, depicts through the eyes of a Roman centurion a civilization on the verge of decline. A Greek clerk takes the philosophical view— Troy fell, Greece fell, Rome will fall.

> "Oh," said Agathocles, "it takes time for the night to fall—that is what people forget. Yes, even the master of your villa may die in peace. But there are still the two spirits in man—the spirit of building and the spirit of destruction. And when the second drives the faster horse, then the night comes on."

In *John Brown's Body* the horses of anger and destruction—Phaeton's horses, "winged stallions, distant and terrible, / Trampling beyond the sky"—have free rein for the majority of the poem. (Benét's original title was *Horses of Anger.*) Reconciliation and hope nevertheless appear at the end. In "The Last of the Legions," written just ten years later, there is no hopeful look forward. "It is time itself we fight," Agathocles asserts, "and no man wins against time." Only the reader's knowledge that in another thousand years London will be a great city mitigates the emptiness of the story's conclusion.

"The Last of the Legions" closes Benét's second collection of short stories, *Tales before Midnight.* An equally worried story, "Into Egypt," opens it. "Into Egypt" does not look backward, however, but focuses on events in contemporary Europe. Its insight into the Nazi destruction of the Jews is all the more remarkable for having been written in 1938. Though Benét did not foresee the exact nature of the Final Solution, he saw that there would be one, and he anticipated not only how German officers might participate, but how the world might in part react. Perhaps Benét becomes heavy-handed when at the end of the forced transfer of the Jews out of Germany there appears a small family that disturbs the officer in charge—a husband with a wife riding a donkey and holding a baby whose hands show the marks of stigmata.

The psychology of the officer is convincingly drawn throughout the story, both his struggle not to see as individuals those who pass through his checkpoint and his nostalgia for the Christmas celebrations of his childhood. The appearance of the Holy Family at the end may well be his guilty dream as he finally realizes that it is not the Jews who are accursed, though his nationalism says they are. "The shame belonged to the land that had driven them forth—his own land. He could see it growing and spreading like a black blot—the shame of his country spread over the whole earth."

Also related to "The Last of the Legions" is "By the Waters of Babylon," which foresees not the fall into ruin of Roman Britain but the fall into ruin of America, specifically New York City. Written earlier than "Into Egypt," in 1937, "By the Waters of Babylon" anticipates atomic warfare, though the secret Manhattan Project that would first develop atomic weapons had not yet begun. The story's narrator is a boy from a primitive society who undertakes a vision quest to the forbidden Place of the Gods at the mouth of the great Ou-dis-sun river. He travels first on foot then by raft as he nears the forbidden place.

I saw both banks of the river—I saw that once there had been god-roads across it, though now they were broken and fallen like broken vines.

Very great they were, and wonderful and broken—broken in the time of the Great Burning when the fire fell out of the sky. And always the current took me nearer to the Place of the Gods, and the huge ruins rose before my eyes.

Yet "By the Waters of Babylon" is more hopeful than "The Last of the Legions." Though there has been great destruction and humanity's progress seems to have been lost, those who have survived are human, we're told, and they will build again.

Benét's poetry at this time, collected in *Burning City* (1936), reflects the same anxieties: "Notes to Be Left in a Cornerstone," "Litany for Dictatorships," "Ode to the Austrian Socialists," the nightmare poems. Even the short story "All Around the Town," with its celebration of the workers who built New York City, ends elegiacally: "When they bomb the town to pieces, with their planes from the sky, there'll be a big ghost left. When it's gone, they'd better let the sea come in and cover it, for there never will be one like it in the ages of man again."

Yet Benét's faith in the strength of humanity perseveres in the face of human weakness and destruction. The scientist in "The Blood of the Martyrs" does not think of himself as strong or heroic. He'd rather be left alone. He'd rather not suffer the confinement and beatings inflicted on him by the new regime. And in the end he is shot. But he does not give in; he does not agree to sacrifice science to the demands of propaganda. "But I am a biochemist," he protests. "I do not know how to look for the virtues of one race against another, and I can prove nothing about war, except that it kills. If I said anything else, the whole world would laugh at me."

Benét's faith, finally, is not just faith that people like the scientist will refuse to go along with the barbarism of totalitarianism; it is the scientist's faith that the whole world will reject such notions as racism and dictatorship. At the time of his death in 1943 this question was still unresolved, as the forces of democracy waged war with the forces of totalitarianism. Though the war was won, the question persists; as long as it does, the imagination, craftsmanship, and humanity of Stephen Vincent Benét will remain relevant.

Selected Bibliography

WORKS OF STEPHEN VINCENT BENÉT

POEMS

Five Men and Pompey: A Series of Dramatic Portraits. Boston: Four Seas Company, 1915.

Young Adventure: A Book of Poems. New Haven: Yale University Press, 1918.

Heavens and Earth: A Book of Poems. New York: Henry Holt, 1920.

Tiger Joy: A Book of Poems. New York: Doran, 1925.

Ballads and Poems 1915–1930. Garden City: Doubleday, Doran and Company, 1931. (A selection from Benét's earlier collections.)

A Book of Americans. New York: Farrar & Rinehart, 1933. (With Rosemary Benét.)

Burning City: New Poems. New York: Farrar & Rinehart, 1936.

NARRATIVE VERSE

John Brown's Body has had numerous editions, many of them significant for introductions and in some cases annotations. A portion of *Western Star,* incomplete at the time of Benét's death, was published from his manuscripts. A different portion has since been included in Townsend Ludington's *The Devil and Daniel Webster and Other Writings.*

John Brown's Body. Garden City: Doubleday, Doran and Company, 1928. First edition.

———. New York: Farrar & Rinehart, 1928. Introduction by Henry Seidel Canby.

———. Edited by Mabel A. Bessey. New York: Rinehart, 1941. Introductory essay "The Coming of the American Civil War" by Bert James Loewenberg. (An edition intended for high school and college students, with apparatus including a cast of characters, individual episodes indicated by subheadings, and notes that often show a bias not true to Benét's intentions.)

———. New York: Heritage Press, 1948. Introduction by Douglas Southall Freeman. Illustrations by John Steuart Curry.

———. New York: Holt, Rinehart and Winston, 1968. Introduction and notes by Jack L. Capps and C. Robert Kemble. (The best edition for scholars, with introduction and notes by two faculty members of the United States Military Academy, maps, bibliography of historical works consulted by Benét, and line numbers.)

———. New York: Holt, Rinehart and Winston, 1969. Introduction by Bruce Catton.

———. New York: Book-of-the-Month Club, 1980. Introduction by Archibald MacLeish. Illustrations by Barry Moser.

Western Star. New York: Farrar & Rinehart, 1943.

NOVELS

The Beginning of Wisdom. New York: Holt, 1921.

Young People's Pride: A Novel. New York: Holt, 1922.

Jean Huguenot. New York: Holt, 1923.

Spanish Bayonet. New York: Doran, 1926.

James Shore's Daughter. Garden City: Doubleday, Doran and Company, 1934.

SHORT STORIES

Thirteen O'Clock: Stories of Several Worlds. New York: Farrar & Rinehart, 1937.

Tales before Midnight. New York: Farrar & Rinehart, 1939.

Twenty-Five Short Stories. Garden City: Sun Dial Press, 1943. (Reprints the stories from *Thirteen O'Clock* and *Tales before Midnight,* with "My Brother Steve" by William Rose Benét.)

The Last Circle: Stories and Poems. New York: Farrar, Straus and Company, 1946. Introduction by Rosemary Benét. (Published posthumously. Includes twelve poems.)

LETTERS

Selected Letters of Stephen Vincent Benét. Edited by Charles A. Fenton. New Haven: Yale University Press, 1960.

Stephen Vincent Benét on Writing: A Great Writer's Letters of Advice to a Young Beginner. Edited by George Abbe. Brattleboro, Vt.: Stephen Greene, 1964.

OTHER WORKS

"The Magic of Poetry and the Poet's Art." In *Compton's Pictured Encyclopedia,* vol. 11. Chicago: Compton, 1936.

The Headless Horseman. Boston: Schirmer, 1937. (Libretto. Based on Washington Irving's "The Legend of Sleepy Hollow.")

The Devil and Daniel Webster. New York: Farrar & Rinehart, 1939. (Libretto. Based on his short story.)

"My Most Unforgettable Character," in *Reader's Digest* 37:113–116 (October 1940). (Memoir of his father.)

A Summons to the Free. New York: Farrar & Rinehart, 1941.

"Daniel Webster." In *There Were Giants in the Land: Twenty-Eight Historic Americans as Seen by Twenty-Eight Contemporary Americans.* New York: Farrar & Rinehart, 1942.

"A Creed for Americans." In *The Democratic Tradition in America.* Edited by Clayton E. Wheat. Boston: Ginn and Company, 1943.

America. New York: Farrar & Rinehart, 1944. (History.)

We Stand United and Other Radio Scripts. New York: Farrar & Rinehart, 1945.

EDITED COLLECTIONS

Selected Works of Stephen Vincent Benét. 2 volumes. New York: Rinehart, 1942. Introduction by Basil Davenport. (Volume One: Poetry contains the complete *John Brown's Body,* seventy-two poems, including "American Names," "Freedom's a Hard-Bought Thing," and "Ode to Walt Whitman," plus the radio play "Listen to the People." Volume Two: Prose contains the complete *Spanish Bayonet* plus twenty-two stories.)

Stephen Vincent Benét: Selected Poetry and Prose. New York: Rinehart, 1942. Edited with an introduction by Basil Davenport. (Good one volume edition intended for college students.)

The Devil and Daniel Webster and Other Writings. New York: Penguin, 1999. Edited with an introduction by Townsend Ludington. (Contains both prose and verse, including selections from *John Brown's Body,* alternative material from the manuscripts of *Western Star,* numerous stories and poems, and a half-dozen essays and letters, as well as a selective bibliography.)

MANUSCRIPTS

Benét's papers and manuscripts, as well as broadsheets, chapbooks, and other special editions, can be found in the Beinecke Rare Book and Manuscript Library at Yale University.

BIBLIOGRAPHY

The only comprehensive bibliography of both primary and secondary materials is by Gladys Maddocks, published in 1951–1952. More recent citations, though not exhaustive, can be found in Ludington (above). Useful annotations can be found in the bibliography of Stroud (below).

Maddocks, Gladys Louise. "Stephen Vincent Benét: A Bibliography." *Bulletin of Bibliography and Dramatic Index* 20:142–146 (September 1951), 158–160 (April 1952). (Does not list individual poems, though it does list individual stories, articles, reviews, forewords, and introductions.)

CRITICAL AND BIOGRAPHICAL STUDIES

Alldredge, Charles. "American Beginnings." *Nation,* July 31, 1943, p. 132.

Bacon, Leonard, et al. "As We Remember Him." *Saturday Review of Literature* 26:7–11 (March 27, 1943). (Reminiscences by fourteen contemporaries, including Archibald MacLeish, Muriel Rukeyser, and Thornton Wilder.)

Benét, Laura. *When William Rose, Stephen Vincent, and I Were Young.* New York: Dodd, Mead, 1976.

Benét, William Rose. "My Brother Steve." *Saturday Review of Literature* 24:3–4, 22–26 (November 15, 1941). (Reprinted in *Twenty-Five Short Stories.*)

Benét, William Rose, and John Farrar. *Stephen Vincent Benét.* New York: Saturday Review of Literature, 1943. (Reprints "My Brother Steve" together with Farrar's "For the Record" and includes a bibliography.)

Engle, Paul. "The American Search." *Poetry* 63:159–162 (December 1943).

Fenton, Charles A. *Stephen Vincent Benét: The Life and Times of an American Man of Letters, 1898–1943*. New Haven, Conn.: Yale University Press, 1958.

La Farge, Christopher. "The Narrative Poetry of Stephen Vincent Benét." *Saturday Review of Literature* 27:106–108 (August 5, 1944).

Moffet, Judith. "Stephen Vincent Benét: An Appreciation on the Centenary of His Birth." *American Poet* 30–33 (fall 1998).

Monroe, Harriet. "A Cinema Epic." *Poetry* 33:91–96 (November 1928).

Tate, Allen. "The Irrepressible Conflict." *Nation*, September 19, 1928, p. 274.

Stroud, Parry. *Stephen Vincent Benét*. New York: Twayne, 1962.

Zabel, Morton. "The American Grain." *Poetry* 48:276–282 (August 1936). (An influential review which countered the generally favorable responses of Monroe and Tate and established the critical rejection of Benét that has generally been accepted since. Discusses only Benét's poetry, without reference to *John Brown's Body*, thus focusing on what in hindsight is the weakest component of Benét's work, though the component Benét himself thought most important. Zabel's view is further limited by critical standards not relevant to Benét's best gifts.)

—PAUL JOHNSTON

Michael Chabon

1963–

*N*IGHTLY, UNDER A tented blanket, a twelve-year-old Michael Chabon would pore over a heavily creased map—one of those brightly colored cartoon souvenir maps that Disney distributes to its Orlando visitors to help them navigate the often baffling walkways of its magic kingdoms. He had brought the map back to his Maryland home from what would turn out to be his family's last vacation, an excursion to Disney World. Even as his parents' marriage did a torturously slow-motion crash and burn into the apparently inevitable sundering of divorce, the boy would be sustained by plotting an imaginary escape, a flight into a furtive magic kingdom of his own devising, an elaborate underground world of passageways beneath the theme park. As Chabon states in "Disney of My Mind," found on his website, that subterranean refuge would contain other desperate children, "hidden in the corners and stairwells and leafy shadows of Disney World"; children similarly blindsided by the unexpected; children, already nostalgic, who had learned that the best times had somehow already passed and who needed a refuge, safe from the "grim-faced men . . . who carried walkie-talkies and did not wear name tags."

The critical element of this adolescent fantasy is surely familiar to readers of the fictions of the grown-up Michael Chabon: the often anxious tension between escape and engagement, between the sweet, centripetal pull of the imagination as a splendid, if imperfect, engine of retreat capable of shaping the most elegant and suasive artifacts and the harsh, centrifugal pull of real life itself recklessly deformed by the crude handiwork of surprise and chance and

unable to coax even the simplest appearance of logic. Indeed, Chabon's first story, an English-class exercise executed on his mother's typewriter when he was only ten, was a dialogue between Captain Nemo, Jules Verne's submarine captain from the science-fiction spectacle *Twenty Thousand Leagues under the Sea,* and Sherlock Holmes, Arthur Conan Doyle's eminently logical detective: a dynamic tension between the exotic and fanciful and the realistic and immediate. The signature characters created by the adult Chabon—Art Bechstein (*The Mysteries of Pittsburgh,* 1988), Nathan Shapiro (in a cycle of short stories collectively titled "The Lost World," and later published in *A Model World,* 1991); Grady Tripp and James Leer (*Wonder Boys,* 1995); Richard Case ("Son of the Wolfman"); Josef Kavalier and Sammy Klayman (*The Amazing Adventures of Kavalier and Clay,* 2000)—feel keenly the pull of the imagination. They are professional fiction writers, inveterate storytellers, committed readers; they work in bookstores, at universities, and in television; they linger preternaturally in libraries. In short they willingly conjure convincing worlds from the easy edifice of words piled atop each other, protective bunkers that provide each with soft prisons. To justify such protective retreats, Chabon proffers a most unsettling vision of the late twentieth century, a world defined by the inability of the heart to find its way to reliability; the emotional terrorism implicit in the cycle of expectation and disappointment of love; the irrevocable, shadowy intrusion of mortality; the clumsy interference of bad luck and the fist-blow of surprise; the pervasive reach of greed; the peculiar woundings exacted by family, the blind handiwork of genetics; the irresistible itch of sexual attraction and the anxious confusions generated by its unpredictable appetites; the inevitability of betrayal by friends and lovers; and ultimately the heavy burden of loneliness.

Indeed, Chabon's narratives are generously littered with victims of brutal surprise, the inelegant shocks that represent the hard vulnerability of people without the protective insulation of the imagination: a child drowns, a young parent drops dead, apparently stable marriages implode in divorce, passion stales like bread left out overnight, a car suddenly veers off the road, a family member commits suicide, casual lovers must confront an unexpected pregnancy while long-suffering parents cannot turn the trick of conception. Like the adolescent Chabon under the tented blanket handling the imminent approach of his parents' divorce by constructing a perfect magic kingdom, Chabon's characters, reeling from the brutal intrusion of surprise, take refuge in protective spaces fashioned by the energy of the imagination.

Chabon, born in the early 1960s, is part of the first generation of American writers raised entirely within the virtual realities of television and cyberspace (he has written three pilots for network dramas and maintains a highly entertaining website). Perhaps because of this his fictions reflect the constant pull of the comfortable shelters of simulated realities: his characters toil on unfinishable manuscripts; they are always reading or on their way to the movies; they indulge a gargantuan appetite for drugs and alcohol; they are accomplished liars and incurable role-players capable of imagining themselves into a variety of attractive personas entirely divorced from reality; they thrive in bookstores, libraries, and universities. Given such disconnection, given such willful flight, Chabon's characters exist in a simplistic either-or dilemma: either indulge elegant private magic kingdoms or accept being ordinary, left

naked amid sheer event. As the adolescent Chabon surely intuited there beneath the tented blanket, any magic kingdom he could conjure would be abundantly more attractive than his own home so inelegantly collapsing into rubble.

The adult Chabon, however, recognizes the impossibility of such refuge and, ultimately, cannot endorse the lure of the imagination and its elegant retreats. But the characters who come to realize the danger in retreat are often leveled by such revelations: they commit suicide; they disappear into addictions; they turn into misanthropic recluses, living suicides surrendered, joyless, alone. Only the rare Chabon character, rocked by events and their unpredictability, nevertheless comes to accept the imperfect world, its brutalities and its wonders. Chabon is not specifically a Jewish writer; he never explores directly the Judaic vision of the late twentieth century as did writers such as Saul Bellow or Philip Roth. He nevertheless draws on his Jewish heritage to offer as exempla of this courageous engagement of this harsh world the European Jewry during the long night of Hitler's Holocaust and, further back historically, the ancient Jews commemorated by the celebration of Passover, which recalls the race's dignity and triumph amid intolerable conditions of enslavement and the horrific threat of ethnic cleansing. That rare willingness to embrace the unavoidable chaos of our existence, to accept vulnerability not as a weakness but as a strength, marks the heroic characters in Chabon's fiction.

His fictions, then, are decidedly intimate. Born too late to explore the existential implications of the gray-flannel Eisenhower boom or to participate in the mass civics lesson executed in the streets during 1960s, Chabon draws on no agenda larger than the intimacy of the shattered psyche. His are intensely private fictions of characters who undergo dramatic moments of interior shattering and often unflattering insight into the nature of their own dilemmas. Like that young boy poring over his theme park map, such characters must then sort from among the possible responses to the mysteries and sorrows, the decidedly human mess of the twentieth-century world. Some escape from its brutality via the imagination; others surrender sourly to its banality; still others exalt in its imperfection.

BIOGRAPHY

Michael Chabon (pronounced "*shay*-bahn") was born May 24, 1963, in Washington, D.C., the first of two sons born to Robert Chabon, a pediatrician for the Public Health Service, and Sharon Chabon, a lawyer. In 1969 his parents moved the family to Columbia, Maryland, a planned community being developed by urban visionaries even as the Chabons (and other pioneer families) were moving in, an experiment in model city living free from the normative blight of older metropolitan areas. Thus, the Chabons had moved into a virtual city, less a place than a theory, whose reality was largely confined to promotional pamphlets, yet another instance in Chabon's experience of the tension between real life and planned retreat. Amid such an unusual environment, Chabon, socially awkward (a "geek" by his own estimation), relished the sweet escape of writing and reading. He especially had a voracious interest in the pulpy narratives of a collection of treasured comic books. That early story of an imagined confrontation between Captain Nemo and Sherlock Holmes garnered not only the plaudits of his English teacher but set in his mind writing as a career. Far from discouraging such an eccentric decision, his parents encouraged their son's interest.

Undoubtedly, the centering trauma of Chabon's childhood was his parents' divorce when Chabon was twelve, a family crisis, he recalls, that caused him anxieties that he never felt comfortable even broaching aloud. After his father moved to Pittsburgh, Chabon summered there for the rest of his adolescence and visited

for holidays. He earned an English degree from the University of Pittsburgh in 1984 and (with his mother then living in Oakland, California) enrolled in the M.F.A. program at the University of California at Irvine, where the company of other fledgling writers was emotionally supporting and the faculty encouraging. One professor, MacDonald Harris, greatly admired Chabon's 1987 thesis, a lyrical narrative about the bittersweet coming-of-age of an economics major during the summer after his college graduation. In the narrative, influenced by Chabon's admiration for F. Scott Fitzgerald's *The Great Gatsby,* Art Bechstein, the son of a powerful Jewish gangster, struggles to come to terms with his own family (conflicted by his father and his ties to the Baltimore mob) as well as with his own sexual identity (contested by two affairs, one a conventional postgraduation romance with a demanding librarian and the other a more fraught relationship with a hip gay man whose trenchant wit and taste for exotica give Art's summer a dangerous depth and unexpected vitality). Without Chabon's knowledge, Harris forwarded the thesis to a New York literary agent who immediately sensed its merit and its commercial possibilities.

Published to glowing reviews in 1988 and hyped by his publisher as a new generation's *Catcher in the Rye, The Mysteries of Pittsburgh* became that rare combination: a work of serious execution and a best-seller. Although acknowledging the bildungsroman genre as the inevitable exercise of too many first-time novelists, critical response generally hailed Chabon's astonishingly dense prose. Unlike either the so-called Brat Pack of 1980s fiction—writers close to Chabon's age such as Bret Ellis Easton and Jay McInerney—or the academically fashionable minimalists, most prominently Raymond Carver, who each drew their stylistic model from Hemingway's stripped-down prose, Chabon, more like John Updike and John Cheever, clearly indulged a love of high-caloric language:

labyrinthine sentences and exotic vocabulary; the spellbinding pull of description; a fondness for the unexpected surprise of metaphor and simile. Chabon himself has cited as influential in his prose style the impeccable sentence constructions of the comic writer S. J. Perelman and the rich opacity and aching lyricism of Vladimir Nabokov. Chabon, only in his mid-twenties, suddenly a best-selling author and gifted with Hollywood good looks, became something of a celebrity. He was selected to be profiled as one of *People* magazine's "Fifty Most Beautiful People of 1988" (an opportunity he declined) and—surely because of the novel's controversial gay love scenes—was tabbed (erroneously) by *Newsweek* as one of the most promising gay writers of the AIDS era, an endorsement Chabon, himself twice-married and the father of three, has called quite gratifying as it indicated that he had managed to capture the difficult anxieties over sexual identity.

Hot property, Chabon began publishing highly successful short stories, many of them in *The New Yorker* (ten of them gathered in *A Model World and Other Stories* in 1991; another nine collected in *Werewolves in Their Youth* in 1999). Chabon found the short-story format agreeable but taxing, particularly the demand to manipulate language and imagery to provide character depth within a story's necessary brevity. Unlike the radical experiments in short fiction conducted by midcentury postmodernists eager to turn stories into testing grounds for language theories (by forcing narratives to acknowledge their told-ness), Chabon's stories recall more the classic story-as-case-study structure pioneered by the turn-of-the century realism of James Joyce and Anton Chekhov and developed by midcentury into the magazine format of writers such as Updike, Cheever, and J. D. Salinger. As character studies of protagonists who are often unattractive misfits in self-indulgent denial about their own mediocrities, the stories provide such central characters with unexpected epiph-anic moments of brutal revelation and the challenge of adjusting to that problematic gift of insight. Tightly crafted, compelled by Chabon's lyrical style, and energized by his knack for rendering everyday objects—a kitchen knife, an ugly gold necklace, a backyard bird feeder—with symbolic resonance, the stories enhanced the status of Chabon as a "promising" talent. "Promising" was an adjective hung often on Chabon by critics who found his writing a bit precious, even slick, and bemoaned a fondness for the exotic self-indulgent thrill of decorative writing at the expense of significant character exploration.

Pressured by such extraordinary success and terrified by the implications of having a national readership (and the attention of critics eagerly awaiting his sophomore offering), Chabon worked with self-conscious dedication (and a handsome publishing advance) on what proved to be a five-year debacle. His ambitious second novel never quite found its way to being about any one thing; instead, Chabon admits on his website, it managed to be about "utopian dreamers, ecological activists, an Israeli spy, a gargantuan Florida real estate deal, the education of an architect, the perfect baseball park, Paris, French cooking, and the crazy and ongoing dream of rebuilding the Great Temple in Jerusalem." Work on what would turn into the four drafts (and nearly fifteen hundred pages) of "Fountain City" was joyless, its many plots and subplots proving to be so architecturally forbidding that, frustrated and burned-out, he eventually dumped the project. Inexplicably, Chabon explains on his website, he sorted through the emotional costs of the bloated and unworkable manuscript and suddenly conceived a scene: "a straight-laced, troubled young man . . . standing on a backyard lawn, at night, holding a tiny winking Derringer to his temple, while, on the porch of a nearby house, a shaggy, pot-smoking, much older man, who had far more reason to want to die, watched him." In short order, he fleshed out the two characters—the one a creepy English major and the other a writing professor mired in an unfinishable manuscript that had swollen to twenty-six-hundred-plus pages. Within months, Chabon delivered to his publishers his long-promised second novel: not "Fountain City," but rather *Wonder Boys,* a comic romp set in the familiar environs of Pittsburgh. Published in 1995, the novel tracks the outrageous events of a single turning-point weekend. Grady Tripp, the frustrated novelist-qua-professor, a forty-ish alcoholic pothead and serial philanderer, must suddenly confront not only the abrupt departure of his wife (his third), who has discovered his infidelity, but also the unexpected pregnancy of his mistress, who happens to be the dean of his college and, furthermore, is married to Tripp's department chair. He must also handle both the visit of his literary agent, a flamboyant gay man who flies in from New York eager for the long-promised manuscript, and the unexpected discovery of the genuine, if untutored, talent of one of his writing students, a disturbing child-man raised largely by films and books whose loose anchorage in the real world has given him a remarkable felicity for pathological lying.

The self-consciously audacious plotline, which comes to involve, among other things, a stolen evening jacket once owned by Marilyn Monroe, a dead malamute, a heisted car, a gorgeous transvestite, a tuba, and several feet of a crushed boa constrictor, moves with cinematic flair and surety and garnered for Chabon immediate critical plaudits as a comic tour de force. (Chabon, perhaps smarting from the unsettling experience of "Fountain City," saw the character of a terminally blocked middle-aged writer more cautionary than amusing.) Given its cinematic sense of scene, its perfectly calibrated dialogue, its poignant comedy, its marvelous cast of characters, and its un-ironic happy ending, the novel was quickly optioned for the movies. The 2000 Paramount film, an intelligent and savvy adaptation directed by Curtis Hanson and starring Michael Douglas, fared indifferently at the box office but revived as a video rental when it was nominated for three Academy Awards.

In June of 1999 *The New Yorker* listed Chabon among the twenty best American writers under forty. Yet Chabon was restless. In an otherwise appreciative review of *Wonder Boys,* the *Washington Post* book critic Jonathan Yardley challenged the young novelist to attempt something a bit grander, more daring than essentially first-person explorations of wealthy, educated characters playing out their quests for identity happily lodged within the comfortable insulation of academia. Chabon took the challenge to heart. He happened to be paging through *Smithsonian* magazine when he chanced upon a feature on Jerry Siegel and Joel Shuster, the creators of Superman, and, more generally, on 1940s Manhattan and the golden era of American comics. A collector of comics as a child (he had, regrettably, sold his most of his massive collection when he was fifteen), Chabon had kept a single box of them. Rereading them now as an adult, marveling over their intricate artwork and wonderfully bizarre plotlines, Chabon tapped his deep love of this distinctly American pop cultural medium and began what would prove to be a massive research investigation into the era and into comics themselves.

Chabon immersed himself in history books, biographies, film studies, art theory, and eventually, as the project began to take shape, war histories, political science texts, and Jewish studies. He walked the streets of Brooklyn to get its feel; he interviewed the comic-book wunderkinds from the 1940s who were still alive. Still smarting from the difficult experience of "Fountain City," Chabon found in the four years of this project a new confidence, its multiple plotlines, massive cast of characters, and nearly fifteen years of action cohering into a satisfying design in which he used the comic-book genre to explore a familiar theme: the role of the imagination, here tested amid an unforgiving twentieth century, represented specifically by the Nazi terrorism against European Jews. But it was primarily a character study. In late 1930s Brooklyn, two young Jewish cousins—one a practicing magician and gifted illustrator who smuggles himself out of Hitler's Czechoslovakia; the other, a warehouse clerk who dreams of being a success and who can effortlessly concoct the most fantastic story lines—invent a successful comic-book superhero. The masked, stern-jawed Escapist issue-to-issue single-handedly defeats the insidious agents of evil stalking the European continent even as the real Hitler and his cohorts grow menacingly virulent.

The work, published in 2000 as *The Amazing Adventures of Kavalier and Clay,* was on a scale Chabon had never attempted, but it nevertheless represented a logical evolution in his confidence in the craft of executing a novel. Having moved from the autobiographical intimacy of *The Mysteries of Pittsburgh* to the first-person projection into the character of the frustrated novelist Grady Tripp, in this work Chabon undertakes a massive third-person exercise with the cultural and historical scope patterned (by Chabon's admission) on texts such as George Eliot's *Middlemarch* and Leo Tolstoy's *War and Peace.* Chabon's novel, like the works after which it is modeled, is self-consciously epic, with multiple points of view, meticulous detailing, historical accuracy (Chabon includes a bibliography), shifting locales and eras (most sumptuously his re-creation of jazzy New York City, awakening from the Great Depression and rediscovering elegance in the months before Pearl Harbor), scenes full of carefully realized secondary characters (including cameos by historical personages such as Orson Welles, New York governor Al Smith, and the surrealist artist Salvador Dali), and above all a compelling story line.

What Chabon found particularly challenging was creating a superhero and attempting to make that creation vivid to his reader through language alone—in mesmerizing interchapters rich with appropriately elevated prose he gives the background story lines of the comics' major characters. As an organizing device, Chabon tracks the contrapuntal narrative lines of the two cousins: one so brutalized by his encounters with history, by his own vulnerability and helplessness (he must leave his family behind in Hitler's Europe) that he is driven into years of seclusion by the sheer futility of his quixotic need to try to defeat evil (like the comic-book heroes he inks); the other drawn to the compelling elegance of pulp fiction plotlines largely because his own life, centrally his relationship with a delinquent father and smothering mother and his growing awareness of his homosexuality, is so fractured and confusing.

Critical response greeted the work as a major publishing event, touting it as a tour de force and linking its confident deployment of historical fact and enthralling fiction, its polished and dense prose line, and its audacious scale to other contemporary works such as *Underworld,* Don DeLillo's massive history of the cold war, and *American Pastoral,* Philip Roth's impassioned look at the impact of the counterculture. Although somewhat discomfited by Chabon's determined movement toward a happy ending and by the odd notion of such rich nostalgia for the 1940s being voiced by a writer born in 1963 (a faux-nostalgia sustained by Chabon's ingestion of an impressive amount of research, documented by the book's hefty bibliography), critical opinion catapulted the book into national prominence, including being short-listed for both the 2000 National Book Critics Circle Award and the prestigious PEN/Faulkner Award for fiction and being awarded the 2001 Pulitzer Prize for fiction. Chabon had clearly arrived as a major player in contemporary American fiction—and he was not yet forty.

THE MYSTERIES OF PITTSBURGH

Much about *The Mysteries of Pittsburgh* (1988) appears to promise head-on engagement, a thinly veiled autobiographical first novel as yet another fledgling M.F.A. turns, according to the prime directive of any undergraduate writing class, to the available materials of his own experience. After all, the character of Art Bechstein (rendered in the persuasive intimacy of the first-person voice) shares much with its creator: both are good-looking, affluent, Jewish; both are recent University of Pittsburgh graduates on the difficult threshold of adulthood; both struggle with a distant father. And, naturally, we expect honest accounting from a character completing a degree in economics. But, as with Nick Carraway, the romantic narrator of *The Great Gatsby,* Art Bechstein gradually reveals himself to be too enamored ("carried away") with the elaborate dodge of the imagination and a bit too comfortable with its strategy of retreat and denial. As with Fitzgerald's novel, here we are in the hands of a manifestly unreliable narrator (not Chabon himself), a character who freely endorses wildly extravagant retreats from fact and who by narrative's end actually cautions us that any recollection of this threshold summer is more than likely a distortion, an elegant exaggeration.

The Mysteries of Pittsburgh, then, is a told-narrative where the central issue is the tale-teller. Art Bechstein has struggled against facticity since the centering cataclysm of his adolescence: his mother's death in an auto accident when he was twelve and his father's subsequent revelation of his long ties to the Baltimore crime syndicate and his underworld life as a gangster known as Joe the Egg (a naive Art had thought his father a professional golfer and amateur painter). Reeling from such intrusive realities, Art had since comfortably insulated himself: he simply never speaks of his mother's death and even now, finishing his college education, when he meets his father for their occasional awkward luncheons the subject of the mob is never brought up, as if his family's considerable wealth had somehow magically accumulated and the shadowy men who come to their table are ordinary business associates. There is no difficult reality Art cannot side-step—he even refashions his suspicions that he might be gay as garden-variety adolescent awkwardness. But such strategic disconnection has come with a price. The summer of his college graduation (a mark of commencement appropriately delayed here as Art works to complete a final term paper—on Freud), Art acknowledges a life spent apart, circumspect, fascinated (even content) by observation, and defined by a refusal to risk. Like Nick Carraway, Art is an entirely self-sustaining narcissist with an alarming disdain for simply being ordinary: in his recurring nightmare, oddly, nothing actually happens; rather it is boredom that terrifies. Rejecting experience, fearing entanglements, relishing the voyeuristic thrill of observing people, Art, completing his classroom education, claims he is now ready to live.

The book opens appropriately with Art lingering on a summer evening in the university library. He chances to meet the mysterious Arthur LeComte, who impulsively invites him to a party. Determined that it is time to live, Art goes along. And ultimately Arthur LeComte, with his splendid talent for origami, will remake Art's sensibility much like the sheets of paper he folds into surprising shapes. Under Arthur's tutelage, Art will be offered three different sorts of life experiences. First, Arthur introduces him to a beautiful librarian he had noticed eyeing Art that evening. The affair with Phlox Lombardi quickly ignites into a conventional post-graduate romance, fiercely erotic initially but quickly moving toward conventional questions of love and commitment. Conventionally attractive, Phlox offers him unexamined devotion and full-tilt sexual exercise (she is a French major). Not surprisingly, she is conventionally abhorred by even the notion of homosexuality—although she will magnanimously "forgive" what she sees as Art's dalliance with Arthur. She is even conventionally conniving: after they fight over Arthur, she lures Art to the library by making an anonymous phone call claiming that a "search and recovery" process for a book he had lost could be initiated only by his coming personally to the library. Once there she conducts the conventional seduction in an isolated study room to convince him to take her back.

If Phlox suggests the conventional, Arthur's boyhood friend, Cleveland Arning, surely embodies its opposite: the freewheeling punk gangster. A renegade Catholic astride a Harley-Davidson motorcycle, Cleveland storms into the narrative tattooed, gargantuan, drunk, irreverent, streetwise. We learn later the painful circumstances behind such audacity—a father bitterly suppressing his homosexuality, an unhappy mother driven, finally, to suicide—but, to Art, Cleveland represents untutored spontaneity and the unrepentant embrace of life. Cleveland's job, collecting the exorbitant interest fees on illegal loans for the local mob, drives him to befriend Art: he wants an introduction to Joe the Egg and the possibility of advancement within the "organization." Indeed, Art will accompany Cleveland on a collection route and see firsthand the seaminess of his family's business, the very reality he had long denied.

While Phlox represents the lure of convention and Cleveland its rejection, Arthur offers to Art the exotic, the forbidden. Like Jay Gatsby, Arthur is a sort of functioning art piece, a persona he has created and sustained by dint of a savvy wit, studied mannerisms and affected elitism, an immense reservoir of pseudo-learning, and a stunning way with dress and appearance. As with Gatsby, we meet Arthur's

roots, in this case his cleaning-lady mother, long after we have come to assume, as Art does, that he comes from upper-class respectability. Pink-skinned with golden stubble, sarcastic, entertaining, Arthur mesmerizes and even excites Art, as he discovers one hot afternoon as he studies Arthur's oiled physique at a country club pool. When they make love, it is a cataclysmic moment in which Art taps, finally, genuine hunger.

Given three such strikingly different life choices, what is surprising (and telling) is that Art ultimately selects none of them. After all, any of the choices would demand engagement and any of them—marriage, crime, or homosexuality—would inevitably diminish into the ordinary. Rather the story of Art's "momentous" summer is given a frame: Art has abandoned Pittsburgh entirely for the sanctuary of life overseas, a flight triggered after watching Cleveland fall to his death after being chased by police after a foiled heist. Art suspects his father might have arranged the ambush, furious over the details of Art's affair with Arthur described in a letter from Phlox that Cleveland had stolen and given to him. But puzzling through such complications would involve for Art the intolerable experience of confronting reality. Indeed, in the hospital following an altercation with the police after Cleveland's killing, Art even raises the suspicion that perhaps his father's connections had something to do with his mother's "accidental" death years earlier. But he is content to hover between possibilities, never resolving these deaths nor bothering to settle his sexual identity; rather he will reside within mysteries, thus neatly ducking the harrowing experience of engagement. Like the Cloud Factory that so fascinates him, a decaying factory that appears to belch out the clouds over Pittsburgh, Art manufactures the airiest of illusions: the beautifully open-ended story he tells. He is, like Nick Carraway, an escape artist. Thus, Chabon's first novel is a sort of anti-bildungsroman, a radical primer in the imagination—the novel's much-admired luxuriant prose line is symptomatic less of Chabon's excess than his character's love of the spell of words—and in the astonishing power of the imperial self to conjure events (given the disturbing closing paragraph, it is uncertain how much of this summer experience actually happened) and thus to escape the too-real within the intricate insulation of the imagination.

"THE LOST WORLD"

Not surprisingly, given Chabon's interest in the tension between escape and engagement, in his follow-up work, "The Lost World," a cycle of five stories, the central character comes to accept the vulnerabilities of engagement. Across five stories that track young Nathan Shapiro's struggles to accept the implications of his parents' divorce, the subsequent reconfiguring of their lives with new lovers, and his own difficult emergence into adulthood, we watch as he invests considerable energy in various retreats (he loves science fiction and James Bond, hangs out in libraries, plays an interplanetary castaway in a neighborhood game, dreams of being a knight errant, and hides behind black-framed glasses, pimples, and a chubby frame) only to make peace, finally, with inevitable realities. He closes in awkward despair, an adolescent already nostalgic for lost worlds (he lives on Les Adieux Circle), a strategy of accommodation to the process of becoming ordinary that represents a decided shift from the easy flight of Art Bechstein but that clearly does not entirely satisfy Chabon. Indeed, Nathan is a critical midpoint on the way to later characters who will come to see the ordinary as sufficiently magic. But we need Nathan Shapiro as corrective to the fantastic extravagance of Art Bechstein.

Nathan begins happy, like all children heading for a dilemma they do not even see coming. It is the summer of his tenth year; his family heads down for its annual summer retreat at Nag's Head. But the reader begins to sense tension in the parents' clipped exchanges, in the muted arguments in other rooms, in the mother's restless explorations of new avenues of self-expression, and, most noticeably, in a confrontation over a kitchen knife in which, when his mother admires the handy implement, the father suggests simply taking it, advice the mother rejects hotly. Appropriately, given the narrative limitations of Nathan's perspective, the reader is never sure of the source of the friction—we only know that something bad is happening in other rooms. During a stroll on the beach, Nathan fashions odd footprints in the wet sand and fools his parents, who try to guess what sort of creature could have left such marks. When, after the stroll on the beach, Nathan is told that the vacation will be cut short, he thinks for a moment it is because of his trick and apologizes, tearfully, for the deception. Later, leaving the cottage, he himself steals the little knife, sure that his mother will blame his father. Thus Nathan determines to create a fight whose origins he understands, in this way asserting control over what is otherwise a helpless and frightening pitch into fathomless anxiety.

In "More Than Human" Nathan must watch helplessly as his father moves out. Clearly the friction of his parents' year-long movement toward divorce has taken its toll. Nathan has grown to feel estranged, a misfit unfit for love. In a poignant moment Nathan, fed on a steady diet of science fiction, asks his father, "If I was a mutant, would you and mom tell me?" In a characteristic strategy of protective retreat, Nathan is sent to the mall on the day his father's belongings are actually moved out. He returns to find only insuperable emptiness, inexplicable abandonment, and space (his favorite television show is *Lost in Space*). As he walks slowly through the new emptiness, he finds crumpled in a wastebasket a list of resolutions his father had made years earlier, promises he made to himself to be more involved with his family, to live better, kinder. Dispatched to the trash, they clearly indicate his father's acceptance of his limitations and his abandoning the fanciful notion that imperfections can be corrected by the bogus act of resolutions. But Nathan misses the point. Nathan tells his father on the phone that night that, as a father, he was the best, and he can come home anytime, a distressingly naive assessment so entirely divorced from reality that even the father mumbles only a curt thanks.

Accepting his father's ordinariness is at the very heart of "Admirals," in which, more than a year after the divorce, Nathan and his younger brother ride with his father and his father's new girlfriend, the bubbly and quite young Anne. When they stop in a posh restaurant, Nathan happens to see in the lounge his mother's new boyfriend, a flashy pilot, deep in conversation with a woman. In the face of such obvious (and casual) betrayal of his mother, Nathan feels like crying. When they leave the restaurant, his father stops a moment in the rain to talk to the striking owner of a flashy sports car, and Nathan must acknowledge that his father suddenly appears small, balding, disheveled—appears, in short, exactly as he is. That night Nathan cannot sleep; he struggles against such unflattering realities and dreams exotically that he is the baby Moses set adrift in the bulrushes, the offspring of unpromising parents, destined nevertheless for greatness, his imagination glorifying his emerging sense of himself as a castaway emotionally abandoned by parents busy going about creating new lives.

Not surprisingly, Nathan's first experience of falling in love ("The Halloween Party") involves an extravagant fantasy: a sweet crush on one of his mother's married friends, a former professional golfer who lives in the neighborhood. When he resolves to declare his love at the woman's neighborhood Halloween party, he devises an overly clever conceptual costume: he wears an ordinary business suit but fashions a hanger to suspend a lightbulb over his head—he will go as a man in the process of having an idea for a costume. Before heading to the party, he accidentally breaks his glasses but decides he sees clearly enough. Reality again rudely intrudes. Nathan's crush is costumed in a black leather bikini, black cape, and boots—suggesting an aggressive sexuality that is entirely unfamiliar to Nathan. He is suddenly a boy at an adult party. Worse, no one understands his costume. In an effort to simplify the outfit, he removes the headgear and now challenges the woman to guess what he is. What he is, of course, is (like his father) simply a guy in a business suit, ordinary and unpromising and (without the lightbulb) clueless.

"The Lost World" completes Nathan's movement into the ordinary. Now sixteen, his mother remarried, his father and Anne expecting a baby, Nathan struggles just to be happy. We find him chugging malt liquor and then, in an effort to rid him of his virginity, being delivered quite naked by his friends to the back door of the house of a girl with a reputation for being easy. The girl, rather, reveals an intriguing complexity. Unperturbed by his nudity, she coolly confides in him that she is on her way the next day to Israel, because her father is determined that she will grow up with a strong sense of her Jewishness. Impressed by the girl's frankness and her beauty, Nathan accepts a sealed letter that she hastily scribbles and promises he will not open it until she is gone. On the way home he hides the letter in a neighbor's bird feeder. Convinced it is a confession of love, he is crushed when he returns for it later and it is gone. Now sure that he has found love, he is surprised weeks later when the letter actually arrives from Jerusalem. Eagerly he opens it, only to find that the message is a taunting reminder of her many other boyfriends and a bland admission only that he had always made her laugh. In addition, the mail brings a coolly polite note from his father assuring Nathan that he will always love him as much as the new child. In dramatic despair, he tears the notes to pieces and informs his mother, even as her new husband is busy spicing Nathan's tuna salad with cut gherkins as a way of expanding his stepson's horizons, that he hates such embellishments. Then suddenly he sees in a melancholic epiphanic moment a life ahead irresistibly mired in routine disappointments and casual betrayals. Friendship and love insufficient, family distant and irretrievable, his imagination exhausted and inaccessible, he resigns himself to making do with an unspectacular adulthood. He gathers up the pieces of the letters and heads for the kitchen, prepared now for a life of tuna salad with gherkins.

WONDER BOYS

For a novel hailed as a fast-paced comic romp, there is something decidedly un-funny about the narrative world of *Wonder Boys* (1995), a terrifying geography where accidents brutalize the unsuspecting; love sours with devastating quickness; suicide proves too tempting; any achievement is blunted by an extravagant fear of failure; betrayal is only to be expected when the heart dares to venture outside its protective isolation; and where, amid the inevitability of such vast loneliness, the sole comfort comes from the cool solace of aesthetic artifacts, from books (writing them and reading them), movies, and records. Approaching forty, Grady Tripp is a fraud; he plays at being a responsible adult, a committed writing teacher, an important novelist completing his anticipated masterwork, a loving husband, a doting lover. His adult life, a carefully sustained art piece, is the terminal point of the logic of escapism implicit in Art Bechstein. Indeed, like that earlier escape artist, Grady Tripp has artlessly constructed the perfect edifice for insulating himself from such terrorism: a novel, in his case an unfinishable behemoth, a massive 2,611-page labyrinth that promises only perpetual care, bound to which, comfortably numbed by his ever-present joints

or his tumblers of liquor, he sustains his self-indulgent free-fall, content to observe the sheer chaos of his life with too-clever befuddlement and self-gratifying confusion. When the guest lecturer at the university's weekend literary festival describes how writers inevitably are disconnected from reality, unconcerned by the real tragedies of real people, content to observe and then recollect such pain into language, Tripp terms such disconnection the "midnight disease." Thus afflicted, he cannot conjure the requisite maturity to take seriously any of the roles he misplays: teacher, novelist, husband, lover. But if he begins his narrative safely enclosed within the fuselage world of his own pleasure prison, he will, by narrative's end, summon the nerve that Art Bechstein ultimately lacks to shatter that protective edifice and to assume the responsibility of engagement. Further, he will touch authentic wonder in the very pedestrian world that so casually crushes young Nathan Shapiro.

At midlife, Grady Tripp (as his last name suggests) has stalled. He is terrified by the experience of vulnerability. As a child, growing up on his grandmother's farm (his mother died from a staph infection she contracted while nursing him, and his policeman father, a crippled war veteran, committed suicide, devastated after he kills a man by mistake), the young Tripp befriended an odd boarder, a pulp horror writer named Albert Vetch, whose wife had been institutionalized after their two sons were killed in a freak fireworks accident. After Vetch's wife committed suicide by drowning, the young Tripp discovered the dead body of Vetch himself, a suicide by gunshot. After such multiple traumas, Grady Tripp has never been able to adjust to the harsh rhythms of change, the implications of loneliness, or the cold inevitability of death. He remembers as a child watching at night as his father slowly stripped off his impressive police uniform, down to his boxer shorts and his prosthetic lower leg, growing smaller, frailer. Horrified by such diminishment into the ordinary, Tripp runs: old enough for college, pumped on Kerouac, he simply leaves his grandmother. Even his three successful novels have featured, he acknowledges, a motif of burial and concealment, fictions in which characters crawl about in underground vaults and caves (shades of Chabon's own childhood Disney World fantasy). Tripp's outrageously zany escapades represent sheer motion without purpose, an exercise in mushrooming absurdity as he struggles to stay in control while each plan he makes goes stunningly awry. Within the first forty pages, he is rocked by a series of surprises. His wife leaves him after discovering his affair. Then at the university reception for the literary festival, Sara, his lover and the chancellor of the university, tells him that she is pregnant. After the reception breaks up, on a whim he escorts James Leer, a creepy (if promising) writing student who has an equally creepy fascination with Hollywood suicides, up to the chancellor's bedroom to show him Sara's husband's prized black satin jacket, worn by Marilyn Monroe. There, Tripp and Leer are attacked by the chancellor's dog, whom the writing student promptly shoots dead. After their panicky escape from the home (Tripp simply stows the dead animal in the trunk of his car), Tripp discovers James has stolen the jacket. In short order, Tripp must suddenly deal with disorder.

The catalyst of his education is the mysterious writing student James Leer, a child-man so entirely devoid of secure contacts with reality that he simply concocts an imaginary life for himself drawn from his own bizarre stories. Never compelled to engage reality, largely because of Tripp's willingness to believe the stories he tells of his impoverished boyhood in a town he simply makes up, James is sustained by his belief that such confections are somehow finer than the tacky ordinary. Addicted to stories, his classroom writing output is prodigious. He

is also mesmerized by films; he especially admires Frank Capra (he has clumsily used needles to cut the name into the back of his hand), with his trademark sentimentality, his unshakeable faith in the essential worth of ordinary humanity—but James himself has resisted any accommodations to the real world. When Tripp finally tracks him down at home, he discovers that James lives in the basement of an upscale suburban house designed like an imposing fortress. He wears ill-fitting red holey pajamas and is surrounded by library books years overdue and Capra memorabilia; he watches a frothy Doris Day movie while he busily hammers out yet another story. The manuscript James lugs about in his frayed backpack is, not surprisingly, a gothic melodrama set in the 1940s, a haunted narrative culled from old movies, replete with murder, incest, arson, and sexual abuse—none drawn from James's own childhood. (We find out when we meet his concerned grandparents that he has been raised amid privilege and love after his wealthy parents were killed in a small plane wreck.) Tripp's agent, who seduces James over the same weekend, reads the manuscript and decides James will be the next wonder boy of the literary world.

The thorough falseness of James's novel stands as counterpoint to the movement upon which Tripp embarks, making his peace with the (extra)ordinariness of a small-town life as father and husband and teacher. Over this eventful weekend, Tripp is forced up against the realization of the threat implicit in the sweet evasions of the imagination, that its indulgence has left him addicted to apartness and the comfort of emotional insulation, unable to bear the routine certainties of time, death, and change. (His blindness to such realities is made clear in the way he treats a bouquet of flowers intended for his wife, Emily—the flowers, tossed absently into the back of his convertible for the long drive out to the country, are slowly plucked down to the stems by the free rush of the wind.) As a contrast to Tripp's inclination to seal himself off from reality, his wife's family is instructive. (Devastated by the revelation of her husband's five-year affair, Emily has—in characteristic Chabon style—retreated, to her parents' farm.) We learn that Emily's (Jewish) parents long ago had suffered the loss of their son in a drowning accident, but, far from allowing such a catastrophe to drive them into despair, they adopted three Korean orphans (among them Emily) and raised them as a "loud, sloppy, jumbled-up, all-surviving family." As if to underscore their strength and unity, they live in a place called Kinship. There, Tripp and James participate in the family's Passover commemoration, with its celebration of the resilience of the Jewish spirit amid intolerable circumstance. Not surprisingly, as the ritual wears on, Tripp drifts off into a pleasing daydream in which he imagines himself (as Nathan Shapiro did) Moses drifting among the bulrushes.

In a series of jolting revelations Tripp adjusts his flawed perceptions. A beautiful student with a crush on him reads his manuscript and honestly assesses its flaws: because he writes stoned, she says, the story lines have no discipline. Then Tripp discerns that his own editor has lost interest in his unfinishable novel and has already turned a greedy eye toward the promise of James Leer. In an elaborate subplot Tripp comes to realize that the convertible given to him is actually stolen and the rightful owners are intent on stealing it back, a tonic lesson in accepting reality. During a Sunday afternoon car chase with the car's legitimate owners, his manuscript, unbound and in the back seat, is scattered into the back alleys of Pittsburgh. His elaborate word-scape crudely gone, and given the oppressive immediacy of Sara's pregnancy, that evening he finally comes to see that it is time to face reality. Disgusted with himself when his editor leaves him behind in the car while he tries to prevent James's expulsion for the theft of the coat, Tripp is moved finally to

tears, a genuine (if modest) show of emotion. Resolutely, he heads for the dean's office and there dramatically accepts responsibility for the weekend's events. Lingering in the hallway outside the office, he realizes that in a single weekend he has lost his publisher, his novel, his wife, his lover, his best students' admiration, his car, and his job. In a final gesture of accommodation, he leans over the stairway balcony and tosses his last bag of marijuana down to the janitor. Even as he does it, he feels dizzy, his heart shudders; he feels himself about to fall over the railing when, with Capraesque flair, Sara out of nowhere pulls him back.

Sara's pregnancy finally completes the journey of Grady Tripp. Recovering from the dizzy spell in the hospital Monday morning, he decides it would be best for Sara if he removed himself from her life and she aborted their baby—another gesture of simplification by retreat and disengagement. On his way out of the hospital, however, he pauses at the maternity ward window, marveling at such stunning miracles. He then goes to Sara's house but is confronted by her husband, armed with a baseball bat, who takes a generous swing at Tripp's head. After the blow, as he walks home in the cleansing rain, he feels clearheaded, "massive and buoyant," until he is picked up—by Sara. In the novel's coda, we learn that Tripp and Sara have married and relocated to Tripp's long-ago abandoned hometown; that his vision, shaken by the bat attack, has now cleared; that he writes a bit, relishes time with his son, teaches part-time, drinks lightly, has forsaken pot, and cautions his writing students against the danger of getting lost in their own fictions. Tripp's is the very life of smallness and routine so feared by Art Bechstein and the compromised life of tuna-salad-with-gherkins so unhappily accepted as inevitable by Nathan Shapiro, a modest celebration of the hard-earned small-scaled wonders of an ordinary life that can terrify, disappoint, but ultimately lift.

WEREWOLVES IN THEIR YOUTH

Given the elegant testimony of the harrowing stories gathered in Chabon's second collection, *Werewolves in Their Youth* (1999), what seems to fascinate Chabon is that stunning moment of irrevocable realization, suggested by the bat swing to Grady Tripp's head, which renders the often unwanted gift of clear sight and makes inevitable the movement toward accepting reality. Characters in these stories have lingered too long within the pleasant shrouds of denial, in worlds of their own construction, and must be hauled out. These stories provide critical counterweight to any assumption that Grady Tripp's happily-ever-after is lightly tendered. Indeed, these unsettling stories, shot through with pain, cannot sustain the lighter touch that so distinguished Chabon's earlier short fictions, the wry, subtle humor, the knowing irony, the quiet exaggerations. Chabon clearly knows the heavy implications of accepting life on its own terms without the gracious makeovers of the imagination, the saving illusions we all fashion to make palatable the emotional devastations we each endure.

Chabon finds parallels between the epiphanic moment of often unwanted insight and the clichéd Hollywood moment when an unassuming man is compelled, helplessly, to undergo the massive physical alterations of becoming a werewolf, a radical moment that is necessary and brutal and that reveals the true, terrifying nature of the man. More to the point, such transformation, once endured, does not permit a return to any assumptions held before—it is final, irrevocable. So clearly engaged within the ordinary, these stories reveal the darker realities of the heart's blind need. In many ways, "Son of the Wolfman," the recipient of a 1999 O. Henry Prize, best suggests the maturity of this second collection, and its luminous theme—the harsh beauty of a world unadorned by the imagination—recalls Grady Tripp's embrace of life's wonder in his recovery of marriage and fatherhood. The story offers a wrenching look at a marriage tested by a wife's decision to carry to term a child she conceived after being raped. Clearly ready to grapple with harsher realities than a midlife Peter Pan's unfinishable manuscript, Chabon here introduces for the first time in his fiction the violence of criminal behavior, the sheer magnitude of the hurt we are capable of inflicting on each other. The tone, thus, darkens. The villain here is not accident or bad luck—rather it is rape and the struggle to accept the implications of our capacity for violence, foreshadowing the massive virulence of Nazi aggression in *Kavalier and Clay*.

When Cara Glanzman decides to keep the baby, the focus of the story shifts to her preparations, her arrangements for a midwife, her birthing classes, her embrace of a healthier lifestyle, her intense dedication to the health of her baby and its tonic effect on her. But it is *her* baby, as her husband, Richard Case, darkly intones at one point, and in muted asides the reader glimpses Richard grappling with the rage he feels toward his wife's attacker and the disturbing sense of disgust he feels for her. He feels alone for the first time in the ten years of their marriage, his carefully arranged world (he works as a television studio cameraman and is adept at the careful packaging implied by framing shots) shattered by the intrusion of violence that has provided the miracle of conception and the promise of life, all the more distressing to Richard because he and Cara for years had struggled but failed to conceive a child of their own. Richard simply cannot fathom this staggering contradiction. He grows taciturn at work. He agrees to photo shoots that are farther and farther from home to distance himself from the pregnancy. He attends to Cara's needs motivated only by duty, absorbed by self-righteous indignation. And in the last week of the pregnancy, he departs in a gesture of callous retreat that recalls Art Bechstein and Grady Tripp, save that now the stakes appear so much higher that such retreat is untenable, even cruel.

Chabon now turns to Richard's reclamation. Weeks later, Richard receives a late-night phone call—his wife, with the baby now long overdue, is desperate to trigger the delivery. She pleads with him to come home. He does, and she asks that he make love to her to stimulate labor. The gesture demands sacrificing his self-serving pettiness and accepting her and the baby as his responsibility, a moment of maturation that Chabon marks with the traditional image of blood-spilling: Richard cuts his finger when he tries to slice open a tube of lubricating oil and ends up in the hospital. Once at the hospital, Cara feels her contractions begin. There is no Capraesque ending—the baby has thick hair, a clear mark of his paternity, and gazes at Richard with pupil-less, emotionless eyes. Chabon refuses to resolve the heartbreaking uncertainties ahead for Richard (and Cara and the child). The world cannot be as neat as Richard's television pseudo-world. "Do you think he's funny-looking?" he asks, searching for confirmation of his fears and justification for another retreat. But after the baby was delivered "with a soft slurping sound," the nurse takes a picture of the newborn and is given the story's closing word, the ambiguously fitting "Beautiful." We are light years beyond Art Bechstein's fabulous retreats, Nathan Shapiro's melodramatic resignation to gherkins in his tuna salad, or Grady Tripp's acknowledgment of the dangerous pull of the imagination. The humane and genuine predicament that Chabon probes in "Son of the Wolfman" presages his next achievement, a work more ambitious than anything he had yet written.

THE AMAZING ADVENTURES OF KAVALIER AND CLAY

In *The Amazing Adventures of Kavalier and Clay* (2000) Chabon moves beyond the negotiations individuals must make without recourse to the splendid and intoxicating refuges of the imagination, to explore the tension between escape and engagement on a cultural and historical scale. As a late-twentieth-century Jew, Chabon turned to perhaps the darkest episode in a bloody century: the insidious rise of the Third Reich and the consequent abomination of the Holocaust. At the same time, he explored a most improbable historical coincidence—that the golden era of American comic books coincided with the emergence of the Nazi menace abroad—to test the viability of the imagination in such a graceless age. Within the narrative, inked cartoons celebrating the hammer strike of good over evil vie with forbidding headlines that appear to confirm the irresistible reach of evil and the impotency of good (most of the novel takes place before Pearl Harbor during the era of American isolationism and proclaimed neutrality). Clearly, Chabon fears that in such a pitched contest, the imagination cannot succeed. Chabon asks, what good can the comic-book creatures of the mind's fancy and their invented worlds do in a world that must, generation to generation, bear witness to our apparently infinite capacity to wound each other? Characters here test the powerful persuasion of escape and the strategies of denial. They succumb to familiar and attractive evacuations: retreating to movie theaters, indulging in drugs and alcohol, maintaining secrets and false identities, engaging in prolific storytelling, even physically going into years of hiding. But by narrative's end, the reach of the imagination is, finally, too limited, and Chabon counsels the need, amid the larger obscenities inevitable in any era, to embrace the magic of the everyday, the difficult complications of love, the imperfect wonder of family, and, ultimately, the unforgiving absolute of death itself.

Not surprisingly, the larger-than-life narrative of Josef Kavalier dominates the text. His flashy persona, cross-continent travel, and audacious gestures of quixotic naïveté (he believes that, like the superhero he draws, he can challenge evil successfully all by himself) overshadow the quieter accommodations to reality being conducted by his long-suffering cousin. After all, Joe Kavalier's life unfolds with the high-octane adventure feel of a serial comic book. Yet there hangs about his character an undeniable sense of flight and escape. Indeed, we are introduced to him as he is dramatically escaping, literally in hiding: in 1939 he secrets himself out of Nazi-occupied Prague by hiding for twenty-seven hours in a trick coffin bound for Lithuania (he was apprenticed as a magician and studied the master Houdini). Once in Brooklyn, with an eye on quick money to help his family follow him to America, Kavalier, a gifted artist, helps his cousin create the comic hero the Escapist, who as part of the League of the Golden Key thwarts the evil machinations of Attila Haxoff and the Agents of the Iron Chains, a thinly veiled allegory for the forces of Hitler. Indeed the commercial sponsors of the comic book's first issue, aware of America's official neutrality, balk over the proposed cover—the masked Escapist landing a haymaker on the jaw of a very recognizable Hitler.

Even as the comics begin to sell (and Hitler's menace grows), Joe contends with the German consulate to arrange passage for his family. He begins an affair with the beautiful Rosa, an avant-garde photographer whose cluttered apartment is decorated by her bizarre, surreal images of ordinary food and whose liberated sexuality ignites Joe's passion. When an indifferent German bureaucrat tells him that his father has died, Joe impulsively runs off to Canada to join the R.A.F., believing he will single-handedly win the war, but he then abandons the plan. Frustrated, he picks fights with German Americans in the streets of New York and even vandalizes the offices of a New York-based pro-German organization. Ultimately, with the help of Rosa, he manages to arrange a crossing for his brother on an unarmed refugee boat. When it is torpedoed by a German U-boat, killing all on board,

he summarily abandons Rosa (even though he suspects she might be pregnant) and his cousin (and their business) and joins the navy, only to be stationed with a handful of other men in the blasted wastes of Antarctica to track German ship movements and monitor radio transmissions. After a fluke malfunction in the radio shack's stove kills all but Joe and a pilot, he nevertheless continues his work and eventually contacts a distant outpost, manned by a lone German geologist, whom he determines he will kill, in grand comic-book style, as revenge for the death of his brother.

After a disastrous flight (in which the pilot dies from a burst appendix), Joe has his showdown and kills the German. Such heroics provide no fulfillment; rather Joe feels a devastation that compels him, after he is rescued, to orchestrate yet another escape once he returns stateside. In ways that recall Nathaniel Hawthorne's tragic Wakefield, Joe entombs himself within walking distance of his cousin's comics business in New York City. In eccentric gestures to ensure his anonymity, for nearly ten years he seldom leaves the rented office he maintains on the seventy-second floor of the Empire State Building (a front that claims to sell vanishing creams); he amasses thousands of comic books that surround him like a bunker; and he dons outrageous disguises when he does venture out. Like Grady Tripp of *Wonder Boys*, Joe occupies his time inventing an enormous manuscript, a two-thousand-page comic book that centers on the Jewish Golem, a gigantic figure fashioned out of river clay and brought to life, according to medieval folklore, by the incantations of a powerful rabbi.

Against such a flashy narrative of exotic escapades, secret identities, and evident derring-do, it is difficult for Sammy Klayman even to register—his story reads like a drab realistic novel set against a comic book. Although his head teems with outrageous tales, his life is achingly dreary. Born in Brooklyn, Sammy is an inventory clerk for a novelty company, although he dreamed of being a novelist or a doctor. Polio rendered his legs permanently weakened. He is the son of an inglorious show-business failure, a father who, billed as the Mighty Molecule, worked the vaudeville circuit as a muscleman and consequently abandoned his family (during a rare visit, Sammy poignantly begs his father to take him along). Fancying himself a savvy entrepreneur, Sammy manages with some degree of chutzpah to sell his boss on the idea of a comic book (independent of actually having an idea for one) as a way to help advertise the company's whoopee cushions and midget radios; he sells the character of the Escapist later for a mere $150 and then watches as the comic grosses millions. Later he endures one failed business after another until he ends up grinding out pulp novels and cheap comic books.

Even as Joe discovers love with Rosa, Sammy, living with his mother, struggles with homosexual impulses he cannot accept. He resigns himself to loneliness until he comes under the spell of a gorgeous radio actor hired to play the Escapist. But even that interlude implodes when they are caught in bed during a raid orchestrated by sympathizers of the pro-Nazi organization Joe had vandalized. Later he finds out his lover has been killed overseas in the Pacific. When his cousin simply disappears after his tour of duty, Sammy bravely assumes responsibility for Rosa's pregnancy and marries her. Like Richard Case, Sammy will raise another man's son. Devastated by poor investments and working feverishly to grind out pulp fictions, he nevertheless raises that child as his own, amid the joys, regrets, and torments of ordinary life, attending to the unglamorous work of household duties and the difficult pretense of husband and father, terrified by the implications of his own secret nightlife of cruising.

When Joe begins to arrange clandestine visits with his son after they meet accidentally in an obscure neighborhood magic shop, Sammy understands that the difficult masquerade of his life must end. Hard on the heels of a lawsuit settlement in which the Escapist character is officially retired (it is judged too close to the copyrighted Superman), Sammy begins to see what is coming when he realizes that his cousin, presumed dead, is very much alive and still in love with Rosa. He must make the most heroic gesture of all: give up the family he created while his cousin withdrew into the exotic retreat of his Empire State Building bunker. When a government subcommittee looking into connections between comic books and teenage delinquency grills Sammy and compels him to admit his homosexuality on live television, Sammy understands, like his cousin, that he can no longer maintain his secret identity.

Although Joe offers to use his considerable savings to bankroll Sammy's dream of owning a comic-book business, Sammy understands that he cannot stay. He says goodbye to his family (when he goes to kiss his son goodbye, the boy is clearly uncomfortable with such intimate contact given his father's revelation) and quietly departs for California (and its comparable freedom) to work in television (like Richard Case, to produce illusions, not live within them), leaving Rosa and Sammy, the new Kavalier and Clay, to realize Sammy's audacious new superhero, the Golem. That willingness to engage difficult realities head-on is a measure of how far Chabon's fictions have matured since Art Bechstein's giddy, self-indulgent escapism, his blithe flight from unpleasant realities. Here the ordinary sustains—in a comic scene, Joe must come to the assistance of Salvador Dali, who attends a cocktail party in an elaborate diving helmet that malfunctions. After Joe frees the struggling artist, Dali gratefully gulps the ordinary air.

Chabon's point, of course, is that it is not easy to celebrate Sammy's lonely life, to find any sparkle in the dreariness of such commonplace sacrifice. Sammy's resilience in the face of emotional catastrophes that do not lose their potency for being ordinary, his determination not to storm off after large-scale foes as his cousin so quixotically does but rather to grapple with the difficult, pedestrian tensions between expectation and disappointment is a kind of heroism too invisible ever to attract a hero's adulation. For comfort, Sammy has had only his remarkable facility for spinning narratives, the inexhaustible imagination that has taken him, despite his crippled legs, to distant galaxies. Art, Chabon concedes, cannot fix the world. Like the magical Golem, a construct of enormous effort and invention, the imagination is "the expression of a yearning that a few magic words and an artful hand might produce something—one poor, dumb, powerful thing—exempt from the crushing strictures, from the ills, cruelties and inevitable failures of the greater Creation."

That is, finally, the difficult wonder of the imagination, not to escort us into protective shelters—that, after all, leads only to emotional disconnection and isolation, and (when they prove no longer tenable) to deep depression, anxieties, even suicide—but rather to make endurable the world we are given to live in, to allow us to pitch a tent amid the emotional terrorisms of the everyday. Here we may conjure, if only for a moment, a magic kingdom (for instance, the interlude spent reading the often spellbinding prose of Chabon himself), but prepared for the inevitable return and ready, in our more Capraesque moments, to feel with the bruising give-and-take of the unpredictable reality the same wonder we felt for the extravagant and too-sturdy private worlds we conjured. The true wonder, Chabon argues, comes only when we fold up the Disney World map, turn off the feeble flashlight, unpitch the blanket, and return to engage a world that can shatter with its beauty and its agonies.

Selected Bibliography

WORKS OF MICHAEL CHABON

NOVELS AND SHORT STORIES
The Mysteries of Pittsburgh. New York: Morrow, 1988.

A Model World and Other Stories. New York: Morrow, 1991.

Wonder Boys. New York: Villard, 1995.

Werewolves in Their Youth: Stories. New York: Random House, 1999.

The Amazing Adventures of Kavalier and Clay. New York: Random House, 2000.

OTHER WORKS
Bumps on My Head (http://www.michaelchabon .com). (Contains essays and unpublished short stories, as well as a discussion of "Fountain City" and a first chapter of that novel.)

CRITICAL AND BIOGRAPHICAL STUDIES

Buzbee, Lewis. "Michael Chabon: Comics Came First." *New York Times Book Review,* September 24, 2000, p. 9.

Contemporary Authors, vol. 139. Detroit: Gale, 1993. Pp. 81–82.

Contemporary Authors: New Revision Series, vol. 57. Detroit: Gale, 1997. Pp. 95–98.

Contemporary Authors: New Revision Series, vol. 96. Detroit: Gale, 2001. Pp. 51–55.

Contemporary Literary Criticism, vol. 149. Detroit: Gale, 2002. Pp. 1–36.

Fowler, Douglas. "The Short Fiction of Michael Chabon: Nostalgia in the Very Young." *Studies in Short Fiction* 32, no. 1: 75–82 (1995).

Gorra, Michael. "Endangered Species." *New York Times Book Review,* January 31, 1999, p. 10. (Review of *Werewolves in Their Youth.*)

Kalfus, Ken. "The Golem Knows." *New York Times Book Review,* September 24, 2000, p. 8. (Review of *The Amazing Adventures of Kavalier and Clay.*)

Mendelsohn, Daniel. "Comics Opera." *New York,* September 25, 2000, p. 63. (Review of *The Amazing Adventures of Kavalier and Clay.*)

Podhoretz, John. "Escapists." *Commentary* 111, no. 6:68–72 (June 2001). (Review of *The Amazing Adventures of Kavalier and Clay.*)

Spiegelman, Art. "Michael Chabon's *The Amazing Adventures of Kavalier and Clay.*" *The New Yorker,* October 30, 2000, pp. 102–103.

Yardley, Jonathan. "Paper Chase." *Washington Book World,* March 19, 1995, p. 3. (Review of *Wonder Boys.*)

INTERVIEWS

Binelli, Mark. "The Amazing Story of the Comic-Book Nerd Who Won the Pulitzer Prize for Fiction: A Conversation with Michael Chabon." *Rolling Stone,* September 27, 2001, pp. 58–62, 78.

Goodman, Bob. "Quixotic Friendships: An Interview with Michael Chabon." *Beacon Street Review* 9, no. 2 (1996). Also available at ⟨http://www.natterbox.com/chabon/chabon1.html⟩.

PW Interviews. "Michael Chabon (*Wonder Boys*): 'Don't Take Advances on Books.'" *Publishers Weekly* 242, no. 15:44 (April 10, 1995).

FILM BASED ON A WORK OF MICHAEL CHABON

Wonder Boys. Directed by Curtis Hanson. Paramount Pictures, 2000.

—JOSEPH DEWEY

Wanda Coleman

1946–

*I*F YOUR PERSPECTIVE on life is one of conservative contentment—that is, if the world and you are on copacetic terms—then the aggressive, provocative, and socially challenging work of the African American writer Wanda Coleman may not be much to your liking. If, on the other hand, you often find yourself troubled by social injustices that will neither resolve themselves nor just go away—such as why wealth is so disproportionately distributed in the United States, or why race and class and gender dictate the perimeters within which individuals must live their lives—then the anger that informs Coleman's work and makes it valuable is well worth close consideration.

An attempt to comprehend the prolific body of work that Coleman has been publishing since the late 1970s must first begin with an appreciation of the author's managing to publish work of any sort, given the particular constraints surrounding her career. In addition to her professional activities as a visiting instructor of English at various colleges and universities in California and as an author, poet, journalist, and novelist, Coleman has been a bartender, a medical transcriber and billing clerk, a secretary, an editor for a men's magazine, a scriptwriter for the soap opera *Days of Our Lives* (for which she won an Emmy Award in 1976), and a performance artist who has delivered over 500 readings across the United States and Australia. Her pursuit of professional writing, however, has frequently conflicted with the need to make a living, as her duties as wife and mother have sometimes required her to forgo literary projects in favor of a steady paycheck, and often in fields unrelated to her occupation as a writer. Cole-

man has never been an "academic poet": her poems are not similar in tone, style, or subject matter to the technically elegant but solipsistic verse typically produced by poets emerging from advanced writing programs since the 1980s. She has essentially been cut off from the so-called network that controls both the dissemination and audience for contemporary poetry. As she lamented in correspondence dated July 29, 2000: "I try to overlook being overlooked/ignored, but it's a huge bitter horse-sized pill I haven't been able to swallow. It's stuck in my throat."

Coleman writes poems about the life-and-death rhythms of the street. Her career is almost a throwback to the nineteenth century, when American writers such as Herman Melville and Walt Whitman received their occupational apprenticeships in the tumult of daily life rather than in the confines of the university. In her prose poem "The Ron Narrative Reconstructions," from the collection *Bathwater Wine* (1998), Coleman sarcastically underscores her continuing professional struggle: "'so tell me,' Federico opens, 'what is it like for a woman to write poetry in America these days?' 'like being trapped in a skidrow men's room,' i quip lamely."

LOS ANGELES IN COLEMAN'S WORKS

To understand the poetry and prose of Coleman, a reader might best begin by appreciating the importance of Los Angeles, the city where she was born and lives and, in various ways, that serves as the backdrop and sometimes the subject of many of her poems, stories, and essays. The city is in fact a recurring character and palpable presence found throughout her work. Over the years Coleman has become one of Los Angeles's great chroniclers, but the city she has steadily described is nowhere to be found in brochures published by the chamber of commerce. Her Los Angeles is more a place of constant struggle and silent suffering; she records the events that take place in the city's shadowed sidestreets and alleyways rather than the glittery dreamscape portrayed by Hollywood, its tabloid press, and fashion magazines.

Coleman's perspective on Los Angeles is as complex as the city itself. Her city is a place that contains the ethnic potential and diversity that is the essence of America. A drive down any of the streets in and around the center of the city reveals signs written in a multitude of languages and alphabets: Korean and Chinese, Vietnamese and Japanese, Russian and Spanish and Arabic. Moreover, the city is also archetypically American in its geographical sprawl, as the metropolis covers 34,000 square miles and is still expanding, spilling over mountains and stretching out into desert. The physical size of Los Angeles and its ethnic multiplicity give this urban landscape its kinetic pulse, and much of Coleman's art has been shaped by such diverse energies. For example, the language she employs in her prose and poetry is the speech of urban life: rhythmical, dynamic, direct. It is tough and street-smart. Her linguistic cadences, grammar, and diction mirror her desire to create accessible work that challenges those readers reluctant to associate literature with the daily language of ghetto life. There exists a sense of breathlessness in her style; like the rhythms of urban black speech, she seeks to record verbatim the dynamics of human interaction and the blood pulse that typifies city life.

In *Native in a Strange Land: Trials & Tremors,* a 1996 collection of essays that reflects upon Los Angeles (its recent history as well as its long-standing status as a cultural epicenter),

Coleman provides, as she puts it in her introduction, "a tour through the restless emotional topography of Los Angeles as glimpsed through the scattered fragments of [her] living memory." Like the rest of us, Coleman is stimulated by the glamour and opportunity that Los Angeles represents both to itself and to the rest of the world. But even more pronounced is her capacity for recognizing that for all its excitement, Los Angeles is a place that excludes more than it includes, deludes more than it illuminates. This observation from *Native in a Strange Land* embodies the core ambivalence that Coleman maintains toward the city: "L.A. to love you is to have my heart split open without the possibility of mending. You hurt me with your poor your alienated your disenfranchised. And yet I still can't leave you. Still can't put you down."

Born on November 13, 1946, to George and Lewana Evans, Coleman was raised in Watts. Her long personal history with Los Angeles has split her as a writer. She seems at once drawn to the city as an overwhelming spectacle, its sense of itself as one of the centers of the universe. But even as she is seduced by Los Angeles, she is compelled to acknowledge the flaws inherent in the object of her love. In the end she appears more inspired by the nightmare than she is by the dream; as in the 1982 film *Blade Runner,* her work recognizes the terrible beauty of the place, its violence, social stratification, and politics of exclusion. She continues in *Native in a Strange Land*: "Loving your money potential. Loving your fame potential. Hating the way you make a sucker pay and pay for a slice of the dream that is never delivered."

Coleman's perspective on Los Angeles reflects her general attitude toward the United States itself, as she sees the city as a kind of American microcosm. As an African American woman who has been influenced by both progressive politics and feminism, her artistic voice has struggled to be heard. Her poems, stories, and essays reveal an America that is anything but accommodating. And her searing observations suggest that the wealth and success that epitomize the public images of both Los Angeles and America are, in truth, illusionary because they are reserved for so very few.

The reality that Coleman chronicles is that not everyone makes it, and not very many who do make it get to keep it. For every fabulous success story, there are graveyards of shattered dreams; for every corporate building, there are hundreds of men and women huddled in its shadows without enough to eat or a place to call home. Coleman often employs the stream of consciousness in both her poems and prose, the language flowing with images of what she sees on the streets after dark. In *Native in a Strange Land* she often stops to observe the ghostlike interactions that take place after middle-class America has gone to bed: "Behind glass and steel skyrises housing corporate kingdoms are impoverished shooting galleries where hypodermics are brandished in full view of anyone driving the back alleys in search of parking. Someone under duress is getting his/her head broken open outside the lobby of a single-occupant residency hotel." Coleman's America belies the image put forward by politicians and patriots, for its truest energies implode within acts of violent self-destruction.

Long before rap artists were lamenting the socioeconomic condition of African Americans and the interrelationship of poverty, crime, and violence, Coleman's art centered upon those sections of Los Angeles and America where hope had vanished. For over three decades she has been publishing work that is angry, politically charged, and sometimes tragically humorous. Her poems, stories, and essays are urban portraits of black struggle, the ravages of poverty, and the quest of women to find dignity in spite of deprivation. Her literary characters and female personae are kindred to those men and women of the underclass who populate the fictions of Nathanael West, Ann Petry, Richard Wright, Edgar Allan Poe, Zora Neale Hurston, and the nineteenth-century naturalists. Like these earlier authors, whom Coleman herself has often cited as influential, Coleman writes to raise society's "window of invisibility," forcing her readers to acknowledge the essential humanity of social outcasts—single welfare mothers, prostitutes, drug addicts, the incarcerated, the unemployed, the homeless.

MAD DOG BLACK LADY

Although Coleman is an editor, dramatist, performance artist, essayist, screenwriter, and social journalist, her most significant literary contributions—in terms of quantity as well as quality—are to be found in the genres of poetry and short fiction, but especially in poetry. Her 1979 volume of poems, *Mad Dog Black Lady,* remains one of the great early publications issued by a twentieth-century poet. Much of the work found in this volume reflects those key elements that compel a contemporary reader to turn to poetry in the first place: an authentic and original voice, musical intonations, an accurate and resonant vision of the world portrayed through unique language, and the employment of imagery that is both startling and enduring. The many other poems that Coleman has published since *Mad Dog Black Lady* can be seen as shoots that have their origins in this collection. Over the years she has experimented with a variety of poetic forms and topics and has even shown a particular fondness for variations on the sonnet, but the best of her poems always seem to return to the dominant themes, imagery, and poetic temperament that characterize the work of *Mad Dog Black Lady.*

The poem "Drone" is a good example of the poet's ability to portray the lives of the underclass and disenfranchised. Its subjects are a medical billing clerk, who is acutely conscious of her own exploitation, and the patients she documents, the problem cases that "most other doctors refuse," who are debilitated by chronic renal failure. The reader is left uncertain who suffers more: the patients who are victimized by their poverty and the hopelessness of their disease or the narrator herself who is trapped by a "subsistence salary" and her workplace alienation.

In the end the office worker shares much in common with the people whose lives she must process: they are both victims of a bureaucratic system that quantifies and numbs their collective humanity. The clerk monitors both a "river of forms," documenting the ceaseless process of dead and dying bodies, and a flow of Medicaid checks that allows "the doctors [to] feed their race horses / and play tennis and pay the captains of their yachts." The title of the poem also resonates in its theme, as a "drone" is a low-pitched continuous sound, a bee that serves the maintenance of the hive yet produces no honey, and a worker engaged in a mindless, repetitive task. Isolated and unable to bring relief to each other, the generic "poor, black or latin" are reduced to the "crisp" charts of their medical files, while the equally anonymous clerk regulates a flow of living dead:

> most of the patients, good patients,
> quietly expire
> i retire their charts to the inactive file
> a few more claims i won't be typing up anymore
> they are quickly replaced by others black, latin or
>   poor
> i make out crisp new charts
> and the process starts all over again

If literature can be said to be about the act of memory, then perhaps no culture has ever needed literature more than the contemporary United States. Its people live in amnesiac times, where the past is either forgotten or reconfigured inaccurately. Coleman's work is a constant reminder of what has been repressed, in American history and in contemporary American society, and of what has been silenced either because of cultural biases, or ignorance, or a specific ideological agenda. Her poetry and prose works hold a mirror up to the nation. They reveal what the nation has chosen to ignore, has failed to address, has deliberately or unwittingly overlooked. In a 1990 interview published in *Black American Literature Forum,* Coleman articulated her self-definition as an artist:

> I'm not writing for people who want to read through my books to feel comfortable. . . . My experience has been a fairly ugly one. I know many others whose lives are also ugly, and I think writing about it is necessary.
>
> In a supposedly great nation like this one, people shouldn't have to feel so dehumanized. That's a disease. That's cancer. That's racism. The body politic of American society has to be healed of that cancer. You have to start somewhere. Let's get those diagnostic studies underway. That's what I'm about.

The poetry in *Mad Dog Black Lady,* and for that matter most of the verse that follows this volume, centers upon survival themes. Although the landscape for these poems is typically an urbanized world where Coleman's female personae are never alone for very long—as they often appear in circumstances in which they are under siege—their sense of psychological isolation is palatable. Typically her first-person female narrators speak with voices that are shaken but undeterred in spite of having to confront compromising situations: as minimum-wage clerical workers, as sexual partners accommodating the quick urges of restive men, as single mothers in search of adequate means to feed children and still pay the rent. The first-person speakers can be said to be representative voices; that is, at the same time that they are part of Coleman's own psyche, they also reverberate with the experience of other women the poet has observed in friendships, on the streets, and in various romantic and occupational situations. In other words Coleman's narrators are simultaneously a part of herself and of the prototypic women struggling under the similar constraints of poverty, racism, and gender inequality.

To underscore the corseted identities of these women, Coleman's narrators often speak without punctuation; in particular, the first-person pronoun "i" is never capitalized in her poetry, revealing the lowly social position her spokeswomen occupy in the eyes of the world as well as their own perceived inferior status. Moreover, the first-person singular voice in her work is rarely limited to a particular individual; her characters come to speak not only for themselves but for an entire race or gender. To survive, these women must rely almost exclusively on their own resources—their intelligence, their angry indignation, their inventiveness, their capacity for endurance—as they know there will be no knights in shining armor appearing on the horizon to effect a rescue.

"Doing Battle with the Wolf," which over the years has become one of Coleman's signature poems from the volume *Mad Dog Black Lady,* uses the metaphor of a wolf to represent white America, an omnipresent and rapacious personification that "has a fetish for black meat and / frequently hunts with his mate along side him." Although set in the city, where a black female narrator goes about a civilized routine of shopping at the supermarket and getting a fill-up at the gas station, the poem maintains a strong undercurrent of primitive terror. It is as if the poem's consciousness belonged to an injured antelope or zebra being stalked on an African plain instead of a contemporary woman living in urban Los Angeles. The abrupt and stark cadences of the poem also highlight its core levels of violence and brutality. Coleman's reliance on hard consonants—"raw hunks of meat skin bone / swallowed / watched as full, the wolf crept away"—tend to emphasize the poem's aggressive themes while likewise deepening the desperate plight of the besieged protagonist. The narrator continually "drips blood" as though wounded (metaphorically

speaking, she is) by the daily systematic draining of her financial and psychological resources. And just as the protagonist finds her symbolic blood everywhere, depositing a trail from her workplace in the morning to her bedroom at night, the wolf is also silently omnipresent, awaiting the moment when she will be most vulnerable and isolated, perhaps after "visiting my man in prison" or "driving the kids to school."

In her essay "Devaluation Blues: Ruminations on Black Families in Crisis" in the collection *Native in a Strange Land,* Coleman argues that the black woman has had to struggle to regain her human dignity especially since "maintaining her self-image as a desirable mate has been a Sisyphean feat. . . . Without her man to 'cover her back,' the unmarried and the unmarriageable Black female was/is particularly vulnerable to the erratic whims of the White male/White society." "Doing Battle with the Wolf" dramatizes this conceptualization through the inclusion of a single black woman who is besieged by the "erratic whims" of an aggressive beast; its fur is "white and shimmers in moonlight/a coat of diamonds / his jaws are power." The white wolf gradually narrows his assault until he comes clawing at his victim's door. But at this point the protagonist is suddenly infused with her own power, transforming herself from the role of victim into an African warrior "armed with my spear inherited from my father as he from his mother." The strength to do battle against the wolf emerges from a familial line that connects the speaker with her great-grandfather's rebellion against the institution of slavery, the psychic powers of her grandmother, and the magic of an African witch doctor. Summoning courage from two fundamental sources—her inherent maternal instincts and her heightened sensitivity to her own black ancestry—the solitary heroine repudiates the passive bleeding that characterizes the earlier sections of the poem:

i open the door
a snarl
he lunges
the spear
against his head
he falls back
to prepare for second siege
i wait
the door will not close
i do not see the wolf
my children scream
i wait
look down
am wounded
drip blood
cannot move
or apply bandages
must wait
wolf howls and the roar of police sirens

It is her duty to defend her children and to assert herself as a representative of black womanhood. But the reality of the wolf's power proves too much. Although the female protagonist strikes the creature once and wounds him, she is unable to triumph over his superior and invisible resources. While she has learned both patience and defiance in her battle, she also knows the wolf is not to be deterred, that he will come again, incensed by her isolation and the scent of her blood. The "roar" of sirens that closes the poem, indistinguishable from the "howls" of the beast, are not indicative of an imminent rescue but rather signal the arrival of the lupine police—the remainder of the pack—perhaps summoned to aid the wolf in subduing his defiant prey.

Like "Doing Battle with the Wolf," many of Coleman's poems are specific reminders of the fragile barriers that separate private and public spaces, the personal and the objective realms. The wolf invades both the narrator's public and private worlds, her trips to the post office as well as to the bedroom, making even a moment's respite impossible. The intersection of these spheres—the personal and the political—is at the core of Coleman's most powerful and insightful work. "Women of My Color," one of the more explicit poems in *Mad Dog Black Lady,* transforms a moment of intimate sexuality into a political statement. The poem begins and ends in an act of fellatio. The graphic sexual refrain "i follow the curve of his penis / and go down" shocks the reader into attentiveness. Oral sex is employed not as an act of granting or gaining intimate (and mutual) pleasure but as a symbol of domination, a not-too-subtle reminder of a black woman's position—social as well as sexual—"on the bottom where pressures / are greatest." What begins as an eroticized event quickly translates into an act of exploitation that is not merely racial but also gender specific; the woman in this poem deliberately blurs any awareness of the color of the penis she is accommodating. Patriarchal authority, whether black or white, is chastised for its need to make woman into "victims" who must "struggle and stay alive":

there is a peculiar light in which women
of my race are regarded by black men
                              as saints
                              as mothers
                              as sisters
                              as whores
but mostly as the enemy
. . . .
there is a peculiar light in which women
of my race are regarded by white men
                              as exotic
                              as enemy
but mostly as whores

it's enough to make me cry
but i don't

following the curve of his penis
i go down

Both races reduce the black woman to stereotyped categories that deny her individuality. Black men, oppressed by the white world and feeling the need to reinvigorate their potency, in turn oppress black women. White men, existing in a cultural vacuum, are even further removed from the real lives of black women, perceiving them either as the "enemy" because they are women or as "exotic" sexual toys. Both white and black male worlds want her "down," conforming to a sexual and economic "curve" where men are able to assert power and pleasure at the expense of her identity. Coleman insists that from either racial perspective, women of color are misrepresented and victimized by men; the narrator's only occasion to exert what remains of her dignity is in her stoic refusal to cry. As in "Doing Battle with the Wolf," Coleman infuses "Women of My Color" with a certain degree of female resiliency. Placed in circumstances—economic, social, racial, and gendered—where there is no possibility for ultimate triumph, her female protagonists struggle to assert a measure of individual self-respect.

MEN AND WOMEN

The natural world is barely present in Coleman's poetry. Occasionally the attentive reader will find mention of a piece of sky or a blast of wind followed by rain, but usually her characters wander a dry and barren landscape where nature has long been displaced by colorless buildings and asphalt streets. As she acknowledges in the poem "Worker," in *Imagoes,* there is "no time to idle in / green pastures or chase stray dogs / through daisy laden fields." In fact, there are very few landscapes that are not manmade in Coleman's poetic universe. The author chooses to turn inward, for human nature is the only nature that appears to interest her. But it is not so much the abstract, or speculative, or even the philosophical dimensions of human nature that are examined in her work, but rather the dimension of human interconnectedness. She is especially attentive to the sexual aspects of human relationships, the glue that either holds them together or cracks, breaking them apart.

Her treatment of sexuality covers a full spectrum of responses, from the genuine fulfillment that emerges from the appreciation of two separate bodies joining together, to the anguish that accompanies sexuality when it is used as a form of manipulation or abuse. In many of her poems, especially her best work, the breakdown of personal and social relationships is attended by a corresponding loss of sexual desire or the violence of its misuse.

Coleman's poetry emphasizes continually the gap, perhaps "chasm" is a more accurate word, separating the worlds of the male and the female. Men and women fail to communicate on a variety of levels in her poetry; indeed, men are characterized as being incapable of empathizing with the emotional, economic, and sexual needs of women. Coleman's female personae therefore assume the daily pain that men—strangers, lovers, blood relatives, faceless representatives of bureaucratic society—force upon them.

"Rape," the most provocative poem in the 1983 book *Imagoes,* indicts the male collusion that is formed to support masculine privilege at the expense of a woman's rights, legal as well as sexual. Coleman elects to tell this story backwards, so that the details of a woman's rape by two burglars begins at the moment two laughing policemen arrive with their insincere pledge to "help" her. Later, the psychiatrist demands with pornographic enthusiasm that the victim "talk about it / tell me every detail." But the most disquieting sequence occurs midway through the poem, when the victim's boyfriend arrives and responds to his girlfriend's violation as though he has been the one personally affronted. His anger is directed not at the woman's assailants but at the victim herself:

> he got indignant. why didn't she call the police
> why didn't she call her mama. why didn't she die
> fighting. . . .

In a bid to reestablish his ownership over her, the boyfriend forces her to have intercourse with him on the exact spot where she was assaulted, essentially raping her again. His own contribution to this woman's defilement can be read both as a desperate attempt to reclaim his dominance in the relationship and as a punishment to his girlfriend for "allowing" her own violation. And perhaps most perverse of all, his demand for immediate sex on the sheets where she was initially raped suggests a masculine identification with the earlier burglar/rapists, who also viewed her body merely as a possession, something else in the apartment to steal or to own.

The men in "Rape" are all joined together in considering the victim's plight as a kind of erotic spectacle, a pornographic fantasy that is contingent on a female's intimate and recurrent violation. This is why Coleman concludes the poem with the sobering rejoinder,

> she picked up the phone

> and made the mistake of thinking the world
> would understand.

Coleman tells this poem in reverse chronological order to help the reader grasp that the act of rape continues long after the perpetrators have "kissed" their victim "goodbye." From the response of bureaucratic authorities (police and psychiatrist), to her boyfriend's reaction, and finally to the burglars who have initiated the poem's action by raping her, it is clear that this woman's body is controlled by everyone except herself. On the other hand, the poem puts forth a more positive, albeit subtle, feminist point, when its victim (like many of Coleman's other distressed women) demonstrates a real measure of self-composure by refusing to panic in the face of her fear and assault. Instead, she uses her considerable powers as a woman to make the rapists "care enough not / to kill me." In spite of her ordeal, she serves as yet another illustration of a Coleman character finding a way to survive the brutality of the world: although

violated and humiliated, she is not destroyed. In correspondence dated July 29, 2000, Coleman commented further on the fecundity of the poem's themes:

> The primary point is that the actual physical rapists are kinder and more gentle than the society that has made [the victim] vulnerable to the rape (represented by the police, the psychiatric doctor, and boyfriend). I'm also making the daring suggestion that the rapists were transformed into lovers during sexual contact. Once they became lovers, they desire to protect her; hence, they return the goods they originally intended to steal.

Violence, the acute sensitivity to economic exploitation, and an explicit examination of sexuality as a means to explore the gender and racial gaps that separate women and men, black and white, are the central themes that distinguish Coleman's early poetry. Her later poems suggest that these problems and issues are still very much with her and us, and that the passage of twenty years has done little or nothing to assuage the social burdens she first described in *Mad Dog Black Lady.* Her 1998 collection of poems, *Bathwater Wine,* which won the Lenore Marshall Poetry Prize (presented by the Academy of American Poets and *The Nation* magazine in 1999), employs stark language, vivid imagery, and explicit sexual content. The dryness, the absence of pathos, the refusal of all idealism, and the indefatigable examination of black suffering connects Coleman's work from the late 1990s to her earliest publications. Whereas in general people, including artists, are thought to mellow with age, her poetry has remained charged with its same passion and outrage. In an era when art so often reflects the general complacency of bourgeois prosperity in the new world economy, Coleman continues to remind readers that not everyone in the United States is awash in dollars and rapture. Coleman's best work always appears on the verge of erupting into some type of violent response to this inequity, yet it seldom does. The poet has learned to exert tremendous control over her emotional subject matter. As in the Harlem Renaissance writer Claude McKay's most memorable sonnets, anger never interferes with Coleman's eloquence; her poems never descend into the realm of blind rage.

BATHWATER WINE AND *A WAR OF EYES*

The first eight poems in *Bathwater Wine* deal with the subject of growing up black and female in an America that has very definite ideals of feminine beauty and its attendant attributes. Like the female protagonist of Toni Morrison's *The Bluest Eye,* Coleman learned quickly and painfully that "only the popular girls get to go to Casablanca" and "only the / girls with amber eyes sit with the swells at Rick's." As much as these poems are about the deep-seated experience of rejection and exclusion, they are also about an emerging sense of selfhood. Like many of the first-person speakers elsewhere in Coleman's poetry, these poems are not narrated from a position of self-pity so much as they are testaments to alternate survival strategies.

The highly competitive girl-women featured in the poems of *Bathwater Wine* may appear initially successful, as in the section entitled "Dreamwalk" ("their starlit eyes / taunt the boys and tease A's out of every teacher's hard / and narrow pen"), but it is also clear that another kind of success awaits them. The speaker's linguistical power of self-expression, for one thing, will soon provide its own degree of influence and ironic comeuppance. And although she will probably never experience the ease with which so-called beautiful women in Western culture come to command sexual attention and exert their authority, the speaker's knowledge will no doubt prove deeper than theirs; it will be earned instead of merely bestowed. This poetic sequence ends with the speaker aware that she is on the cusp of such transformations, that

"something important is going to happen" to her, so she whispers to herself "please hurry."

In the poem "I Died with the First Blow & Was Reborn Wrong" Coleman joins her own frustration at being consistently overlooked as a poetic voice in contemporary America with the "calculated amnesia" that the nation as a whole has historically demonstrated toward blacks and Native Americans. The reigning culture of "straw-blond ambition" has chosen either to ignore the labor and artistry of its minorities or to appropriate it without acknowledging the original source:

you steal the song out of my mouth

take my rhythms as yours
dance my dance
wear my skin to deceive the viewers

To reinforce Coleman's position in this poem, one need only examine the degree to which white artists continue to appropriate the blues tradition in the development of rock and roll—often without allotting much credit to black precursors. The poet's own personal experience mirrors this artistic travesty, for as a black female writer she has endured a double-edged rejection, languishing as her own work has been overlooked by the dominant culture.

perhaps if i had been colored male
a shining whiteness shaft-deep in your sludge pot
perhaps then i would be deemed half-human

In addition to her volumes of poetry, Coleman has also authored a collection of short stories and a novel. *A War of Eyes and Other Stories,* her 1988 short story collection, was deliberately titled to reflect the ways in which human beings are visualized and to reveal the identities—particularly the racial identity—that these people, in turn, assume and project from such visualization. This collection demonstrates once again Coleman's skill at infusing literary constructions with sociological observation and theory. As Coleman herself said in the *Black American Literature Forum* interview, "These stories are about how individuals are defined by the eyes of others, and that it is a war to be seen clearly. This is my single greatest concern as a person and as a writer of literature: how racism affects me."

Coleman's concern is evident most obviously in the fact that this collection features a predominantly black cast. This is important to note not only because the themes of these tales are particularly relevant to blacks but also because the physical blackness of the characters—from the range of skin tone, to the shape of facial features, to the cut and curl of the hair—often signals how these men and women perceive themselves and each other. Indeed, the opening tale in *A War of Eyes,* "Watching the Sunset," examines the unique fate of Mister Wilson, a man who, because of his mixed bloodlines, is trapped between two races: "The Civil War . . . fascinated him. That's where I was lost, he thought. That's where my history begins." That he is by profession a teacher of history only adds to his personal torment by making him that much more aware of his ambiguous location in a racial limbo. His tragic sense of alienation in a culture that, throughout its history, has demanded clearly demarcated color identity and allegiance is reminiscent of William Faulkner's narratives; his isolation is deepened by the loss of his white father and black mother and by his status as an only child. Wilson has tried living with both races, but neither one wholly accepts him. Consequently, he comes to identify personally with the sunset he is watching: a mixture of colors, fading into a "blue-black" night illuminated by "lights that were not stars."

The shadowy world of racial identity, especially as it complicates the lives of urban blacks, is illuminated to a greater or lesser extent in each of the stories in *A War of Eyes.* One of the more expansive and thought-provoking treatments of this theme occurs in the tale "The Screamer," a narrative that centers on Linda, a young woman who is an archetypical Coleman protagonist: black, uneducated, desperate for money, and forced to struggle against social and economic circumstances that are simply too large for her to comprehend, much less surmount. That she is also eight months pregnant only serves to deepen her general anxiety, as she keeps hearing—at least in her own head—a tortured scream from somewhere, "sometimes . . . so loud it seemed to come from within her." It is impossible for Linda to attend to this sound, as it appears to be more of a metaphysical scream, the existential cry of an aching soul.

Linda is employed as a telephone receptionist for an old house painter, Mr. Sims, whose office and career are symbolized by the filthy toilet that Linda refuses to use: "She stood in the door of the closet and looked down at the stool blackened with layers of dirt, grease, paint and the remnants of urine and feces." Like the indigent black men who sometimes help her boss with large painting projects, Linda sees both them and herself as "shadows against a darkening vista of white wall. Painted over by pain and disappointment. *I too am a shadow.*" Linda lives in a world where her pregnancy does not make her more but rather less visible—at least in terms of her psychological identity. She works a job where her employer refuses to pay her the money he owes. Like a shadow himself, he disappears when angry creditors come looking for payment, leaving Linda to absorb their wrath.

As black people struggling to make an honest living in the ghetto, every character in this tale is a "shadow against a darkening vista of white wall." The scream that continually haunts Linda is really the collective shriek of black desperation and rage. As in Ralph Ellison's *Invisible Man,* a classic tale of lost identity, the theme of a "shadow identity" or invisibility connects this tale not only to the other stories in *A War of Eyes* but also to the larger racial protest raised throughout Coleman's oeuvre: that poor black people remain shadows to whites as well as to each other. Coleman suggests that none of her characters in "The Screamer" are free enough to possess the pride of visibility. They are reduced by a scarcity of cash, by unsanitary dwellings, by high rents and not enough good food, and by a fear of the future aptly symbolized in the story's disembodied protest scream—a cry that may finally emanate from Linda's unborn child, who is on the verge of being forced into this world.

As is often the case with Coleman's poetry, *A War of Eyes* contains stories in which individuals are separated from each other rather than connected. In addition to being separated by skin tones and facial features (the legacy of slavery still influences many of these African Americans, making them profoundly aware of their own physical proximity to white culture) and varying degrees of economic disparity, Coleman's characters are also restricted by class and gender barriers. In the story "Ladies" Diane is an affluent and highly educated black social worker who is the therapist for a woman named Rhetta, the latter as much victimized by low self-esteem and poverty as she is by a domineering boyfriend she simply calls "a thug." Diane tries to enlighten Rhetta by empowering her with feminist theory: "This is a new age, Rhetta. A woman is a whole being. Not an addendum—not an extension of a man. But his partner. You have rights and they must be respected—by everyone." However, in spite of her good intentions and her own status as an independent professional woman, Diane is rendered speechless when she visits Rhetta's dilapidated Watts apartment one afternoon and encounters the "massive presence" of her aggressive boyfriend. His physical reality combined with the squalid conditions in the apartment where Rhetta must

live simply dwarf the feminist rhetoric Diane has espoused in group therapy discussion, and she is made to experience intimately the utter futility of any attempt to liberate her oppressed sister.

This tale is a biting satire of academic feminism at its most facile, rendered irrelevant by the flesh-and-blood realism that it often theorizes about and attempts to ameliorate. The abject poverty of Rhetta's world actually mocks and repudiates the shelter and security presumed by Diane in her own world. In effect, Diane has been bleached by her acceptance and participation in a system that has freed her from Rhetta's ghetto life. The story ends abruptly with Diane in desperate flight from the apartment and all that it represents, stopping only long enough to make eye contact with Rhetta, who is standing in the kitchen window "a moment before dropping the curtain," to return to a life without choices, allies, or hope. Perhaps Diane's terror in the face of Rhetta's existence is as much about the therapist's dim recognition that this could easily have been her own condition as it is a rejection of antifeminism.

Although Coleman is acutely sensitive to feminist issues throughout her prose and poetry, she is just as often frustrated in her search for a satisfying alternative to the oppression her female protagonists must endure. "Ladies" describes African American women who are sharply separated by barriers of class and education. Likewise, the title story in *A War of Eyes* argues that race is also a barrier to feminist bonding—that simply sharing the status of mutually oppressed female in a patriarchal culture is not sufficient to bring about interracial unity. In the *Black American Literature Forum* interview, Coleman elaborated upon this position:

The women's movement has refused to come to terms with racism, which it must do if it hopes to be a valid movement. . . . The white women of privilege in this nation must answer to the so-called minority women of America—women of color and poor white women as well. They must acknowledge our experience and needs as different from their own. And until this happens the feminist movement will remain a joke.

In "A War of Eyes" Blue-Eyed Soul-Mama is another of Coleman's well-intentioned liberal feminists. This white woman, who believes in primal scream therapy, initiates a theatrical "war" among individual members of her group therapy session in which "our hatreds, our frustrations, our deep inner madness" will be expressed dramatically; through dance and nonverbal communication the participants will render for themselves "an artistic statement of racial harmony." This worthwhile goal fails to materialize for the narrator of the tale, Doña, "the largest as well as the darkest" female in the group. Doña then deepens the racial divide when she attacks White Deborah, the one white woman "the blacks in our group dislike . . . most because of her arrogance and reserve." At the point in the narrative where Doña is on the verge of capturing White Deborah in a trance-like gaze that is reminiscent of a vampire seducing its victim, Blue-Eyed Soul-Mama interrupts the drama to announce: "War is over!" The last line of this tense psychodrama reveals that White Deborah is Blue-Eyed Soul-Mama's daughter, and that the mother is not willing to risk much if it comes at her daughter's expense. Blue-Eyed Soul-Mama's personal involvement only serves to sabotage the point of this psychological interaction. Her premature interruption of events reveals her own false effort at "racial harmony." As Doña acknowledges, "I am flush with anger and resentment. In my heart I know my siege against her daughter will never be forgotten." The narrative ends abruptly, with the two races more polarized than before, as blacks are once more confronted with whites who change the rules of social engagement to fit their own requirement for survival.

MAMBO HIPS AND MAKE BELIEVE

The novel *Mambo Hips and Make Believe* (1999) is a long, digressive character study of a white woman named Tamala Josephine Fortenot. As the title suggests, Tamala is a voluptuous woman who clings to her dreams even as reality is constantly thwarting her every scheme. Tamala resembles other women found throughout Coleman's canon: although a perpetual victim of sexist and economic oppression, she is not a quitter. And while she has ample reasons to do so, she never surrenders to cynicism or despair.

The novel deliberately avoids a linear approach to the narrative of Tamala's life. While sections occasionally dovetail chronologically, most often there is a collapse in linear time and progression to the point where the reader will find an excerpt from Tammy's adolescent diary juxtaposed with a scene from her later adulthood. The protagonist's great dream is to become a serious writer. For much of *Mambo Hips,* she is engaged in writing, revising, and promoting a family memoir, "Splashing Upward," that she hopes will bring her both fame and fortune. To make a living in the interim, however, she has been forced to devote much of her literary energies to authoring a series of articles for gossip periodicals and soft-core pornographic publications. Tammy perseveres in spite of her loneliness and professional frustrations. Other neophyte writers—especially those with Tamala's great looks and charm— might have abandoned their craft for the job of homemaker or for an occupation that offered better and more regular pay. Tamala persists in her image of herself as a serious writer: "The struggle just to get a typewriter and a place of my own—well, there's been so much sadness of late and so many brick walls."

The novel successfully captures southern California in the 1970s and 1980s, particularly the bar and club scene in Los Angeles, and has a clear sense of period detail, from musical allusions to women's fashion and makeup styles. Against this background Tamala's personal and professional struggles are sharply etched. The narrative relies heavily on Coleman's own experience in the publishing world and her sporadic efforts to find work in Hollywood. The many incidents of backstabbing and manipulation in *Mambo Hips* (from sexual favors to the intellectual plagiarism of ideas) cast Hollywood in the worst possible light.

Tamala's professional efforts are often undercut by her own personal mistakes. Despite her unbridled enthusiasm, provocative fashion sense, undeterred ambition, and sexual chemistry (most of the novel is set in a time before AIDS made such bedroom behavior suicidal), most of her amorous adventures bring her little or no satisfaction: "Grayson [her final lover] was the only relationship in her life which lasted longer than three months." Her love life parallels her dietary misadventures: although she is a diabetic, she drinks alcohol excessively and eats capriciously. Tamala's childlike enthusiasm, loyalty to her friends and family, and dedication to her literary ambitions are all undermined by her inability to take responsibility for her personal life and her stubborn refusal to mature. Thus, what is enticing about this girl-woman also becomes her undoing. Her innocence and enthusiasm teeter precariously on the edge of bimbohood: "It wasn't long before Tamala relaxed into miniskirts and bell-bottomed denims, tight blouses and T-shirts, accenting her outfits with platform heels, outrageous earrings and a sexy anklet. . . . Her starlet's figure drove the fellows wild and they flirted outrageously."

Tamala is a barfly, a waif, and an eternal dreamer who is in love with love. She appears as a prototype for thousands of women who try to make it in Los Angeles every year—women who are neither particularly original nor talented. On the other hand, as her black friend Erlene is quick to point out, Tammy also has soul, and her behavior is seldom malicious. As

she recognizes in a rare moment of self-reflexive honesty: "What I have going for me are deep feelings, a minuscule amount of psychic intuitiveness, a hunger for knowledge, a basically kind and loving nature, and that's about it." Thus, in spite of her many liabilities, both professional and personal, Tammy's character engages the reader. Her commitment to family and friends is never as superficial as the rest of her life appears to be. She is genuinely concerned about the welfare of her psychologically disturbed brother, Davey, and she is the only member of the Fortenot family who bothers to attend her brother Matt's funeral after he commits suicide.

More than anything else, Tammy's is a sad life, and her efforts to sustain it with dreams of "make believe" are simply overwhelmed by the imposition of fate, reality, or the cruel machinations of others. Tammy is a postmodern version of Stephen Crane's Maggie, girl of the streets. Trapped in the history of a dysfunctional family and the hard facts of her own poverty, she struggles to find someone or something to serve as a rudder in her life. Still, she spends most of the novel adrift, searching for The Big Score—an article in a major publication, a windfall inheritance, movie rights for one of her unpublished books, a winning lottery ticket—anything to get her beyond the daily desperation that defines her existence.

And yet Tamala remains one of Coleman's most endearing protagonists. Unlike Crane's Maggie, she draws solid women to her side, a community of females who support her as she travels down a river of sorrow. The men in her life—her brother Matt, Slattery, her father, and all her sexual partners, even the one she appears to love, Grayson—remain underdeveloped and unsavory characters who never provide her with the material and spiritual things she needs to survive and flourish. Coleman's obvious interest is in the women of this novel. The men in it emerge as little more than cardboard figures, rather than fully developed characters. While the males in this novel abuse Tamala sexually or deliberately choose to distance themselves from her deepest needs, her female friends are a constant and loyal source of strength—this in spite of Tamala's frequent errors in judgment. The best of these girlfriends is Erlene, a black poet and single mother who in many ways is a foil for reading Tammy: both share a similar quest to be recognized as writers, both are fiercely protective of one another, both have been victimized by many of the same institutions, businesses, and individuals.

All the chapters in *Mambo Hips,* even those lacking scenes from their twenty-year friendship, conclude with a letter written by Tamala to Erlene. These letters, usually no more than a page or two in length, often comment on a particular moment in Tammy's life. Their contents reveal Tamala's commitment to her writing projects as well as the genuine affection she feels toward her girlfriend. Most important, the letters highlight the one relationship that has remained a constant in Tammy's otherwise lonely existence—her relationship with Erlene. But Erlene, who is also interested in the Los Angeles party scene and its attendant sexuality, at least stops to consider the implications of her behavior. She represents the woman Tamala could have become with smarter choices and a greater level of resistance against the tyranny of men. As Tamala confesses in one of her letters to Erlene, "I am nearly constantly fighting obstacles, either externally or internally. The internal are the worst, exacerbated as they are by the external."

Tamala is a practicing Buddhist. Her religion is the means by which she tries to recenter an existence that is often on the verge of spinning out of control. Unfortunately, Tammy is no closer to attaining nirvana at the end of her life than she is at any other point prior to that. The religious faith and peace she seeks is an anathema to the Hollywood lifestyle she likewise craves. Thus, these spiritual pursuits are effectively consigned to the perimeters of her daily behavior; Buddhism never does help much in stabilizing her personal life or in finding an "alternative Path" that leads beyond the avarice and ambition of California capitalism. It is as if the tenets of Buddhism, like the example that is set forth by Erlene, remain a distant goal for Tamala—a place she wants desperately to get to but never can.

Coleman's characters struggle against circumstances that engulf them. The dual burdens of sexism and racism keep her women confined to subservient lives. For them, happiness and self-determination are distant ideals, at the pole of some distant horizon. More than mere stories of existential despair, these poems and prose narratives are also portraits of endurance. They do not romanticize women by forging them as models of feminist enlightenment or self-sufficient beings who revel in their independence. Rather, Coleman's work is about survival—what a woman must do to survive in a world that seeks constantly to steal her individuality and humanity. Like Camus's Sisyphus, Coleman's female protagonists have been cursed by the gods; however, the vast majority of them also refuse to surrender to despair, suicide, drug addiction, or institutionalization. Her characters take us, finally, beyond brutality to fierce dignity.

Selected Bibliography

WORKS OF WANDA COLEMAN

POETRY

Art in the Court of the Blue Fag. Santa Barbara, Calif.: Black Sparrow Press, 1977.

Mad Dog Black Lady. Santa Barbara, Calif.: Black Sparrow Press, 1979.

Imagoes. Santa Barbara, Calif.: Black Sparrow Press, 1983.

Heavy Daughter Blues: Poems and Stories, 1968–1986. Santa Rosa, Calif.: Black Sparrow Press, 1987.

The Dicksboro Hotel & Other Travels. Tarzana, Calif.: Ambrosia Press, 1989.

African Sleeping Sickness: Stories and Poems. Santa Rosa, Calif.: Black Sparrow Press, 1990.

Hand Dance. Santa Rosa, Calif.: Black Sparrow Press, 1993.

American Sonnets. Kenosha, Wis.: Woodland Pattern/Light & Dust Press, 1994.

Bathwater Wine. Santa Rosa, Calif.: Black Sparrow Press, 1998.

Mercurochrome: New Poems. Santa Rosa, Calif.: Black Sparrow Press, 2001.

OTHER WORKS

"The Time Is Now." *The Name of the Game.* Directed by Nicholas Colasanto. Universal City Studios/NBC-TV, 1970. (Television series episode.)

24 Hours in the Life of Los Angeles. Text by Wanda Coleman and Jeff Spurrier. Edited by Klaus Fabricius and Red Saunders. New York: Alfred van der Marck Editions, 1984. (Essay collection.)

A War of Eyes and Other Stories. Santa Rosa, Calif.: Black Sparrow Press, 1988. (Short stories.)

Earthbound in Betty Grable's Shoes: The Selected Poems of Susannah Foster. Edited by Wanda Coleman. St. John, Kans.: Chiron Review Press, 1990.

Native in a Strange Land: Trials & Tremors. Santa Rosa, Calif.: Black Sparrow Press, 1996. (Essay collection.)

Mambo Hips and Make Believe. Santa Rosa, Calif.: Black Sparrow Press, 1999. (Novel.)

Love-Ins with Nietzsche: A Memoir. Fresno, Calif.: Wake Up Heavy Press, 2000. (Essay collection.)

FILMS AND DISCOGRAPHY

Mad Dog Black Lady. Eugene, Ore.: Produced and directed by Jeff Land and Scott Grant. 1985. (60-minute film.)

Black Angeles. Lawndale, Calif.: New Alliance, 1988. (Spoken word CD and cassette.)

Berserk on Hollywood Boulevard. Los Angeles: New Alliance/Idiot Savant Records, 1991. (Spoken word CD and cassette.)

Black & Blue News. Los Angeles: BarKubCo/Idiot Savant/Widowspeak Records, 1991. (Solo spoken word CD and cassette.)

High Priestess of Word. Lawndale, Calif.: BarKubCo/New Alliance, 1991. (Solo spoken word CD and cassette.)

Twin Sisters. Lawndale, Calif.: New Alliance, 1991. (Spoken word CD and cassette.)

Our Souls Have Grown Deep Like the Rivers: Black Poets Read Their Works. Edited by Rebekah Presson Mosby and Al Young. Los Angeles: Rhino Entertainment Company, 2000. (Audioanthology.)

CRITICAL AND BIOGRAPHICAL STUDIES

"Coleman, Wanda." *Contemporary Authors.* Vol. 119. Detroit: Gale Research, 1987. Pp. 65–66.

Comer, Krista. "Revising Western Criticism through Wanda Coleman." *Western American Literature* 33:356–383 (winter 1999).

George, Lynell. "A Perversion of Dreams and Other Truths." *Los Angeles Times,* January 5, 2000, p. E1.

Hacker, Marilyn. "The 1999 Lenore Marshall Prize." *The Nation,* December 6, 1999, pp. 44–47.

Magistrale, Tony. "Doing Battle with the Wolf: A Critical Introduction to Wanda Coleman's Poetry." *Black American Literature Forum* 23:539–557 (fall 1989).

Pinkley, Diane. "Poet-Warrior: A Review of Wanda Coleman's *Bathwater Wine.*" *Meat Whistle Quarterly* 2:44–47 (winter 1998).

Russell, Caryn. "American Artifacts of Heartbreak and Racism: *A War of Eyes and Other Stories.*" *High Plains Review* 4:264–269 (1989).

Schwalberg, Carol. "Wanda Coleman: *Native in a Strange Land.*" *Poets & Writers Magazine* 26:46 (September/October 1998).

INTERVIEWS AND CORRESPONDENCE

Bush, Rebecca. "Wanda Coleman: Featured Poet." *Slack* 25–32 (1994).

Coleman, Wanda. Written correspondence from the author to Tony Magistrale, dated July 29, 2000.

Levine, Rachel. "A Conversation with Wanda Coleman." *ACM/Another Chicago Magazine* 35:210–235 (1999).

Magistrale, Tony, and Patricia Ferreira. "Sweet Mama Wanda Tells Fortunes: An Interview with Wanda Coleman." *Black American Literature Forum* 24:491–507 (fall 1990).

—TONY MAGISTRALE

Harry Crews

1935–

In HIS 1954 autobiography, Emmett Kelly, whose doleful Weary Willie redefined the circus clown, eloquently described his character as "a sad and ragged little guy amid the happy noise of the circus who is very serious about everything he attempts—no matter how futile or how foolish it appears to be [*recall the classic bit with Willie trying to mop up the spotlight*]—who finds the hard way that the deck is stacked, the dice frozen, the race fixed and the wheel crooked." What might appear one of the more curious enterprises in southern novelist Harry Crews's long, often eccentric career was an aborted project in the late 1980s to write the screenplay of a biographical movie about Kelly. But the interest is perhaps not so odd. Given the casual excesses—the "happy noise"—of Crews's hurdy-gurdy fictive world, his soulful central characters are rather like Weary Willie: isolates who introduce a deep touch of understatement amid such spectacle excess, who struggle with resilient heart to assert a semblance of dignity by performing an idiosyncratic ritual—for instance, karate, bodybuilding, hawk training, football, acrobatics—amid the wider craziness that threatens to diminish such rituals into absurdity. Thus, Weary Willie—and the circus itself—may help locate the fiction of an elusive writer whose nearly four decades of work have raised only questions over where such an intriguing figure rightly belongs.

The artistic evolution of Harry Crews begins, curiously, with a Sears-Roebuck mail-order catalog. Growing up amid the depression-era poverty of a south Georgia farm, the young Crews was enthralled by the catalog. He would sit for hours paging past images of perfect people and would invent secret lives and fantastic adventures for them. Crews has often commented on this passion for invention despite growing up in a rural outback largely without books (save the Bible and the catalog); how, in the absence of radio or newspapers, he learned the art of storytelling by listening to his family of back-porch raconteurs; how, by age seven, he was writing down his own stories; how, at thirteen, he wrote his first novel (a detective story); how later he taught himself the discipline of blocking out a story by painstakingly dissecting model novels (most prominently Graham Greene's *The End of the Affair*); how he had written (and discarded) four complete novels even before his first was published; how his need to write alienated him from his own rural roots (a farm family unable to understand how a man could be paid for "lying"), from his wife and children, and even from the academic community that, since the 1950s, had given him whatever tenuous sense of home he had managed to secure.

Simply put, Crews loves stories. Typing furiously at his 1920s Underwood, fashioning his tight little worlds, Crews demands that readers step into his novels much as they would step under the big top: willing to suspend the expectations of more modest realism (a circus, after all, is not a theater) and to accept self-justifying audacity. Crews does not tell stories—he stages them. Unlike other southern writers so expressly bound to postage-stamp back lots of a recognizable Deep Dixie or the postwar realistic writers of his generation (John Updike, Philip Roth, John Cheever) given to

BELMONT UNIVERSITY LIBRARY

capturing the sound and press of specific geographies, Crews's fictive world is defiantly made-up, conjured out of an excessive, exuberant imagination and thus populated not by the pedestrian sorts likely to be shopping at the Winn-Dixie but rather by the eccentric sorts so casually existing as part of a circus environment. What is remarkable about Crews's fiction is not his much-vaunted output but rather the disparity, even the tension, between the life lived and the books written. Despite his prodigious output, Crews has never drawn from his own considerable life story: the painful estrangement from his rural family; the drowning death of his first son and the consequent shattering of his marriage; his awkward fit into the academic world; the terrifying distance between himself and the God he was raised to trust existed; his frantic decade-long struggle to find his way into print; his costly addiction to pills and alcohol—none of it finds record in his fiction. Rather, like that boy sitting in the red Georgia dirt spellbound by a mail-order catalog, Crews turns to the enthralling circus world of his invention. Like the circus, his fictive worlds are magic evasions, artful dodges. Where is Crews country? Where do his outlandish characters belong? They belong nowhere but in the world Crews himself creates. Caught up in the delight of shocking, the license to exaggerate, the sheer need to stun, Crews, like a circus manager too fond of spectacle excess, finds himself often accused of slick showmanship, cheap effects, and crass manipulations. And reading too much Crews can create the suffocating strangeness of being locked in a circus that never folds, never closes. But if the carnival excess distracts, the clowns amid Crews's circus world ultimately compel, his engrossing central characters' gestures at dignity stand (like Kelly's Weary Willie) against and amid the ludic exaggerations of the larger narrative contexts and provide Crews's fiction its unsuspected humanity.

LIFE

Harry Eugene Crews was born June 7, 1935, near Alma in the cotton and tobacco belt of south Georgia on the edges of the backwater wastes of the Okefenokee Swamp. The second surviving son of Ray Crews, a hardworking sharecropper, and Myrtice Crews, a loving mother (whom Crews would idolize long into his adult life). Crews endured a childhood marred by emotional and physical traumas and defined by a struggle to belong somewhere. Overworked by a lifetime of backbreaking farm work, his father, Ray, died in his sleep when Harry was not yet two—at age thirty-one, his heart simply gave out. Harry was sleeping in the same bed. His mother soon married Ray's brother, Pascal, the only father Crews would know, a heavy drinker who would become abusive during his binges. In his autobiography, Crews recalls, "Every night I lay in bed trembling, thinking, this time he's gonna kill mamma. Her screaming and begging ripped and shook through the house as he beat her and beat her, usually stopping only when he got too tired to go on."

But Crews would learn suffering firsthand. At five, he endured a mysterious fever during which his legs suddenly curled up painfully and uselessly and then, after six weeks of bed rest, just as mysteriously uncurled and slowly returned to full use. It was most likely infantile paralysis, although Crews has suggested it might have been a stress reaction to his turbulent home life. Then, within the year, during a game of crack-the-whip, he fell into an open tub of boiling water in which his mother was dipping and skinning slaughtered hogs. He would recall that once pulled from the tub he tugged the skin of his hands off "like a wet glove." But more profound pain awaited the young Crews. When he was six, his mother, fearful of her husband's violence, took her two sons south to Jacksonville, Florida, where she found work in a cigar factory. Evicted within a year from their apartment, the family returned to Bacon County only to return to Florida later, a shuttling back and forth that would become a pattern for Crews's childhood.

In 1953 Crews graduated from high school (the first in his family to do so) and, desperate to get out of Georgia, joined the U.S. Marines (his older brother was already serving in Korea). Because the cease-fire suspending the war was signed in July, Crews never served overseas. But during his three years' service he responded to the discipline of the corps, which would later help in his fanatical commitment to the physical demands of writing. Further, he took advantage of military camp libraries to begin an ambitious reading program. "I did my time in the Corps with a book always in hand," he has said. After completing military service in 1956 and briefly returning to Georgia, Crews enrolled at the University of Florida at Gainesville under the GI Bill. Well-read but not accustomed to the academic environment (an adviser suggested he might pursue trade school), after just two years he packed up a new motorcycle and headed West with one hundred dollars to his name. For eighteen months, he roamed from Canada to Mexico ("If you can cook or tend bar, you can work in any city in this country") eventually returning ("purified and holy") to the university. There, he came under the mentoring of the southern novelist and essayist Andrew Lytle, whose temperament and background could not have been more different from Crews's but who found in Crews's fledgling writing the promise of serious craft and a flair for character. Lytle would become a surrogate father for the young Crews. In his senior year (January 1960), Crews married Sally Ellis, a sophomore English major who had tutored him through a difficult semester in Spanish. They had a son, Patrick, born in September of that year. By then, Crews had taken a job teaching junior high school English in Jacksonville. Still burning to write and finding high school teaching uninspiring, he returned

to Gainesville and quickly earned a master's degree in English education. Troubled by his own manic pursuit of his writing and by the demands of his schooling, Crews found little time for the responsibilities of his family. He and Sally divorced in 1961, and she left with their son for Dayton, Ohio. When Florida's Creative Writing Department turned down his application for entrance into its graduate creative writing program, Crews moved south in 1962 to teach freshman English at the Junior College of Broward County (now Broward Community College) in Fort Lauderdale. Now with a stable income, he persuaded his wife to give their marriage a second chance. A second son, Byron, was born in August 1963. Then on July 31, 1964, Patrick Crews, aged three, drowned in a neighbor's pool. Crews himself pulled his son from the pool but was unable to revive him. Guilt scarred Crews deeply (he claims never to have visited his son's grave). He came to feel that his marriage reconciliation had, in effect, lured Patrick to his death and that his commitment to writing had taken time from his son now irretrievably lost. Ultimately, he and Sally would divorce again, although he has stayed close to Byron and counts their relationship as central in his emotional life.

By his own account, during the mid-1960s amid such devastating emotional upheavals, Crews wrote "like a house on fire," cranking out hundreds of stories (all rejected) and drafts of four different novels. In 1963 Crews published his first story in the *Sewanee Review,* a prestigious academic journal then edited by Lytle. In "The Unattached Smile," a sailor on liberty in Puerto Rico gets involved with a prostitute whose haunting smile reminds him of his sister in ways that hint of incestuous undercurrents. Although a second story, "A Long Wail," was accepted soon after by the *Georgia Review,* Crews entered a long stretch of much writing and little publication. Compelled to write but growing more certain that, as he began his thirties, he would never succeed, Crews began ingesting amphetamines and Wild Turkey bourbon to help him through nightlong bouts of creativity before returning to the classroom by day. Finally in 1968 he found a publisher for *The Gospel Singer,* a disturbing southern gothic in which a celebrity evangelist is lynched by a rabid mob after he admits his own moral failings. Critical response was encouraging. In 1968, with the quick follow-up acceptance of what Crews considers his best novel (the grotesque comic allegory *Naked in Garden Hills,* 1969), Crews accepted a teaching position in the creative writing department at the University of Florida, paradoxically the same department that had earlier denied him admission. Although never comfortable within academia ("it's like swimming in a sea of gumdrops"), he discovered a flair for the classroom and enjoyed the rewards of encouraging students and their apprentice efforts.

Now secure in a livelihood, Crews began publishing novels at a remarkable rate—nearly a novel a year for the next ten years. Each novel would shock readers and critics alike, uncertain exactly how to appreciate the bizarre fictional landscape of Crews's black comic vision, a bleak landscape peopled by the misshapen who struggle to achieve dignity, where sexual excess and horrific violence are the status quo. His books unsettled ("if you want to write about sweetness and light, get a job at Hallmark," he told Tammy Lytal and Richard Russell in an interview)—and he became something of a cult figure, his books never selling well and never attracting the sort of academic treatment of more erudite writers of his generation yet managing to encourage fierce loyalty among his fans. He became a regular faculty member at the Bread Loaf Writers' Conference where his charismatic readings entranced a generation of younger writers. In 1972 he was awarded the National Institute of Arts and Letters Award for Fiction. In 1975 he began a long, lucrative association

as a contributor to both *Playboy* and *Esquire,* finding in their men's magazine format an attractive forum from which to project his evolving sense of himself as a macho man's man, hard-drinking and hard-driving, irreverent and straight-talking, writing essays about cockfighting and carnival workers, gator poachers and dogfights. But it is Crews, as the recording consciousness, who inevitably emerges as the dominant character. In the haunting essay "Climbing the Tower" (1977), Crews, describes visiting the University of Texas for a literary conference, where he sits, quite drunk, under the same clock tower where in 1966 Charles Whitman had opened fire on the campus below. In a moment of striking honesty, Crews writes of his own identification with that tormented, alienated gunman as a way to explain his approach to character-driven fiction and the experience of slipping into the skin of a character, no matter how repellent.

This penchant for identifying with the repellent climaxed with the stunning, controversial *A Feast of Snakes* (1976), in which the frustrations and shattered dreams of a former high school football player explode in a bloody shooting spree at novel's end. Its horrific climax, its unforgiving look at the hopelessness of the American Dream (published at the height of the Bicentennial hoopla), and its claustrophobic feel of inevitable disappointment had left Crews, as artist, at his own dead end. Its publication would close Crews's frenetic decade of novel writing; he would not publish another novel for ten years. His lifestyle contributed to this hiatus: his addictions to speed and Valium and to alcohol consumed his energy. He turned to film projects, some based on his own novels (a natural evolution given his cinematic sense of scene, his gift for dialogue, and his natural talent for storytelling). None would be made. Clearly his most significant endeavor of this period was his 1978 autobiography, *A Childhood: The Biography of a Place,* a turning-point achievement in which Crews exhumed memories of his Georgia upbringing and directly confronted realities he had largely avoided in his extravagant fictions. Such excavation, however, drove Crews deeper into his addictions, and stories of Crews's outrageous, self-destructive behavior began to circulate. He would in mid-decade begin a series of difficult treatment programs for substance abuse until, he stated to Joann Biondi in an 1990 interview, he was at last, clean and sober: "Oh, God, I miss it. I wish I could kick back with a martini almost every day at about four in the afternoon. But I can't."

He would return to fiction in the late 1980s, including a 1989 two-act drama titled *Blood Issue* commissioned for the Actors Theatre of Louisville, Kentucky, which marked the first time Crews used elements of his own life as part of his writing. In a wrenching family drama reminiscent of Tennessee Williams, an alcoholic writer revisits his Georgia farm home and learns difficult truths about his father. Perhaps reflecting the dramatic changes within his lifestyle, Crews's post-rehab novels, most notably 1992's compelling *Scar Lover,* while still centering on offbeat, darkly comic characters, move beyond the often gratuitous violence and lurid sexuality of his earlier works toward endings that are, without irony, affirmative, even tender, as characters learn the difficult necessity of trust and friendship. In the early 1990s Crews began to relinquish his teaching load until in 1997 he retired. Nearing seventy, Crews clearly began to ponder his own mortality while, as he has often told interviewers, feeling lucky after a lifetime of hard living just to have the opportunity to do such pondering. In addition to completing work on the second projected volume of his autobiography (to be titled *Assault of Memory*), Crews has published two novels since his retirement that are decidedly valedictory. One (*Where Does One Go When There's No Place Left to Go?* 1995) is a postmodern romp in which he imagines he is kidnapped by his own characters and spirited off to Disney World, where, in a most appropriate landscape of artifice and imagination, the aging writer, in effect, looks back on a gallery of characters more real to him than people he had met. The other (*Celebration,* 1998) is a sobering meditation on death and the indignities of aging that focuses on the decrepit tenants of a Florida trailer park momentarily revived by the striking presence of an exotic young woman. Death, he once told Mary Voboril in an interview, holds no great terror—"I don't like funerals, don't like memorials, don't like eulogies, and so in my will, when I die, however I die, I am to be taken posthaste to the nearest crematorium and burned up without anybody seeing me . . . and my ashes taken to the Little Satilla River [in south Georgia] to feed the fishes": the sharecropper's son home at last.

A WRITER DIFFICULT TO PLACE

Like that sharecropper's son who never quite felt at home anywhere, Crews's extravagant fictions are difficult to place. Some see Crews, born in 1935 and so defiantly proud of his rural Georgia roots, as the redneck branch of the family of post–World War II writers who deployed cartoon characters in improbable and baroque plotlines to chronicle both the alarming collapse of the postwar promise of American power amid the early frost of the cold war (with its terrifying premise of imminent nuclear apocalypse) and then the difficult adjustments to a succession of national traumas: the rifle shots in Dallas; the noise, waste, and pain of Vietnam; the bloody street-birth of civil rights; the absurd realpolitik of the Nixon White House, each played out against the emerging intellectual void fostered by a generation's addiction to television and the dehumanization implicit in the techno-culture of the emerging computer age. Like Crews, these writers—Thomas Pynchon,

Ken Kesey, Norman Mailer, Kurt Vonnegut—sustained a profound anxiety over the self-apparent wasteland of midcentury America and, despite a shared sensibility of black comedy, an unshakeable despair over the possibility of redemption in a culture so death-soaked and so devoid of purpose.

Others detect in Crews more a shattered religious sensibility and connect him to the mid-century struggle of writers such as Samuel Beckett and Graham Greene to live in a world that had outlived its Creator, the struggle of the flesh to assert a redeeming sense of the spiritual, to reclaim the privileged position as creation and the satisfying reassurance it brings of purpose, order, and dignity. Unlike the fictions of fellow southerner Flannery O'Connor, to whom Crews is often aligned, Crews can find no conviction save his own certainty (born of his Baptist upbringing) that humanity could not be born simply to chance. In his first published interview, with Anne Foata, Crews argued, "The most awful thing that I can imagine . . . is to be cut loose from the universe, to be cut loose from the fact that rocks fall when you drop them, that stars move in a certain pattern, to be cut loose from all that and have no sense that it is all working somehow." Without validation of the soul, his characters are left in an untenable posture: slightly more evolved than animals, torn by temptations and bloodlusts, vulnerable to the roiling whims of chance. Like Graham Greene (whose influence Crews often cites), Crews challenges his characters, violent and lustful, to preserve a sense of sin, to sustain an uncompromising sense of guilt in a larger cultural context where actions appear to exist in a consequence-free environment. Institutional religion itself found wanting, his characters seek alternative validation. Supremely they pursue athletic endeavors where they elevate physical fitness to spiritual status—it is the best we have in the absence of what we so desperately seek. That such a strategy can never work is finally

the great sorrow at the center of Crews's religious vision.

Perhaps irresistibly given Crews's much-documented rural Georgia upbringing and his consistent interest in southern characters and southern locales, his work has often been placed geographically (despite his frequent objections). In this reading Crews is seen as the leading voice of the New South, the so-called Grit Lit generation that found unworkable the elegant, Faulknerian sensibility of the Deep South as a lost agrarian aristocracy steeped in its history and proud of its rootedness. For Crews, the rural South is more a brutal environment, a savage naturalistic world whose barely literate inhabitants struggle day to day for sustenance and have little claim to dignity. Given the economic boom of the Sun Belt, Crews's fiction is especially interested in the shift from rural to urban as prosperity and cultural refinement marginalize a rural population driven to pursue economic livelihoods within an urban landscape, not really belonging anywhere. Crews has often cited as a defining epiphanic moment his decision, in the late 1960s, to stop denying his own upbringing as a sharecropper's son and to accept without shame that his artistic vision, despite his evolution into a university professor, would always reflect that world. As stated in his autobiography, "Once I realized that the way I saw the world and man's condition in it would always be exactly and inevitably shaped by everything which up to that moment had only shamed me, once I realized that, I was home free."

Still others find in Crews's over-the-top fictional sensibility the broad, savage touch of the satirist, defiant, angry, uncompromising, unforgiving. Deeply dissatisfied with his own cultural moment, unable to afford the niceties of subtlety, Crews pillories with heavy-handed directness his culture's erotic fascination with machines, its mercenary lusting after profit, its crass consumer mentality, its shallow intellectuality, its fascination with the pornography of violence, its happy freefall into moral relativism, and the sheer lack of awareness of its own precarious position. His anger unleavened by nuance and uneasily direct, he seethes like Jonathan Swift or Nathanael West or, more directly influential to Crews, like Hunter S. Thompson, gonzo journalism's hip guru of toxic rage, and Walt Kelly, the creator of the southern bayou comic strip *Pogo,* whose unassuming folksiness masked stinging lampoons of cold war insanities. Like those curmudgeony voices, Crews clearly disdains his own culture, where diligence and discipline are unrewarded, where the worst rise inexorably to positions of authority, where the higher virtues of love and trust and belief are hopelessly unworkable, where wisdom is replaced by easy platitudes, and where inevitably the best are driven to suicide, madness, or inglorious retreat.

And there are those who would prefer not to place Crews at all, but rather to relegate him to the margins, dismiss him as a minority enthusiasm, at best a literary curiosity (like the carnival attractions he so often chronicles), at worst a cult figure among the anti-intellectuals who disdained the midcentury postmodernists who reconfigured the novel by using fiction itself as a testing ground for language theories and whose experimental work, in turn, required elaborate commentary for even professional readers. These anti-intellectuals found in Crews a bracing antidote to such contrived, difficult tomes: they welcomed his clipped, accessible prose; reader-friendly symbolism; pitch-perfect ear for dialogue; compelling plotlines; and characters caught up in moral dilemmas where good and evil shift uncertainly, all done with a biting comic sensibility and an irreverent willingness to indulge the grotesque and the lurid.

But this same generous embrace of Crews-in-the-margins has also led to a mainstream perception of Crews as a promising middling

talent wasted by his own excessive indulgence of alcohol and drugs, by a personal lifestyle frittered in a faux-Hemingway fondness for macho thrills, and by a mercenary pursuit of publication. Thus, he becomes a sort of Wal-Mart Norman Mailer, a bargain-basement Hemingway (or a glorified Mickey Spillane): a tough-guy posture, a swaggering macho cliché pounding out novels that strain to shock with unmotivated violence and a titillating soft-porn kinkiness. Irredeemably misogynistic, this Crews fashions women characters who exist either as two-dimensional centerfold fantasies or as calculating menaces who coolly eviscerate their unsuspecting men. In this reading Crews is dismissed as a celebrity too fond of his own ego, conducting, for more than twenty years, a performance-art piece named Harry Crews: the hard-core guys' guy, motorcycle enthusiast, jock, barroom raconteur with stints in jail, whose scarred body testified to a life on the edge; whose elbow tattoo of a hinge served as a not-too-subtle reminder of his excessive drinking; whose earring, menacing moustache, and any one of a number of deliberately audacious hair styles from shaved head to Mohawk sustained an intimidating persona enhanced by a perpetual scowl and laser-eyes and complemented by a no-nonsense interview style salted generously with expletives and backwoods one-liners. Himself less a novelist, more a caricature, his deliberately exaggerated fictions bear all the literary weight of comic strips.

So then where *does* Harry Crews belong? His books have found sustaining life neither in bookstores nor classrooms. He does not belong in either of the principal camps of postwar American fiction: his works are not satisfyingly realistic, slice-of-life narratives with recognizable characters in recognizable landscapes whose recognizable dilemmas help explicate the difficult struggles of the day-to-day; nor are they audaciously postmodern, sophisticated *textes* that gleefully detonate themselves by exploiting with unsettling and often gaudy awareness the fiction-making process itself. He is neither a self-manufactured celebrity (à la Mailer or Gore Vidal or Truman Capote) nor is he "neglected" with that implied status of being the special project of enthusiastic academics. Although part of the generation that came of age during the liberal era of midcentury, with its high-minded rhetoric of social and political consciousness, and an eyewitness to the tectonic changes in the Deep South during the mid-1960s, Crews is neither a social activist nor even comfortable with the idea of agenda-driven fiction bent on preaching to its cultural moment. Crews, then, seems doomed to linger in the uneasy between, between realism and postmodernism, between respectability and popularity, between reputation and celebrity, between heavyweight and lightweight, uncertain over just where he belongs.

Like the circus itself, a Harry Crews novel belongs only in the space it defiantly provides itself, the space it defines by its own gaudy and elaborate rules, a protected environment that welcomes only that audience willing to accept its terms. Crews's novels are undeniably scored to the calliope's trill. The novels function like intensely compelling circus worlds peopled by the exaggerations appropriate to the managed spectacle of the circus, with its staged brutalities, its heavy-handed craziness, and its defining imperative to startle. Each novel is a closed system that skews the recognizable world. Thus, even the noblest characters, locked within such a claustrophobic environment of spectacle, can never hope to achieve reliable heroism; their every dilemma appears contrived, every horror stage-managed, every defeat strikingly vaudevillian, any triumph seriously qualified by the ongoing circus world. Even their occasional deaths are tidily insulated as ironic.

Characters then are trapped within Crews's fictive world itself, caged (one of Crews's favorite metaphors) within a narrative world of effortless exaggerations and routine absurdities. Like Kelly's Weary Willie, within such carnival texts, Crews's central characters struggle to maintain a modicum of control and dignity by pursuing a slender obsession, an audacious ritual that, played out against and amid the circus world of the larger text, gives the characters a resonant humanity singular within the carnival texts. These clowns-in-the-text include a fanatic bodybuilder, an obsessive dieter, a karate enthusiast, an amateur hawk trainer, a midget masseur, a koan-spouting weightlifter, a record-setting high school football star, a gifted gospel singer, a man who attempts to consume a car, a genetic mishap who balances on his finger, a glass-jawed boxer able to knock himself out cold. These central characters then become Weary Willies who, amid the greater noise of the circus, assert what Crews has often described in his own central characters as the "heroism of senseless acts." And yet these clowns-in-the-text resist our sympathy because, like all clowns, they defy mimesis and remain contrivances; they are distant and isolated, less people, more fascinating objects (imagine seeing a clown in full regalia at a shopping mall). After all, locked within the circus itself, clowns can never achieve genuine heroics but can only hope for survival; they are outrage without consequence, suffering without relevance, flesh-and-blood cartoons. By similar logic, as long as Crews's characters remain within the circus texts, they are similarly fated. The true heroics among Crews's characters are only those few Crews dares to free, characters who at the close of their novels step entirely out of the antic narrative world itself. With such open-endings, these characters slip free of Crews's stage-managed circus world to engage the freewheeling vulnerabilities of the everyday.

It may be helpful to use Crews himself as parallel enterprise. After all, for nearly twenty-five years, Crews, locked safely within the protective circus-space of the university, played the irreverent clown, the redneck-with-tenure, a public performance piece enhanced by his own outrageous sense of costuming and energized by his drug and alcohol abuse. It was a convincing act, complete with stints in jail, obligatory barroom fights, a brief gig as lead singer in an alternative thrash club band (The Harry Crews Band), a compelling cameo in a Sean Penn film (*The Indian Runner,* 1988*),* appearances on Manhattan talk shows as a sort of rural curiosity, and a plethora of apocryphal stories of outrageous drunken readings-qua-performances at assorted literary conferences. Only after Crews himself underwent detoxification in the late 1980s did he himself depart this circus, abandon his act to face clean and sober the vulnerabilities of the everyday. It is tempting to use Crews's 1978 autobiography as a cathartic experience. After years of outrageous narratives heady with unapologetic excess, in the graphic honesty of the autobiography Crews himself stood finally outside his own act, suddenly exposed, the "I" he had neatly skirted through twenty years of writing. Perhaps not surprisingly in the novels published since his detoxification, Crews appears more willing to extend generous emancipation to his central characters, to endorse the need to risk the very movement into the everyday he himself accepted. As Crews has said in the *Palm Beach Post* of his own detoxification, "Taking the world entirely straight, with no buzz at all, man, that's hard duty."

"Good fiction," Crews argued in a seminal 1990 interview with A. B. Crowder, "is there to make you breathe with another human being, bleed with him, to suck you out of your skin for a little while and put you in somebody else's skin." If then his fictions are best approached as character studies, what do his central characters share? To provide a pathway through three decades of Crews's novels, this essay will focus on the dozen central characters he has fashioned, excluding only the 1995 novel *The Mulching of*

America, a misdirected heavy-handed lampoon of corporate America that manipulates a series of two-dimensional characters involved in door-to-door soap selling, a satiric contrivance that by Crews's own admission got out of his control. By arranging his characters not chronologically but rather thematically, it is possible to trace a career-long interest in the struggle to accept the imperfect flesh and its necessary vulnerabilities within an unscripted world. From the implosion of Joe Lon Mackey (*A Feast of Snakes,* 1976) to the reclamation of Pete Butcher (*Scar Lover,* 1992), these characters can be grouped into three areas: those who succumb to the hot lure of the flesh and who, as little more than animals, are terrified by the brutal play of chance and who move inexorably toward messy death; those who try to control the flesh by abandoning the complications of connection, who distance themselves from the everyday, and who are left alive but decidedly, coolly, alone; and those who come hesitatingly to accept the flesh as the sole avenue to the saving touch of others and who necessarily come to accept the uncertain flux of a world engineered by chance. They alone step free of the circus world of the Crews novel and move by narrative end into an (un)easy freedom.

THE ANIMALS

We begin with Joe Lon Mackey, Crews's purest animal. Two years beyond the promise of his small-town high school football career (he graduated virtually illiterate), whatever expectations he had managed to define have been cashiered swiftly by forces entirely unlike the uniformed opponents of his glory days; he is left to howl, literally, in his rage. Married to a woman already collapsed into dreariness, sentenced (at age twenty-two) to a life term in a double-wide trailer, finding purpose difficult to sustain with two squealing babies, a slovenly wife with bad teeth, and a job that includes renting port-a-potties and running moonshine, he exists solely in a brutal present (the past too dead, the future too predictable): love is only the tearing relief of satisfaction (in a brutal, animalistic interlude, he cheats on his wife with an ex-girlfriend, now a cheerleader at the University of Georgia); anger is best expressed by punching something or somebody; escape is compelled by the grim consumption of cheap alcohol. Crews sets Joe Lon amid the circus excess of the town's autumn Rattlesnake Round-up Weekend, which without irony includes both a beauty contest and gruesome dogfights and climaxes with a diamondback roundup and barbeque. Joe Lon is the least attractive of Crews's clowns largely because his act is long over—his football records are already being eclipsed. He is left alone, bored and dreamless; worse, he disdains love—it was the lure that had trapped him into marriage, it had driven his mother to suicide when she found herself unable to leave his violent father. Joe Lon's shockingly quick explosion at the end—in a spare half page, he shoots four revelers, including his ex-girlfriend—is as pointless as the sick exhibitions of dogfighting that his father stages. It is a misdirected gesture at the sort of control he had felt on the football field, the sort of control from which his tawdry life had so completely slipped free. After the shooting spree, the shocked revelers toss Joe Lon, appropriately helpless, into the rattlesnake pit where he dies gruesomely.

A parallel fate awaits Stump, the proprietor of a Florida trailer park for old folks in *Celebration* (1998). A veteran haunted by memories of Korea, one hand chopped off by a corn picker, Stump (like Joe Lon) has abandoned any assumption that life might delight and now moves through each day sustained by routine, deadened by alcohol, and livened only occasionally by the joyless friction of sex. He lives surrounded by the stink of mortality, hemmed in by the infirm left to die in excruciating slow motion.

The novel tracks the tectonic impact of Too Much, a stunningly erotic woman-child who, at eighteen, generates (as her nickname indicates) energy sufficient to rejuvenate the entire trailer park. Homeless after the grandfather who raised her dies (and thus familiar with helplessness and the shatteringly quick stroke of death), she moves in with Stump. He and Too Much indulge what Stump terms their "circus act": in the bathtub, she pleasures herself by the slow stimulations of his stump, thus turning the ugly and useless into the magical and beautiful. Audaciously, she decides to provide the retirement folks with a May Day celebration, that ritual welcome to the tonic energy of spring, complete with a costumed dance around a maypole. Terrified only by boredom and the easy logic of surrender, Too Much coaxes the resisting residents to pursue the "chance of ultimate possibility," the tantalizing notion that life can continually surprise and delight. One by one they rediscover long-ignored talents, revive dormant emotions, and reestablish themselves as a community. The novel moves toward the May Day celebration as the giddy residents (costumed in ways that recall moments when they were happiest), dancing and singing, feel empowered and alive. Except for Stump. He cannot accept the implications of such revival ("Why couldn't they all accept that the next thing for all of them was death?") and reduces Too Much to an itch he hungrily scratches. Undeterred, the celebrating old folks drag him to their maypole, hoist him up, and happily wrap their ribbons around his suspended body until, finally, they twist the ribbons around his face and (we assume) suffocate him.

Unlike Joe Lon and Stump, their most vital years so unavailable, Dorothy Turnipseed (*Body,* 1990) is at the peak of her physical prowess. A hard-training bodybuilder, Dorothy has sculpted the sort of muscled frame that has placed her in a position to compete for Ms. Cosmos, a prestigious bodybuilding title. Along the way, she has in effect re-created herself into a sustained performance-art piece she has fancifully renamed Shereel Dupont. Her fierce dedication to burning out the fat in her body has left her consumed with self-justifying narcissism that does not permit others into her suffocating sense of ego (her ongoing affair with her trainer is curiously passionless; indeed, they make love as a way to burn off water weight). Like Joe Lon and Stump, she is fixated on the physical plane, her vision stubbornly horizontal. She is consumed by the control implied by her training regimen. Crews cautions such control is illusory. First, Dorothy's coarse hill family, including an old flame, unexpectedly invades the glamorous beach hotel where the competition will be staged and shatters her focus. Then in the competition she finishes second. Unable to accept such a setback, Dorothy slices her own wrists in a final gesture of control, thus destroying the finely sculpted (albeit empty) frame into which she had placed her entire trust. Like Joe Lon Mackey and Stump, Dorothy indulges the sterile illusion of self-sufficiency—the clown consumed by her act, unwilling to accept the untidy realities beyond the circus itself.

Unlike these three characters, the nameless Gospel Singer of Crews's first novel in 1968 negotiates a more complex interaction between interior and exterior. Along with his gorgeous looks, his effortless charisma, his potent sexuality, and the intoxicating spell he evokes with his singing, such an attractive form encases an evolving sensibility, a nascent conscience, that causes him to question the legitimacy of his own celebrity even as the crowds swell and he himself succumbs to the blandishments of fame. There is much of the circus atmosphere in Crews's depiction of the revival circuit (indeed, a carnival show actually follows the Gospel Singer to take advantage of the crowds that his revivals attract). Yet, the sheer need of his audience begins to sour his initial enjoyment of the

lurid excess of stardom: money, fame, women. "The hopeless, hopeful faces feeding on words, but mostly feeding on him, the Gospel Singer, on the beauty of his face and the beauty of his voice." He begins to feel the hard loneliness of the spotlight, the inaccessibility of his family (the plot revolves around his annual return to his small Georgia hometown and his confrontation with a girl he had "ruined"). Stricken by the plight of a longtime friend, a black man who sits in the local jail accused of raping and killing that same woman and who, although innocent of the rape, faces the certainty of lynch-mob justice because of that presumed violation, the Gospel Singer begins to feel the need to cleanse the excess of his own behavior. When his fanatic followers decide that he should heal infirmities and even convert souls, he acts to stop the madness. He attempts to save his friend by announcing to his congregation that the woman was not a desecrated virgin but rather a woman of decidedly loose morals, initially corrupted by him. In a dramatic turn, he then admits, "I caint do nothing but sing gospel songs and lay your women, your wives and mothers and daughters." Stunned by his honesty, the mob beats him and then lynches him along with his friend. In his final breath, the Gospel Singer asserts a final pathetic gesture of control by cursing them all to hell, unable to forgive their actions or accept his own evident helplessness.

THE COOL AND ALONE

Four other characters in Crews's works exhibit what the previous four so staunchly deny: need—the awkward sensibility, ignited in the flesh, that the self cannot suffice. Yet here that generous impulse outward backfires and leaves each one devastated. They accept cool isolation within Crews's circus world, a place apart, like clowns amid the circus, clinging only to their act and the slender protective hermetic space they inhabit.

The gargantuan millionaire Mayhugh Aaron Jr., known as the Fat Man (*Naked in Garden Hills,* 1969) is rent by the savage pull of need—specifically, a homoerotic impulse felt long ago in college for a long-distance runner. When he attempted to act on this compelling need, it backfired, and he departed the university to accept a long life of cooled loneliness entombed (along with a midget manservant) within a magnificent house built high above the town of Garden Hills, itself ironically built at the bottom of a massive abandoned mining pit. His spirit denied, he sustains it by binge reading; his flesh denied, he sustains it by binge eating, weight-gain drinks complemented by massive, and ironic, ingestions of diet supplements as his bulk swells to a monstrous six hundred pounds. He is flesh out-of-control. The novel thus plays out the catastrophic implications of mismanaging natural resources such as love and need—Garden Hills itself had been ravished by the strip-mining tactics of a phosphate conglomerate. The mining boom gone, Dolly, a savvy entrepreneur who learned early the hard cash value of her uncanny sex appeal, determines that the town's future rests on her ambitious plans to convert an abandoned phosphate factory into a tacky go-go club in which local girls, desperate for money, would be hoisted up to dance seductively in garish cages. On a crash diet (yet another futile exercise in control), Fat Man, wracked by hunger, goes to the club, compelled by the aroma of food. In ways that recall Joe Lon and Stump, the drunken revelers first beat and strip him and then trap him by baiting one of the go-go cages with a rib roast. Howling, they hoist him over the dance floor to become a grotesque curiosity, a permanent exhibit, at last beyond the complications of living, a clown left locked in center ring.

If Fat Man is destroyed because he struggles to control the pull of the flesh, Marvin Molar (*The Gypsy's Curse,* 1974) too readily concedes to its pull: he falls under the erotic spell of the sexually charged Hester. Their love is grotesquely mismatched. Hester is a perfect, if empty, form (serially promiscuous, she feels connection only via her ability to excite men). Marvin is a grotesque form—unable to talk (the roof of his mouth has a hole), unable to hear (an accident at the age of ten), unable to walk (his legs are withered). Abandoned by his horrified parents, Marvin has been raised at a rundown gym by a generous community of misfits—a retired stuntman and two punch-drunk ex-prizefighters. Marvin, little more than an elaborate torso, lives every moment aware of the flesh and its limitations. He trains fanatically in the weight room seeking in a developed musculature the control and design nature had so completely denied him. He works as an acrobatic attraction: using his incredible upper-body strength, he twirls on his fingers for small appreciative audiences. He prides himself on his self-possession, his massive strength, and his self-sufficiency—until he meets Hester.

When Hester moves into the gym temporarily, the men find themselves suddenly competing for her attention. Hester enjoys baiting the men, upsetting their routine (she does housekeeping naked), playing to their masculine pride. When Hester reestablishes ties to a former lover, a Greek with a perfect body who dismisses Marvin as a freak, Marvin is ravaged by jealousy. Unlike the pain of his workouts, this is unasked-for, uncontrollable agony. At novel's end, he dispatches Hester with a hatchet and calmly anticipates a lengthy jail term where caged, like Fat Man, he will finally be beyond the complexities of love. The flesh here cannot redeem—indeed the title refers to a curse that in effect wishes only that the cursed find love.

If flesh denied slowly consumes Fat Man and flesh indulged destroys Marvin, Herman Mack (*Car,* 1972) introduces into Crews's argument the possibility of turning away from the flesh entirely—and turning rather to an object, a reflection, Crews hints darkly, of the twentieth-century consumer society and its fierce materialism. At age thirty, Herman, shy and awkward, has lived without the distraction of sexual love—he has never recovered from a preadolescent crush on a neighborhood girl killed in a bizarre accident in the Mack family's vast auto junkyard. Now, consumed by a fascination with the sheer power of the car that has been central to his family's livelihood, he concocts an outrageous ambition: he will actually eat a car, a 1971 Ford Maverick, in the ballroom of a downtown Jacksonville hotel. He becomes something of a national celebrity as the curious flock to watch him ingest (and then pass) sterilized half-ounce lumps of the car, a sort of auto-erotic fantasy.

When it becomes apparent (his insides are being shredded) that Herman cannot complete the stunt, he turns to the sterile consolations of a hotel prostitute, Margo, so soured on physical love that she has turned herself into a sex machine in the hopes that she "could get rid of fucking by fucking everybody." Together, they find a solace uncomplicated by passion, denied the ignition of the flesh. The novel closes with Herman and Margo encaged in their own way: leaning on each other in the front seat of a wrecked touring car under a tunnel of rusting junked cars in the family's auto graveyard, listening to the thunder of the car crusher—a disturbing tableau that suggests only stasis, mock-happiness, and paralysis. Herman and Margo deny the flesh, and they end alone—with each other.

George Gattling (*The Hawk Is Dying,* 1973) is a tempting figure. Unlike the isolates we have seen, he appears to be the heroic solitary self. He does not end up dead or caged. Unlike them, George, at midlife, has achieved remarkable material success: up from an impoverished rural Georgia childhood, he now owns a car upholstery business. But success has given him no pleasure, nor does his conventionally lavish subdivision home or his conventionally beautiful lover. George is haunted by boredom over a comfortable life that appears to offer nothing to complain about. "I'm at the end of my road," he thinks. "Work hard, they say, and you'll be happy. Get a car, get a house, get a business, get money. Get get get get get get get. Well, I got. And now it's led me where everything is a dead-end." George understands that if God only existed, the world would stun with purpose, but, without that steadying center, life is a pointless vacuum.

When an autistic nephew drowns in a freak waterbed accident, George acts on his accumulating despair. He turns to the medieval art of training hawks, traps a number of them before he finds the perfect red-tail, and then endures the considerable pain and frustrations involved in mastering the fierce raptor. He is obsessed by the creature, its power, its freedom, its majesty. In the novel's dramatic closing scene George takes his hawk to the countryside near the gravesite of his nephew and has the hawk attack and kill a rabbit, a clean act of choreographed butchery that has the design and purpose so entirely lacking in his dead-end suburban life. George and the hawk thus create a community. Yet we leave George frozen in a tableau, awaiting, arm outstretched, the return of the hawk, his newfound community at best ambiguous. After all, in breaking the bird's spirit and forcing himself into its primitive reality, George refuses to grapple with the emptiness in his everyday life and prefers controlled pain (he chains the bird night and day to his wrist) rather than confronting the far less tidy pain that eats away his contentment. Richly satisfied by his own little drama of manning a hawk, impressed by its logic of control, he deftly avoids confronting the genuine vulnerabilities of a life that continues its curiously purposeless drift—his is a cage of a much different sort, the enclosing sustenance of problematic self-content.

THE SAVING TOUCH OF OTHERS

But if Crews imprisons, he as well frees. The final five characters this essay will examine—drawn, with two exceptions, from Crews's post-recovery fictions—reveal his willingness to educate his characters in the necessary pull of want, the grace possible in the struggle to find significant others. And those willing to be a part of relationships that move from friendship, to marriage, to the most complex arrangement of all, the family, learn as well that such imperfect arrangements draw their strength from their ability to survive (rather than contest) a world decidedly beyond our control. And these are the characters Crews generously sets free.

This Thing Don't Lead to Heaven (1970), dedicated to Crews's son Patrick, confronts head-on the most terrifying reality of the flesh: the fascism of mortality. It is a contested text: characters wrestle with the inevitability of death and the irresistible magic of defying its pull, the belief systems we have constructed to avoid accepting its reality (a traveling casket salesman euphemistically terms graves "garden plots"; a local preacher passes out brochures that reassure "There Is No Death"). Cursed in the womb (literally, by a one-eyed woman who touches his mother's swollen belly), Jefferson Davis Munroe is a genetic mishap, a dwarf who looks like a child "taken apart and then hurriedly and unskillfully put back together." He yearns only to be normal. Abandoned even by the circus (he is thrown off a train near Cumseh, Georgia), he is hired by Axel Gates, who runs a Senior Club, a euphemism for a retirement home. Adept at the art of massage therapy, J. D. becomes the home's therapeutic masseur, his hands able to coax temporary relief, ironically, through an ordeal of considerable pain. J. D. himself comes under the haunting spell of Carlita Rojas Mundez, a Haitian woman who was on her way to employment in Atlanta when she was abandoned accidentally by her bus in Cumseh. J. D. comes to believe Carlita possesses voodoo sufficient to

make him grow; for her part, Carlita believes the tiny man possesses powerful magic. Because Carlita cannot speak English, their attempts to communicate are unworkable. When a rest home resident lies near death, the two meet in his room. In their jumbled attempts to communicate he tries to get her to bring the old man back to life to indicate her power; but she thinks she wants him to kill the old man to prove her love. When she tries to smother him, the old man suddenly revives and fends off her attack. Later, as the resident inevitably surrenders to death, J. D. understands there is no magic—only the physical reality of his malformed stature and his tremendous need for Carlita. And that is magic enough. He decides to leave with Carlita for Atlanta (although Axel cautions the urban world is unforgiving). It is enough that he decides to depart Cumseh and, by extension, head out of Crews's tight fictive world. On his way to the bus station, J. D. accidentally drops his knapsack and breaks his bottle of massage oil—indicating that the strategy of easy escapism is over. We are uncertain of his fate—only that, with Spanish-English dictionary in tow, he now has strength sufficient to face it and the love of a strong woman to share it.

In *Karate Is a Thing of the Spirit* (1971), Crews examines a less improvised exit by focusing on a more involved sort of relationship. The novel centers on a lifelong drifter named John Kaimon who joins (and ultimately departs) a renegade karate commune operating in an abandoned motel in Fort Lauderdale. Haunted by memories of his mother's violent death and his father's consequent insanity, Kaimon has sought only refuge from such misfortune in the pseudo-consolation of community (he has experimented with hippie communes and biker gangs out West). In joining the fanatic karate community, run like a zealous military camp by a former used-car dealer, Kaimon hopes to find yet another sanctuary. Initially he resists the asceticism and rigors of the trainees and the physical pain of the ritual practices—passersby gawk at the trainees exerting themselves at the bottom of the hotel's empty pool. But he falls under the considerable spell of Gaye Nell Odell, a former beauty queen and current karate machine who helps Kaimon learn the mental and physical discipline of the sport and the endurance of pain that (unlike the sufferings of the larger world) is caused and controlled. He gradually gives in to the commune mentality. After he and Gaye Nell share intimacy (as part of his training, she attacks him when his injured hands are bandaged as a lesson on how to divorce feeling from passion), she tells him she is pregnant. When the consummate fanatic Gaye Nell engages the camp master in a karate exercise in which he must repeatedly kick her stomach, Kaimon realizes she is trying to lose the baby. Disillusioned by such a level of narcissistic intensity, Kaimon abandons his belief in their system (and in any system) and realizes that he believes only in her and their child—accepting the imperfect flesh and the vulnerabilities of the real world. Accompanied by Gaye Nell, he hotwires the commune's microbus and, during a beach beauty contest that degrades into a frightening circus of drunken excess, they depart the novel's (and the novelist's) reach. That is magic—and mystery—enough, lovers ready to engage without script the roiling unfolding of the everyday, hard-eyed and hand in hand.

Eugene Biggs (*The Knockout Artist,* 1988) is the first Crews character to depart not just from but rather toward. From the beginning, Biggs is a genuine sideshow attraction—both cursed and blessed with a glass jaw, he delivers self-inflicted knockout punches in fancy ballrooms for the entertainment of bored New Orleans elite coolly searching for the odd thrill. A curiosity that becomes a sensation, he even serves as the subject of a psychology dissertation written by his lover, an earnest academic so detached from her heart that she dictates observations about Biggs's behavior even while they make love. In a book whose central character's act so crudely parodies resurrection (he drops cold to the floor before being revived), Crews moves to offer this Weary Willie genuine resurrection, reclamation from this dead-end spectacle excess, this artificial world where he is trapped and degraded by the mercenary whims of the rich (Biggs is fond of lingering at the city zoo to watch the magnificent lions).

That tawdry circus world—with its sexual bizarreries, its casual indulgence of drugs and alcohol, its blithe amorality, and its obsession with money—is expertly satirized by Crews when Biggs visits the yacht of a shadowy tycoon known as Oyster Boy, who wants to acquire Biggs to help bring along a promising fighter. Biggs accepts the offer and is given an opportunity he was denied—as a young fighter, he was simply abandoned by his trainer after losses stemming from his freakish jaw. He meets Jacques Deverouge, a Cajun man-child who works as a janitor, and rediscovers the clean glory of training the body into a functioning whole. When he is asked to set up a fight that he knows is beyond the skill of his pupil, he refuses to participate in the intrigue, sick finally of defeat, tired of the cold logic of exploitation and exhibition. And when he discovers his lover's serial infidelities, Biggs trades his BMW for a motorcycle and prepares to head back home to rural Georgia, its no-nonsense realities of day-to-day survival reassuringly free of the amoralities of the cosmopolitan wasteland. Before he leaves he cautions Jacques, "You got to get out, too. Everybody you've met, everybody . . . is bad, bad news from the ground up. . . . They locked into whatever they locked into, but you ain't locked into it." In a move of compelling compassion, Biggs invites Jacques to leave with him—they have no money, no plans, no future, only (as Jacques points out) their fists. That difficult affirmation of genuine vulnerability, that willingness to depart the artificial cage of their comfortable circus world, that need for a significant other to engage the everyday directly salvages Eugene Biggs.

But it is not enough. Crews understands that the heart, that haunting pull of the flesh, cannot be sublimated entirely in camaraderie and male bonding. Duffy Deeter, in *All We Need of Hell* (1987), struggles within the complications of marriage itself. A successful Jacksonville lawyer from rural Georgia roots, he is flesh-bound (a weekend athlete with a taste for the controlled pain and ordered competition of games), death-soaked (he conjures fantasies of Nazi concentration camps while he makes love), anxious (he drinks heavily), and distant from those he cannot bring himself to love: a wife he is divorcing (who cleans out his bank account and is sleeping with his own law partner); a fat son whose sluggish lifestyle offends him; and a stunning mistress (improbably named Marvella Sweat), a gum-cracking philosophy student and cocaine addict. Like all of Crews's clowns, Duffy's life has become a performance piece. He believes in tight control—he derives his philosophy from Zen—and believes that interior calm can be maintained only by abandoning the will to interfere, a passionless doctrine that has convinced him of the strategic need to resist compassion as well as passion (he blasts Hitler speeches on his car's tape deck). His reclamation begins, ironically, with a fierce handball showdown with a stranger, a massive former football player named Tump Walker, who attacks Duffy when he senses he is losing. Their friendship, however, leads Duffy to understand the complicated network of love, that control and order (that Zen-like calm he so relishes and upon which he expounds at tedious length) comes at too high a cost: estrangement from the world (living a few feet off the ocean, he closes his windows and listens to tapes of the surf). He comes to accept the difficult reality of how little we control (catching his wife in bed with his law partner, he only spanks the man) and the dangerous illusion that anyone can live apart from the untidy world. With Tump's help, he discovers unsuspected depths to his son and the rich reward of friendship itself—a man does not have to carry "his own shit alone." And most dramatically he prepares at novel's end to reconcile with his wife, forsaking the itch-and-scratch endgame of his mistress. With their son, the two head off for south Florida for a second-chance weekend, the difficult affirmation of vulnerability, of forgiveness, and of the need we have each for the other that only begins with tearing hunger of the flesh.

Eugene Biggs discovers the comfort of friendship; Duffy Deeter revives the support of marriage. Still, Crews offers a summa character—Pete Butcher in 1992's *Scar Lover*—whose commitment comes ultimately from affirming the most complicated human community of all: the blood family. Of those characters Crews cares enough to free from the circus world of his own invention, Pete Butcher at narrative's end goes the shortest distance (only down the block to a local park), but he surely comes the farthest. And with Pete, it is not how far he travels at the end but rather with whom he travels: a younger brother he had accidentally injured years earlier with a hammer, causing catastrophic brain injury sufficient to institutionalize the boy and driving Pete into depths of guilt, blame, and rage. Terrified by the implications of living in a world prone to such accidents (his parents were subsequently killed in a truck accident hauling livestock to sell to help defray the brother's medical costs) and estranged from an older brother, Pete has shut down his heart, refused friendships; he works unloading boxcars for a Jacksonville paper company, where he is locked within the confines of the hot, narrow car, like a caged animal.

Distance has always been comfort for Pete—he was, we are told, a baby given to projectile puking—until he meets the enigmatic Sarah, who tells him right off that she is in the incipient stages of breast cancer (her mother has already undergone a mastectomy). Terrified again by the freewheeling exercise of chance, he bails on her even when he rushes her to the emergency room when she feels weak. Pete is content with the illusion of self-sufficiency until he loses his job and finds himself forced to lean on the unexpected kindness of Sarah's family, who take him in. Pete accepts an offer from Sarah's father to work with him at his lumberyard; he is horrified when, on his first day of work, Sarah's father drops dead from a heart attack as they are cutting a tree together.

In the difficult adjustment to that death, Pete begins to understand the futility of control, and he realizes that recasting accidents as his fault is an assertion of egotism that only justifies the comfort he takes in his isolation. Pete commences a trajectory arc away from the bunker-self. Crews does not spare us the reminder that we are flesh—the family intrigues to liberate the father's body from a funeral home and in the process we are escorted through a roomful of corpses awaiting the gruesome ritual of preparation. But Crews will not permit the simplistic dismissal of the flesh. When the family conducts a sort of amateur cremation of the father in the woods, Pete (whose surname ties him to flesh) notices how sweet the flesh smells. In an epiphanic rush, Pete realizes the breathtaking depth that love gives to the imperfect flesh. He turns to Sarah. He accepts a place in Sarah's family, accepts the responsibility for the mother's medical care, even thwarts a scheme to defraud her out of her insurance.

Sarah's mother affects the reunion between Pete and his brother, a difficult and awkward moment that leads, ultimately, to Pete, in tears, kissing the brother's scarred head, thus assuming responsibility for the accident without indulging the elaborate theatrics of blame. With the brother asleep nearby, Pete and Sarah make love, and in the morning Pete begins the difficult work of the commitment his brother represents: together they head for the park to play catch. Pete departs the circus world of Crews's creation, ready to engage the world he has too long denied, the world of brutal accident that is tolerable, Crews ultimately concedes, only when it is shared. Taken out of the context of Crews's considerable body of fiction, such an ending can smack of unearned sentimentality. But within the difficult struggle back to Joe Lon Mackey, this is a spare possibility within an unforgiving world—a world never more than a book away from leveling Crews's next central character.

CREWS'S PLACE IN LITERATURE

Where then does Harry Crews belong? Is he indeed *sui generis*? Certainly, his central characters are not unique in the canon of the American literary imagination. The American imagination has often focused on clown-in-the-circus figures who pursue a small measure of dignity amid the noise and distractions of their narrative worlds; characters who, overwhelmed, finally abandon their "act" for the wider pleasure of engaging the unscripted world outside the closed stage of their narratives, have, in essence, stepped free of their own narratives. From Huck Finn to Harry Angstrom, from Tom Joad to Yossarian, from Nick Carraway to Big Chief Bromden, from Caddy Compson to Dean Moriarty, characters have been expelled from fictive worlds more toxic than nurturing, their creators (and readers) content to watch them disappear into a horizon that promises only the difficult vulnerability the rest of us accept every day.

What *is* decidedly unique about Crews, however, is his refusal to allow his characters to step free alone. Given a man so engaged in creating a public persona of he-man Hemingwayesque alienation and who so often declaimed on the cultivation of interior stamina and individual endeavor (expounding on the virtues of long-distance running, motorcycling, weight-lifting, and the martial arts—as well as on writing itself), Crews has produced a body of fiction that moves unerringly to counsel that this shattered, absurd world, cut free of its sponsoring Creator, is inexplicably better shared: with lovers, with friends, with family.

That sort of counsel is salvaged from cliché and sentimentality largely because it comes from a writer who has himself struggled with the complications of distance since that long-ago childhood morning when he awakened to find his young father dead beside him. This affirmation of others, then, resonates because it comes from one who has found awkward the trick of intimacy, whether with his blood family, his university colleagues, his own family, or ultimately even his readers (not only did he create the elaborate smokescreen of his persona, but he also produced off-putting fictions that denied the confessional impulse and deliberately indulged gratuitous violence and lurid sexuality and centered on the misshapen and the deformed); it comes from a writer who has struggled a lifetime to find a way to trust his own heart to any community larger than himself. Enthralled by the easy suasion of the imagination, coaxing entire worlds into place with frenetic commitment; sustained for more than twenty years by the aggressive illusion of self-sufficiency compelled by an assortment of addictions; and satisfied by years of playing a persona that allowed him to avoid honest confrontation with himself, Crews came finally to offer in his fictions the modest benediction of connection. Perhaps the only writer similar to Crews within his generation is the short-story writer Raymond Carver, whose writings after his own recovery from alcohol addiction in the mid-1980s tapped a similarly luminous conclusion: the rich possibility of confluence, empathy, and compassion, the sheer wonder of the need we have each for the other amid a terrifying, if wondrous, world of chance and surprise.

Selected Bibliography

WORKS OF HARRY CREWS

FICTION

The Gospel Singer. New York: Morrow, 1968.

Naked in Garden Hills. New York: Morrow, 1969.

This Thing Don't Lead to Heaven. New York: Morrow, 1970.

Karate Is a Thing of the Spirit. New York: Morrow, 1971.

Car. New York: Morrow, 1972.

The Hawk Is Dying. New York: Knopf, 1973.

The Gypsy's Curse. New York: Knopf, 1974.

A Feast of Snakes. New York: Atheneum, 1976.

The Enthusiast. Winston-Salem: Palaemon Press, 1981. Limited edition, later published as the first five chapters of *All We Need of Hell.*

All We Need of Hell. New York: Harper & Row, 1987.

The Knockout Artist. New York: Harper & Row, 1988.

Blood Issue (staged 1989). In *Southern Playwrights: Plays from the Actors Theatre of Louisville.* Edited by Michael Bigelow Dixon and Michele Volansky. Lexington: University of Kentucky Press, 1996. Pp. 27–75.

Body. New York: Poseidon, 1990.

Scar Lover. New York: Poseidon, 1992.

The Mulching of America. New York: Simon & Schuster, 1995.

Where Does One Go When There's No Place Left to Go? London: Gorse, 1995. (Published in a single volume with *The Gospel Singer.*) Northridge, Calif.: Lord John Press. 1998. (Limited edition.)

Celebration. New York: Simon & Schuster, 1998.

NONFICTION AND COLLECTIONS

A Childhood: The Biography of a Place. New York: Harper & Row, 1978.

Blood and Grits. New York: Harper & Row, 1979. (A collection of previously published [with one exception] magazine essays.)

Florida Frenzy. Gainesville: University Press of Florida, 1982. (Previously published work centered on Florida.)

Two by Crews. Northridge, Calif.: Lord John Press, 1984. (Limited edition, includes two nonfiction pieces previously published in *Playboy*: "The Violence That Finds Us" [September 1983] and "The Buttondown Terror of David Duke" [February 1980].)

Madonna at Ringside. Northridge, Calif.: Lord John Press, 1991. (Limited edition, previously published essays.)

Classic Crews: A Harry Crews Reader. New York: Poseidon, 1993. (Includes entire texts of *A Childhood; The Gypsy's Curse; Car;* and two essays, "Fathers, Sons, Blood" [about his son's drowning death] and "Climbing the Tower.")

"Assault of Memory." *Southern Quarterly* 37, no.1:124–138 (fall 1998). (First two chapters of the second volume of Crews's autobiography.)

CRITICAL STUDIES

Bledsoe, Erik, ed. *Perspectives on Harry Crews*. Jackson: University Press of Mississippi, 2001. (Essays originally published in *Southern Quarterly* special issue on Crews [fall 1998].)

Carter, Nancy Corson. "1970 Images of the Machine and the Garden: Kosinski, Crews, and Pirsig." *Soundings: A Journal of Interdisciplinary Studies* 61, no.1:105–22 (1978).

Covel, Robert C. "The Violent Bear It as Best They Can: Cultural Conflicts in the Novels of Harry Crews." *Studies in the Literary Imagination* 27, no. 2:75–86 (fall 1994).

DeBord, Larry W., and Gary L. Long. "Harry Crews on the American Dream." *Southern Quarterly* 20, no. 3:35–53 (spring 1982).

———. "Literary Criticism and the Fate of Ideas: The Case of Harry Crews." *Texas Review* 4, no. 3–4:69–91 (fall–winter 1983).

Guinn, Matthew. "Arcady Revisited: The Poor South of Harry Crews and Dorothy Allison." In his *After*

Southern Modernism: Fiction of the Contemporary South. Jackson: University Press of Mississippi, 2000.

Jeffrey, David K., ed. *A Grit's Triumph: Essays on the Works of Harry Crews*. Port Washington, N.Y.: Associated Faculty Press, 1983.

———. "Murder and Mayhem in Crews' *A Feast of Snakes*." *Critique: Studies in Modern Fiction* 28, no.1:45–54 (fall 1986).

Long, Gary L. "Naked Americans: Violence in the Work of Harry Crews." *Southern Quarterly* 32, no. 4:117–130 (summer 1994).

Noble, Donald. "The Future of Southern Writing." In *The History of Southern Literature*. Edited by Louis D. Rubin Jr. Baton Rouge: Louisiana State University Press, 1985. Pp. 578–588.

Papovich, J. Frank. "Place and Imagination in Harry Crews's *A Childhood: The Biography of a Place*." *Southern Literary Journal* 19, no.1:26–35 (fall 1986).

Schafer, William J. "Partial People: The Novels of Harry Crews." *Mississippi Quarterly: The Journal of Southern Culture* 41, no.1:69–88 (winter 1987–1988).

Seelye, John. "Georgia Boys: The Redclay Satyrs of Erskine Caldwell and Harry Crews." *Virginia Quarterly Review* 56, no. 4:612–626 (autumn 1980).

Shelton, Frank W. "A Way of Life and Place." *Southern Literary Journal* 11, no. 2:97–102 (1979).

Shepherd, Allen. "Matters of Life and Death: The Novels of Harry Crews." *Critique: Studies in Modern Fiction* 20, no.1:53–62 (September 1978).

INTERVIEWS

Bledso, Erik, ed. *Getting Naked with Harry Crews: Interviews*. Gainesville: University Press of Florida, 1999. (Includes interviews by Joann Biondi, A. B. Crowder, Anne Foata, Tammy Lytal and Richard Russell, and Mary Voboril.)

Hiaasen, Scott. "The Fierce and Funny World of Harry Crews." *Palm Beach Post,* May 15, 1994, p. 1J.

—JOSEPH DEWEY

Mark Doty

1953–

*I*N HIS POEM "Chanteuse," from the 1993 collection *My Alexandria,* Mark Doty refers to the Greek poet Constantine Cavafy as having "no other theme / than memory's erotics." The same can be said of Doty's own work, which focuses on transient beauty, a theme that is no surprise given the circumstances of his life. Central to his work and life has been the long struggle to come to terms with the death of Wally Roberts, his partner of twelve years, who died from complications of AIDS in 1994. His two most well-known books, *My Alexandria* and the prose memoir *Heaven's Coast* (1996), are informed by his life as a gay man and by the AIDS epidemic. His honesty about his homosexuality as well as the pain he and Roberts suffered because of AIDS has meant that in addition to being known as a graceful craftsman, Doty is viewed as an activist and as a role model for younger gay writers. Mark Wunderlich situates Doty as

> the first post-Stonewall gay poet to emerge as a major voice in American letters. His predecessors, such as James Merrill, William Meredith, and Richard Howard, had all favored a more privileged tone and vocabulary [and] . . . occluded references to homosexuality. . . . Simply by being open about his sexuality . . . Doty created a new model for gay and lesbian poets and poetry.

Such authenticity in terms of his sexual orientation was, at first, difficult for Doty, as he writes in the autobiographical essay "A Reader's Tale." In his late teens and early twenties, he looked for a way to write poetry about his own experiences within the established literary tradition: "I wanted a poetry that would tell it 'straight' and yet still be poetry as I understood it, still feel rich and musical and capacious, not confined to a narrow range of erotic expression."

Although Doty is perhaps best known for writing about the AIDS crisis, his poetics has also been noted for the way it is infused with a carpe diem approach to life. The things Doty treasures most are changeable—human and animal relationships, physical landscapes—and Doty has therefore looked to art as a way to frame his experience and preserve the moment. In referring to a painting in *Still Life with Oysters and Lemon* (2001), he explains, "the overall effect, the result of looking and looking into its brimming surface as long as I could look, is love, by which I mean a sense of tenderness toward experience, of being held within an intimacy with the things of the world." Although Doty realizes that death is a part of life, he admits in *Heaven's Coast,* "That design—ferocious wisdom, implacable light, time's ineluctable unfolding—is too large and brilliant for us to see." Yet, he writes in "Atlantis" that he wants to make "this gesture / toward the restless splendor."

BIOGRAPHY

Doty was born in Maryville, Tennessee, on August 10, 1953, to Ruth Stephens and Lawrence Woodworth Doty. He has one older sister. As Doty writes in *Firebird* (1999), his memoir of childhood, "My sister's only two when the war [World War II] ends; my parents begin their wanderings in the towns of Tennessee. Then there's that little boy, stillborn, little occasion for grief. . . . He has a little headstone somewhere, to this day I don't know where. And then me." Because Doty's father was an army engineer, the family was often relocated, living in Tennessee, Texas, Florida, Arizona, and California. Doty remembers the family moving thirteen times before he went to high school. As a result of these moves, Doty admits in "A Reader's Tale" that he was "an outsider kid":

When other people looked at me, I knew what they saw: stranger, sissy, bookworm, four-eyes, no-good-at-sports, fatty. But inside me there was something else, a shining self, alive with nobility and tenderness, and a great deep longing for something unsayable, and questions that couldn't be answered, and a deep connection to the secret heart of the world. And if nobody looking at me could see that, then the books I loved knew it was there, because they shone that sort of light back to me; they knew about that light, and they dwelt there, too, far more purely than I ever could.

Because his sister was considerably older than Doty and left home early, most of Doty's childhood experiences were defined by his relationships with his parents, primarily his mother. Doty says in *Firebird,* "My mother taught me to love the things that would save me." Yet the relationship was troubled. She was an alcoholic, she was lonely, and she had difficulties with Doty's homosexuality. One day when she was drunk she pointed a loaded gun at him and attempted to kill him but failed because she had trouble unlatching the safety. During Doty's early twenties, she died from the complications of advanced alcoholism.

Doty experimented with drugs, dropped out of high school and never returned, took some classes at the University of Arizona, and married the poet Ruth Dawson, twenty years older, in 1971. Dawson taught at Drake University in Des Moines, where Doty eventually received a degree in 1978. While in Iowa the two published under a single name, M. R. Doty, not only single poems but also three chapbooks, *An Alphabet*

(1979), *An Introduction to the Geography of Iowa* (1979), and *The Empire of Summer* (1981). Doty writes in "A Reader's Tale," "In retrospect I am deeply embarrassed by this; I regret that it ever happened . . . that I took advantage of the convenience of disappearing into a collective nom de plume. The fact is that I wrote all of the poems in all three of the chapbooks with the exception of a single piece at the end of *An Introduction to the Geography of Iowa.*" Ruth Dawson and Mark Doty divorced in 1980.

After his divorce, Doty traversed two of the major turning points of his life: his graduate school experiences at Goddard College, which were so intense that Doty began to see a therapist, and his coming out as a gay man. Shortly thereafter, in the early 1980s, he moved to New York and met Wally Roberts, a window dresser, with whom he lived for twelve years in Boston; Montpelier, Vermont; and Provincetown, Massachusetts. "Wally tested positive for HIV in 1989," Doty explains in "A Reader's Tale." Doty tested negative. "We did not know what the news meant, exactly; there was no knowing just what to expect, or when, and at the same time we both felt that we knew perfectly well what this knowledge predicted." Roberts died at their home in Provincetown in January 1994.

Doty has spent most of his adult life as a college professor, teaching at Goddard, Sarah Lawrence, and the University of Houston. After Wally Roberts' death, he met Paul Lisicky, a novelist, with whom he has formed another lasting relationship and continues to live, at least part of the year, in Provincetown.

Doty says, in "A Reader's Tale," "I feel, as a writer, unfinished, and I think I am lucky to feel so." Along with *My Alexandria* (1993)—which in the United States was a National Poetry Series selection, won the National Book Critics Circle Award and the Los Angeles Times Book Award, and also became the first American book ever to win the London Poetry Book Society's

T. S. Eliot Prize—Doty's full-length collections of poetry include *Turtle, Swan* (1987); *Bethlehem in Broad Daylight* (1991); *Atlantis* (1995), which won the Ambassador Book Award, the Bingham Poetry Prize, the *Boston Review* Poetry Prize, and the Lambda Literary Award; *Sweet Machine* (1998); and *Source* (2001). His nonfiction prose includes *Heaven's Coast* (1996), which won the PEN/Martha Albrand Award for best book of nonfiction; *Firebird* (1999); and *Still Life with Oysters and Lemon* (2001). In support of his work, he has received both the National Endowment for the Arts and Guggenheim Fellowships.

TURTLE, SWAN AND *BETHLEHEM IN BROAD DAYLIGHT*

Turtle, Swan and *Bethlehem in Broad Daylight* were both originally published by David Godine, in 1987 and 1991, respectively, then reissued by the University of Illinois Press in a combined volume in 2000. There are slight differences between the reissue and the earlier editions, including notes, corrected errors, and a few added lines. Because many critics see the two as leading to *My Alexandria*, it is appropriate to talk about them together. The reissue, which Doty considers the corrected text, is quoted here.

Pat Monaghan and David Baker sum up the range of critical response to Doty's early work. Whereas Monaghan, writing in *Booklist,* commends Doty's craftsmanship and "resonant passion," Baker has complained that Doty seems distanced from his material, that "his narrative drive turns frequently into lineated prose; his speaker often prefers detachment and judgment over involvement and sympathy."

In both books Doty's poetic approach is already evident: long poems; disparate images and events in which Doty finds a connection; a circularity of presentation. In an interview with Eloise Klein Healy, he explained that the way in which he "braids" his material mirrors the way his mind works: "so much of the self is always elsewhere." In addition, he wanted to give a sense of the "layered richness of consciousness" and of "scale" through "accumulation." Within the particulars of executing these conscious strategies, Doty establishes his signature themes: memory, desire, and beauty, all accompanied by loss.

The title poem, "Turtle, Swan," which interrelates the images of a swan, a turtle, and a male lover at a movie theater, is a good early example of Doty's approach and thematic concerns. The swan, which the speaker sees on the way home from work, is described in terms of its awe-inspiring appearance and strength:

> the word [swan] doesn't convey the shock
> of the thing, white architecture
> rippling like a pond's rain-pocked skin,
> beak lifting to hiss at my approach.
> Magisterial, set down in elegant authority . . .

While such meticulous attention would lead the reader to believe that the swan would be the subject of the poem, Doty instead leaves the swan and turns his attention elsewhere—both in time and space. He sees a large turtle whose lack of speed makes it a target for children,

> for kids who'd delight in the crush
> of something slow with the look
> of primeval invulnerability. . . .

When his lover sees a turtle shell in a neighboring town, the speaker is worried that this turtle might be the one he saw earlier but rationalizes that it could not have traveled so far. The last important image involves a movie theater, in which the speaker is looking for his lover: "I saw straight couples everywhere, / no single silhouette who might be you." The images of the swan and turtle are then brought back as the speaker contemplates mortality:

> . . . I only know that I do not want you
> —you with your white and muscular wings

that rise and ripple beneath or above me,
your magnificent neck, eyes the deep mottled
   autumnal colors
of polished tortoise—I do not want you ever to
   die.

The poem's closing words are typical of Doty's propensity for crystallizing his main point in a ringing statement at the end of a poem.

While *Turtle, Swan* emphasizes memory and loss, it also underscores the importance of things—not in their accumulation or monetary value, but in their ability to last. From the mother's wish to be viewed in the same way as the father's tools ("Gardenias"), to the speaker's view of his neighborhood—"One house after another; permanence lay in things" ("Horses")—to the speaker's envisioning of the domestic images of Emily Dickinson's life ("Late Conversation"), Doty's characters use things not only to ground their lives but also to frame their lives and give symbolic value to them.

Doty makes connections with an unlikely range of people and creatures—the smallest horse in the sideshow of a circus, Shakers, the Greek poet Constantine Cavafy—in a fashion that reflects his belief that we are all a part of the design of the earth and, in our idiosyncrasies, have something to reveal to each other. A poignant example of this conviction is illustrated in the poem "Charlie Howard's Descent," which memorializes Howard's murder in Bangor, Maine, in 1984. The poem shows Howard's grace and sense of forgiveness as he is thrown from a bridge into a river by three teenage boys. Howard, who has endured a difficult life because of his homosexuality, rises up out of the water as a transcendent spirit and says,

it's all right . . . he knows
they didn't believe him
when he said he couldn't swim,
and blesses his killers

in the way that only the dead
can afford to forgive.

As painful as life's experiences can be, Doty ultimately chooses compassion and wonder. The critic Deborah Landau has rightly described him as "a poet who envisions sustaining moments despite great suffering and offers his readers 'a way to continue.'"

In *Bethlehem in Broad Daylight,* Doty focuses on similar subjects, such as memory and transformation, and also writes increasingly about his life as a gay man. The critic Penny Kaganoff has pointed out the way that Doty uses "classical imagery to imbue his subjects with the unreality of myth and the inexorability of history." At the same time, the poetry exhibits a preoccupation with the "shimmer" of life, which is often associated with a new way of seeing something. This "shimmer" can take its form in variety of ways: the longed-for effect of a drug, "the window / where RESIDENTIAL shimmers" ("Harbor Lights"), the ceremonial objects of Masons ("The Ancient World"), the wonder of a field trip ("The Garden of the Moon"), or dramatic presentation ("Isis: Dorothy Eady, 1924"). In addition to the shine itself and its power of transformation, Doty's poems contain the sense that beauty in the world stands for something beyond the moment, something almost revelatory.

Doty writes increasingly about sexuality: one key element of this is risk. When a man named Peter is killed while he is wearing a paper doll crown ("Tiara"), the speaker is stunned when "someone said he asked for it." This statement makes the speaker ponder the whole notion of "asking for it." If it is longing that makes us "ask for it," the speaker concludes that what Peter has died for is something that we all live for: "ravishing music." Doty told Deborah Landau that the poem "is an elegy for a friend of mine who was a drag queen, always out in clubs. . . . After he died someone said at his wake, 'Well, he asked for it.' I was filled with rage at that ridiculous notion that we invite our own oppression as a consequence of pleasure."

Doty also writes of a risk-taking mentor, James L. White, who wrote about his homosexuality in his collection *The Salt Ecstasies*. In "Paradise," an homage to White, Doty interrelates ideas of beauty, seeing, and risk in much the same way as he interrelates images and events. In section 2 of the poem, Doty uses the image of blind children in a blue room to suggest a seeing beyond the literal: "It's the same / with longing," and he continues,

> It isn't even a question,
> whether the subject or object
> of desire is made more beautiful.

In addition, he uses the image of a text—and increasingly does so in his work—in order to "read" the world. In section 3, the speaker describes

> the breathtaking fall from self
> . . . .
> [like] blind readers who disappeared,
> for a while, into the text.

At the end of the poem, the speaker admits that he would not have chosen life as a homosexual, yet he has found a way to transform the ugly labels of his culture into something meaningful. White, as a role model, helped to bring the speaker to this transformation.

MY ALEXANDRIA

Doty's next book also included such a transformation, for which critics praised it. *My Alexandria* appeared in 1993 and chronicled Doty and Roberts' struggle with AIDS. Roberts died shortly after the book's publication. In a foreword to the book, Philip Levine, who chose *My Alexandria* for the National Poetry Series, set the tone for the critical discussion of the collection, writing,

> In the search for his Alexandria, the holy city of the imagination where he might find love, transcendence, and beauty, the poet has gone into the actual cities of the world where he has found us, the unloved, the dying, the survivors, among the wreckage of our lives. The courage of this book is that it looks away from nothing.

While critics have compared Doty to Walt Whitman, Hart Crane, James Merrill, Constantine Cavafy, Wallace Stevens, and Elizabeth Bishop, Vernon Shetley adds Robert Frost, citing Frost's "plain spoken intensities" and praising Doty's "accessibility and immediacy." Deborah Landau sees Doty as "reimagining the terms used to describe . . . [the] destruction [of AIDS] and envisioning possibilities for political, sensual, and spiritual redemption." With such universal praise for the book, its only criticisms had to do with the length of the poems and the depressing subject matter.

A recurrent image in *My Alexandria* has to do with the importance of the gestures human beings make in their lives. In "Days of 1981," a poem addressing the freedom of life before AIDS, a boy gives a bartender an offering of flowers, and these flowers frame the speaker's sexual "flowering": meeting someone in this same bar and afterward having sex. The speaker thinks that he is in love, and at first he treasures the ceramic heart the man gives him. Later in the poem he realizes that his emotions have led him not only to a misreading of the relationship but also to a misinterpretation of the quality of the art. The speaker finally realizes that the gestures are important in and of themselves.

"Human Figures" continues this preoccupation with the gesture, underscored by voyeurism. While on a bus in San Francisco, the speaker watches a man who is doing something furtive in his lap—it turns out, he is creating human figures out of newspaper—and from this scene the speaker makes an association to a time he saw a homeless man in Boston bleeding all over a bench and sidewalk. In both cases the speaker "didn't want to look" but does anyway, wanting to "read" the situation. The poem, through its variety of texts—twisted human shapes, a newspaper (the *Boston Globe*) stained with the blood of the homeless man, the poem itself—illustrates in both private and public ways the connections humans have with one another. Moreover, it raises the issue of how humans implicate themselves by involvement through the simple acts of seeing and reading. Once something is seen or understood, how is it possible to turn away?

A longer poem, "The Wings," looks at a world understood through the knowledge of AIDS, using images of angels to underscore the interrelationship between heaven and earth. Roger Gilbert places the poem in the context of other 1990s poetry using religious iconography; Gilbert points out that "Doty's interest in his angel is not merely poetic . . . but deeply personal" because the speaker's—in this case, Doty's—lover is HIV positive. In the poem, the speaker attends an auction with his lover, where he notices a boy who waits for his parents, transformed by a book. He goes on to see the boy as an angel; when he takes some snowshoes his father has purchased and "slings them both / over his back" he is "suddenly winged." This angel transmutes later into one of the angels from Wim Wenders' film *Wings of Desire* (in the film angels yearn to walk among humans once again because they miss life—precisely because it does not last). The speaker and his lover collect lovely objects throughout the poem; this process of collecting is juxtaposed against the AIDS quilt, with its mementoes stitched in place to emblemize a life. In light of these losses, the speaker, who is a teacher, is amazed by his students when "they wonder why the poet we're reading's / so insistent on mortality," and he offers up his observations of earthly angels, "the light-glazed angel / in the children's bodies." He also imagines an angel leaning over his sick loved one, saying that the beauty of life is in death,

your story, which you have worn away
as you shaped it,
which has become itself
as it has disappeared.

"Brilliance," another poem that explores living in the shadow of AIDS, emphasizes choosing life even in the face of death. In this poem a man does not want to own anything because he knows he is going to die, but, when his caretaker suggests that he get some goldfish, he is persuaded.

Yes to the bowl of goldfish.
Meaning: let me go, if I have to,
in brilliance. . . .

Ultimately the speaker correlates this man's desire with a Zen master's concern for a fawn, into which he is reincarnated. The speaker speculates, then, about the dying man becoming the goldfish:

is he bronze chrysanthemums,

copper leaf, hurried darting,
doubloons, icon-colored fins
troubling the water?

This transformation through longing is important to Doty, who told Eloise Klein Healy that he views desire as "the most powerful force in human life."

Two poems, "Night Ferry" and "Becoming a Meadow," use textual motifs in order to reconstruct reality. The night ferry, which travels in the dark, creates a limbo for travelers, as they are suddenly outside their familiar framework, aware of the process of journey in a way that they would not be in their ordinary lives—the journey is a "text" that has special poignancy given the circumstances of Doty's and Roberts' life together. The speaker says,

. . . The narrative

of the ferry begins and ends brilliantly,
and its text is this moving out

into what is soon before us
   and behind: the night going forward,

sentence by sentence, as if on faith . . .

"Becoming a Meadow" connects beach life, text life, and love life into an epiphanic wave. The thinking process of the poem starts with a phrase that the speaker hears when he enters a Provincetown bookstore: *"becoming a meadow."* The rest of the poem is not only about that process but also about becoming the ocean.

And if one wave breaking says
You're dying, then the rhythm and shift of the whole
says nothing about endings . . .

If life may be compared to an ocean, the individual waves are only part of a whole, and the whole is what the poet wishes to keep in mind, not just death but the entire interrelationship of life and death.

The last poem in the collection, "Lament-Heaven," attempts to find beauty in death and has a difficult time doing so. At first the speaker asserts that

. . . I think
this is how our deaths would look,
   seen from a great distance,

if we could stand that far
   from ourselves: the way birch leaves
     signal and flash . . .

He also uses the image of "lights along the shore" being extinguished, and asks,

. . . If death's like that,

if we are continuous,
   rippling from nothing into being,
     then why can't we let ourselves go

into the world's shimmering story?
   Who can become lost in a narrative,
     if all he can think of is the end?

The speaker also consults a Ouija board but is ultimately dissatisfied with this project because the "guiding spirit" is elusive, and in a variation of Yeats's "How can you tell the dancer from the dance?" Doty asks,

. . . Strip something
of its mortality, and how do you know
   what's left to see?

The speaker then looks to religion for answers, the message in Sing Sing of a man who writes that *"God's not dead. I can 'feel' him / all over me."* The speaker cannot make the same claim, although he does feel a "godliness" when he visits a church. What transforms his experience is the rapturous violin music of a twelve-year-old girl in the church: "I would have lived in that music," he declares. Such epiphanic moments give us a connectedness with other people and transform reality,

. . . canceling out
the whine of the self
   that doesn't want to be ground down,

answering the little human cry
   at the heart of the elegy,
   Oh why aren't I what I wanted to be,

exempt from history?

Although Doty understands that people will die, he also realizes that music cannot be made without people. It is as if he takes the reader by the collar and asks,

Do you understand me?

I heard it, the music
   that could not go on without us,
   and I was inconsolable.

It will take time for him to arrive at a more peaceful acceptance.

ATLANTIS

In his next collection, Doty turns to the physical landscape to escape from the pain of the loss of his lover. *Atlantis* elicited almost universal critical admiration when it appeared in 1995. Published after Wally Roberts' death (although most of the poems were written when Roberts was still alive), the book is dedicated to Roberts and gives the impression of being an extended elegy. Critics admired the specificity of the details in the poems: Patricia Hampl wrote that "when [Doty] sees the ocean—the salt spray hits you," and Frank Allen noticed that many of the poems resembled still lifes. (Allen here anticipates an increasing preoccupation with Doty, culminating six years later in the prose work *Still Life with Oysters and Lemon.*) In the *Yale Review,* Willard Spiegelman commented on the musicality of the work, contending that Doty's sensitivity to sound and image was "stronger than almost any other poet of his generation." "Perhaps the book's best splendor," said Hampl, "is the seemingly casual, immediate voice which manages to engage us in a story whose end the poet refuses to see as horrific, even as he fiercely exposes its heartbreaking details."

Atlantis is divided up into five sections, with the title poem in the center of the book. Because this poem is about Roberts, its placement underscores the centrality of grief. Yet in much of the book Doty addresses life instead of death, or, more precisely, he addresses how life and death are not opposites, but part of a continuum.

"What we don't name we have a harder time seeing," Doty maintained in his interview with Eloise Klein Healy, and this idea is treated in the opening poem of *Atlantis,* a poem titled "Description," in which he writes, "I love the language / of the day's ten thousand aspects." He ponders the poet's credo that the universal is realized through particulars and feels the situation is not so simple, emphasizing the "blur of boundary." In Doty's view, it is not that details are a passageway into the universal, or a way of translating the universal; rather they are an interactive part of the universal. For Doty, this suggests a way in which to understand death. Just as the landscape's beauty becomes a part of us as we experience it and name it, so human beings die and yet live on through others who remember them and honor them.

"A Green Crab's Shell," one of Doty's signature poems from the collection, discusses this point more directly. The carapace of the crab is left—its inner parts eaten by a gull—and yet its interior is astonishingly beautiful: "a shocking, Giotto blue." The speaker muses in the poem,

Not so bad, to die,

if we could be opened
into *this*—
if the smallest chambers

of ourselves,
similarly,
revealed some sky.

In talking with Bill Moyers about the poem, Doty acknowledges his debt both to Rilke and "the great Renaissance painter Giotto [di Bondone], whose frescoes make use of this sock-you-in-the-eyes blue which represents heaven. It is one of that intensity and power" (*Fooling with Words*). Readers and listeners find the poem powerful; audiences often applaud it individually at readings.

"Grosse Fuge," which addresses a friend's dementia from AIDS, does so in the context of nature and music. By interweaving details about learning Beethoven with re-learning the world's beauty through its constant surprises—springlike weather in the fall—Doty underscores the poignancy of his friend Bobby's disease as Bobby loses the sense of who he is while others begin to forget him because he has AIDS. One of the most moving details in the poem is Bobby's statement,

My mother . . . doesn't want me
crying in the house; she doesn't want
my tears around.

The speaker comments, "How are we to read / this nameless season—renewal, promise, / confusion?" and continues, "No way to *know* what's gone." Just as the confusion of the season mirrors the new confusion of Bobby's life—not only his dementia but also the response of others to him—learning the music of Beethoven is like learning the landscape of AIDS: "Like trying to familiarize yourself, / . . . with the side of a mountain." Or, as Bobby himself says, describing the boxes that swim around him at night, "*In one of those . . . is the virus, / a box of AIDS. And if I open it . . .*"

Yet in the midst of this overwhelming knowledge, there is life: Bobby is "well enough / to be a bitch" and "In the wet black yard, / October lilacs." This surprising relationship—death-in-life—is what we have. As Doty writes,

What can you expect, in a world that blooms
and freezes all at once?
There is no resolution in the fugue.

Since Bobby died before Wally, this poem also gives a momentum to Doty's understanding of AIDS as he moves toward the central poem of the collection, and, of course, in his own life to the harrowing effects of that illness.

In "Long Point Light," Doty uses an image of increasing significance to him—the lighthouse—to mark the segue between life and death. While at other times (for instance, in speaking with Eloise Klein Healy), Doty uses the lighthouse to discuss the past—speaking of how one's life looks different from different points in the lighthouse—in this poem he uses it as a code and a marker of a boundary, a metaphor for heaven. At first he postulates,

. . . Sometimes I think
it's the where-we-will-be,
only not yet, like some visible outcropping

of the afterlife . . .

Yet how do we humans speak of the afterlife? We cannot, and so Doty gives the lighthouse its own voice, which brings the poem back to the living, and the responsibility of the living:

Here is the world you asked for,
gorgeous and opportune,

here is nine o'clock, harbor-wide,
and a glinting code: promise and warning.
The morning's the size of heaven.

What will you do with it?

The six-section poem "Atlantis" addresses head-on the grief that haunts the book and uses the image of dogs as its framing device, as well as the motif of dreams. In the first section, "Faith," Doty recounts a recurring dream in which he is walking with Wally and their dog, Arden, is either killed or severely hurt. This dream becomes a way of talking about AIDS. As Doty explains,

Soul without speech,
sheer, tireless faith,
he is that-which-goes-forward,

black muzzle, black paws
scouting what's ahead;
he is where we'll be hit first,

he's the part of us
that's going to get it.

Now, outside the dream and with Wally gone, Doty finds himself fearful for his dog when they go for walks, admitting, "I didn't know who I was trying to protect."

In the second section, "Reprieve," he explains how he wanted to believe that the news of Wally's diagnosis was simply a bad dream. He remembers how he used to teach writing workshops to children, and they liked stories to end with "It was all a dream." They are wise, he realizes, in emphasizing "waking"—a return to life. That wisdom, for Doty, has a hard edge. When later in the poem Wally describes a dream of being invited to go dancing with the dead, and admits he is not ready yet, Doty can offer merely this small comfort: "*it was only a dream.*"

The next three sections see death in a more positive way. In section 3, "Michael's Dream," Michael dreams of his lover, Randy, moving from his earthly form into "*a shining body, brilliant light.*" Through that description Doty grasps, both literally and figuratively, the beauty of Wally's body that contains this "*shining,*" this heavenly light. In section 4, "Atlantis," he looks to the physical landscape of the beach in Provincetown to stress the "ongoingness" of life; he uses the image of the lost city of Atlantis to illustrate both what is lost and what will last: "the lost world / rising from the waters again." In section 5, "Coastal," he speaks of a girl who tries to save a sick loon, and he uses her as a stand-in for himself, saying,

> Foolish kid,
>
> does she think she can keep
>   this emissary of air?

The last section, "New Dog," is reminiscent of his earlier poem "Brilliance" in its emphasis on hope. When two friends explain that they cannot keep their cocker spaniel, Wally expresses a desire to adopt the dog, and Doty admires his attachment to the world. When the friends find that they cannot part with their pet after all, Doty goes to an animal shelter and finds Beau "too big, wild, / perfect." When he brings the dog home, Doty is astonished that

> . . . though
> Wally can no longer
> feed himself he can lift,

his hand, and bring it
to rest on the rough gilt

flanks . . .

By the poem's end, Doty brings this gesture to its natural culmination, writing admiringly of the way Wally in his illness can embrace life so fully:

> . . . all
> he is now, this gesture
> toward the restless splendor . . .

The emphasis on the positive moments gleaned from the tragedy of AIDS marks a transition for Doty. In the process of understanding his own grief and moving on from it, he seems to see himself as part of a larger community. He also has more fun. "Crêpe de Chine," in which he uses the bravado of drag to emphasize the city's abundance, is an excellent example:

> and I'm hearing the suss of immense stockings,
> whispery static of chiffon stoles
>
> on powdered shoulders
> click of compacts, lisp and soft glide
> of blush. And I'm thinking of my wig,
>
> my blonde wig . . .

In speaking of a baker's display, he says, "I want to wear it" and goes on to say of the city: "That's what drag is: a city / to cover our nakedness." In the essay "A Reader's Tale," Doty describes this poem, as well as "Homo Will Not Inherit," as "more public and performative, less intimate in tone."

Yet "Homo Will Not Inherit" has a much different mood. On a religious handout, someone has printed the message: "HOMO WILL NOT INHERIT. *Repent & be saved.*" The shock of this announcement angers the poet, and he goes on to outline what he *will* inherit: "the margins / which have always been mine." Through sexuality, he says, he has "been possessed of the god myself,"

> . . . I have been an angel

for minutes at a time, and I have for hours
believed—without judgement, without
  condemnation—
that in each body . . .

is the divine body . . .

There is a fullness, a richness of experience in his life that he does not find in organized religion:

> . . . I'll tell you

what I'll inherit, not your pallid temple
but a real palace, the anticipated
and actual memory, the moment flooded

by skin and the knowledge of it . . .

He announces, "I'm not ashamed / to love Babylon's scrawl. How could I be?"

After discussing both the intimate and communal, Doty in the collection's final poem emphasizes the theme of the permeation of boundaries. In "Aubade: Opal and Silver," a poem written just a week before Wally Roberts' death, dogs play a role once more, as a way of interpreting the link between this world and the next. With Doty's two dogs, Beau and Arden, playing in falling snow, an iridescent curtain seems to fall on the day, and their moving forms, gold and black, seem to travel between the falling snow and the sky as if between two worlds. Doty writes,

> . . . this fabric's
spun of such insubstantial stuff

it doesn't quite conceal the other world.
Can't we see into it already, a little? . . .

HEAVEN'S COAST

Heaven's Coast, published in 1996, revealed that in addition to being a gifted poet, Doty could be a compelling practitioner of the memoir. In a review titled "Speak, Gay Memory," David L. Kirp discusses the way Doty's memoir finds a place with other memoirs by gay men, like *Truth Serum,* by Bernard Cooper, and *Geography of the Heart,* by Fenton Johnson, which chronicle "lovers . . . either dead or dying. . . . They reach past AIDS to show how the lives of contemporary gay men . . . are actually lived." Kirp finds special praise for Doty's "precise economy of language," underscoring that "he has a gift for coaxing insight from the seemingly commonplace." While Doty joked with Eloise Klein Healy that moving from poetry to prose "feels like a form of cross dressing," he explains in "A Reader's Tale" that he "was conscious of a tension between the desire to speak as an advocate and as a representative of a group to write a love story about two men whose lives were devastated by the epidemic and to remain stubbornly true to the particularities of individual experience. I believe this was the energizing conflict."

A picture of Doty and Roberts taken in 1992 precedes the text in the book. The photograph shows the two obviously in love and also obviously in the throes of Wally's disease. They both look fragile and tired. But if *Heaven's Coast* is a death story, it is equally a life story. The book is framed by the knowledge of life after Wally, although the book was written as a journal to chronicle this crisis. The memoir also allows Doty to revisit events and examine how his memory reshapes them differently, as he readdresses some subject matter that he has already addressed in poems.

Doty's approach, while clear and exact, at the same time works in the way memory works: in an associative and, at least in Doty's case, a poetic manner. One example serves to emphasize this technique. In the chapter "Cold Dark Deep and Absolutely Clear" Doty describes an encounter with seals, and the strangeness of this encounter frames a series of other seal observations. Because Doty "has always associated seals with Wally," these experiences gain power, especially one with a dead seal: "I want to caress it [the seal]; I want to lie down beside it. . . . I held Wally's body for a long time, and I could feel as I did, as I let my hands know him for the last time, that the body was moving away from me, sinking into itself." In the next chapter, "Seal Coda," he admits,

> I'd made the seals into metaphor, made them my seals. . . . But there, half covered by sand, lay another seal. . . . *Make all the meaning you want,* Death says, *shape it how you will. Open the limits of your thinking or feeling, make room for me, accommodate how you will, nothing touches the plain truth of me.*

Among the images and metaphors Doty uses to shape his grief and memory, an important device is landscape. One particularly moving section involves a Boston neighborhood where he lived with Roberts. (Doty makes references to events and details that will be familiar to those who have read *My Alexandria.*) Doty writes, "that which we leave behind is transfigured in us, too; my city's a location of memory and desire, and I can plot in this neighborhood points of rapture and longing and wonder. Here a corner where a particular magnolia, in flower, tattooed the sidewalk, and us with the shadows of its blooms. . . . Here the portico of a church—little private space—we'd duck inside to kiss." As he moves through the points of his nostalgia, he is particularly touched by their room: "nocturnal, radiant, passionate." He recounts one time when the snow blew inside: "We were englobed, inside the shook heart of a paperweight. Our room, which already felt outside the rush and pour of things, seemed still further set aside in space and time. In memory that snow springs still; our laughter and our wonder in the storm's interior, lovers suddenly stunned." In both Doty's poetry and prose, memory—together with art—has the transform-

ing power to create something lasting.

Another notable section is "A Visit with Bill," which shows the importance of being surrounded by loved ones and loved objects. Bill, who has AIDS, is being taken care of by his lover, Phil, who has made of the hospital a home. Striking about the section is "a mint-green chenille bathrobe piped, like a birthday cake." This gorgeous, over-the-top bathrobe says something about the lushness of the care with which Phil surrounds Bill, or, as Doty points out, "it feels like a room whose glow is filtered through figured silk." The beauty of their relationship makes it possible for Doty to re-live the beauty of his last days with Wally.

At the time of Wally's death, Doty was aware of the intimacy and intensity of their relationship:

> I was never this close to anyone in my life. . . . I know I am going to be more afraid than I have ever been, but right now I am not afraid. I am face to face with the deepest movement in the world, the point of my love's deepest reality—where he is most himself.

At the end he says to Wally, "*You go easy, babe, go free. . . . Go easy, but you go.*"

While he admits, "there is no consolation," he learns to go on, although he sees Wally everywhere—in scents, in experiences of lavish beauty, in the world. One pivotal moment occurs during a healing massage; another occurs during a walk with his dogs. When he sees a coyote, he thinks of Wally:

> Like the seals, the coyote stared back at us, and I could imagine in that gaze Wally's look toward home—his old home—from the other world: not sad, exactly, but neutral, loving, curious, accepting. . . . I am going on, the gaze said, in a life apart from yours, a good life, a wild life, unbounded.

This seems to be what Doty needs to understand, and it leaves him thinking, "I'm alive with a strange kind of joy."

SWEET MACHINE

Sweet Machine, a poetry collection published in 1998, holds on to this moment of joy. The book is dedicated to Paul Lisicky, Doty's partner since 1996. In addition to writing poems that are more joyful, Doty has said that he was attempting to write poems that "turn more towards the social, to the common conditions of American life. . . . I'm trying to talk about public life without resorting to public language." At the same time, the poems reflect the restlessness of the poet during this phase of his life, a time when Doty and Lisicky moved often. Doty also points out that the poems illustrate "breakage, contradiction, disruption." In short, they are poems of transition.

Desire animates the poems of *Sweet Machine,* which are prefaced by an epigraph from Hart Crane: "Thou canst read nothing except through appetite." Where critics have found fault with this collection, it has been for the poems' extravagance and for a relaxed style of writing that, one critic argued, would have been improved with some extensive editing. Furthermore, Doty's inclusion in this volume of two poems cast as direct responses to his critics have struck some readers as inappropriate. William Logan in the *New Criterion,* while acknowledging Doty's eminent talent among his generation of poets, was among those who criticized Doty's excesses of language, declaring, "You can take only so much pizzazz. At the drop of a hat he's seized by rapture—and that's just in daily life. When it comes to sex he's Judy Garland bursting into song."

Sweet Machine begins with an attention to art and beauty, "the lavish wardrobe / of things" ("Favrile"). Part 1 of "Where You Are" splits in half on the page, as if Doty's new way of seeing must be reflected in a new way of creating, and physically representing, the poem on paper. Doty's preoccupation with art and beauty is not new; but here he is more concerned with their ethereality, as in "Fog Suite," concerning a folding screen:

> I take fog as evidence,
>
> a demonstration of the nothing
> (or the nothing much)
>
> that holds the world in place.

In two poems, both entitled "Concerning Some Recent Criticism of His Work," he addresses the fact that his poetry is too preoccupied with *"Glaze and shimmer, / luster and gleam."* His first answer is playful, that a drag queen cannot have "too many sequins"; his second is more serious. He can't see anything else, asking, "what's the world but shine / and seem?"

While he does address the dead—Bobby in "One of the Rooming Houses of Heaven," dead friends and loves in "Emerald"—his strategy seems to be revision and experimentation. Art becomes more personally symbolic. "Murano," written for Lynda Hull (also released as its own book from the Getty Museum in Los Angeles and which, although lovely, has been criticized for its odd relationship between pictures—of Venetian glass from the museum's collection—and text), and "Thirty Delft Tiles," written for James Merrill, use art to stand in for people, as if it can bear a suffering that the actual human beings cannot. At the same time these poems emphasize the vulnerability, imperfection, and wonder of these two particular people. Doty asserts that Hull is living on as "glass," whereas Merrill is the teacup,

> —nothing delicate but thick, and cracked,
> and crazed with tea-stained lines where stress
>
> had split the glaze, rough spots
> where the cup was glued and dropped
>
> and glued again: nothing you'd expect
> to bear the tongues of angels,
>
> but isn't that always the way?

In addition, Doty includes a selection of poems on his dogs. "Retrievers in Translation," "Golden Retrievals," and "Shelter" all focus specifically on the actual experiences of dogs. While "Retrievers in Translation" uses the translator's sense of beauty to "translate" the text of the dogs' lives—"the crowded world / says, *Here, look here,* and yields a confusion / of silk particulars"—"Golden Retrievals" is written from the point of view of Doty's dog Beau. In a sonnet, Doty has Beau explaining his relationship with his master:

> . . . This shining bark,

> a Zen master's bronzy gong, calls you here,
> entirely, now: bow-wow, bow-wow, bow-wow.

This poem has had a range of responses, with William Logan calling it "awful" and Bill Moyers telling Doty that "in one of my favorite poems you let your dog do the naming." Doty replied that the poem was written for an anthology, *Unleashed,* including poems written from a dog's point of view. "I thought, I'd never write a poem that way," Doty told Moyers. "About a week later, Beau and I were out for walk in the woods, and I started picking up these signals. . . . What can I say? He's fond of puns. He wanted to dictate this sonnet." Lastly, "Shelter" uses the experiences of dogs in an animal shelter to stand for how we all are eager to live and be loved:

> . . . don't we want
> to be delivered again,
>   even knowing the nothing

> love may come to?
>   O Lucky and Buddy and Red,
>   we put our tongues to the world.

"In Mercy on Broadway" he addresses another experience of seizing the moment, although here the setting is the corner of Eighth Avenue and Broadway in New York City, where Doty is being offered one of a dozen or so turtles. Mark Wunderlich says of the poem: "'Mercy on Broadway' . . . acts as a bridge, linking Doty's previous work with his new artistic ambitions. . . . The poem becomes a meditation on finding the will to start over, but it also functions as a love song for the noise and chaos of street life. . . . In his masterful poem, Doty combines the vast and the very small, what's impersonal and what is deeply felt." He understands that the fate of the turtles will not be good, and yet he understands that their situation is like any of ours:

> . . . Listen, I've seen fever
> all over this town, no mercy, I've seen

> the bodies I most adored turned to flame
> and powder, my shattered darlings

"I don't think these turtles / are going to make it," he speculates. But "maybe an hour / on Broadway's jewel enough." In taking this carpe diem approach, he can appreciate not only what he's had but also what he has:

> I've been lucky; I've got a man

> in my head who's spirit and ash
> and flecks of bone now, and a live one

> whose skin is inches from mine.

Just as Walt Whitman writes about archetypal experiences grounded in New York, so does Doty.

FIREBIRD

Firebird, published in 1999, takes Doty back to the memoir, where he moves to the difficult terrain of childhood. "The book is very much concerned with experiences of being enchanted and entertained," Doty told Brad Crawford of *Writer's Digest.* "It's definitely not the sort of memoir that wants to traffic in portrayal of pain. It's story of relative triumph." While the book addresses the difficulties of Doty's life—his mother's alcoholism, his father's emotional distance, his own inability to deal with his homosexuality—and readers have been drawn to the courage of this memoir, Doty himself has emphasized that he was interested more in the method of writing the book than in the actual specifics of his biography, claiming that what actually happens in a writer's life is the least important part of a memoir. Indeed, the craftsmanship of *Firebird* has been widely acclaimed.

The title of the book comes from what Doty has described as a defining moment of his life, when Igor Stravinsky's "Suite from the Firebird" was played in his fourth-grade classroom, and he felt transformed. In the memoir he recalls how he did an interpretative dance that transcended time and space: "*Here* is who he is, swelling, taking form, the real body, triumphant boy, the bird in the fullness of its light, larger, empowered. . . . Unsayable movement, given form, in the body of a heavy little boy no longer weighted, without limit, hardly held to earth at all."

The book speaks to the power of transcendence over circumstance, but it does not flinch from painful experiences—the loneliness of the youthful outsider, who moves from school to school as his father changes government engineering jobs; the desperation of a fourteen-year-old who is dragged to the barbershop to have his long hair shaved and then attempts suicide; the difficulties of a gay boy who has no gay role models to look to: "Where would I begin to talk to this man, the first gay person I've ever met who actually says he's a gay person?" Doty shares his discussions with his mother about his sexuality. When she finds gay pornography in the house, she asks him, "How would you like a stick up your ass?" to which he

replies, "Well, is that so different from what a man and a woman do?" "No, no it's not," she replies. "The woman's part is no good." During another drunken conversation, she attempts to kill him with his father's gun, and Doty remembers, "Maybe I'm thinking I won't miss it, this sorry stubborn queer flesh, maybe I'm thinking nothing at all, merely empty, ready to receive what my mother offers."

Doty finds his escape through art, particularly writing. After Doty's acting teacher passes his poems to her friend, the poet Richard Shelton, Shelton asks to meet Doty. The two become friends, and Doty values Shelton's encouragement of his writing and admires how Shelton and his wife, Lois, a musician, place art at the center of their life together. Doty realizes that there is a way to live as an artist. He visits Shelton and his wife at their home, where, he says, he stood "transfixed, imagining what it would be like to have these people for parents, suddenly full of envy for their son, feeling I've been permitted entrance to a life so far from anything I've known." Because *Firebird* is framed by the adult experience of Doty's success as a published poet, including the triumph of winning the T. S. Eliot prize, the fragility of his early artistic self comes across as especially poignant. This self is shaped by "twin poles": "A boy lifted by music, his body become aerial and bright as the phoenix that music portrays— and that boy, years later, turning to ash, held in the sights of his mother's gun." Overall, memory, whether good or bad, is a strength: "*What we remember . . . can be changed. What we forget we are always.*" In short, Doty asserts, "I believe that art saved my life."

STILL LIFE WITH OYSTERS AND LEMON

In *Still Life with Oysters and Lemon* (2001) Doty examines art itself. He uses the painting of that title by Jan Davidsz de Heem, a seventeenth-century Dutch still life painter, as a way to examine the importance of things in our lives and the resonance of those things—their ephemerality, as well as permanence. As Doty explains in the book, "To think through things, that is the still life painter's work—and the poet's."

In comparison with the clear, though very different, uses of the memoir in *Heaven's Coast* and *Firebird,* it is much more difficult to categorize the genre of *Still Life with Oysters and Lemon.* It is not a memoir, though it uses memoir. It is not a poem, although it uses the language of poetry. It is not only about art, although it uses art as its starting point. The book begins with an epigraph by Virginia Woolf—"Life which is so fantastic cannot be altogether tragic"—and this insistence on the beauty of life, particularly as triggered through objects, is at the heart of the book. Doty uses these objects as opportunities for artistic reverie, and in doing so gives a sense of the meaning of those objects to him. Granted, objects have always been important to Doty, but here meticulous attention to the smallest of details—whether in paintings or memory—gives a different sense of proportion to the object and heightens it.

Take his feelings about his grandmother, for example. Rather than starting with the person, he uses objects and his emotional response to those objects in order to give a sense of his relationship with his grandmother. The object with which he begins is a peppermint:

> Hypnotist's wheel, red whirl blazoned on a hard white candy ground, spinning even when it isn't moving; that's the life of the spiral, it seems to whirl even when it's at rest. . . . [The peppermints] emerge, one after the other, endless, pouring out. . . . But the dark from whence they emerge is the unfathomable void of my grandmother's glossy black pocketbook.

Throughout the text Doty juxtaposes his attention to still lifes with his personal attention to memory, and while he brings the same descriptive eye to each, part of the struggle is to articulate the life of art, on the one hand, and the art of life, on the other—or in other words, to give a sense of the influence of ephemeral, living moments in art, and of the influence of the permanence of objects in life. Objects are the transition from one level of experience (art) to another (life): "There is a Japanese word [*sabi*] for things made more beautiful by use, that bear the evidence of their own making, or the individuating marks of time's passage: a kind of beauty not immune to time but embedded in it."

The object is valuable to Doty for several reasons: "first, [as] a principle of attention, simply that"; second, because of "a faith in the capacity of the object to carry meaning, to serve as a vessel"; third, as "permanent intimacy." As Doty writes, "I becomes an eye." What becomes important is not just the object, but the experience of that object, or as Doty explains, "What is documented, at last, is not the thing itself but a way of seeing—the object infused with the subject. The eye moving over the world like a lover."

He uses the still life to explain not only what is important to him about this form of art, but about art in general, and his own art, poetry: "The great still lifes of the seventeenth century are full of individual differences. . . . And yet there is no sense here of a drive toward personality. . . . There is an odd quality of egolessness." In terms of art and poetry, he ponders their "use" and finally decides that both are "advocates of intimacy, as embodiments of paradox, as witnesses to earth, here, this moment, now. Evidence, thus, that tenderness and style are still the best gestures we can make in the face of death."

SOURCE

Source (2001) continues both Doty's sense of the gesture and his movement toward a more public self. The epigraph, by Walt Whitman, says something about this shift: "Men and woman crowding fast in the streets, / if they are not flashes and specks, what are they?" Whitman has always been a model for Doty, and Doty's work increasingly focuses on the place of the individual among the multitudes and the richness of the human continuum.

Critical response to the book has emphasized this shift to the collective, to what Stephen Whited has called "a shared emotional experience." While the animating spirit of Whitman is at the heart of the book, and "Letter to Walt Whitman" is arguably the central piece of the collection, destined to become a classic, Doty starts first by turning his attention to unlikely subjects, not only in terms of his own writing but also in terms of poetry itself. Just as in *Sweet Machine* Doty pushes the boundaries of form, here he pushes at the boundaries of subject matter, risking bathos in order to give attention to minute details that under other lights would get little, if any attention. Doty ponders the death of a baby rabbit, admitting, "And here comes / the *So?* of poetry"; he looks at a bag of goldfish ("Fish R Us"); he looks at the stain left by the heads of men who work out in a gym, "halo / the living made together" ("At the Gym"). After taking on the enormity of the AIDS crisis in previous poems, he attempts to give voice to the least of us as well as the least observed.

The irony is that, in "Manhattan: Luminism," he then addresses Manhattan, one of the most written about of places, discussing it not so much in terms of landmarks, but in terms of the details of individual experience: signs and a florist's window, a mirror, a child who presses her face against the face of an elephant in a video store poster; pigeons. The poem is representative of this collection's preoccupation with looking at how individualized detail becomes archetypal and shared; as the poem reaches its last section, it uses a second-person

strategy, inviting the reader to partake of the experience. Doty writes,

> . . . You were afraid
> you were edgeless, one bit
> of light's indifferent streaming,
>
> and you are—but in a way you also
> are singled out, are, in the old sense,
> a soul, because you have heard
> the thrilling, deep-entering rumple
> and susurrus of the birds . . .

In "Letter to Walt Whitman," Doty pays homage to the many others who have paid homage to Whitman, although Allen Ginsberg's "A Supermarket in California" would be the most familiar to readers. Ginsberg addresses the discomfort Whitman would feel with modern life on the West Coast—out of Whitman's home territory (and across the country, no less)—but it is precisely to Whitman's home territory that Doty returns. Doty in the poem apprehends Whitman through the objects in his house (he and Paul Lisicky make the journey to Camden, New Jersey, Whitman's last home), but also through the message of his poetry. Ginsberg believes that Whitman would feel anachronous in 1950s America; by contrast, Doty argues that at the beginning of the twenty-first century Whitman's assertions have reached a culmination—"delight in the beauty of boys," "men held in common by our common skin"—of which Whitman would have approved. He admires Whitman's courage in writing about his sexuality:

> . . . to mistake the nipple
> for the soul, souse of ejaculate
> for the warm rain of heaven. It stops
> my breath, to think of what you said.

The beauty of what Whitman has shared with Doty can be reciprocated through Doty's observations of the diverse beauty of America's people (even given overpopulation and pollution), of nature, and of his relationship with Paul, a relationship that in Whitman's time would have been "erased."

One other long poem, "An Island Sheaf" (also published as a chapbook with Dim Gray Bar Press), is a series of takes on Key West and pays homage to another of Doty's poetic mentors, Elizabeth Bishop; the shift in perspectives and emphasis on small details mirror Doty's approach in *Still Life with Oysters and Lemon*. The piece, which is in five sections, is painterly and addresses with fine detail the natural phenomena of Key West. The section names—"Sea Grape Valentine," "Watermelon Soda," "Elizabeth Bishop: *Croton*," "Hesperides Street," and "Catalina Macaw"—say something about the ways in which Doty changes emphasis and frame in order to give a multilayered approach to his poem. "Sea Grape Valentine," made up of short lines of Bishopian description, makes the case for the lasting quality of the sea grape,

> this fallen valentine,
>
> candybox token
> veined in hot gold,
> its tropic wax
>
> embalmed and blazing?

By contrast, the watermelon soda of section 2 is the setting for a crab, and Doty muses,

> Strange island,
> to yield a walking
>
> hot-pink soda can
> inhabited by a lucky,
> Modernist crab . . .

While the sea grape lasts, the crab—and soda can—disappear by the next day.

Section 3, which again uses intensity of focuses, addresses a watercolor by Bishop entitled *Croton*. The section's theme is about the relationship of things to their context—in this case, a leaf to its surroundings—and says

something about Bishop's sense of exile. Section 4 is more narrative, with Doty associating the picture of a coffee can with his own surroundings and appreciating the walk home in a kind of paradise, musing, "Any kingdom's imagined, / must be, before it's inhabited." Along with astonishing beauty, however, we find decay: "That means love the rot black / in the tree-trunk crack"—and this awareness is an important part of Doty's project. The poem ends with "Catalina Macaw," a parrot whose fierce presence says *yes* to life.

At the end of the book, Doty once again turns his attention to what is of value, what lasts. In "Brian Age 7" he is amazed by the passion—and especially, the pleasure—of a boy who draws himself with an ice cream cone. Although Doty himself is a firm believer in the craft of a poem, he is here concerned with the joys that sustain us. In "Essay: The Love of Old Houses" Doty writes of his love for this house in Provincetown, explaining

> . . . why I like old houses best:
>
> here it's proved that time requires
> a deeper, better verb than *pass*;
> it's more like pool, and ebb, and double
> back again, my history, his, yours . . .

"Source," the title poem of the collection, uses a moment in time in order to consider this idea of permanence. In thinking of horses he has passed by on the way to town and then returned to see, he admits,

> Experience is an intact fruit,
> core and flesh and rind of it; once cut open,
> entered, it can't be the same, can it?
>
> Though that is the dream of the poem . . .

While the poem creates something lasting, it is something different from the lived moment:

> . . . The poem wants the
> impossible;
>
> the poem wants a name for the kind nothing
> at the core of time.

The horses in their enthusiasm and beauty—in addition to being a symbol of passion—summarize for Doty what life ultimately is all about: "pleasure / and sunlight," the road into and out of it, "the source of spring." When asked by Eloise Klein Healy what he wanted out of life, Doty did not hesitate: "More of it."

Selected Bibliography

WORKS OF MARK DOTY

POETRY

An Alphabet: Poems. Ithaca, N.Y.: Alembic Press, 1979. (Chapbook published with Ruth Dawson under the name M. R. Doty; all poems by Doty.)

An Introduction to the Geography of Iowa. Fort Kent, Maine: Great Raven Press, 1979. (Chapbook published with Ruth Dawson under the name M. R. Doty; only one poem—"On an Article in the *Des Moines Register* Which States That There Are Only Four American Chestnut Trees in Polk County, That One of These, in My Front Yard Has Died—by Ruth Dawson.)

The Empire of Summer. Birmingham, Ala.: Thunder City Press, 1981. (Chapbook published with Ruth Dawson under the name M. R. Doty; all poems by Doty.)

Turtle, Swan. Boston: David R. Godine, 1987.

Bethlehem in Broad Daylight. Boston: David R. Godine, 1991.

My Alexandria. Urbana: University of Illinois Press, 1993.

Atlantis. New York: HarperPerennial, 1995.

Favrile. New York: Dim Gray Bar Press, 1997. (Chapbook.)

Island Sheaf. New York: Dim Gray Bar Press, 1998. (Only 125 copies of this chapbook were printed, each autographed by Doty.)

Sweet Machine. New York: HarperFlamingo, 1998.

Murano. Los Angeles: J. Paul Getty Museum, 2000.

Turtle, Swan and Bethlehem in Broad Daylight. Urbana: University of Illinois Press, 2000.

Source. New York: Harper, 2001.

NONFICTION

Heaven's Coast: A Memoir. New York: HarperCollins, 1996.

Firebird: A Memoir. New York: HarperCollins, 1999.

Still Life with Oysters and Lemon. Boston: Beacon Press, 2001.

ESSAYS

"The 'Forbidden Planet' of Character: The Revolutions of the 1950s." In *A Profile of Twentieth-Century American Poetry.* Edited by Jack Meyers and David Wojahn. Carbondale: Southern Illinois University Press, 1991. Pp. 131–157.

Introduction to *Syzygy* by Sarah Brock. Landisburg, Pa.: Pine Press, 1995. (Winner of the 1995 Blue Mountain Poetry Award Chapbook Series.)

"Is There a Future?" In *In the Company of My Solitude: American Writing from the AIDS Pandemic.* Edited by Marie Howe and Michael Klein. New York: Persea, 1994. Pp. 3–17. (This piece became the prologue to *Heaven's Coast.*)

"A Reader's Tale." In *Contemporary Authors,* vol. 161. Detroit: Gale, 1998. Pp. 99–113.

"An Exile's Palm." In *Here Lies My Heart: Essays on Why We Marry, Why We Don't, and What We Find There.* Edited by Deborah Chasman and Catherine Jhee. Boston: Beacon Press, 1999. Pp. 129–156.

"The Panorama Mesdag." In *Drawing Us In: How We Experience Visual Art.* Edited by Deborah Chasman and Edna Chiang. Boston: Beacon Press, 2000. Pp. 125–134.

"Rooting for the Damned." In *The Poets' Dante.* Edited by Peter S. Hawkins and Rachel Jacoff. New York: Farrar, Straus and Giroux, 2001. Pp. 370–379.

CRITICAL AND BIOGRAPHICAL STUDIES

Allen, Frank. Review of *Atlantis. Library Journal,* August 1995, p. 79.

Baker, David. "Smarts." In his *Heresy and the Ideal: On Contemporary Poetry.* Fayetteville: University of Arkansas Press, 2000. Pp. 119–136.

Freeman, Chris. "Art That Saves." *Gay and Lesbian Review* 7, no. 2:52 (2000). (Review of *Firebird: A Memoir.*)

Gilbert, Roger. "Awash with Angels: The Religious Turn in Nineties Poetry." *Contemporary Literature* 42, no. 2:238–269 (2001).

Hampl, Patricia. Review of *Atlantis. Commonweal,* December 1, 1995, p. 20ff.

Jarraway, David R. "'Creatures of the Rainbow': Wallace Stevens, Mark Doty, and the Poetics of Androgyny." *Mosaic* 30, no. 3:169–183 (1997).

Kaganoff, Penny. Review of *Bethlehem in Broad Daylight. Publishers Weekly,* October 12, 1990, p. 57.

Kirp, David L. "Speak, Gay Memory." Review of *Heaven's Coast. The Nation,* July 15–22, 1996, pp. 33–38.

Landau, Deborah. "'How to Live. What to Do?' The Poetics and Politics of AIDS." *American Literature* 68:193–225 (1996).

Logan, William. "Sins and Sensibility." Review of *Sweet Machine. New Criterion* 17, no. 4:1 (1998).

Marcus, Peter. "Reflections on Intimacy." *Gay and Lesbian Review,* September 2001, p. 42. (Review of *Still Life with Oysters and Lemon* and *Murano.*)

Monaghan, Pat. Review of *Bethlehem in Broad Daylight. Booklist,* November 5, 1990, p. 596.

Moyers, Bill, ed. "Mark Doty." In *Fooling with Words: A Celebration of Poets and Their Craft.* New York: Morrow, 1999. Pp. 46–68.

Shetley, Vernon. "Poetry in Review." *Yale Review* 81, no. 4:138–156 (1993). (Review of *My Alexandria.*)

Spiegelman, Willard. "Poetry in Review." *Yale Review* 84, no. 2:160–183. (Review of *Atlantis.*)

Steinberg, Sybil, and Jonathan Bing, eds. "Mark Doty." In *Writing for Your Life #3.* Wainscott, N.Y.: Pushcart Press, 1997. Pp. 86–90.

Swiss, Thomas. "Coming to Terms." *Poet and Critic* 13, no. 2:20–21 (1982). (Evaluation of early chapbook poems by Doty; the issue includes early poems by Doty.)

Whited, Stephen. Review of *Source. Book,* January–February 2002, p. 73.

Wunderlich, Mark. "About Mark Doty: A Profile." *Ploughshares* 25, no. 1:183–189 (1999).

INTERVIEWS

Bing, Jonathan. "Mark Doty: The Poet's Idea of Order on Cape Cod." *Publishers Weekly,* April 15, 1996, pp. 44–45.

Crawford, Brad. "Mark Doty's Healing Laughter." *Writer's Digest,* November 1999, pp. 8ff.

Healy, Eloise Klein. *Mark Doty.* Videocassette. Directed by Dan Griggs. Lannan Foundation, 1997.

Moyers, Bill. *Lucille Clifton and Mark Doty.* Videocassette. Directed by Catherine Tatge. Thirteen/WNET, 1999.

—*KIM BRIDGFORD*

Stephen Dunn

1939–

STEPHEN DUNN IS a thoughtful poet, a ruminator. Right from the start of his poetic career there was a tone of mildly amused quasi-objectivity and a fascination with everyday life. One pictures him slowly turning his life in his hand like a man staring into one of those crystal globes with a snow scene inside. But he almost always sees more than what is apparently there. In his best poems he sees beyond the snow, the little sled, the scraggly tree. He glimpses, for a brief moment, in the energy that develops between the lines of his poem, the disjunction between the snow and the feeling or memory; he sees the passing, strange, and yet ordinary truth of our lives.

In the course of his thirty-year writing career, Dunn's poetry has grown in depth, breadth, and skill. Beginning in 1974 with *Looking for Holes in the Ceiling,* Dunn has published eleven books of poetry. When he won the Pulitzer Prize for poetry in 2001 for his collection *Different Hours* (2000), Dunn commented, "I probably couldn't have written it earlier in my career. I hope it withstands the scrutiny of the Prize." These two humble statements sum up Dunn's long-standing attitude toward his work. In the realm of poetry, he is a long-distance runner, and the idea that he "couldn't have written it earlier" is part of his sense of writing as a process, a large endeavor, requiring many years to reach fruition. Past sixty when he won the prize, his attitude of hoping that his work "withstands the scrutiny" is one he cultivates. This is a poet fond of understatement, of the small dramas of domestic life, and one who approaches the larger topics—love, death, fidelity, life's meaning—with humility and irony.

Dunn was something of a surprise as the Pulitzer winner that year; his reputation has been a quiet one. He is better known among poets than he is to the larger reading public, and his work is not as widely anthologized as that of other poets of his generation, such as Galway Kinnell or Sharon Olds. Although he receives very respectful reviews in literary journals and the *New York Times,* his clear, conversational poetry does not seem to excite in critics the same level of intellectual engagement as that of Mark Strand or John Ashbery. When he was interviewed by Elizabeth Farnsworth for the *News Hour with Jim Lehrer* on April 26, 2001, Dunn responded to her comment that his poetry is "so eloquent about the most ordinary things" by saying: "I've always tried to take on the dailyness of our lives, which I think is mysterious. . . . Whenever I've been able to arrive at clarities about that which is elusive about dailyness, that has pleased me." As the bard of "dailyness," Dunn carved out a significant place for himself in the last quarter of the twentieth century in the United States. His fellow poet Gerald Stern has written of Dunn on the book jacket of *Landscape at the End of the Century* (1991), "He is a magnificent poet," and the critic Stephen Cramer wrote in *Poetry* magazine, "Stephen Dunn has quietly become one of our major poets of disabused wisdom." But it has been a slow process.

BACKGROUND

Stephen Dunn was born in Brooklyn, New York, on June 24, 1939, into a sometimes struggling salesman's family—his father, Charles Francis

Dunn, sold vacuum cleaners, and his mother, Ellen Dorothy Fleishman, was a homemaker. Dunn grew up in Queens, New York, where he was very aware of himself "as a Catholic in the Jewish section of Forest Hills," which was then a "relatively safe middle-class neighborhood." But he knew that just a few blocks in any direction, other ethnic groups dominated: the Italians to the south; beyond Continental Avenue, to the east, "the harmless Protestants"; and to the west "poorer kids and their street gang, the Gauchos." He goes on in this essay, "Stepping Out" (from *Walking Light,* 1993), to assert that "every neighborhood has bullies, and I'm convinced that they watch how we walk. In Forest Hills, shufflers were in deep trouble, as were the pigeon-toed. Kids who walked like ducks were doomed." And so, as a kid, Dunn "tried to cultivate a walk" that would not give him away, a walk that "was somewhere in between 'walking tall,' like the best movie heroes, and walking quietly, like a medium-sized animal. . . . Above all, I tried not to let my false confidence ring false." This exaggerated self-awareness of adolescent male status reminds one of the young Alexander Portnoy in Philip Roth's novel *Portnoy's Complaint* (1969).

By the time Dunn was fourteen he was five feet, eleven inches tall, and as a teenager he discovered the joy of basketball, happily shoveling snow off the schoolyard concrete in winter in order to shoot hoops. He claims basketball as his "first love" or even, he is willing to assert, his religion. When he writes prose on this subject it has the clarity of poetry, as in "Basketball and Poetry: The Two Richies" (from *Walking Tall*): "Sometimes I played in the dark, a distant streetlight the only illumination." Having survived the masculinity tests of his boyhood, Dunn attended Hofstra University in Hempstead, New York. There he played basketball on a team with a 25–1 record, majored in history and English, and received his bachelor's degree in 1962. He played professional basket-ball for one season (1962–1963) with the Williamsport Billies in Williamsport, Pennsylvania. Dunn often compares poetry and sports, particularly basketball. He likes to see links between the two endeavors, pointing out in "Basketball and Poetry" that "in basketball it's common to play with people better than you. To grow up on the schoolyards in Queens was to know something about hierarchy and pecking orders." For poets, then, the great opponent or teammate might be William Butler Yeats, and like the less skilled ballplayer, the poet must continue to keep writing "in the face of such greatness." In both cases, Dunn claims, "there's much to be said for obsessiveness and stubbornness."

Ultimately, Dunn feels that the most important thing that poetry and basketball have in common is "the possibility of transcendence," an idea that he shares with John Updike in *Rabbit Run* (1960). There, too, sports—the sheer bliss of playing—could catapult one into a transcendent realm. It is a kind of male, magical initiation rite for those who rise above the crowd. Once, some years after his Billies days, when Dunn was playing in the *Long Island Press* League, he had an amazing night on the court when he scored 45 points. As he wrote twenty-five years later in "Basketball and Poetry," "On that evening I was better than myself. Every previous hour on a basketball court, all my muscle memory, all my ability, converged that evening with dream."

When Dunn won the Pulitzer Prize, *Sports Illustrated* ran a short piece in which Alfred Kim noted that Dunn had played basketball "at Hofstra in the '50s" and that he uses "sports in his work as a metaphor for the travails of everyday life." Shortly after his brief foray into professional basketball, as well as a six months' stint on active duty in the U.S. Army, Dunn entered corporate America, taking what he refers to as "a high-paying job" as copywriter at the National Biscuit Company in New York City (1963–1966). This work involved touting commercial baked goods, a trade he came to find discomfiting. In his poem "The Last Hours" (from *Different Hours*), Dunn looks back at this time and writes:

> I'm twenty-five, on the shaky
> ladder up, my father's son, corporate,
> clean-shaven, and I know only what I don't want,
> which is almost everything I have.

So when his boss offers him a promotion, a new office, and a raise, all he can think is

> . . . I'm translating
> his beneficence into a lifetime, a life
> of selling snacks, talking snack strategy,
> thinking snack thoughts.

Leaving the office that day, he knows he will quit.

Surely that experience as a young man working in the advertising world left its mark on Dunn's view of society. Twenty years later, when he was writing nonfiction on his life and work, he was compelled to point out in "The Good and Not So Good" (from *Walking Light*) that "The truth always is a little strange because the conventional world has little interest in the truth, and regularly accepts packaged versions of it." That image of the "packaged versions" of the truth comes from advertising, the great packager of false visions, and Dunn had been, if only briefly, of the devil's company. So he tends to be even more committed to truth seeking than some of his contemporaries who are further removed from, and therefore less implicated in, the world of business. As he writes in "Bringing the Strange Home" (from *Walking Light*), "I'm just interested in those poems that manage to cut through passable truths or to another level of truth and connection. . . . We need to find and champion the poems that are true to the ambiguity of experience." Dunn firmly believes that "it is a desirable, subversive act to replace what passes for truth with a more

accurate/deep approximation, whether the subject is a dinner party or poverty" ("The Good and Not So Good"). As he points out in "Stepping Out," "we live with various mystifications—like religious dogma or government-speak—against which almost any honest poem is a corrective."

During his several years in the corporate world, Dunn was taking writing workshops at the New School for Social Research (1964–1966). On September 26, 1964, he married Lois Ann Kelly (with whom he had two daughters). During the mid-1960s, Dunn and his wife spent a year in Cadiz, Spain, while he attempted to write a novel, which he later declared to Robert Strauss "wasn't any good." When he returned to the United States in 1967, he took a job editing *Flying* magazine in New York City. Upon the advice of a friend who read his poetry, Dunn applied to the creative writing program at Syracuse University, where he studied with Philip Booth, Donald Justice, and W. D. Snodgrass and received a master's degree in 1970.

While he was a graduate student Dunn began teaching, consistently wearing black shirts to avoid disclosure of his intense nervousness, which caused embarrassing underarm sweat stains. Dunn was delighted to discover that the freshmen were more insecure than he was. He had been shy and silent much of his life, so this entry into teaching marked a significant change. As he acknowledges in *Walking Light,* "It was a fine surprise that I had things to say to them." He was thirty years old before he felt ready to put in his "two cents worth" in Booth's graduate poetry workshop. Looking at what he labels "A History of My Silence," Dunn concludes, "If anything has, poetry has given me the confidence to speak." He quickly adds, "Nevertheless, I prefer a dark booth in the corner of a dark bar, one chosen person across from me."

Dunn went from Syracuse to Minnesota, where he was an assistant professor of creative writing at Southwestern State University (1970–

1973). He writes of this time in a poem called "The Sexual Revolution," in *Different Hours:* "we lived on the prairie amid polite / moral certainty," outside the range of the "faraway friend [who] wrote / to say the erotic life / was the only life. Get with it, he said." During those three years in the Midwest, living about thirty miles from the poet Robert Bly's farmhouse, Dunn was finding and honing his poetic voice and vocation. According to Dunn, "Bly was a big influence on everybody in those days, especially his translations and his thinking about the Deep Image," a term coined by Bly to describe a method for evoking strong feelings. It proved useful for Dunn to live for several years in the starkly cold landscape of Minnesota, away from his eastern ties. Once he returned east, he settled in New Jersey for the long term.

Dunn has had a dual career since that time: college professor and serious poet. He took a job at Stockton State College in southern New Jersey in 1974 and has been teaching there ever since, rising to the position of Distinguished Professor of Creative Writing at what today is called the Richard Stockton College of New Jersey. As his reputation has grown, he also has held visiting professorships at the University of Michigan, Princeton University, Syracuse University, and Columbia University. He is the winner of numerous writing awards and grants, including the Academy of American Poets Award, the New York Poetry Center's "Discovery '71" Award, several National Endowment for the Arts fellowships, a *Transatlantic Review* fellowship, the Theodore Roethke Prize from *Poetry Northwest,* numerous Yaddo writing fellowships, a Guggenheim Fellowship, an Academy Award in Literature from the American Academy of Arts and Letters, and, of course, the Pulitzer Prize for Poetry.

In an interview with Robert Strauss of the *New York Times,* Dunn said, "That I do teach at Stockton has been noted lately as somewhat special and it very well may be. Since the Pulitzer, I have been offered a chair at a major university, which I have turned down. I have grown comfortable here." So he teaches and he writes, and he does not expect to grow rich. "I suppose now I will get some money in speaking fees, but, let's be real, I will be teaching again in the fall. This is not pro basketball."

CRITICAL APPRAISAL

Dunn generally defies categorization, but if he belongs to any school of poetry, it would be among what David Baker calls, in *Heresy and the Ideal: On Contemporary Poetry,* "the wistful, plaintive, or melancholy voice" of the "recent Romantic lyric." Baker says of this kind of poetry, to which he also ascribes the work of Linda Gregerson, Sharon Olds, and Robert Hass, "Its fundamental method is the plain style, its frequent mode the personal anecdote." He goes on to say specifically of Dunn's work, "He brings important news, and warning, from the nearly paralyzed districts of American suburbia and middle-age." Baker states "Dunn is wonderful because, unlike many, he writes with powerful and astute ironies: a deep sense of terror yet a resonant spiritual investment; an available, charming voice capable of great intimacy or confessional revelation." Clearly, Dunn's star is rising in the American poetic firmament.

The tone with which critics describe Dunn's work is generally appreciative—and certainly more so since he won the Pulitzer—yet somehow, over the years, also mildly damning, as if Dunn's very sanity annoyed some of them. According to Robert Miltner, writing in *Contemporary Authors:*

> Dunn writes poetry that reflects the social, cultural, psychological, and philosophical territory of the American middle class; his poems are considered intelligent and given neither to postmodern pessimism nor contemporary experimental excess. In

his lyrical poems, Dunn is often his own protagonist, narrating the regular episodes of his growth both as an individual and as part of a married couple.

The words critics choose to describe Dunn's work can be quite niggling in their implications: "level-headed," "consistent," "conversational," "pleasing," and "friendly." Over and over, Dunn's focus on domestic subjects is praised, but the very consistency of relegating him to the realm of the "domestic" and the "suburban" suggests that some critics find in Dunn a lack of passion, strangeness, transcendence. Those who want to find him safe, however, are missing very central implications of his poetry. Read closely, his voice is often dangerous, subversive, and cunning. Such critics are not wrong in seeing Dunn as the bard of the domestic world, but they underestimate that world, the one in which, in fact, most of us live in our comfortable Western societies. If it is from within our shared, common state that Stephen Dunn contemplates life, then he is speaking from a familiar place but often with a far deeper and more unsettling vision than we commonly allow ourselves.

As a poet, Dunn regularly peels back the masks of the domestic and the ordinary to reveal other meanings, other possibilities. Through his eleven volumes of poetry he has employed differing strategies in this ongoing quest, and the very titles of his works, among them, *Not Dancing, Local Time, Landscape at the End of the Century,* suggest the various vantage points of his inquiry. G. E. Murray writes of his "fearless insights into the riches and ravages of middle age" and Emily Nussbaum of how he balances "effortlessly between the casual and the vivid" and of his gift for mapping out "the subtle mordant shifts of adult morality." The poet laureate Billy Collins, in a blurb from the book jacket of *Different Hours,* says of Dunn, "The art lies in hiding the art . . . and Stephen Dunn has proven himself a master of concealment."

If there are basically two critical camps in the assessment of Dunn's work—those many who applaud and those few who damn—they are split along the issue of what it means to be "ordinary." Writing in *Publishers Weekly,* Jeff Zaleski condemns Dunn's recent poetry as describing "the travails of ordinary people in language not only simplified but generalized." He adds, "Many poems try so hard for their transparency that they become predictable, so hard to be representative that their speakers seem too normal to be true." This is about as harsh as any critic is with Dunn, and it is a not a widely held view. It would be difficult to determine in contemporary America exactly who the "ordinary people" are, the ones Zaleski thinks that Dunn is chronicling. It is hard to support a reading of Dunn's work in which his speakers are "too normal to be true." So often they live multiple lives with manifold truths and lies, distracted by weather and women, patience and the void.

Those poets who appreciate Dunn's artistry write of his "easy, conversational music, composed of one exactly right word after another" (Alicia Ostriker on the book jacket to *Different Hours*), of how "his poems would not be so strikingly naked were they not so carefully dressed" (Billy Collins on the book jacket to *Different Hours*), of how he provides "straight wisdom, wisdom not sweetened and diluted with sanctimony but shots of the original stuff, a brand which clears the head with a jolt and which may even be useful" (Jonathan Holden in *Western Humanities Review*). On the whole, respect for Dunn's craftsmanship and vision have grown over the past three decades, and we can expect more critical attention to his work in this post-Pulitzer phase of his career.

INDIVIDUAL COLLECTIONS

The opening poem in Dunn's first collection, *Looking for Holes in the Ceiling,* is entitled

"What" and begins, "What starts things / are the accidents behind the eyes," a recognition that could be applied to the body of his work. He is fond of accident and recognizes the possibilities of illumination in the uncharted course; as he points out in this poem, one can even ponder "your transplanted life-line going places / in someone else's palm." Dunn writes with a young voice here, the man still finding himself, defining himself, seeking to know and spy. Often the imagery is of a male in hiding: in "Rapist," he is "the man crouched behind a bush"; in "In Certain Places at Certain Times There Can Be More of You," "there were too many masks. / They each fit tightly around my face"; in "A Man Waiting for It to Stop," he is at a bus stop, and so he considers the act of waiting and how he will take the bus to "The last stop, / the neighborhood / where he never grew up." The poems, then, become ways of constructing an adult persona with which he can live. He compares his own masculinity to that of blue-collar men and begins the poem "At Every Gas Station There Are Mechanics":

> Around them my cleanliness stinks.
> I smell it. And so do they.
> I always want to tell them I used to box . . .

He playfully suggests that if these manly mechanics were to claim that he could not have his car back, that it belonged to them, he would meekly acquiesce, "And then I would walk home, / and create an accident."

Robert Wilson praised *Looking for Holes in the Ceiling* in *New Letters* as "a crash course in survival" and as "poems which seem to strike a blow for life," noting that Dunn does not offer his readers "ready-made answers." Already his style in this collection reveals those traits that he would continue to fine-tune over the next decades: the short line; the clear, grammatical thinking; the vernacular, plain-speaking voice; the strong ordinary images, infused with the slightly mocking and undercutting perceptions

of "what ifs." Clarity is a given in Dunn's poetry, at least on the surface. Underneath, strange fishes may be swimming about, sometimes little darting piranhas with quick, deadly mouths that take deeper, more devastating bites than one first suspects they might. It is his talent to disguise the sense of danger that hovers around the edges of his poems. Dunn's visual, sensual perception is acute; in "Fat Man, Floating," he notes, "Small waves drag their tongues / across his body."

Again and again in this collection, Dunn reaches out to define himself, sometimes with the outrageous and somewhat absurd bravado of the young: "I am the bomb inside a stone. / I am a tongue surrounded by teeth" ("Monologue on the Way Out"). In "Biography in the First Person," he is more direct: "All my uncles / were detectives. My father a crack salesman." He continues, "I am none of my clothes. / My poems are approximately true." This last statement is a wonderful credo for Dunn. Yes, his poems are true, real, authentic, but "approximately" so, leaving him wiggle room of wide latitude. Later in the poem he warns: "Be careful: / I would like to make you believe in me." Partly this is his poet voice and partly his teacher voice because, as a teacher, he recognizes how easily students fall in love with that charismatic charmer at the front of the room. "When I come home at night after teaching myself / to students," he admits, "I want to search the phone book / for their numbers, call them, and pick their brains." He is wise enough to see that he is "teaching myself," and the idea is a little scary—because, after all, one does not want to lose the "self," give it away, or even "teach" it to others. But at this time, in his early thirties, when he has begun to teach, Dunn is enjoying the complexity of the process. In "Decisions to Disappear," he reveals, "I often imagine myself absent, / on the tip of somebody's tongue."

In "On Hearing the Airlines Will Use a Psychological Profile to Catch Potential Skyjackers," he prophetically declares himself a skyjacker who has been caught and admits his motivation:

> the plot to get the Pulitzer Prize
> in exchange for the airplane,
> the bomb in my pencil,
> heroin in the heel of my boot.

Of course, this criminal vision is a far-fetched joke in the early 1970s. Dunn enjoys playing with fantasies, so that as the media probes for his possible motivation—perhaps childhood deprivation? He imagines his response:

> "There is no one cause for any human act,"
> I'll tell them, thinking *finally,*
> a chance to let the public in
> on the themes of great literature.

In "Carrying On" he wishes to ask "madmen" why he feels the bones in his nose would be crushed "by the invisible glass" if he "were to walk into an opening anywhere." Such a desire, late in this collection, suggests the ongoing nature of Dunn's discomfort with ordinary life, that slightly shaky feeling of a man who wonders "if words make anything happen." It is a state of imbalance that suits a poet; it is the itch at the base of the brain that demands scratching. Sometimes his writing makes sense and then "for days I'm able / to pull rabbits out of the thinnest afternoons." The final poem in the collection is "How to Be Happy: Another Memo to Myself," in which he maps out the possible routes to satisfaction, emerging finally with the reminder, "there are few pleasures / that aren't as local as your fingertips." This is the man who went on to write ten more volumes of poetry—for the most part on those very local pleasures, although like any honest pilgrim he often lost his way and wondered where the pleasures went.

His next collection, *Full of Lust and Good Usage* (1976), begins with several poems about living in a small town in a cold part of the country, his feelings of disjunction and strangeness and an awareness of the commitment to repression in all around him. He writes in "Beneath the Sidewalk,"

> So much has been held in,
> so much has seeped through
> the soles of our shoes,
> that half our lives are beneath the sidewalk.

We suspect that "soles" may be a pun and that it is the soul of the place that Dunn finds arid. Insomnia seems to afflict those living there, and in his poem "For the Sleepless," the speaker walks at night to his window, "my nakedness / with me like an angry friend." Writing in *Parnassus,* Cheryl Walker calls *Full of Lust and Good Usage* "a man's book," and she goes on to suggest that he "follows in the metrical footsteps of Mark Strand." "What makes this a man's book," Walker explains, "has nothing really to do with lust, . . . but rather with that certain sense of ease which is everywhere in spite of the uneasiness Dunn talks about. This kind of ease is still unavailable to most women."

Only occasionally is Dunn provoked into humor, as in the poem "Prairie Life: A Citizen Speaks," which begins:

> We live here, open to the wind and dust.
> When a bitch is in heat
> the scent carries so far
> dogs we've never seen show up
> like gunfighters.

For all Walker's inference of masculine ease, there is actually a suggestion that Dunn is waiting for his life to happen, as if he were stuck in a timeless, eventless place: "I have walked back to my house / thinking how fine, yet incomplete my life is." In "Truck Stop: Minnesota," he gets a slightly sour look from the waitress, feels estranged, and at the same time declares:

> She is the America I would like to love.
> Sweetheart, the truckers call her.
> Honey. Doll.

And she smiles at them while the alienated speaker finds himself "full of lust and good usage, lost here."

Dunn introduces the subject of gambling, about which he has written memoir material, in the poem "The Big Winner Rises Late": "here I am / this big winner of small games." He characterizes himself as "this coxcomb of the prairie strutting / in front of my bay window," and even his victory at poker reminds him of the ridiculousness of his posture, so that the very birds are laughing. If he was defining himself in his first book, he is reinterpreting his gestures in the second. He comes face to face with this subject in "California, This Is Minnesota Speaking," directed to a childhood friend who is now a doctor running a nude therapy group on the West Coast:

> I tell him I've been to the edge
> of myself a few times,
> and the atmosphere there is rarified
> and terrifying.

The speaker asks what it is like to live on the edge, the way his way-out friend does, and the friend replies, "save your romantic bullshit / for some midwesterner." This startles the speaker into recognizing the safety of his position:

> solid ground beneath me, never a chance
> that the wild gesture you begin on Tuesday
> will be more than thin air
> on Wednesday.

His friend talks about

> the price
> of ecstasy,
> the fact that there's no middle
> where he is.

Listening to him on the phone, hearing the seagulls cry in the background, the speaker wants "to let myself drift / out of control." This is a yearning that shows up fairly regularly in Dunn's poetry in one version or another from book to book because, for the most part, Dunn has apparently led the safe life, as most people do. We expect insanity from poets, and this places a special pressure on him, writing in the 1970s, still so dominated by the mythic madness of Sylvia Plath, Anne Sexton, and Robert Lowell (two of the three died by suicide and the other of a heart attack at sixty). After he has returned to the East Coast, Dunn writes "Letter to Minnesota," enjoying being back but also recognizing the kind of Midwestern innocence he has lost. He finds that "I, as always, am somewhere / in between myself and the dreams of myself." In the middle section of the book, there is suddenly a new awareness of bodies: bodies in bed, the pregnant body of his wife, human bodies, animal bodies, "a quiet ceremony of tongues" ("Those of Us Who Think We Know"), along with "jelly fish running out / of breath on the sand" ("The Dark Angel Travels With Us to Canada and Blesses Our Vacation"), and sitting in a bar with "the musk of sex still on him" ("In the Afternoon"). It seems to be a kind of magic time, connected with love and fecundity and nature. His two daughters are born, and he celebrates them in "For Fathers of Girls":

> Suddenly we are fathers
> of girls: purply, covered with slime
>
> we could kiss. . . .

The life lived close to nature and the daily confrontations with herons and cranes ultimately lead him to wonder in "A Private Man Confronts His Vulgarities at Dawn":

> . . . how
> to cherish all of this,
>
> and just how many debts
> a body is allowed.

In the book's final section, he seems to be summing up who he is at that moment in time, starting with deaths and how he has greeted them in his life to date: "And always the stillness that is not / a stillness when the news comes" ("Deaths"). He then writes poems about his grandmother's stroke and his father's death and, in "Grandfather," about his grandfather, who would read and drink gin at night "until numb enough to sleep," leaving as his legacy the image of "the tough guy / who read books." Dunn is gathering his family wisdom, so that "Rewrite" begins, "Our children cannot save us," moving on in the next stanza to the recognition that "we must not try to save them." He is on some kind of quest, and it requires odd gestures, as in "The Visitant":

> You try to shake the hand of the small boy
> who lives within you,
> but it's buried in the deep
> debris of adulthood

His imagery grows richer in this attempt, finding on revisiting his old home

> . . . locks strewn on the floor,
> keys still in them like men
> who've had heart attacks in women.

In his next two collections, *A Circus of Needs* (1978) and *Work and Love* (1981), Dunn continues his quest for the meaning of things—not the obvious meaning, of course, but the meaning that requires hard work and honesty to uncover, a meaning that is slightly uncomfortable. As a father he is aware of how the changing world may affect his sleeping child, recognizing in "Midnight" that

> Someday I'll have to tell my daughter
> about the Bronx
> before she walks through it,
> though the Bronx might be everywhere
> by then.

And for him, the Bronx has become "The larvae of thieves in the gutters." In "Essay on Sanity"

he is continuing to find out who he is and what he believes: "I am tired of hearing the insane / lauded for their clear / thinking." In "The Rain Falling Now," he tells us that what interests him is animals "that stare from the darkness, / the ones that hold back." This personae ("I") is both Dunn and not Dunn, for as he said in an interview for *Cortland Review:* "Because I've most often composed poems in the first person, it's been crucial to think of myself as a fictionist as opposed to someone who's just eliciting what's happened to him." He goes on to explain, "I use the vehicle of the first person to help make credible what might be the experience of others or some conflation of my own experiences glazed by imagination." But, most important, he asserts, "At all cost, I try to avoid the solipsisms of the untransformed self."

Still, it seems as if in these collections he is telling us more about himself and those around him. In "My Brother's Work" he writes:

> My brother who will not leave
> his job wonders how Gauguin left
> the world and found himself
> on the other side of it.
> "What *balls,*" he says, "braver
> than a suicide."

In the poem "Hard Work 1956," about working at a Coke plant at the age of seventeen, he brings us the parental wisdom: "hard work, my father said, / was how you became a man." These are pieces of personal life transformed in context into the large puzzle of life. He even addresses the reader in "Poem for People Who Are Understandably Too Busy to Read Poetry":

> You see, I want this poem to be nicer
> than life. I want you to look at it
> when anxiety zigzags your stomach
> and the last tranquilizer is gone.

Dunn is a very conscious poet, in what he reveals and what he does not reveal. He is a man who will later claim, "I never discuss my own life without a mask. And there's often a mask beneath the mask."

Not Dancing came out in 1984 and continues Dunn's fascination with polarity and opposites, as in the opening poem, "Corners," about the meaning of corners:

> I've sat in corners at parties hoping for someone
> who knew the virtue
> of both distance and close quarters, someone with a
> corner person's taste
> for intimacy, hard won, rising out of shyness
> and desire.

This is the essence of Dunn: the desire for both distance and close quarters. As he says in "Blues for Another Time,"

> I knew twins who hated each other,
> but wore matching clothes.
> That's the way things are, I know.
> That's as clear as they're likely to get.

In "Legacy," Dunn is still taking up the legacy of his original family, still dealing with his long dead father:

> Nights he'd come home drunk
> mother would cook his food
> and there'd be silence.
> Thus, for years, I thought
> all arguments were silent
> and this is why silence
> is what I arm myself with
> and silence is what I hate.

He recognizes the dangers of these experiences of family intimacy and family despair. "The Routine Things Around the House" begins,

> When mother died
> I thought: now I'll have a death poem.
> That was unforgivable.

The plight of the poet can be located in this excessive self-consciousness and hyperaware-

ness of possible betrayals. Dunn addresses this very issue in an essay titled "Degrees of Fidelity" in the *Mid-American Review:* "My experience as both a writer and a reader has convinced me that most poems about family should be put in a locked cabinet. . . . Beware the poet who values content more than handling of content, a danger especially present in our most personal poems." He also realizes, "The dead free us as much as the living constrain us." Ultimately, it would seem, Dunn can have it both ways: "As poets our fidelity to people we know is always complicated by our fidelities to the poem . . . not to mention to truth itself."

Published in 1986, *Local Time* begins with "Round Trip," a nine-page poem, which is long for Dunn. The journeys are several: out to the prairie, back to the east, into the city (where he is mugged), and then in "a rented cabin up north." But that summary takes into account only the physical level, and Dunn's poem suggests that we read the metaphysical in the physical "because mood invents landscape," and therefore the flatness of the prairie can turn "irredeemable" until finally one wishes "for an edge again." The protagonist of this poem, the "I" voice, is engaged in "trying to build / a house of cards amid a house / of people." But he comes to recognize, "One should be alone / to build a house of cards":

> . . . One should have none
> of the clutter that comes
> from living a life.

Of course, he is engaging in playful allegory. Everything means something in this story. And within the story he imagines other stories, stories within stories, like the traveler on a ferry making a dull trip off-season but knowing that when the story is told,

> . . . We'll make our friends
> wish they were us, we'll replace experience
> with what we say.

This poem guides us toward an understanding of art: the reordering, the disguises, the mixed motivations, and the subtle shifts. This cunning is not merely for purposes of misleading "our friends" or other people; rather it is part of the strategy for holding things together in an unsafe and precarious world. In the final section of the poem, for example, someone he knows has died, and he receives three phone calls informing him. In his poem "Halves," Dunn writes of how we lie in bed awake in the morning, but

> We keep out eyes closed as long as we can,
>   hang on to the vestiges
> of night as if we were balancing
>
> two delicate and always vanishing halves.

It is this liquid sense of life's endless slippage that exists in many of Dunn's poems through the years.

Several poems in this collection take up the theme of what goes on between men and women, their closeness and their incomprehension. In "He/She," Dunn writes of the woman, perhaps his wife, who

> . . . argues beyond winning,
>   screams indictments
>   after the final indictment.

It is as if she does not know the rules of fair combat, does not know what he learned in the schoolyard: "you choose carefully, or you choose war" and "one word too many meant / broken fingers, missing teeth." In "After the Argument" he admits they have a "stupid / unspoken rule": whoever speaks first loses. And so they dance around each other, sleep for a night in different rooms, although they cannot "stand hating / each other for more than one day." The poem "Long Term" turns on the idea that "everything that can happen between two people / happens after a while."

Dunn even has a poem, not one of his best, on the unspoken subject of menstruation, called "The Gulf." He remarks how

>   it enters his life
> monthly like a bill from an old creditor
>
> who sometimes overcharges. . . .

Dunn is the sensitive and confused male in this series of poems. His behavior is not so sensitive that he might not be perceived by women as overly reserved or incapable of understanding female issues—typical complaints lodged against men—but it is sensitive in his very recognition of his role as insensitive male. These poems manifest attitudes and issues particularly tied to their time, when, after women's liberation, all the old bargains between men and women were being renegotiated.

Between Angels (1989) is organized in three sections, labeled "Leavings," "Variations," and "Urgencies." There is a playful tone throughout much of this collection that is not always successful; certain poems begin to sound a little too self-assured and at the same time distant. Frequently, in the second section, Dunn uses "he" instead of "I" in the little tales he relates. The reader suspects it is still "I" but a protected ego, one that disowns the seriousness of the discoveries in such poems as "The Man Who Closed Shop," "Letting the Puma Go," "Luck," and "His Music." At his best, in poems like "On the Way to Work" or "Tenderness," he continues to develop the speaker who is really an adventurer, willing to be hurt and therefore alive to possibility. Dunn's most successful poems are not merely neat or clever, but rather they are trips down a road with no road signs. In "On the Way to Work" a driver discovers someone ahead of him with the bumper sticker "Life is a bitch. And then you die." He wants to see who it is, and he speeds up and finds a woman in her forties, smoking. She has short hair, no makeup, and "A face that had been a few places / and only come back from some." The speaker is moved:

> . . . I smiled
> at her, then made my turn
> toward the half-life of work.

Thus he echoes her sentiment "Life is a bitch," but now they must part. "And I had so much to tell her / before we die," sensing that for them there would be no knowing where such talk would stop. The poem has the feeling of Robert Frost's "Road Not Taken," in an infinitely more ironic mode.

In "Tenderness," Dunn tells the story of an early romance; he was twenty-three and the woman thirty-four, mother of two and wife to a man in prison who had abused her. As Dunn writes: "All she knew of tenderness / was how much she wanted it." He comes to her relatively inexperienced sexually but ready to learn "What it feels like to feel just right." She is pleased with him as a lover, finding him tender, and he admits, looking back,

> . . . I think it was terror

> at first that drove me to touch her
> so softly . . .

But he moves on to selfishness, recognizing the benefit to himself of provoking her loving response; finally, he tells us his tenderness became "motiveless in the high / ignorance of love." The phrase "the high ignorance of love" is one of those moments when Dunn's poetry takes a leap cognitively and emotionally. He shows us what we somehow already know: that love is ignorant. In that ignorance, rightly respected, lies bliss. He notes that when that relationship ended, "I had new hands and new sorrow," and as a man he had changed, not in the direction of heroism but toward knowledge.

In this collection Dunn is trying to figure out through poetry just what it means to be human and therefore flawed. In a poem entitled "Kindness," he wonders just how self-motivated kindness is, whether in Manhattan or the cold, desolated winters of Minnesota. Soon he announces, "Kindness of any kind shames me" because it reminds him of what he has not done. He does not stop there; he remembers a woman whom he once met in Aspen who was so kind that he was compelled to test her, driving her at last to cut him off. After thinking about the poet James Wright's remark that the hearts of men are merciless, he decides that "any kindness is water turned / to wine." Ultimately, he ends up questioning the worthiness of the recipient because the stranger in him knows "what strangers need." The twisting and turning of this poem are characteristic Dunn, the man who seeks to see all sides of a subject before he lands. Even his landing, at last, is open to interpretation. He is not seeking the easy or comfortable answer. This may explain the title poem, "Between Angels," a kind of metaphysical position he finds absurd because it places him always between choices. There is the sense that he both minds and does not mind being thus stuck, that he "cannot bear / living like this" but also that "everything's true / at different times," so he can indeed bear it.

Landscape at the End of the Century (1991) is an uneven collection, often expressing that sense of transience and mild foreboding suggested by the title. Time is passing, but these poems ask, What does it mean? In his first poem, "Allegory of the Cave," he refers to the sunlight "and violence of history, encumbered / by knowledge." This is our contemporary human plight, and, as he says in "Update," "once upon a time / there was a God." In the same poem, addressed to Herman Melville's character Bartleby the scrivener, Dunn points out from a future vantage point,

> and here's what you've spawned:
> drop-outs, slackards,
> and a kind of dignity, . . .

He concludes in his explanation of our times:

It's the end of the century;
almost everyone dreams of money
or revenge.

Now there is cynicism as well as truth. Dunn's dark vision of that overused concept the "American Dream" boils down to dollars and rage. If one were to have watched television or read the newspapers around 1990, Dunn's lines would probably have represented a fair assessment of the culture.

In such a mood Dunn is still very aware of his own truths and is ready to tell them without mystery. In "What They Wanted," he says, "I told them: find out who you are / before you die," a message that goes back to Socrates and the ancient Greeks. "I said life is one long leave-taking," another perception not centered on either money or revenge. In fact, money and revenge seem to be the furthest things from his consciousness. Rather, he is a seeker after experiences that are much more delicate, humorous, even outlandish. When he is out on the road or at the mall, he hopes to discover "an equal lover / of the discordant." "I'd rather be related to that punky boy / with purple hair," he asserts,

than talk with someone who doesn't know
he lives
in "*Le Siècle de Kafka,*" as the French

dubbed it in 1984. . . .

In this poem, "Smiles," he is at a time of life when the absurdity of things is starting to overwhelm him, and he is stuck in a particularly foolish bureaucratic snafu. He finds that the solution that pleases the state is why he is lonely

for the messiness of the erotic, lonely

for that seminal darkness that lurks
at birthday parties, . . .

This poem pulls various motifs together in an effective recognition of how fragile life is and therefore how delicious in its fragmentation and yearning.

Occasionally, there is a poem simply too obvious or repetitive of old themes and perceptions, like "Ordinary Days" or "Working the Landscape," which reads more like an essay than a poem. This is always the risk: that the poet will grow too fond of his own perceptions and ignore the ambiguities that lead to genuine revelation. Happily, these slips into the predictable or the overly clever are rare, and a poem like "After the Resolution" redeems the whole collection. Here he plays with the idea of wanting to live his life as if he had only one year left. In this mood, "his work, for example, / awaited him like an open mouth." But soon he discovers something deeper, "the call of sleep," which he finds "nearly as strong / as death." Awake from his dreams, in an ecstasy of commandment breaking,

He wanted to steal other men's wives.
He wanted to pick locks
and enter and destroy and rearrange.

As the poem builds toward his conclusion, he returns to a favorite motif, "Doesn't the soul tire / of decency?" It is only midday, and he finds that he needs courage even to get dressed. Looking outside, he sees the poem's final image,

. . . A few cruel birds
took over at the feeder,
bluer and handsomer than all the rest.

He achieves here the felt experience of life; he does not arrive at a moral place or a great insight. Instead, he recognizes his own dark side and desires and then sees, perhaps, in the handsome bluebirds something that speaks to him—something he does not need to name.

In 1994 Dunn's publisher, Norton, brought out *New and Selected Poems: 1974–1994,* an indication of his increasingly significant place in the poetry world. Dave Smith wrote in *New England Review,* "Those who have known Dunn's books will welcome this omnibus of artful talk. Those just discovering him will have the best of it." Daniel Hoffman commented for the book's jacket, "Stephen Dunn is one of the most accessible and pleasure-giving poets now writing. His work is inimitable." The new poems are few, mainly "The Snowmass Cycle," which Dunn has admitted in an interview is one of his personal favorites. It is a series of mountain-inspired meditations, in which he observes himself and the outer world. The subjects include retreat, solitude, and the body, with such perceptions as this:

I knew a man who said he could dominate
solitude. In other ways, too,
he was a fool.

He closes with a certain kind of knowing:

Before a person dies he should experience
the double fire
of what he wants and shouldn't have.

He has earned this affirmation from his willingness to experience the empty and the full, the pretty and the corrupt, the "chosen uprootedness, soul shake-up, / every day a lesson" that marks this cycle.

Dunn's 1996 collection *Loosestrife* opens with two epigraphs, the second of which, from the modern dancer and choreographer Martha Graham, reads, "There are times when we find no warmth in our culture and then we become a little mad with the desolation of the heart." This recognition of certain "times" apparently spoke to Dunn in his early fifties. The book is divided into four sections but opens with a poem set off by itself, "Solving the Puzzle." In it the speaker throws one puzzle piece away to make the other pieces fit. He interprets this letting-go gesture as meaning "No expectation of success now, /

none of that worry." These lines reek of both middle-aged rationality and Graham's "desolation of the heart." Lowering expectations—is that the name of the game in midlife?

The poems that follow suggest a kind of self-assessment that goes with reordering priorities and throwing puzzle pieces away. After all, as that poem concludes:

Something in the middle, though,
was missing.

It would have been important once.
I wouldn't have been able to sleep
without it.

We must conclude that now he can sleep with the imperfect puzzle. His sleep is sometimes disturbed, however, as in the poem that begins:

Just before he woke a voice said,
"You've been a coward
in matters of the heart."

This poem, called "The Voice," scratches away at this insecure feeling, this sense of diminishment that can come to one between sleeping and waking.

In a poem appropriately titled "Diminuendo," he suggests, "each felt the dull courage that comes / from caring less." A couple sits at a café, "neither fully present," and his

. . . mind cut loose
from his heart
like a dingy in cold, still water.

Here is one of those perfect Dunnian images: exact, alive, and perceptive. There is a new, more sophisticated tone here, as the couple sits on until

A sudden breeze uplifted their napkins,

but that was all there was of action.
It was time to go;
one of them, soon, would say so.

That biting rhyme at the end is almost Henry Jamesian in its unsaid saying. The poem presents the horror show of life lived in the diminuendo mode, a modern reworking, perhaps, of Robert Frost's "Oven Bird" (which ends, "The question that he framed in all but words / Is what to make of a diminished thing"). And as Dunn continues to pursue these unspoken rules of diminished life, the next poem, "After Making Love," opens with the remark "No one should ask the other / 'What were you thinking?'" He suggests that all one will hear about is the past "or the strange loneliness of the present." He goes on to admit, "Some people actually desire honesty," but then he dismisses them:

They must never have broken

into their own solitary houses
after having misplaced the key,

never seen with an intruder's eyes
what is theirs.

Here Dunn enters the somewhat disorienting world of Raymond Carver's short fiction: in Carver's story "Neighbors," a couple does intrude into their neighbors' home, trying on their clothes, drinking their liquor, and fantasizing on their bed while supposedly engaged in apartment watching and cat care. Both Carver and Dunn recognize the vaguely underwater quality of life in America, the slightly surreal world of marriage and divorce (although Dunn is a long married man).

It seems that at this point in his poetic career Dunn is also ratcheting up his poetic style. He writes in "Alert Lovers, Hidden Sides, and Ice Travelers: Notes on Poetic Form and Energy" (from *Walking Light*), "Form to me implies an alertness to the demands of your material and an orchestration of effects. It is some happy combination of the poet's intent and the poem's *esprit*. . . . And we'd like to have some control after we lose control." In the poem "Tucson," he writes of a bar fight:

> . . . I'd forgotten
> how fragile the face is, how fists too
> are just so many small bones.
> The bouncer waited, then broke in.
> Someone wiped up the blood.

He is bathing in alliteration here. The speaker's friend comments, "it's a good fighting bar, you won't get hurt / unless you need to get hurt." This collection is filled with such gems. Dunn's style is stripped down and utterly effective. David Baker sees in *Loosestrife* "a darker book than his others, and the flower of its title, the purple loosestrife, is a pertinent totem," because, as a rugged, beautiful, non-indigenous plant, it has become "a contagious invader, hated by gardeners, taking over suburban wetlands." Dunn's poetry, Baker says, makes known the "terror . . . of a similar invasion into privacy and coherence. . . . The most revealing invasions of Dunn's cosmos are those brought about by self-knowledge." Baker is alert to a continuing theme in Dunn's work, evident right from the first collection: the self confronted with the self.

The tone of the *Loosestrife* poems is complicated; there is the usual digging and asking questions, but the mode is more critical even than usual, more aware of life's judgments. To the question concerning what he would give "to be perfectly understood," the response is this: "Who would want to know me then, / he thinks, who could forgive me?" As Baker points out, the self-knowledge in Dunn's work is "likely to yield shame, guilt, meagerness of spirit." It is not a state of mind, however, in which he stays. As Baker insightfully notes, "Being opposed has become Dunn's trademark circumstance— that is, being resisted or contested, as his many poems of invasive damage establish, but also of being doubled, being composed of contrary wills or fates." This being the case, Dunn is always looking to the opposite meaning of anything he first encounters, as in these lines from "Ars Poetica":

> I'd come to understand restraint
> is worthless unless
> something's about to spill or burst . . .

In "Heaven," he explicitly states, "It always made perfect sense, / feeling things at least two ways." Occasionally, Dunn makes reference to what is going on in the world at large, images from the television:

> Bosnians, Sudanese, flicker into our lives,
> flicker out. To think of them is to lose
> any right to complain.

Where he lives, he observes on a more mundane level in the poem "Parameters," "All of us separating our trash— / no easier way to feel virtuous." Dunn refuses the easy solutions of the late twentieth century; in a poem addressed to an unknown recipient, "Because You Mentioned the Spiritual Life," he announces, "The spiritual life, I'm thinking, is worthless / unless it's another way of having a good time." In the midst of "Fishing boats and sea air," he will not pretend to any spiritual longing that rises above the earthly pleasures. The closest he can come is peeling an orange and acknowledging, "What a perfect thing an orange is / to think about." This poem ends with the Zen perception "Moments / are what we have."

The collection itself concludes with the long work "Loosestrife," a poem in ten parts. Dunn's poems generally run about a page to a page and a half in length, so this one steps outside his usual method. It is a meditative poem, moving back and forth between nature and weather on the one hand and the human response to them on the other: the man in the landscape. The landscape here is South Jersey, and where Dunn lives is marshland not far from the ocean or from Atlantic City, with its slums and casinos.

He takes us through the winter, an oddly warm one, and the spring. He is aware of changes in himself and those around him: "Our hearts: / caged things, no longer beating / for the many." In a sense he takes a journey through the weather and the landscape to comprehend the meaning of this time and place. When a false spring arrives in March, the daffodils are deluded into blooming too soon and meet their death in a frost. He notes of the humans, "we stripped down, got colds." And from this, the shared plight of the humans and the daffodils, he recognizes:

> Heraclitus, I want to say, I've stepped
> into the same stream twice,
> and everything felt the same.

Finally, the speaker moves toward reconciliation. In response to a student's query about why he, the well-known poet, goes on living in South Jersey, he replies: "Because it hasn't been imagined yet." He understands that "Where he saw nothing, I saw chance." Being Dunn, however, the speaker is not sure that he has talked long enough to get it "true."

In 1998 Dunn published an uncharacteristic work, a collection of what he called "Prose Pairs" in a book entitled *Riffs & Reciprocities*. These brief prose pieces—each a single paragraph in length—came out of a request from a friend. As the work developed, he began to see the paired paragraphs as extensions of his poetry; here, too, he tries "to pin down an abstraction or breathe a personal life into it," as he says in the introduction. He goes on to say, "I was attracted by such vehicles for meditation and exploration, and the compositional pressures they exerted to make every sentence count." It is as if he is falling into competition with himself, the lone basketball player shooting hoops. Because they are pairs, part of the fascination is "with how I might make different ideas, claims, and stories rub up against and inform each other." It was a spontaneous process: "I rarely began a paragraph knowing what the next paragraph would be."

This format turned out to be peculiarly suited to Dunn's mind given that his poetry reveals an ingrained tendency to look at almost anything from at least two angles, and often those angles prove to be opposites. He gets to play with all the crazy and sane ideas passing through his consciousness; like a jazz musician, he goes on riffs. His paragraph on "Technology" concludes, "The light bulb changed the evening. The car invented the motel." This blaze of solid recognition leads in its paired piece, "Memory," to this admission: "More and more I forget what I need, and remember what I'd like to forget." Then he passes on to "Memory's law: what we choose to say about our past becomes our past," a particularly enlightening perception for a poet.

In the year 2000 Dunn published *Different Hours*, the collection that won him the well-deserved Pulitzer Prize. After all, he has carved out a large territory of serious American poetry, which is also sometimes vastly amusing and witty and honest beyond the norm. His style has not changed a great deal over the years, but he has honed it to a more consistent, fine patina of control and simple elegance. G. E. Murray writes in *Southern Review* of Dunn's "conversational style, no doubt hard-earned, but in its effect so casual, apropos and compelling that it quietly surrounds the reader with recognitions that both inform and surprise." Murray also mentions "the continuing tensions that make Dunn's insights so viable" and, "as always, a delightfully taut lyricism." Writing in *Poetry*, Bill Christophersen finds in Dunn's poetry "an unpretentious language that nonchalantly invests the mundane with meaning." He comments on how a "distrust of truth, self, and other would-be absolutes nags at the speaker. . . . In *Different Hours* the chaotic world beyond the topiary intrudes repeatedly, schoolyard murders and friends' divorces crowding in on the speaker's awareness."

Most critics hear Dunn's voice in *Different Hours* resonating with a lifetime's experience, and yet it maintains its modesty. In fact, one could call Dunn a genius of modesty. He is like a fine instrument whose sound has improved with the years. This is clearly his best collection to date. The tone in these poems ranges from the sadly wise ("More and more you learn to live / with the unacceptable," from "Before the Sky Darkens") to the boldly assertive ("I've had it with all stingy-hearted sons of bitches. / A heart is to be spent," from "Sixty") to the gently world-weary ("Mendacity and love, high spirits / and gloom—nothing was new," from "Emperors"). Generally, there is a slight smile curling his lips, an acceptance of life in all its complexity and disappointment. Henry David Thoreau once wrote, "The mass of men lead lives of quiet desperation." For Dunn the truth lies well short of desperation. He sees life as a kind of long game in which one adopts various strategies for survival, and he does not wish to pretend otherwise.

The collection closes with a poem entitled "A Postmortem Guide," in which he makes an advance request to his eulogist:

> Do not praise me for my exceptional serenity.
> Can't you see I've turned away
> from the large excitements,
> and have accepted all the troubles?

It takes a brave and perhaps stubborn man to lay claim to such a legacy, but it is in "all the troubles" that life exists for most of us, and certainly those of us past the age of thirty-five. He goes on to suggest that for accuracy's sake, the eulogist should say "that [he] rarely went as far as [he] dreamed." Always, Dunn is compelled to be honest, to avoid the falsely heroic, the inauthentic.

CONCLUSION

Stephen Dunn stands, deep in his poetic career, as the long-distance runner who has prevailed.

Certainly, he has used his life as the raw material of his art, but he has artfully achieved a voice that goes beyond the purely personal to the unpretentiously archetypal. That is no easy task. As he wrote in his essay "Degrees of Fidelity," "The need to suppress can be the impetus to transformation, to ingenuity, to the virtue of indirection." What has consistently marked his poetry is a reverence for the truth, however messy or ignoble; the belief that a poem finds its wisdom in the course of being written; the use of clear, strong, ordinary language for non-ordinary perceptions; a love of storytelling; a sense of humor and irony that colors almost all he writes, even his most serious work; a delight in discovery of the surprises that lie in store for the metaphysical adventurer; and, finally, a refusal to back away from the painful, the conflicted, or the disappointing.

Because he is a man, the significance of being male in the twentieth century often seems to be the subtext of his poems. Whether the issue is relationships and attractions to women (and these are the subjects as well as the asides of numerous poems) or sports or driving or gambling or yard work, we feel his masculine angle of vision. It is not so much that he has a position on what it means to be male but rather that, as a male, his culture and his anatomy, of course, shape him in certain specific ways. Still, he is certainly not any sort of male stereotype. There is scant braggadocio in his work. He is too smart, too humble, and too self-aware for that.

In fact, Dunn is consistently bright, well read, witty, urbane, and conscious of life's complexity. He is hardly the ordinary man, yet when he writes his poetry, he gives himself over to his quest to say the thing truly, and he consequently eschews the overly clever, the arch, or the purposely mysterious. When he writes about nature, there is usually a human being in the picture. When he writes about human relationships, his speakers are inextricably immersed in the tasks of daily life. He still tends to walk lightly (like the title of his essay collection); such walking is his characteristic posture, physically and metaphysically.

Selected Bibliography

WORKS OF STEPHEN DUNN

POETRY

Looking for Holes in the Ceiling. Amherst: University of Massachusetts Press, 1974.

Full of Lust and Good Usage. Pittsburgh: Carnegie-Mellon University Press, 1976.

A Circus of Needs. Pittsburgh: Carnegie-Mellon University Press, 1978.

Work and Love. Pittsburgh: Carnegie-Mellon University Press, 1981.

Not Dancing. Pittsburgh: Carnegie-Mellon University Press, 1984.

Local Time. New York: William Morrow, 1986.

Between Angels. New York: Norton, 1989.

Landscape at the End of the Century. New York: Norton, 1991.

New and Selected Poems: 1974–1994. New York: Norton, 1994.

Loosestrife. New York: Norton, 1996.

Different Hours. New York: Norton, 2000.

PROSE

"Relations." In Philip E. Booth, *Trying to Say It: Outlook and Insights on How Poems Happen.* Ann Arbor: University of Michigan Press, 1996. (A 1985 interview of Booth by Dunn.)

Riffs & Reciprocities: Prose Pairs. New York: Norton, 1998.

Walking Light: Essays & Memoirs. New York: Norton, 1993. Expanded edition, Rochester, N.Y.: BOA Editions, 2001.

"Degrees of Fidelity." *Mid-American Review* 21, no. 1:69–72 (fall 2000).

CHAPBOOKS

Five Impersonations. Marshall, Minn.: Ox Head Press, 1971.

Winter at the Caspian Sea. With Lawrence Raab. Aiken, S.C.: Palanquin, 1999.

CRITICAL AND BIOGRAPHICAL STUDIES

Baker, David. *Heresy and the Ideal: On Contemporary Poetry.* Fayetteville: University of Arkansas Press, 2000.

Christophersen, Bill. "Down from the Tower: Poetry as Confabulation." *Poetry* 179, no. 4:217–225 (January 2002).

Corn, Alfred. "Between Angels." *Poetry* 155, no. 4:289–291 (January 1990).

Cramer, Steven. "Paying Attention—*Landscape at the End of the Century* by Stephen Dunn." *Poetry* 159, no. 2:111–116 (November 1991).

Doak, SuAnne. "Stephen Dunn." In *Dictionary of Literary Biography: American Poets Since World War II,* 2d series, vol. 105. Edited by R. S. Gwynn. Detroit: Gale, 1991.

"Dunn, Stephen." In *Contemporary Poets,* 5th ed. Edited by Tracy Chevalier. Chicago: St. James Press, 1991.

Holden, Jonathan. "Stephen Dunn and the Realist Lyric." In his *Rhetoric of the Contemporary Lyric.* Bloomington: Indiana University Press, 1980.

———. "Recent Poetry." *Western Humanities Review* 39, no. 2:162–164 (summer 1985).

———. *Style and Authenticity in Postmodern Poetry.* Columbia: University of Missouri Press, 1986.

Kim, Alfred. "Word for Word." *Sports Illustrated,* April 30, 2001, p. 28.

Kitchen, Judith. "New and Selected Poems." *Georgia Review* 49, no. 2:509–511 (summer 1995).

Krauss, Jennifer. "The Home and the World." *New Republic* 194, no. 22:39–41 (1986).

Kriegel, Leonard. "Urban Reflections: *Walking Light: Essays and Memoirs.*" *Sewanee Review* 102, no. 2:36–37 (spring 1994).

Kronen, Steve. "Earthly Quires." *Kenyon Review,* n.s., 13, no. 3:166–168 (summer 1991).

Libby, Anthony. "One Gives Us 'Happiness'; the Other, 'Gluttony.'" *New York Times Book Review,* January 15, 1995, p. 15.

Miltner, Robert. "Dunn, Stephen." In *Contemporary Authors,* New Revision Series, vol. 53. Detroit: Gale, 1997.

Murray, G. E. "The Collective Unconscious." *Southern Review* 37, no. 2:404 (spring 2001).

Nussbaum, Emily. "Different Hours." *New York Times Book Review,* August 19, 2001, p. 17.

Pack, Robert, and Jay Parini. *Introspections: American Poets on One of Their Own Poems.* Hanover: University Press of New England, 1997. (Includes a chapter by Stephen Dunn on his poem "The Guardian Angel.")

Smith, Dave. "Dancing through Life among Others: Some Recent Poetry from Younger American Poets." *American Poetry Review* 8, no. 3:29–33 (May–June 1979).

———. "Can We Talk? Welcome Poetries of Dunn and Dobyns." *New England Review* 17, no 2:147–165 (spring 1995).

"Stephen Dunn." In *Contemporary Literary Criticism,* vol. 36. Detroit: Gale, 1986.

"Stephen Dunn." *Richard Stockton College* (http://www2.stockton.edu/sdunn/).

Vendler, Helen. "In the Zoo of the New." *New York Review of Books,* October 23, 1986, p. 47.

Walker, Cheryl. "Premature Celebrations." *Parnassus* 6, no. 1:198–207 (fall–winter 1977).

Wilson, Robert F., Jr. "The Survival School of Poetry." *New Letters* 41, no. 4:103–107 (summer 1975).

Wojahn, David. "Short Reviews." *Poetry* 165, no. 4:221–224 (January 1995).

Yenser, Stephen. "Recent Poetry: Five Poets." *Yale Review* 68, no. 4:557–577 (summer 1979).

Zaleski, Jeff. "Different Hours." *Publishers Weekly,* November 20, 2000, p. 66.

INTERVIEWS

Dacey, Philip. "Interview with Stephen Dunn." *Cortland Review* (http://www.cortlandreview.com/features/00/03/index.html?jump), March 2000.

Farnsworth, Elizabeth. "Pulitzer Prize: Poetry." *Online NewsHour* (www.pbs.org/newshour/bb/media/jan-jun01/dunn_04-26.html).

Kitchen, Judith, and Stan Sanvel Rubin. "Only the Personal Matters: A Conversation with Stephen Dunn." *Literary Review* 30, no. 4:559–570 (summer 1987). Reprinted as "'Accumulating Observations': A Conversation with Stephen Dunn." In *The Post-Confessionals: Conversations with American Poets of the Eighties.* Edited by Earl G. Ingersoll, Judith Kitchen, and Stan Sanvel Rubin. Teaneck, N.J.: Fairleigh Dickinson University Press, 1989.

Pinsker, Sanford. "Acts of Clarifications: A Conversation with Stephen Dunn about Process and Poetry." *Missouri Review* 7, no. 1:59–68 (1983). Reprinted in his *Conversations with Contemporary American Writers.* Amsterdam: Rodopi, 1985.

Strauss, Robert. "Poets and Pulitzers, Such Is the State's Fate." *New York Times,* May 27, 2001, sec. 14, p. 3.

Thorndike, Jonathan. "Mysteries of the Main Highway." *Associated Writing Programs Chronicle* 25, no. 2:1 (1992).

—*VICTORIA D. SULLIVAN*

John Fante

1909–1983

*O*NCE ALMOST FORGOTTEN but today widely embraced in an international posthumous revival, the gritty and poetic novels and short stories of John Fante continue to carve out for their author an increasingly prominent niche in the pantheon of American literature. Two decades have passed since the independent California publisher Black Sparrow Press began to reissue Fante's early works, some of which had been out of print for more than forty years at the time of the writer's death in 1983. In those two decades Fante's reputation as one of the great outsider figures of twentieth-century letters, and as an unheralded forerunner of important subsequent literary developments, has steadily deepened and spread. The phenomenon of this revival is made all the more noteworthy by the virtual absence heretofore of corporate publishing support or academic canonization. Until the end of the twentieth century readers found their way to Fante largely on their own, by word of mouth and via the enthusiastic passing along of this or that dog-eared title from hand to hand and friend to friend. Now, at last, critical consensus is catching up with the popular conviction that John Fante's time finally has arrived.

In particular, *Ask the Dust* (1939), third in the quartet of novels known as the "Saga of Arturo Bandini," continues to establish itself as a modernist masterpiece, worthy to stand alongside the best work of such peers as Nathanael West and Sherwood Anderson. A tragicomic *künstlerroman* that is by turns hilarious and appalling, the novel blends a savage love story drenched in racial tensions and religious guilt with a self-reflective account of its impoverished and occasionally delusional young writer hero as he struggles against the economic, romantic, and literary odds in the garden-jungle of depression-era Los Angeles. The novel also offers readers an emotional tour de force of charged and nervy language that evokes an inspired, uncanny immediacy. As such, *Ask the Dust* captures the dizzying effects of youthful longing and despair that characterize the novel's protagonist, twenty-year-old Arturo Bandini. Those effects also are associated with the City of the Angels—the paradoxical city of concrete and dreams, smog and yearning—through which Arturo moves and with the soul of which his own soul must wrestle: "Los Angeles, give me some of you! Los Angeles come to me the way I came to you, my feet over your streets, you pretty town I loved you so much, you sad flower in the sand, you pretty town."

As impetuous and rhapsodic as it is plaintive and bittersweet, as violent as it is romantic, the book, in its bruising comedy, speaks to anyone who knows how it feels to be young and ablaze with unrequited desire, not to mention vaulting pride, worming shame, and the rest of youth's contradictions. Readers, in turn, respond. Speaking hyperbolically perhaps, but with the force of conviction—and on behalf of like-minded readers both here and abroad who would rush to agree—the renegade street writer Charles Bukowski once hailed *Ask the Dust* as the finest novel written in all time. Another aficionado of Fante's time and place, the screenwriter Robert Towne (famous for the 1974 movie *Chinatown*) has called *Ask the Dust* the best piece of fiction ever written about Los Angeles.

Such heartfelt encomiums aside, it is clear that many years after Fante died a washed-up B-movie scenarist, the distinctive voice of his published prose continues to influence younger generations of readers and writers, who revere him as the father and, indeed, the patron saint (as the novelist and screenwriter Michael Tolkin has called him) of the so-called Los Angeles school of writing. Fante also is recognized for several ancillary achievements. Perhaps first among them is the historically significant contribution Fante made to American regional and ethnic literature. In such clear-eyed depictions of early twentieth-century Italian-American family life as his first published novel, *Wait until Spring, Bandini* (1938), and the stories of his two collections, *Dago Red* (1940) and the posthumous *Big Hunger: Stories 1932–1959* (2000), it is now clear that Fante was breaking important ground toward the later maturation of a culturally diverse national literature. Throughout his life he would continue writing about the Italian-American experience, its joys and catastrophes and their frequently operatic intersections. His late novel *The Brotherhood of the Grape* (1977), one of his funniest, treats the Italian-American theme with special poignancy.

A second area in which Fante excelled was his satiric writing about Hollywood. Throughout his career Fante remained as much an outsider in the world of film as he did in Los Angeles literary circles. The critic David Fine observes, in *Imagining Los Angeles: A City in Fiction*, that Fante was, strictly speaking, "neither a Hollywood novelist . . . nor one of the hard-boiled boys in the back room," the critic Edmund Wilson's term for such Los Angelesque writers as Raymond Chandler and James M. Cain. And yet, thanks precisely to this marginalized position, Fante offers an original perspective upon the enterprise that through the years has seduced and compromised, if not destroyed, so many writers. In *Full of Life* (1952), he confects a

benign view of the screenwriting life, but in the late novella *My Dog Stupid* (in *West of Rome*, 1986) and in his last novel, *Dreams from Bunker Hill* (1982), he lays bare the absurd indignities to which a serious writer can be subjected when succumbing to the blandishments of inflated wages and industrialized glamour endemic to the industry. In these respects Fante knew whereof he wrote, for he suffered much those same indignities during a sporadically lucrative but mostly unfulfilling forty-year career as a contract screenwriter in Hollywood.

A third subtheme that weaves throughout the main of Fante's fiction has to do with Roman Catholicism—the conflicts, comedies, and consolations engendered by Mother Church. A youthful apostate from the faith of his birth, Fante never really broke free from his Catholic roots; indeed, he died in the good graces of the church, anointed with the oil and blessed with the holy water of the last rites. The tensions caused by this lifelong ambivalence inform virtually all of his works. As their titles suggest, many of his short stories deal directly—and seriocomically—with this ambivalence: "Altar Boy," "First Communion," "The Road to Hell," "The Wrath of God," "Hail Mary," "A Nun No More," and "My Father's God," among others. It is likely, in fact, that the deeply Catholic nature of Fante's whole body of work accounts at least in part for his long neglect in the eyes of critics, whose historical blind spot needs at last to be named and corrected.

The themes of the Italian-American ethnic experience, of Hollywood and Catholicism, are inextricably intertwined throughout Fante's oeuvre. It is in his trademark treatments of alienated youth and romantic overreaching set in the hard, yet palmy city of Los Angeles, however, that Fante's most important achievement arguably lies. In such tortured, exultant, and ultimately affecting confessional novels as *The Road to Los Angeles* (1985) and *Ask the Dust*, as well as in several of his other key works,

Fante can be said to have foreshadowed the Beat writers of a later era. He also must be acknowledged—though not in all cases of extra-literary excess held culpable—for tracing a direct line to what might be called the contemporary anti-school of letters once practiced most notoriously by Charles Bukowski and still today by an international cadre of Fante admirers in thrall to his on-the-pulse way of writing.

No matter how accessible and straightforward that way may appear, it must not be assumed that Fante was a natural, much less a naive writer. The chains of influence that lead forward from his work to the present moment connect backward as well. Specifically, Fante's early immersion, on the one hand, in certain mystical traditions of Roman Catholicism and his lifelong indebtedness, on the other, to such nineteenth-century masters of errant consciousness and psychological point as Fyodor Dostoyevsky and the Norwegian writer Knut Hamsun loom equally large in Fante's literary formation. Still, despite the depth and the breadth of his self-education in books, Fante was first and foremost an autobiographical writer. He unabashedly held up the mirror of his writing to the tumult of his own experience to focus the facts and then fictionalize the truth. And for Fante the truth always lay in the emotion. Thus, while his narratives of fractious home life and heady artistic ambition may appear to transcribe the unmediated realities of the life he lived, care must be taken to avoid identifying too closely the life and the works.

The reason for this caveat is that Fante also was unabashed and, indeed, frankly shameless about changing the realities of his experience to fit the aesthetic and, at times, the crudely commercial needs of his fiction. As a professional writer of fiction, of course, he had the perfect right to do so. At times, however, he went so far as deliberately to confuse the two, leaving it to others after him to tease out the distinctions. To appreciate the point and counterpoint of this writer's accomplishments, it becomes crucial to know the key events and dramatic contours of his life, for the life and the works help illuminate each other in sometimes surprising, always rewarding ways.

EARLY YEARS

John Thomas Fante was born on April 8, 1909, in Denver, Colorado, the eldest child in a poor Italian-American family of three sons and one daughter. His mother, Chicago-born Mary Capolungo Fante, was a pious and unassertive woman who suffered much at the hands of her alcoholic and spendthrift husband, Nicholas Peter Fante. A bricklayer by trade, the elder Fante was a native of Italy's mountainous Abruzzi region, the son himself of an alcoholic itinerant knife grinder. Fleeing the poverty of their homeland, Fante's father followed his father to America in 1901. For the next several years he shuttled between the "Mile-High City" of Denver and the upstart town of Boulder thirty miles to the north, finding enough work in the building trades eventually to bring his mother and sister to join him and his father. Though reunited, theirs remained a family torn by strife, for not only were father and son frequently drunk and in trouble, but the mother also was a hysteric given to frequent screaming tirades against America, where she felt imprisoned by the New World strangeness of it all.

In his first published novel, *Wait until Spring, Bandini,* John Fante etched his paternal grandmother in fictional acid as young Arturo's maternal grandmother, the embittered and vituperative Donna Toscana. In that same novel he presented rounder, more sympathetic versions of his father and mother in the respective figures of Svevo and Maria Bandini, the short-tempered bricklayer with a weakness for wine and women and his long-suffering, prayerful wife. In fact, Fante's childhood home life provided him with the foundations for many of the characters, settings, and situations to which he would return repeatedly in his fiction. Although he did not begin writing until he was in his early twenties, Fante blotted up the experiences of his formative years in a way only born writers seem to do.

Among these experiences was that of the dire poverty caused by his father's profligate ways. An inveterate gambler whose prowess at cards dwindled the more he drank, and vice-versa, Nick Fante's losing habit was responsible for the chronic lack of funds and even food that his wife and children were forced to endure. A lifelong brawler as well—as late as the age of sixty-two he was arrested for stabbing another man in a barroom fight—the elder Fante also could be publicly uncouth to his neighbors and physically brutal to the members of his own family. Although he earned decent wages and a well-deserved reputation for the quality of his masonry and his willingness to work hard, in many ways John Fante's father lived down to the image of the dissipated Italian—the "wop," the "dago," the "greaser"—then prevalent in racist attitudes of the day. The younger Fante thus learned at an early age the sting not only of American poverty but also of American prejudice. Growing up in Colorado at a time when that state's elective politics were infested with active Ku Klux Klansmen who hated the region's burgeoning immigrant Italian population as much as they hated the foreignness of Roman Catholicism, Fante had to withstand the triple brunt of his poverty, his ethnicity, and his faith. He would bear the scars of these experiences throughout his life, and his fiction would reflect them as well.

Despite constant financial hardships, Fante's mother saw to it that her children received a formal Catholic education at Boulder's Sacred Heart of Jesus School. There, Fante was inculcated with the tenets of the faith as well as the fundamentals of reading, writing, and arithmetic by the strict Sisters of the Blessed Virgin Mary.

He served as an altar boy, played sports, got in fights, and was in all a normal enough youngster, exhibiting no signs of early genius. His innate intelligence did show enough promise, however, that upon graduating from Sacred Heart he was accepted into Denver's pricey Regis High, a rigorous Jesuit prep school that agreed to a lower tuition in exchange for the promise of Nick Fante's bricklaying services. True to his ways, unfortunately, his father failed to uphold his end of the bargain. John Fante compensated for the shame of being his father's son by developing a ferocious competitive streak, first on the playing fields of the school's football and baseball teams and later in the boxing ring.

Counterbalancing this physical drive was the life of the spirit to which Jesuit tradition led Fante. During his grammar school years under the nuns, Fante learned all the popular Catholic devotions—confession, Holy Communion, the Mass, the rosary—but in his four years at Regis he absorbed the deeper habits of mind of Jesuit contemplative practice laid out in *The Spiritual Exercises* (1548), the influential meditation manual written by Ignatius of Loyola, founder of the Society of Jesus. As the critic Jay Martin has pointed out, the disciplined shaping of an interior life rich with the made structures of narrative contemplation later informed Fante's characteristic style of storytelling. Martin's observation leads to a striking assessment: "If Eliot and Stevens are our major American meditative poets, Fante is our major meditative novelist."

In the beginning Fante did well at Regis. While there, he also felt the call of the priesthood, and for a time he planned to follow up his high school graduation in 1927 by enrolling in the Jesuit seminary in Florissant, Missouri. Before he graduated, however, his faith was shaken by a perceived betrayal that contributed to his eventual estrangement from the church. One of the priests on the faculty, a trusted confidant to Fante, evidently one day made the mistake of calling him a wop, and Fante never forgave him. Fante's sensitivity to the issue of racial prejudice, coupled with a prickly awareness of the class tensions embodied by his presence at Regis among so many sons of privilege, soon drove him away from the church and toward an increasingly alienated rebelliousness. Following graduation—his ranking in the lowest third of the class attributable largely to his rejection of the Jesuit program—he moved back to his family's home in Boulder, where frictions between his father and mother were higher than ever.

An aimless Fante spent a couple of years alternating between reluctantly assisting his father at work—carrying hod, cleaning up job sites, so much backbreaking, brainless labor—and halfheartedly pursuing his formal schooling at the University of Colorado in Boulder. Unmoored from the stabilizing structures of his religion and the guidelines of Jesuit methodology and increasingly disturbed by the deterioration of his parents' marriage, Fante sought refuge elsewhere. He poured all five feet, three inches of himself into the physical rigors of the boxing ring, where, during Saturday night club fights, he routinely dished out ruthless beatings against larger, heavily favored opponents. And yet he also found his way to the public library in Boulder, where he undertook an equally aggressive self-education. Hungry to fill the emptiness inside him, he devoured the classics of philosophy, history, and literature. Without knowing exactly what he was doing, he was preparing himself, body and soul, for the coming decision to become a writer. Before he could make that decision, however, Fante had to suffer the other determinant betrayal of his young life, even more devastating to Fante than the first.

After years of neglecting the family with his drinking and gambling, Nick Fante finally deserted his wife and four children for another woman. With their mother on the verge of a nervous breakdown and the Great Depression bearing down upon them, the younger Fantes were left to fend for themselves. Unemployed, having flunked out of college, and increasingly estranged from the life all around him, John Fante found himself suddenly the man of the house. To his credit, if only in his way, the twenty-year-old Fante lived up to the Italian tradition that held the eldest son responsible for his family's welfare in the event of a father's death, disability, or disappearance. Rather than remaining in Boulder, the site of so much family suffering, Fante set out hitchhiking to California.

After a desperate period of vagrancy and starvation, he embarked on a series of odd jobs as an unskilled laborer in the warehouses and the fish canneries of the Los Angeles harbor. Like his father before him, he worked hard, and soon he was able to send for his mother and siblings to join him. Even as he eked out support for his family, however, Fante was developing a set of personal characteristics that would plague both himself and those around him for the rest of his life. Equal parts resentment, defensiveness, and braggadocio, this quirky bundle of explosive—and implosive—traits would also come to characterize the fictional alter egos that soon were clamoring to be created, most notably that of Arturo Bandini.

EARLY CAREER

Soon after moving to the West Coast, Fante began writing in earnest. He was encouraged in this direction by H. L. Mencken, with whom Fante had initiated a lopsided correspondence in 1930. Prolific author, iconoclastic editor of *American Mercury,* and perhaps the nation's most influential man of letters at the time, Mencken responded laconically but with warmth to Fante's effusive and hot-blooded missives. Soon he came to occupy in the young writer's mind the double role of literary mentor and surrogate father. At Fante's most extreme, and signaling a deep-seated need to fill the void of his forsaken faith, the headlong young scribbler referred to Mencken in one letter as "the man who replaced the God Almighty in my heart." For his part, the understanding Sage of Baltimore kept Fante's hopes alive even while, in his professional role as editor, he politely rejected manuscript after manuscript. Increasingly obsessed with becoming a great writer, Fante persisted to the point of self-neglect. In one letter to Mencken, he described himself as "crazy with poverty and worry." In another he reported that while producing 150,000 words in one thirty-day siege of work he had lost thirty pounds, or a pound a day. Fante's commitment finally paid off when Mencken accepted his first story for publication. "Altar Boy" appeared in the August 1932 issue of *American Mercury,* and Fante's career, if only modestly, was launched.

"Altar Boy" is emblematic of many of the stories that Fante wrote throughout the 1930s. In it the young Jimmy Toscana tells of his rascal's experiences in Catholic grammar school and at home in the Boulder of Fante's boyhood. Sacrilegious mischief in church and classroom leads to petty after-school theft and the subsequent terrors of the confessional, as well as fear of a violent father. The story's tone is doubly ironic, for while church teachings and practices offer sturdy targets for satire as so many superstitious foibles, the narrator remains oblivious to his own naïveté, which is clearly conveyed to the reader. Thus, for example, when Jimmy tells of his mother's crying over his disappointment at getting a cheap secondhand bicycle for his birthday rather than the shiny new one he has been praying for, he ascribes her tears to mere religious sentimentality and not to the obvious hurt she feels for her beloved son in the face of his father's inability to be more giving.

Jimmy Toscana's narration is a central element unifying many of Fante's early stories. Whether or not Jimmy is named, however, all of the early stories are told in the same first-person voice of a young boy who shares not only Jimmy's rough-and-tumble outlook but also his interest in and sensitivity toward the fragile life of his family. The influence of Sherwood Anderson's *Winesburg, Ohio* (1911) is evident in the unpolished tone of this voice, the sensibility of which nevertheless evolves from the ironic lack of self-consciousness of "Altar Boy," "The Still Small Voices," "Jakie's Mother," "Horselaugh on Dibber Lannon," and "My Mother's Goofy Song," among others, to the growing self-awareness of "The Odyssey of a Wop," "Home, Sweet Home," "The Wrath of God," and "Hail Mary."

In "A Kidnaping in the Family" the speaker recalls an oedipal juncture with his parents that illuminates the interrelationship of innocent boy, uncaring father, and martyr-like mother. In an old trunk in his mother's bedroom the boy finds a photograph that enchants him. The photograph shows the boy's mother a week before she married, looking fresh and young and beautiful. Now worn down by the vicissitudes of a loveless marriage, the mother finally gives in to her son's insistence that she tell the story of his father's courtship. The story she tells, however, is so romantically exaggerated, so much like a fairy tale, that the reader is left to understand the truth that eludes the little boy, namely, that the sweet lie he has been told could be contradicted no more bitterly than by the reality of his mother's life. The story within the story of "A Kidnaping in the Family" sums up the relation between Fante's life and much of his life's work: fiction at once conceals and reveals the truth.

Like several other pieces dating from the early to the mid-1930s, "Bricklayer in the Snow" and "Charge It" are studies that eventually led to *Wait until Spring, Bandini.* In these stories the basic family unit of Fante's fiction—poor working-class Italian-American father, mother, and children—is depicted against the sometimes comical, sometimes wrenching conditions of their lives together. When the mortar-freezing Colorado winter makes work impossible for the bricklayer father of the former story, the laughable aspects of his irascibility turn first to brooding and then to bouts of violent frenzy that terrorize his wife and children. "Charge It" draws out the consequences of the father's unemployment in excruciating detail. In this story, also set in a cruel Colorado winter, the mother must go yet again to the neighborhood grocer to beg for basic foodstuffs to feed her children. As seen through the eyes of her eldest son, who narrates the story, the mother's shame is cause for a simmering anger at the inequities all about him. Like the story's point of view, which shifts between son and mother, this anger is not as sharply focused as it will come to be once the carefully rewritten story material finds its true expression as part of *Wait until Spring, Bandini*.

While he was developing his craft in such dress-rehearsal exercises as "Bricklayer in the Snow" and "Charge It," Fante also produced numerous first-rate stories that continue to stand on their own, including "A Wife for Dino Rossi," "Home, Sweet Home," "A Bad Woman," and "Washed in the Rain." Two of these tales, "One of Us" and "The Odyssey of a Wop," bear especially telling parallels to the underlying biographical facts. "One of Us" recounts the story of the death of Jimmy Toscana's closest cousin, a boy so similar to Jimmy in mien and manner that the two are known as the Twins. Early-twentieth-century Italian-American burial customs are brought paradoxically to life in the story's vivid rendition of the boy's wake, with the narrator's double laid out on a bed of ice in an open coffin in the middle of the family living room. Ten years before Fante wrote this story, his own Twin, a look-alike cousin named Mario

Campiglia from whom the young Fante had been inseparable, had been killed in an automobile accident. Fante had been haunted ever since by the mirror image of his own flesh and blood lying dead before him. Like many of his other stories, "One of Us" can be read on one level as Fante's way of dealing with deep-rooted experiences of psychological trauma by means of the age-old transformation of pain into art.

So, too, with "The Odyssey of a Wop." Here the narrator is older, having recently graduated from an unnamed Jesuit high school in Denver. In a series of thematically linked vignettes, the narrator recalls his unhappy education, from early childhood onward, in the harsh realities of American racism. Not least among these realities is the self-loathing with which he and his family must struggle as the objects of so many Italian-oriented acts of race baiting. Perpetrating these assaults are neighbors, classmates, a teacher who is also a priest—echo of Fante's time at Regis—co-workers, employers, and random passersby: a broad enough spectrum of American society to engender in the narrator a suspicion of the culture at large. As is typical in Fante's work, however, it is with himself and his own wounded feelings that the narrator is most concerned. More extensive social critique is left for the reader to extrapolate from the sharply individualist focus of Fante's perspective.

"The Odyssey of a Wop" moves from Colorado to Los Angeles, where, following his parents' reconciliation, Fante himself moved in 1933. Living alone in a series of cheap downtown rooming houses in the dilapidated area known as Bunker Hill, Fante endured a brief but memorable period of real poverty. During this time he became intimate with the seedy bars and desperate denizens of L.A.'s skid row, storing up the atmospherics for later use in his fiction. Even as he kept one eye on the long-range novelist's career that he imagined for himself while honing his early story-writing skills, he also was watching out for his more immediate needs. He thus did not hesitate when, on the basis of his reputation as a promising young author, he was offered a screenwriting contract with Warner Bros. in 1934. Soon Fante was pulling in the considerable depression-era salary of $250 per week by churning out what he would always consider mere Hollywood "piffle." His conscience was eased somewhat by the encouragement of Mencken, who pragmatically advised him to take advantage of the Hollywood system while he could. Thus began the lifelong fork in Fante's career that kept him divided between writing for a buck and writing, as Arturo Bandini puts it in *The Road to Los Angeles,* "for posterity."

THE SAGA OF ARTURO BANDINI

Arturo Bandini is Fante's most celebrated creation, the alter-ego protagonist of a four-novel cycle that includes *Wait until Spring, Bandini, The Road to Los Angeles, Ask the Dust,* and *Dreams from Bunker Hill.* These novels were written and published far out of sequence. Considered in the order given here, as well as in contextual relation one to another, they trace the developing line of Arturo's experiences, from the misadventures of a poverty-stricken boy in Colorado to the ordeals of an obsessed young writer in the lower depths of Los Angeles and, later, a failed contract scenarist in Hollywood.

In *Wait until Spring, Bandini* Arturo is introduced in his early adolescence, a pre-coming-of-age time in which he is forced to come of age by a crisis in the life of his family. Significantly, both family and crisis are modeled on Fante's own. When Svevo Bandini deserts his wife, Maria, and their three young sons for the wealthy Widow Hildegarde, first-born Arturo's world is turned upside down. It is winter in Boulder, always the hardest season for Maria but this year beyond even her formidable

powers of endurance. Normally warm and full of life despite the enormity of her husband's shortcomings, the abandoned wife and mother falls into an alarming state of emotional shutdown from which Arturo resolves to save her.

The novel's tripartite plot alternates between Svevo, Maria, and Arturo in their respective story lines, with Arturo's ultimately synthesizing the other two. Along the way Fante braids masterly characterizations with affecting interaction among the novel's principals, all against a thoroughly realized American backdrop. Thus, the comedy of Arturo's native-born exasperation at his father's old-world habits—slurping eggs through his mustache and swilling red wine—has its dramatic payoff in Svevo's self-incriminating befuddlement when faced with the class-defining delicacy of the Widow Hildegarde's tea and cookies. Not so delicate is the encounter that Maria must undergo with the heartless grocer, Mr. Craik, in a scene that fulfills the early promise of "Charge It." Even as the grocer doles out niggardly portions of cheap meat and flour against the hopeless arrears of her "wop" husband's line of credit, he belittles Maria for the very poverty from which she comes to him for help, further complicating her emotional crisis.

As with the themes of ethnicity and class, so, too, does the theme of religion play a central part in Fante's first published novel. Nuns drill their charges in the subtleties of the catechism, Maria prays her rosary until the beads shine, and the haunting peal of the chimes from the parish church that Svevo helped build with his own hands resonates with multiple meanings. For his part, Arturo is obsessed to the point of comical scruple over the problem of sin in all its variety: "Venial sins? Mortal sins? The classifications pestered him. The number of sins . . . exhausted him; he would count them to the hundreds as he examined his days hour by hour." And yet, when he discovers that the only way he can get his parents back together is by willfully committing a sin, he does not shrink from doing so. Like Huck Finn's decision to go to hell for helping the runaway slave Jim gain his freedom, Arturo's decision to save his family is steeped in the complex ironies of moral seriousness.

Those ironies deepen in *The Road to Los Angeles*. No longer an innocent young boy full of good intentions, the Arturo of this novel is eighteen, cynical and hopelessly entangled in the thickets of a harrowing passage from adolescence to adulthood. It should be noted that *The Road to Los Angeles* was the second novel Fante wrote under contract to the publisher Knopf, but as the first had been rejected in 1934, Fante was still writing in the novice's hope of using his fiction to tell the absolute, lacerating truth. Owing to his raw treatment of such controversial topics as race, sex, and religion, however, in 1936 Knopf also rejected this book, and Fante returned his attention to the stories that would become the more readily acceptable *Wait until Spring, Bandini*. Half a century ahead of its time, *The Road to Los Angeles* would not be published until 1985, three years after Fante died. It remains to this day an entrancing performance of manic energy and stylistic bravado, still capable of shocking.

Working on this book throughout the mid-1930s, Fante poured all of his frustrations and dreams into the combustible figure of eighteen-year-old Arturo Bandini. In the aftermath of his father's unexplained and strangely unmourned death—a telling imaginative response to the infidelity of Fante's own father—Bandini now works a series of ever more demeaning jobs in the Los Angeles harbor area to support his mother and younger siblings. His true ambition, however, is to be "the greatest writer the world had ever known." Here the lifelong influence on Fante of Knut Hamsun's great novel *Hunger* (1890), about a desperate young man bent on becoming a great writer, asserts itself for the first time. Like the pathetic hero of Hamsun's

masterpiece, Arturo, too, suffers from a pathological compulsiveness; soon his ambition deteriorates into a series of impossible fantasies that Arturo inflicts on anyone unlucky enough to cross paths with him. In his mind he writes earthshaking sociological treatises, philosophical tracts, and fictional epics that earn him a Nobel Prize. Such grandiose thinking enables him to survive humiliation after humiliation—as ditchdigger, dishwasher, warehouse flunky, grocery clerk, and fish cannery worker, not to mention self-abusing lover of pulp magazine pornography—but only at the cost of his connection to basic human sympathy. Cut off from fellow feeling for everyone around him and increasingly paranoid about his own ethnicity, Bandini sinks lower and lower into defensively racist behavior, verbally assaulting the "Spick sluts" and "slimy Oriental[s]" with whom he works at the cannery when they scoff at his literary pretensions.

Now an aggressively lapsed Catholic on a personal crusade against all religion, Bandini has become a sworn acolyte of the German nihilist thinker Friedrich Nietszche. As such, he rejects the common decencies as so much bourgeois claptrap, substituting for them a derisive mélange of mismatched ideas about the rights and privileges of the Superman-self. The contrast between, on the one hand, Bandini's ranting proclamations of his presumed superiority—to his terrorized mother and sister, to his bemused co-workers at the cannery, to uninterested strangers on the street—and, on the other, his increasingly abject failures provides the novel with much of its humor, which is thoroughly black and sardonic. Other stories dating from this period, and similarly raw in subject and tone, include "To Be a Monstrous Clever Fellow," "I Am a Writer of Truth," and the as yet unpublished "Fish Cannery."

By the time Fante came to write *Ask the Dust* during several months of hard-worked inspiration early in 1939, he was a seasoned professional and thus able to fit the extremity of his artistic vision within the demands of the literary marketplace. That extremity again plays itself out in the figure of Arturo Bandini. Now twenty years old and living alone in a rented room on Los Angeles's Bunker Hill, Bandini is striving to achieve his ambitions as a writer in the real world. True, that world still consists of much giddy dreaming about the tyro author's longed-for future success. At this point Bandini has published a single short story, "The Little Dog Laughed," in the revered J. C. Hackmuth's *American Phoenix,* a thin disguise for H. L. Mencken's *American Mercury.* Far from preventing fantasies of fame and fortune, this solitary success fuels those fantasies all the hotter. But unlike the utterly solipsistic Bandini of *The Road to Los Angeles,* the Bandini of *Ask the Dust,* while still an often overbearing egotist, also now grapples with the problem of human relationship and even romantic intimacy.

At the center of *Ask the Dust* and its saga of one young writer's frustrating fulfillment is the doomed love story of Arturo Bandini and Camilla Lopez. A poor but beautiful Mexican waitress with a fiery spirit and a temperament as mercurial as Bandini's, Camilla provides not only an attractive object for the young man's excessive romanticism but also a projected target for his own unresolved racial conflicts. Thus, in one breath Camilla is Bandini's "Mayan Princess," whereas in the next she is a "filthy little Greaser." Having learned firsthand the harsh effectiveness of racist epithet from his own experiences growing up, Bandini uses Camilla's aboriginal otherness to displace his own sense of displacement in a culture dominated by WASP attitudes and values. Despite this twisted objectification, he can stop himself neither from loving her nor from feeling remorse at his seemingly remorseless cruelty. Tossing in bed one night after yet another misguided attack on Camilla, Bandini recalls "the folks back home,"

> and I was miserable, for tonight I had acted like them. Smith and Parker and Jones, I had never been one of them. Ah, Camilla! When I was a kid back home in Colorado it was Smith and Parker and Jones who hurt me with their hideous names, called me Wop and Dago and Greaser, and their children hurt me, just as I hurt you tonight. They hurt me so much I could never become one of them, drove me to books, drove me within myself, drove me to run away from that Colorado town, and sometimes, Camilla, when I see their faces I feel the hurt all over again, . . . and when I say Greaser to you it is not my heart that speaks, but the quivering of an old wound, and I am ashamed of the terrible thing I have done.

Although Bandini speaks these words only silently and to himself, the feelings they evince are a far cry from his true heartlessness in *The Road to Los Angeles.* While it is just as daring an act of high-wire writing as that novel, *Ask the Dust* is also a far more studied achievement in the nuances of a character's evolution. Moreover, the deceptive simplicities of *Ask the Dust* in terms of both plot and prose mask structural elegances and emotional depths accomplished only in very great novels. Despair as he might about his failures with Camilla, about his dead-end situation, about his lack of stature and height and cold cash, again and again Bandini rises and soars on the hopeful rhapsodies of his own voice and nowhere more so than in his amateur's passion to write a great novel of his own:

> Six weeks, a few sweet hours every day, three and four and sometimes five delicious hours, with the pages piling up and all other desires asleep. I felt like a ghost walking the earth, a lover of man and beast alike, and wonderful waves of tenderness flooded me when I talked to people and mingled with them in the streets. God Almighty, dear God, good to me, gave me a sweet tongue, and these sad and lonely folk will hear me and they shall be

happy. Thus the days passed. Dreamy, luminous days, and sometimes such great quiet joy came to me that I would turn out my lights and cry, and a strange desire to die would come to me.

Thus Bandini, writing a novel.

Combining realistic urgency and poetic power, *Ask the Dust* stands as testimony to a talent that was coming into the fullness of an original American voice. In this, his third novel Fante had found his métier. He had embodied a character, the inimitable Arturo Bandini; ensouled a setting, the unattainable City of the Angels ("Los Angeles, give me some of you!"); and animated a theme, the irrepressible desire for love and beauty in a world that lacks too much of both. When the novel appeared in November 1939, critical responses were generally warm—the *Atlantic Monthly* offered up a positive comparison to the German writer Johann Wolfgang von Goethe's *Sorrows of Young Werther* (1774)—but *Ask the Dust* never matched the modest financial success of *Wait until Spring, Bandini* one year earlier.

The year before that, in 1937, Fante had married poet Joyce H. Smart, the beautiful blond Stanford University–educated daughter of an established northern California Anglo-German Protestant family. Because of the clash of their cultures and individual temperaments, however, the marriage was a turbulent one from the start. As time passed, Fante began to exhibit more and more of the faults that had made his own father an unsatisfactory husband, drinking and gambling to excess with such friends as the MGM story editor Ross B. Wills and the Los Angeles social activist and historian Carey McWilliams. As if acknowledging a fascination with his darker side, Fante identified these two in the dedication of his story collection *Dago Red* as "good friends, evil companions."

In three consecutive years Fante had published three first-rate works of fiction, evidence of a staggering creative pace. Now, at the onset of World War II, he embarked on a project that he felt certain would launch him into the front ranks of American writers, an epic novel that would do for the exploited Filipino migrant workers of the West Coast what John Steinbeck's *Grapes of Wrath* (1939) had done for their Oklahoma dust bowl counterparts. Toward that end he wrote two fine short stories, "Helen, Thy Beauty Is to Me—" and "Mary Osaka, I Love You," meant to fit into the novel. When Fante's editor at Viking rejected the first ninety-three-page manuscript of "The Little Brown Brothers" with the advice that Fante stick to the familiar material on which his reputation was building, Fante was crushed. His extended reaction amounted to a years-long binge of drinking, gambling, and golf. What little focus he had retained while working a brief stint for the San Francisco branch of the Office of War Information writing radio propaganda was now gone, and he resigned himself to doing Hollywood stoop labor on so many forgettable studio assignments. Earlier in the decade, Fante had worked on one very promising film project, *It's All True,* a daring semidocumentary omnibus conceived by the actor and director Orson Welles. But following the unprecedented success of *Citizen Kane* (1941), Welles was entering the long downward slide of his own career, and the project, including Fante's contribution, came to nothing.

In all, the 1940s passed in a blur. By the time the decade was over, Joyce had presented Fante with three children, two sons and a daughter, with another son soon to come. Thanks to a modest regular income from property Joyce had inherited, they all lived in a handsome house in a good part of Los Angeles, where Fante was reduced to writing formulaic stories for slick women's magazines—when he wrote anything at all. Although he had been on the verge of a major literary breakthrough at the beginning of the decade, by the dawn of the 1950s his books were all out of print, and Fante himself was nearly a forgotten entity.

LATER YEARS

Tensions between Fante and his wife came to a head in 1950, when Joyce issued an ultimatum: either start writing again or leave. Surprising even himself, Fante harnessed his concentration and quickly wrote a new novel about Arturo Bandini, now a prosperous Los Angeles screenwriter happily married to a beautiful blond Protestant wife who is pregnant with the couple's first child and also in the comical process of converting to Catholicism. When the termite-ridden kitchen floor of their California dream home collapses beneath her, the protagonist's colorful Italian bricklayer father moves in to make repairs, and the novel ends in a joyful resolution of faith, hope, and love.

The sunny domestic comedy was about as far removed from reality as Fante could have made it. True, Joyce had become a Catholic in 1948, but as she makes clear in *Selected Letters,* virtually everything else about their relationship was in shambles, and both "Joyce and Fante remained scarred by this period for the rest of their married life." Nevertheless, *Full of Life* appealed widely to readers, and for the first and only time in his career Fante had a best-seller. One reason for the book's success was the shrewdly marketed interest generated by the ambiguity of the protagonist's name. When his editor suggested a bait-and-switch tactic that he thought would improve sales by leading readers to take the novel for autobiography, Fante agreed to change the names of his central characters from Arturo and Emily Bandini to John and Joyce Fante. The formerly headlong young author bent on telling only the truth was now a wily pro, using his own name to manipulate the fictional pretense of nonfiction and pocketing the profits.

When Fante sold the film rights to *Full of Life,* he moved his family to a sprawling ranch home in the remote privacy of Point Dume, a beautiful spot on the Malibu coastline where theirs was the only house for miles around. It was the early 1950s, a disastrous time for the many writers then suffering the effects of the Red Scare and congressionally sanctioned communist witch-hunts. By contrast, having never involved himself closely in politics—"I shall not dirty my hands trying to save the masses," he once had written Mencken—Fante was entering an extended period of relatively steady employment with a number of major film studios.

Although he continued to be attached to mostly inferior projects, in 1956 Columbia Pictures released the film version of *Full of Life,* which, like the novel before it, proved a hit; for his own screenplay adaptation Fante was nominated for a prestigious Writers Guild Award. Having experienced hunger firsthand, Fante now valued the middle-class appurtenances of a living wage, but he never pretended to enjoy the process much less the profession of screenwriting, which he considered mere work for hire. Even when, in the late 1950s, his rising reputation took him to Italy and France to write film scripts for Dino De Laurentiis and Darryl F. Zanuck, Fante remained a novelist at heart, contemptuous of the film industry and those writers who subordinated themselves as artists to its box-office bidding. Naturally, this contempt cut both ways, for as long as he was not writing novels himself, Fante also was tormented with a gnawing sense of failure that he masked with a frequently abrasive demeanor.

These tensions sharpen the sad comedy of *My Dog Stupid,* the short novel that Fante worked on sporadically in the mid- to late 1960s. Henry Molise is a sold-out novelist turned screenwriter living out his late middle age on Malibu's Point Dume and facing the fact that he is past his breadwinning prime. Unable to get a studio job, saddled with four difficult teenage children, and married to a loving wife whom he nevertheless has grown too used to, Molise dreams of escaping his troubles by absconding to Italy, but he cannot bring himself to act out the fantasy.

When an oversexed lost dog strays into his life, Molise takes what solace he can in identifying with the beast while suffering the loss, one by one, of his brood of children as they grow up and leave home. Callused on the outside but sensitive within, Molise recognizes that to "write one must love, and to love one must understand." In the end, that is the life-enabling recognition shot through *My Dog Stupid,* an unsentimental love for family earned through the compassionate understanding of all the foibles that make any family its own deepest source of heartache.

Finishing *My Dog Stupid* was a personal triumph for Fante, for he had proved to himself that he could still write a novel. The triumph was short-lived, however. Even though he tried hard to place the book, he could not find a publisher, and the manuscript went into the same set of overstuffed file drawers that held the manuscript of *The Road to Los Angeles* and a growing number of aborted novels, unpublished stories, and rejected film scripts, teleplays, and treatments. Fante continued to take filmwriting jobs when he could get them, but for a man of his age in the so-called New Hollywood of the 1960s and 1970s, such jobs were increasingly hard to come by. Although he had been given the diagnosis of diabetes in 1955, Fante had done little to curb his appetite for rich foods and alcohol, and his health was beginning to deteriorate. In 1974, when the idea for a book that he had been struggling to write for more than twenty years again seized his imagination, he went back to the well of his artist's desire and produced one of his finest novels.

The Brotherhood of the Grape takes up once more with writer Henry Molise. Whereas, in *My Dog Stupid,* Molise had fantasized perversely about deserting his beautiful and loving wife, he now is forced to leave her in their Malibu ranch home while he travels to northern California in a quixotic bid to patch up the absurd half-century-long lovers' quarrel of his aging parents.

Again the comedy centers on the frailties of family and, in particular, the failing health of Nick Molise, Henry's incorrigible father, who refuses to acknowledge his own mortality and continues to drink and lay brick as he always has. Although Henry has come to save his parents' marriage—his mother claims to have found another woman's lipstick on her husband's underwear—the reluctantly dutiful son allows himself to be cajoled into helping Nick erect a brick smokehouse up in the Abruzzi-like mountains of the Sierra Nevada. There he watches his father die, or rather, as he soon comes to realize, he experiences a vision of the death that lies waiting within each precious second of life:

> Then a peculiar thing happened. My father died. We were working away, swirling in mortar and stone, and all of a sudden I sensed that he had left the world. I sought his face and it was written there. His eyes were open, his hands moved, he splashed mortar, but he was dead, and in death he had nothing to say. Sometimes he drifted off like a specter into the trees to take a piss. How could he be dead, I wondered, and still walk off and pee? A ghost he was, a goner, a stiff. I wanted to ask him if he was well, if by any chance he was still alive, but I was too tired and too busy dying myself, and too tired of making phrases. I could see the question on paper, typewritten, with quotation marks, but it was too heavy to verbalize. Besides, what difference did it make? We all had to die someday.

Later in the novel old Nick does indeed die, but the family survives, as intact as such a fractured family as the Molises can be, thanks to the profoundly comical emphasis on hope and love that pervades every sadness in the book. While the domestic comedy of Fante's earlier *Full of Life* has been branded "dishonest" by the critic Richard Collins, no such charge can be made against *The Brotherhood of the Grape,* which honestly earns its laughs—and its readers' admiration—every step of the way. One reader who especially admired the book was the filmmaker Francis Ford Coppola, who expressed his feelings by publishing the novel in his short-lived magazine *City*. Warmly prefaced by the screenwriter Robert Towne, who in 1971 had optioned the film rights to *Ask the Dust, The Brotherhood of the Grape* ran in five consecutive serial installments of *City* during the summer of 1975. When the book appeared in hardcover two years later, the novelist Larry McMurtry was moved in a *Washington Post* review to make favorable comparisons with both Dostoyevsky's *Brothers Karamazov* and Shakespeare's *King Lear*.

Despite all the creative energy that Fante had poured down the sinkhole of Hollywood script-writing over the years, he had rebounded to write a first-rate novel—and this time to see it published. His fiction had come a long way from the callow teeth-baring excesses of *The Road to Los Angeles;* indeed, viewed in the long context of his developing artistry, *The Brotherhood of the Grape* is not only Fante's most mature work but also his most generous and wisest.

FINAL YEARS

Although such prominent film talents as Coppola and Towne were demonstrating their appreciation for Fante during the 1970s, the largest part of this late interest in his work must be credited to the American small-press legend Charles Bukowski. Already famous internationally for his street-tough poems and novels of the American underside, the prolific Bukowski, in his 1978 novel *Women,* dropped an admiring aside about Fante. When Bukowski's publisher, John Martin of California's Black Sparrow Press, followed up on the hint and found a copy of *Ask the Dust* to read, he decided immediately to republish the book, convinced that here was a neglected American masterpiece. By this time Fante had fallen victim to the ravages of diabetes. After several painful operations he had lost his eyesight, and he soon also lost his legs

in a ghastly series of amputations. But Fante was so buoyed by the news of his early work's rediscovery that he set to work on one last novel.

The result was *Dreams from Bunker Hill*. Dictating the novel to Joyce, who took it all down in longhand on yellow legal tablets, the blind Fante returned in his mind to the time of his youth, when he was poor and struggling to become a writer in downtown Los Angeles during the bitter time of the depression. He also was returning to the figure of Arturo Bandini, the lightning rod for his most electrifying literary successes. Originally entitled "How to Write a Screenplay," *Dreams from Bunker Hill* traces Bandini's comical peregrinations from a pay-by-the-week rented room hard by the mean streets of skid row to the tawdrier haunts of Hollywood. Along the way Bandini works his way up from his job as a busboy in a downtown deli to a position as editorial assistant at a crooked literary agency and soon to a contract as an overpaid but frustrated screenwriter at Columbia Pictures. There on the lot among the real-life likes of the writers Ben Hecht, Dalton Trumbo, Nathanael West, and Horace McCoy, Bandini soon sees through the sham of Hollywood glamour and wishes for "the reality of Bunker Hill."

First, however, he must endure a gauntlet of embarrassments, insincerities, and outright betrayals at the hands of his employers, his colleagues, and his friends. When Helen, his beloved desk clerk at his beloved rooming house, breaks off their affair because she no longer can bear the sadness of being with a man thirty years younger than she, Bandini flees the maddening distractions of Hollywood for the idyllic refuge of Terminal Island in Los Angeles Harbor, where he rents a lonely little seaside cottage. There, amidst picturesque sandy beaches and pure ocean air, he resolves to get back to his serious writing. But one flight leads to the next in this novel, and when that resolution fails, Bandini returns to the Colorado town of his boyhood for a joyous reunion with his family. The most notable element of this reunion is the presence of Bandini's father: no longer dead or absent or, even worse, merely unbearable, as in so many other of Fante's works, the father here is central to the joy of Bandini's homecoming. He is evidence of the imaginative reconciliation Fante was driven to enact in his final novel between the two figures at greatest odds with each other in his earlier works. And thus one vital circle completes itself.

More vital still is the circle of Bandini's odyssey as a writer, for his real homecoming does not take place until he returns from Colorado to his cherished room in the Filipino hotel on Temple Street—"the smallest, most uninviting room in Los Angeles"—and begins again to write. Having forsaken the false attractions of Hollywood and at last having felt the true embrace of his family, Bandini is now ready to do what he is meant to with his life, namely, to write with the full measure of his heart:

> My thought was to write a sentence, a single perfect sentence. If I could write one good sentence I could write two and if I could write two I could write three, and if I could write three I could write forever. . . . I sat erect before the typewriter and blew on my fingers. Please God, please Knut Hamsun, don't desert me now. I started to write. . . . A man had to start someplace.

These were the last words of fiction Fante would ever write for publication. He was by now an old man and very ill; following the completion of *Dreams from Bunker Hill,* his health rapidly deteriorated, and he lived out his final agonizing months in the Motion Picture Country Home in Woodland Hills, California, where he died of pneumonia on May 8, 1983. After a funeral mass in the traditional Latin at Our Lady of Malibu church, what little remained of his once fiercely athletic body was buried on an obscure hillside in Culver City's Holy Cross Cemetery. More important than such obituary

details, however, is the fact that despite impossible odds he had survived to write the fourth and final installment in the Saga of Arturo Bandini, half a century after he had started it. What is more, he had lived to conclude his cycle in the hopeful, forward-looking tone of a writer whose spirit, in defiance of everything, remained strong and even young to the finish.

In his introduction to the 1980 republication of *Ask the Dust,* Bukowski celebrated the power of that spirit. He recalled the "wild and enormous miracle" that he experienced upon discovering Fante's masterpiece in the stacks of the Los Angeles Public Library when, like Arturo Bandini, Bukowski himself was a poor young man struggling to find his own voice as a writer. In 1995 a three-day conference devoted exclusively to John Fante took place at California State University, Long Beach—in effect, confirming the power that Fante's works still exert upon readers. The first of its kind, this event drew scores of writers, filmmakers, artists, and scholars from many parts of the United States and from as far away as Italy, France, and Romania. While richly various perspectives were expressed both in formal presentations and spontaneous discussions, agreement was unanimous that the legacy of John Fante is a living legacy and as such deserving of serious critical attention.

Of course, readers who already had embraced Fante on their own, and especially those multitudes in Europe who had made him a posthumous best-seller in such countries as France, Germany, and Italy, needed no such academic imprimatur to confirm their enthusiasm. Surely it was no accident that the film adaptation of *Wait until Spring, Bandini* (1990) was directed by a Belgian, Dominique Deruddere, or that the award-winning film documentary on Fante, *A Sad Flower in the Sand,* was written and directed by Jan Louter, a Dutch resident of France. Moreover, in 2000 a double issue of the Amsterdam-based literary journal *Bunker Hill* was devoted to John Fante. Closer to home, thirty years after discovering *Ask the Dust* while doing background research into 1930s Los Angeles for *Chinatown,* the American screenwriter Robert Towne announced his intention to direct a film from his own screenplay adaptation of *Ask the Dust.* The actors John Turturro and Peter Falk also engaged to develop *My Dog Stupid* for film. Meanwhile, in a notable reversal of the decades-long neglect suffered by Fante's works at the hands of major American publishers, *The John Fante Reader* appeared in 2002 from the William Morrow imprint of Harper-Collins, the sort of big-house celebratory compilation of a life's worth of works typically reserved for only the most widely acknowledged "major" writers. Finally, indeed, John Fante's time has arrived.

What connects this belated but inexorable gathering of minds is the lasting shock of surprise and recognition that continues to spread outward from Fante's body of work. Genuine art, the novels and short stories that he left behind—and that were almost consigned to oblivion—are with us still, if anything more vital than ever. Two late stories come to mind in this regard, cautionary tales and yet also passionate affirmations of the gamble and the gift of life as Fante envisioned it.

In "My Father's God," the young boy who narrates the story observes his father's desperate efforts to avoid having to make his first confession in more than thirty years. Pressed to do so by a zealous new parish priest, the boy's father, Nick, wheedles a special dispensation to write out his sins rather than recite them aloud in the feared "box" of the confessional. When, after days of blackening sheet after sheet, Nick finally finishes writing, he thrusts the sulfurous narrative upon his son and orders him to deliver it. "Guard it with your life," Nick warns his son—and we feel the awesome weight of responsibility that John Fante assumed in becoming a confessional writer, forever pressing himself to deliver the truth even when he was making it up and flailing himself when he failed.

Then again, in "The First Time I Saw Paris" an older version of Fante's classic protagonist, now a successful and worldly screenwriter, has his complacency shattered by the sight of a weeping old woman, "the oldest and lousiest and ugliest human being" he has ever beheld, standing still and alone amidst an uncaring stream of fashionable Parisian pedestrians. He tries to put the old woman out of his mind, first attempting to rationalize away the troubling sympathy that assails him and then knocking back a defensive highball and another. But try as he might, he cannot escape the sense of holiness surrounding her, and he finds himself wondering "suddenly frightfully could she be a saint, because it was possible because saints can be the strangest of people in the damnedest of places." John Fante's achievement is to have reminded us of as much. He leaves us with that incandescence.

Selected Bibliography

WORKS OF JOHN FANTE

NOVELS
Wait until Spring, Bandini. New York: Stackpole Sons, 1938. Reprint, Santa Barbara, Calif.: Black Sparrow Press, 1983.

Ask the Dust. New York: Stackpole Sons, 1939. Paperback edition, New York: Bantam, 1954. Reprint, Santa Barbara, Calif.: Black Sparrow Press, 1980.

Full of Life. Boston: Little, Brown, 1952. Paperback edition, New York: Bantam, 1953. Reprint, Santa Rosa, Calif.: Black Sparrow Press, 1988.

Bravo, Burro! With Rudolph Borchert. Illustrated by Marilyn Hirsh. New York: Hawthorn Books, 1970.

The Brotherhood of the Grape. Boston: Houghton

Mifflin, 1977. Paperback edition, New York: Bantam, 1978. Reprint, Santa Rosa, Calif.: Black Sparrow Press, 1988.

Dreams from Bunker Hill. Santa Barbara, Calif.: Black Sparrow Press, 1982.

1933 Was a Bad Year. Santa Barbara, Calif.: Black Sparrow Press, 1985.

The Road to Los Angeles. Santa Barbara, Calif.: Black Sparrow Press, 1985.

Prologue to Ask the Dust. With etchings by John Register. Santa Rosa, Calif.: Black Sparrow Press, 1990. (Limited edition of the impassioned synopsis Fante wrote in 1938 of *Ask the Dust*.)

SHORT STORIES

Dago Red. New York: Viking Press, 1940. (Contains "A Kidnaping in the Family," "Bricklayer in the Snow," "First Communion," "Altar Boy," "Big Leaguer," "My Mother's Goofy Song," "A Wife for Dino Rossi," "The Road to Hell," "One of Us," "The Odyssey of a Wop," "Home, Sweet Home," "The Wrath of God" and "Hail Mary.")

The Wine of Youth: Selected Stories. Santa Barbara, Calif.: Black Sparrow Press, 1985. (Contains all the stories from *Dago Red* and seven later stories: "A Nun No More," "My Father's God," "Scoundrel," "In the Spring," "One-Play Oscar," "The Dreamer" and "Helen, Thy Beauty Is to Me—.")

The Big Hunger: Stories 1932–1959. Edited and with a preface by Stephen Cooper. Santa Rosa, Calif.: Black Sparrow Press, 2000. (Contains "Horselaugh on Dibber Lannon," "Jakie's Mother," "The Still Small Voices," "Charge It," "The Criminal," "A Bad Woman," "To Be a Monstrous Clever Fellow," "Washed in the Rain," "I Am a Writer of Truth," "Prologue to *Ask the Dust*," "Bus Ride," "Mary Osaka, I Love You," "The Taming of Valenti," "The Case of the Haunted Writer," "Mama's Dream," "The Sins of the Mother," "The Big Hunger" and "The First Time I Saw Paris.")

COLLECTED WORKS

West of Rome. Santa Rosa, Calif.: Black Sparrow Press, 1986. (Contains the novella *My Dog Stupid* and the long story "The Orgy.")

The John Fante Reader. Edited by Stephen Cooper.

New York: William Morrow, 2002. (Contains a selection of stories, novel excerpts and letters.)

CORRESPONDENCE

John Fante and H. L. Mencken: A Personal Correspondence 1930–1952. Edited by Michael Moreau and Joyce Fante. Santa Rosa, Calif.: Black Sparrow Press, 1989.

John Fante: Selected Letters, 1932–1981. Edited by Seamus Cooney. Santa Rosa, Calif.: Black Sparrow Press, 1991.

FILMS

Dinky. Screenplay by Harry Sauber from a story by John Fante, Frank Fenton, and Samuel Gilson Brown. Warner, 1935.

East of the River. Screenplay by Fred Niblo from a story by John Fante and Ross B. Wills. First National, 1940.

The Golden Fleecing. Screenplay by Marion Personnet, Laura Perelman, and S. J. Perelman from a story by John Fante, Frank Fenton, and Lynn Root. MGM, 1940.

Youth Runs Wild. Screenplay by John Fante with additional dialogue by Ardel Wray from a story by John Fante and Herbert Kline. RKO Radio, 1944.

My Man and I. Screenplay by John Fante and Jack Leonard. MGM, 1952.

Full of Life. Screenplay adaptation by John Fante from his novel. Columbia, 1956.

Jeanne Eagels. Screenplay by John Fante, Daniel Fuchs, and Sonya Levien from a story by Daniel Fuchs. Columbia, 1957.

Walk on the Wild Side. Screenplay adaptation of Nelson Algren's novel by John Fante and Edmund Morris. Columbia, 1962.

The Reluctant Saint. Screenplay by John Fante and Joseph Petracca. Davis-Royal Films International, 1962.

My Six Loves. Screenplay by John Fante, Joseph Calvelli, and William Wood from a story by Peter V. K. Funk. Gant Gaither/Paramount, 1963.

Maya. Screenplay by John Fante from a story by Jalal Din and Lois Roth. King Brothers/MGM, 1966.

Something for a Lonely Man. Screenplay by John Fante and Frank Fenton. Universal Television, 1968.

Wait until Spring, Bandini. Screenplay by Dominique Deruddere from the novel by John Fante. Basic Cinematographica, 1990.

BIBLIOGRAPHY
Mullen, Michael. "John Fante: A Working Checklist." *Bulletin of Bibliography* 41:38–41 (March 1984).

CRITICAL AND BIOGRAPHICAL STUDIES
Bukowski, Charles. "Preface." In *Ask the Dust.* Santa Barbara, Calif.: Black Sparrow Press, 1980.

Collins, Richard. "Stealing Home: John Fante and the Moral Dimension of Baseball." *Aethlon: The Journal of Sport* 12, no. 1:81–91 (summer 1995).

———. *John Fante: A Literary Portrait.* Toronto and Buffalo, N.Y.: Guernica, 2000.

Cooper, Stephen. "John Fante's Eternal City." In *Los Angeles in Fiction: A Collection of Essays,* rev. ed. Edited by David Fine. Albuquerque: University of New Mexico Press, 1995. Pp. 83–99.

———. "Madness and Writing in the Works of Hamsun, Fante and Bukowski." *Genre* 19:19–27 (1998).

———. *Full of Life: A Biography of John Fante.* New York: North Point Press/Farrar, Straus & Giroux, 2000.

Cooper, Stephen, and David Fine, eds. *John Fante: A Critical Gathering.* Madison, N.J.: Fairleigh Dickinson University Press, 1999. (Contains the editors' introduction and eleven essays by participants in the 1995 John Fante Conference at California State University, Long Beach.)

"Fante, John." In *Twentieth Century Authors: A Biographical Dictionary of Modern Literature.* Edited by Stanley J. Kunitz and Howard Haycraft. New York: H. W. Wilson Co., 1942. Pp. 433–434.

Fine, David. "Down and Out in Los Angeles: John Fante's *Ask the Dust.*" *Californians* 9, no. 2:48–51 (September–October 1991).

———. "John Fante." In *Dictionary of Literary Biography. Vol. 130, American Short-Story Writers Since World War II.* Edited by Patrick Meanor. Detroit: Gale, 1993.

———. *Imagining Los Angeles: A City in Fiction.* Albuquerque: University of New Mexico Press, 2000.

Gardaphe, Fred L. "Breaking and Entering." *Forkroads* 1, no. 1:4–14 (fall 1995).

Gordon, Neil. "Realization and Recognition: The Art and Life of John Fante." *Boston Review* 18, no. 5:24–29 (October–November 1993).

———. "Shanghaied in Tinseltown." *Salon* (http://www.salon.com/books/feature/2000/05/12/fante).

Kordich, Catherine J. *John Fante: His Novels and Novellas.* New York: Twayne Publishers, 2000.

Martin, Jay. "John Fante: The Burden of Modernism and the Life of His Mind." In *John Fante: A Critical Gathering.* Edited by Stephen Cooper and David Fine. Madison, N.J.: Fairleigh Dickinson University Press, 1999.

McMurtry, Larry. "John Fante's *The Brotherhood of the Grape*: A Small-Town Italian Family in Vivid Focus." *Washington Post,* March 21, 1977.

Pleasants, Ben. "Stories of Irony from the Hand of John Fante." *Los Angeles Times Book Review,* July 8, 1979, p. 3.

Spotnitz, Frank. "The Hottest Dead Man in Hollywood." *American Film* 14, no. 9:40–44, 54 (July–August 1989).

Tayler, Christopher. "Bandini to Hackmuth." *London Review of Books,* September 21, 2000, pp. 28–29.

Ulin, David L. "Back from the Dust." *Los Angeles Times Book Review,* May 14, 1995, p. 9.

Wills, Ross B. "John Fante." *Common Ground* 1:84–90 (spring 1941).

—STEPHEN COOPER

Cristina García

1958–

CUBAN-AMERICAN NOVELIST Cristina García is one of the first U.S. Latinas to attain both mainstream and critical success with her fiction. As such, she belongs to an elite cadre that includes Sandra Cisneros, Ana Castillo, Esmeralda Santiago, and Julia Alvarez, among others. García's ascent in American literary culture is nothing less than remarkable. Four years from the time she decided to quit her career in journalism to write fiction, García's first novel was published to wide acclaim.

THE MAKING OF A NEW YORKER

García was born in Cuba on July 4, 1958, a fact that the writer pondered in a 1999 article titled "Star-Spangled," published in *The Washington Post Magazine:*

> I was born on the Fourth of July in Havana, six months before Cuba was turned upside down by Fidel Castro's revolutionary government. . . .
>
> A hundred miles away . . . the United States was celebrating its 182nd birthday. Feliz cumpleaños, yanquis! But what did this have to do with me? Nothing. Not yet, anyway. In fact, nobody in my family could have imagined just how much and how soon it would have everything to do with us.

García's father, of Spanish and native Guatemalan ancestry, was born in Central America. García described her mother, in a 1994 interview with Iraida H. López, as "Cuban, Cuban, Cuban . . . all the way!" When Fidel Castro seized power in Cuba—establishing a military state and prompting the mass exodus of political refugees—García's family was divided. With the exception of her mother, her maternal family championed Castro's cause and remained in Cuba. Her father's family chose to emigrate, and according to García, as quoted in a 1992 article by Cynthia A. Kirkwood, "My mother joined my father's camp. So we were politically polarized." In "Star-Spangled" García explained that whenever her mother "received a letter from her mother, my Abuela [grandmother] Gloria, a rarity in itself, it would be dated something like: 'May 11th, 1968, Year of the Heroic Guerrilla,' or 'December 14th, 1972, Year of Socialist Emulation.' This would drive my mother to paroxysms of fury."

The family left Cuba in 1961, when García was two; she has no childhood memories of her country of origin. Eventually, the family established themselves as entrepreneurs, owning retail businesses including a restaurant, where the writer helped out in her adolescence. Unlike many Latino writers who were raised in predominantly Hispanic communities in the United States, García grew up, as she stated in the interview with López, "with Irish, Italian, and Jewish kids. My family used to live in a Jewish neighborhood in Queens. . . . Then we moved to a mixed neighborhood in Brooklyn Heights. I went to high school in Manhattan and all my classmates were Irish and Italian." Despite the absence of Hispanics in her community, García recalls that being Cuban was "a family affair." She credits her mother with instilling in her a Cuban sense of tradition, particularly through language. "I didn't grow up sensing that I was inferior or that Spanish wasn't as good as English," she told López. "My mother was very adamant about language and understood how language and culture go hand in hand. She made a very strong effort to make sure we knew we were Cuban."

In "Star-Spangled," García admits that she was "an exasperating kid," who "didn't like or want to go and play outside with the other kids." She says that her mother had to lock her out of the house to force her to play outdoors with the other children in the neighborhood. García preferred to stay inside, reading "or gaz[ing] at the Woolworth reproductions of Renoir paintings that hung in our living room, and mak[ing] up stories about the rosy-cheeked subjects."

An avid reader, García was also a strong student. After attending Catholic schools through high school, she earned undergraduate and graduate degrees from elite institutions. In 1979 she was awarded a bachelor's degree from Barnard College in political science, with a concentration in international politics. Two years later she received a master's degree in international relations, with a concentration in European and Latin American politics and economics, from the School of Advanced International Studies at Johns Hopkins University.

Once in graduate school, García's aspirations of working for the foreign service dissipated when she found herself at odds with the nation's conservative political atmosphere during the 1980s and the presidency of Ronald Reagan: "With a Republican administration in Washington, work at an international agency didn't appeal to me," she told López. To help support herself while in graduate school, García worked part-time as a copygirl for the *New York Times*. Upon her graduation, she set out for Germany, where she had accepted a marketing position with Procter and Gamble. Unhappy in this job, García returned to the United States and used the connections she had made at the *New York Times* to obtain a job with the *Knoxville Journal,* after a short internship at the *Boston Globe.*

In 1988 García accepted a transfer to *Time's* Los Angeles bureau, where she was reunited with her boyfriend, Scott Brown, also a journalist for *Time.* However, her experiences with Miami's Cuban enclave ultimately led García to confront the issues surrounding her identity. She took a five-month leave of absence from *Time* and enrolled in a women's writing course through UCLA's extension school. As she told Joseph M. Viera, for her, writing fiction was

> ultimately a reconciliation. As a journalist for many years, I was always writing other people's stories. . . . In a strange way [writing fiction] was an opportunity to tell the truth through lying. By making up stories, you have a billion variables at every juncture. You have so much freedom that you end up having to tell the truth amidst the fabulations.

In this writing workshop, García discovered the character who shapes her first novel, Celia del Pino: as quoted in Kirkwood, García had "a strong image of an old woman, all dressed up with drop pearl earrings, wearing makeup and her hair done. It was the middle of the night. She had a pair of binoculars, and she was searching the sea for invaders. And I said, 'Who is she?'" The answer came as she worked on the manuscript for what would become her first novel, *Dreaming in Cuban* (1992).

One month after leaving *Time,* García participated in a writers' workshop in upstate New York, where she met the writer Russell Banks. After reading fifty pages or so of her manuscript, he suggested that García contact his literary agent upon the project's completion. García worked feverishly over the course of the next three to four months, finished the novel, and sent it to Banks's agent, Ellen Levine, who sold the book to Sonny Mehta, editor in chief at Alfred A. Knopf, within a month.

With the advance money that she received from Knopf, García traveled to Hawaii to join Brown, who had begun a fellowship at the University of Hawaii. There, García revised her novel, preparing it for publication. As quoted in Kirkwood, García explained, "During the final month, I was working 18-hour days on the book. . . . I was totally frazzled. The night before I sent it off . . . I was up round the clock." She wrote and rewrote parts of the novel "hundreds of times." Upon completing the final draft, García remembers bursting into tears, thinking, "If I had kept up any longer at that pace, I would have had to have been hospitalized. The last month or two, I was like a crazed person."

Six months after finishing *Dreaming in Cuban,* on December 8, 1990, García married Scott Brown. In 1992, on the day she learned that her novel had been nominated for the prestigious National Book Award, she went into labor to deliver a child; she named her daughter Pilar, after the book's protagonist.

DREAMING IN CUBAN

Upon García's publication of *Dreaming in Cuban* in 1992, the literary critic Michiko Kakutani, writing in the *New York Times,* hailed the writer and her book:

> Ms. García stands revealed in this novel as a magical new writer. . . . She has tackled the large historical theme of political and spiritual exile . . . using the much abused form of the family epic, and she has produced a work that possesses both the intimacy of a Chekhov story and the hallucinatory magic of a novel by Gabriel García Màrquez.

Publishers Weekly concurred with Kakutani's assessment, further underscoring the similarities between García's prose and that of the magical realists: "Embracing fantasy and reality with equal fervor, García's vivid, indelible characters offer an entirely new view of a particular Latin American sensibility." Reviewer Thulani Davis, writing for the *New York Times,* noted that "Ms. García's novel and her characters' sense of their own lyricism . . . make her work welcome as the latest sign that American literature has its

own hybrid offspring of the Latin American school."

Dreaming in Cuban, the first noted bildungsroman by a Cuban-American woman, serves as a cornerstone in this body of literature as well as the greater U.S. Latino canon. García's deviation from a traditional, or anti-Castro and anti-communist, Cuban-American political agenda; exploration of "self" that includes Cuban sensibilities without excluding an American national identity; and concentration on female characters mark this novel as a radical shift from what had been historically produced by Cuban-American writers of her generation.

Dreaming in Cuban is told without sequence, in random order, structured as if a dream. As such, it presents a challenge in terms of the text's structure. García employs multiple narrators whose voices are predominantly female. While men are represented, they are secondary characters defined by their relationships with their female relatives. García has been criticized for this, illustrating the complexities involved in gender and politics with respect to the Cuban and Cuban-American cultures, which have traditionally subjugated women. García was quoted in Kirkwood as saying that the novel is "an exploration of the very different ways you can be Cuban." In her interview with López, she described it as a highly autobiographical novel on an emotional level, the writing of which allowed her "to excavate new turf, to look at the costs to individuals, families, and relationships among women of public events such as a revolution."

The story opens with the scene that García wrote during her UCLA fiction workshop in April 1972, as Celia del Pino, the family matriarch, equipped with binoculars and wearing her best dress and leather pumps, watches the Cuban coast for *yanquis,* American invaders. As the novel unfolds, we learn that after the death of her husband, Jorge, Celia committed herself completely to the "social experiment" that is Cuba. Celia's past is vague and told only in sketches, but her story is replete with unfulfilled expectations. Before marrying Jorge del Pino, Celia worked in a department store in Havana, selling photographic equipment, mostly to American tourists. It was there that she met the love of her life, Gustavo Sierra de Armas, a married Spanish lawyer. The two embark on an illicit—and forbidden—romance that ends abruptly when Gustavo returns home, abandoning her. Years later Celia is still obsessed by her romance with Gustavo, having turned the short affair into a romantic delusion that torments her.

In Gustavo Sierra de Armas we find the manner in which men are portrayed in the text—sacred, distant, and unreliable. Although Gustavo's presence is solely manifested through Celia's love letters and memories, these facilitate the movement of the novel. Further, they establish a precedent by which women must pay a price, physically, emotionally, and psychologically, if they dare to rebel against the constraints of their gender as dictated by their culture. In contrast, the men are given carte blanche to do as they please, while being extolled and privileged despite their flaws.

Interestingly enough, it is at Jorge del Pino's suggestion, during his courtship of Celia, that she begins writing to her lover: "'Write to that fool,' Jorge insisted. 'If he doesn't answer, you will marry me.'" Celia does marry Jorge del Pino; however, this relationship is destined for problems. Celia's mother- and sister-in-law are characters of classically evil proportions. When Celia becomes pregnant, her mother-in-law, Berta Arango del Pino, asks accusingly: "How many more mouths can my poor son feed?" Celia's sister-in-law, Ofelia, appropriates Celia's stylish clothing and shoes, claiming that Celia will be unable to wear such a wardrobe once the child is born. It is at this point that Celia wishes for a male child: "If she had a son, she would leave Jorge and sail to Spain, to Granada. She would dance flamenco, her skirts whipping a thousand crimson lights. . . . One night, Gustavo Sierra de Armas would enter her club, walk onstage, and kiss her deeply to violent guitars." However, Celia resolves to remain in her marriage should she bear a daughter: "She would not abandon a daughter to this life," to a Cuban culture that privileges males.

Celia's pregnancy is not a happy one. Jorge, a traveling salesman, leaves his wife for long stretches with his sister and mother. Before giving birth, Celia's deteriorating psychological state is apparent in a letter to Gustavo when she charges Berta and Ofelia with "poison[ing] [her] food and milk." She writes: "The baby lives on venom." When Celia's hopes of escape are shattered by the birth of a daughter, Lourdes, she suffers a mental breakdown. Celia holds the child by one leg and announces to Jorge, "'I will not remember her name.'" She is sent to an insane asylum, where isolated and shunned, Celia continues to write Gustavo, telling him, "They burn my skull with procedures. They tell me I'm improving."

After Celia's return home and the birth of a second child, another daughter, her mental health seems to have been restored. She appears hopeful about her responsibilities as a mother to her daughters, and in a letter to Gustavo she reveals her intentions: "I've named my new baby Felicia. Jorge says I'm dooming her. She's beautiful and fat with green eyes that fix on me disarmingly. I'll be a good mother this time." Celia seems to have accepted motherhood as she settles into her new home on the beach, but her dreams are not completely fulfilled until she gives birth to a son, Javier.

The reader is given very little information about the del Pino household during the children's early years, except for brief excerpts, told in epistolary form. Trapped by her society and her marriage, Celia continues a fantasy relationship with her former lover, a silent, adulterous rebellion on her part. Gradually, her letters to Gustavo take a more political turn, and the children's adolescent rebellions parallel Castro's rise to power and its subsequent effects on the family.

The novel begins to focus on Cuba's political disarray, laying a foundation for the upheaval that will ensue and the divergent stances that the family will take. In a letter to Gustavo dated September 11, 1940, Celia writes:

> I'd forgotten the poverty of the countryside. From the trains, everything is visible: the bare feet, the crooked backs, the bad teeth. At one station there was a little girl, about six, who wore only a dirty rag that didn't cover her private parts. She stretched out her hands as the passengers left the train, and in the bustle I saw a man stick his finger in her. I cried out and he hurried away. I called to the girl and lowered our basket of food through the window. She ran off like a limping mongrel, dragging it beside her.

The passage continues, emphasizing the fact that female children are not protected in Cuban culture. Moreover, it is obvious that Celia's sensibilities are touched by the injustice and abuse that she encounters in her country. Celia knows that Cuba is in dire need of gender, social, and economic reform, all of which Castro's revolution promises to bring about. Because of the revolution, Celia is able to be political, although Jorge, who represents the "old" traditional values and mores, does not appreciate his wife's outspoken involvement. Celia must keep her enthusiasm for the anticipated revolutionary upheaval to herself; Jorge will not allow any references to the revolution in his home.

Celia is acutely aware of the social ills and disparities that plague Cuba. She has vested interests in a new political system that can offer her freedom and accessibility to power, a voice within a social structure repressive to women, a release from her depressed role in a stifling patriarchy. She abhors the immorality of starving children and the island's social and economic disparities. With Jorge's death, all obstacles to Celia's involvement in Castro's government are removed, and she serves as a judge in a neighborhood committee dedicated to solving family disputes. As a judge, Celia offers intriguing punishments to those defendants found guilty. For example, in a case in which a husband was accused of seducing another woman, Celia sentences the man to work for a year as a volunteer in the state-run nursery in Santa Teresa del Mar, assigning him chores that have traditionally been reserved for women:

> The nursery is short-staffed, and our *compañeras* need help changing diapers, warming milk, washing linen, and organizing the children's playtime. You will be the first man to ever work there, *compañero,* and I will be checking up to see that your behavior is one of a model Socialist man in all respects.

Celia's judgment is an unambiguous assertion of equality. Her fervent dedication to the revolution, however, is interrupted when her son, Javier, returns from Czechoslovakia, destitute after his wife abandons him for a Russian professor. Her decision to forgo her involvement in the revolution to care for her son is a clear juxtaposition of the role forced on her by the old Cuban society and the role she has chosen as an active revolutionary.

Felicia Villaverde, the child Celia had vowed to love, is revealed in the novel through the visions and dreams she recounts, as well as from the stories told by other characters, Herminia Delgado in particular. These intermittent sections of the novel are relayed primarily through memory. Jorge had warned Celia that naming her second daughter Felicia (which means "happiness") would bring the girl bad luck, but Celia disregarded this admonishment. The naming of Felicia was inauspicious; no female child had a chance at happiness on the island then, given its cultural and political history, and despite Celia's attempts to be a better mother to this daughter, Felicia was doomed from the start.

Felicia becomes best friends with a girl of African descent, Herminia Delgado, the daughter of a priest of the Santeria religion. Felicia is attracted to the African-based religion, and this attraction and her relationship with Herminia amount in the novel to a severing of her ties with the dominant, European-based Cuban society.

As a young woman, Felicia rebels against social mores. Against her father's wishes, she marries the biracial Hugo Villaverde, an abusive philanderer who impregnates and then abandons her. On Christmas Eve, Felicia delivers twin girls, whom she names Luz (Light) and Milagro (Miracle). Her husband appears periodically, leaving despair and disease in his wake: we learn that Hugo "returned on several occasions. Once, to bring silk scarves and apologies from China. Another time, to blind Felicia for a week with a blow to her eyes. Yet another, to sire Ivanito and leave his syphilis behind."

The reader next sees Felicia when her three children are older. She is alienated from her daughters due to her mental instability, and her relationship with a five-year-old Ivanito borders on the incestuous. Intuiting that Celia is seeking to separate her from Ivanito, Felicia plans a double suicide. As she and her son finish dinner, Felicia "crushes pink tablets" onto their ice cream, claiming the concoction will "give [them] strength." Felicia then carries her son upstairs and places him in bed beside her. She tells him, "Close your eyes, *mi hijo.* Be very still," and the two fall asleep together, wrapped in each other's arms.

Celia has a premonition, a dream, that something is wrong at the house on Palmas Street, where she herself had suffered a breakdown, and notes on her arrival there that the house "has brought only misfortune." Celia finds mother and son in time to save them, and Ivanito is sent away to boarding school, where he can be "integrated" with other boys his own age. Felicia is deemed an "unfit mother" and sent to the work camps in the Sierra Maestra.

After being released from the labor camps, where it was intended she be reformed into a "New Socialist Woman" of the revolution, Felicia seeks the help of a Santeria priest for advice in finding another husband. The *santero* tells Felicia, "What you wish for, daughter, you cannot keep. It is the will of the gods." Felicia defies the *santero*'s warning and falls in love with a restaurant inspector, Ernesto Brito. Four days into their relationship, he is killed in a grease fire, and Felicia once again suffers a breakdown, blaming Castro—El Líder—and his political corruption for Ernesto's death.

When the reader next finds Felicia, she is living in an amusement park with a man named Otto. An unspecified amount of time has elapsed. Felicia suffers from amnesia but gradually begins to experience faint memories. While having sex with Otto, she remembers her son, Ivanito. Although Otto treats Felicia with respect and kindness, she is incapable of receiving this love, and one night after the park has closed, she lures him onto a roller coaster and pushes him to his death.

Felicia returns home and tells Herminia what she has done. At this point in the novel, Felicia wholeheartedly devotes herself to Santeria. However, at a time when Felicia should ideally obtain happiness, Herminia observes that she is dying:

> I've seen other *santeras* during their first year. They are radiant. . . . But Felicia showed none of these blessings. Her eyes dried out like an old woman's and her fingers curled like claws until she could hardly pick up her spoon. Even her hair, which had been as black as a crow's, grew colorless in scruffy patches on her skull. Whenever she spoke, her lips blurred to a dull line in her face.

Felicia has fulfilled her father's prophecy of being doomed. She has failed to be a wife, a mother, a *compañera*; quite simply, there is no place for her in Cuban society.

Lourdes, Celia del Pino's oldest child, is the daughter Celia had hoped would be a boy. Her beginnings are difficult, foreshadowing a life that is filled with mother/daughter conflict, yet she is determined to exert control over everything in her path. Lourdes's initial reunion with her mother is not a happy one. After Celia is released from the asylum, her frail emotional condition dictates that the del Pino family move to Santa Teresa del Mar. While Celia resumes her role as mother, it is no surprise to the reader that Lourdes is distant toward her. She clearly prefers her father. In fact, Lourdes's relationship with Jorge deepens until the two become inseparable. Little information is given about the del Pino family's lives until Lourdes becomes a young woman and is being courted by Rufino Puente, a young aristocrat. As Lourdes prepares for her marriage, Jorge becomes jealous of Rufino and blames himself for the fact that he is losing his daughter to another man.

When the wedding occurs, it is not an idyllic conjoining of two families. Dona Zaida, Lourdes's mother-in-law, is eerily reminiscent of Jorge's mother, who inflicted such suffering on Celia. However, Lourdes is not destined to repeat her mother's fate. In fact, after her honeymoon, much to Dona Zaida's horror, Lourdes decides to take an active part in her husband's business. She "reviewed the ledgers, fired the cheating accountant, and took over the books herself." Lourdes, however, is not able to conquer the more formidable foes presented in the Cuban Revolution. In one of the most pivotal scenes in the novel, a series of events ensues that transforms Lourdes from a headstrong woman into a resolute and determined fighter. To wit, at the beginning of Castro's reign, a pregnant Lourdes is thrown from a horse. She suffers a "sharp, round pain" in her chest, but manages to walk for nearly an hour until she reaches help, then borrows a horse and rides to Rufino's rescue, as he is held at gunpoint by two soldiers of the revolution. Lourdes's victory is short-lived; she suffers a miscarriage, losing a child that she is convinced is her much-longed-for son. Lourdes blames the despised soldiers, the hated Castro for the loss, and the family leaves Cuba.

After arriving in Miami, it is Lourdes who defines the goals for exile. She and her husband buy a used Chevrolet, and Lourdes tells Rufino that she wants to go "where it's cold." As they drive up the East Coast, Lourdes continues to say "colder," until they arrive in New York, where it is finally "cold enough." Lourdes is not only able to adapt to North American society—she thrives. Obviously competent in business affairs—she managed her husband's ranch in Cuba better than the professionals Rufino hired—Lourdes opens and operates an establishment that she names Yankee Doodle Bakery. She wants to be the proprietor of a chain of bakeries. Like Celia, who was rejuvenated by her physical work in the sugarcane fields, which was required of all Cubans after Castro's ascent to power, Lourdes's self-confidence is restored through her work. Not only does Lourdes take care of herself and her family, but she offers her services to her new country. She volunteers with the police department, acting as a watchwoman for her neighborhood.

In direct contrast to Lourdes is her husband, Rufino. In fact, Lourdes recognizes that her husband is all but inept in exile: "Something came unhinged in his brain that would make him incapable of working in a conventional way. There was a part of him that could never leave the *finca* [ranch] or the comfort of its cycles, and this diminished him for any other life. He cannot be transplanted." When Lourdes tries to put Rufino to good use in the bakery, she loses her patience with him: "As handy as he is for some things, he couldn't get the hang of the pastry business, at least not the way

[Lourdes] runs it." Lourdes is at odds with her husband and the role he plays in her life.

In the United States, Lourdes is only truly comfortable with her father, Jorge, who, even after his death, appears periodically to his daughter in the form of a spirit. Jorge visits Lourdes "on her evening walks home from the bakery, and whispers to her through the oak and maple trees. His words flutter at her neck like a baby's lacy breath." Jorge is proud of Lourdes's "tough stance on law and order, identical to his own." In fact, he encourages Lourdes to join the auxiliary police force so that she can prepare herself in case of a Communist invasion. Upon his advice, Lourdes plans the opening of her second bakery in New York and moves toward establishing herself as a zealously patriotic American.

Gradually Jorge's visits become less frequent, and Lourdes grows anxious, knowing that she will have to mourn his death once again: "He complains of an energy waning within him, and is convinced that the time he's stolen between death and oblivion is coming to an end." In one of his last visits to his daughter, Jorge assures Lourdes that he did love Celia and that Celia loved Lourdes. Jorge tells Lourdes of Felicia's death in Cuba and urges for family unity, advising his daughter to travel to Cuba to face her mother: "Please return and tell your mother everything, tell her I'm sorry. I love you, *mi hija.*"

Pilar Puente, the amalgam of all that has come before her and all that may yet be for the Cuban-American woman, is Lourdes's daughter and Celia's granddaughter. Not only must she navigate an emotional relationship between these two important women, her identity hinges on the successful reconciliation of what they represent. Born in Cuba but raised and educated in the United States, Pilar is a member of the "1.5 generation" that the sociologist Rubén Rumbaut, in an essay included in the 1991 text *Refugee Children: Theory, Research, and Ser-*

vices, edited by Frederick L. Ahearn Jr. and Jean L. Athey, described as "children who were born abroad but are being educated and come of age in the United States." Pilar's plight is made all the more difficult because, as Gustavo Pérez Firmat explores in his seminal *Life on the Hyphen: The Cuban-American Way* (1994), Pilar belongs to an "intermediate immigrant generation" which was "born in Cuba but made in the U.S.A."

Pilar searches for the components of self, language, spirituality, morality, and place in what she herself identifies as a purgatory of biculturalism. Pilar must synthesize the past with the present, the Cuban with the American. Her predecessors' problems and challenges seem almost one-dimensional in light of Pilar's daunting task. For example, Celia can only be Cuban, and Lourdes can only be American. And Felicia, the only other family member who endeavors to combine the old with the new—Santeria with Catholicism, Afro-Cuban with white, sexuality with love—is driven insane. Pilar's challenge is a formidable one.

The reader is first introduced to Pilar early in the novel when Celia del Pino, Pilar's grandmother, thinks about the grandchild who was forced out of her arms when Lourdes decided to immigrate to the United States. Of the letters she sends her grandmother, Celia notes: "Pilar, her first grandchild, writes to her from Brooklyn in a Spanish that is no longer hers. She speaks the hard-edged lexicon of bygone tourists itchy to throw dice on green felt or asphalt." This lost language indicates to Celia the cultural displacement that has occurred because of the political conditions in Cuba. For Pilar, Cuba remains etched in her mind free from the lexicon and the contamination of the Communist state—but this image of Cuba is illusory.

Despite the loss of identity she suffers because of her immigration to the United States, Pilar holds vivid memories of her birth country, strongly connecting her to her homeland, a Cuba to which she longs to return. Pilar's confusion about her forced emigration is exacerbated by her close relationship with her grandmother, despite geographical and political divides: "Pilar keeps a diary in the lining of her winter coat, hidden from her mother's scouring eyes. In it, Pilar records everything. This pleases Celia. She closes her eyes and speaks to her granddaughter, imagines her words as slivers of light piercing the murky night." In this respect, Celia and Pilar share writing as a common bond: they both record their experiences and feelings—Celia, in her clandestine letters to her first lover, Gustavo, and Pilar, in the journal she conceals from Lourdes. As Celia performs as her generation's historian through the letters she writes Gustavo, Pilar, too, acts as a historian, with her journal entries capturing the experiences of the "1.5 generation." It is in these writings that both Celia and Pilar are able to express themselves.

Another interesting aspect of the relationship between Pilar and Celia is their ability to communicate with each other telepathically. Pilar reveals: "Abuela Celia and I write to each other sometimes, but mostly I hear her speaking to me at night just before I fall asleep. She tells me stories about her life and what the sea was like that day. . . . Abuela Celia says she wants to see me again. She tells me she loves me." It is through this communication that Pilar maintains her interest in Cuba, and, to Lourdes' dismay, she threatens to return.

And so mother and daughter, often violently disparate, voyage to Cuba, where the last part of the novel takes place. By this time both Pilar and Lourdes, who was told by an apparition of her dead father to return to Cuba, feel that it is time to go home: it is a time for reconciliations, for facing the past and the truth, and for final goodbyes. On the trip to Abuela Celia's house, Pilar notices four fresh bodies floating in the Straits of Florida, rafters killed in their despera-tion to flee the country. Pilar recognizes that this is not the Cuba of her memory.

Pilar uses her time in Cuba to ponder the vagaries that have rendered her family asunder: "We're all tied to the past by flukes. Look at me, I got my name from Hemingway's fishing boat." While in Cuba, Pilar recognizes that "Cuba is a peculiar exile, I think, an island-colony. We can reach it by a thirty-minute charter flight from Miami, yet never reach it all." It is also during this visit that Pilar realizes that she is no longer part of Cuba's culture. Even the Spanish language spoken by her and her mother is "another idiom entirely."

Pilar ultimately acknowledges that her idea of Cuba has been falsely colored by her joyous childhood, a time that no longer exists: "I have to admit it's much tougher here than I expected." While contemplating what her life would have been like had she remained in Cuba with her grandmother, Pilar admits that she misses the United States and its freedom. She concludes, "I'm afraid to lose all this, to lose Abuela Celia again. But sooner or later I'd have to return to New York. I know now it's where I belong— not *instead* of here, but *more* than here." Pilar's home is in the United States as a bicultural member of society, as a Cuban-American woman, and so one voyage ends and another begins.

THE AGÜERO SISTERS

After the success of *Dreaming in Cuban,* García did not want to write a sequel to her first novel or replicate it. As she explained in an interview in the late 1990s with Bridget Kevane and Juanita Heredia, the idea behind *The Agüero Sisters* (1997) was to explore "Cuban history without necessarily focusing on the watershed of the revolution. . . . I wanted a different landscape and scope." Still living in Hawaii at the time she wrote the novel, García, who resided on the edge of a swamp, began to acquaint herself with the island's natural landscape. Of the experience, García recalled in the same interview: "What I didn't know was that it was a migratory paradise for wintering birds from Alaska. I ended up getting binoculars and a little inflatable canoe and was up in the mornings checking out the birds." She was inspired by this new interest and began research into the natural landscape at the University of Hawaii. There, she accessed the collections on Cuban history, particularly the holdings on travels to the island by naturalists who explored Cuba's flora and fauna.

In her second novel, as she said in an interview for the online Ballantine's Reader's Circle, García also wanted to "explore loss, extinction, and the nature of memory." She was curious about how history is made, especially the way in which families construct their own histories. In particular, García continues, she was influenced by a visit her mother made to Cuba to visit her sister, García's aunt:

It was supposed to be a six-month honeymoon reunion for the two of them but it ended after only a month with much acrimony on both sides. I didn't witness the reunion, but for years afterward I heard each sister complaining about the other. That got me thinking about what happens to siblings and family when they've been apart for a long time and how they go about reconciling what divided them in the past and in the present.

The Agüero Sisters, a culmination of these musings, is the story of the half sisters Constancia and Reina Agüero and their quest to discover the circumstances of their mother's mysterious death more than forty years earlier. García told Joseph M. Viera in a 1998 interview that the novel

was my way of exploring the nature of family myth, the way, I'm sure, all of our families, through various ways, create a history for ourselves, just the way nations do. . . . This was my way of exploring . . . where the truth lies, how people within a family, within a country, in vari-

ous sorts of ecological settings, compete for their versions of events.

Avoiding grand, nostalgic, archetypal constructions of an idyllic Cuba, García assumes the role of cultural reader and interpreter in her fiction as she reconstructs a more plausible, more responsible, account of Cuban history than that which has often been perpetuated by the hegemonic exile community of Cuban Miami. Quite simply, Cuba—pre- as well as postrevolution—is never rendered as the utopian paradise familiarly found in Cuban-American fiction. Instead, García delves into Cuba's colonial history and forces her readers to boldly confront race issues that remain deeply embedded in the nation's highly mythologized past.

In *The Agüero Sisters* the island's natural history is revealed through Ignacio Agüero, Constancia's father and Reina's stepfather, who serves as an intermittent narrator. In the interview with Viera, García explained that Ignacio's journal entries trace "the sad exploitation of the country's natural splendor—the effects of history and politics in Cuba."

Behind [Blanca], a sudden whirring arose, a soft breath at the nape of her neck. . . . She turned to alert her husband and found him staring at her, fixed as a muscle behind his double-barreled gun.

At the sound of the shot . . . Blanca Agüero collapsed with an unexpected violence, half sliding into the rippling marsh.

Ignacio Agüero waited until nightfall, watched and waited until a lone red-tailed hawk soared above them in the sky. Then he carried his wife seventeen miles to the nearest village and began to tell his lies.

This prologue establishes the parameters of the novel's plot: the Agüero sisters, Constancia and Reina, must piece together the circumstances of their mother's death. To complicate matters, readers learn that Ignacio has told his daughters differing accounts of Blanca's death, which they, in the remainder of the novel, must reconcile with the truth.

A force to be reckoned with, Reina is portrayed in this novel as immune to manipulation and exploitation by the men in her culture. Instead, García subverts the conventional historical structures of oppression, permitting Reina to dominate the men around her: "The most daring of her colleagues," García writes, "call her Compañera Amazona, a moniker she secretly relishes. Often, Reina selects the smallest, shyest electrician in a given town for her special favors, leaving him weak and inconsolable for months."

In El Cobre, Reina's job is to repair the "prehistoric" electric pump that "has electrocuted two men since mid-November. Now not even the most skillful electricians will go near it." As García tells the story of how Reina attempts to fix this pump, she includes details about Cuban history:

> Reina is the first to reach the mouth of the copper mine. It is an amphitheater of decay. In the seventeenth century, slaves extracted enough ore from the mine to meet all of the country's artillery needs. A hundred years later, they turned on their masters with muskets and machetes and, eventually, through the intervention of the Bishop of Santiago and La Virgen de la Caridad del Cobre herself, were declared free citizens.

Suddenly, in an inexplicable accident of nature, which "occurs so fast that nobody present can describe the events accurately or in sequence," Reina is injured when "the ground begins to shudder and fissure," and she is thrown into a ceiba tree, landing "forty feet high in the tree's uppermost branches." She suffers a broken nose, two broken thumbs, and a loosened tooth in the incident and then is apparently struck by lightning. At this point, the chapter closes, and the next time Reina appears, she is in the hospital, recovering from multiple skin grafts.

The novel then moves to New York City, again in 1990, where we are introduced to Constancia, Reina's older sister. She is busy selling cosmetics, "staving off women's little everyday deaths," at a Manhattan department store. Constancia is described as her sister's complete opposite:

> She is fifty-one years old, but her skin is soft and white. Her dark hair is arranged in a French bun, and her nails are lacquered to match her carnelian lips. Constancia is partial to Adolfo suits, which set off her petite figure, and she completes every ensemble with a short strand of pearls.

Constancia's husband, Heberto, owns a tobacco shop in Manhattan, where "sales double whenever Constancia is on duty." Heberto is planning to retire to Key Biscayne, near Miami, in the coming month, but Constancia is apprehensive about the move. In particular, "when silence surrounds her, the temptation to remember is too great." In this section of the novel, Constancia's daily thoughts are punctuated with fleeting memories of Cuban life. The plot is developed further when readers learn that Constancia's mother, Blanca, abandoned her daughter when she was five months old.

While Constancia plans her move from New York to Miami, her half sister, Reina, remains in a Cuban hospital, convalescing from her injuries. There, Reina observes other patients "cursing the revolution and El Comandante [Castro] himself." Once a firm believer in Castro, Reina has become disenchanted with Cuba's "social experiment": "Ten years ago, Reina wouldn't have put up with their blaspheming. Now she doesn't even flinch." To make matters worse, Reina learns that her thirty-two-year-old daughter Dulcita ("Dulce"), desperate to leave the socialist state, is planning to escape Cuba by marrying a sixty-four-year-old Spanish airline-reservations clerk. Reina's world appears to be collapsing before her.

Restless in Key Biscayne, Constancia is having difficulty adjusting to the climate of Florida and the Cuban exile community: "Constancia doesn't consider herself an exile in the same way as many of the [Miami] Cubans. . . . In fact, she shuns their habit of fierce nostalgia, their trafficking in the past like exaggerating peddlers." Constancia's discomfort in Miami sparks additional painful memories of her life in Cuba. At this point in the narrative, we learn that Constancia's mother returned to the Agüero home when Constancia was three: "Mama returned, eight months pregnant and bruised. There were terrible welts on her body, and one eye was swollen shut, but Mama did not cry or complain. Constancia remembers wishing her mother would leave and never come back." Despite Constancia's wish, Blanca remains, and Constancia's half sister, Reina, a dark-skinned child, is born. This new member of the family proves to exacerbate Constancia's alienation from her mother. After Reina's birth, Constancia constantly aggravates the baby, and her actions have consequences: "After Mama threatened to leave again, Papi took Constancia to stay on Abuelo Ramón's ranch in Camaguey. It was supposed to last only the summer. It endured for the next six years. . . . She never shared a home with her parents again." When Blanca dies in 1948, Constancia, then six years old, is reunited with her father and half sister. Now middle-aged, Constancia muses over her past and wonders why Reina inherited "their past—Papi's stuffed birds and bats, his books, the family's photographs—while Constancia managed to receive nothing at all?"

Reina, having returned to her apartment in Vedado after her prolonged hospital stay, also ponders her life, the present and the past. She remembers asking her mother "why Constancia had been sent to live so far away. But her mother told her only that she and her sister were meant to live apart." Reina also recalls seeing her dead mother at the funeral parlor. Disobeying her father, Reina slipped away, and in her explorations she makes a discovery: "In the last embalming chamber, her mother lay on a rust-

ing pedestal, her throat an estuary of color and disorder, as if a bloody war had taken place beneath her chin." Alone in her apartment, it becomes clear to Reina that Cuba holds nothing for her, and she resolves to emigrate.

Constancia is haunted by her younger days in Cuba. She remembers her father telling her of her mother's accidental drowning. She also recalls Ignacio telling her a different version of Blanca's death:

Their mother had shot herself in the Zapata Swamp, he said, aimed the gun at her own throat. He made Constancia promise never to tell Reina, that the secret would only reopen wounds. This frightened Constancia more than his original version, because now she knew she couldn't rescue Papi, knew for certain that he would die next.

Disturbed, Constancia suffers a strange dream, and upon awaking,

she switches on her vanity mirror, finds her face in disarray, moving all at once like a primitive creature. . . .

Constancia takes a deep breath . . . Then she checks the mirror again. Her face has settled down, but it appears different to her, younger, as if it truly had been rearranged in the night. She rubs her eyes, pinches her cheeks. . . . Then it hits her with the force of a slap. This is her mother's face.

Distressed, Constancia visits Oscar Piñango, a Santeria priest, who turns to his divining shells: "The shells never lie," he says. The pattern in which the shells fall offers a message that "doesn't waver: *oddi*, where the grave was first dug, where the grave was first dug."

Heberto, oblivious to his wife's turmoil, leaves with La Brigada Caimán on a clandestine mission to free Cuba. Constancia, bored living the life of the typical, retired Cuban woman in South Florida, turns entrepreneur, launching a new line of cosmetics, Cuerpo de Cuba, aptly named Body of Cuba. They are sold in royal-blue bottles, "with a label featuring a cameo of her mother's face (now her own)." Constancia's products are overwhelmingly popular with the Cuban exile community, in large part because they capitalize on nostalgia. In the meantime, Constancia seems to be regressing through time as she dresses in thrift-store finds in the styles of the 1940s, seemingly evolving into her mother.

In the midst of this transformation, Constancia receives a telegram, informing her that her sister Reina has finally been granted permission to emigrate from Cuba and will be arriving in Florida in a day. Bringing a suitcase filled only with "her father's mementos—taxidermic bats and birds, a few books and clothes, the framed photograph of her mother," Reina is finally reunited with her sister in Miami, where she begins her new life as an exile. Upon seeing Constancia at the airport, Reina is stunned by her sister's resemblance to their mother: "Reina couldn't help it—she studied her sister's face like a blind woman, tried to read with her hands the grace and terror that lay hidden there." Reina is so mesmerized by her sister's face that she sleeps with Constancia for several nights, "listening for messages from the dead."

In Miami, the Agüero sisters begin to discuss their past lives, searching for a congruent truth that both can accept. Constancia insists that she does not like to "romanticize the past," while Reina retorts, "I guess it's less painful to forget than to remember." Tension begins to rise between the two sisters, especially in regard to their divergent pasts and their differing versions of their mother's death.

As Reina explores the Miami area, she functions as a cultural commentator, taking note of the myriad obsessions with Cuba that characterize the exile community in Miami:

Reina likes to listen to the reactionary exile stations in Miami best. They play the best music and the most outrageous lies on the air. She's amused by their parading nationalism, like a bunch of roosters on the make. . . .

The minute anyone learns that Reina recently arrived from Cuba, they expect her to roundly denounce the revolution. . . . These pride-engorged *cubanos* want her to crucify El Comandante, repudiate even the good things he's done for the country. . . .

El exilio, Reina is convinced, is the virulent flip side of Communist intolerance.

Shortly thereafter, the exile news media announces that the militant group Heberto belongs to has landed on Cuba's shores, and some members have perished in their effort to free Cuba: "The reports are conflicting, but this much Constancia knows to be true: that at Varadero Beach, forty-four men in guerrilla fatigues died storming the Hotel Bellamar." Constancia also knows that Heberto is reported among those presumably missing or dead. Angry, Constancia wants to lash out at Reina; she "wants to shatter Reina's confidence, to tell her how their mother returned to Havana eight months pregnant, big with another man's child." Constancia is continually disturbed by her memories of Cuba and her family. She turns to the Santeria priest, who "tells Constancia that . . . in Cuba, the secrets will lie buried in their original grave." Constancia now knows that she must make a pilgrimage to her homeland to discover the truth.

Before the narration of Constancia's return to Cuba, Ignacio's most revealing journal entry is presented. It tells of Blanca's mysterious disappearance from the home when Constancia was an infant. It also offers an explanation for Blanca's return, eight months' pregnant, to the Agüero household. In June of that year, Blanca gave birth to "another man's baby, twelve pounds strong, nutmeg brown." It is further revealed that Reina's father was "a giant mulatto. . . . He had a broad, smooth face and eyes that suggested a touch of oriental blood."

The novel culminates with Reina and Constancia traveling in Heberto's boat from Key Biscayne to Key West, where Constancia "plans to charter a fishing boat there that will take her to Cuba," fulfilling the *santero's* instruction. The sisters are still at odds. Reina is angry at Constancia for painting Heberto's boat with flowers in order "to promote her new perfume: Flower of Exile." Yet she is supportive of Constancia's quest and gives her sister a regulation jumpsuit so that Constancia will better fit in with the Cuban people.

Upon her arrival in Cuba, Constancia confirms her husband's death, pays the mortician six-hundred American dollars to cremate his body, and takes off with his ashes in an empty cold cream jar. Upset because her cellular phone does not work and she cannot contact the United States to check on her business, Constancia nevertheless manages to return to her uncles' ranch. There she finds a buried copper box that contains a worn bit of bone and a stack of her father's last papers. The novel ends with Constancia learning the truth in her father's own words: *"I did not plan what happened in the Zapata Swamp. You must understand this."*

As with her first novel, García's *The Agüero Sisters* was well-received upon its release in 1997. While virtually all reviewers praised the novel, Ilan Stavans, writing for *The Nation*, criticized García for writing "the same book twice. Not word for word . . . but she has become her own imitator, however deftly." Although Stavans esteems the book as "wonderful," he claims that "it is not a wonderful second book," as it covers "the same ground as its predecessor without taking new risks, without expanding into new horizons."

In contrast, Sue Miller, in a review written for *Newsweek,* called the book "a superb second novel. . . .With sensual prose and a plot that captures the angst of the Cuban diaspora, García seductively draws us in and refuses to let go." Deirdre McNamer, writing for the *New York Times,* agreed, calling García "a strikingly deft and supple writer, both in her sensibilities and her language. She has a talent for the oblique

that allows her to write what amounts to a family saga by focusing not on the strict beat that constitutes conventional plot but on seemingly offhand memories and exchanges." *Publishers Weekly* noted that "García gives us beautifully nuanced portraits of riven people, separated by more than an ocean. . . . [Her] lushly vibrant prose evokes a tropical atmosphere and a seething sexuality, both steamily intensified by santero rituals and mystical phenomena."

CONCLUSION

By the age of forty-five, García had won several coveted awards for her work, including a National Book Award nomination for *Dreaming in Cuban,* a Guggenheim Fellowship, a Hodder Fellowship at Princeton University, a Whiting Writers' Award, and the Heidinger Kafka Prize for Fiction for *The Agüero Sisters.*

Aside from her two novels, García has published a nonfiction book, *Cars of Cuba* (1995), that documents the aging automobiles in contemporary Cuba, and two short stories that have appeared in literary anthologies: "Tito's Goodbye" and "Inés in the Kitchen." In regard to the latter story, García has said that she salvaged it from a dead novel she attempted to write, following *Dreaming in Cuban.* The piece tells the story of Inés, a woman who finds herself constricted by marriage. "I think in some ways," commented García in the interview with Kevane and Heredia, "I was writing about my own stifled feelings in my marriage. But it was also about what I saw around me, cousins of mine getting married, moving to the suburbs, having, as that old phrase goes, quietly desperate lives." As for her writing habits, García admits to having a ritual that "must be inviolate"; thus, she maintains a separate office outside of her house, a sacred sanctuary, with no telephone, no way of communicating with the outside world, no way of interrupting her work. There, she spends five to six hours,

Monday through Friday, reading and writing. García begins by reading poetry (Octavio Paz, Pablo Neruda, and her beloved Wallace Stevens) for two hours before writing.

At the turn of the twenty-first century, García, who is divorced from Brown, is living in California with her daughter. Her third novel, a story with an Afro-Chinese-Cuban male protagonist, is forthcoming. García has visited Cuba regularly since her first return in 1984. Like her fiction, she transcends politics and national borders. What remains most important about García are her attempts to break down artificially imposed, man-made boundaries and delve into the human conditions and relationships that link us all.

Selected Bibliography

WORKS OF CRISTINA GARCÍA

FICTION

Dreaming in Cuban. New York: Knopf, 1992.

The Agüero Sisters. New York: Knopf, 1997.

"Tito's Goodbye." In *Iguana Dreams: New Latino Fiction.* Edited by Delia Poey and Virgil Suárez. New York: Harper Perennial, 1992. Pp. 75–80.

"Ines in the Kitchen." In *Little Havana Blues: A Cuban-American Literature Anthology.* Edited by Delia Poey and Virgil Suarez. Houston, Tex.: Arte Público, 1996. Pp. 152–157.

NONFICTION

Cars of Cuba. With Joshua Greene and D. D. Allen. New York: Abrams, 1995.

"Star-Spangled." *Washington Post Magazine,* July 18, 1999, pp. W21+.

CRITICAL AND BIOGRAPHICAL STUDIES

Alvarez-Borland, Isabel. "Displacements and Autobiography in Cuban-American Fiction." *World Literature Today* 64:43–48 (1994).

———. *Cuban-American Literature of Exile: From Person to Persona.* Charlottesville: University Press of Virginia, 1998.

Brogan, Kathleen. "From Exiles to Americans: 'Recombinant' Ethnicity in Cristina García's Dreaming in Cuban." In her *Cultural Haunting: Ghosts and Ethnicity in Recent American Literature.* Charlottesville: University Press of Virginia, 1998. Pp. 93–128.

Caminero-Santangelo, Marta. "Contesting the Boundaries of Exile Latino/a Literature." *World Literature Today* 7, no. 3:507–517 (2000).

Davila, Florangela. "Cristina García Identifies with Her Characters." *Seattle Times,* June 17, 1997, p. C1.

Davis, Rocio G. "Back to the Future: Mothers, Languages and Homes in Cristina García's *Dreaming in Cuban.*" *World Literature Today* 74, no.1:60–68 (2000).

Davis, Thulani. "Fidel Came Between Them." *New York Times,* May 17, 1992, section 7, p. 14. (Review of *Dreaming in Cuban.*)

Duany, Jorge. "Neither Golden Exile nor Dirty Worm: Ethnic Identity in Recent Cuban-American Novels." *Cuban Studies* 23:167–183 (1993).

Fusco, Coco. *English Is Broken Here: Notes on Cultural Fusion in the Americas.* New York: New Press, 1995.

Iyer, Pico. "This Earthly Island." *Time,* May 12, 1997, p. 88.

Kakutani, Michiko. "The Dreams and Yearnings of a Family of Exiles." *New York Times,* February 25, 1992, p. C17. (Review of *Dreaming in Cuban.*)

———. "Letting Fantastic Events Echo Life's Uncertainty." *New York Times,* May 27, 1997, p. C16. (Review of *The Agüero Sisters.*)

Kanellos, Nicolás, ed. *Biographical Dictionary of Hispanic Literature in the United States: The Literature of Puerto Ricans, Cuban Americans, and Other Hispanic Writers.* Westport, Conn.: Greenwood, 1989.

———. *The Hispanic Almanac: From Columbus to Corporate America.* Detroit: Visible Ink, 1994.

Kirkwood, Cynthia Adina. "A Cuban Odyssey: It Took a Trip to Havana to Piece Cristina García's History and Literary Quest." *Los Angeles Times,* August 30, 1992, pp. 7+.

Luis, William. *Dance Between Two Cultures: Latino Caribbean Literature Written in the United States.* Nashville, Tenn.: Vanderbilt University Press, 1997.

McCracken, Ellen. *New Latina Narrative: The Feminine Space of Postmodern Ethnicity.* Tucson: University of Arizona Press, 1999.

McNamer, Deirdre. "World of Portents." *New York Times Book Review,* June 15, 1997, p. 38.

Miller, Sue. *Newsweek,* April 28, 1997, p. 79. (Review of *The Agüero Sisters.*)

Publishers Weekly, March 10, 1997, p. 48. (Review of *The Agüero Sisters.*)

Publishers Weekly, January 13, 1992, p. 46. (Review of *Dreaming in Cuban.*)

Rumbaut, Rubén. "The Agony of Exile: A Study of the Migration and Adaptation of Indochinese Refugee Adult and Children." In *Refugee Children: Theory, Research, and Services.* Edited by Frederick L. Ahearn Jr. and Jean L. Athey. Baltimore, Md.: Johns Hopkins University Press, 1991.

Sachs, Lloyd. "Illuminating the Shadows: Author Explores Myth and Reality." *Chicago Sun-Times,* June 10, 1997, p. 35.

Sachs, Susan. "Immigrant Literature Now About More Than Fitting In." *New York Times,* January 9, 2000, section 1, pp. 21+.

Stavans, Ilan. "Swooning in Cuban." *Nation* 264, no. 19:32–34 (May 1997). (Review of *The Agüero Sisters.*)

Stefanko, Jacqueline. "New Ways of Telling: Latinas' Narrative of Exile and Return." *Frontiers: A Journal of Women Studies* 17, no. 2:50–69 (1996).

Vasquez, Mary S. "Cuba as Text and Context in Cristina García's *Dreaming in Cuban.*" *Bilingual Review* 20, no. 1:22–27 (1995).

Viera, Joseph M. "Matriarchy and Mayhem: Awakenings in Cristina García's *Dreaming in Cuban.*" *Americas Review* 24, nos. 3–4:247–258 (1996).

INTERVIEWS

"A Conversation with Cristina García." *Ballantine Reader's Circle* (http://www.randomhouse.com/BRC/garcia.html).

Kevane, Bridget, and Juanita Heredia. "At Home on the Page: An Interview with Cristina García." In *Latina Self-Portraits: Interviews with Contemporary Women Writers.* Albuquerque: University of New Mexico Press, 2000. Pp. 69–82.

López, Iraida H. "'. . . And There Is Only My Imagination Where Our History Should Be': An Interview with Cristina García." *Michigan Quarterly Review* 33, no. 3:605–617 (1994).

Viera, Joseph M. "Exile Among Exiles: Cristina García." *Poets and Writers* 26, no. 5:40–45 (September/October 1998).

Vorda, Allan. "A Fish Swims in My Lung: An Interview with Cristina García." In *Face to Face: Interviews with Contemporary Novelists.* Edited by Allan Vorda. Houston, Tex.: Rice University Press, 1993. Pp. 62–76.

—JOSEPH M. VIERA AND DEBORAH KAY FERRELL

Charlotte Perkins Gilman

1860–1935

"Work." This single word served as a beacon, a signal flag for all that Charlotte Perkins Gilman did and all that she believed. To be a complete person, she wrote, one must have some sort of meaningful, self-defining work, and one must have the freedom of choice to determine for herself the nature, scope, and range of that work, unencumbered by social traditions, prejudice, or gender expectations. The answer to what was commonly referred to in the nineteenth century as the "woman question," Gilman believed, was not to be found in women's suffrage, in equal education, or in equality under the law, though she worked for all these causes at various times in her life and thought them important. Rather Gilman held that the economic imperative—the ability to earn one's five hundred guineas, as Virginia Woolf would later write—enhanced one's value in a patriarchy, which ultimately brings one a sense of self-worth as well.

Born on July 3, 1860, in Hartford, Connecticut, Charlotte Anna Perkins, from early childhood on, felt herself destined for important deeds, coming as she did from one of New England's most illustrious families, the Beechers. Her great-grandfather was Lyman Beecher, the family patriarch, and she was the great-niece of Harriet Beecher Stowe, the preacher-reformer Henry Ward Beecher, the suffragist Isabella Beecher Hooker, and the author-educator Catharine Esther Beecher. Her uncle was Edward Everett Hale, an author and Unitarian clergyman married to her father's sister Emily, while Charlotte Perkins Gilman's father, Frederick Beecher Perkins, somewhat cold and distant, became a scholar and librarian of minor impor-

tance. Gilman would lament in a letter (reprinted in *A Journey from Within,* 1995) after his death, "So able a man—and so little to show for it."

Gilman was the third and last child of Frederick and Mary Perkins. The oldest son, Thomas Henry, died in infancy, and the second son, Thomas Adie, was born the year before Gilman. Mary Perkins' health was precarious, and Frederick Perkins left home shortly after Gilman's birth, when her mother was told that having another child would be ill-advised. Thereafter Gilman's father was only "an occasional visitor," as Gilman would later write in her autobiography, *The Living of Charlotte Perkins Gilman* (1935), "a writer of infrequent but always amusing letters with deliciously funny drawings, a sender of books, catalogues of books, lists of books to read," but never a real presence in her life. "By heredity," she admitted, "I owe him much; the Beecher urge to social service, the Beecher wit and gift of words and such small sense of art as I have; but . . . I have missed the education it would have been to have grown up in his society."

Growing up without his society meant a childhood filled with memories of railroad journeys, extended visits with relatives and friends, and always the specter of mounting debts and poverty. Watching her mother grieve for a lost husband and have to depend on the beneficence of family and friends became shaping events in Gilman's life. She recalled that her "mother's life was one of the most painfully thwarted I have ever known. After her idolized youth, she was left neglected. After her flood of lovers, she became a deserted wife. The most passionately domestic of home-worshiping housewives, she was forced to move nineteen times in eighteen years." Her mother was trained as a musician yet sold the piano to pay for food when Gilman was two; she never had another. Mary Perkins detested debt, but debt followed her everywhere she moved: "Absolutely loyal, as loving as a spaniel which no ill treatment can alienate, she made no complaint, but picked up her children and her dwindling furniture and traveled to the next place."

After thirteen years of such a life Mary Perkins divorced her husband, thinking to free him to marry another since he would not be a husband to her. Thereafter, however, Frederick Perkins and his family bitterly resented her: "So long as 'Mary Fred' was a blameless victim they pitied her and did what they could to help, but a divorce was a disgrace." Yet Gilman's mother loved Frederick Perkins until her death in 1893. Living with her daughter in Oakland, California—just across the bay from where Frederick worked as director of the San Francisco Public Library—Mary greatly desired to see him. "As long as she was able to be up," wrote Charlotte, "she sat always at the window watching for that beloved face. He never came."

To her daughter, Mary Perkins' life became an emblem for all that was wrong with the lives of nineteenth-century women. Relegated solely to the domestic sphere, fated to endure one pregnancy after another, dependent upon a husband for one's livelihood and social status, a woman like Mary Perkins had little for which to hope when the marriage contract failed or went awry. It was a flawed system of which young Gilman wanted no part. Other lessons learned from her mother's failed life developed in Gilman a stoic self-control and self-denial accompanied by an extraordinary longing for affection. Gilman wrote in her autobiography that her mother judiciously determined that her children would not suffer lost affection as she had, and the remedy was to condition them against affection: "She would not let me caress

her," wrote Gilman, "and would not caress me, unless I was asleep. This I discovered at last, and then did my best to keep awake till she came to bed, even using pins to prevent dropping off, and sometimes succeeding." When her mother then came into her room to see that she was tucked in, she pretended to be asleep: "how rapturously I enjoyed being gathered into her arms, held close and kissed."

Yet for one whose life would shape her work, Gilman had an imaginative and intellectually rich childhood. With only four years of formal schooling, she thrived on the stimulus of the extraordinary parlor conversation of the Beechers and the Hales. At seventeen she requested a reading list from her father that would facilitate her understanding of human history, as she "wished to help humanity." The books she read included some of the heroines of history, and at an early age she was interested in the variety of self-help programs that were currently in vogue, joining the Society for the Encouragement of Studies at Home and attending lectures by the likes of Oliver Wendell Holmes. She wrote about these formative years: "I figured it out that the business of mankind was to carry out the evolution of the human race, according to the laws of nature, . . . [and that] we are the only creatures that can assist evolution." Social evolution, she came to see, was "to be in human work," and one's first duty was "to find your real job, and do it."

She also learned during these formative years how important to her peace of mind physical exercise was, a facet of healthy life too often ignored in the social conditioning of young girls. She discovered the power of her own will as well, recalling in later years one of those defining moments when her will was tested against her mother's. In the fall of 1873 Mary Perkins had moved herself and her two children to a cooperative housekeeping group managed by a Dr. and Mrs. Stevens and inhabited by an odd array of esoterics and Swedenborgians, who more amused Gilman and her brother Thomas than inspired them. Gilman was commanded by her mother to apologize to Mrs. Stevens for some infraction that she did not commit, and she refused. Gilman's mother, a severe disciplinarian, demanded the apology or else her daughter "must leave." Gilman, again refusing to compromise her adolescent integrity, quietly looked at her mother and said: "I am not going to do it,—and I am not going to leave you— and what are you going to do about it?" Gilman's mother's response was to strike her daughter, but Gilman recalled, "I did not care. . . . I was realizing with an immense illumination that neither she, nor any one, could *make* me do anything. . . . one could not be coerced. I was born."

From the beginning, necessity inspired Gilman to find ways to earn her keep, though she later wrote that the "lack of money never impressed" her much. An artistic nature and some training at the Rhode Island School of Design provided her with the skills to turn her considerable artistic talent to profit, painting advertising cards for Kendall's Soap Company. She was once encouraged to devote herself to painting professionally and told that she could make a fine living painting still life, but she wrote: "This seemed to me a poor ambition, not conducive to my object—the improvement of the human race."

During these teen years several close relationships developed that remained with her throughout her life: her intense and deep friendship at seventeen with Martha Luther, whose engagement in 1881 caused her considerable pain, and her relationship with Grace Channing, granddaughter of William Ellery Channing. Grace Channing would be an important presence throughout the twists and turns of her life. Of her friendships with women Gilman would write to her cousin and later husband, George Houghton Gilman: "I have an intense and endless love for women, partly in reverence for their high

estate, partly in pity for their blind feebleness, their long ages of suffering." Writing to Luther in 1881 she questioned why her contemporary world "so confounded love with passion that it sounds to our century-tutored ears either wicked or absurd to name it between women?" Advising Luther to destroy her letters, Gilman understood even at twenty-one the gossipmongering and titillating nature of people: "What horrid stuff these letters would be for the Philistines!"

On January 10, 1882, Gilman wrote in her diary that she had been invited to visit "Mr. Stetson's studio . . . and eke to an art thing tomorrow night." Almost a year later she wrote despondently about Mr. Stetson: "I am weak. I anticipate a future of failure and suffering. Children sickly and unhappy. Husband miserable because of my distress. . . . Let me keep at least this ambition; to be a good and a pleasure to *some* one, to some others, no matter what I feel myself." Despite Gilman's better judgment, fears, and forebodings, Charles Walter Stetson swept his way into her life, proposing just two and a half weeks after he first set eyes on her. An up-and-coming young painter, unusually handsome, a combination of "Byron and Brando," as Gilman biographer Ann Lane has written, Stetson had an extraordinary physical appeal to Gilman. She wrote in her autobiography of this dashing young man's effect on her: "He was quite the greatest man, near my own age, that I had ever known. He stood alone, true to his art. . . . There was the natural force of sex-attraction between two lonely young people, the influence of propinquity." Despite Stetson's appeal, Gilman was ambivalent about their relationship from the beginning, seeing all the signs that she would never be able to have a great work and Stetson too.

Finally after "a terrible two years," according to her autobiography, she reluctantly consented to marry Stetson. There had been a mighty struggle between the two, and he had won his Pyrrhic victory. About the time of Stetson's first proposal Gilman had listed all the "reasons for living single" in her diary. The tenor of the rocky two-year relationship before their marriage can be observed in their diaries and letters as a war of wills punctuated by such incidents as the time Gilman declined a friend's gift of Walt Whitman's *Leaves of Grass* (later to become a favorite volume) because Stetson had disapproved of the explicit sexual references in the poem "Song of Myself." After the event the two parted company for more than five weeks. Arguments were interspersed with periods of closeness and the kinship of two immensely talented young people who felt overwhelming physical appeal for each other. On one occasion Stetson wrote the following manifesto, reprinted in Gilman's diary: "I hereby take my solemn oath that I shall never in future years expect of my wife any culinary or housekeeping proficiency. She shall never be required, whatever the emergency, to DUST."

After they were wed on May 2, 1884, by Stetson's father, a Baptist minister, there was only a semblance of truce, for Gilman was just beginning to come into her own at the very point that Stetson was expecting her to become his. Just a few months before, she was notified of her first publication, the poem "In Duty Bound," published in the *Woman's Journal* and later in her collection *In This Our World* (1893). Her reading during this time included John Stuart Mill's *On Liberty* and *The Subjection of Women,* which could not have left her with a settled mind as she interacted with Stetson, whose notions about young women's behavior were conservative and outspoken. At the same time, he was just beginning to have some tangible success with his own work. She reflected in her autobiography on this period: "I think Walter was happy. A most successful exhibition in Boston had established him more favorably and enabled him to meet domestic expenses; and an order for a set of large etchings was added."

Stetson's diaries during the period of courtship and early marriage (published in 1985 as *Endure: The Diaries of Charles Walter Stetson*) are telling as he charts his progress toward "domesticating" Gilman. He proudly notes that his love is transforming her, that she seems less willful, daring, and independent, that she is "more like what is best in other women— thoughtful, bland, gracious, humble, dependent." He marked the degrees that her will slowly bowed to his, that her pride began to dissipate; and he proudly declared, as if some momentous milestone in their relationship had been achieved: "She wants to be treated more as a child now than a woman."

By the time Gilman gave birth to her daughter Katharine just ten months after marrying, she had plunged into deep gloom and nervous exhaustion. As she recalled in her autobiography, her "steady cheerfulness, the strong, tireless spirit sank away. A sort of gray fog drifted across [her] mind, a cloud that grew and darkened." This was a period of profound gloom: "I, the ceaselessly industrious, could do no work of any kind. I was so weak that the knife and fork sank from my hands—too tired to eat." She lay on the "lounge and wept all day." Never before physically ill in her life, she found with her always a "constant dragging weariness miles below zero. Absolute incapacity. Absolute misery. To the spirit it was as if one were an armless, legless, eyeless, voiceless cripple." Called to serve humankind, she could not even serve herself. And of her daughter, whom she nursed for five months, she recalled, "I would hold her close—that lovely child!— and instead of love and happiness, feel only pain. The tears ran down on my breast. . . . Nothing was more utterly bitter than this."

It was almost as if she had foreseen this scenario in her poem "In Duty Bound," written a few months earlier:

A narrow house with roof so darkly low
  The heavy rafters shut the sunlight out.
One cannot stand erect without a blow:
    Until the soul inside
    Shrieks for a grave, more wide.
. . . .
           . . . It takes supernal strength
To hold the attitude that brings the pain.
And they are few indeed but stoop at length
    To something less than best,
    To find in stooping, rest.

Such stoic coming to terms with one's lot, however, was not to be in real life. It was obvious that the "nervous prostration" that her physician had diagnosed was not going to disappear on its own. Thus she was ordered to wean Katharine and go away for a time. Her dear friend Grace Channing, now living in Pasadena, had asked Gilman to join her family for a short visit during the winter of 1886. So traveling across the country, stopping in Ogden, Utah, for a brief stay with her brother Thomas and in San Francisco for a short visit with her father, she met Channing and found "paradise." She writes in her autobiography: "I recovered so fast, to outward appearance at least, that I was taken for a vigorous young girl. Hope came back, love came back, I was eager to get home to husband and child, life was bright again."

Gilman was always extremely generous toward Stetson, writing in her autobiography: "A lover more tender, a husband more devoted, woman could not ask. He helped in the housework more and more as my strength began to fail." Her diary records Stetson's unfailing devotion, his offer to let her "go free," his desire to do whatever was necessary to lift the dark and fearsome cloud. For the next year Gilman struggled valiantly to engage herself both in work and in motherhood. She continued to exercise, write, paint, and become involved in women's issues. Her diary records reading Elizabeth Barrett Browning's *Aurora Leigh* with Stetson in September, a story of a young woman's struggle to reconcile being an artist

with domesticity, which probably brought Gilman little sense of relief. A few months later Stetson brought home a copy of Margaret Fuller's *Woman in the Nineteenth Century*, which they read together, and shortly after that, *The History of Womankind in Western Europe*, but his efforts were more perfunctory than sincere. Additionally he worried that too much reading on her own might be harmful. In February of that year (1887) Alice Stone Blackwell had asked Gilman to manage a woman's suffrage column in the Providence newspaper, and she agreed to do it. She had recently met Blackwell (daughter of feminist icon Lucy Stone) and her husband, their egalitarian relationship standing in sharp contrast to her marriage. She wrote a play, articles on dress reform, and poetry, trying hard to reconcile domesticity with work. At length, again on the verge of nervous exhaustion, with talk of "pistols and chloroform," she prepared to journey to the Philadelphia clinic of Dr. S. Weir Mitchell, whose treatment of postpartum depression and female "hysteria" was touted as state of the art at the end of the century. A few days before leaving she wrote in her diary an apostrophe to Stetson: "I asked you a few days only before our marriage if you would take the responsibility entirely on yourself. You said yes. Bear it then."

S. Weir Mitchell was hailed as the best "nerve specialist" in the country; he accepted Gilman's case with unwavering confidence, certain that he could cure her depression and what she thought might be brain fever. He assured her that he had treated women like her before, informing her of the two types of people plagued with "nervous prostration," which Gilman recalled in her autobiography: "the business man exhausted from too much work, and the society woman exhausted from too much play." After ascertaining that her case was "hysteria" rather than "dementia" he prescribed a strict regimen:

> I was fed, bathed, rubbed, and responded with the vigorous body of twenty-six. . . . After a month of

this agreeable treatment he sent me home, with this prescription: "Live as domestic a life as possible. Have your child with you all the time. . . . Lie down an hour after each meal. Have but two hours' intellectual life a day. And never touch pen, brush or pencil as long as you live."

Gilman wrote that she returned home after a month of this treatment, diligently followed Mitchell's instructions, and "came perilously near to losing my mind." Her description of the months that followed her trip to Philadelphia ring remarkably familiar to anyone who has read "The Yellow Wallpaper": "I made a rag baby, hung it on a doorknob and played with it. I would crawl into remote closets and under beds—to hide from the grinding pressure of that profound distress." Then in a moment of "clear vision," without blame and without quarrel, she and Stetson agreed to divorce. It was clear that if she "went crazy," she later wrote, "it would do my husband no good, and be a deadly injury to my child." For the first time in four years of marriage Gilman felt the shroud begin to lift.

"THE YELLOW WALLPAPER"

Written directly from her experiences with Stetson and Dr. Mitchell, "The Yellow Wallpaper" originally appeared in the January 1892 issue of the *New England Magazine.* William Dean Howells, eventually to become Gilman's dear friend, had given the story to the editor of the *Atlantic Monthly,* who declined to publish such a disturbing piece of writing. When finally this remarkable story did find a publisher, Gilman was never actually paid the forty dollars the story was to have brought (her agent was supposedly paid but she never received the money), but Howells later asked to include it in a collection he was arranging called *Masterpieces of American Fiction.*

A classic in American fiction, "The Yellow Wallpaper" is an extraordinary piece of writing, artfully written yet serving clearly Gilman's straightforward aesthetic philosophy, as described in her autobiography: "In my judgment it is a pretty poor thing to write, to talk, without a purpose." The story, originally designated as a gothic tale, is about a young woman, a writer, a creative individual who has recently given birth and is struggling against postpartum depression. The protagonist, who is also the narrator, has been relegated by her physician-husband, John, to the upstairs nursery of a rented mansion while their own home is renovated and while she recovers from nervous exhaustion and "hysteria." John is a paragon of proper Victorian manly virtues—attentive, watchful . . . controlling. He is also "practical in the extreme" and a creature of facts rather than feelings, a man who "has no patience with faith, an intense horror of superstition" and, as the narrator notes, who "scoffs openly at any talk of things not to be felt and seen and put down in figures." Suffice it to say that John is a fitting symbol of the patriarchy. His sister, staying with the couple to help manage the household, functions as "keeper of the patriarchy" (Gilman was acutely aware that women often served to undermine any "sister" nonconformists). The narrator muses about her sister-in-law: "She is a perfect and enthusiastic housekeeper, and hopes for no better profession." Both husband and sister-in-law believe that the narrator's writing has been the chief source of her illness, and from both she must hide her creative efforts as she whiles away the days in the nursery. The dilemma in which the narrator finds herself is thus both an emblem for nineteenth-century woman and for the female artist, specifically the creative woman who attempts to reconcile domesticity and her work.

As the narrator remains, day after day, isolated behind the closed doors of the nursery, she becomes transfixed by the strange pattern of the wallpaper in the room, at first disturbed and appalled by its color and pattern but later mesmerized and obsessed. As time passes she observes that a particular spot on the paper appears to be in the shape of a "woman stooping down and creeping about behind the pattern." The figure behind the pattern appears more clearly at night in the moonlight (a Romantic metaphor for both madness and creativity, lunacy and illumination). Eventually the narrator becomes completely absorbed in contemplating the paper—its smell permeates the house, the fabric rubs off on her clothing, and always the specter of the figure behind the pattern haunts her imagination. At times during the daylight she notices the figure skulking about, creeping down the shaded lanes of the garden or in the dark niches of the grape arbor: "I don't blame her a bit," muses the narrator. "It must be very humiliating to be caught creeping by daylight! I always lock the door when I creep by daylight." At length she attempts to free the woman from behind the paper, and on the day before the family is to leave the house, John comes home to find her "creeping" in circles about the nursery, surrounded by a mass of torn wallpaper. The narrator tells her husband, "I've got out at last . . . in spite of you and Jane. And I've pulled off most of the paper, so you can't put me back!" With that John faints, and she continues to creep in circles about the room, crawling directly over his prostrate body—having at last escaped her stifling, confining existence through her very madness.

What is particularly brilliant about the story is the multifaceted, rich symbolism of the yellow wallpaper, which is an overt metaphor for the stifling, smothering lives of nineteenth-century women trapped by limiting social expectations and narrowly defined roles. However, the paper is also a metaphor for women's text and for women's art, considered by nineteenth-century patriarchal society as atypical and substandard. It is no accident that the speaker is a writer, an artist stifled by her situation and the well-meaning help of family and friends. The speaker says of the paper, with its "uncertain curves," "outrageous angles," and "contradictions" of design, "I know a little of the principle of design, and I know this thing was not arranged on any laws of radiation, or alternation, or repetition, or symmetry, or anything else that I ever heard of." Clearly Gilman crafted two dimensions to the story: the stifled mother and wife, discouraged from achieving any useful work, and the female artist whose work was judged as atypical and inferior by masculine critics of the day. The wallpaper serves also as an emblem for the "subtextual" quality of women's writing, particularly women's writing in the nineteenth century.

INDEPENDENCE AND A WOMAN'S WORK

In later years, Gilman wrote to her cousin Houghton Gilman that "to live steadily at an equal distance. . . . kills me. That is why 'wife' is a word unknown to me, and must be always." During the long, bleak winter of 1887–1888, the letters of Grace Channing were all that raised Gilman's spirits. The following summer she traveled to Bristol, Rhode Island, to stay for a while with Channing who was visiting there. The two wrote a play together, and Gilman determined to accompany Channing when she returned to Pasadena in October 1888. To afford the trip and to start a new life with her daughter Katharine, Gilman sold her property, paid her debts, and, saying goodbye to Stetson, left for California on October 8. By Christmas Stetson, having difficulty reconciling himself to the breakup of their marriage, followed. Gilman was adamant that they separate, however, and Stetson, with her blessing, turned increasingly to Channing for sympathy and consolation. Eventually, after his and Gilman's divorce in 1894, Stetson would marry Grace Channing.

During that "first year of freedom," as Gilman recalled in her autobiography, she wrote "some thirty-three short articles, and twenty-three poems, besides ten more child-verses," as well as plays with Channing. Gilman also became active in community theater and performed regularly. During the next year her energy level was very high despite the economic worries, and she seemed to come into her own as a writer. A high point of accomplishment, she recalled, was receiving a note from Howells praising her poem "Similar Cases." "We have nothing since the Biglow Papers," Howells wrote, "half so good. . . . And just now I've read in *The Woman's Journal* your 'Women of To-day.' It is as good almost as the other, and dreadfully true." Gilman wrote a summary of the year 1890 in one of her diaries, noting that the period had been "cruelly hard" yet "a year of great growth and gain. My whole literary reputation dates within it—mainly from 'Similar Cases.' Also the dawn of my work as lecturer." The next year she recorded in her diary a profound compliment from her uncle Edward Everett Hale: "You are getting to be a famous woman my dear!" The transformation had begun; she had become a writer, and she was free.

Over the next decade Gilman established her literary and activist reputation; became one of the most important female lecturers in the country; edited a major publication, the *Impress*; published a favorably reviewed collection of poems, *In This Our World* (1893); and wrote and published her magnum opus, *Women and Economics* (1898). On a personal level the decade was propitious as well, with the events of her life always shaping her ideas and her writing. California at this time was, as she recalled, "a seed-bed" for new ideas and forward thinking, particularly in the area of labor and economics.

One day while riding a bus she met a woman who invited her to speak at the Nationalist Club of Pasadena. The Nationalist clubs and their publication were the chief organs for the social doctrines of Edward Bellamy, whose book *Look-ing Backward* espoused his socialist, utopian theories of cooperative social change. The Nationalists repudiated Marxist doctrine that advocated class struggle and violent change, focusing instead on eliminating social injustices and economic disparities through democratic processes and the "evolutionary" molding of human nature through education and peaceful change. Gilman tried to make a distinction between her brand of socialism and that of Marx, writing in her autobiography that her "Socialism was of the early humanitarian kind, based on the first exponents, French and English, with the American enthusiasm of Bellamy. The narrow and rigid 'economic determinism' of Marx . . . I never accepted." She also made clear that her main socialist interest was "in the position of women, and the need for more scientific care for young children." Gilman always thought that women's economic independence was "of far more importance than the ballot."

As lecture engagements increased and essays and poetry found their way into publication, "Mrs. Stetson's" activism increased. She organized a number of women's congresses in California, where she met Helen Campbell, Jane Addams, and Susan B. Anthony, all becoming lifelong friends, as would the activist daughters of Lucy Stone and Elizabeth Cady Stanton. She also met in 1891 two women who would become personally important in her life, Harriet ("Hattie") Howe, Nationalist program chair, and Adeline ("Delle") Knapp, a reporter for the *San Francisco Call*. That year she had begun divorce proceedings against Stetson, and her mother had come to live with her. Thus by September 1891 Gilman, her mother, Katharine, and Knapp began living together. In February the following year they moved to a boarding-house at 1258 Webster Street in Oakland. The owner, a Mrs. Palmer, shortly turned over the daily running of the house to Gilman, who would draw upon those experiences in her later novel *Benigna Machiavelli* (1914). As Gilman's responsibilities increased and her mother grew more feeble, Howe too came to live at the boardinghouse to help with the work.

All during this time Gilman continued to write. Hattie Howe remembered her friend as an extraordinarily dynamic and charismatic speaker as well. In an essay she wrote after Gilman's death (reprinted in *Critical Essays on Charlotte Perkins Gilman,* 1992), Howe described Gilman as a slender woman, even smaller behind the podium, but with an unforgettable presence: "Such eyes, magnetic, far reaching, deep seeing, nothing could be hid from such eyes, and a Voice, clear, compelling, yet conversational, easily reaching to the farthest end of the hall, entirely devoid of effort."

Gilman's relationships with Howe and Knapp have been the focus of much biographical attention. Certainly her diaries reveal a closeness that is unusual even within the confines of overly affectionate Victorian relationships typical of nineteenth-century women. Her friendship with Knapp was more volatile and short-lived but more intense than her relationship with Howe. Shortly after meeting Knapp, Gilman wrote: "Go and lunch with Miss Knapp. I love her." As she wrote of going on a boat ride with her new friend, her words were unusually sensual—"a calm, delicious night, warm, starlit, with the light-engirdled bay all smooth, and we two happy together. She spends the night." At times when Knapp was away on a journalistic assignment, Howe filled the void of affection: "Read poetry to Hattie in the evening and make love to her." However one interprets such confessions, it is certain that because of these relationships Gilman's burden of caring for her mother, who had been diagnosed with cancer, was lightened somewhat, despite the frequent quarrels with Knapp, whose lifestyle and habits were incompatible with those of Gilman. On March 7, 1893, Mrs. Perkins passed away after

a long and difficult illness. When Knapp left for the last time on July 15, 1893, an exhausted Gilman wrote, "It is a great relief to have her go."

Increasingly Gilman became involved in more reformist organizations, including the Pacific Coast Women's Press Association (PCWPA) for whom she edited a small paper, the *Impress,* transforming it into a family weekly. She also belonged to the Woman's Alliance, the Economic Club, the Ebell Society, the State Council of Women, and others. During these years (1893–1895), she viewed herself principally as a philosopher rather than a reformer, writing in her autobiography: "My business was to find out what ailed society, and how most easily and naturally to improve it."

In April 1894 Gilman's divorce decree was finally granted. A few months earlier Grace Channing had visited, and Gilman had spoken with her about Katharine's staying for a while with her and Stetson. Katharine was nine now, and Gilman's work was becoming ever more demanding, with long periods traveling and lecturing. The steady life that Stetson and Channing could provide was admittedly more settled and healthier for the child than what Gilman could offer her. "Giving up" her daughter was perhaps the most painful act of her life and certainly drew down the wrath of friends and foes alike, yet she knew that it must be done. Looking back on the event she wrote in her autobiography

> Since her second mother was fully as good as the first, better in some ways perhaps; since the father longed for his child and had a right to some of her society; and since the child had a right to know and love her father . . . this seemed the right thing to do. No one suffered from it but myself.

The parenting relationship that Gilman, Channing, and Stetson forged was remarkable, as revealed in letters included in *The Diaries of Charlotte Perkins Gilman* (1992). Shortly after

Katharine's arrival at her father's home, Stetson wrote to Gilman:

> She sits at arm's length from me—oh so beautiful! It makes tears fill my eyes—drawing for you. . . . No two persons could be more companionable than we are. I know what she wants before she says it. . . . truly, dear, I do not see how I can ever let her leave me again. . . . I wish we could have her *together*.

Gilman was always particularly appreciative of Grace Channing for her care of Katharine, writing some years later to her ex-husband, "I am unceasingly grateful to Grace for being what she is—have been ever since I knew her."

Katharine's memories of both her "mothers" were positive, and through living with her father, traveling to Europe, and receiving his encouragement she developed the artistic talents she had inherited from both parents. However, Gilman was haunted and guilt-ridden that Katharine had gone to live with her father, expressing in 1897 to her cousin Houghton Gilman how much she missed her child: "This baby down stairs makes me think of Kate so. Kate when she was little and O so lovely! . . . it aches and aches. I wish—no I don't wish a thing." Though Katharine would spend long vacations with her mother and would later live with her for periods of time, Gilman confessed to her cousin: "You see I can't even let myself go toward Katharine, for the simple reason that it hurts so. And pain—emotional pain—means madness. I *can* not suffer any more. The spring is broken. To think much of her is to want her."

Gilman was always bitter over the way many of her California friends and the public in general reacted to the decision she and Stetson made to share Katharine. She sarcastically recalled in her autobiography that while reporters and interviewers continued for years to question her about their decision and about her personal life, she had yet to read a single article in the media entitled "Should Artistic Men Marry?"

In the summer of 1895 the *Impress* folded and, at the invitation of Jane Addams, Gilman left California to travel to Chicago. Addams was one of the country's leading reformers and activists, having established Hull-House as a settlement house offering community support services. For a short time Gilman lived at Hull-House, participating in the community and learning much from the wide array of reformers and thinkers drawn to Addams. Gilman later referred to Addams as "a truly great woman. Her mind had more 'floor space' in it than any other I have known." Addams asked Gilman to take over the management of a new settlement house in a place called "Little Hell" on Chicago's north side, but still fearful of her occasional emotional unsteadiness, she declined, suggesting her mentor and mother-figure Helen Campbell for the task. She did, however, attend the January 1896 Suffrage Convention in Washington and there meet Lester F. Ward, who had written to her praising "Similar Cases." Ward, whom Gilman had long admired, was one of the leading thinkers in the new field of sociology and a Reform Social Darwinist. His ideas were immensely influential on Gilman's writing.

On July 8 Gilman sailed for England to attend the International Socialist and Labor Congress as a delegate from California, this trip abroad to be one of many in the succeeding years. She made many valuable contacts while there and visited her English publisher, T. Fisher Unwin, who had recently published the British edition of her collection of poems, *In This Our World*. She met the playwright George Bernard Shaw and other Fabians and became close friends with the family of the poet William Morris, particularly his daughter May, who became a lifelong friend. She found herself known and admired in England and returned to America to commence what she referred to as her "wander years," an "at large" delegate in the business of the world. The closest she came during this time to a "home" was the New York boardinghouse that belonged to her stepmother (Frederick Perkins had remarried an old flame, Frankie Johnson, whom he had known before Mary Perkins). Gilman relished the opportunity to develop a relationship with her stepmother and stepsisters and even with her father, who was in declining health. In 1897, the following year, she began two important projects: getting reacquainted with her cousin Houghton Gilman and putting to paper a body of ideas that had been distilling for sometime in her mind—*Women and Economics.*

WOMEN AND ECONOMICS

The first draft of the most important book Gilman would write was finished in just seventeen days and written in five different houses. As was usually the case in Gilman's writing during this time, ideas were first expressed in lecture form and then in written form, with little revision and in the same straightforward style as she spoke. However, these particular ideas had been fermenting for years, a brew derived from original thought as well as from a variety of general influences (Charles Darwin, Ward, Bellamy, Olive Schreiner, even Whitman and Ralph Waldo Emerson). Gilman was not in the habit of compiling bibliographies, and indeed, beyond study in general philosophy and sociology, her ideas were original or derived from the copious conversations that she enjoyed in the reformist circles in which she lived and worked. After Mary Wollstonecraft's *Vindication of the Rights of Woman,* Mill's *The Subjection of Women,* and Fuller's *Woman in the Nineteenth Century,* Gilman's *Women and Economics* is one of the most important and original contributions to feminist thought before the twentieth century. In her insistence that woman's economic dependence on man was at the root of her servitude and excessively sexualized social role, Gilman was much ahead of her time, particularly in an age that still believed that political enfranchisement would secure gender equality.

Gilman began her argument by asserting that human beings are the "only animal species in which the female depends on the male for food, the only animal species in which the sex-relation is also an economic relation." Yet she insisted that women did in fact render economic service through their domestic duty, but they were rarely compensated for that service. Women were likewise seldom encouraged to find useful nondomestic work for the period before and after their maternal service: "A human female, healthy, sound, has twenty-five years of life before she is a mother, and should have twenty-five years more after the period of such maternal service." Women were instead, argued Gilman, encouraged to become parasitic creatures, whose living is obtained by the exertions of others.

Drawing upon her understanding of Darwinian determinism, Gilman asserted that "the human female was cut off from the direct action of natural selection, that mighty force which heretofore had acted on male and female alike . . . developing strength, developing skill, developing endurance, developing courage." Nineteenth-century women erroneously saw their "economic profit" as coming solely through the "power of sex-attraction," and that fact dominated every aspect of their lives. Just as Wollstonecraft found the female to be constitutionally and mentally inferior as schooled by eighteenth-century society, so too did Gilman: "Man has advanced, but woman has been kept behind. . . . By experience she is retarded." But woman's inferior condition she lays squarely at the feet of patriarchal society: "No wonder that our daily lives are full of the flagrant evils produced by [women's] unnatural state. No wonder that men turn with loathing from the kind of women they have made."

Gilman observed both sexes as debilitated by such a system whose result was an unnatural emphasis on the "sex relationship." Woman "gets her living by getting a husband," Gilman wrote. Man "gets his wife by getting a living. It is to her individual economic advantage to secure a mate. It is to his individual sex-advantage to secure economic gain. The sex-functions to her have become economic functions." To focus female energy in such a limited way or to forgo that bountiful energy which might be channeled to areas of social good was a waste; by the same token, woman's influence in the traditional working world would serve to balance the overabundance of male aggression in what was traditionally designated as solely his sphere. Gilman wrote, "Between the brutal ferocity of excessive male energy struggling in the market-place as in a battlefield and the unnatural greed generated by the perverted condition of female energy, it is not remarkable that the industrial evolution of humanity has shown peculiar symptoms."

To those who charged that such economic equality would "unwoman" the female Gilman responded that work inculcates personhood and a sense of one's usefulness to society. With characteristic talent at "turning the question," Gilman argued that it is not, for example, "being a doctor that makes a woman unwomanly, but the treatment which the first women medical students and physicians received was such as to make . . . men unmanly." To counter those who would assert that woman's subjugation had the advantage of keeping her at home to preserve the cohesiveness of the family unit, Gilman declared such logic specious—indeed the real reason for woman's subjugation and sex differentiation was simply to maintain the sexual and domestic services she provided. The consequences of the traditional nineteenth-century division of labor were a variety of types of personal deceit and perversions both in men and in women. A healthier state for both sexes would be to have woman "stand beside man as the comrade of his soul, not the servant of his body."

HOUGHTON AND RESOLVING THE UNRESOLVABLE

The two central controlling emotions throughout Charlotte Perkins Gilman's life were the need for love and the need for work, and until she knocked upon the door of her cousin's Wall Street law office the afternoon of March 8, 1897, both appeared unresolvable. She recalled in her autobiography that she stood before her young cousin that day and asked, "You haven't the slightest idea who I am"—to which Houghton Gilman replied, "Yes I have, you're my Cousin Charlotte." Two days later he repaid the visit, and Gilman wrote in her diary that evening: "Houghton Gilman calls. Like him." They began to go about together to plays and museums, and as Gilman recalled, "This was the beginning of a delightful renewal of earlier friendship, still continuing." Theirs was thus a "friendship," as William Godwin once said of his relationship with Wollstonecraft, which melted into love.

If Walter Stetson were uniquely ill-suited for Charlotte Perkins, Houghton Gilman was happily uniquely right. He was a kind, supportive, gentle, unassuming, and intelligent man. She did not write a great deal about their relationship in her autobiography but to state simply that they "were married—and lived happy ever after. If this were a novel, now, here's the happy ending." The volume of her letters to him, however, records their deep affection and the singular care that both took in coming to terms with their love and attempting to forge a relationship that would both suit and last.

To be fair, Gilman had repeated the warning to her new suitor that she had written to Stetson almost twenty years before declaring that as much as she loved him, she loved "WORK better, & I cannot make the two compatible." She cautioned, "Think another year dear boy. And—much as I love you—do not [let] your final decision be influenced by fear of its effect on me. . . . feel *free* to decide." Her love letters to Houghton Gilman, seven years her junior, record the difficult three-year struggle for both as they agonized whether marriage was the right thing to do. Writing to him in 1899 she declared without guile, "My position is this. First last and always I must so live as to do my work. . . . I shall have rooms of my own." That they eventually came together so compatibly was due to Houghton's willingness to accept Gilman as she was (something Stetson was not able do) and Gilman's candor in dealing with Houghton. She wrote to him: "Mine is a self-absorbed and other-people-absorbing nature—I am apt to encroach. . . . You must not let me swallow you—pour my life and affairs all over you. I don't *mean* to be selfish and exacting, but I fear I am."

Gilman tried to convince her cousin that she could never be a domestic woman; she had already unsuccessfully tried that route. She wrote in an early love letter: "Houghton—as you value my life, my sanity, my love; use your clear mind and strong will to work out such plan of living as shall leave me free to move as move I must. You will have to give up a certain ideal of home; I shall have to give up even more." She wanted him to understand her faults as well as her finer points: "My charms are essentially transient—I'm awfully nice for a while. But you hold me and I spoil on your hands!" She warns him in the same letter, "My love for you is a poor thing. It was not great enough in the first place to protect you from my own selfish longing for somebody to love me and care for me."

Houghton Gilman was certainly human enough to have his own doubts about the monumental step they would take on June 11, 1900. Particularly he worried about being overshadowed by his wife, about being left in the lower gallery as she soared on to fame, about never quite measuring up professionally to her. Yet he succeeded where Stetson failed because his love was unselfish enough to accept her unconditionally and to attempt sincerely to understand her range of ideas and ideals. He asked her to suggest books to read, reacted to her writing, and attempted to enter into her sphere of understanding, and she repaid him with her undivided concern and admiration. Writing to him in 1897 she reflected, "How kind your eyes are. . . . You looked at me in a way that stays." Houghton was willing simply to be there for her, and that was quite enough. "I *cannot* give you all—or even much," she wrote to him in the year before they married. "It is simply that you will be there to come back to—and O how *glad* I shall be to come back!"

A NEW BEGINNING

The year 1900 was happy and personally fulfilling in a variety of ways. Gilman wrote in her diary at year's end: "I am happy & content. Houghton—Katharine—Home." As to her professional plans for 1901 she resolved, "May I grow stronger and do good work in spite of my happiness!" Her new beginning with her new husband in many ways marked a fresh start with her daughter as well. Two years before, thirteen-year-old Katharine had come for a long summer visit with her mother in the resort town of Cold Spring Harbor, Long Island. There mother and daughter renewed their relationship, and Gilman's diaries and letters are filled with blissful comments about how good it was to have Katharine again, what a sweet, beautiful, and empathetic child she was. Gilman wrote to Houghton, "If I cry—she cries. . . . I spoke lightly . . . [of her] abundance of other parents; and she said promptly that none of them were as nice as I was! Last night, cuddling me closely, she inquired why it was that one's mother was better than anything else in the world." Yet despite the joy of being with Katharine again, the emotional pressure caused old haunts within to resurface, and she wrote to Houghton: "I felt very weak Monday morning, and low. . . . like the passing of a black cloud."

By the end of August the strain was clear and present, and it was with some relief that the visit ended and Katharine left to rejoin her father and stepmother in California.

After Gilman and Houghton were married she seemed better able to cope, and her daughter, then fifteen, came to live with them in New York. With Houghton to help, Gilman was better able to integrate work and family, and when she was away on an extended lecture tour, her old friend and mentor Helen Campbell came to stay with Katharine and Houghton. The Gilmans lived in New York from 1900 until 1922 in successive apartments during an extraordinarily productive period. In 1902, after a serious illness with scarlet fever, Katharine joined Stetson and Channing in Italy to study art, with Gilman visiting her daughter after her 1905 international tour. This visit must have been particularly satisfying for Katharine, who had the opportunity to show her mother the country that had become her home.

Though she did not actually receive much financial return from *Women and Economics,* Gilman did establish both her place in the publishing world and her international reputation. Based upon the extraordinary popularity of this book she received a five-hundred-dollar advance on her next, *Human Work* (1904), which in her autobiography she called "the greatest book I have ever done, and the poorest." She uncharacteristically revised and rewrote *Human Work,* never completely satisfied with the book, though it was important for developing several new ideas. For one, she articulated in it her conception of society as an "organic" unit which functions as a living organism, in which one poisoned aspect affects all other parts. One's "highest duty," she wrote, is to recognize these organic relationships and "to find and hold our proper place in the Work in which and by which we all live." In particular she returned to the idea that female servitude and woman's sex-based economic function are

in themselves a "social disease," and the woman "who makes her living by marriage" is essentially a "prostitute."

While revising *Human Work,* Gilman wrote and published two other works: *Concerning Children* (1900) and *The Home* (1903). *Concerning Children* is a wonderful blending of sociological theory about the home and a practical approach to child rearing. Gilman believed that children were not merely individual members of a family group but formed a permanent and distinct class and should be respected and nurtured with that fact in mind. Certainly a child needs the love and kindness which the home provides, but the self-sacrificing mother, Gilman believed, only produces selfish children. Gilman also challenged the traditional Victorian attitude toward rearing children in the "habit of obedience"; conditioning them to reason and to think for themselves made more sense to Gilman. "It is a commonplace observation," she adds, "that the best children—i.e., the most submissive and obedient—do not make the best men [or] . . . the best citizen[s]."

The Home develops the central thesis that as society has evolved the home has remained stagnant. Men have ranged freely and developed the modern industrial age while women have remained "home-bound" and ignorant not "necessarily of books, but ignorant of general life." An interesting essay that follows this line of thought is "Domestic Economy," published in *The Independent* (June 16, 1904). Here Gilman examined the inefficiency of the typical one-woman/one-home household and in particular the ideal—and to her mind false assumption—that a husband and wife are equal partners, his wife, in her fashion, "doing just as much as he . . . for the success of the firm." Gilman maintained that it is a "waste" for "half the people of the world," regardless of their potential talents or intellectual capacity, "to wait upon the other half, thus limiting the output of their labor." Gilman posited instead a revisioning of the home and cooperative home economy in which professional men and women would render their abilities and talents to the work world while skilled home workers provided services allowing the day-to-day functions of the home to carry forth. In the same fashion professionals would also teach and care for small children.

THE *FORERUNNER* YEARS AND AFTER

As the first decade of the new century drew to a close, Gilman continued to write in the same prolific fashion as before, but she began to encounter difficulty placing essays and books with publishers and journals. In her autobiography, she recalled a conversation she had sometime before November 1909 with Theodore Dreiser, then on the *Delineator* staff, who looked at her from across his desk and said, "You should consider more what the editors want." Taking his words more to heart than he could have imagined she determined to become her own editor and publisher, embarking on an entirely new venture—the publication of her own monthly magazine, *Forerunner*, "written," as she said, "entirely by myself." Each issue contained one installment of a novel, the serial publication of a polemical piece, a short story, articles of various length, poems, verses, book reviews, and other types of writing. It was a huge undertaking, one that she sustained for seven years.

Another idea lay behind her foray into publishing: she understood that the writing of nonfiction had its limitations and that stories and novels which dramatically illustrated her ideas might reach a broader audience. Certainly she continued to produce philosophic and sociological studies—*The Man-Made World* (1911) examined the effects of masculine dominance on the family, art, literature, education and religion; *Our Brains and What Ails Them* (1912) looked at social problems resulting from people trained not to think logically; and *Social Ethics* (1914) explored the ethical weaknesses of organized patriarchal religion. However, by this point in time, it seemed to Gilman that fiction might touch the heart strings and accomplish more with the masses than nonfictional appeals to logic.

Gilman was candid about her writing, declaring in her autobiography that hers was "not, in the artistic sense, 'literature.'" As far as method was concerned, her goal was simply "to express the idea with clearness and vivacity, so that it might be apprehended with ease and pleasure." Certainly her assessment is true for the majority of fiction she wrote for *Forerunner*; however, some of the stories recall the fine writing of "The Yellow Wallpaper." For example, "If I Were a Man," printed in *Physical Culture* in 1914, is a delightful piece of satire utilizing the technique of "gender cross-fire," allowing women to see how the other half lives. In it Gilman also made a statement of what for her would be a kind of androgynous ideal: a woman's consciousness in a male body and with male freedom. Other interesting short stories published in the *Forerunner* are "The Cottagette" (August 1910), dramatizing how domesticity robs a woman of her life; "Making a Change" (December 1911), portraying a musician-mother who nearly loses her mind until allowed to reclaim her talent; "Turned" (September 1911), a powerful story of marital betrayal and a wife's befriending the compromised servant girl; and "The Unnatural Mother" (November 1916), a metaphor for Gilman's personal sacrifices in which a good mother sacrifices her life in order to save her town during a flood, only to be judged harshly by the townspeople for "abdicating" her responsibilities to her child.

Several longer works of fiction, all but one published in the *Forerunner*, exhibit Gilman's virtuosity in terms of genres and styles, as well as provide fairly good storytelling—these are

Benigna Machiavelli, the science-fiction fantasy companion volumes *Herland* (1915) and *With Her in Ourland* (1916), and the detective novel *Unpunished* (1997). Benigna Machiavelli is a non-traditional heroine who determines to forge her own way in life, using whatever Machiavellian methods she can muster. The story is told from the point of view of a precocious adolescent, and Gilman is able to direct a good deal of pointed satire at the patriarchy in this picaresque survival novel. Some of the more interesting ideas explored in the novel deal with Gilman's awareness of the "reality" created through literature. For example, early in the story Benigna observes that the world needs "good people with brains, not just negative, passive, good people, but positive, active ones, who [give] their minds to it." Indeed, she adds, what the world needs is a "good villain," and she makes up her mind to become one. Thereafter Benigna "plays" her life as a heroine in a novel of her own making. Another associated motif is the actor/player theme, which serves as a metaphor for the flexibility and imagination that one needs for survival in this world.

Unpunished is a dark satire in the guise of a detective mystery. It tells the story of a villainous male authority figure and symbol for the patriarchy who happens to be a lawyer, Wade Vaughn—a man whose public face is the benevolent patron caring for his stepdaughter and dead wife's disfigured sister, Jacqueline Warner. His private face, though, is that of a sadistic blackmailer, a powerful individual who thrives on controlling those around him at the expense of human decency. Vaughn's murder opens the novel, and we learn in bits and pieces the nature of his crimes, as husband and wife detective team, Bessie and Jim Hunt, unravel the mystery in a manner later made popular by the *Thin Man* detective stories. The quick-paced, upbeat dialogue provides an interesting counter to the noir satire. The book provides an exposé on domestic violence and also presents some

extremely modern feminist ideas—for example, the importance of "telling one's story" or, as Carolyn Heilbrun would say, "writing one's life" as both a therapeutic and shaping reality. Gilman presents some powerful symbols: the "will" as a metaphor for the patriarchy's control of women, Jacqueline's physical deformity as an ironic contrast to Wade Vaughn's moral deformity, and the "mask" (Wade's figurative mask and Jacqueline's literal) as a metaphor for social deception. The story has many fascinating turns of plot, with the resolution of the murder providing a surprising denouement.

Two of Gilman's most important books printed in the *Forerunner* are the satirical science-fiction fantasy *Herland* and its sequel, *With Her in Ourland.* While these works provide some of Gilman's best writing, they also evince some characteristics that critics have observed mar her work: ethnocentrism and chauvinism. While the occasional ethnic slights and comments certainly detract from the body of Gilman's work, it is important to place Gilman's ethnocentrism within the context of the Social Darwinism and intelligentsia circles of her time, when talk of "race" superiority and ethnic characteristics were common. It is also important to understand that a different benchmark of political correctness was current at the turn of the century and that Gilman was often very blunt, seldom cloaking her ideas in softening language. It should be noted, as well, that comments which make us uncomfortable are often spoken by fictional characters we should not readily assume to be Gilman's center of intelligence. We should consider also the whole body of Gilman's work, as well as her personal life and actions. As Gilman biographer Ann Lane has noted, "Charlotte's was the only voice raised at the 1903 convention of the National American Woman's Suffrage Association against a literacy requirement for the vote."

As satire, which is essentially the way both *Herland* and *Ourland* should be read, these two books fall within a genre in which Gilman exhibits considerable skill. Following the tradition of Jonathan Swift and Samuel Johnson she employs the convention of cultural crossfire in both works. She allows her innocent ingenue—in most cases Herlander Ellador—to react to the young men who serve as foils and presents American culture and traditions for Ellador (and us) to observe and assess freshly without blinding cultural biases. The technique works well in *Herland,* which owes much to Swift's *Gulliver's Travels,* and to a lesser extent in *Ourland,* a modern rendition of Johnson's *Rasselas.*

Gilman uses many traditional rhetorical strategies of satire to expose the patriarchy: ironic inversion, as the men are viewed as sex objects in *Herland,* and cultural crossfire, as the societies of *Herland* and America are contrasted. In the process the overmasculinized system with its "sexuo-economic" values, which in large part Terry represents, is seen for what it is. At one point in the story Terry despairs over the women he sees in Herland: "They've neither the vices of men, nor the virtues of women—they're neuters!" The narrator assesses Terry's biased point of view: "Terry did not like it because he found nothing to oppose, to struggle with, to conquer. 'Life is a struggle, has to be,' he insisted. 'If there is no struggle, there is no life—that's all.'" Because the world of Herland is centered on children, a nurturing, cooperative spirit rather than a competitive spirit drives society. Yet Gilman does not necessarily portray *Herland* as the definitive model, as the sequel *Ourland* makes clear.

With Her in Ourland carries the story from the world of women back to the men's world. Jeff chooses to remain in Herland with Celis, preferring the world of women to the aggressive, competitive, and flawed patriarchy. Terry is cast out of Herland for his antisocial behavior when he attempts to take his unwilling bride Alima in a boorish fashion. Van and Ellador choose to leave Herland of their own accord, as Ellador wishes to study Van's world to see if Herland might be improved. The couple travels through a broad range of patriarchal countries, and Ellador is anxious to see firsthand the European conflict brewing in France and Germany in 1915.

The last years of Gilman's life were as the first, busy with work and writing, for she was prolific until the end of her life. Even after the *Forerunner* folded she continued to produce, contributing in 1919 and 1920 over three hundred articles to *New York Tribune* syndicates, including the *Baltimore Sun* and the *Buffalo Evening News.* Other major works were still to follow: *His Religion and Hers* in 1923 and her autobiography, *The Living of Charlotte Perkins Gilman,* which was published posthumously in 1935. When Walter Stetson died in 1911, Grace Channing and Katharine moved near the Gilmans' New York apartment. Katharine went on to become an artist like her father, eventually setting up a studio near both mothers in New York. After she married F. Tolles Chamberlin, a painter and sculptor, she moved to her beloved Pasadena and had two children.

In 1922 Gilman and Houghton moved from New York to Norwich Town, Connecticut, to live in Houghton's family home, sharing the house with Houghton's brother and wife, an unhappy arrangement with which they coped with marginal success. However, Gilman's letters and autobiography suggest that all her years with Houghton were happy ones, and she worried after learning of her breast cancer diagnosis that he would be alone when she died. In 1934 Houghton suffered a cerebral hemorrhage, and she remembered in her autobiography, "Whatever I felt of loss and pain was outweighed by gratitude for an instant, painless death for him, and that he did not have to see me wither and die—and he be left alone." Afterward she flew to Pasadena to be near Katharine, and Channing joined her in a little house next to Katharine.

Unwilling to repeat the circumstances of her mother's illness and believing to the end that she was master of her fate, Gilman, with the blessing of those she loved, took a lethal dose of chloroform and died on August 17, 1935.

Selected Bibliography

WORKS OF CHARLOTTE PERKINS GILMAN

FICTION

What Diantha Did. In *Forerunner* 1 (1909–1910); New York: Charlton, 1910.

The Crux. Serialized in *Forerunner* 2 (1911); New York: Charlton, 1911.

Moving the Mountain. In *Forerunner* 2 (1911); New York: Charlton, 1911.

Herland. New York: Pantheon, 1979; Mineola, N.Y.: Dover, 1998.

The Charlotte Perkins Gilman Reader: The Yellow Wallpaper and Other Fiction. Edited with introduction by Ann J. Lane. New York: Pantheon, 1980.

Benigna Machiavelli. Santa Barbara: Bandanna, 1994.

"The Yellow Wall-Paper" and Selected Stories of Charlotte Perkins Gilman. Edited by Denise D. Knight. Newark: University of Delaware Press, 1994.

Unpunished. Edited by Catherine J. Golden and Denise D. Knight. New York: Feminist Press, 1997.

With Her in Ourland: Sequel to Herland. Westport, Conn.: Greenwood, 1997.

POETRY

In This Our World: Poems. Oakland, Calif.: McCombs & Vaughn, 1893; Boston: Small, Maynard, 1898; New York: Arno, 1974.

The Later Poetry of Charlotte Perkins Gilman. Edited by Denise D. Knight. Newark: University of Delaware Press, 1996.

NONFICTION

Women and Economics: A Study of the Economic Relation between Men and Women as a Factor in Social Evolution. Boston: Small, Maynard, 1898; Mineola, N.Y.: Dover, 1998.

Concerning Children. Boston: Small, Maynard, 1900.

The Home: Its Work and Influence. New York: McClure, Phillips, 1903.

Human Work. New York: McClure, Phillips, 1904.

The Man-Made World; or, Our Androcentric Culture. In *Forerunner* 1 (1909–1910); New York: Charlton Co., 1911.

Our Brains and What Ails Them. Serialized in *Forerunner* 3 (1912).

Social Ethics. Serialized in *Forerunner* 4 (1914).

His Religion and Hers: A Study of the Faith of Our Fathers and the Work of Our Mothers. New York: Century, 1923.

The Living of Charlotte Perkins Gilman: An Autobiography. New York: Appleton-Century, 1935; edited with introduction by Ann J. Lane, Madison: University of Wisconsin Press, 1990.

Charlotte Perkins Gilman: A Nonfiction Reader. Edited by Larry Ceplair. New York: Columbia University Press, 1991.

The Diaries of Charlotte Perkins Gilman. Edited by Denise D. Knight. 2 vols. Charlottesville: University Press of Virginia, 1994. (An abridged version was published in 1998.)

A Journey from Within: The Love Letters of Charlotte Perkins Gilman, 1897–1900. Edited by Mary A. Hill. Lewisburg: Bucknell University Press, 1995.

OTHER WORKS

The Forerunner 1–7 (1909–1916). Reprint, with introduction by Madeleine B. Stern, New York: Greenwood, 1968.

BIBLIOGRAPHY

Scharnhorst, Gary. *Charlotte Perkins Gilman, A Bibliography.* Metuchen, N.J.: Scarecrow, 1985.

CRITICAL AND BIOGRAPHICAL STUDIES

Degler, Carl N. "Charlotte Perkins Gilman on the Theory and Practice of Feminism." *American Quarterly* 8:21–39 (spring 1956).

Golden, Catherine, ed. *The Captive Imagination: A Casebook on The Yellow Wallpaper.* New York: Feminist Press, 1992.

Hill, Mary A. *Charlotte Perkins Gilman: The Making of a Radical Feminist, 1860–1896*. Philadelphia: Temple University Press, 1980.

———. *Endure: The Diaries of Charles Walter Stetson*. Philadelphia: Temple University Press, 1985.

Karpinski, Joanne B., ed. *Critical Essays on Charlotte Perkins Gilman*. New York: G. K. Hall, 1992. (Includes Harriet Howe's essay, "Charlotte Perkins Gilman—As I Knew Her," pp. 73–84.)

Knight, Denise D. "The Reincarnation of Jane: 'Through This'—Gilman's Companion to 'The Yellow Wall-Paper.'" *Women's Studies* 20:287–302 (1992).

———. *Charlotte Perkins Gilman: A Study of the Short Fiction*. New York: Twayne, 1997.

Lane, Ann J. *To Herland and Beyond: The Life and Work of Charlotte Perkins Gilman*. New York: Pantheon, 1990.

Meyering, Sheryl L., ed. *Charlotte Perkins Gilman: The Woman and Her Work*. Ann Arbor: UMI Research Press, 1989.

Scharnhorst, Gary. *Charlotte Perkins Gilman*. Boston: Twayne, 1985.

—SYLVIA BAILEY SHURBUTT

James Jones

1921–1977

YOUNG NOVELISTS-TO-BE ARE sometimes so attuned to the nature of their yearning for immortality that they become uncanny forecasters of the path their literary fortunes will follow. As a nineteen-year-old army private stationed in Hawaii in 1940, James Jones began writing autobiographical stories in the manner of his recently discovered idol, Thomas Wolfe. He included an excerpt from one of these stories in a 1941 letter to his brother Jeff (published in *To Reach Eternity: The Letters of James Jones*, 1989). In the passage, Jones hinted at his own goals and ambitions as a writer in terms that offered fitting tribute to his literary output in the years to come:

> He wanted to be the voice that shrieked out the agony of frustration and lostness and despair and loneliness, that all men feel, yet cannot understand; the voice that rolled forth the booming, intoxicating laughter of men's joy; the voice that richly purred men's love of good hot food and spicy strong drink; men's love of thick, moist, pungent tobacco smoke on a full belly; men's love of woman: voluptuous, throaty voiced, silken-thighed, and sensual.

More than any other literary figure of the post–World War II generation, Jones remained, by and large, a man's writer. One might narrow this description even further to include men who came of age during the war, especially those who fought overseas and held stubbornly to a sensibility shaped by that transformational experience, even in the face of profound social change in the decades following.

Jones is known primarily for his war novels, brutally realistic depictions of the military's debilitating effect on individual worth and the traumatizing nature of battle. An appreciation for the significance of Jones's themes—the terrifying sense of anonymity the war instilled in those who fought, the war's influence on postwar American society—is certainly not limited to male readers. Yet his attempt to engage readers' sympathies is peculiarly male. In the film version of Jones's second novel, *Some Came Running* (1958), Frank Sinatra, in the role of the main character Dave Hirsh, periodically refers to "dames" in the long-suffering, condescending manner prevalent in Hollywood movies of the 1940s and 1950s. The term strikes contemporary viewers as humorously anachronistic. They can only imagine it being used ironically today, if indeed it would be used at all. Jones's mode of perception bears that same out-of-date manner. Still, there is undeniable power and insight in his portrayal of men trying to maintain a sense of individual autonomy as they fight the powers of organization and control that seek to eliminate that autonomy. The men must also fight their own natures as they deal with the consequences of their battles with a society that increasingly surrenders its independence to government and corporate forces of authority and conformity, in exchange for the economic benefits of the postwar consumer society.

The curious thing about the aggressively male orientation of Jones's work (many critics charged that Jones was incapable of creating a credible female character) is that he attempted, in his fiction, to redefine the masculine identity men had inherited for generations and that constituted a unique aspect of the American character. In a December 1963 article for *Esquire,* he attacked the macho code promulgated by Ernest Hemingway, this despite the fact that Hemingway was an obvious influence on the way Jones portrayed men and women. As a survivor of the battle of Guadalcanal, Jones saw firsthand the connection between such masculine codes and the circumstances of war; he also saw the irrelevance of such codes in the struggle of states' competing industrial and technological capabilities, in which men are merely statistics in a war of machines.

Jones's work overall presents a thematic split. Outside of his war novels, he published a number of books that deal primarily with the relationships between men and women, concentrating especially on sexual dynamics. He felt that American attitudes about sex were hopelessly mired in hypocritical notions about morality, often influenced by religious beliefs, and that what Americans said and wrote about sex in no way corresponded with what they actually did in their sexual lives or how they felt as sexual beings. But Jones's approach to this material is one-sided. Although he wished to impart a new kind of male identity, the novels demonstrate a narrative ease only with respect to the relationships between men. When Jones addresses men vis-à-vis women he flounders, primarily because his presentation of sexual dynamics appears outdated and his conception of women severely limited. Women are portrayed primarily as sexual beings in relation to men, which makes it difficult for readers to envision a new male identity, since that identity makes no allowance for women as independent selves with the capacity to create fulfilling and spiritual lives not tied to men. Readers expect novels from the past, even great novels, to reflect outmoded mores. But Jones's domestic novels appeared at a time when American sexual and gender attitudes underwent profound change, and although he eagerly adopted more explicit language in matters of sex, his philosophy remained tinged with the "dame" mentality.

Jones believed that critics missed the point in his depictions of men and women. The relationships between men, he claimed, demonstrated the destructiveness of male bravado, making strong emotional and spiritual connections between men and women impossible and resulting in sex being simply a means of exercising power. Critics, however, generally felt that Jones postured along the same macho lines he was supposedly attacking. In novels like *Some Came Running* and *Go to the Widow-Maker* (1967) readers can easily feel as though Jones's sympathies lie with the very male characters, activities, and attitudes he is actually using to demonstrate the weaknesses of traditionally masculine characteristics. This confusion may result, in part, from Jones's narrative approach. He often mixes straight omniscient narrative with the more internal perspective of characters in a way that makes it difficult to separate what is the narrator's point of view (and perhaps Jones's) and what comes from a character's perspective (which might well be the opposite of Jones's). The same approach does not appear as troublesome in the war novels because there Jones's narrative attitude is consistently in line with what his characters think and believe.

Another possible explanation for the "two James Joneses"—the one who wrote well-received and appreciated war-related novels and the one whose domestic novels were frequently reviled—is the fact that Jones was not afraid to embody the contradictions of human behavior in his characters. As a Jones biographer, Frank MacShane, pointed out in regard to Jones's fiction overall, "What endures is the depiction of actual life, for it alone can encompass contradictions and reconcile opposites, which by definition a strict philosophy cannot do." This can make it difficult for readers to determine what "philosophy" Jones wishes to convey about relationships between men and women, but

Jones was more interested in showing how people actually behave than in presenting characters that follow a pattern of activity consistent with a philosophical point of view. Readers might well feel some doubt, however, as to whether what Jones saw as the truth about how people behave is consistent with what they experienced in their own lives, or whether Jones's "truth" transcends the parochial concerns of a particular time and place in American social history.

The dichotomies at the heart of Jones's fiction reflect dichotomies within the man himself. A researcher into his personal life comes continually upon references to his gentleness and kindness as a human being. Yet there are also aspects of his life which indicate that Jones had not escaped the masculine trap he wrote so compellingly about. It can be hard to reconcile the fact that the man who began his literary career by publishing *From Here to Eternity* to almost universal acclaim in 1951, followed it in 1958 with *Some Came Running,* a book that was just as universally condemned as subliterate, a monstrosity. What emerges from Jones's fiction, though, is a comparable inability on the author's part to reconcile the two sides of his nature—the boisterous, hard-drinking he-man and the tender, affectionate family man. Jones's subconscious artistic impulses usually served the former more effectively than the latter, especially when it came to examining the psychological pressures exerted on the masculine psyche by war. But if Jones was not able to present the transformation of male identity as convincingly as he illustrated the characteristics of that identity, his work nonetheless provides a kind of case study on the *need* for redefinition. Jones asked what it meant to be a man at a time when most fictional and social analyses focused on the shift occurring in what it meant to be a woman. If nothing else, Jones's fiction gave those involved in the women's movement a revealing, psychologically complex look at what

they were up against. Interestingly, in many respects Jones felt himself to be on their side.

THE EVOLUTION OF A WRITER

Jones was born into a well-to-do family in the small Midwestern town of Robinson, Illinois, on November 6, 1921. His paternal grandfather, George W. Jones, was a successful lawyer who had discovered oil on his property outside Robinson, and who owned a mansion that stood prominently on the town's Main Street, a symbol of the family's burgeoning fortunes. His four sons—one of whom was Ramon Jones, James's father—inherited his wealth after his death, but much of the money was invested in a Chicago utilities company wiped out by the stock market collapse of 1929. The big house on Main Street, which had become home to Ramon's family, was sold and the nearby house that the Joneses moved into reflected their significantly reduced circumstances. The change affected the family profoundly.

Ramon Jones, a dentist, had been dominated by his father while growing up; as an adult he grew increasingly dependent on alcohol. He married Ada Blessing, an attractive and vivacious woman, in 1908 and the two had three children: a son, Jeff, born in 1910; James, born eleven years later; and a daughter, Mary Ann, born in 1925. Ada Jones had a difficult time coping with the family's economic decline, and that, coupled with Ramon's alcoholism, created an environment of bitterness and hostility in the Jones household. James's relationship with his mother was especially troublesome because she often vented her dissatisfaction with her circumstances and her husband, James's father, on him. Jones dealt movingly with his childhood and with his ambivalent feelings toward his mother in a number of short stories included in the collection *The Ice-Cream Headache, and Other Stories,* published in 1968. He never lost the bitterness he felt over his mother's treatment of him and his father. Ada Jones died of congestive heart failure (which eventually killed James as well) in March 1941, while James was stationed in Hawaii. The turmoil in Jones's family life was compounded a year later when his father committed suicide.

After an undistinguished high school career, during which James earned a reputation as a roughneck, he enlisted in the U.S. Army Air Corps, no doubt to escape both his parents' household and the stifling social niceties of the American Midwest. Sent to Hawaii, he arrived there in 1940 and took the unusual step of transferring from the air corps to the less prestigious infantry, a move he provides some explanation for in his fictional treatment of the transfer in *From Here to Eternity*. The switch necessitated his move to Schofield Barracks, which he later made famous. While there he met the various characters whose fictional incarnations would populate the world of his first novel, most notably Robert E. Stewart, a bugler and boxer who served as the inspiration for Robert E. Lee Prewitt.

Growing up in Robinson, Jones had spent a considerable amount of time at the public library near his house. To make more bearable his stay at Schofield, he visited the base library often and there discovered the 1929 novel *Look Homeward, Angel* by Thomas Wolfe. As Jones stated in a conversation with Willie Morris shortly before Jones's death in 1978 (the interview was edited by R. T. Kahn for publication in *Bookviews*), "That crazy boy and his crazy family and his drunken father and miserly mother [were] so like myself and my own family that I discovered I'd been a writer all along without really having realized it." In many letters to his brother Jeff, Jones recorded his own pursuit of the writing trade shortly after his encounter with the Gant family in Wolfe's novel. His efforts were largely autobiographical and very much in the Wolfean manner.

They were soon interrupted, however, by the December 7, 1941, Japanese attack on Pearl Harbor, which Jones witnessed. In the immediate aftermath of the attack, Jones and his comrades made ready for an expected Japanese invasion, establishing defensive positions throughout the island of Oahu. But when no attack materialized, the company returned to normal duty, with the added anxiety of awaiting inevitable orders to ship out and engage enemy forces in combat. During the lull while the fate of his division, the Twenty-fifth Infantry, was decided, Jones enrolled at the University of Hawaii, taking classes in composition and American literature.

Jones's company shipped out for the western Pacific island of Guadalcanal in December 1942 to participate in what became the first successful American offensive of the war. MacShane emphasizes that Jones's few months on Guadalcanal "fundamentally changed his life." In fact, "Exposure to ghastly experiences gradually changed the values and attitudes of all the men," a theme that haunted Jones's fiction throughout his career. The most obvious and painful lesson of Jones's combat experience was that in the face of modern technological warfare, soldiers die random, meaningless, and anonymous deaths.

Jones was hit by the fallout from a mortar shell fairly early in the Guadalcanal campaign, but the head injury was not serious and he soon returned to duty. The rigors of battle exacerbated an old ankle injury, however, and eventually he removed himself from the field, reporting to the hospital in March 1943. After surgery and a stop in New Zealand, he shipped home to San Francisco in May to recuperate. Part of the first wave of American wounded returned from battle, Jones soon found himself in a Memphis veterans' hospital, where he encountered what MacShane describes as "a full range of horrors."

Like many returned vets, Jones found it difficult to reorient himself to life stateside. He grew angry and bitter at what he saw as the war profiteering taking place in the new consumer society. He was also uneasy about the shifting sense of personal morality brought on by a wartime mentality. Most of all, he recognized a divide between himself and all those at home who had no idea what he, and other combat veterans, had been through. Jones later vented his frustration along these lines in a 1963 article titled "Phony War Films" for the *Saturday Evening Post,* wherein he attacked the way in which American cinema presented war to its citizens, writing that Americans in general "had no concept of—the random quality of cipherdom, the totally arbitrary, numerical killing upon which . . . modern 'industry-oriented' warfare [is] built . . . [or] of the regimentation of souls, the systematized reduction of men to animal level, the horror of pointless death, the exhaustion of living in constant fear."

After a three-month period of drinking, fighting, and carousing with what seemed to him an inexhaustible supply of available women, Jones was declared fit for duty and sent to Camp Campbell in Kentucky. But his attitude problems persisted and he went AWOL on numerous occasions while stationed there. During the first of those unsanctioned leaves, which occurred prior to his arriving at Camp Campbell, Jones returned home to Robinson, Illinois, and between drinking bouts made the acquaintance of Lowney Handy, a woman known about town for befriending veterans, especially troubled veterans, and the woman who would alter the direction of Jones's life and the nature of his fiction. Well-read and harboring literary aspirations of her own, when Lowney Handy discovered that Jones wished to write, and that he had some talent for it, she, with the aid of her husband, Harry Handy, offered him guidance and support, eventually becoming a pivotal element in the creation of *From Here to Eternity.*

First, though, Jones had to deal with the army. After being busted to private and then promoted again to sergeant, Jones became incensed at the treatment accorded a Jewish officer in his company and went AWOL for the final time in May 1944. He headed to Indianapolis, where he worked on a novel he had begun, *They Shall Inherit the Laughter,* that dealt with veterans returning from the war. Lowney Handy eventually tracked him down, talked him into going back, and then worked on his behalf to get him out of the army for good. Jones spent time in the stockade at Camp Campbell before being transferred to the prison ward of the hospital as a psychiatric patient. He was eventually diagnosed as suffering from "psychoneurosis" brought on by his military service and granted an honorable discharge in July 1944.

Once discharged, Jones made a visit to the home of Thomas Wolfe in Asheville, North Carolina, before returning to Robinson and moving in with the Handys. There he continued work on his novel. From the start, Jones's arrangement with the Handys was unusual. He and Lowney were sexual partners, apparently with Harry's knowledge and compliance. The Handys borrowed money to build an extension on their house that provided a space for Jones to work. The three lived together amiably, not caring what the residents of Robinson thought of their unorthodox trio.

Lowney also exerted a strong influence on Jones's writing. Schooled in a philosophy that combined the tenets of theosophy and occultism with American transcendentalism, Lowney helped Jones, first and foremost, get rid of his undirected anger and channel his energies in a more positive and productive manner. John Bowers, who became a member of the artists' colony Jones and Handy later established to help develop other young writers, saw this as Lowney's primary contribution to Jones's evolution as a novelist. As Bowers wrote in a short memoir published in "Glimpses" in the *Paris Review*:

> [Lowney] got to Jones fairly early and tried to get him to write about things he knew and that were meaningful to him and to go deeply within himself, wrestle with it, and get it on paper. In that she was a marvelous literary influence. Otherwise, who knows. Whatever he would have done—potboilers, poetry—I don't think it would have been as forceful or as meaningful unless Lowney had originally tackled him. She got him to find his true voice.

Although Jones's relationship with Handy eventually soured and her effect on his work became less salutary, she played a prominent role in his early novels, most importantly *From Here to Eternity*.

Once finished with *They Shall Inherit the Laughter,* and feeling as though he needed more of an educational foundation to support his work, Jones went to New York and enrolled at New York University. While there, he showed his manuscript to an agent, who rejected it, recommending substantial revisions. Undeterred, Jones decided to pursue the editor who had been so vital to Thomas Wolfe's development as a novelist, the venerable Maxwell Perkins at Charles Scribner's Sons. Perkins, too, rejected *They Shall Inherit the Laughter,* but saw something in it that suggested to him that Jones had what it took to be a successful author. So when Jones, who had gone back to work on his original manuscript, later mentioned in a letter to Perkins an idea he had for a novel about the peacetime army prior to American involvement in World War II, the editor was interested. He optioned the unwritten book for $500, the first money Jones made as a writer. Jones abandoned *They Shall Inherit the Laughter* and went to work on what became *From Here to Eternity*.

Thus began a years-long process of work and travel, where Jones alternated between working in his study at the Handys', wintering in Florida, and taking to the road with a jeep and trailer that Harry Handy helped him to buy, writing at trailer courts across the United States. *From Here to Eternity* emerged slowly from Jones's tortuous process of continual rethinking and revising. Jones remained in contact with Perkins, whose excitement grew when he saw the work-in-progress begin to come together. When Perkins died in June 1947, Burroughs Mitchell took over editorship of the project, guiding the book through the remaining years of its composition and finally its publication. To make it through periods of weariness with the seemingly never-ending task of finishing the novel, Jones sometimes turned to writing shorter fiction, producing stories culled from the abandoned *They Shall Inherit the Laughter.* His first published piece, in fact, was a short story entitled "The Temper of Steel," which appeared in the *Atlantic Monthly* in March 1948. Other stories based on his childhood and military experiences appeared sporadically in the years following.

Jones finished *From Here to Eternity* in February 1950. The prepublication process included a thorough review of Jones's extensive use of barracks language. He wanted the book to be blunt and realistic in presenting the way that soldiers act, think, and speak, but that meant breaking new ground in what publishers, and their lawyers, would allow into print. Jones was adamant, however, that Scribners avoid censorship of the kind that had led to the substitution of *fug* for the more colorful word it so unsatisfactorily masked in Norman Mailer's *The Naked and the Dead* (1948). Despite some editorial tinkering, *From Here to Eternity* maintained its gritty and authentic diction. As George Garrett concluded in a 1984 biography of Jones, the language used in the novel "had seldom been seen in popular American fiction and never before with such overt emphasis. . . . For better and for worse, the American novel was never to be as inhibited as it had been before."

THE GUN AND THE BUGLE

Jones's war trilogy—*From Here to Eternity, The Thin Red Line* (1962), and *Whistle* (1978), and sometimes understood by critics to extend to a fourth novel, *The Pistol* (1959)—presents a powerful fictional illustration of what Jones identified in the nonfiction text *WWII* (1975) as the "evolution of a soldier." In his 1981 biography of Jones, James Giles offers a thorough analysis of how Jones's theory of military evolution plays out in the novels making up the trilogy. Of *From Here to Eternity*, Giles asserted, "Jones believed that the crucial evolutionary step came when individual combat soldiers submerged their own individuality into a necessary mass anonymity." The process of submersion even prior to participation in World War II creates the primary tension in *From Here to Eternity* between a soldier's effort to maintain his individuality and personal dignity and the army's attempt to make him conform to its hierarchy of authority and pattern of regimentation.

The initial reviews of *From Here to Eternity*, and various analyses since, have disagreed on various aspects of Jones's accomplishment, but on one point they are unanimous—that Jones conveys a remarkable documentary sense of what life was like in the peacetime Regular Army prior to World War II. In the process, Jones also reasserted the value of social realism in American fiction. Largely through the accumulation of details over 860 pages, Jones's presentation gives a sharply defined picture of the enlisted man's daily struggle with the forces of loneliness, sexual frustration, and financial hardship, as well as with the cynicism bred by the army's irrational way of doing things. This is additionally seasoned with what Ned Calmer, writing in the *Saturday Review* in 1951, referred to as the novel's "spectacularly indecent vocabulary."

The book's success rests largely on its two main characters. Private Robert E. Lee Prewitt is a soldier's soldier but also a man who refuses to compromise his personal integrity for the sake of advancement within an army system that is often corrupt and inefficient. The novel begins, in fact, with Prewitt's transfer from the Bugle Corps back to straight duty at Schofield Barracks, having refused to serve with the Corps after being denied the rank of First Bugler for someone of clearly inferior ability. Sergeant Milton Anthony Warden understands fully the nature of Prewitt's objection to army decision-making but addresses his own frustration with the system from within its hierarchy as a noncommissioned officer, bending and manipulating the system so that he maintains a sense of his own dignity and protects men like Prewitt from themselves. Warden can see that Prewitt is bent on self-destruction, "trying to live up to a romantic, backward ideal of individual integrity."

Prewitt's need for individual acknowledgment puts him on a collision course with the army he serves, in the person of General Sam Slater, a voice of the technological age. Slater explains to his subordinate officers how in the past, authority could be exerted by appealing to men's sense of honor, patriotism, and service. But, he goes on, the machine age has

destroyed the meaning of the old positive code. Obviously, you cannot make a man voluntarily chain himself to a machine because its [*sic*] "Honorable." The man knows better.

. . . So you have no choice but to make him afraid of *not* chaining himself to his machine. You can do it by making him afraid of his friends' disapproval. You can shame him because he is a social drone. You can make him afraid of starving unless he works for his machine. You can threaten him with imprisonment. Or, in the highest efficiency, you can make him afraid of death by execution.

Evidence of this strategy as employed by the military and by American society more generally appears throughout Jones's fiction, providing the impetus for conflict within his male characters, who struggle to establish identities free of the coercive exercise of authority. Their efforts often lead to precisely the kind of masculine bravado and macho posturing that Jones suggests men must escape. But, as Prewitt recognizes after fighting with Bloom, a member of his own company, the two men battle each other because "it was so much easier than trying to find the real enemy to fight, because the real enemy the common enemy was so hard to find since you did not know what it was to look for it and could not see it to get your hands on it."

The real enemy might be hard to identify, but it often appears to take the guise of women in *From Here to Eternity.* Prewitt's and Warden's attempts to accommodate individualism within the structure of an arbitrarily authoritarian organization like the army are male pursuits. Any attempt by women to restrict the men's freedom serves to align them with the enemy powers against which the men are fighting. The novel's plot turns on the dual story lines of Prewitt's confrontation with the army and the love interests of Prewitt and Warden. Prewitt falls in love with a whore named Lorene, whose real name is Alma, and Warden seduces Karen Holmes as an act of vengeance against her husband, Captain Holmes, but then finds that he too is in love. Discovering what love means to the two men propels the affairs forward within the larger narrative concern of life at Schofield Barracks. Prewitt and Warden find that the individual freedom and personal integrity they strive for, in their distinctively different ways, leave little room for the emotional and spiritual bonds associated with love. The best women can hope for, in the end, is to play the noble role, according to the men, of satisfying the men's sexual needs.

One consistent note of reservation in the reviews of *From Here to Eternity,* beyond the recognition of a crudeness in its style, was that the novel showed real power when it came to documenting army life with vivid, realistic details but often faltered when it wandered into the realm of ideas, or philosophized about the social and historical milieu it sought to depict. Nevertheless, it was a philosophical transformation that had brought the book into being. Lowney Handy had much to do with this. When critics attack the awkward philosophizing within *From Here to Eternity,* they often focus on the stockade section, in which Prewitt comes under the influence of fellow prisoner Jack Malloy and his theory of passive resistance, a frame of mind born of Malloy's previous involvement with the Wobblies, members of the socialist labor union the Industrial Workers of the World. Prewitt's out-of-body experience while in the prison's infamous Black Hole is directly attributable to Malloy's magnetic pull. Critical objections to this section have seen it as an intrusion. And it does reflect the hodgepodge of ideas on Eastern religious systems and the occult that Lowney Handy tried to inculcate into her students at the Handy Colony, and that Jones himself later repudiated, although they still played a significant role in his second novel, *Some Came Running.*

Even so, the sympathy with which Jones conveys the stubborn and fractious Prewitt to his readers might well be the result of Jack Malloy's basic tenet about his "new religion"— that "God is growth and evolution." As Stephen Carter argues in *James Jones: An American Literary Orientalist Master* (1998), the implication of Malloy's proselytizing becomes obvious for Prewitt: "'If God is Growth and Evolution, then there is no need for the concept of forgiveness. . . . if evolution is growth by trial and error, how can errors be wrong? since they contribute to growth?'" This view of life and God offers Prewitt a new way of perceiving his own experience and is part of the tender force by which *From Here to Eternity* compels readers' participation in the narrative. Jones may have returned from the war, in the words of a *Life* magazine writer, as a "whimpering neurotic," but his exposure to a new way of understanding what happened to him while in the army made *From Here to Eternity* possible.

In an obituary tribute to Jones published in the *New York Times Book Review* in June 1977, his friend Irwin Shaw characterized Jones's work as being about "the conflict between the gun and the bugle." This phrase offers an apt way to visualize the tension between Jones's recognition of the violence and ugliness that is part of the human character and his seemingly contradictory understanding of the struggles human beings undergo to discover and assert a better part of themselves. Jones never flinched from showing what sons-of-bitches people can be, but he also tempered those moments with scenes such as the one in which Prewitt plays the bugle for his company in *From Here to Eternity.* In the words of Ihab Hassan, in *Contemporary American Literature: An Introduction, 1945–1972,* Prewitt performs as if he is "putting all human suffering into the clear, intolerable note of his bugle blowing Taps."

FROM HERE TO CELEBRITY

Published in January 1951, *From Here to Eternity* was an immediate sensation. Jones's novel accomplished the dual task of giving a detailed insider's look into military culture while also presenting "a great simple truth," as Joan Didion termed it in a 1977 article in *Esquire,* that "the Army was nothing more or less than life itself." The novel received laudatory reviews, with only a few dissenters. Most critics treated it as a work of substantial artistic merit, even when acknowledging a certain raggedness in technique. The book became that rare case in which a monumentally successful best-seller is accorded respect for its artistry as well; *From Here to Eternity* won the National Book Award for fiction in 1952. An Academy Award–winning movie version followed in 1953.

The book's critical success meant that Jones was taken seriously as an artist, most notably by other novelists, while its popular bonanza made him a wealthy man and an international celebrity. Jones reveled in both facets of his career, making his next move somewhat surprising. He returned home to Robinson, and to Lowney Handy, and began work on a second novel; he also aided Lowney's plan to develop a community in which young writers like Jones would be given the support and guidance they needed to become successful authors. The practical and spiritual master of the enterprise would be Lowney herself. Even before this time, Handy had adopted other protégés that she schooled in her unique brand of literary spiritualism, but she and Jones now set out to formalize the arrangement and build a campus of sorts where their academy of young writers could flourish.

Jones invested a considerable portion of his financial windfall from *From Here to Eternity* in the Handy Artists Colony, which set up shop on some land the Handys owned in Marshall, Illinois, not far from Robinson. Lowney instituted a spartan regimen for her literary charges, enforcing it with a fierce authoritarianism. The daily routine included strict dietary and exercise components, in addition to waking before dawn to begin writing on an empty stomach. Afternoons were set aside for physical labor, much of it devoted to building up the colony grounds. One of the cornerstones of Handy's approach to writing was to have colonists copy long passages verbatim from works of fiction she deemed worthy, Hemingway and F. Scott Fitzgerald among her favorites, in order to impress a sense of style on her students.

Ultimately, the Handy Artists Colony subsisted on the credibility, and money, Jones lent it. Both were put in jeopardy as the relationship between Jones and Handy deteriorated. When Jones made his final break from Lowney, which more or less coincided with his finishing *Some Came Running,* the colony died a fairly quick death. In 1957 Jones married Gloria Mosolino, an actress and would-be writer he met in New York. When Jones did finally leave Robinson, and Lowney, after a violent confrontation between Lowney and Gloria, he broke contact with his former mentor and lover, completely and permanently.

The creative offspring of their partnership remained, however. And it suffered a fate comparable to the broken relationship. The 1,266-page *Some Came Running* appeared in January 1958 and met a fusillade of critical scorn. It tells the story of Dave Hirsh, a war vet and writer who returns to his small Midwestern hometown, in part to even the score with his brother, who chased him away many years before after Dave got one of the local teenage girls pregnant. Dave's plans are upset, however, by his meeting a local female college professor and by his involvement in the wild partying lifestyle of the town's social undesirables, the leader of whom is Bama Dillert, a professional gambler who becomes Dave's confidante.

Critics found much in the book worthy of attack. The relationship between Dave and Gwen French, an English professor, came under fire for stretching the bounds of credulity. Dave wants to sleep with Gwen but believes she will not sleep with him because she is a guilt-ridden nymphomaniac, who now wishes to abstain from sex as an act of penance for her past behavior. Gwen wants to sleep with Dave but believes she cannot because despite her pretense at vast sexual experience she is actually a virgin. The randy and sexually uninhibited behavior of Jones's working-class characters also caused reviewers concern, as did the tedium of his naturalistic approach. Hirsh's arrival in Parkman, Illinois, taking place over a single day, required 200 pages of narration, lending credence to Norman Mailer's 1959 characterization of the book's "caterpillarish" pace.

The most strident objections to *Some Came Running* focused on its prose. Critics, by and large, detested Jones's experimental approach to narration, where in addition to capturing the colloquial nature of his characters' speech he carried those colloquial forms over into the narration itself. The result was often long passages of awkwardly constructed sentences, full of redundancies and littered with adverbs, a style even his editor, Burroughs Mitchell, later described as "irritating." Jones also did away with apostrophes for almost all contractions (something he did to a lesser extent in *From Here to Eternity*), and although he made it clear that the grammatical lapses were intentional, Jones never offered a reason for the practice, assuming, apparently, that readers would figure that out for themselves. Most readers probably concluded, as did Harvey Swados, writing in the *New Republic* in 1958, that it was a "maddeningly pointless and irritating rebellion against the apostrophe."

Critics assumed that Jones was incapable of writing with sustained coherence, and even took Scribners to task for allowing such an abomination to be published. In 1958 a *Time* critic assessed the prose of *Some Came Running* by noting that "Choctaw rather than English would appear to be [Jones's] first language." Of all the darts fired at the massive novel, the one that seems most representative of the phenomenon surrounding it was a *New Yorker* reviewer's assessment that the book was "thrillingly bad." Jones had expected some kind of critical backlash, given the phenomenal success of *From Here to Eternity,* but nothing could have prepared him for the level of vituperation that *Some Came Running* generated. He defended the artistic integrity of the novel throughout his life, maintaining that it was one of his best books and that critics had misunderstood and underestimated both its vision and its technique.

Jones had monumental ambitions for *Some Came Running*. What makes the novel so maddening is that he both fulfills and undermines those ambitions in about equal measure. The novel provides a remarkably in-depth sense of its small-town milieu; one undeniable quality of the book is that readers come away from it feeling as though they have *lived* with its inhabitants. That may turn out to be exactly what readers dislike, given that Jones exposes the self-delusion that guides how most of the characters conduct their lives. Not surprisingly, much of the delusion centers on sexual attitudes and behavior, as those expose, often in self-destructive fashion, the lies and hypocrisies embedded within daily living. Jones also shows how self-delusion moves from the personal to the social level, so that society itself operates on the principle of the believed lie.

Maxwell Geismar, writing about Jones in his 1958 text *American Moderns: From Rebellion to Conformity,* concludes by observing of *Some Came Running* that "we can put it down as a kind of spiritual documentary whose value or lack of value will have to be appraised in the light of the future." If the novel is resurrected from the oblivion it resided in at the beginning of the twenty-first century, it will no doubt be because of its unsentimental delineation of the spiritual climate in small-town America immediately after World War II. But the appreciation of its accomplishment will continue to be qualified by the recognition of its obvious stylistic deficiencies.

The good will Jones had created with readers through *From Here to Eternity* saw to it that *Some Came Running* sold well despite its reviews, a pattern that held throughout Jones's career. For a writer so unmistakably identified with the American character, Jones's response to the critical failure of *Some Came Running* proved curious. He and his new wife left the country, moving to Paris, where they lived and raised two children on the Île St.-Louis for sixteen years. Before leaving, Jones made his only real public reply to the critics of *Some*

Came Running by publishing the short novel *The Pistol* in January 1959. In what he termed a "deliberately symbolic" work in the European mode, Jones demonstrated that he was capable of writing lucid and controlled prose. Although the book was widely admired, Jones himself did not find its symbolic and minimalist approach particularly satisfying and returned to the larger canvas of social realism. *The Pistol* did, however, recapture for him some of the literary prestige he had so painfully forfeited with *Some Came Running.*

The Pistol records the experiences of Private Richard Mast, who in the confusion of the Pearl Harbor attack makes off with a pistol that had been signed out to him for guard duty. Once the attack subsides and the army must deal with its tragic consequences, no one appears interested in tracking the pistol down. Mast himself covets the weapon for the comfort it provides. "The world was rocketing to hell in a bucket," he thinks, "but if he could only hold onto his pistol, remain in possession of the promise of salvation its beautiful blued-steel bullet-charged weight offered him, he could be saved." The thought makes clear that although Mast envisions his pistol as saving him from a particular fate—being sliced in two by a Japanese soldier wielding a samurai sword—the gun represents a form of salvation from the ensuing horror of the war itself. And Mast is not alone in seeing the gun as such a talisman. His fellow soldiers attempt to secure it for themselves, the story developing as a series of episodes in which Mast seeks to maintain possession despite these attempts.

A sense of helplessness in the face of a seemingly indifferent controlling force unites the men despite their selfish (human) natures. As Giles notes, "One of Jones's main concerns in the novella is to depict the selfishness of the human ego, especially when faced with extinction. Nonetheless, the gradual revelation that each seeker of the pistol has a common fantasy of extinction and views the weapon as a talisman of salvation indicates a potential for communion." Such a view highlights a crucial paradox at the heart of Jones's approach to war, and in his fiction more generally. Individuals resist, sometimes to the death, the assertion of authority over their lives, so that they can remain separate from others and therefore independent, free, autonomous; yet the assertion of authority exploits what Giles calls the "potential for communion" to such a degree that human beings form intense emotional bonds in spite of themselves and their yearnings for self-determination. The phenomenon goes a long way toward explaining Jones's lifelong love-hate relationship with the U.S. Army.

Jones went to work on *The Thin Red Line* (1962) after settling in Paris. Based largely on his own experiences in the South Pacific, the novel follows C-for-Charlie Company from the troop ship as it arrives at Guadalcanal to relieve the marines who had made the first advance there, then through its initial encampment and first taste of battle, and finally as it overcomes the remaining Japanese positions, securing the island for the Allies. Jones delved into the individual motivations and psychological responses of the men as they encounter the horrors of war, but many critics have noted over the years that the real central character of the novel is the company itself as it makes its advance, battling an unforgiving climate and unfriendly terrain as well as a fierce and well-entrenched enemy.

Readers of *From Here to Eternity* could recognize characteristics in the men of C-for-Charlie Company that harked back to the earlier novel. In creating *The Thin Red Line,* Jones wanted to follow the soldiers introduced in his first novel as they made the transition from peacetime career men to hardened combat veterans. In fact, as originally conceived, *From Here to Eternity* had a three-part structure; the story began in Hawaii, followed the soldiers

through the war, and finished with the men's difficult adjustment to postwar life in the United States. Jones did not get very far with *From Here to Eternity* before realizing he could not do the entire scheme. Instead, he broke the three parts into separate novels that spanned his career as a writer.

But Jones felt strongly that to preserve the narrative integrity of *From Here to Eternity,* Prewitt had to die, which obviously meant that Jones could not follow this character from Hawaii to Guadalacanal. So, as he explained in an author's note in *Whistle,* he decided to create new characters, but characters who would share traits with their previous incarnations, and he gave them names that echoed their former selves. Hence, Private Prewitt became Private Witt, Sergeant Warden became Sergeant Welsh, and Mess Sergeant Stark became Mess Sergeant Storm in *The Thin Red Line*; and then Bobby Prell, Mart Winch, and John Strange, respectively, in *Whistle.* The choice proved fortuitous because it not only allowed Jones to create artistically self-contained separate novels as he also traced his characters' evolution from book to book but also emphasized the degree to which these men were completely transformed by their experiences in war, essentially becoming different people at the different stages of their lives.

In "Jones's *The Thin Red Line*: The End of Innocence," published in 1964 in the *Revue des Langues Vivantes,* Paulette Michel-Michot delineates how the individuals in C-for-Charlie Company react to their first exposure to combat and what motivates their behavior at each newly horrifying stage of battle. What makes *The Thin Red Line* so memorable is the unique nature of each soldier's combat experience. The hero of the book may be C-for-Charlie Company, but that does not mean that individuals fade into a collective identity. As Michel-Michot suggests, however, they do share the common experience of crossing the line that separates the human from the animal. To survive their introduction to what Jones refers to as "the darker, nether side of patriotism," the men enter into "battle numbness," shutting down their emotions for the sake of getting the job done and succumbing to "a crazy sort of blood lust, like some sort of declared school holiday from all moral ethics." Such a psychological and emotional descent may foster success on the battlefield, but it has debilitating personal consequences for those so affected. "In the long run," writes Michel-Michot, "[it is] a psychologically destructive process which for ever changes human beings."

The soldiers make other discoveries and express other dimensions of their personalities in the face of combat as well. They head off to battle believing, for instance, that they act as free individuals. But one of the soldiers, Private Doll, asks himself a question before the troop ship has even landed at Guadalcanal that reverberates throughout the rest of the book: "What made men do it? . . . What kept them there? Why didn't they just up and leave, all go away?" Each man's response to these questions emerges as he confronts the stark realities of war, but each must also wonder the degree to which that response reflects freedom of choice. Sergeant Welsh, after prolonged exposure to enemy fire, must first admit that he is "scared shitless," and second, acknowledge that he is "afflicted with a choking gorge of anger that any social coercion existed in the world which could force him to be here."

Another recurring motif in the soldiers' reflexive reaction to combat is the repressed sexuality it unleashes. When a group of soldiers find the tattered, bloody remains of American khaki in the jungle, their first visceral indication of what awaits them, they respond with breathless, pointless, nonsensical commentary, but there

> was a peculiar tone of sexual excitement, sexual morbidity, in all of the voices—almost as if they

were voyeurs behind a mirror watching a man in the act of coitus; as though in looking openly at the evidence of this unknown man's pain and fear they were unwillingly perhaps but nonetheless incontrollably seducing him.

The link between sex and the accruing horrors of combat expresses itself throughout the ensuing battle in the psychological motivations by which the men force themselves to continue. Questions about the complex and often bizarre nature of American sexuality, particularly male sexuality, and how it is bound up with the American tradition of intense masculinity, preoccupied Jones throughout his career. No doubt his need to explore that dimension of human behavior in his fiction had its origin in what he experienced and what he witnessed as a soldier, especially a soldier under fire.

The Thin Red Line communicates in stark, bold terms the metamorphosis imposed on men by combat. When it appeared in 1962 it was received warmly, the critics recognizing that Jones's unique talents seemed especially suited to the emotional and psychological intricacies of men bound together through military service.

AN AMERICAN IN PARIS

With the success of *The Thin Red Line,* Jones turned his attention to his new hobby and obsession, scuba diving. He described his initial involvement in what he referred to as skin diving in a June 1963 *Esquire* article, and then reported on further underwater adventures in a piece for the *New York Times Magazine* in 1965. Both were nonfiction preludes to the novel he was working on called *Go to the Widow-Maker,* which was published in 1967. In a deliberate move away from his previous preoccupation with war and the military, Jones brought together his new love for scuba diving, the tumultuous break from Lowney Handy, and the subsequent adjustment to married life. He also explored the masculine bravado that played so large a part in the scuba diving subculture, examining how it collides with the main character's attempt to forge a loving and spiritual partnership with his new wife.

Go to the Widow-Maker, like *Some Came Running,* was soundly trashed by critics. If anything, the attacks were even more vicious because reviewers had come to see *Some Came Running* as an anomaly in the face of Jones's two fine follow-ups. But the complaints about *Go to the Widow-Maker* echoed those concerning the former book—that the entire 618-page novel was overwrought, the prose execrable, the psychological insights laughable, and the characters both unbelievable and morally reprehensible. Jones's fiction outside of the military-related novels had the persistent and ultimately damning quality of generating conclusions among critics that were exactly the opposite of what he claimed were his intentions as a writer. Many read *Go to the Widow-Maker* as endorsing the macho worldview of a character such as scuba instructor Al Bonham (and it *is* fairly easy to come away from the book sharing that point of view), but Jones saw Bonham, finally, as a pathetic embodiment of all that is wrong with the masculine identity.

Most of the novel focuses on the conflict between the masculine fraternity of scuba divers and the values that this fraternity represents, and the famous playwright Ron Grant's relationship with Lucky Videndi, which pulls him away from the camaraderie of his male diving (and drinking) buddies. All of Jones's novels, with the exception of *A Touch of Danger* (1973), contain the buddy element—men gathering with men, usually around a bottle, and establishing loving connections through shared participation in manly rites and rituals. Ron recognizes such a bond after an encounter with a nurse shark in which he and three other men expose themselves to a potentially dangerous situation but can only

laugh about it immediately afterward: "He felt, and it was shared, a real warmth of really deep affection for all three of them. And he didn't need to be ashamed of it. It was something you could never explain to any woman and, he realized, something no woman would ever be able to understand." Jones's seemingly sympathetic portrayal of Ron and his diving comrades in such scenes makes it difficult to discern his intention as anti-chauvinistic, even though he also depicts Ron's fear of being considered a coward and other motivations as underlying his ultramasculine behavior.

The love triangle involving Ron, Lucky, and Carol Abernathy also creates confusion for readers, in terms of what Jones wishes to say about traditional masculine virtues. Lucky's behavior in the aftermath of finding out that Ron has lied to her about the extent of his involvement with Carol brings into question whether she actually is capable of being the means by which Ron can evolve beyond the masculine code represented by the diving fraternity. In their seemingly endless and tediously described battles, Ron and Lucky both become repugnant to readers.

One of the distinctions that mark the decade between *Some Came Running* and *Go to the Widow-Maker* is illustrated by Jones's sexual frankness in the latter book. His explicitness in describing the activities and attitudes of Ron and Lucky illustrates the advance in what publishers would allow into print, an advance that Jones helped pave the way for with *From Here to Eternity.* But in *Go to the Widow-Maker* such narrative liberty seems a mixed blessing. There are times when Jones's directness serves a valuable purpose, as when he connects Ron's exploration of a sea cave with the sexual vitality that such adventure inspires within him. But at other moments, rather than using the freedom with words to pursue meaningful dimensions of sex and sexuality, Jones appears instead to simply revel in saying things that have not been said in mainstream works of fiction before.

Jones's crudity will always have its defenders, applauding the author's achievement in a realm of verisimilitude that many writers eschew—and rightly so. Plenty of Americans, and American readers, share the vocabulary and language that Jones has so often been criticized for. Jones always had a large regular audience despite negative reviews; the author himself expressed surprise at the degree to which the people he talked to after he moved back to the United States in the 1970s accepted his work on its own terms and understood what he was attempting to do. Chances are, those readers responded to Jones's novels much in the manner that Tom Carson did when he reassessed the viciously maligned *Some Came Running* in the *Village Voice Literary Supplement* in 1984 and declared, "What a fucking great book."

As a measure of the critical lambasting that Jones's nonmilitary novels suffered over the years, consider Kenneth John Atchity's indignant eruption in 1972 while reviewing Jones's 1971 novel *The Merry Month of May* for *Mediterranean Review*: "I have often wished that the God of Books would grant to each reviewer, once in a lifetime, the right to have any writer taken out of circulation and quietly strangled—without any question, any explanation. Jones would be my choice." What fueled such negative critical response was that Jones had pretensions to literary greatness. If he had been a common variety hack content to remain within the boundaries of his cordoned-off wing of the literary exhibition hall, he probably would have been politely tolerated and perhaps even appreciated for his obvious talent at rendering scenes in keenly observed, vivid detail. But the fact that he meant to be counted among those in the main showroom was simply more than many critics could bear.

Jones remained a best-selling author, despite taking his lumps from critics, a state of affairs

that must have generated many sighs of relief at his new publishing house, Delacorte Press. It had taken a sizable sum for Delacorte to lure Jones away from Scribners, where he had an amiable relationship with Burroughs Mitchell and felt an emotional attachment first engendered by Perkins. Jones repaid Delacorte's investment by remaining popular, but *Go to the Widow-Maker* was the first in a series of three novels that proved to be critical failures.

Before publishing the second of those three novels, Jones gathered the stories for *The Ice-Cream Headache, and Other Stories,* using them as the immediate follow-up to *Go to the Widow-Maker* in 1968. *The Ice-Cream Headache* brought together all of the short fiction Jones had written up to that point, published or not, plus the title story Jones wrote especially for the volume. Even though most of the stories were written early in Jones's career, *The Ice-Cream Headache* served a purpose similar to *The Pistol* after *Some Came Running,* reasserting Jones's ability to work within the limits of a traditional genre and to do so with a tighter control of language than was evident in *Go to the Widow-Maker.* Once again, Jones illustrated with a shorter work that his choices as a writer were just that, choices, and not the weaknesses of someone who did not know what he was doing, as critics complained.

Although Jones had been planning a follow-up to *The Thin Red Line* to complete his war trilogy, he kept putting it aside in favor of other projects. Sometimes these included work on screenplays, largely unproduced, that helped to pay for his Paris home and his comfortable European lifestyle. That Paris home put him right in the thick of the student rebellion of 1968, which became the basis for *The Merry Month of May,* published in 1971. The prose in *The Merry Month of May* was noticeably more controlled than in *Go to the Widow-Maker.* But this time critics took Jones to task for the overall conception of the book and what they perceived as the confused morality at the center of it. Jones felt, again, that critics missed the point—that their objections were precisely what he was getting at concerning the breakdown of moral values in the name of personal freedom.

Jones attempted in *The Merry Month of May* to unite the events of the 1968 May student rebellion with the disintegration of an American family living in Paris by showing the destructive effects of total personal liberation without regard to the needs of family or community. Not surprisingly, many of those who objected to the novel did so on the basis of the graphic sexual content involving Harry and Louisa Gallagher, their son Hill, and a black bisexual woman, Samantha Everton, whom all three end up sleeping with. Giles describes Samantha as "one of the most unfortunate characterizations in all Jones's fiction," and she does come uncomfortably close to being a caricature, opening Jones to charges of both racism and homophobia. Readers might also sympathize with John W. Aldridge's complaint in a 1971 piece for *Saturday Review* that Jones's exploration of sexual dynamics in the book seems premised on the "simple raunchy fascination of it all."

The examination of the student uprising, on the other hand, seems too sketchy and impressionistic to give a true sense of what was going on and, more importantly, why. Jones describes some of the battles between students and police and notes the way that the physical environment of the city was affected by the hostilities, but he provides very little about the intellectual and philosophical basis for the revolt. And this makes it difficult to discern what links the Paris uprising to the fortunes of the Gallagher family, besides the dumbfoundingly amoral behavior of Samantha Everton. Readers see the students participating in a kind of free-for-all of sex and politics, a free-for-all that middle-class liberals like Harry Gallagher get caught up in, while the larger historical and philosophical dimensions of events are curiously absent.

The Merry Month of May marks Jones's first attempt at a first-person observer-narrator, the pleasantly unctuous Jonathan (Jack) James Hartley III—a failed poet and novelist, currently the editor of a literary review in Paris. Hartley is the most interesting aspect of the novel because he raises intriguing questions not only about Jones's attitude toward the student protest in Paris but also about how Jones saw himself in relation to the students. In his introduction to *The Almost Revolution* (1969), a nonfiction account of the May rebellion by Allan Priaulx and Sanford Ungar, Jones mentions that his sympathies lay with the students, although he found himself commiserating with the police as well. A similar ambivalence appears in Jack Hartley—intellectually, he knows that as a good liberal he should be on the side of the students, but emotionally he finds himself feeling detached from if not downright antagonistic to the students' demands.

Jack Hartley represents the most controlled and consistent use of a narrator in Jones's fiction. Hartley also has a fascinating relationship to his creator because he embodies so many of Jones's idiosyncrasies. If, as one critic suggested, he is Jones's alter-ego, he presents a provocative glimpse into how Jones might have been struggling with his own growing conservatism, especially in response to the liberation movements of young people in the late 1960s and early 1970s. Further and more direct evidence of his antipathy toward the counterculture appears in his next novel, *A Touch of Danger.*

Jones's first attempt at genre fiction, *A Touch of Danger* is a private detective novel in the tradition of Raymond Chandler and Dashiell Hammett. Jones admitted in a 1973 *Publishers Weekly* interview with Barbara Bannon that Lobo Davies, the book's aging, grumbling narrator, "thinks a lot of the ways I think." In fact, Jones was surprised that he ended up putting so much of himself into Davies; his original intent was to "write a private eye yarn just for fun." The result, he thought, was a genre novel with literary merit, although most critics did not agree when the book appeared.

The novel follows Lobo Davies as he vacations on the Greek island of Tsatsos and gets entangled in a drug smuggling operation that caters to the idle rich on the island, as well as to a community of young hippies who have asserted squatters' rights on a huge abandoned construction site overlooking the sea. Through Davies, Jones registers again his feelings about the aimless, irresponsible, and hypocritical behavior of those in the counterculture. But an even greater contempt in *A Touch of Danger* is reserved for those of wealth and privilege, who use their social and financial position to subvert the rule of law for their own advantage, not caring who is hurt or destroyed in the process. Jones had expressed a similar kind of outrage in one of his first short stories, "The Way It Is," back in the 1940s, prior to publishing *From Here to Eternity.*

A Touch of Danger exudes, through Lobo Davies, a world-weariness that is in keeping with the traditions of the private eye genre Jones emulated. But there is a more personal dimension to the weariness as well. Jones was feeling his age, having turned fifty and having suffered his first serious attack of the heart problems that would eventually kill him. The tone of his response to such events in his own life is evident in Lobo's reaction to the vain posturing of Pekouris, the island police chief:

> He was the personification and spit and image of my picture acquired over 50 years of what the whole human race stood for and was worth. . . . It was a pretty dismal image to put up against 50 years. If you couldn't laugh at it, you would want to go away and shoot yourself.

Although *A Touch of Danger* demonstrated that Jones could work effectively within the detective genre, it did not contribute much to

his prestige as a serious writer of American fiction. Many reviewers saw Jones as slumming in the genre domain, wasting his considerable talents rather than tackling the large, serious novels that *From Here to Eternity* and *The Thin Red Line* had led them to expect from the author. In fact, the series of novels from *Go to the Widow-Maker* to *A Touch of Danger,* covering most of the years of Jones's residency in France, led to one of the conundrums of Jones's career: What effect, if any, did his removal from the United States in 1959 have on his abilities as a writer?

Norman Mailer went on record in the *Paris Review* in 1987, declaring that Jones

> made a terrible mistake leaving America. It was the fundamental error of his life. His roots were here. He wrote best about the country. . . . Going to France, he dried out his taproot. He got into the literary world in the worst way. He was the literary celebrity of Paris for many years.

Jones's friends and contemporaries, William Styron and Irwin Shaw, both disputed the notion that Jones lost his creative magic by moving to Paris. Styron points to *The Thin Red Line,* which was written in Paris, as evidence to the contrary. But in *The Thin Red Line* Jones reflected back on his military service for the book's narrative power, whereas novels like *Go to the Widow-Maker, The Merry Month of May,* and *A Touch of Danger* depend on Jones's view of contemporary reality as he then lived and felt and thought about it. Ironically, Jones himself pointed to the troubles inherent in the kind of lifestyle he adopted after moving to Paris during a 1962 radio interview with Leslie Hanscom. When asked from where a writer draws his material, Jones observed that

> American writers, once they become writers and become reasonably successful . . . stop being people and . . . become writers. In this way they sort of cut off their own material. Society and

themselves sort of cut it off so they return to their youthful experiences before they became "writers" in order to find material.

Jones's Paris novels show him approaching his material from the point of view of someone who had become very much an insider, while the power of Jones's early fiction rests in large part on its fellow feeling for those on the outside. In "James Jones and Jack Kerouac: Novelists of Disjunction," an essay published in 1963 in *The Creative Present,* edited by Nona Balkian and Charles Simmons, David Stevenson contends that "Jones depicts the disjunctive relationship which his central characters have with a traditional, half-mythic America by creating and eulogizing a whole subculture in black-and-white opposition to the accepted one." One reason for readers' interest in Jones's early fiction, Stevenson continues, is that his characters "tempt us to be aware of the intensity of our generation's and our own personal unease with the kind of world we do inhabit. . . . Because they are outsiders by choice: they like it that way." The appealing subversive quality Stevenson mentions does not exist in the trio of novels cited above, although each has other less powerful qualities that recommend themselves to readers.

TAPS

Following the relative disappointments of *Go to the Widow-Maker, The Merry Month of May,* and *A Touch of Danger,* Jones returned to the original source of strength in his writing, the war. A sense of his own mortality may have pushed him in that direction. In the summer of 1970 he suffered his first major episode of congestive heart disease. And as his health deteriorated over the years following, a sense of urgency about getting back to the long-delayed last installment of his war trilogy weighed on him.

Before undertaking *Whistle* in earnest, however, Jones committed to two nonfiction projects that helped shape his frame of mind for the final book. The first, in 1973, was an assignment from the *New York Times Magazine* to go to Vietnam and report on the waning days of U.S. involvement in the war. He later expanded his observations and published *Viet Journal* in 1974, which included an epilogue, "Hawaiian Recall," describing his return to Schofield Barracks and other locales featured in *From Here to Eternity* as he made his way back from Indochina. It is fitting that Jones should conclude his visit to Hawaii by remarking, "I had come back hoping to meet a certain twenty-year-old boy, walking along Kalakaua Avenue in a 'gook' shirt . . . but I had not seen him." His just completed travels throughout Vietnam, largely in the company of army brass, demonstrated how far this soldier had come. *Viet Journal* seems a calculated antidote to the general perception of the military and of the Vietnamese, particularly the Viet Cong and North Vietnamese, then being presented through the media. Jones admits to his army chaperone in Vietnam, General Mike Healy, that he both loved and hated the army, and if his two lengthy war novels had emphasized what he hated to a greater degree than what he loved, *Viet Journal* conveys more about what he found appealing in army life.

Partly this is due to the treatment he received from army officers, who viewed Jones as someone who understood the nature of military service and war, and would likely give the army a fairer shake than it typically received from the media back home. At a time when most news reporters found it nearly impossible to travel around Vietnam, the army made its helicopters available to Jones, taking him into sensitive and dangerous areas. Jones also clearly admired the behavior demonstrated by the officers he encountered—their intelligence, their courage, the graceful way they practiced the manly pursuits of cigars, booze, and poker. *Viet Journal* contains none of the withering contempt for the officer corps so evident in *From Here to Eternity* and *The Thin Red Line*. Jones's general approach to his material and his intellectual motivation while in Vietnam can be detected in the tone of his summary judgment of an evening spent in the company of a group of officers: "I had looked closely and I could not see one man among them who even looked like he might be involved in a military-industrial conspiracy to take over the United States."

Jones carried the sense of reconnecting with his military past evident in *Viet Journal* over into his next project, the impressive *WWII*. The book's graphics editor, Art Weithas, gathered many of the best artistic renderings from the war by those artists actually in the field, for which Jones agreed to write accompanying text. In addition to providing cogent descriptions and analyses of the book's images, Jones propounds his theory of "the evolution of a soldier," the process by which an ill-prepared and scared young kid becomes an effective warrior in combat—and the concomitant cost to his sense of self and humanity—followed by the extreme difficulty of returning to any semblance of normal civilian life after the war. Jones offers by way of example his own experiences in the South Pacific and return stateside after being wounded, which paint a revealing picture of how he transformed his life into fiction, particularly for *The Thin Red Line* and the yet-to-be-published *Whistle*. Finally, Jones's work in *WWII* gives readers a terse, lucid, and compelling history of the European and Pacific campaigns. One can hardly think of a better, more appropriate way than *WWII* for Jones to prepare for his final fictional battle—the completion of his army trilogy as his own life was ending.

Jones moved back to the United States in July 1974, partly to relieve financial pressures he experienced as a result of the high cost of living in Paris, partly to reconnect with the sources of his most powerful fiction. He accepted a position as writer-in-residence at Florida International University for the 1974–1975 academic year, and by all accounts was a dedicated and effective teacher. University budget problems prevented Jones's contract from being renewed, so he packed up his family again and moved from Miami to Sagaponack, Long Island, where he remained for the rest of his life, establishing friendships with other writers, most notably with Willie Morris.

After publishing *WWII* to much fanfare and universally appreciative reviews in 1975, Jones set to work on *Whistle,* spurred on by his worsening physical condition. Knowing that his time was short, Jones intensified his work on the book, putting in ten- to fourteen-hour days, determined to have it finished before he was no longer capable of writing. He did not quite make it. In early May 1977 Jones's health took a final turn for the worse. He was a few chapters short of finishing *Whistle,* so he dictated his ending to Willie Morris at the hospital, asking that Morris see to it that the book was published in finished form. Jones died on May 9, 1977. His body was cremated and buried in the old graveyard in Sagaponack.

After consulting with fellow writers and friends of Jones's, including authors Irwin Shaw, William Styron, and Peter Matthiessen, Morris decided not to write the final chapters of *Whistle* but simply to transcribe what Jones had left him of his plans. Although the last three and a half chapters demonstrate a loss of narrative fullness as a result of this approach, the ending maintains a feeling of Jones's presence and the novel overall seems complete. It concerns the fate of four men from the Twenty-fifth Infantry who fought together at Guadalcanal and New Georgia in the South Pacific and have returned home wounded or ill, winding up in the same army hospital in Tennessee for their recuperation.

Whistle returns to some of the themes Jones initially explored in the abandoned novel *They Shall Inherit the Laughter* after his return from the South Pacific. It also contains aspects of wartime and postwar civilian life that went into *Some Came Running.* The main characters are recognizable as well from previous incarnations—Mart Winch as Warden/Welsh from the preceding novels, Bobby Prell as Prewitt/Witt, John Strange as Stark/Storm, and Marion Landers as Corporal Fife in *The Thin Red Line,* a character who most resembles Jones himself. The four battle-scarred men from C-for-Charlie Company try to maintain the vital connecting spirit engendered by their shared trauma overseas but find it increasingly hard to do so in the face of life back in the States. The wartime economic boom has Americans feverish for the money and commodities that a secure job provides. Casual sex fueled by a limitless supply of alcohol has the vets themselves spending their time at local hotels, where the women are as eager to participate in the relaxed wartime standards of morality as any of the soldiers. A couple of the men find wives and families leading different and separate lives now, making a return to what they left behind near impossible. The relationships that do exist between the men and women in the book are calculated for short-term profit or pleasure. The soldiers returned from war are left wondering what they sacrificed their minds and bodies for while overseas.

Jones contended in his 1963 article "Phony War Films" that rather than "develop[ing] and enlarg[ing] human character, through the exercise of personal courage . . . modern warfare destroys human character." The tragic consequences of such destruction are everywhere evident in *Whistle.* Bobby Prell, the war hero whose battle-scarred legs are saved from amputation, engages in a disastrous marriage and becomes a government spokesperson touring the United States to tell his story and sell war bonds. He dies, more or less intentionally, in a bar fight. Marion Landers, recognizing the collapse of the fellow feeling that had held the men of the company together, walks into the path of a speeding car. John Strange decides to return to overseas duty but finds he cannot go through with it, cannot "watch the young men be killed and maimed and lost," cannot be "witness again to all the anguish and mayhem and blood and suffering," so he leaps from a troop ship that is carrying him to Europe. And Mart Winch, failing in his attempt to rescue the remnants of his command from their own memories, succumbs to the madness that had threatened his stability even as far back as his prewar experiences in *From Here to Eternity.*

Most of what Jones wishes to impart in *Whistle* about wartime loss and social transformation is carried through the cold and selfish and brutally pragmatic relationships between men and women. The novel is permeated with the desperate, pleasure-seeking commingling of bodies, often described in clinical or near pornographic fashion. The women, especially, many of whom have husbands in service overseas, are aggressive in communicating their desires in bed. Jones seems particularly preoccupied with oral sex in *Whistle,* seeing in most of the women's desire for cunnilingus not only a sea change in moral values but also a shift in the balance of power between men and women, a shift his male characters find very disturbing.

The heavy sexual component in *Whistle* reflects reality as Jones lived it when he returned from Guadalcanal and spent months recuperating from ankle surgery in a Memphis army hospital. But exactly what he intends for it to show can be hard to decipher, especially when you consider *Whistle* within the larger context of Jones's exploration of American sexual mores throughout his fiction. He obviously wanted to demonstrate something about the breakdown of moral values brought on by the war; that seems inherent in the almost sadistically detached manner with which bodies come in contact with each other in the novel. But one of Jones's bedrock principles throughout his career was that Americans were sexually immature and hypocritical, a maladjustment created most often by puritanical religious beliefs.

This creates confusion about whether Jones wishes ultimately to condemn or sanctify the evolving sense of morality in the United States as a result of the war. Such confusion could, however, be at the heart of the four soldiers' inability to reintegrate into the lives they left behind before the war. In the service, they met with sexual frustration at almost every turn, the repressed sense of that frustration exploding in a frenzy of sanctioned violence during combat. They have grown committed to a masculine ideal based on that very kind of association of sex with battle. Theoretically, one would expect them to welcome a new standard of behavior that removes the surface hypocrisy and acknowledges sex as the expression of natural instincts rather than an operation in scaling socially ingrained barriers. But when presented with that possibility, they are left wondering what such a shift means with respect to their masculine identities. In such a context, what defines them as men? This might explain where Landers lays the blame for the disintegration of what remains of C-for-Charlie Company near the end of the novel:

> In each case it was a woman who had pulled them away. Females. Pussy. Cunt. Had split the common male interest. Cunt had broken the centripetal intensity of the hermetic force which sealed them together in so incestuous a way. Their combat. Cunt vs combat. In his cups Landers decided he had discovered quite by accident the basic prevailing equation of the universe.

Expressing an important philosophical dimension of *Whistle* in so crass, so crude, so vulgar a manner as "cunt vs combat" has not helped win James Jones admirers in an age of enlightened gender politics since his death. Even at the time the book appeared, Pearl Bell took Jones

to task in *Commentary* for his stridently masculine approach:

> It was as if his idea of the fearlessly aggressive virility that distinguishes men from boys had become frozen for the rest of his days by the army's unyielding maleness, which ritualized not only the soldier's performance of his duty and the punishment of his derelictions, but his drunkenness and whoring, his obscenity, his deeply private longings and distemper. If the army was the only milieu in which Jones felt at home as a writer, it was because that fine-tuned machine of war, that honeycomb of rules and traditions and regulations, provided with a rigidly stable point of personal, sexual, and social reference, the unalterable measure by which he could grasp and judge the world at large.

Perhaps Jones did only feel at home when writing about the army, but his nonmilitary fiction at the very least shows him struggling with the kind of fearlessly aggressive virility that Bell acknowledges the army probably imposed on him.

But even in that struggle Jones met criticism akin to Bell's, and not just from women. Writing of *Go to the Widow-Maker,* a book that attacked the issue of masculine identity head-on, Wilfrid Sheed surmised that the book "makes sense only if we read it as the further adventures of the Jones enlisted man who began life in *From Here to Eternity* and was forged and twisted into adulthood in *The Thin Red Line.*" That, of course, is exactly who Jones was. And millions of other men shared his experience, forging and twisting their adult identities from the crucible of the army and World War II.

In an appreciative assessment of *The Thin Red Line* included in *The American Novel since World War II* (1969), edited by Marcus Klein, Saul Bellow makes an incisive observation about Jones's combat soldiers as "reveng[ing] themselves on the slothful and easy civilian conception of the Self." This idea of an oppositional self-concept instilled by military service explains perhaps why a later generation of writers including Tim O'Brien and Philip Caputo, who underwent their own transformations of self as a result of exposure to the military and to war, found much to admire in *Whistle*. It also helps explain how L. J. Davis's 1978 review of the book can begin with the statement, "[Jones's] ideas concerning American womanhood are egregious when they are not positively insulting," and yet still later accommodate the following conclusion about Jones's grasp of the "common professional soldiery" from World War II: "With its peculiar crude power, James Jones's voice is the best and truest they will ever have."

Whistle appeared in 1978 and was lauded for bringing to a close the journey of a group of army infantry soldiers from before the outbreak of World War II, through their testing in battle, and finally to their disastrous return to a world they no longer recognized as home. According to Jones, writing in an author's note in the novel, the trilogy that took him almost thirty years to complete, and upon which he knew his posthumous reputation as an author would rest, said "everything I have ever had to say, or will ever have to say, on the human condition of war and what it means to us, as against what we claim it means to us."

That fictional legacy appeared to fade in the decades following Jones's death, despite periodic reminders of his place in the annals of postwar fiction. Shortly after Jones died, Willie Morris published a book-length tribute, *James Jones: A Friendship*, in which he declared that the war trilogy constituted "three of the finest novels in American literature." In 1979 NBC paid its own tribute to *From Here to Eternity*, using it as the basis for a six-hour miniseries broadcast over three evenings, starring Natalie Wood and William Devane. Public television contributed a documentary, *James Jones: Reveille to Taps*, shown in 1985 and 1986. The mid-1980s also saw two biographies of Jones produced, adding to Giles's book-length critical treatment of his fiction that appeared in 1981. A collection of Jones's letters and an anthology of his war writings appeared in 1989 and 1991, respectively. Despite this persistent activity on his behalf, Jones's place in the American pantheon continued to slip. Of the war novels, only *From Here to Eternity* maintained a steady presence on fiction shelves at bookstores, although with Terrence Malick's 1998 remake of *The Thin Red Line* and a general resurgence of interest in World War II after Steven Spielberg's *Saving Private Ryan* (also 1998), a trade paperback reissue of the war trilogy was undertaken by Delta in 1998 and 1999.

As for Jones's nonmilitary novels, they have disappeared entirely from public and literary consciousness. Tinged with the singular perspective of a generation that came of age during the war, and especially of the men of that generation, they strike a contemporary reader as jarringly dated. Other authors evolved away from that unique wartime perspective as time passed and the American identity transformed itself. Jones witnessed that change, yet held firm to his own postwar sense of things and of relationships between people. Where that may have hurt his domestic fiction, it gave unusual force to his novels about war, even as he looked back on it fifteen or thirty years later. *From Here to Eternity, The Pistol, The Thin Red Line,* and *Whistle* remain provocative indictments of the absurdities of military service and the horrors of armed conflict. "This small-town boy from Robinson, Illinois," Willie Morris wrote for the *Paris Review* in 1987 of Jones's evocation of the World War II era, "has given us this stunning corpus of work, perhaps the most significant and distinguished corpus of work there is on that catastrophic set of years. . . . A substantial part of great writing is carrying the news from one generation to the next. Jones's war work has certainly done that."

Selected Bibliography

WORKS OF JAMES JONES

BOOKS

From Here to Eternity. New York: Charles Scribner's Sons, 1951.

Some Came Running. New York: Charles Scribner's Sons, 1958.

The Pistol. New York: Charles Scribner's Sons, 1959.

The Thin Red Line. New York: Charles Scribner's Sons, 1962.

Go to the Widow-Maker. New York: Delacorte Press, 1967.

The Ice-Cream Headache, and Other Stories: The Short Fiction of James Jones. New York: Delacorte Press, 1968.

The Merry Month of May. New York: Delacorte Press, 1971.

A Touch of Danger. New York: Doubleday, 1973.

Viet Journal. New York: Delacorte Press, 1974.

WWII. Graphics Direction by Art Weithas. New York: Grosset and Dunlap, 1975.

Whistle. New York: Delacorte Press, 1978.

The James Jones Reader: Outstanding Selections from His War Writings. Includes excerpts from first unpublished novel, *They Shall Inherit the Laughter,* and other unpublished work from the 1940s. Edited by James R. Giles and J. Michael Lennon. New York: Birch Lane Press/Carol Publishing Group, 1991.

ARTICLES

"Living in a Trailer." *Holiday,* July 1952, pp. 74–76, 78–79, 81, 83, 120.

"Too Much Symbolism." *Nation,* May 2, 1953, p. 369.

"Phony War Films." *Saturday Evening Post,* March 30, 1963, pp. 64–67.

"Flippers! Gin! Weight Belt! Gin! Faceplate! Gin!" *Esquire,* June 1963, pp. 124–127, 129–130, 132, 134, 136–139.

"Letter Home: Sons of Hemingway [Pamplona, Spain]." *Esquire,* December 1963, pp. 28, 30, 34, 40, 44.

"Letter Home [Alexander Calder's studio]." *Esquire,* March 1964, pp. 28, 30, 34.

"Letter Home [Skiing in Klosters, Switzerland]." *Esquire,* December 1964, pp. 22, 24.

"Why They Invade the Sea." *New York Times Magazine,* March 14, 1965, pp. 47, 49–50, 52, 55.

"James Jones." In *Authors Take Sides on Vietnam: Two Questions on the War in Vietnam Answered by the Authors of Several Nations.* Edited by Cecil Woolf and John Bagguley. New York: Simon and Schuster, 1967. Pp. 143–144.

Introduction to *The Almost Revolution* by Allan Priaulx and Sanford J. Ungar. New York: Dell, 1969.

NOTEBOOKS, CORRESPONDENCE, AND MANUSCRIPTS

Charles Scribner's Sons Collection, Princeton University Library, New Jersey. Includes Jones's correspondence with Scribners.

Handy Writers' Colony Collection, University of Illinois at Springfield. Includes typescript of *They Shall Inherit the Laughter* and Jones's letters to Lowney Handy.

Humanities Research Center, University of Texas at Austin. Includes manuscripts, correspondence, business papers, and notes.

Rare Book Collection of the Beinecke Library, Yale University, New Haven, Connecticut. Includes manuscripts, notebooks, and letters.

To Reach Eternity: The Letters of James Jones. Edited by George Hendrick. Foreword by William Styron. New York: Random House, 1989.

BIBLIOGRAPHY

Hopkins, John R., ed. *James Jones: A Checklist.* Foreword by James Jones. Detroit: Bruccoli-Clark/Gale Research Company, 1974.

CRITICAL AND BIOGRAPHICAL STUDIES

Adams, Richard P. "A Second Look at *From Here to Eternity.*" *College English* 17:205–210 (January 1956).

Aldridge, John W. "The War Writers Ten Years Later." In *Contemporary American Novelists.* Edited by Harry T. Moore. Carbondale: Southern Illinois University Press, 1964. Pp. 32–40.

———. "Twosomes and Threesomes in Gray Paree." *Saturday Review,* February 13, 1971, pp. 23–26.

———. "The Last James Jones." *New York Times Book Review,* March 5, 1978, pp. 1, 30–31.

Atchity, Kenneth John. "The Merry Month of May [rev.]." *Mediterranean Review* 2, no. 2:46–47 (winter 1972).

Bell, Pearl K. "The Wars of James Jones." *Commentary* 65:90–92 (April 1978).

Bellow, Saul. "Some Notes on Recent American Fiction." In *The American Novel since World War II.* Edited by Marcus Klein. Greenwich, Conn.: Fawcett Premier, 1969. Pp. 159–174.

Bowers, John. *The Colony.* New York: Dutton, 1971.

Burress, Lee A., Jr. "James Jones on Folklore and Ballad." *College English* 21:161–165 (December 1959).

Calmer, Ned. "The Real Enemy Is Hard to Find." *Saturday Review,* February 24, 1951, pp. 11–12.

Caputo, Philip. "An Eloquent Farewell to Arms." *Chicago Tribune Book World,* February 19, 1978, p. 1.

Carson, Tom. "The Hell with Literature: James Jones's Unvarnished Truths." *Village Voice Literary Supplement,* September 1984, pp. 1, 18–20.

Carter, Steven R. *James Jones: An American Literary Orientalist Master.* Urbana: University of Illinois Press, 1998.

Davis, L. J. "G.I. Jones: The End of the Epic." *Washington Post Book World,* March 12, 1978, pp. E1–E2.

Dempsey, David. "Tough and Tormented, This Was the Army to Mr. Jones." *New York Times Book Review,* February 25, 1951, p. 5.

———. "By Sex Obsessed." *New York Times Book Review,* January 12, 1958, pp. 5, 32.

DeVoto, Bernard. "The Easy Chair: Dull Novels Make Dull Reading." *Harper's,* June 1951, pp. 67–70.

Didion, Joan. "The Coast: Good-bye. Gentleman-ranker." *Esquire,* October 1977, pp. 50, 60–62.

Fiedler, Leslie. "James Jones' Dead-End Young Werther: The Bum as American Culture Hero." *Commentary* 12:252–255 (1951).

Fussell, Paul. *Wartime: Understanding and Behavior in the Second World War.* New York: Oxford University Press, 1989.

Garrett, George P. *James Jones.* San Diego, Calif.: Harcourt Brace Jovanovich, 1984.

Geismar, Maxwell. "James Jones: And the American War Novel." In his *American Moderns: From Rebellion to Conformity.* New York: Hill and Wang, 1958. Pp. 225–238.

Gelsanliter, James. "Remembering James Jones." *Writer's Yearbook* 53:74–79, 91 (1982).

Giles, James R. *James Jones.* Boston: Twayne, 1981.

Glicksberg, Charles I. "Racial Attitudes in *From Here to Eternity.*" *Phylon* 14:384–389 (1953).

"Glimpses: James Jones, 1921–1977." *Paris Review* 29, no. 103:205–236 (summer 1987).

Griffith, Ben W., Jr. "Rear Rank Robin Hood: James Jones's Folk Hero." *Georgia Review* 10:41–46 (1956).

Hassan, Ihab. "The War Novel." In *Contemporary American Literature 1945–1972: An Introduction.* New York: Frederick Ungar, 1973. Pp. 64–66.

Hendrick, George, Helen Howe, and Don Sackrider. *James Jones and the Handy Writers' Colony.* Carbondale: Southern Illinois University Press.

Hicks, Granville. "James Jones's *Some Came Running*: A Study of Arrogant Primitivism." *New Leader,* January 27, 1958, pp. 20–22.

James Jones: Reveille to Taps. PBS television documentary. Produced by J. Michael Lennon and Jeffrey Van Davis. Springfield, Ill.: Sangamon State University, 1984.

Jones, Ernest. "Minority Report: *From Here to Eternity.*" *Nation,* March 17, 1951, pp. 254–255.

Krim, Seymour. "Final Tribute: The Eternal American Soldier." *New Times,* June 10, 1977, p. 76.

Kunitz, Stanley, ed. "Jones, James." *Twentieth Century Authors: A Biographical Dictionary, First Supplement.* New York: Wilson, 1955. Pp. 500–501.

Lardner, John. "Anatomy of the Regular Army." *New Yorker,* March 10, 1951, pp. 117–119.

Lydon, Michael. "A Voice Against Anonymous Death." *Atlantic,* September 1991, pp. 119–122.

Macauley, Robie. "Private Jones's Revenge." *Kenyon Review* 13:526–529 (summer 1951).

MacShane, Frank. *Into Eternity: The Life of James Jones.* Boston: Houghton Mifflin, 1985.

Michel-Michot, Paulette. "Jones's *The Thin Red Line*: The End of Innocence." *Revue des Langues Vivantes* 30:15–26 (1964).

Mitchell, Burroughs. "Eternity and Afterward." In his *The Education of an Editor.* Garden City, N.Y.: Doubleday, 1980. Pp. 57–81.

Morris, Willie. *James Jones: A Friendship.* Garden City, N.Y.: Doubleday, 1978.

O'Brien, Tim. "Every Soldier, Coming Home." *Saturday Review,* April 15, 1978, pp. 76–80.

Perkins, Maxwell. Various letters addressed to James Jones. In *Editor to Author: The Letters of Maxwell E. Perkins.* Edited by John Hall Wheelock. New York: Charles Scribner's Sons, 1950. Pp. 273–274, 295–299.

Shaw, Irwin. "James Jones, 1921–1977." *New York Times Book Review,* June 12, 1977, pp. 3, 34–35.

Sheed, Wilfrid. "The Jones Boy Forever." *Atlantic,* June 1967, pp. 68–72.

Shepherd, Allen. "'A Deliberately Symbolic Little Novella': James Jones's *The Pistol.*" *South Dakota Review* 10, no. 1:111–119 (spring 1972).

Stevenson, David L. "James Jones and Jack Kerouac: Novelists of Disjunction." In *The Creative Present: Notes on Contemporary American Fiction.* Edited by Nona Balakian and Charles Simmons. Garden City, N.Y.: Doubleday, 1963. Pp. 193–212.

Styron, William. "A Friend's Farewell to James Jones." *New York,* June 6, 1977, pp. 40–41.

Sunseri, Alvin. "Quiet Desperation: The Career of James Jones." *North American Review* 264:56–59 (summer 1979).

Volpe, Edmond L. "James Jones—Norman Mailer." In *Contemporary American Novelists.* Edited by Harry T. Moore. Carbondale: Southern Illinois University Press, 1964. Pp. 106–119.

Whipple, A. B. C. "James Jones and His Angel." *Life,* May 7, 1951, pp. 143–157.

Wood, Thomas J., and Meredith Keating. *James Jones in Illinois: A Guide to the Handy Writers' Colony Collection.* Springfield, Ill.: Sangamon State University, 1989.

INTERVIEWS

Aldrich, Nelson W., Jr. "James Jones." In *Writers at Work: The Paris Review Interviews,* Third Series. Edited by George Plimpton. New York: Viking, 1967. Pp. 231–250. Originally published in *Paris Review* 20:34–35 (autumn/winter 1958–1959).

Bannon, Barbara A. "Story Behind the Book: *A Touch of Danger,*" *Publishers Weekly,* May 7, 1973, pp. 38–39.

Goodfriend, Arthur. "The Cognescenti Abroad II: James Jones's Paris." *Saturday Review,* February 1, 1969, pp. 36–38.

Hanscom, Leslie. "The Writer Speaks: A Conversation Between James Jones and Leslie Hanscom." In *James Jones: A Checklist.* Edited by John R. Hopkins. Detroit: Bruccoli-Clark/Gale Research Company, 1974. Pp. 6–18.

Kahn, R. T. "James Jones: A Talk Before the End [conversation with Willie Morris]." *Bookviews,* June 1978, pp. 6–7.

Lasky, Michael S. "James Jones Has Come Home to Whistle." *Writer's Digest,* October 1976, pp. 22–26, 52.

Moffett, Hugh. "Aging Heavy of the Paris Expatriates." *Life,* August 4, 1967, pp. 30–34.

"Two Writers Talk It Over [transcribed conversation with William Styron]." *Esquire,* July 1963, pp. 57–59.

Viorst, Milton. "James Jones and the Phony Intellectuals." *Esquire,* February 1968, pp. 98–101, 131–132.

FILMS BASED ON THE WORKS OF JAMES JONES

From Here to Eternity. Directed by Fred Zinnemann. Screenplay by Daniel Taradash. Columbia, 1953.

Some Came Running. Directed by Vincente Minnelli. Screenplay by John Patrick and Arthur Sheekman. MGM, 1958.

The Thin Red Line. Directed by Andrew Marton. Screenplay by Bernard Gordon. Security/ACE, 1964.

From Here to Eternity. Television miniseries. Directed by Buzz Kulik. NBC, 1979.

A Soldier's Daughter Never Cries. Fictional treatment of Jones's family life in Paris and after moving back to the United States, based on a novel by his daughter, Kaylie Jones. Directed by James Ivory. Screenplay by James Ivory and Ruth Prawer Jhabvala. Universal, 1998.

The Thin Red Line. Directed by Terrence Malick. Screenplay by Terrence Malick. Twentieth Century Fox, 1998.

—BRIAN KENT

Mary Karr

1955–

THE NARRATOR OF *Don Quixote* says that his hero was born in a village "the name of which I have no desire to recall." Mary Karr insists on calling her Texas hometown "Leechfield," a name clearly invented for its unpleasant connotations. The daughter of J. P. (Pete) and Charlie Marie Moore, Mary Marlene Karr was born in Groves, Texas, on January 16, 1955. Her sister, Lecia, who is two years older, is an important figure in Karr's immensely successful memoirs, *The Liars' Club* (1995) and *Cherry* (2000). Groves (pop. 16,744 in 1997) was originally called Pecan Groves, but it no longer has a pastoral reputation. The notorious chemical Agent Orange, used during the Vietnam War as a defoliant, was manufactured there; the city is part of the greater Port Arthur area, a region filled with petroleum refineries and chemical plants. Karr has been merciless toward the area in her memoirs, describing it as socially and intellectually backward as well as polluted. Others have shared her view: the region has been described disparagingly in numerous biographies of the singer Janis Joplin, who grew up in Port Arthur. Joyce Carol Oates devotes much of her review of Karr's *Cherry* to a list of horrors she experienced living for eight months in the region in 1961 and 1962, citing pollution, dead snakes, rats, and roaches as physical ordeals, and cultural sterility and racism as psychological ones. Karr has given a mythic status to the area: it is probably just as well that she has spared it the obloquy of calling it by its actual name. Her May 2001 essay, "Memories of East Texas," in *Architectural Digest* has a relatively positive view of the tract house and working-class neighborhood in which she grew up, so she may be mellowing about Leechfield.

She left Groves in 1972 and went with six male friends to Los Angeles, seeking the turned-on, dropped-out lifestyle she had read about in *Rolling Stone* magazine and Tom Wolfe's *Electric Kool-Aid Acid Test.* After adventures in the hippie and surfing scenes in California, in 1972 she entered Macalester College in St. Paul, Minnesota, where she spent two years before dropping out to travel. She became interested in the antiapartheid movement and as a result met the African-American poet Etheridge Knight in Minneapolis. She considers Knight her first poetry mentor. In 1979 she obtained an M.F.A. degree at Goddard College, an innovative school where she met writers like Geoffrey and Tobias Wolff, whose memoirs influenced her own. In 1987 her first collection of poems, *Abacus,* appeared in the venerable Wesleyan University Press Poetry Series, a frequent starting point for young poets in America. She married the poet Michael Milburn in 1983 and had a son, Dev Milburn, in 1986. She and Milburn divorced in 1991.

She has lived a life typical of a creative writing professor, teaching at such places as Emerson College, Tufts, and Harvard. At the time of this writing, she was Jesse Truesdale Peck Professor of Literature at Syracuse University. She has won numerous awards, including the Whiting Writers Award from the Mrs. Giles Whiting Foundation in 1989 and the Carr P. Collins Prize from the Texas Institute of Letters in 1996 for *The Liars' Club.* She has held fellowships from the National Endowment for the Arts and the MacDowell Colony. Her first collections of poetry, *Abacus* (1987) and *The Devil's Tour* (1993), were well-received, but fame came with *The Liars' Club: A Memoir* in 1991. The book was on the *New York Times* best-seller list for almost sixty weeks, and it has been credited with creating the so-called memoir boom, which became the subject of a special issue of the *New York Times Magazine* in 1996. *Life* magazine included her in Jen Dorman's 1998 photo essay "Strong Women," where a photograph of Karr shows her sitting on a pool table in "Sadie's Place" in Syracuse, captioned by a glib comment on her ability to always land on her "Manolo Blahnik spike heels," presumably the ones she is wearing in the picture.

ABACUS

Karr's poems fall into the American mainstream, the kind of accessible and carefully crafted poetry that flourishes in university M.F.A. programs. Her poems are brief, rooted in specific situations, and the style is clear. She uses metaphors skillfully, and she has a gift for bringing a poem to a striking conclusion. Her work shows the influence of the confessional poets of the 1960s, a "boom" in poetry started by Robert Lowell's *Life Studies* (1959), a collection in which Lowell wrote about his highly dysfunctional family. The prose section of that book, "91 Revere Street," is an important precedent for Karr's memoirs. The contrast is worthy of note: Lowell's family was patrician and he could call himself a "Mayflower screwball," whereas Karr's background is Texas working class. Lowell only wrote one brief prose work dealing with his family. Karr would eventually use the confessional approach in her full-length memoirs.

The confessional stance relies on frank, even shocking, revelations about self and family. Addictions, mental illness, and family conflicts abound in confessional poems: the works of John Berryman, Anne Sexton, and Sylvia Plath,

as well as Lowell, are typical of the mode. Such poetry often violates the usual proprieties of taste. And the proprieties of literary style are stretched in the quest to convey extreme situations. The poet may repel rather than move the reader if brutal frankness becomes mere brutality of tone and diction. The love Karr expresses toward her family members generally prevents her from seeming exploitative of their weaknesses.

It would be rash to assume that all of her work is autobiographical, but a number of poems in her three collections correspond to people and situations in the memoirs, and she often dedicates poems to family members. She begins *Abacus* with a group of highly introspective poems. The first work, "Magnifying Mirror," is built on a moment when the speaker looked into a mirror in her mother's purse and found her face very large. Later, we are told, the speaker learned to hate her face and saw it as very large. The fact that the mirror was taken from her mother's purse is significant: she says that she imitated her mother's taste in high heels and her taste for alcohol and men. The speaker had to pay a psychiatrist "to puff me up again." The question posed by this poem is valid for all of Karr's work: "Magnifying Mirror" asks whether "birth," a kind of fall from the womb into fear and imperfection, should be overcome by looking out into the world or into the self. The answer implied by her work as a whole is that both methods are needed: her opus employs both viewpoints, sometimes dealing primarily with the self and at other times with the people and situations that impinge on it. A fascination with mirrors need not lead to narcissism.

The mirror image in the opening poem inclines the reader to see the succeeding poems in *Abacus* as explorations of the writer's personality, though the next poem, "Diogenes Invents a Game," adopts the mask of a created speaker, a fictional modern-day namesake of the ancient Greek philosopher Diogenes. The real

Diogenes was a fanatical seeker of the truth who was called a "Cynic," meaning a dog, because he lived such an austere life, sleeping in a wooden tub. Karr's persona is certainly cynical and world-weary. The six poems in which Diogenes appears do not really present him as a distinctive character, though he is clearly disillusioned, the benign face of cynicism. In "Diogenes Invents a Game," the speaker copes with the darkness of the world by playing with a mattress button at night. The poem turns into a parable when the mattress button falls into a web where the deluded spider treats it as prey. The spider, too, creates "a little web against the dark."

The most interesting poems in the first section of *Abacus* draw on Karr's knowledge of a Texas milieu. "A Ballet in Numbers for Mary Ellen" uses imagery from ballet classes to discuss a friend's mental breakdown. In "Taking Out the Lawn Chairs," she looks at the lives of a Texas family, the Perrys, with details of life in Texas: bluetick hounds, pecans, summer heat so severe that the speaker wakes with "snails of sweat" on her lower lip. "Aunt Gladys" deals with the lives of country relatives, and "The Lynched Man" describes a child's encounter with the dead body of hanged man. In "Vampire," a poem that perhaps owes a debt to the late poems of Sylvia Plath, Karr dramatizes self-loathing by presenting the protagonist through imagery of werewolves and vampires. The poem never explains just what the vampire woman feels guilty about. The section ends with two moving poems about her father's fatal illness, a subject she returns to in *The Liars' Club*. In "Vigil," she presents a bleak picture of sitting with her sister in the hospital room, playing "honeymoon solitaire" and washing down aspirin with coffee as the father "poked the plastic / oxygen tent to see where he stopped and we began," metaphorically a crucial problem for children as well as parents. In "Perspective: Anniversary D-Day," she makes her first

effort to write about a scene that will have great importance in *The Liars' Club*: the opening of her father's old footlocker. In the poem, she reads the father's letters in an attempt to understand his past. The poem concludes with a bleak scene of rolling her unresponsive father in his wheelchair back to bed in the nursing home: he is beyond response and his mattress seems a raft on which he is already embarking.

The second section of *Abacus* is devoted to love poems, mostly in urban settings like Paris. The language is often sensuous: "I slithered out / of my black dress like a python," she says in "My New Diet." The emotions are intense: longing, regret, and anger, as well as eroticism, run through the poems. The book gets its title from lines in "The Distance," which describe stringing a necklace with stones given by the lover, making a kind of abacus of love and hate. Perhaps the finest of them is "Exile's Letter," a poem with delicate, almost subliminal echoes of Chinese poets like Li Po (who wrote a poem by this title). The opening image of shaping a boat out of pages of the poem itself is a common one in Chinese lyrics. The mask of Diogenes is worn very lightly in "Diogenes Tries to Forget": the narrator craves pecan pie, an image out of a Texas background.

The poems in the third section of *Abacus* are varied in subject but generally dark in mood. The two poems about a father who is rather clearly Karr's easily dominate the section. "Witnessing My Father's Will" uses the occasion to cast doubt on the powers of language, a difficult theme for a poet. The father's apathy makes communication seem helpless, and his "theory / that theories are garbage" makes the poet share his tendency to think in shrugs, which are a cynical though perhaps stoical gesture. The other father poem, "Home during a Tropical Snowstorm I Feed My Father Lunch," builds a chilled winter setting that is grotesque for the Gulf coast of Texas. Karr uses the setting for a poem of powerful emotion: the daughter attempts to feed the parent and has to free his throat of meat that is choking him. He responds by biting her, hard. The incident is even more effective when reported in *The Liars' Club,* where it comes near the end of a book that has superbly established the father's character, the daughter's character, and the complexity of their relationship.

THE DEVIL'S TOUR

Karr has written a long essay, "Remembering James Laughlin," about her friendship with the founder-editor of the book publisher New Directions. In 1991 he solicited a manuscript from her at a time when her career and personal life were at low points. She flourished under his encouragement, and she says that poets get little encouragement. "Poetry is a humiliating art: Practiced in isolation, it draws those isolate by nature, then offers them few public arenas for reward." At a time when she felt that she was in a "spiritual quagmire," Laughlin's letters and conversations increased her sense of worth and sharpened her knowledge of literary history, especially since Laughlin was personally acquainted with important modernists he published, like Ezra Pound and William Carlos Williams. She suggests that poets today are not sufficiently interested in the history of their art.

With *Abacus,* Karr demonstrated her promise. In *The Devil's Tour,* her first book with New Directions, the promise is fulfilled. The technique is more confident, and she demonstrates skill in the use of stanza forms, especially three-line units. The book manages to be more introspective but less self-centered. The tour of the title is, she says on the back cover, a tour of the human skull: the mind, which she says (quoting Milton's Satan), "can make a hell of heav'n' or a heav'n of hell. I myself am hell." To speak of oneself as hell puts her in the tradition of confessional poetry, but she speaks for more than herself. She demonstrates a knowl-

edge of natural history, science, and history that keeps the book from being merely a set of personal reflections, and she creates compelling characters, like a priest who hears the confession of Don Giovanni, and a child evangelist who grows up to be a heartless seducer, alienated from the people to whom he preaches.

The cover of the volume has a memento mori design by Hermann Strohbach. The memento mori is an object reminding the one who contemplates it of the inevitability of death: a skull is a favorite example. The illustration by Strohbach depicts scenes from human life with a central image of two skeletons holding up a mirror in which a skull is reflected. Under it a demure young woman sits. The inscription beneath the illustration is in Greek and Latin, translated on the back cover as "Hither you come: behold what you are, what you will be, or were. / For this mirror the inscription will be, 'Know thyself.'" The tone of the book is somber—not always funereal, but, like John Webster in T. S. Eliot's poem "Whispers of Immortality," Karr knows "the skull beneath the skin." Images of skulls abound. One poem, "Disappointments of the Apocalypse," is about the end of the world. Another poem is about the plagues of the Middle Ages.

There are more personal reflections on death. "In Illo Tempore" re-creates a hospital visit to a dying friend who cannot speak but still hums Schubert. At first the poet and her husband, Michael, wear rubber gloves and paper masks and gowns, but finally they strip off these barriers to contact and oil the friend's hands and comb his hair. The husband makes the occasion a genuine meeting with the inarticulate friend by bending close to his ear and naming the notes and rests in the Schubert song. The death of the friend is dealt with at length in several poems in Michael Milburn's own poetry collection, *Such Silence* (1989). Milburn also has a poem about Pete Karr entitled "Her Father's Letters," In another poem, Karr writes an elegy, "Post-

Larkin Triste," for the English poet Philip Larkin, a writer who was also much concerned with death. Larkin is the subject of an essay she published in *Seneca Review* not long after his death. Elegies are a traditional way for poets to affirm the value of their art by saluting a fellow writer. Karr's opening line speaks of experiencing a cold New England wind on the day Larkin died, an echo of the opening of W. H. Auden's famous elegy, "In Memory of W. B. Yeats": "O all the instruments agree / The day of his death was a dark cold day." She makes a poem out of not having met the poet she admired. Larkin was notoriously private and hated meeting other poets, so she respected his integrity by not meeting him, except in written words. In her poem, she suggests that this meeting was the equivalent of the time Larkin listened to William Wordsworth's poetry in his "bubble" of a car and wept.

The poet, according to Wordsworth's 1800 preface to *Lyrical Ballads,* is "the rock and defence of human nature," and two poems in *The Devil's Tour* assume that role. In "Average Torture," Karr dissects the mundane and boring routines that human beings fall into. Her evocation of quiet desperation is so strong that it serves as a warning. In "All This and More," she provides the "devil's tour" of hell of her title, suggesting that hell is not a place of physical torture (molten lead and giant pliers) but an immersion in a media-dominated reality. In her vision, the damned sit in overstuffed armchairs with antennae screwed into their heads, watching television parodies of their lives. "Small but Urgent Request to the Unknowable" searches for a redeeming goodness within the mind, a nugget of kindness surviving the evolution of the cortex as a mechanism for survival in a Darwinian world. The poem is a forerunner of her subsequent poems of religious search.

Evolution and its discontents are a subject of a number of the poems, like "Erectus," which looks at the evolution of the brain in *Homo sa-piens,* and "Against Nature," which conflates biology and the story of the fall of man. In "Against Nature," she celebrates the emergence of human values from the Darwinian world. The memento mori tradition uses the skull to remind us that we are mortal, but Karr varies it by reminding us that the skull of Mozart was crowded with angels as he wrote his *Requiem.* "Day-Care Field Trip: Aquarium" uses sea creatures in tanks as a way to talk about our own evolution: the miniature sea of the aquarium is a good microcosm for symbolizing larger questions of value. She imagines human ancestors watching children as they themselves look with open mouths at primitive creatures. A less successful poem about the movement of human history, "The Unweepables," commemorates lost and battered women but remains too abstract in its presentation.

The day-care poem is one of several that grow out of the experience of motherhood. "Soft Mask" introduces her son into her body of work through an ultrasound picture. "Croup" deals touchingly with a child's illness. The less personal "Parents Taking Shape" considers the shifting perspectives on parents as a child grows up. The beneficent parents seem monstrous after the child's intelligence develops, and he feels emotionally torn between them, a situation that Karr explores more personally in her memoirs. In "Sad Rite," the speaker traces the emotional effects of abortion rather than of motherhood, conveying the grief of a woman who tries to escape the aftermath of the experience by going to a bar. The agony of the speaker is conveyed by an image of a blood-red moon. In Karr's carefully planned collection, the moon image is picked up in a positive way in the ultrasound poem, where the unborn child's face is imagined in a window with a background of blooming trees and a blood-red moon.

The book has a number of poems on the poet's parents, a subject with a permanent place in her work. "The Legion" foreshadows *The*

Liars' Club, describing the bar where her father and his friends would drink and talk. The poem expresses grief for a father who metaphorically orphaned his daughter by wandering "fearful in his skull" as he sat in the bar, his attention given over to the bar and his friends, who are described without malice as "aging boys." The poem lacks concrete details of the conversations he had over Lone Star beer, but *The Liars' Club* fills in that gap brilliantly. The other father poem, "Accusing Message from Dead Father," describes a phone call from the father in a dream. It has a guilt-ridden description of taking her father to a home after he became incapacitated. The intimate details of the helpless father's body (his penis lies slack along his leg, and his daughter must carry bottles of "warm piss") are typical of confessional poetry since Robert Lowell's *Life Studies,* which dealt with the deaths of his parents with unprecedented frankness. Sharon Olds's work similarly abounds with such descriptions.

More interesting are the two poems about her mother. Karr is fascinated with the imagery of eyes as well as skulls. "Her One Bad Eye," which is dedicated to her mother, builds its exploration of their frustrated relationship through the situation of a corneal transplant. In a convoluted comparison, Karr says that just as the new cornea does not contain memories of what the donor saw, her mother's mind cannot

. . . recount

to me her life's saga
in a way that makes sense.

So mother and daughter are dead to one another. The other poem, "Mass Eye and Ear: The Ward," also deals with her mother's eyes, a moment of looking closely at them while lighting a cigarette for her mother in the hospital. Part of the moment is the recollection of finding her mother's seven wedding rings in the attic, the epiphany that forms the climax of *The Liars'*

Club. The poem ends with a brilliant image of seeing her mother through a "bridal veil" of cigarette smoke.

Karr frames *The Devil's Tour* with two poems marking epochs in her life. The opening poem, set in her East Texas childhood, is "Coleman," an elegy for a friend who found life in the Port Arthur area intolerable. She recalls him at a moment when at fifteen he slipped under an oilfield fence and rode the bobbing pump like a rodeo horse, a superb scene. Persecuted for nonconformity, Coleman ostensibly died in a hunting accident, but the narrator suspects it was suicide. She leaves the area, choosing not to be destroyed, knowing that the oil-field bronco could not be broken. Her subsequent career recalls a line from Auden's elegy for Yeats: "Mad Ireland hurt you into / poetry." Mad Leechfield, her hometown as she conceives of it, hurt Karr into poetry also. The poem at the end of the book marks another departure. In "Divorce," she explores the breakup of a marriage by describing the day that students helped move possessions out of the house. The poem ends with the speaker saying, "I didn't know what could happen next."

THE LIARS' CLUB

For Mary Karr herself, what happened next was astonishing. She was successful as a poet, in the way that most poets in America are successful: she had respectable publications, reasonable financial rewards through grants and jobs. But she was not famous: few poets in America can hope to be. Her memoir changed that situation, making her a best-selling author and a public figure. An enormous amount of information is available about the writing of *The Liars' Club* and the effects of fame on the author. Much of this material is available on the Internet, and it varies wildly in accuracy. A reliable online "Reading Group Guide" includes biographical information, a long interview, a reprint of an article by Karr on memoirs, and a set of study questions. The article, now entitled "The Family Sideshow," is a slightly revised version of "Dysfunctional Nation," her coda to the special issue of the *New York Times Magazine* on the memoir boom, a publishing frenzy that she helped to create. She distills her observations about the appeal of memoirs, views gathered when she made public appearances and talked to many readers. Karr suggests in "The Family Sideshow" that the dysfunctional family is in fact the American norm in the baby-boom era and that readers are interested in reading about other "whacked-out families" (the racy idiom is typical of Karr) and are able to draw empowerment from seeing that others have survived. In a long essay, "All Our Lost Children: Trauma and Testimony in the Performance of Childhood," Patricia Pace uses the book to illustrate the linkages of trauma and emerging subjectivity in the child. She notes that Karr's work deals with emblematic "events of our time—alcoholism and mental illness, separation and divorce, family secrets, survival." Its success is therefore not surprising.

Her most considered comments on memoirs appear in a long essay published in *Parnassus,* "A Memoirist's Apology." In it she observes that her first memoir came in a financial crisis after a divorce. She likes to say in interviews that she needed to buy a secondhand Toyota. The necessity created a virtue: she found that the family experiences haunting her poetry could be dealt with more amply in the prose form of a memoir. She distrusts prose, with its wealth of information, because she is devoted to the short poem, for which music is supreme. But she admits that information—exposition, character development—is suited to prose. Information makes the poem sag, as she puts it. She concedes that prose enabled her to deal with the central tragedy of her mother's life, the loss of two children to a husband who kidnapped them. She observes that her subjects have

always chosen her, and readers of her poetry know that family dysfunction haunts her lyrics. In *The Liars' Club,* she finds ways not to exorcise the ghosts of the past but to bring them into the light.

She did not come to memoir with naive notions of simply telling her experiences. In the interview on the "Reading Group Guide" website, she mentions that she taught courses on memoir at Syracuse University, and she praises Maya Angelou (whom she read as a junior in high school), Frank Conroy, Maxine Hong Kingston, John Edgar Wideman, and Tobias and Geoffrey Wolff among modern American autobiographers. She can also cite St. Augustine and Rousseau. A writer she particularly admires, Harry Crews, wrote a gritty narrative set in Florida, *Childhood: Biography of a Place,* which must have encouraged her to portray East Texas as "the Ringworm Belt." In "The Family Sideshow," she praised Michael Herr's "psychedelic" account of the war in Vietnam, *Dispatches.* She found it more revealing than the many volumes of objective records compiled from official sources. Karr believes that readers can accept an honest subjectivity in autobiography.

One dimension of her writing barely visible in her poetry is a powerful ability to use the spoken idiom. Karr, a Texan, grew up with the racy southern idiom that grounds utterance in vivid and physical expressions. In an interview that appears as part of the online Reading Group Guide to *The Liars' Club,* she observes that the idiom of her book is primarily her father's. He was a refinery worker who grew up in East Texas, in the "Big Thicket" region around Jasper, and strong rural speech came easily to him. She gives as an example (used in other interviews) the expression "it's raining like a cow pissin' on a flat rock." Her mother, a former art student who read widely in literature and philosophy, contributed an early interest in the arts to Karr, but the earthiness of the book is a salute to her father, and many of the finest passages in the book are tall tales he recounts among his drinking buddies, the "liars' club" of the title. Karr, like other contemporary memoirists, is aware that truth is difficult to establish from the subjective viewpoint of a narrator involved with the action. Calling her book *The Liars' Club* enables her to point out that we all embroider our stories, even those that express our most profound experiences. One of the writers she most admires is Mary McCarthy, whose *Memories of a Catholic Girlhood* constantly worked to correct her memories of childhood experience.

The first section of Karr's book, "Texas, 1961," begins dramatically with one of her earliest memories, a kind of primal scene that it took her years to understand. The reader is drawn into a mysterious situation: the seven-year-old Karr is being questioned by the sheriff about possible harm done to her or her sister, Lecia, aged nine. The situation is left unclear for almost 160 pages, though it emerges quickly that the mother has had a nervous breakdown. Eventually the reader learns that the mother, Charlie Marie, had called the family doctor and claimed to have killed the children with a butcher knife, though she in fact only threatened them with it. Karr follows the opening scene with an account of the illness of Charlie Marie's own mother, who owned a cotton farm near Lubbock. Karr writes harrowing scenes of cancer and the painful, mutilating treatments for it. Grandmother Moore's cancerous leg was treated with mustard-gas injections and had to be amputated after gangrene developed. The grandmother, with her increasingly irrational behavior and artificial leg, is seen by the child as almost a monster.

Karr is extremely frank about the fear and repulsion she felt toward her grandmother, making her into a grotesque character, but she points out that her sister had very different memories of the woman. She puts emotions into her work

that most people try to deny or conceal: the frankness was there in her more confessional poems but not in such disturbing detail. As she says, the memoir offers information. When Karr was a student at Goddard College, she came to know Geoffrey and Tobias Wolff, siblings who wrote about their own dysfunctional families in *The Duke of Deception* (1979) and *This Boy's Life* (1989), respectively. Tobias Wolff was her colleague at Syracuse University for years. In "A Memoirist's Apology," Karr mentions the advice given her by Tobias Wolff, who advised her to conceal nothing, to take no care for her own dignity: he told her to just tell the stories. She has often alluded to this advice in interviews, mentioning that she posted it over her computer during the writing of *The Liars' Club*.

She manages to present her parents with affection in spite of their flaws. The father drank hard and got into fights, but there is no question that he loved his family. The mother, described in Leechfield parlance as "nervous," was eccentric, bad-tempered, and dependent on alcohol and drugs. A spendthrift, she wasted almost a million dollars inherited from her mother. She sometimes disappeared at night and her preteen children had to go find her. She was immensely interested in the arts and had talent herself. When she died in 1997, Karr scattered her ashes behind the Metropolitan Museum in New York City. The parental quarrels were ferocious. But the narrator's affections are strong. Her sister, Lecia, as happens often in troubled families, is prematurely capable of dealing with family crises, especially ones involving the mother. In both of her memoirs, Karr presents Lecia as a personality whose qualities contrast sharply with her own, much like a character foil in drama. Lecia is socially confident and grows up committed not to the arts but to making money.

Karr portrays a family rent by its own conflicts but capable of dealing fiercely with the outside world, gaining a reputation for eccentricity in the neighborhood. The mother could make scathing comments to nosy neighbors. Karr says that she herself once shocked the Dillards next door by swinging upside down naked in a window. She also describes using her air rifle against neighbors who ridiculed her when Charlie Karr was committed for a while after the knife incident. Her father was given to punching people. His fights were brief, Karr says in *The Liars' Club*: he would hit the man, and the man would fall down.

The father's tall tales to the Liars' Club in the "Texas, 1961" section are fine re-creations of the ambiance of southern storytelling, worthy of being classed with the tales in William Faulkner's *The Hamlet*. Karr summons up the lively interplay between the teller and the listeners, letting each story unfold with comments and responses from the audience. The tales usually have some lesson among the drollery: the time the young Pete Karr went out to make a purchase and did not return for years makes a comment on ambivalence about home, and the story of a couple so antagonistic that the husband finally sawed their house in two is a wry commentary on marriage. The great set piece is the narrative of the supposed suicide of Pete Karr's father. The father was still alive, of course: the story is a fabrication but moves the audience with its tragic force. It comes after Pete's mother-in-law has suffered a drawn-out agonizing death and suggests that a quick violent death is preferable to the obscenity of a life preserved in agony and mental confusion.

There are brilliant episodes representing real life rather than lies. The flight of the women of the family to escape Hurricane Carla, one of the great storms of the twentieth century, is an episode of novelistic force. Charlie Karr drives her daughters to Pete's family in Jasper under terrible conditions. The time when Lecia was stung by a Portuguese man-of-war at the beach is suitably painful to read. The seven-year-old Mary's rape by a teenage boy in the neighborhood has a tremendous force through its reti-

cence: the actions are described objectively though not graphically, the pain of the experience is implied but not made explicit. The scene is actually more powerful than the detailed description of oral sex forced on her by a male baby-sitter in the "Colorado, 1963" section. The terrible quarrels leading up to Charlie Karr's mental breakdown are harrowing. Once she tries to drive the whole family off the Rainbow Bridge, the highest in the region, and they are saved when Pete knocks her unconscious and takes control of the car. The breakdown culminates in her mother's burning the family mementos and threatening the children with the knife. Another crucial scene is Karr's memory of opening her father's footlocker after his death (a kind of flash-forward in the narrative, part of the attempt to understand him). The scene balances the crucial episode in the third and last section, "Texas Again, 1980": Karr searches the attic for documents about her father to support a veteran's claim and comes across her mother's seven wedding rings, which hold the key to her mother's character. The contents of the footlocker include old bills and a pistol with a bullet in the firing chamber. They do not explain the man's character. His tall tales revealed more of his thinking than such traces.

The second section, "Colorado, 1963," deals with the mother's decision to settle in a little town in Colorado and buy a bar (a disaster for an alcoholic!) with part of her large inheritance from her mother. The father will not give up his job and a divorce ensues. The mother marries the bartender, Hector, one of the more laughable wicked stepfathers in world literature. The stepfather is not quite as detestable as the similar figure in Tobias Wolff's memoir, *This Boy's Life,* but only because he is more pathetic than evil. The Colorado days explore the complications of divorce for children, the divided loyalties that arise at times like Father's Day. The Colorado sojourn comes to an end after a fight between the mother and stepfather, which almost ends in violent death: Charlie Marie pulls a gun on Hector and the daughters have to calm the situation, another example of their being forced into behaving maturely beyond their years, a common pattern in dysfunctional families. Lecia, ever the rescuer, calls her father and demands plane tickets home for herself and Mary. A hilarious set of errors in travel connections ensues, involving an accidental trip to Mexico. The original marriage is reestablished after Charlie Marie and Hector come to Leechfield to pick up some of Charlie's clothes. Pete beats Hector up and then has a happy reunion with his former wife, who shows great craftiness in dealing with the sheriff over the assault on the miserable Hector.

The final section, "Texas Again, 1980," deals with the father's death and the revelation of a family secret that has been the cause of the family's dysfunction. The decline and death of Karr's father was the subject of powerful poems in *Abacus,* notably "Home during a Tropical Snowstorm I Feed My Father Lunch." The scene of the daughter attempting to feed her recalcitrant father, in which the father bites his daughter as she tries to clear a plug of food from his throat, is more detailed and therefore disturbing in the prose narrative. And along with the graphic details of the incident, the reader has the whole context of the father-daughter relationship to give weight to the events. The father's final illness leads to Karr's discovery of her mother's wedding rings. Confronted with the rings, the mother takes tranquilizers and goes to bed. Eventually, however, her daughter gets the truth out of her, in a fine scene set in a Mexican restaurant, where over margaritas (the scene is appropriately salty and soppy) the family secret emerges. The mother married at age fifteen and had two children, Tex and Belinda. She went with her family to New York, where she studied art, to the disapproval of her husband and mother-in-law. One day she returned to the apartment and found her children

gone. She eventually tracked them down but was pressured into giving them up. Her subsequent series of marriages was a quest to find a man who could help her win the children back. This scene of confession ends the memoir on a note of hope, as Karr and her mother leave the restaurant feeling purged by the revelation of the truth.

Karr's first memoir was generally well-received by critics. "This Personal Maze Is Not the Prize," a review article by Eric Murphy Selinger in *Parnassus,* traces connections between Karr's poems and the autobiography. Even more helpfully, he puts Karr's work in the context of other confessions by poets, beginning with William Wordsworth's verse memoir, *The Prelude,* and continuing to recent books by William Corbett and Thylias Moss. He believes that such memoirs serve as a letter of introduction to the writer's second self as a poet. This approach values *The Liars' Club* without losing sight of the poems that Karr published in the years before and after her first memoir. William Harmon's very long review, "Mary Karr, Mary Karr, Mary Karr, Mary Karr," is, as the title implies, an encomium, but he does scrutinize the style and plausibility of her memoir, finding some shortcomings in both. On the whole, like Selinger, he puts the memoir in the context of her poetry, linking themes in *The Liar's Club* to *Abacus* and the 1998 collection *Viper Rum.* He suggests that the memoir may become a classic. He particularly relishes her ability to evoke childhood through the sense of smell.

VIPER RUM AND "AGAINST DECORATION"

Selinger and Harmon both praise Karr's polemical essay of 1990, "Against Decoration," first published in *Parnassus* and then reprinted in her third poetry collection, *Viper Rum.* The controversial article is directed at several targets. Primarily she attacks what she calls "the assembling neo-formalist canon," as represented by several anthologies, most notably Robert Richman's *The Direction of Poetry: Rhymed and Metered Verse Written in the English Language since 1975*. She singles out several poets as engaging in what she calls "highbrow doily-making" in the late-twentieth-century poetry scene—for example, James Merrill and Amy Clampitt—and she analyzes their poems mercilessly, seeing them as "purple" and baroque. She states her own artistic credo indirectly when she says that the neoformalists commit two sins: "absence of emotion" and "lack of clarity." For her, "to pay so little attention to the essentially human elements of a poem makes a monster of poetry's primary emotional self, its very reason for being, so that the art becomes exclusively decorative and at times grotesque." She complains that poems in *The New Yorker* are mostly trivial, full of references to botany. Her own poems, in the early collections and in *Viper Rum,* are certainly full of emotion and are written with great clarity.

When Karr singles out deconstruction as an encouragement of decorative poetry, she is less convincing than when she analyzes poetry she considers flawed, and her attack on excessive metaphor is based on an odd reading of Aristotle. She claims that he considered metaphor merely the seasoning for the meat, but in the *Poetics* he said, "the greatest thing by far is to be a master of metaphor. It is the one thing that cannot be learned from others; it is also a sign of genius, since a good metaphor implies an eye for resemblance." He made similar claims for metaphor in the *Rhetoric*. In his review of *Viper Rum,* Robert MacDowell suggests that Karr's critique of neoformalism is historically inaccurate.

The good rebel eventually gets welcomed into the establishment. Many of the poems in *Viper Rum* were published in *The New Yorker,* and Karr continues to contribute to that magazine. Reviewing the collection, Barbara Jordan suggests that Karr's models are Larkin and Seamus Heaney. Certainly Larkin is a presence. In Jordan's words: "Like him, she has an unwavering eye for details, and an ability to make that detail betray its circumstance." Both poets are acutely aware of the waste and despair in human life. Larkin is not thought of as a confessional poet, but in his late work he could be remarkably frank about his unhappiness and his fear of death.

In *Viper Rum,* Karr continues to explore her personal life through brilliant poems about her parents and other poems about her past struggles with alcohol. She also introduces religious themes into her work for the first time. The book has a technical ease, dominated by poems in three-line stanzas, often run-on, which organize perceptions without fitting them too rigidly into formal patterns. One poem, "Incant against Suicide," is even a sonnet, though an unrhymed one. The image of the skull recurs in the poems as a reminder of mortality and as the theater of consciousness.

The title poem, one of Karr's most complex works, uses a jungle setting to commemorate the successful struggle against alcohol. A coral snake is caught by a waiter in the lodge where the speaker is staying. Placed in a Hellmann's mustard jar, the snake represents the poisons ingested by alcoholics. The owner of the lodge then brings out the viper rum, a gallon jug containing not only rum but also a python. The speaker remembers a past life damaged by alcoholism, nights spent standing at the sink drinking, "my head hatching snakes." Somehow the addiction was overcome:

What plucked me from that fate

can't yet be named, but I do reverence to it
every day. . . .

The speaker declines to drink in the lodge, leaving her shot glass at the table turned upside down. Another poem, "Limbo: Altered States," uses another scene of temptation as a vehicle for remembering the past: the drinks cart comes during an airplane flight, and the opportunity to backslide must be rejected.

The book has a number of family poems, especially about the poet's mother, who died in 1997. "Beauty and the Shoe Sluts" describes her mother looking over a collection of dancing shoes to see which ones will fit the daughter, who quotes lines from the *Bacchae* of Euripides: "Will they ever come to me again, / the long, long dances?" The mother's response is, "No, / praise God and menopause, they won't." The valedictory tone of this poem is echoed in one of her longest poems, "Lifecycle Stairmaster." A return to Texas prompts the poet to contemplate the life cycles of her family as she uses the aptly named machine in her sister Lecia's luxurious house. Her mother sits nearby reading a mystical text, *The Cloud of Unknowing*. She falls asleep at the book. The poet realizes the irony of the moment: that she is exercising to avoid that terminus of death toward which her mother moves. Her father reached that end already, and she speaks of seeing his "chlorine-scented ghost" by the swimming pool. In a burst of Texas detail, she describes her sister's cornbread and chili, dishes familiar from her childhood, when her father would cook them: another way of making him a presence in the work. The poem ends with the family being "clapped to our chairs for grace," a quiet use of the religious-faith theme in the book. "The Invention of God in a Mouthful of Milk" is a less elaborate poem, a recollection that the aged mother was the poet's avenue to life. The first image of a deity was the mother who nursed her. She has two touching poems about her father, both addressed to him, but her mother is the conspicuous presence in her collection.

The mother is now subject, another poem says, to "Four of the Horsemen (Hypertense and Stroke, Coronary Occlusion and Cerebral Insult)." The poem contemplates the mother watching television, wielding her remote control imperiously. Karr has never lost her awe for her mother, although she is acutely aware of her shortcomings as a parent. The mother has undergone drastic medical treatment: her heart was "reamed" by a surgeon who pried open her chest and stapled it shut afterward. These graphic details are countered by the wisdom of the Stoic philosopher Epictetus, who, she says, taught us that we are "meat hunks" and must learn to bear suffering. Karr manages to undercut this somewhat pretentious allusion by observing her mother's skeptical attitude toward caution: she "scorns delivered wisdom" and still smokes heavily. The poem ends on a powerful note: the poet puts her ear to her sleeping mother's chest as if to "power up" (one of several brilliantly chosen verbs in the poem) her heart. But in her mother's heartbeat she hears the approach of the four horsemen of illness referred to in the title of the poem. A poem like this one is in the lineage of Robert Lowell's *Life Studies*: frank, straining against propriety in tone, and shocking in diction and subject matter. Like Lowell, she has some lapses: in "The Last of the Brooding Miserables," she describes a friend's suicide by saying that he shut the garage door and "sucked off the family muffler," a gratuitous sexual image. The poem is cast as a prayer but has some awkward references to Marcus Aurelius unmediated by the irony that lets her put the self-denying Epictetus in a poem about a chain-smoking mother.

The book has considerable variety: love poems and social satires mingle with poems about family and religion. The religious theme is the real innovation in her subject matter. She has written an essay for *Vogue* ("Houses of the Spirit," 1995) about her turn to Catholicism, which came after several years of searching for a religion after her young son asked to go to church. One poem, "The Wife of Jesus Speaks," is a defiant application of shockingly explicit language to Christ. It is spoken posthumously by the imagined wife of Jesus, who has committed suicide. The diction is full of missteps, like the casual reference to the "Roman bastards" and the graphic description of a sexual union between the wife and Christ. Judging from the *Vogue* article, her quest has not been easy: after her six-year-old son asked to go to church, she spent years going with him to a variety of churches (and even a synagogue and Zen center) before finding that Catholicism satisfied her needs. Other poems dramatize traditional struggles of the soul with nascent religious faith. "The Grand Miracle" shows the speaker struggling with doubt and winding up at the altar "for bread and song." In the *Vogue* essay, she talks in a similar way about the host as "a wafer of light" laid on the tongue. The poem entitled "Christ's Passion" contemplates the crucifixion and ends with "I can only hope," which can be read to stress hope or offhandedness.

The final poem, "Chosen Blindness," gathers up themes and motifs from the collection, dealing as it does with her love for the son to whom it is dedicated, her remembered struggles with alcohol, and her growing religious conviction. The poem is in three parts. The first part talks about her blindness to flowers, a minor thing, but related suddenly to her years of drinking when she could look out on a meadow and see nothing because she was ingesting poison. The second part of the poem describes going to church and links the experience with her ancestors, who struggled to cope with the poverty of the Dust Bowl until the rains returned. Rain, of course, suggests spiritual renewal. The third section of the poem has a startling memory of a time the poet set out to commit suicide, leaving a note for her infant son on the glowing computer screen. Now he is old enough to help her hold the hymnal, and a different kind of glow concludes the poem, something internal.

In two uncollected poems from *Poetry* magazine, Karr explores devotional themes more fully. "Descending Theology: Christ Human" considers the incarnation and makes the thoroughly orthodox point that the incarnation of Christ makes possible a union of Christ and the fallen human being. We are far from "The Wife of Jesus Speaks" in this poem. "Descending Theology: The Garden" retells the story of Christ's betrayal in the garden of Gethsemane, emphasizing his compassion for Judas, an example of unlimited love. The life of the poem dwells in the fine creation of the scene, both the foreground of disciples sleeping on the ground, "wrapped in old hides," and the greater sweep of the oasis of Gethsemane around which "the cracked earth radiated out for miles."

CHERRY

In another uncollected poem, "The Choice," the poet talks about her vocation. She begins with a tribute to Wordsworth, a poet who made art out of his life. She remembers going to his house in the Lake Country and looking at "a child's stumpy desk" with the poet's initials. Later, fired by this encounter, she decided to pursue graduate work in writing. She told "the resident genius" that "given the choice between being writing and being / happy" she would pick the latter. The reply was, *"Don't worry, you don't have that choice." Cherry* is a Joycean memoir of Karr's emerging artistic consciousness, a kind of *Portrait of the Artist as a Young Woman,* as Sanford Pinsker has observed in the *Georgia Review.* Karr's work is a nonfiction version of the bildungsroman, the novel showing the growth of a personality, or to be more precise, it is a *kunstlerroman,* a work showing the formation of an artist. She aims at extreme realism in her story, as shown by the title, one of several words in the book that refer to the female genitals. As a synonym for the hymen, the word "cherry" implies inexperience, and the book shows the initiation of the heroine into several aspects of life. The book is dedicated to a number of friends and to St. Jude, patron of lost causes, a wry way to convey that her struggles in adolescence must have made her feel like her situation was hopeless.

She begins the work with a prologue that chronologically is at the end of her narrative: she departs from home and Leechfield at seventeen with six male surfer friends. The departure was brought on by ennui and a craving for experience, and the following narrative, which stretches from her grade school days into high school, shows her steadily increasing dissatisfaction with the horizons of her small city. She also shows how she became aware of a world elsewhere through reading and contacts with high school friends who were budding intellectuals. The prologue, written like much of the book in the second person (for distance) and the present tense (for immediacy) shows where her family had gotten by 1972: her father was turned inward and apathetic; her mother was, if not apathetic, at least indifferent to her daughter's departure. Sister Lecia, who, in one of Karr's brilliant metaphors, spent much of her time looking as if she belonged on a parade float, had more or less disowned the family, pretending that she was orphaned.

After the prologue, the narrative unfolds in a pattern of school experiences, from alienation in grade school to deeper alienation in high school. The critic Don Graham wrote a long article for *Texas Monthly* on *Cherry*, "The Pits," in which he complained about the year-by-year tendency of the narrative, which certainly lacks the artful leaps in time that characterize *The Liars' Club*. The narrative pattern is a venerable one, found in innumerable memoirs and autobiographical novels, but in *Cherry* the reader's familiarity with Karr's life is a problem: we already expect the protagonist to be an outsider at school, and the first chapter in the section called "Elementary's End" begins predictably with her exclusion from a group of fifth-grade girls at a skating rink. She turns to books that summer, finding solace in E. E. Cummings'

poetry, the Tarzan books, and Harper Lee's *To Kill a Mockingbird*, which portrays a small town more malign than her own.

Such a narrative usually presents at least one confidante, and in *Cherry* the narrator becomes close to Clarice Fontenot, who is fourteen years old to her eleven. Clarice is a rebel, and one of the best scenes in *Cherry* presents her ascent of a goalpost where she takes off her pants and "undersancies." Later Karr herself crusades for a first bra by riding her bicycle topless through the neighborhood, a scene that echoes her exhibitionism in the window in *The Liars' Club*. Her exhibitionism is self-defeating, particularly when she performs it in front of the Cleary family: John Cleary is the important first romantic crush experienced by the narrator.

Karr has said in numerous interviews that one of her purposes in *Cherry* was to find a language for talking about the sexuality of young women, a subject she feels has been neglected. Karr says in the online guide to *Cherry* that she thinks teenage boys want to "boff" girls "into guacamole," whereas girls feel much less focused sexual emotions. In *Cherry*, she strives not only to evoke the traditional emblems of romance, like roses, but also to provide a vocabulary for body states. She uses terms like "cool light" and refers to the solar plexus region of the body to indicate a sexuality not confined to the genital area. In one of the most amusing scenes of the book, she describes being asked in seventh grade to massage the legs of John Cleary, with whom she was smitten, in the presence of his family: his tendons were cramped by football practice. The scene is remarkably droll, as the narrator's sexual excitement grows and grows. She discovers when she returns home that she has indeed been physiologically excited. But boys are more clearly "hardwired to procreate," in her vivid phrase, and the narrator approaches sex cautiously. When her full sexual initiation comes, much later—from someone named Phil—the event is presented in a de-romanticized way (the narrator being hyper-sophisticated as well as nervous), with her female friends Meredith and Stacy in the next room for what might be called moral support.

This being the 1970s under consideration, the characters are more interested in drugs than anything else. According to Karr: "If there was any place worthy of escape in the seventies, it was Leechfield with its mind-crushing atmosphere of sameness." Short of heading to California or some other exciting place, the method of escape is through drugs, though she tried another fad of the time, transcendental meditation. One common complaint by reviewers was that *Cherry* is another narrative of coming of age in the hippie period. There are two set pieces about drugs: the inevitable drug bust and a bad trip in a seedy club called Effie's Go-Go. The drug bust ends serendipitously, when Karr's mother comes to the jail and discovers that the judge is an old friend of hers.

More interesting than the narrator's drug experiences are her literary ones. Her high school friend Meredith knows lengthy passages of poetry by heart, and she and Mary even admire the same obscure poem by Howard Nemerov. Another friend, Stacy, knows more about T. S. Eliot than either of them. Karr makes it clear that allusions to Gerard Manley Hopkins and John Berryman came naturally to her mind. But young Karr also cultivated a circle of rebellious friends, Gulf Coast imitators of California surfers. They offered complete acceptance, which, she says, warmed her countercultural heart. When Karr's interest in high school activities like the girls' drill corps plummets (she comes to see the drill corps as an absurdity, young women marching in silver fur costumes), her decision to leave it is punished by the school officials, who place her in remedial classes because she has failed to show maturity.

The climax of the work is the bad acid trip at Effie's Go-Go, a nightmare of paranoia and danger, though nothing terrible happens to Karr or her companions, Augustus Maurice, a gay misfit, and "Miss Ann," who was a "Jesus freak," as the slang of the time put it. They encounter a number of black people who appear menacing and sexually ambiguous, but the line between reality and drug hallucinations is a wavering one. Karr's language mimics the confusion of the acid trip. Her puzzling experience leads to an epiphany afterward, when she discusses it with Meredith. Karr tells her friend that she has to conclude that "there's no place like home." Meredith reminds her that the phrase comes out of *The Wizard of Oz* and offers her Froot Loops in a Mickey Mouse bowl. The narrative hedges her final revelation with pop-culture irony, as if Meredith were playing the Wizard to Karr's Dorothy. The final insight Meredith gives her is that she remains "your Same Self"; Karr's Same Self reflects some principle of unity in all the transformations she has been undergoing while growing up. This revelation has a touch of hippie mysticism, like the sayings of Ken Kesey and his Merry Pranksters recounted in the 1970s book that inspired Karr's escape to California, *The Electric Kool-Aid Acid Test*. But Karr claims that the insight sustains her through shape-shifting in the future.

Karr's second memoir reached the best-seller lists and receive a number of enthusiastic reviews, but it also had a fair number of dissenters. The parents whose conflicts were so fascinating in the first book were not very visible, some reviewers complained. She used many of her best anecdotes in the first book, leading Lily Burana to comment in the *Village Voice Literary Supplement* that "there's less shrimp in this batch of gumbo." Other reviewers disliked works of teenage angst or hippie coming-of-age narratives. The dominance of second-person narration irritated some commentators, like Valerie Sayers in *Commonweal*, who said that this was "a device I'd hoped had been left behind in the 80s." The reception in Texas was harsh in several cases, as in Don Graham's "The Pits," with its complaints about the simplicity of a structure that traces its heroine's life grade by grade. Clay Reynolds, a Texas novelist, questioned the accuracy of some of the details of language and setting. Certainly the first book has a more impressive structure, with its leaps in time, and the presentation of the Charlie and Pete Karr conflicts through the viewpoint of a perceptive child makes *The Liars' Club* a distinctive book.

Other reviewers had praise for *Cherry*, however, including Sara Mosle, who suggested in the *New York Times* that the *Liars' Club* succeeded because of its "riveting particularity"—Karr's family being so extraordinary—whereas "Karr's stunning new sequel," *Cherry*, succeeds for its universality, its exploration of "every adolescence." Sanford Pinsker admires *Cherry* for its bildungsroman quality, the way that the narrator's artistic growth is traced in the work, which outweighs the book's teenage angst in his view: "In this sense, *Cherry* is only marginally about hankering to have big hooters and a hunk for a boyfriend, or about being deflowered: the book is about the interior parts of Mary Karr that responded to the magic of language well used." Debate is likely to continue, and careful analysis of the books will eventually replace the visceral reactions of the reviewers.

Karr has hardly exhausted her material: another memoir may follow. One of the poems in *Abacus*, "For My Children," crams a whole memoir of her California days into a page and a half: sleeping "in a pink Lincoln Continental on blocks / in a deserted lot," bodysurfing by day and taking LSD at night. These days ended when she left for home and then college. Whether or not she continues to write memoirs, her commitment to poetry is strong. In "Negotiating the Darkness, Fortified by Poets' Strength," an article about the aftermath of the September 11, 2001, terrorist attacks, she told

the readers of the *New York Times* that lyric poetry offers "relief—if not actual salvation—during catastrophic times." She observes that after the tragedy she and many others, by no means all of them poets, exchanged poems constantly. She affirms the value of poetry, extolling its power of consolation and its economy. She says it requires hubris to write knowing that few poems reach greatness, but she sees "a joy in the absurdity of one's enterprise" and she accounts for that joy by the "true wonder at poetry's redemptive power." The poet feels that she is bringing a Little Leaguer's bat "into the cathedral of Yankee Stadium," but she feels awe at the cathedral, her term for the collective monument of poetic tradition. The maturity of her recent poetry indicates that she should be able to hit many home runs during her career: her batting average has been improving steadily.

Selected Bibliography

WORKS OF MARY KARR

POETRY

Abacus. Middletown, Conn.: Wesleyan University Press, 1987.

The Devil's Tour. New York: New Directions, 1993.

Viper Rum. New York: New Directions, 1998. (With an afterword, "Against Decoration.")

MEMOIRS

The Liars' Club: A Memoir. New York: Viking, 1995.

Cherry. New York: Viking, 2000.

ESSAYS

"Missing Larkin." *Seneca Review* 18:79–92 (1987).

"Against Decoration." *Parnassus: Poetry in Review* 16:277–300 (1990).

"Houses of the Spirit." *Vogue,* March 1995, pp. 104, 118, 124.

"A Memoirist's Apology." *Parnassus: Poetry in Review* 20:96–107 (1995).

"Tell-all Tales." *Harper's Bazaar,* June 1995, pp. 78–79.

"Dysfunctional Nation." *New York Times Magazine,* May 12, 1996, p. 70.

"Remembering James Laughlin." *Parnassus: Poetry in Review* 23:13–23 (spring–summer 1998).

"The Hot Dark." *The New Yorker,* September 4, 2000, pp. 42–49.

"How to Read 'The Waste Land' So It Alters Your Soul Rather Than Just Addling Your Head." Introduction to *The Waste Land and Other Writings by T. S. Eliot.* New York: Modern Library, 2001. Pp. ix–xxvii.

"Memories of East Texas." *Architectural Digest,* May 2001, pp. 56, 60.

"Negotiating the Darkness, Fortified by Poets' Strength." *New York Times,* January 14, 2002, section E, p. 1.

OTHER WORKS

"The Cowboy on Mama." *Esquire,* March 1995, pp. 133. (Short story.)

"The Choice." *The New Yorker,* November 26, 2001, pp. 86–87. (Poem.)

"Descending Theology: Christ Human," and "Descending Theology: The Garden." *Poetry* 179:144–145 (December 2001). (Poem.)

"Reading Group Guide: *The Liars' Club.*" Includes "The Family Sideshow," "Discussion Questions," "Author Biography," and "Author Interview." (http://www.readinggroupguides.com/guides/liars_club.html).

"Reading Group Guide: *Cherry.*" Includes "Introduction," "About Mary Karr," and "An Interview with Mary Karr." (http://www.penguinputnam.com/static/rguides/us/cherry.html).

CRITICAL AND BIOGRAPHICAL STUDIES

Atlas, James. "The Age of the Literary Memoir Is Now." *New York Times Magazine,* May 11, 1996, pp. 25–27.

Ballantyne, Sheila. "The Thousand-Yard Stare." *New York Times,* July 9, 1995, pp. 8–9.

Barber, David. "Body and Soul." *Poetry* 164:164–168 (June 1994).

Bristow, Jennie. "Teenage Confessions." *New Statesman* 130:51 (June 25, 2001).

Dorman, Jen M. R. "Strong Women." *Life,* January 1998, pp. 80–84.

Draper, Robert. "Mary Karr." *Texas Monthly,* September 1996, pp.106–109.

McDowell, Robert. "Expansive Poetry." *Hudson Review* 51:792–803 (winter 1999).

Mosle, Sara. "Highway Out of Town." *New York Times Book Review,* October 22, 2000, p. 10. (Review of *Cherry.*)

Mutter, John. "Authors at NACS Discuss Memoirs, Personal Journeys." *Publishers Weekly,* May 26, 1997, pp. 32–34.

Pace, Patricia. "All Our Lost Children: Trauma and Testimony in the Performance of Childhood." *Text and Performance Quarterly* 18:233–247 (1998).

Powers, Elizabeth. "Doing Daddy Down." *Commentary,* June 1997, pp. 38–41.

Tresniowski, Alex. "Dispatch from a Combat Zone." *People Weekly,* September 23, 1996, pp. 95–96.

"True Confessions: A Special Issue." *New York Times Magazine,* May 12, 1996. (Commentary on Mary Karr and the "memoir boom.")

BOOK REVIEWS

Burana, Lily. Review of *Cherry. Village Voice Literary Supplement,* October–November, 2000, p. 93.

Churchill, Sue. Review of *Viper Rum. Southern Humanities Review* 34:97–100 (winter 2000).

Dingus, Anne. "Family Karr." *Texas Monthly,* July 1995, pp. 78–81. (Review of *The Liars' Club*).

Graham, Don. "The Pits." *Texas Monthly,* October 2000, pp. 70–74. (Review of *Cherry*).

Gray, Paul. "Texas Teen." *Time,* October 23, 2000, p. 82. (Review of *Cherry.*)

Harmon, William. "Mary Karr, Mary Karr, Mary Karr, Mary Karr." *Southern Review* 33, no. 1:150–155 (winter 1997). (Review of *The Liars' Club.*)

Ivins, Molly. "Ezra Pound in East Texas." *The Nation,* July 3, 1995. (Review of *The Liars' Club.*)

Jones, Malcolm. "Bobby Socks, Hard Knocks." *Newsweek,* October 2, 2000, p. 174. (Review of *Cherry.*)

Jordan, Barbara. Review of *Viper Rum. Chicago Review* 44:213–218 (1998).

Kakutani, Michiko. "They're Liars, and That's Just the Least of Their Problems." *New York Times,* May 26, 1995, p. C28. (Review of *The Liars' Club.*)

Katrovas, Richard. "History and the Transpersonal Talent: Or, 'I'm Just Tired of Reading Guys.'" *New England Review and Bread Loaf Quarterly* 11:340–350 (spring 1989). (Review of *Abacus.*)

Oates, Joyce Carol. "Pilgrim's Progress." *New York Review of Books,* November 2, 2000, pp. 30–32. (Review of *Cherry*).

Pinsker, Sanford. "Citizens of Somewhere Else: Memoir and the Sense of Place." *Georgia Review* 55:162–170 (spring 2001). (Review of *Cherry.*)

Reynolds, Clay. Review of *Cherry.* *Southwestern American Literature* 26:125–127 (spring 2001).

Sayers, Valerie. "Tattletale." *Commonweal,* November, 3, 2000, pp. 27–28. (Review of *Cherry*).

Selinger, Eric Murphy. "This Personal Maze Is Not the Prize." *Parnassus: Poetry in Review* 24, no. 2:77–117 (2000). (Review of *The Liars' Club.*)

Shulman, Alix Cates. "Hungry for More." *Women's Review of Books,* December 2000, pp. 19–21. (Review of *Cherry.*)

Smith, Patrick. "What Memoir Forgets." *The Nation,* July 27, 1998, pp. 30–34. (Review of *The Liars' Club.*)

Wakefield, Dan. "Speak, Memory!" *The Nation,* January 8, 2001, pp. 35–38. (Review of *Cherry.*)

INTERVIEWS

Garner, Dwight. "A Scrappy Little Beast." *Salon* (http://www.salon.com/may97/karr970521.html).

Hogan, Ron. "Mary Karr." *The Beatrice Interview* (http://www.beatrice.com/interviews/karr/).

Kanner, Ellen. "Mary Karr: Remembering the Agonies and Ecstasies of Adolescence." *First Person Bookpage* (http://www.bookpage.com/0010bp/mary_karr.html).

Olsson, Karen. "Refinery Daze, Part Two." *Texas Observer,* December 8, 2000, pp. 18–20.

—BERT ALMON

Larry Levis

1946–1996

NOT YET FIFTY, Larry Levis died of cardiac arrest on May 8, 1996. In an interview with Christopher Buckley for *Quarterly West,* the Pulitzer Prize–winning, senior American poet Philip Levine commented:

> There was no one quite like Larry as a poet or as a person. I think he was easily the best poet of his generation, [and] at times I truly believe he was writing the best poems in the country. Many of the poets I've talked to since his death feel the same way.

During his life Levis published five books of poetry, three poetry chapbooks, a book of prose fiction, and many essays on contemporary poetry and poetics. Shortly after his death the posthumous book *Elegy* (1997)—essentially complete when he died and then edited for publication by Levine—was published by the University of Pittsburgh Press, which later brought out *The Selected Levis* (2000). Poets and readers of poetry knew Levis' prose works as well, among them his critical essays for *Field,* his piece on war poetry and other essays in *American Poetry Review,* and *Black Freckles* (1992), his award-winning book of what he chose to call fiction. Levis' prose, like his poetry, was inventive in style, poignant in the deep humanity of its subjects, and arresting in its imagination. His voice was at once powerful and modest. Early in his career he developed a directness and candidness of psyche and style that came across in his voice whether he was writing poetry or prose.

In 1989 Levis wrote an essay for *Pacific Review,* later published in *On the Poetry of Philip Levine: Stranger to Nothing* (1991), in which he paid homage—with great humor, sincerity, and precise memory—to his teacher. Levis writes engagingly about Levine's achievement, his importance as a poet, teacher, and friend. The essay also explains what it means to be given the gift of poetry, to realize at an early age how important a life of art can be, and then to pursue that life. Characteristically modest, Levis gives much credit to others as he offers a perspective on his own formation as a young poet.

In poetry or prose, Levis' work had what might be called an intimate sense of detachment—a voice or stance that allowed him to examine himself as an objective character in the world he knew and thus write about the most personal events and aspirations in an objective, factual style. This combination avoided sentimentality and at the same time allowed his poems to carry great and immediate emotional weight. (The autobiographical piece he penned in 1996 for the *Contemporary Authors Autobiography Series* speaks almost as much about others—his parents, the workers on his father's farm in Selma, California—as about Levis himself.) In the essay on Levine, he refers to his high school friend Zamora, managing to deflect the spotlight from himself and focus it on the ideas he is writing about. Zamora is almost a guardian angel, a guide, but one sure to keep a hopeful young poet's feet on the ground:

> For two years, largely in secret, I read and reread Eliot, and I told no one of this. But finally one afternoon in journalism class, while the teacher was out of the room, Zamora stretched out, lying

over three desk tops, and began yelling at the little evenly spaced holes in the plyboard ceiling: "O Stars, Oh Stars!" The others around us talked on in a mild roar. Then Zamora turned to me and said: "I saw that book you always got with you. Once again, guy, I see through you like a just wiped windshield." There was this little pause, and then he said, "What is it, you wanna be a poet?" I said, "Yeah. You think that's really stupid?" His smile had disappeared by the time he answered, "No, it isn't stupid. It isn't stupid at all, but I'd get out of town if I were you."

Zamora would resurface a few years later in one of Levis' most brilliant poems, "Caravaggio: Swirl & Vortex," from his fifth book, *The Widening Spell of the Leaves* (1991). He was an important friend, a down-to-earth muse who supported a young poet in choosing the direction for his life. Levis knew early on that his life would be given to poems, and he gave it without qualification. For him there was no other course. He concluded his essay on Levine with this paragraph:

> Whenever I try to imagine the life I might have had if I hadn't met Levine, if he had never been my teacher, if we had not become friends and exchanged poems and hundreds of letters over the past twenty-five years, I can't imagine it. That is, nothing at all appears when I try to do this. No other life of any kind appears. I cannot see myself walking down one of those streets as a lawyer, or the boss of a packing shed, or even as the farmer my father wished I would become. When I try to do this, no one's there; it seems instead that I simply had never *been* at all. All there is on that street, the leaves on the shade trees that line it curled and black and closeted against noon heat, is a space where I am not.

One of Levis' main gifts was his intense and specific imagination—his power to conceptualize, to extend narrative and supposition out into the likely realms of imagination and then bring it all back to an accessible and experiential base, an emotional and human level that moved the reader and made sense. Every image or vision from the imagination was there to serve the rush

and resonance of experience. Whenever a more abstract or conceptual image was needed in a poem, that abstraction, that laconic reaction to absence, was always anchored to some specific place, to some common action in the world. Levis conveyed the feeling with an authenticity that convinced a reader that he had seen it, that he knew it firsthand. The small farming community of Selma, California, is not far from Fresno. There are streets in Fresno, with their shade trees closed against the noon heat, where, without his poetry, Levis is not.

EARLY LIFE

Levis was born on September 30, 1946, at St. Terresa's Hospital in Fresno. His father, William Kent Levis (called "Kent"), and his mother, Carol Clement Mayo, owned a farm in Selma, an agricultural community just south of Fresno. Larry, one of three children, was among the fourth generation on the farm, which was started by his great-grandfather Levis and farmed by his grandfather and father. Levis' father passed away in the late 1980s, but his mother continued to live on the farm. Levis' father was Irish-French and his mother's family was from San Francisco; her father was a restaurateur who once owned the Valley Grill in Fresno.

Levis attended grammar school in a four-room schoolhouse a mile south of the family farm; there was an outside building for lavatories and a wooden shedlike building where teachers parked their cars. This was early California architecture, with a bell tower on top of the "garage" and palm trees and pepper trees in the yard. (The scene is described—with some embellishment—in Levis' prose poem "Schoolhouse," found in the chapbook *The Leopard's Mouth Is Dry and Cold Inside,* 1980). Levis graduated from Selma Union High School and wanted to attend the University of California at Berkeley; however, a low grade in a photography class kept him from Berkeley, and he enrolled at Fresno State College, where he met and studied with Philip Levine.

After graduating with his B.A. in English from Fresno State in 1968, Levis enrolled at Syracuse University in New York State and received an M.A. in creative writing in 1970. For the next two years he was an instructor in the English Department at California State University, Los Angeles. He then returned to graduate school, earning a Ph.D. in Modern Letters from the Department of English at the University of Iowa in 1974. From 1974 to 1980 Levis was a professor in the English Department at the University of Missouri, Columbia. He later moved to take a position in the M.F.A. and Ph.D. creative writing program at the University of Utah, where he became director of the program. In 1992 Levis accepted a senior position in the English Department at Virginia Commonwealth University in Richmond, teaching in the M.F.A. program there until his death.

In 1969 Levis married Barbara Campbell; they were divorced four years later. In Iowa, he met and married the poet Marcia Southwick, and they had one son, Nicholas. They divorced in 1983. Six years later Levis married Mary Jane Hale, but they were divorced a year later.

In 1971 Levis received the YM-YWHA Discovery Award. Two years later he was awarded the first of three National Endowment for the Arts grants in poetry. Levis won a Guggenheim Fellowship in 1983, followed five years later by a Senior Fulbright Award in creative writing to Yugoslavia; he also received an individual artist grant from the Virginia Commission on the Arts. The critical responses to Levis' work over the years echo a consensus among most practicing poets, who praise it for its brilliance and poignancy, its humanity, its arresting inventiveness, and its importance. *Wrecking Crew* (1972), the poet's first book, received the U.S. Award of the International Poetry Forum. Levis' second book, *The Afterlife* (1977), was the Lamont Poetry Selection of the Academy of American Poets. *The Dollmaker's Ghost* (1981) was chosen by Stanley Kunitz as the winner of the open competition in the National Poetry Series. Levis' next two major collections were *Winter Stars* (1985) and *The Widening Spell of the Leaves* (1991). His posthumous book, *Elegy,* appeared in the fall of 1997.

Despite prizes, publishing successes, and the sheer daring and brilliance of his work, Levis' writing is not included in the anthologies that define the last three decades of the twentieth century—*The Norton Anthology of Modern Poetry* and A. Poulin Jr.'s important *Contemporary American Poetry,* to name two. Such omissions speak volumes about the politics of contemporary poetry. Larry Levis wasn't a "networker"—he did not promote himself. He was satisfied simply by writing and submitting his poems. He was serious and solitary about his writing. He had modesty and integrity. The work was the thing.

WRECKING CREW

Levis' first collection, *Wrecking Crew,* is a book of short poems employing a disembodied voice and distilled imagery. That imagery sometimes verges on the surreal, possibly showing the influence of the many Spanish poets Levis had read. Though imaginative and inventive, these poems do not really contain indications of what was to come in this poet's career. In the style of much of the 1970s, the poems were driven by surface surprises of imagistic pronouncement and unpredictable phrasing. Most of the poems worked against their titles. However, the most substantial poems, "Fish" and "The Poem You Asked For," are not completely in that style. "Fish" offers a concrete base of experience from which the poem rises:

> The cop holds me up like a fish;
> he feels the huge bones
> surrounding my eyes . . .

The speaker has been arrested and is being man-handled by the cops. From there the imagination enters, but in a truly lyric sense, and then it jumps into images not manufactured for their own brilliance but to express the poet's emotional and existential condition:

> Now, I must
> go on repeating the last, filthy
> words on the lips
> of this shrunken head,
>
> shining out of its death in the moon—
> until trout surface
> with their petrified, round eyes,
> and the stars begin moving.

Interestingly, "The Poem You Asked For" is a kind of proem to the volume, set off from the rest to open the book. Its method is an obvious personification, yet above the invention and the humor of the poem there is the vision of the speaker. He is someone who knows what a poet is up against wrestling the imagination for his life, a writer who lives on his talent knowing he can be deserted by it, knowing that the reception of his work is at best fickle. But he stays engaged with the work and survives on his wit and an attitude that will not allow sentimentality, one that shows strength in detachment from, and yet reverence for, the muse. The "You" in the title can be read as both You the reader and You the colloquial address to the speaker himself:

> Finally I cupped it in
>
> my hands, and carried it gently
> out into the soft air, into the
> evening traffic, wondering how
>
> to end things between us.
> For now it had begun breathing,
> putting on more and
>
> more hard rings of flesh.

> And the poem demanded the food,
> it drank up all the water,
>
> beat me and took my money,
> tore the faded clothes
> off my back,
>
> said Shit,
> and walked slowly away,
> slicking its hair down.
>
> Said it was going
> over to your place.

Even this early on, some quintessential Levis comes through—the perfect insolent gesture, the wit and humor. The poem walking "slowly away, / slicking its hair down," is a quintessential bit of Levis imagination, as he pushes the zany personification beyond any expected levels.

THE AFTERLIFE

The Afterlife is Levis' important breakthrough book. While a number of its poems are still in the more imagistic vein of earlier work, there are poems in this book unlike anything else anyone was writing, poems that would define the range and originality of Levis' vision. While at Iowa from 1972 to 1974, Levis wrote, essentially, his second book of poetry, his Ph.D. thesis entitled *SIGNS*, but that manuscript never saw publication. In putting together *The After-life*—his actual second book—Levis kept the twelve-sectioned poem entitled "Linnets" and five other poems from *SIGNS*. Interestingly, three poems from *SIGNS* were also saved for his third book, *The Dollmaker's Ghost*. The original moves and imaginative conceits in such poems as "The Double," "Rhododendrons," and "The Morning after My Death" were yet to be written when Levis completed *SIGNS*; together with "Linnets" they later establish the bench-

mark of Levis' voice and style in *The Afterlife.*
K. K. Merker at Windhover Press in Iowa City
was paying close attention to this new work and
published *The Afterlife* in a letter press edition
of 175 copies and submitted it to the Lamont
Award competition for 1976. Winning that
award ensured the book a trade edition from the
University of Iowa Press in paper and cloth.

"Linnets" is the final poem in *The Afterlife,*
and it had been published earlier in an issue of
Field, attracting a good deal of attention in the
poetry world. It was a poem that took big risks
in style, form, and statement. A number of the
sections moved in the bright and almost arbitrary
imagistic style of much of the poetry of the
1970s, yet Levis' imagistic sections were clearly
sewn to theme. The linnets were almost totems
for poetry, for the mortality and weight of the
world against art, the voice, the life. The poem
opens narratively, its first three sections in fact
being prose poems, with the poet's brother
shooting a linnet with a shotgun. The fourth
section then shifts to lines and non-narrative
images of death. The poem wheels out widely
after that, across the earth, into the imagination,
and comes back finally to the brother and family where it began. The focus moves from the
avowed subject to tangentially related subjects
that reinforce the prevailing mood. Although
scenes shift, the undercurrent of narrative
remains strong, and the imagistic textures
contribute to the fabulistic whole. As an elegy
for us all, the poem mocks us, it mocks God's
beneficence, it shows God's weakness. The
smallest life is important and holy; the birds
come back at the end of the poem when we
disappear. The linnets will go on singing despite
our death, and then there will be a silence that
erases our presence. This is the final section of
the poem:

> This is a good page.
> It is blank,
> and getting blanker.
> My mother and father

> are falling asleep over it.
> My brother is finishing a cigarette;
> he looks at the blank moon.
> My sisters walk gravely in circles.
> My wife sees through it, through blankness.
> My friends stop laughing, they listen
> to the wind in a room in Fresno, to the wind
> of this page which is theirs,
> which is blank.
>
> They are all tired of reading,
> they want to go home,
> they won't be waving goodbye.
>
> When they are gone,
> the page will be crumpled,
> thrown into the street.
> Around it, sparrows will be feeding
> on bits of garbage.
> The linnet will be singing.
> A man will awaken on his deathbed,
> not yet cured.
>
> I will not have written these words,
> I will be that silence slipping around the bend
> in the river, where it curves out of sight among
>   weeds,
> the silence in which a car backfires and drives
>   away,
> and the father of that silence.

In this poem Levis establishes a symphonic
movement and strategy for his imagination. The
twelve sections of the poem move in a theme,
variation, and recapitulation format between
narrative, lyric, and imagistic accretion. Years
later he would write more exclusively in that
vein in *The Widening Spell of the Leaves* and in
his posthumously published *Elegy.*

Equally important in *The Afterlife* are the
"moves," the imaginative leaps, and the voice
that the best poems in this book would establish.
"The Double" is one of the primary examples
of this original intensity, of a rhetoric of the
imagination that allows the vision to go further
and the scene and its emotional impact to
include more. Levis' logic and concentration in
the vignette rivet the reader deeper into the

poem and its moment in time; the vision of the poem is intensified by such specificity and directed focus. This style of poem pushes beyond the exact detail of nostalgia or startling image and goes two or three steps further into the lives that are gathered to indict the time, place, and concept coursing beneath it all. Here is the second stanza:

> I remember watching wasps
> on hot evenings
> fly heavily over chandeliers
> in hotel lobbies.
> They've torn them down, too.
> And the elderly drunks
> who seemed not to mind anything,
> who seemed to look for change
> in their pockets, as they gazed
> at the girl in the Pepsi ad,
> and the girl who posed for the ad,
> must all be dead now.

The poem drives beyond the drunks alone who might be emblem enough to the old-fashioned Pepsi ad, and then further to imagine the girl who posed for the ad, three steps in specific conceptualization beyond where most would take it. Levis has, in their mortality, an empathy for them all, and his voice—wistful, resigned, clipped as if adding yet one more remembered detail or inevitability—gives us a tone, a texture of pathos. The rhythm of resignation in the lines, in their declaration, in their detailed imagination, ring with authenticity. Levis holds up a lost moment briefly to the light.

By stanza three we see that it is the poem itself which is the other, the "double." Levis developed that mirroring reflex long before postmodernism became fashionable. It is the poetry which takes up so much space in the psyche. The poem is the second soul, this impending shadow of the psyche. Through the language of experience, he offers a scene so precisely rendered, so common and accessible, that we feel it with him. The third stanza tells us that this is in fact a "love poem" to his life,

> like the man chain smoking
> who discovers he's
> no longer waiting for anyone,
> and goes to the movies
> alone each Saturday, and grins,
> and likes them.

This double, this poem, has weight and presence in the world, and the poet has stood

> in its shadow, the way I stood
> in the shadow of a dead roommate
> I had to cut down from the ceiling
> on Easter break, when
> I was young.

> That night I put my car
> in neutral, and cut the engine
> and lights to glide downhill
> and hear the wind rush over
> the dead metal.
> I had to know what it felt
> like, and under the moon,
> gaining speed, I wanted to slip
> out of my body and be
> done with it.

The image of "dead metal," of the car gliding down the dark hill, at once alive and moving and "dead," perfectly captures what it might be like to be in the body and out of it at the same time. The poem ends with a man, grown old, alone after all his friends have died, going to the piano:

> certain that no one will
> overhear him, though he plays
> as loud as he can,
> so that when the dead come
> and take his hands off the keys
> they are invisible, the way air
> and music are not.

The dead move past air, past music in the world. And where did this poem begin? "Out here, I can say anything." At once direct and intimate and distanced and disembodied: this is the voice

Levis has developed, the voice of a man who shrugs his shoulders and tells the truth with all the empathy and wonder he can. In this poem Levis sees himself as a character, and he examines his past, his experience, objectively. In this way, given the subject of death and the "other" in art, he never allows the poem to become emotionally soft or predictable.

This view of the self—the desire to escape the past and yet to know it as well—surfaces in the poem "Rhododendrons." The voice now sees the bigger picture. It has grown beyond the immediate concerns of youth and yet is not sure of the course of this life:

> I laugh,
>
> but I don't know.
> Maybe the whole world is absent minded
> or floating. . . .

There is a distance, a detachment in looking back at another earlier version of oneself to see what it all could mean. Levis here makes one of the best and most original moves in the book:

> I want to be circular;
> a pond or a column of smoke
> revolving, slowly, its ashes.
>
> I want to turn back and go up
> to myself at age 20,
> and press five dollars into his hand
> so he can sleep.
> While he stands trembling on a street in Fresno,
> suddenly one among many in the crowd
> that strolls down Fulton Street,
> among the stores that are closing,
> and is never heard of again.

Going back up to himself at twenty—with this gesture Levis achieves a distance that holds off the romanticizing of youth, and yet the genius of it is the implicit, simple, and intimate affection he has for that character. He does not want to make some grand gesture; he wants to do

something small, give him five dollars to make life a little easier. The specificity of the place stops time, holds the moment and the emotion in a clarifying light.

"The Morning after My Death" begins with the spirit speaking, as one might surmise from the title, but what he has to say is surprising:

> How little I have to say;
> How little desire I have
> To say it.

It would be difficult to think of another poet who, beginning with this book, looks so consistently into the metaphysical, yet a metaphysical continuum that is entirely secular—there is not all that much, it seems, beyond this world. So much for metaphysical pronouncements. The second section of the poem moves to the mundane world, which marches on with, yes, Souza to offset the secular darkness, the flat facts of death, and the small life that feeds off it:

> Far off, a band is playing Souza marches.
> And as the conductor, in his sun stained
> Uniform, taps his baton for silence, and all
> Around him the foliage is getting greener,
> Greener, like the end of things,
> One of the musicians, resting
> His trumpet on his knee, looks around
> A moment, before he spits and puts the horn
> Into his mouth, counting slowly.
>
> And so I think of the darkness inside the horn,
> How no one's breath has been able
> To push it out yet, into the air,
> How when the concert ends it will still
> Be there, like a note so high no one
> Can play it, or like the dried blood inside
> A dead woman's throat, when the mourners
> Listen, and there is nothing left but these flies,
> Polished and swarming frankly in the sun.

Given the frankness of the presentation here, the reader has no trouble following the imaginative leap that takes the poem into the darkness inside the horn. Only on second thought do we realize how unexpected that leap actually is. Levis is both bold and believable. His voice is given wholly to living and to indicting every daily denial of life.

THE DOLLMAKER'S GHOST

The secular metaphysical cast of *The Afterlife* carries over to *The Dollmaker's Ghost,* expanded largely into other lives and into elegy. The first section pays homage to Levis' father and the hard life on the farm in Selma. He moves into his father's thoughts, imagining how he'd almost like to be done with his hard life, or at least for life to be somehow simpler. The presence of the poet in these poems is almost one of a ghost witnessing, standing to the side of others' lives, listening to their thoughts. He enters the mind of the young woman in an Edward Hopper painting; writes of the lives of such diverse literary figures as Weldon Kees, Miguel Hernandez, and Anna Akhmatova; and writes poems for his grandparents and the Polish poet Zbigniew Herbert. In the poem "García Lorca: A Photograph of the Granada Cemetery, 1966," Levis begins with a photograph of the Spanish poet and dramatist Federico García Lorca in the ossuary at Granada and then turns the piece into a love poem for his wife:

> And though your long bones
> Have nothing to do with Lorca, or those deaths
> Forty years ago, in Spain,
> The trees fill with questions, and summer.
> He would not want, tonight, another elegy.
> He would want me to examine the marriage of wings
> Beneath your delicate collar bones:

Lorca is present only to bring Levis closer to his own presence, shared with his wife. Thus a poem of death, or ghosts, becomes a poem of love, or the living. The end of the poem is ethereal, evanescent:

> And here is our dark house at the end of the lane.
> And here is the one light we have kept on all year
> For no one, or Lorca,
> And now he comes toward it—
> With the six bulletholes in his chest,
> Walking lightly
> So he will not disturb the sleeping neighbors
> Or the almonds withering in their frail arks
> Above us.
> He does not want to come in.
> He stands embarrassed under the street lamp
> In his rumpled suit . . .
>
> Snow, lullaby, anvil of bone
> That terrifies the blacksmith in his sleep.
>
> Your house is breath.

The title poem in part four imagines the ghost of a dollmaker speaking and the poet overhearing him as he is parked by the bank of the Missouri River. The majority of poems in this book, however, are set in and around Fresno. He comes back to himself at the end of the book, almost a spirit, and, as in the first section in which he revisits his parents' farmhouse and farm, these poems try to preserve, to freeze time. "Some Ashes Drifting above Piedra, California," begins with the declaration:

> There is still one field I can love;
> There is still a little darkness in each furrow
> And each stump.
> Behind it
> You can sit down and begin to doubt
> Even the hair on the backs of your hands—
> And what you see now is nothing:
> It is only
> The scrubbed, wooden sink inside this shack
> Abandoned by farm workers,

From this simple declaration the poem moves on to consider the question of doubt: doubting the value of life. He considers the life of a rancher and a farm worker, and then tells of two lovers who drowned in the canal:

> Now they are these words.
> And now, if I strike a match

To offer you
This page burned all the way
Into their silences,
Take it—
While your hair dies a little more
Into the day,
While the sun rises,
These two will be ashes in the palm of my hand,
Stirring a little and about to drift
Easily away, without comment,
On the wind.

The reader feels that the poem is indeed being offered out of the palm of the poet's hand, so immediate and intimate is its tone. The poem begins by doubting "even the hair on the backs of your hands" and here extends a hand full of ashes—perhaps a circular journey beginning and ending not in affirmation but its opposite. The bitterly compassionate tone implicates the reader in a resigned view of mortality.

In the book's last and most powerful section, the poems open with statements such as this one, from "For a Ghost Who Once Placed Bets in the Park"—

To become as pure as I am,
You will have to sit all day in a small park
Blackening one end of Fowler, California.

His stance is fresh, inviting—the reader indeed desires to become that pure. In "To My Ghost Reflected in the Auxvasse River," the opening lines lead us to the specific and mundane—but exact—logic of the imagination, the little trail of the ordinary that can confront the burden of limited belief. Again, he's addressing the other, singing an elegy for each half of the soul and, by implication, for us all.

I'm tired of praising the dead
Tired of ghosts.
I am just sitting in my yard, watching
Thin clouds move above me,
And the grasses all bending in one direction.
This wind has no friend but me;

It is Spring,
And I am addressing you, Spirit,
Because the wheat ripens for no one,
Not for the sky,
Not even for you,
And you, who do not believe in words,
Care less for my life than for a broken comb
  you've left
In a movie theater, or in a bar.

Levis wrote convincingly of the spirit, of its possibilities but also its limitations. His imagination was so specific, it was almost as if he had seen it, his metaphysical constructs so unelaborate and functional that they are chilling to the reader who has grander ideas. His writing life was given in large part to figuring out the condition most of us find ourselves in, body and soul. In doing so he avoided the obvious or easy path for his confrontations, or pain, or elegiac occasions. He found holiness in the ordinary, the commonplace. "The Spirit Says, You Are Nothing:" concludes *The Dollmaker's Ghost*. The poem speaks a little of the writing life and more so of the great angst and longing for life itself; it speaks of the waste of a life and cherishes then the body in its ordinary habits and blindness to time. These are the last two sections, the spirit speaking to the body:

By now you are lying so still
You think you can rise up, as I can,
Without a body,
And go unseen over the still heads of grasses,
And enter the house
Where your wife will not look up from the letter
She is writing,
And your son goes on sleeping—
A thimble of light spilling into the darkness.
But you do not move.   And this
Is about stillness, now:
How you remember strolling alone, at seventeen,
Through the dusk of each street,
How you liked the wind reddening the face
Of a drunk, who,
In the last days of his alcohol, reeled
And stared back at you,
And held your gaze.

How all you remember of New York is
That man,
Who would not have read this poem,
Or any poem,
And who once dreamed
That a speck of white paint on a subway platform
Would outlast
Everyone he knew.
    *
But you were young, and you had
Plenty of time:
Going west,

You slept on the train and did not smile.
Under you the plains widened, and turned silver.

You slept with your mouth open.

You were nothing,
You were snow falling through the ribs
Of the dead.

You were all I had.

Levis' ability to begin with some small ordinary element around him and move it logically, necessarily, and imaginatively to a larger question, a more metaphysical vision or speculation, is another of his poems' great virtues. In this, he is not unlike the seventeenth-century metaphysical poets in their yoking of disparate imagery for unified effect. In *Winter Stars,* "South" is a prime example of this ability to expand from an ordinary particular to larger themes. Indeed, "South," a long poem in sections employing the theme-and-variation mode, contains many of the characteristic elements of the best of Levis' work. Ultimately about the loss of youth, the poem opens:

I will begin with this moth,
Its tan wings as unchanging
As the palm fronds that must still
Hang above the room I slept
In as a child. . . .

In the course of the poem the imagery returns to the moth as emblem and touchstone. The narrative line of the poem follows the poet back to his eighteen-year-old self, whom he visits and whose actions, aspirations, and confusion he evaluates, as well as the outcome years later. He also looks at the lives of others. This is an inclusive poem that whirls and bastes and finds its way back to the beginning with gravity and grace. "Some Grass along a Ditch Bank," not as long as "South," also begins with the commonplace and moves to the story, or elegy, of a life: "I don't know what happens to grass / But it doesn't die, exactly." The closure this poem achieves, as in much of Levis' work, is much larger and more meaningful than one could have predicted from the opening.

Other poems in *Winter Stars* are direct, poignant elegies. "Those Graves in Rome," which remembers the Romantic poet John Keats and his friend Joseph Severn, both buried in the Protestant graveyard just outside the wall around Rome, begins thus:

There are places where the eye can starve,
But not here. Here, for example, is
The Piazza Navona, & here is his narrow room
Overlooking the Steps & the crowds of sunbathing
Tourists. . . .

The poet also remembers walking the streets of Rome with his friends. He muses on the human hope to preserve a little of ourselves with stone and markers. He finds another emblem to reinforce the subject:

           . . . Among such friends,
Who never allowed anything, still alive,
To die, I'd almost forgotten that what
Most people leave behind them disappears.
Three days later, staying alone in a cheap
Hotel in Naples, I noticed a child's smeared
Fingerprint on a bannister. It
Had been indifferently preserved beneath
A patina of varnish applied, I guessed, after
The last war. It seemed I could almost hear
His shout, years later, on that street. But this

Is speculation, & no doubt the simplest fact
Could shame me. . . .

That fingerprint becomes as great an emblem of death (maybe greater, for all our collective anonymity) as the grave markers of Keats and Severn.

"Oklahoma" is a poem about separation from his wife, with the landscape of the dust bowl serving as the counterpart to marital disintegration.

> Often, I used to say: I am this dust; or I am this
>   wind.
> And young, I would accept that. The truth is, it
>   was never the case.
> I have seen enough dust & wind by now to know
> I am a little breath that always goes the distance
> Longing requires, & to know even this will fail.
> The truth is, dear friends, we fall apart;
> And for mysterious reasons, not entirely clear to
>   us,
> We choose to live alone. The truth is,
>
> We do *not* choose, & do not fall apart. But *are*
>   apart. . . .

In the best of Levis poems—and this is one of them—a reader never questions that he is arriving at a truth. As his work progressed—indeed as this poem progresses—we see Levis even more aware of the limitations of his own art and psyche. He is "on to himself" here and manages to arrive at that point in art where the artifice seems to disappear and we hear an inspired, direct, true voice, a voice of honest humility that will risk everything.

This directness is a sign of great maturity, something found in the works of Levine, Gerald Stern, Yehuda Amichai, Wislawa Szymborska, and Czeslaw Milosz, to name a few. His work had a great modesty but also a great passion—a passion derived from such close and empathetic observation, from the perfect detail and image. Responding to a Levis poem, many readers feel that he genuinely was speaking to them, as he meant to. His poems were never self-aggrandizing, and never did they adhere to some current style or call attention to their own surfaces. Here is the end of "Oklahoma":

> I rise, & put on my precisely faded jeans, a black
>   Hawaiian shirt
> With ridiculous light yellow roses, & sharp-toed
> Cowboy boots.
>   Style, after all, is a kind of humor,
> Something truly beneath contempt,
>
> Even here, on the southern plains, in Oklahoma
>   City.
>
> Though something, beneath the armor we put on,
> Is always missing, the trouble with this wind
> Is that it drives the land away: These raw cuts
> In the red dirt of the roadside almost speak for
>   themselves.
> Are they painful? They look as if they once were.
> Someday, see for yourself, & take care when you
> Do so. Look closely, but take care.
> And put your arms around each other's waists so
>   you don't
> Slip through to anything truer
> Than you meant to be.
>
> The earth, for example, has often been a lie.
>
> And the wind its rumor.
>
> Together once, they drove all
> The better people away.

The title poem, "Winter Stars," begins with an incident the poet remembers in which his father broke up a fight between one of the workers on the ranch and the worker's father. Levis' father was ill, slipping out of this life, in a place that was also disappearing—rural California. The poet is trying to make sense of the past and the present. The stunning scene conveys the almost hopeless feeling attending the death of one's father, trying to reason past the pain of life and death:

> If you can think of the mind as a place
>   continually

Visited, a whole city placed behind
The eyes, & shining, I can imagine, now, its end—
As when the lights go off, one by one,
In a hotel at night, until at last
All of the travelers will be asleep, or until
Even the thin glow from the lobby is a kind
Of sleep; & while the woman behind the desk
Is applying more lacquer to her nails,
You can almost believe that the elevator,
As it ascends, must open up on starlight.

I stand out on the street, & do not go in.
This was our agreement, at my birth.

He finds the perfect analogy of mind as city to convey what this loss might feel like—how ordinary in its mundane detail of course, how exact in its equation of distance and disregard. The poet is out on the street; the elevator goes up to the stars perhaps; there is all this sky, it seems, between father and son, all the distance the last few steps of which cannot be crossed in this life. Yet something may yet come right, if the "agreement" is not only upheld but understood.

And for years I believed
That what went unsaid between us became empty,
And pure, like starlight, & it persisted.

I got it all wrong.
I wound up believing in words the way a scientist
Believes in carbon, after death.

Tonight, I'm talking to you, father, although
It is quiet here in the Midwest, where a small
 wind,
The size of a wrist, wakes the cold again—
Which may be all that's left of you & me.

When I left home at seventeen, I left for good.

That pale haze of stars goes on & on,
Like laughter that has found a final, silent shape
On a black sky. It means everything
It cannot say. Look, it's empty out there, & cold.
Cold enough to reconcile
Even a father, even a son.

Life finally comes down to more than your art, or is worth every bit of your art. Emptiness, cold, and silence are found to have substance, to render some kind of embrace, to communicate.

THE WIDENING SPELL OF THE LEAVES

In *The Widening Spell of the Leaves,* Levis shows his mastery of the mid-length and longer poem. A sequence of seven long poems makes up almost half the book. The imagination is more inclusive than ever before and spins and reaches far to bring in elements that amplify and charge the life the poet is examining in his work. There is a varied cast of supporting characters: the poets François Villon and Samuel Taylor Coleridge, the painters Caravaggio and Rembrandt, the jazz musicians Charlie Parker and Miles Davis, Levis' old high school pal, Zamora, and a guardian angel with one wing. The lives of others, famous and not, open a window onto a common humanity. In "Slow Child with a Book of Birds," Levis looks at that child's perception, he looks at his own, he looks at the birds "endangered like all else," and somehow, like that simple child, wants to come to the end of the day with "no regrets." In these poems the deeply personal is melded with the esoteric and popular culture, such as a hit song from the 1960s, is melded with considerations of high art. All elements, common or elegant, are pulled in by the voice, given equal dignity and attention.

With signature daring, Levis opens the book with the line "Sooiee, pig pig pig." This is the starting point of an impressionistic narrative of childhood in which he would refuse to eat the dinner set before him on the table. The journey from earliest childhood memories continues through to the last poem in the book, "At the Grave of My Guardian Angel: St. Louis Cemetery, New Orleans." In the cemetery the poet has come across a gravestone bearing his name and the dates 1947–1949; there is a small beaten figure of an angel on the grave. He states, "For it is all or nothing in this life, for there is no other." He speaks to this frail double, this half angel with only one wing, and coaxes it to head back to California, "The Mojave one way; the Pacific the other," protected by—the down-to-earth Levis touch—a seatbelt:

> At least we'll have each other's company.
> And it's not as if you held your one wing, tattered
>   as it was, in contempt
> For being only one. It's not as if you were
>   frivolous.
> It's not like that. It's not like that at all.
> Riding beside me, your seat belt around your
>   invisible waist. Sweet Nothing.
> Sweet, sweet Nothing.

The effort at consolation, of the angel as much as of himself, teeters on the edge of the abyss.

"Caravaggio: Swirl & Vortex," the second in the sequence of seven poems from the second section of the book, tells of Caravaggio's life and examines one of his paintings, in which David holds the head of Goliath. The poet examines his own life in light of the painter's, and muses also on the loss of Zamora's life in Vietnam. Caravaggio used himself as a model for many of his paintings, and the David in this painting resembles Caravaggio at a younger age; the Goliath is the painter in his early thirties, worn and a little dissipated, not fated to live much longer. The poet remarks that his high school pal Zamora, his—to some extent—guardian angel, looked a bit like Caravaggio:

> I had a friend in high school who looked like
>   Caravaggio, or like Goliath—
> Especially when he woke at dawn on someone's
>   couch. (In early summer,
> In California, half the senior class would skinny-
>   dip & drink after midnight
>
> In the unfinished suburb bordering the town,
>   because, in the demonstration models,

> They filled the pools before the houses sold. . . .
>   Above us, the lush stars thickened.)
> Two years later, thinking he heard someone call
>   his name, he strolled three yards
>
> Off a path & stepped on a land mine.

Levis moves from there to the Vietnam War Memorial, which he so accurately interprets as a "one of the styles of Hell," then back to his youth and Zamora, then finally back to Caravaggio. Far from an art history lesson, Levis' observations on Caravaggio reveal the grit of living and lead him to mourn the senselessness of early death, the obscenity of war, the tragedy of wasted talent. The longer, loose lines create a music of thought as they push toward a clarity of vision:

> My friend, Zamora, used to chug warm vodka
>   from the bottle, then execute a perfect
> Reverse one-&-a-half gainer from the high board
>   into the water. Sometimes
> When I think of him, I get confused. Someone is
>   calling to him, & then
>
> I'm actually thinking of Caravaggio . . . in his
>   painting. I want to go up to it
> And close both the eyelids. They are still half
>   open & it seems a little obscene
>
> To leave them like that.

By this point Levis had developed a syntactical rhythm that would accommodate his asides, a way of taking everything in and erupting in arresting suppositions. Throughout Levis' work, wit and irreverence fully balanced pathos. It was this that made Levis' voice unique in American poetry.

PROSE WORKS

Levis' prose is equally direct and modest, equally personal, yet original and striking in its thinking. His essays on poetics truly deserve to be read and reread. A substantial selection of them have been gathered in *The Gazer Within, and Other Essays by Larry Levis* (2000), and another book of his prose, combined with a selection of critical essays about his achievement as a poet, was compiled for publication by the University of Georgia Press. His essays are brilliant yet practical, helpful to those interested in writing poetry or simply in reading it. Levis was well read and well educated, but he wore his knowledge lightly—he was a writer, a thinker who never came across as superior.

"Eden and My Generation," an essay that appeared in *Field* in 1982, discusses landscape, exile, and loss in poetry. He explains his generation's break from the moderns and earlier contemporary poets and offers insights into the works of Robert Hass, David St. John, Thomas Lux, and others. He examines the sources for poetry and how those sources may differ even among poets in the same generation. Loss and a sense of place—indeed, loss of that place—are of central importance: Levis points out, for example, that Gary Soto's San Joaquin Valley is not the same landscape as his San Joaquin Valley.

What is it, then, that one loses? That everyone loses? Where I grew up, the specific place meant everything. As a child in California, I still thought of myself, almost, as living in the Bear Flag Republic, not in the United States. When I woke, the Sierras, I knew, were on my right; the Pacific was a two-hour drive to my left, and everything between belonged to me, *was* me. I was astonishingly sheltered. It was only gradually that I learned the *ways* in which place meant everything, learned that it meant 200 acres of aging peach trees which we had to prop up, every summer, with sticks to keep the limbs from cracking under the weight of slowly ripening fruit. It meant a three-room schoolhouse with thirty students, and meant, also, the pig-headed, oppressive Catholic church which, as far as I could determine, wanted me to feel guilty for having been born at all. . . . I rejoiced when I read that [the nineteenth-century French poet Arthur] Rimbaud (at fourteen!) called his home town of Charlesville a "shit-hole"—even when the desire to get away was strongest, I was dimly aware that my adolescent hatred of the place was transforming it, was slowly nurturing an Eden from which I was already exiling myself. After I had left for good, all I really needed to do was to describe the place exactly as it had been. That I could not do, for that was impossible. And that is where poetry might begin.

The essay is at once a kind of primer for younger poets and a valuable historical document regarding the evolution of letters in America.

Two years earlier Levis wrote "Some Notes on the Gazer Within" for the *Field Guide to Contemporary Poetry and Poetics* (1980). This is a lyric essay about the process of writing poetry, about landscape as a source for his work, and about the work of other poets. "What interests me here is a deeper poetics," he writes, "one that tries to grasp what happens at the moment of writing itself." The urge to look inward "is to encounter, at least on some very honest days, my own space; it is to discover how empty I am, how much an onlooker and a gazer I have to be in order to write poems." Certain elements of the landscape and, as he puts it, the "human landscape," help to place him in the context of both space and time: "the asylum, the steel mill, the cemetery, the ghost on the riverbank, the dying resort beside the unfading Pacific are locations, for me, of a human fertility within time." He concludes:

Gazing within, and trying to assess what all this represents, I find I've been speaking, all along, about nature, about the attempt of the imagination to inhabit nature and by that act preserve itself for as long as it possibly can against "the pressure of reality." And by "nature" I mean any wilderness, inner or outer. The moment of writing is not an escape, however; it is only an insistence, through the imagination, upon human ecstasy, and a reminder that such ecstasy remains as much a birthright in this world as misery remains a condition of it.

Black Freckles, a collection of eight prose pieces, appeared in 1992. In his autobiographical essay for the *Contemporary Authors Autobiography Series,* Levis says of the collection: "I also wrote a book of prose, or stories as they may be. . . . It freed me from any illusion that I might 'try fiction.'" Nevertheless, *Black Freckles* won the Western State Book Award for short fiction. The pieces are not character- or plot-driven but rather are propelled by ideas, sensations, emotions. They have the same introspective and lyrically candid voice as Levis' poems, perhaps just a few degrees more discursive and direct. Some of the pieces lean more toward the mythic or surreal. All of them seem to carry the pressure of the poet's own voice, his own life history, so that "fiction"—even where events recognizable from the poet's life have been embellished or exaggerated—does not in the end seem an apt term for them at all. The title of the most engaging essay, "A Divinity in Its Fraying Fact," is composed much in the manner that most of the titles of *The Widening Spell of the Leaves* and *Elegy* are. This prose comes very close to his poetry:

If your name was Ramon or Coronado or Xavier, or if they simply called Dead Rat (pronounced Debtrat, *y rapido*), and if you had just stepped onto the high rung of a ladder to pick early Santa Rosa plums, and if you happened to peer out, over the trees and into the pool, you would not know exactly what to do because you would believe that you had just seen a woman hosing down a patio while a dead man lay beside her. And each time you glanced over at them again, he would be slightly bluer in hue, and, as the afternoon wore on, he would slowly become paler and bluer until he seemed mottled, like a trout.

In addition, the rhythms, imagery, economy of diction, and thematic focus seem closer to poetry than to prose. In most of these pieces, nothing really "happens." The lyric impulse of the writer is to respond to the past, to the emotional traffic of his life, and make some sense of it.

In the winter 1996–1997 *Quarterly West* interview, Philip Levine spoke about Levis' last book:

He had a huge voice. I think there's so much invention, vitality and imagination in his work. There are so many different landscapes in the work, there's such an intensity—emotional intensity—so many surprises, such daring. I have found his mature work so inspiring; it's shown me the value of not finding your niche and getting cozy in it. In these new poems once again Larry was journeying out, trying to create a kind of poem that didn't exist until that moment. The daring, the sheer inventiveness, the power of these poems is going to shock a great many people.

A poet's voice is a measure of his soul, the music of the life to which he aspires. It establishes and sustains a discrete vision. The majority of poems in Levis' posthumous book, *Elegy,* take the reader on such emotional and stylistic journeys as Levine describes. The book's last and longest poem is "Elegy Ending in the Sound of a Skipping Rope," a poem issuing largely from Levis' Fulbright visit to Yugoslavia. He begins the first stanza of the first section by considering the portraits on the daily devaluing currency, the *dinar.* Note the delicacy and exactness of the couplets and single lines:

All I have left of that country is this torn scrap
Of engraved lunacy, worth less now

Than it was then, for then it was worth nothing,
Or nothing more than

The dust a wren bathes in,

. . . .

The characters met on faint blue paper.
They were thin as paper then.

They must be starving now.

The commitment to close observation serves as counterpoint to the personal and more discursive rhythms of memory and meditation. The entire poem—fourteen pages—exhibits such an economy of expression that each image seems held up to the light, to the dust of time. In many instances, these last poems are harrowing meditations on the specter of death. In his Afterword to *The Selected Levis,* David St. John said it best: Levis "believes in the simple dignity of human beings, and what we constantly discover in these poems is [his] hope in a desperate tenderness that might rescue us from our notions of oblivion."

One of the short poems in *Elegy* that best conveys this important theme in Levis' work is "Photograph: Migrant Worker, Parlier, California, 1967." Levis has discovered this photograph at an art opening. He wants to save the man in the picture, Johnny Dominguez, from becoming merely a subject for art. He wants to rescue his dignity:

> As for the other use, this unforeseen
> Labor you have subjected him to, the little
> Snacks & white wine of the opening he must
> Bear witness to, he would remind you
> That he was not put on this earth
> To be an example of something else,
> Johnny Dominguez, he would hasten to
> Remind you, in his chaste way of saying things,
> Is not to be used as an example of anything
> At all, not even, he would add after
> A second or so, that greatest of all
> Impossibilities, that unfinishable agenda
> Of the stars, that fact, Johnny Dominguez.

"Elegy with a Thimbleful of Water in the Cage" is another of the daring poems to which Levine referred. It offers the scope of the poet's vision, his understated spiritual hope, his unmitigated love of the particulars of this world. The first section of the poem coupled with the coda of the last two-lined section could well be Levis' own elegy:

> It's a list of what I cannot touch:
>
> Some dandelions & black eyed susans growing
> back, like innocence

> Itself, with its thoughtless style,
>
> Over an abandoned labor camp south of Piedra;
>
> And the oldest trees, in that part of Paris with a
> name I forget,
> Propped up with sticks to keep their limbs from
> cracking,
>
> And beneath such quiet, a woman with a cane,
>
> And knowing, if I came back, I could not find
> them again;
>
> And a cat I remember who slept on the burnished
> mahogany
> In the scooped out beveled place on the counter
> below
>
> The iron grillwork, the way you had to pass your
> letter *over* him
> As he slept through those warm afternoons
>
> In New Hampshire, the gray fur stirring a little as
> he inhaled;
>
> The small rural post office growing smaller, then
> lost, tucked
> Into the shoreline of the lake when I looked back;
>
> Country music from a lone radio in an orchard
> there.
> The first frost already on the ground.
>
> *
>
> I pass the letter I wrote to you over the sleeping
> cat & beyond
> The iron grillwork, into the irretrievable.

Selected Bibliography

WORKS OF LARRY LEVIS

POETRY
Wrecking Crew. Pittsburgh, Pa.: University of Pittsburgh Press, 1972.

The Rain's Witness. Iowa City: Southwick Press, 1975. (Limited letter press edition; this poem first appeared in *Field* as "Linnets.")

The Afterlife. Iowa City: Windhover Press and University of Iowa Press, 1977. (Limited letter press edition. Trade edition published by the University of Iowa Press, 1977.)

Larry Levis. Kansas City, Mo.: New Letters, 1977. (Sound recording originally broadcast in October 1977.)

The Leopard's Mouth Is Dry and Cold Inside: Prose Poems by Marcia Southwick and Larry Levis. St. Louis, Mo.: Singing Wind Press, 1980. (Limited edition chapbook.)

The Dollmaker's Ghost. New York: E. P. Dutton, 1981.

Sensationalism. Iowa City: Corycian Press, 1982. (Limited letter press edition.)

Winter Stars. Pittsburgh, Pa.: University of Pittsburgh Press, 1985.

The Widening Spell of the Leaves. Pittsburgh, Pa.: University of Pittsburgh Press, 1991.

Elegy with a Thimbleful of Water in the Cage. Richmond, Va.: Laurel Press, 1996. (Limited letter press edition.)

Elegy. Edited with a foreword by Philip Levine. Pittsburgh, Pa.: University of Pittsburgh Press, 1997.

The Selected Levis. Afterword by David St. John. Pittsburgh, Pa.: University of Pittsburgh Press, 2000.

FICTION, ESSAYS, AND CRITICISM

"Some Notes on the Gazer Within." In *A Field Guide to Contemporary Poetry and Poetics.* Edited by Stuart Friebert and David Young. New York: Longman, 1980. Pp. 102–123.

"Some Notes on Grief and the Image." In *Of Solitude and Silence: Writings on Robert Bly.* Edited by Richard Jones and Kate Daniels. Boston: Beacon Press, 1981. Pp. 170–174.

"Eden and My Generation." *Field* 26:27–47 (spring 1982).

"War as Parable and War as Fact: Herbert and Forché." *American Poetry Review,* January–February 1983, pp. 6–12.

"Strange Days: Zbigniew Herbert in Los Angeles." *Antioch Review* 45, no. 1:75–83 (winter 1987).

"Not Life So Proud to Be Life: Snodgrass, Rothenberg, Bell, and the Counter-Revolution." *American Poetry Review,* January–February 1989, pp. 9–20.

"Philip Levine." In *On the Poetry of Philip Levine: Stranger to Nothing.* Edited by Christopher Buckley. Ann Arbor: University of Michigan Press, 1991. Pp. 337–343.

Black Freckles. Salt Lake City, Utah: Peregrine Smith Books, 1992. (Fiction.)

"Larry Levis." In *Contemporary Authors Autobiography Series, Vol. 23.* Farmington Hills, Mich.: Gale Group, 1996. Pp. 181–192. (Autobiographical essay.)

The Gazer Within, and Other Essays by Larry Levis. Edited by James Marshall, Andrew Miller, and John Venable, with the assistance of Mary Flinn. Ann Arbor: University of Michigan Press, 2000. (A collection of Levis' major essays on contemporary poetry.)

New Virginia Review 11, no. 1 (April 2001). (A special issue dedicated entirely to Larry Levis and including many essays about his life and his work.)

CRITICAL AND BIOGRAPHICAL STUDIES

Andrews, Tom. "The World as I Found It." *Ohio Review* 57:172–177 (1997).

Bargen, Walter. "Larry Levis and Walter Bargen: A Conversation." *Pleiades* 19, no. 2:65–83 (summer 1999).

Bell, Marvin. *Missouri Review* 5, no. 3:35–66 (1982). (Interview.)

Bender, Sheila. "Heart in the Presence of Oblivion." *Poet Lore* 87, no. 1:56–58 (spring 1992).

Buckley, Christopher. "A Conversation with Philip Levine." *Quarterly West* 43 (1996–1997). (Twentieth anniversary issue.)

———. "Larry Levis: The Poet and His Prose." *New Virginia Review* 11, no. 1 (April 2001).

Dana, Robert. "What Does It Mean, American? The Poetry of Larry Levis." *North American Review* 278, no. 1:45–46 (January–February 1993).

Kelen, Leslie. "After the Obsession with Some Beloved Figure: An Interview with Larry Levis." *Antioch Review* 48, no. 3:284–299 (summer 1990).

"Levis, Larry (Patrick)." *Contemporary Poets*. 6th ed. Detroit: St. James Press, 1996.

Molesworth, Charles. *New York Times Book Review,* August 23, 1981, p. 12. (Review of *The Dollmaker's Ghost.*)

Philips, Robert. *Hudson Review* 51, no. 2:449–451. (Review of *Elegy.*)

St. John, David. "Elegy for an Elegist." *New York Times Book Review,* May 3, 1998, p. 35.

Sandy, Stephen. *Poetry* 140:293 (August 1982). (Review of *The Dollmaker's Ghost.*)

Selman, Robyn. "Role Call: The Many Lives of Larry Levis." *The Village Voice,* December 1991, p. 31.

Smith, Ellen. "The Margin as Frontier: The Widening Spell of the Line." *Denver Quarterly* 28, no. 3:97–104 (winter 1994).

Tammaro, Thom. *Library Journal* 110:130 (June 1, 1985). (Review of *Winter Stars.*)

Whedon, Tony. "Three Mannerists." *American Poetry Review,* May–June 1998, pp. 41–47.

Wilson, Eliot. *Black Warrior Review* 24, no. 2:172–176 (spring–summer 1998). (Review of *Elegy.*)

Wojahn, David. "Survivalist Selves." *Kenyon Review* 20, no. 3–4:180–190 (summer 1998).

Zimmer, Paul. "Elegy." *Gettysburg Review* 11, no. 3:528–530 (autumn 1998).

—CHRISTOPHER BUCKLEY

Paule Marshall

1929–

*I*F THE PURPOSE of narrative is to "to give point to our labors, exalt our history, elucidate the present, and give direction to our future," as Neil Postman writes in *The End of Education* (1995), then Paule Marshall's fiction offers a grand narrative. In an interview with Sabine Bröck, Marshall stated that she is concerned about a "non-acceptance of ourselves" within the Black community. This is, as she explained in an interview for *Matatu,* a self-disregard that must be combated because "Cultural revolution is about how you see yourself." She emphasizes the way Ralph Ellison's essays taught her that "there is a whole culture, a whole field of manners about Black American life that has to be first of all acknowledged and celebrated." Given the "severing" and "separation" imposed by "slavery and colonialism," and "notions of inferiority [imposed] on us as a people," she asks, "How can we . . . create—out of this horror—a personality which would be positive and assist us to erect a new society, a new nation?" Marshall believes that a writer's job is "to create new images that will overcome the negative psychological images we have because of our history." Thus her readers begin a satisfying spiritual quest toward a reconception of past, present, and future.

In Marshall's fiction, the spiritual quest is often represented by physical journeys: the forced journeys from Africa, the purposeful journeys from a Caribbean island to the United States, the vacation trip from New York back to the American South or to an island homeland, and the half-day's pilgrimage from one island to another. From these physical journeys characters rediscover strength and resiliency, find new opportunities and choices, become aware of historical continuities, and discover a new pride or willfulness. Some characters—such as Merle in *The Chosen Place, The Timeless People* (1969) and Reena in *Reena and Other Stories* (1983)—plan to travel to Africa; their shorter journeys have awakened them to the need for even greater reconciliations with the past, or they desire to see a place, as Reena does, where "black people . . . have truly a place and history of their own and . . . are building for a new and, hopefully, more sensible world."

What makes Marshall remarkable is her ability to express both these individual, psychological journeys and the way they are interdependent with broader social and economic developments. As she stated in her interview with Bröck, in her first novel, *Brown Girl, Brownstones* (1959), she "wanted to tell the story of a young woman in relation to her community," the Black community, not just the "larger oppressive racist society." This interest in the multiple influences on an individual's life may explain her artistic attraction to Thomas Mann, who, she said in her interview for *Matatu,* "handles so well the full-blown, the large-scale novel" and "was such an expert at handling this great mass of material." Her ambitious novel of Third World development, *The Chosen Place, The Timeless People,* portrays one of the most memorable characters in literature, Merle Kinbona. *Daughters* (1991) is both the story of a woman's progress toward independence and the story of Triunion and Midland City's political and socioeconomic journeys. *The Fisher King* (2000) is a distillation of a complex community's influences on an eight-year-old boy. As Marshall stated in her *Matatu* interview, she thus achieves her goal of writing "fully delineated human being[s]" and also having them "serve as symbols of principles." And the reinvigorated hopes of her characters offer hope for our world community.

When her characters' hopes are not renewable, Marshall is interested nonetheless. Dorothy Hamer Denniston in *The Fiction of Paule Marshall* concludes that Marshall "was intrigued with people who in their later years seemed unfulfilled." This interest is most clearly seen in *Soul Clap Hands and Sing* (1961): the main characters of all four stories are elderly, unhappy, and unable to change. It is also evident in *The Fisher King,* in which two elderly great-grandmothers cannot relinquish their prejudices against each other. As their great-grandson knows, however, "With some people, especially when they reach a certain age, part of them, the good part, couldn't always control the bad things other parts of them were saying or doing." He concludes, "What he must do, then, was to pay attention to . . . her good part, and not to what came out of her mouth. That way he could still love her." Marshall's characters come to understand one another; if one of them cannot overcome personal limitations and renew herself, others will make allowances, and thereby sustain the possibility of love in the world.

In the introduction to her short story "To Da-Duh, In Memoriam" (in *Reena and Other Stories*), Marshall writes that she is "an unabashed ancestor worshipper." At age nine, Marshall spent a year living with her grandmother, nicknamed Da-Duh, in Barbados: "It was as if we both knew, at a level beyond words, that I had come into the world not only to love her and to continue her line but to take her very life in order that I might live." The significant ancestor appears in one way or another in almost all of Marshall's work: in the "unquestioning love"

of one character in *Brown Girl, Brownstones;* in the "great breast [that] . . . had been used it seemed to suckle the world" of a character in *The Chosen Place, The Timeless People;* and in Great-aunt Cuney, in *Praisesong for the Widow* (1983), who pulls Avey Johnson back to her ancestral homeland and toward the revitalization which ensues from that journey. In contrast, the characters who run away from their pasts, erase it from their memory, or divorce themselves from their own history are destitute, unfulfilled, and subsumed by goals and adopted personas alien to them.

As immediate ancestors, Marshall's fictional mothers tend to have the same attitude as Great-aunt Cuney: instead of being adoring caretakers, these mothers challenge their daughters to live up to their dreams and potential. "Unnatural" in that they encourage independence at a young age, let their children lead self-determined lives, and sometimes even challenge them through what seems like disagreeable antagonism, these apparently cold mothers are favorably contrasted against the smothering mother and spoiling caretakers of Primus MacKenzie in *Daughters* (1991). These challenging mothers exemplify the way that Marshall sees ancestry: as potentially enabling instead of limiting. Awareness of one's past, participation in one's community, and acting on one's responsibilities to that community challenge one to become whole, a theme explored by the critic Joyce Pettis in *Toward Wholeness in Paule Marshall's Fiction.*

Marshall's male characters rarely achieve such wholeness, perhaps because of their need to make it in "this man's country." But the main ideological criticism that Marshall has received about her treatment of black male characters has not come from readers protesting those that have assimilated and become economically successful, such as (in *Daughters*) Ursa's father Primus MacKenzie, her boyfriend Lowell Carruthers, and Midland City mayor Sandy Law-son. In fact, Marshall does tend to make this kind of success look like failure. Instead, according to Denniston, Marshall's "strong, capable, independent, [and] assertive" female characters have led some critics to charge that "Marshall perpetuates the myth of the emasculating or castrating black woman." Marshall responds in her interview with Bröck that "Black women historically have been strong, have had to be strong, and that strength is a positive feature and that strength does not take away from their 'womanly qualities,' their ability to be tender, to be emotional, giving creatures." Joyce Pettis proposes that "Sons of the community are tractable in Caribbean neocolonialist and American postslavery games of political domination" while "Daughters are more likely to have attained spirituality and are also more likely to return their service to the community." She confirms Marshall's own emphasis—made most explicit in *Daughters*—on "black male and female partnership . . . as essential to salvaging and preserving the community."

Marshall seems to appreciate the power of synergy, not only between women and men but also among multiple identities. As an African American and African West Indian, Marshall has three conflicting identities, which she turns into a celebration of the multiple strengths of each. She remembers feeling comfortable in both worlds until she noticed the conflicts between them. In her *Matatu* interview she says that she sees "similarities—they are all the same culture with some variations on the theme." Marshall continues, "This is what my work is about—to bring about a synthesis of the two cultures and in addition, to connect them up with the African experience." Thus she has been difficult to categorize as an Afro-American or an Afro-West Indian writer. She is less a chronicler of local differences than a visionary of a world culture under assembly.

MARSHALL'S BACKGROUND

Valenza Pauline Burke was born in New York to Ada and Samuel Burke on April 9, 1929. Both her parents emigrated from Barbados earlier that same decade, and they lived in a Brooklyn neighborhood of West Indians. At age nine she spent a year with her grandmother in Barbados, and the visit inspired her to write some early poetry. While her youthful characters are often outspoken and spirited, Marshall remembers a childhood of being seen and not heard. She was a bookworm, reading English novels by Charles Dickens, William Makepeace Thackeray, and Henry Fielding. Her accidental discovery of Paul Laurence Dunbar was an inspiration because she had finally discovered a black writer and because Dunbar increased her appreciation for the wonderfully expressive and creatively resistant language that she heard when serving tea and cocoa to her mother's friends at the kitchen table. The stylistic and political lessons she gleaned from these women "who talked endlessly, passionately, poetically, and with impressive range" are described in her essay "From the Poets in the Kitchen," from *Reena and Other Stories*: "the best of my work must be attributed to them; it stands as testimony to the rich legacy of language and culture they so freely passed on to me in the wordshop of the kitchen."

Marshall started at Hunter College majoring in social work, which, Denniston points out, was one of the two professions—the other being teaching—considered appropriate for educated black women at the time. After a hiatus because of lengthy illness, Marshall transferred to Brooklyn College, changed her major to English literature, and graduated cum laude, Phi Beta Kappa, in 1953. She held many jobs during the next couple of years, including working as a librarian for the New York Public Library. Between 1953 and 1956 she worked her way from research assistant to part-time journalist, and eventually to full-time journalist, for *Our*

World, which she described in an interview with Pettis as being "in a serious competition with *Ebony* at the time" and filled with "lots of stories about black entertainers." She told Pettis that the need to "knock out the copy" at the magazine trained her to produce text, although she admitted in another interview, with Bröck, that she still tends to be "a very slow, fussy, meticulous kind of writer." During this time Marshall traveled to the Caribbean and South America on assignment, gathering more observations and experiences for her future career as a fiction writer.

In 1957 she married Kenneth Marshall, a psychologist, and gave birth to a son within a couple of years. Unwilling to use all her time mothering, and in spite of her husband's dissapproval (foretold in her 1954 short story "The Valley Between" in *Reena and Other Stories*), Marshall found a babysitter and rented a small apartment in which to write. Four years after *Brown Girl, Brownstones* was published, in 1963, she divorced Kenneth Marshall and began teaching at various colleges. In 1970 she married a Haitian, Nourry Ménard. She has taught at the University of California, Berkeley, the Iowa Writers' Workshop, the University of Massachusetts (Boston), as well as at Columbia, Yale, Oxford, Cornell, Michigan State, Virginia Commonwealth, and New York Universities.

Marshall has also been the recipient of many awards and fellowships. A Guggenheim Fellowship in 1960 aided her in writing *Soul Clap Hands and Sing,* which was awarded the Rosenthal Award from the American Academy of Arts and Letters in 1961. She has received the Ford Foundation Grant for Poets and Fiction Writers (1964–1965), the National Endowment for the Arts and Humanities Award (1967–1968 and 1978–1979), the CAPS award (1974–1975), and Smith College's Tribute to Black Womanhood Award (1983). *Praisesong for the Widow* was awarded the Columbus Foundation's American Book Award in 1984. She has also received the Langston Hughes Medallion Award (1986), the New York State Governor's Arts Award for Literature (1987), the John Dos Passos Award for Literature (1989), and was a PEN/Faulkner Award Honoree (1990). She was granted the esteemed MacArthur Fellowship for lifetime achievement in 1992. In 2001 she won the Black Caucus of the American Library Association's Literary Award for fiction.

BROWN GIRL, BROWNSTONE

Marshall, who got through adolescence reading at the library, began to wonder why she did not see someone like herself, a "young urban Black woman," reflected in anything she was reading. Gwendolyn Brooks's *Maud Martha* (1953) was the closest thing she found. Marshall imagined an "ordinary" protagonist, too, and, as she explained to Bröck, she did not want her protagonist to

> go through all of those terrible things that are supposed to happen to Black people, to young Black women. She is not raped by her father, or her stepfather, or her mother's boyfriend, she does not witness physical brutality between her mother and father, she is not, in other words, a social statistic.

All that, Marshall wants to remind us, is "not the total story" of the Black community, emphasized, she believes, to "discredit" that community. Marshall, in contrast, started producing fiction that Helene Christol describes as being "not only built upon qualities that characterized earlier black women's fiction" but also "anticipated key features of the black women's novel that would only burst fully into blossom and mature in the 1970s and 1980s."

The emotional, intellectual, and physical growth of a girl from age ten to twenty, especially the complexity of growing up in her household of contrasts and conflicts, is at the center of Marshall's first novel. Marshall dedicates *Brown Girl, Brownstones* to her mother, and the cluster of issues she takes up and mulls over in this rich narrative involves a daughter's relationship to each of her parents. When the novel opens, Selina Boyce loves her father above all else. Usually found in the sunroom, Deighton Boyce is often half-studying for, half-dreaming of, a better future. When he inherits two acres in Barbados, his dreams turn to gardening and the big white house he intends to build, "A house to end all houses!" Selina's mother, Silla, however, has a different purchase in mind—the brownstone they currently lease. She will turn to trickery to get what she wants, poisoning an already disintegrating marriage and turning her youngest daughter against her.

Silla and Deighton have planted their dreams in different soil, and they are at odds in most other ways as well. Deighton, on the one hand, is free with money, moves easily in his stylish clothes, looks for pleasure, and often gets it. Silla, on the other hand, invests all her energies in achieving a propertied future. She works hard, speaks harshly, angers easily, and fights for what she wants: "Her lips, set in a permanent protest against life, implied that there was no time for gaiety." While Deighton's style appeals to Selina, this same easy style allows him to walk away from her. Silla's fierce selfishness disgusts Selina, but it manifests in Selina's determination to find and reach her own goals. The contrast between Silla and Deighton develops into a contrast between Brooklyn and Barbados, and it becomes an investigation of the complexities of being a black immigrant in America: adopting competitive economic values, struggling to prevent white responses from destroying one's humanity and individuality, living up to one's responsibilities to the past and the future.

Marshall is well known for her ability to capture the human voice, and Silla's censorious voice dominates the story (including many epigraphs). Silla's dangerous voice is emphasized when Miss Suggie tells Selina to comb her hair "before your mother come and put that mouth of hers 'pon you." Silla's voice is critical of other characters for their sensuousness, their uselessness in old age, their lack of firm direction, and their lovingly taking on more responsibility than necessary. But her mean-spiritedness inspires sympathy and understanding in the context of one unattributed epigraph: "*Of all things upon the earth that bleed and grow, a herb most bruised is woman.*" Marshall's understanding of Silla is wide-ranging and subtle, not limited to the few strands of Silla's complicated personality but conveyed by Marshall's representation of Silla's original deep love for Deighton and its bewildering decline, her ambition, her desire to give her daughters a better childhood than her own, her inability to understand her daughters' lives and the death of her son, and her reluctant acknowledgment that she had to become something she hates in order to get ahead. The critic Eugenia C. DeLamotte has characterized Marshall's invocation of Silla's speech and the way that speech represents "a tragic metamorphosis—the corruption or distortion of a woman's power."

Marshall also traces the parents' relationship with each another, documenting its loving sympathy as well as the meanness that can grow out of frustrated love. Silla has changed and Deighton has not, perhaps because he cannot, perhaps because he intends to return to Barbados eventually anyway. He is a visitor, even an illegal immigrant, whereas Silla is setting down roots in her new home. Marshall captures their differences, the divide that has grown between them, in an early scene, when Deighton is watching his wife and yearning for a reconciliation. They joke together, but he nonetheless sees her "resolute mouth." He loves her and yet sees "her resentment . . . her eyes hardening and her face shutting like a door slammed on him." She cannot understand him either, asking "But be-Jesus-Christ, what kind of man is you, nuh? . . . He ain got nothing and ain looking to get nothing."

Surrounded by people with different values and goals, each vying for her attention and loyalty, Selina remains loyal to her own gradually forming dreams. Selina sees what happens when other people give up their dreams. Deighton's dreams have been deferred to the point of disappearance; he gives up his family and his love of sensation for the "dull," "dazed," even "blind" passivity offered by Father Peace, who claims to be god on earth. Selina's boyfriend Clive, cynical and disengaged at age twenty-nine, is unable to pick himself up by the bootstraps. His will was destroyed by retrieving dead bodies in the Pacific, by the sight of death in that beautiful setting, and by his mother's powerful hatred and literal destruction of his art, which is the stuff of his own dreams. Although Selina is academically successful and hardworking, Silla is enraged by her daughter's sympathy with all that is antipathetic to her own brutal drive for material success.

Selina's goals have been influenced by many people, and her mother finds this intolerable. Selina becomes friends with Suggie, a boarder in her family's house, a woman who escapes into sensual love on her weekends off from her weekday, sleepover job taking care of some white children. Selina listens to the stories of Miss Mary, an elderly white lady who was a boarder in the brownstone long before the Boyces moved in. Selina is sympathetic with her father, whom she sees as a man with grand ideas but no success, who is unable to finish what he starts, and whose failures have been brought about by the conflicts between his own love of life and the racism he has faced in the United States.

Silla wants her daughter to share her own dreams, and she strives to get rid of all her competition. She brutally erases Suggie, Miss Mary, and Deighton from her daughter's life: she has Suggie evicted, scares Miss Mary into dying, and has Deighton deported to Barbados, although he avoids reaching his homeland (and confessing the failures he had already hoped to shed through Father Peace) by jumping from the ship and drowning. But Selina is more like her mother than Silla knows: Selina will not be moved, and she will stick to her own dreams as stubbornly as Silla sticks to hers.

Selina gradually comes to understand her mother, to sympathize with her, but her mother's brutality makes her lose the daughter that she has been striving to steal back from her husband all these years. Selina decides to strike out on her own, perhaps as a dancer on a cruise ship so she can visit Barbados. She has lost her father and her friends, and she has left her boyfriend because he cannot escape his own powerful mother. She refuses, however, to be forced to live out her mother's dreams: she will not become a doctor nor pretend any longer that she sympathizes with Silla's business association. Her potential return to Barbados symbolizes a return to much that her mother has rejected, much that her father and Suggie loved and yearned for, and affirms the value of personal and family history and place that Miss Mary's wandering descriptions of her past has inspired. Selina, then, participates in the American "tradition of progress," rebelling against her mother as her mother rebelled against her own forebears. To her mother Selina says, "I'm truly your child," and Silla responds, "G'long! You was always too much woman for me anyway, soul. And my own mother did say two head-bulls can't reign in a flock."

SOUL CLAP HANDS AND SING

The theme that Marshall emphasizes in the four stories collected in *Soul Clap Hands and Sing,* a theme that she certainly began to explore in her earlier novel, is the sad and sometimes irremediable transformation of a person into someone else, either purposefully or accidentally. Marshall says she was interested in writing about male characters after critics of her first novel wondered if she could. She took this as a challenge and, as she told Pettis in their interview, also wanted to deal with the question of how to find "a way to live fully." Because Marshall sees women as "agents of change," her women characters act as catalysts that force her male characters toward realization.

The final story of the collection, "Brazil," has no true main character because the protagonist, Heitor Baptista Guimares, has lost himself in his stage identity, The Grande Caliban, and cannot remember the peasant and restaurant worker he once was. Heitor searches for himself under the makeup, but all he finds is a face "without expression, bland." Marshall writes, "Caliban might have become his reality." Perhaps even worse, Heitor realizes that he cannot see Caliban as of his own making. Instead of retiring a successful, self-made man, he sees that various people around him imagined his life for him: they saw his potential stardom, assigned him a new name, and made up the choreographed moves that have become his signature. His fame has erased all previous memory of him: the villagers in his home have clipped newspaper photos for so long that all they can envision is Caliban. The owner of the restaurant in which Heitor used to sweep the tile floors has recovered those floors with linoleum, hung a portrait of Caliban on the wall, and renamed the restaurant O Restaurante Grande Caliban. Heitor's show partner, and even his wife, do not recognize his real name. Heitor Baptista Guimares has disappeared, and Caliban can only hope that his old self will "emerge into consciousness" as the mountains around Rio seem to suddenly come into view.

Marshall's epigraph from Yeats's "Sailing to Byzantium" expresses the shared theme of these stories: "An aged man is but a paltry thing, / A tattered coat upon a stick, unless / Soul clap its hands and sing." The main characters of all four stories are middle-aged or elderly men who, in spite of whatever success they might have

achieved, have sold or accidentally lost their souls through carelessness or small compromises and can no longer "clap hands and sing." Mr. Watford in "Barbados" has lived in the United States as a ghost, "closeted" and "detached," making money and saving it only to return to Barbados and live as an alienated old man. Marshall writes, "He had never lost the fear that if he lived too fully he would tire and death would quickly close the gap. His only defense had been a cautious life and work." The story ends with his inability to notice his own feelings, to express them as anything but anger, "crumpled" under insults, and "moaning."

Similarly, in "Brooklyn," Max Berman is an aging French literature professor who has lost his job because of the accusation that he had been a communist. Marshall makes clear that his fault was not in being or not being a communist, but rather in not taking any political position seriously and having "withdrawn into a modest cynicism." He had become such a ghost that "he had begun to think of his inquisitors with affection and to long for the sound of their voices. They, at least, had assured him of being alive." By the end of the story, Max realizes he will never know all the people, including not least himself, that he has "wronged through his indifference." One of these people is an attractive African American student, Miss Williams, whom he encourages to "try something new and bold," but only because he is making sexual advances to her. Shocked, Miss Williams has an epiphany: she will "do something," she will "begin," and wonders if André Gide might have been right: "Maybe in order for a person to live someone else must die." To her Gide's "book seems to say that the only way you begin to know what you are and how much you are capable of is by daring to try something, by doing something which tests you."

The protagonists in *Soul Clap Hands and Sing* are unwilling to take on the challenges that would have given them life. In "British Guiana"

Gerald Motley has drunk his life away. On awakening, to what becomes the last day of his life, he is pulled between "the fabulous form of some dream" and ordering another rum drink. Consistently irreverent, aware of his wasted promise, and "indifferen[t] to the colony's troubles" (among other things), he did what was expected of him. He took the jobs offered by relatives and "married the fair-complexioned daughter of a highly respected Georgetown family." Drowning his potential in drink, he has managed to scare off his respectable wife but still does not full-heartedly turn to any of his own passions. In addition, Motley has a young and promising, but cynical, protégé, Sidney Parrish, who seems to be quickly developing the same deadening attitude that has crippled Motley. Mr. Motley will not be saved, but he sets up Parrish for a challenging job, perhaps releasing him from Motley's own fate. The story of Motley's last day also tells the story of how one man never quite forced himself to live.

The men of *Soul Clap Hands and Sing* and Marshall's other works, who have lost themselves or who have failed to achieve their dreams, blame the women around them. In the novel *Brown Girl, Brownstones,* Deighton has every right to blame his wife for making it impossible for him to go home and relax on his two acres; however, his history of not finishing what he begins suggests that he might never have built his house. In her short stories, too, Marshall's male characters have themselves to blame and yet manage to find female scapegoats. The most interesting scapegoat is Sybil Jeffries, who has a "long, bold affair" with Gerald Motley in "British Guiana." When choosing between striking out on his own in his career or settling into a sinecurial position that allows him to be "the first colored man in the West Indies to hold this high a position in broadcasting," Motley goes instead on "an overland trek" "into the bush." When he leaves the marked trail, he "felt a terror that had been the most

exquisite of pleasures" and "the bush had closed around him, becoming another dimension of himself, the self he had long sought." But Sybil "placed herself between him and what could have been a vision of himself"; she insists they leave the jungle, and he decides to take the job in broadcasting (and starts drinking). Perhaps Sybil is to blame, but she manages to move on to success in Jamaica.

The anger in the other stories of *Soul Clap Hands and Sing* is simpler, more direct, and yet probably less deserved. The Grande Caliban strikes his female partner, destroys her apartment, and scares his completely innocent wife (who is failing to save him with her youth and her resemblance to the Virgin Mary). Mr. Watford's housekeeper makes him realize how much he appreciates companionship, but she inconveniently hates him. Marshall makes it clear that these men have no right to blame women as much as they do, and she goes so far as to claim that their very inability to live fully is demonstrated by their inability to love. They all use women and let them go, without making commitments. In "Brooklyn" Max Weber remembers his wife: "She had been a gift—and her death in a car accident had been a judgment on him for never having loved her, for never, indeed, having even allowed her to matter."

THE CHOSEN PLACE, THE TIMELESS PEOPLE

In this longer work Marshall creates a beautiful and heartbreaking mix of characters, complicated in themselves and also in their diverse relationships with one another, the past, and their environments. Inspired by "a group of social scientists from the States" and "their reaction to and relations with local people," Marshall writes a novel on a topic somewhat overlooked in fiction: the rich interaction between a development team and the people living in the place they are trying to "improve." She explores the reasons development projects tend to fail, the complicated racial attitudes and historically founded blindnesses and false assumptions that seep through into even the best intentions on both sides, the competition between remembering the past and working toward a better future, and much more. In *The New York Times Book Review* in 1969 Robert Bone called *The Chosen Place, The Timeless People* "the best novel to be written by an American black woman, one of the two important black novels of the 1960s (the other being William Demby's "The Catacombs"), and one of the four or five most impressive novels ever written by a black American." In the novel, fully drawn diverse characters, including a WASP woman, a Jewish man, a West Indian woman, and others, interact with one another. In 1970 Bell Gale Chevigny wrote that she "know[s] of no serious contemporary novel attempting this synthesis—it almost constitutes a new form."

The novel is set on a fictional Caribbean island, Bourne, and a couple of locations on the island express its whole messy history. Sugar's Nightclub represents all corners of the triangle trade: Africans, sugar, and rum. What was once a barracoon (slave barracks) became a sugar warehouse and is now a bar that serves rum, rum, and more rum. Women still sell themselves there. Black islanders have become diabetics from drinking too much rum, their own bodies containing and representing all three corners of the triangle trade.

Sugar's Nightclub is also a mishmash of the world's cultures; perhaps Marshall is attributing responsibility for the triangle trade all over the globe. In a couple of paragraphs of description, Marshall mentions Buddha, Jesus, a Teddy Bear, the Eagle, a Chinese dragon, a mosque, a broken ram's horn, and the Nicene Creed. Miscellaneous beliefs are represented by knickknacks left behind and never retrieved by the revelers who have populated the nightclub over the years. Through these references Marshall may be suggesting that people worldwide have left their faiths behind in irresponsible revelry, leaving their most valuable possessions forgotten on the walls of a cheap bar, and thus injuring our collective humanity. Later the novel alludes to the Birmingham church bombing, connecting the loss of spirituality to the suffering of blacks. Marshall may concur with Reena, the title character of an earlier short story, who says, "frankly, I question whether I want to be integrated into America as it stands now, with its complacency and materialism, its soullessness."

A main character of *The Chosen Place, The Timeless People,* Merle Kimbona, is another of Marshall's strong women. Merle's bedroom, like Sugar's nightclub, holds an accumulation of the past: pictures of slave ships, slaves working in the cane fields, and plantation owners hunting. It also contains furniture from her father's house (himself a planter who had "sired . . . forty-odd children"). She has tried to put some order to it all, but so far has failed. Marshall writes, "It [the bedroom] expressed her: the struggle for coherence, the hope and desire for reconciliation of her conflicting parts, the longing to truly know and accept herself." Over the course of the novel Merle discovers a way to handle this miscellany, to recognize her past without letting it paralyze her.

White characters are also shown to be unable to divorce themselves from their pasts. Harriet is a capable, orderly woman who has left her first husband, a nuclear scientist, because she no longer wants to be an accessory to the earth's complete destruction. Forgetting this husband, she also tries to ignore the source of her money and her family's power: her Anglo-Saxon roots, her family's involvement in the slave trade, and other backroom deal making. She is kind, interested, polite, always appropriate, strong-willed, and smart. She marries Saul, a Jewish anthropologist, and plans to help him save the world. She also manages many unpleasantnesses by ignoring them: she gave "the impression of someone who had been inoculated against the effects of the sun, heat, dust, and glare." She "appeared immunized" to everything around her, but she cannot escape her past; she sees her mother's servants in the black women around her. She likes the Bourne islanders as long as they let her help them, show some appreciation, make some attempt to let her know that she is making a difference, but they do not, and she can only wait so long.

Gradually Harriet is affected: she gets a scar, gets shadows under her eyes, begins to go gray. When she is swept away by a group of rowdy black men with their own agenda at Carnival, she becomes enraged at their unwillingness to listen to her. When she finds out that Saul has become more intimate with Merle than she had imagined, she is shaken enough to express her emotions to both of them. They respond to her new openness with sympathetic understanding, but Harriet then reverts to her ancestor's tricks: buying and manipulating people. She tries to pay Merle to go far away, and she uses her connections in upper crust Philadelphia to have Saul removed from his job. When Saul shouts, *"What is it with you and your kind, anyway?"* he connects her to the ancestry she thought she could escape. Harriet would like to live separately, in the private space between the tacky, rich partyers and the poverty-stricken Bournehills people. She would like to live with her class prerogatives but also with conscience. Marshall seems to argue that this is not possible; the ocean in which Harriet disappears may be the only place in between.

The Chosen Place, The Timeless People is especially intriguing in that it continually points off the page, to that which is beyond expression. Saul cannot understand why the people of Bournehills seem stuck in time. He constantly wonders what he is not understanding, what people are not telling him. He tries to discern the nameless and intangible reason that development will not work here. DeLamotte, who explores the many roles of silence and speech in Marshall's fiction, points to the power of certain silences in this novel. She also notes that Merle is "always speaking and withholding her truth at the same time" and that nobody listens to her anyway: when she teaches the island's history at school, she is fired.

Marshall suggests that outsider development projects ignore the fact that the people have already found ways to handle their own problems, that through their long experience they have worked out solutions that take into account cultural, personal, situational, and many other types of variables, which no outside developmental anthropologist can appreciate. Marshall offers a conservative critique of a liberal reformation that has systematically neglected the wisdom and spiritual essence of tradition and local customs.

PRAISESONG FOR THE WIDOW

The much briefer and more personal treatment of this widow is quite different from the encyclopedic discussion of the development of Third World nations, but in both cases Marshall is interested in the relationship between history and development, whether it is on a personal or national scale. Marshall's work seems to have become more essential, here distilling the ideas in *Chosen People* into the story of one woman, Avey Johnson. She refines the tragic history, the undying but quiet hope, into the empty rum keg that is played at the "Big Drum" she attends and which she describes as "the bare bones of a fete. The burnt out ends." Marshall writes, "It was the essence of something rather than the thing itself."

But Avey sees that this essence is what she needs, and she devotes her future to it. Like Coleridge's ancient mariner, she plans to speak up: about the excursion, her great-aunt, and her ancestors. She will catch "those young, bright, fiercely independent token few" young black professionals "As they rushed blindly in and out of the glacier buildings, unaware, unprotected, lacking memory and a necessary distance of the mind (no mojo working for them!), she would stop them . . . before they could pull out of her grasp." Marshall promotes the idea that a person must remember and maintain his or her genetic and social history in order to best step forward toward the future. The loss of that past, either deliberately or accidentally, leads one to stagnation, blindness, sickness, and a disconnection from the people who provide a viable eco- or social system.

At the beginning of *Praisesong for the Widow*, Avey escapes her itinerary on the *Bianca Pride*, a Caribbean cruise ship, to go ashore in Grenada. By chance she accompanies a group of "out-islanders" on their yearly pilgrimage to their home island of Carriacou. She has gradually become more and more alienated from her "Halsey Street" history, a history of working hard but staying poor, living on the fifth floor of a walk-up, and dancing lovingly and spiritedly with her husband. Now she has become a self-contained woman who represses herself in more ways than one. She is like the ship, "sleek, imperial, a glacial presence," and she is self-conscious about anything that reminds whites that she is black. She wears "muted colors" and "appropriate" clothes which are always "in good taste." She has a "carefully barred gaze" and a "folded-in lip," which allows her to hide "the spillover of raw pink across the top" of her underlip. Even her body is obliged to efface its identity.

Similarly, early on her husband also tactfully tries to hide his own abilities; he runs the office but has "to be careful not to make it appear so." His single-minded push to succeed at college, in multiple jobs, and in entrepreneurship when nobody would hire him, by moving to the suburbs, and with the slow killing of his happy side, is captured in his comment: "If it was left to me I'd close down every dancehall in Har-

lem and burn every drum!" In this way he erases his only solace, which is to return home after a day at the office "and let Coleman Hawkins, the Count, Lester Young (old Prez himself), The Duke—along with all the singers he loved: Mr. B., Lady Day, Lil Green, Ella—work their magic, their special mojo on him." After such a session, Avey remembers that "his body as he sat up in the chair and stretched would look as it if belonged to him again."

In spite of the difficulties at Halsey Street, especially the economic troubles that led to marital problems and attempts to abort their third child, Avey feels "like a secret tippler" because the "memories of that earlier period were a wine she could not resist." They were happy alone and then with their first child. Growing away from that period, Jerome fighting every moment to succeed, and Avey guiltily encouraging him because she knows her own angry words initiated this sudden change in him, they lose themselves and their love: "Love like a burden he wanted rid of. Like a leg-iron which slowed him in the course he had set for himself." Here Marshall highlights the link between what sustains and what restrains.

Like Jerome, Avey begins "to regard the years there [on Halsey Street] as having been lived by someone other than herself." Avey sees herself in mirrors and does not immediately recognize herself. When she stares at Jerome in his coffin she sees another face, the one "with the tight joyless look" and which now seems triumphant, having killed Jerome years before. Marshall is suggesting the form of murder—or suicide or schizophrenia—that comes with rejecting one's past.

What transforms Avey is the complete purging of what came between her early life and her present: having "money in the bank," her hat and gloves, and a house in North White Plains. In one upsetting dream, she is dressed up to go "the annual luncheon . . . given by Jerome Johnson's lodge" when her aunt appears and beckons to her. Her stubborn refusal, in spite of all kinds of silent coaxing on her aunt's part, ends with her "fur stole like her hard-won life of the past thirty years being trampled into the dirt underfoot." In a section titled "Lavé Tête" Avey's "mind, like her pocketbook outside, had been emptied of the contents of the past thirty years during the night, so that she had awakened with it like a slate that had been wiped clean, a *tabula rasa* upon which a whole new history could be written." Avey also purges herself physically on the boat ride, and she gradually comes to see herself as part of a community linked by threads instead of divorced from these islanders. In seeking desperately to distance herself from the legacy of black enslavement, she has replicated the crime against a black multi-generational continuity implicit in slavery. By the end of the novel, however, she begins paying reparations, by paying attention to her youngest daughter and the future she embodies.

DAUGHTERS

In *Daughters,* Marshall seems to try to pull people back into themselves, into achieving the dreams they have given up, or following their heritage in one way or another. Ursa Bea, the main character, worries that she has become a "YRUM in blackface," YRUM meaning "the Young and the Restless Upwardly Mobiles." When she finds that she is just too successful in a "National Consumer Research Corporation," she daringly quits and begins freelancing a study on Midland City, New Jersey. Her longtime boyfriend has given up his rewarding work as a minority recruiter to work at a frustrating private sector job that takes over his life and changes his face to one of misery. Her father has started out his political career with the goal of improving the island of Triunion, but he has had to make so many compromises that he no longer recognizes his own original goals. Her mother, an American who moved to Triunion to live

with her husband, compromises her expectations when it comes to her marriage but stubbornly holds on to her political ideals. She encourages Ursa in her new work, secretly enables the election of a younger politician to take her husband's place, and implants in her daughter the emulation of two local freedom fighters, Congo Jane and and Will Cudjoe. Ursa's friend Viney, who compromised herself over and over to find a "useful" and good (not perfect) man, finally chooses to become pregnant alone.

Marshall evokes sympathy for all the characters, even those who would betray their own people's birthrights (such as Ursa's father, Primus Mackenzie, who secretly tries to give the beach on government lands to the resorts) or those who would waste time in a "static" relationship or job. Ursa finally sympathizes with the woman who has been her father's "Number Two" wife, and she begins to understand that she can never quite understand, and perhaps has no right to understand, what holds her parents together. In short, Marshall expands her readers' love for human beings trying their best and correspondingly contracts her readers' tendencies to be judgmental about other people's complicated lives. Her view of human conduct is agnostic but affectionate.

In this vein, the book explores mothering. Many of the Triunion women see Ursa's mother, Estelle, as "unnatural" because she sent Ursa off to the United States as soon as she could. But Estelle wants her daughter to be American, to wear an afro and short pants instead of frilly dresses, and to understand the fight for civil rights in the United States that crippled Estelle's brother. Estelle wants her daughter to be independent, not to hang on to her lifelong nanny as her husband seems to do. Estelle does not write Ursa long letters, and she does not demand that Ursa return home to visit. It is only when she enlists her daughter in helping her overthrow her husband's election that Estelle calls Ursa home, and in this, too, she is encouraging her daughter in a surprising act of defiance.

Like Estelle with Ursa, Viney wants her son, Robeson, to grow up to be a strong and special man, like his namesake, Paul Robeson. But her determination to raise him as a boy who expects the same rights as whites is shaken when, at age twelve, he is wrongly arrested for trying to steal cars. He tries to explain that he was only reading the speedometers through the windows and imagining where the cars have traveled, but the officer will not listen. Robeson shouts about his rights. Handcuffed and pushed into a squad car, the boy's confidence is shaken, and his mother fears that the way she is raising him is not preparing him for the world in which he lives. Viney says she might now understand why some mothers are "so quick with that hand":

> Maybe it's their way of teaching them how to behave around the Pirellis [the arresting police officer] out there. That might be part of it. So they'll know better than to go up in some white cop's face talking about their constitutional rights and running the risk of being blown away. Maybe I haven't been teaching Robeson what he really needs to know.

The episode makes Viney wish Robeson had a father standing there for him at the police station, suggesting the necessity for cooperation between black men and women.

Daughters had opened with Ursa remembering her horrible experience in college, when she wanted to write her senior thesis on "the general nature of gender roles and relationships," examining "the relatively egalitarian, mutually supportive relations that existed between the bondmen and women and their significance for and contribution to the various forms of resistance to enslavement found in the United States and the Caribbean." Her professor unjustly found this topic unacceptable, but Ursa is now getting a second masters and is about to begin writing her thesis on the topic after all. Her interest is inspired by Congo Jane and Will Cudjoe, "Coleaders, coconspirators, consorts, lovers, friends. You couldn't call her name without calling his, and vice-versa." They are her mother's heroes, and Ursa's heroes, and they model the early cooperation between Estelle and Primus to win elections and improve Triunion, and now between the upstart candidate and his partner and wife. But Viney cannot find a "useful" man to pair up with. She says,

> I'm gonna tell you, "The woods are on fire out here," my granddaddy used to say, "and we need everybody that can tote a bucket of water to come running." He used to say that all the time, talking about the situation of Black Folks in this country, you know, and the need for all of us to stand up and be counted. To be useful. And one day I took a good look at Willis Jenkins and knew he was not one of those Folks. He might be bright, talented, good to look at, great in bed, someone who knew how to talk the talk in order to get over, but he wasn't really useful. Because Willis Jenkins wasn't about to tote so much as a thimbleful of water anywhere, for anybody, not even for himself if his own patch of woods was on fire.

Black solidarity, across national and gender lines, is the key in a world controlled by a white elite. Marshall emphasizes the range of experience shared by blacks in America and in the West Indies. As in *Praisesong*—where so many ideas, events, or moments in history are linked or approximately equated to so many other ideas—in *Daughters* Ursa is always "seeing double." When she drives into Midland City, and finds herself on an overpass above a black neighborhood, she sees "Triunion all over again!" Remembering an expensive road that bypassed Armory Hill, she wonders, "Where am I? Which place? What country? Is there no escaping that island?" In both places rich whites, whether tourists or suburbanites, are able to get where they want to go without seeing the city itself and its people. In Midland City, the road not only bypasses that neighborhood but also destroys it.

The fight in Midland City is compared to all sorts of wartime resistances and atrocities: Mae Ryland calls herself "a gook," and Ursa thinks portions of the city look like Dresden or "a bombed-out section in Beirut." Mae is coming up with a "Marshall Plan" for the neighborhood, and Marshall imagines "More detox, more rehab, more outreach and job training than you could shake a stick at. More housing, clinics, schools, factories, daycare . . . You name it." Ursa feels overwhelmed with what she thinks of as double exposures: "Everything— elections, roads, the South Ward [in Midland City], Armory Hill, the PM [her father], the Do-Nothings, Sandy Lawson [the mayor of Midland City who seems to have sold out], the white people-them! still running things in both places—everything superimposed on everything else. Inseparable. Inescapable. The same things repeated everywhere she turned."

The answer to this repetition, the key to the future, and the combined work of black men and women, is rebirth, and childbirth, both literal and figurative, permeates the novel. Estelle has many, many "slides" (miscarriages) before she has Ursa Bea. The novel begins with Ursa's second abortion, thoughts of which reoccur throughout the novel. She keeps wondering whether the doctors did anything, whether she is still carrying the baby. Her mother comments that she is relieved her daughter has not become "a veritable baby-making machine." Viney, who became pregnant through artificial insemination, is raising a son in Paul Robeson's image. Ursa's unfinished work is most obviously her thesis on Congo Jane and Will Cudjoe, the birthing of an erased history, the history of the people who birthed her. Marshall's epigraph reads

Little girl of all the daughters,
You ain' no more slave,
You's a woman now,

She shows her women characters making choices, not under command and not even controlled by their own habit or reflex. They are dancing forward, spontaneously but certainly not effortlessly, taking the paths they deem right or necessary. After watching her father's defeat in the election, Ursa plans her trip back to New York and a long bath. "That before anything else," but there will surely be much else.

THE FISHER KING

In *The Fisher King* Marshall is more encyclopedic and more essential all at once. This novel, much shorter than several earlier ones, manages to communicate the complexity of four generations of Brooklyn dwellers, several of whom were unwillingly linked through a romantic triangle involving a "homegrown Romeo and Juliet" and a "foster care, City child without any background or family." Thus the people who would disdain one another's ways—the "Americans" and the West Indians and the people with no known history except a troubled mother named Dawn—are drawn together, although they do not let this fact force them to bury their real and imagined differences.

Bowing respectfully to James Baldwin's short story "Sonny's Blues," Marshall's long-dead hero is Sonny-Rett Payne, a man who alienates his mother and brother by playing "Sodom and Gomorrah music." Born Everett Payne, he is renamed when he plays "'Sonny Boy Blue' like it had never been played before": he "put a hurtin' on" that "hokey-doke, Tin Pan Alley tune, . . . made it his tune, his song," and left everyone dumbstruck. The protagonist in this novel, however, is Sonny-Rett's eight-year-old grandson, also named Sonny. He is a boy who has never had a family because his grandparents are dead, his "girl-mother" ran away, and his African father was deported from France because he was *sans papiers.*" While Baldwin's Sonny lives in Harlem instead of Brooklyn, their music is crucial to both performers, their music expresses both pain and pleasure, they use drugs, and they have a difficult relationship with their brothers. Sonny's brother in Baldwin's story begins to appreciate the music Sonny plays, but in Marshall's novel, Edgar DeCorsey Payne comes to appreciate and understand his brother's music only after Sonny-Rett's mysterious death in a Paris Metro station.

As in the Arthurian fisher king legend, Edgar Payne has missed his first chance at fulfilling his redemptive quest but is still trying. Having passed up his chance to care for Sonny-Rett's daughter, Jo-Jo, he is intent upon caring for the son she had before she disappeared. Similarly, now that his own daughter is divorced and in law school, he is caring for her two children. He says, "Alva and I are back to being parents in our old age. But we don't mind. In fact, we're doing a much better job this time around. We didn't do so good with our daughter. But then she was a handful." Making up for the past in another way, Edgar is also working through the private sector to accomplish what Robert Kennedy, for whom he worked, had proposed before his assassination: a "Marshall-type plan" called the Central Brooklyn Renewal Project. Edgar now heads "The Three R's Group of Central Brooklyn," the goals of which are "Reclamation. Restoration. Rebirth." Also like the Arthurian fisher king, Edgar can see the terrible and wonderful in the same things, his credo being "Nothing's pure. Nothing's wholly selfless."

Hattie, who raises Sonny, knows this to be true, and she too is trying to make up for the past. Hattie, the "City child" friend of his grandparents, has always been "fathermothersisterbrother" to Sonny. She also raised his mother, furnished Sonny-Rett and Cherisse's home in Paris, and kept the family finances as the "materfamilias." She raised JoJo, whom she lost, and she is making up for it with Sonny. Sonny was a "gift," "The outward and visible sign of [Sonny-Rett, Cherisse, and JoJo's] continuing presence. It contained all three of

her loves." Many of these terms invoke the Christian symbolism attached to the fisher king, but Hattie is at a disadvantage in this struggle over Sonny because she is not quite family.

The influence of the Arthurian legend of the fisher king is also evident in the castles that young Sonny draws. Worried that he will lose everything he loves, he imagines that his grandfather is in the castle and he draws himself in armor outside, as protector. His famous grandfather, then, is no longer quite dead to him. He dreams of finding his mother and tracing his father to wherever he might be in Africa. Hattie is really all he has, and she is old, a tender point with him. Thus Marshall shows the fears of loss and abandonment of a child lacking a network of dependable people. Sonny's own mother, JoJo, seems to have fallen apart because everything she depended on, her whole limited world, "had suddenly proved unreliable, untrustworthy, and therefore somehow worthless." The people Sonny depends upon seem to be at least as tenuous: an elderly woman who is addicted to drugs and works at an exotic dance club that gets shut down unpredictably, and an even older alcoholic woman. Edgar and the United States offer Sonny greater stability, not only because of numbers but also because of variety: cousins his own age, two albeit somewhat unstable great-grandmothers, an uncle and aunt, and a divorced cousin in law school. Not all of these people will disappear at the same time, and not all them will leave him destitute; some are financially well-off and each has learned to "cut-and-contrive" in a different way.

The real difference in *The Fisher King* is probably brought about by Marshall's choice of a child protagonist. The child character forces Marshall's symbolism to be more light-handed. Instead of the main character seeing everything double, as in *Daughters,* Sonny sees from a simple perspective. There are many parallels drawn: between club owners and plantation owners, between needless hatreds among blacks in France and the United States, between the treatment of black female dayworkers and the treatment of domestic pets, between the woods surrounding Edgar's "magazine house" on Long Island and the Berlin Wall. But these are more subtly drawn, not emphasized and reiterated, because Sonny does not quite have the capacity to see and articulate them.

Marshall's strength as an observer of subtle human foibles remains strong through *The Fisher King*. She catches the vanity that will not let a woman have a breast tumor removed through surgery, the tragedy of an old woman saying, "the world don' have no uses anymore for someone like me," the way one old woman who hates another actually also cares for her, and the fact that sometimes old people cannot control the bad parts of themselves and need excusing. She notes the way people insist on feeling superior to others, one character describing the United States as "A country where everybody always running from the next body feeling they's better." She speaks up against people having to work too hard and being treated too inhumanely, all for a living of which they can never be sure.

Those who are healthy, powerful, and prosperous have an obligation to provide both means and meaning to the others. By alluding to the "Marshall Plan"—the European Recovery Program by which the United States injected thirteen billion dollars into Europe's economy between 1948 and 1951—in both *Daughters* and *The Fisher King*, Paule Marshall recommends her own narrative method of reclamation, reconstruction, and rebirth. In a 1996 interview with Angela Elam she stated,

Perhaps, a young black woman, a young black man, who is searching for self will come across one of my books, and see himself or herself and perhaps even their world, reflected in a truthful and complex way. I believe that seeing oneself reflected truthfully in the literature is a kind of empowering act. It not only gives you a sense of your right to be in the world—this is one of the fantastic things that literature can do—but it also gives you, then, the power to move to the next phase. From your own personal empowerment, you can begin to mobilize, to really bring about the liberation of your community.

Selected Bibliography

WORKS OF PAULE MARSHALL

NOVELS AND SHORT FICTION
Brown Girl, Brownstones. New York: Random House, 1959.

Soul Clap Hands and Sing. New York: Atheneum, 1961.

"Return of the Native." 1964. Reprinted in *Sturdy Black Bridges: Visions of Black Women in Literature.* Edited by Rene-app Bell et al. New York: Anchor Books, 1979. Pp. 314–321.

The Chosen Place, The Timeless People. New York: Harcourt, Brace & World, 1969.

"Some Get Wasted." In *Harlem U.S.A.* Edited by John Henrik Clarke. New York: New American Library, 1970. Pp. 136–145.

Praisesong for the Widow. New York: Plume, 1983.

Reena and Other Stories. Old Westbury, N.Y.: Feminist Press, 1983.

Daughters. New York: Atheneum, 1991.

The Fisher King. New York: Scribner, 2000.

OTHER WORKS
"The Negro Woman in Literature." *Freedomways* 4:20–25 (1966).

"Shaping the World of My Art." *New Letters* 40, no. 1:97–112 (October 1973).

"Characterizations of Black Women in the American Novel." In *The Memory and Spirit of Frances, Zora, and Lorraine: Essays and Interviews on Black Women and Writing.* Edited by Juliette Bowles. Washington, D.C.: Institute for the Arts and Humanities, Howard University, 1979. Pp. 76–79.

"Islanders of the Bed-Stuy: The West Indian Zest to 'Buy House' Rejuvenates a Community." *New York Times Magazine,* November 3, 1985, pp. 179–182.

"Black Literature in the '90s: The Past as Prologue to 'The New Wave.'" *Defining Ourselves: Black Writers in the 90s.* Edited by Elizabeth Nunez and Brenda Greene. New York: Peter Lang, 1999. Pp. 25–33.

CRITICAL AND BIOGRAPHICAL STUDIES

Alexander, Simone A. James. *Mother Imagery in the Novels of Afro-Caribbean Women.* Columbia: University of Missouri Press, 2001.

Billingsglea-Brown, Alma Jean. *Crossing Borders Through Folklore.* Columbia: University of Missouri Press, 1999.

Brathwaite, Edward. "West Indian History and Society in the Art of Paule Marshall's Novel *The Chosen Place, The Timeless People.*" *Journal of Black Studies* 1, no. 2:225–238 (December 1970).

Bröck, Sabine. "Transcending the Loophole of Retreat: Paule Marshall's Placing of Female Generations." *Callaloo* 10, no. 1:79–90 (winter 1987).

Brown, Lloyd W. "The Rhythms of Power in Paule Marshall's Fiction." *Novel* 7:159–167 (winter 1974).

Busia, Abena P. A. "What Is Your Nation? Reconnecting Africa and Her Diaspora through Paule Marshall's *Praisesong for the Widow.*" In *Changing Our Own Words: Essays on Criticism, Theory, and Writing by Black Women.* Edited by Cheryl A. Wall. New Brunswick, N.J.: Rutgers University Press, 1989. Pp. 196–211.

Christian, Barbara. "Ritualistic Process and the Structure of Paule Marshall's *Praisesong for the Widow.*" *Black Feminist Criticism: Perspectives on Black Women Writers.* New York: Pergamon, 1985. Pp. 149–158.

——. "Paule Marshall." *Black American Writers.* Edited by Valerie Smith. New York: Charles Scribner's Sons, 1990. Pp. 289–304.

Collier, Eugenia. "The Closing of the Circle: Movement from Division to Wholeness in Paule Marshall's Fiction." *Black Women Writers (1950–1980).* Edited by Mari Evans. Garden City, N.J.: Anchor, 1984. Pp. 295–315.

Cooke, John. "Whose Child? The Fiction of Paule Marshall." *CLA Journal* 24, no. 1:1–15 (1980).

Coser, Stalamaris. *Bridging the Americas: The Literature of Paule Marshall, Toni Morrison, and Gayl Jones.* Philadelphia, Pa.: Temple University Press, 1994.

DeLamotte, Eugenia C. *Places of Silence, Journeys of Freedom: The Fiction of Paule Marshall.* Philadelphia, Pa.: University of Pennsylvania Press, 1998.

Denniston, Dorothy Hamer. *The Fiction of Paule Marshall: Reconstructions of History, Culture, and Gender.* Knoxville: University of Tennessee Press, 1995.

Gikandi, Simon. "The Circle of Meaning: Paule Marshall, Modernism, and the Masks of History." In *Of Dreams Deferred, Dead or Alive: African Perspectives on African American Writers.* Edited by Femi Ojo-Ade. Westport, Conn.: Greenwood Press, 1996. Pp. 143–155.

Hathaway, Heather. *Caribbean Waves: Relocating Claude McKay and Paule Marshall.* Bloomington: Indiana University Press, 1999.

Kubitschek, Missy Dehn. "Paule Marshall's Women on Quest." *Black American Literature Forum* 21, nos. 1–2:43–60 (spring–summer 1987).

Kulkarni, Harihar. "Paule Marshall: A Bibliography." *Callaloo* 16, no. 1:243–267 (winter 1993).

McCluskey, John, Jr. "And Called Every Generation Blessed: Theme, Setting, and Ritual in the Works of Paule Marshall." In *Black Women Writers (1950–1980).* Edited by Mari Evans. Garden City, N.J.: Anchor, 1984. Pp. 316–334.

Macpherson, Heidi Slettedahl. "Perceptions of Place: Geopolitical and Cultural Positioning in Paule Marshall's Novels." In *Caribbean Women Writers: Fiction in English.* Edited by Mary Condé and Thorunn Lonsdale. New York: St. Martin's Press, 1999. Pp. 75–96.

Nazareth, Peter. "Paule Marshall's Timeless People." *New Letters* 40, no. 1:113–131 (October 1973).

Olmsted, Jane. "The Pull to Memory and the Language of Place in Paule Marshall's *The Chosen Place, The Timeless People* and *Praisesong for the Widow.*" *African American Review* 31, no. 2:249–267 (summer 1997).

"Paule Marshall: The Fiction Writer." A special section on Paule Marshall. *Callaloo* 6, no. 2:21–84 (spring–summer 1983).

Pettis, Joyce. *Toward Wholeness in Paule Marshall's Fiction.* Charlottesville: University Press of Virginia, 1995.

Rose, Toby. "Crossroads Are Our Roads: Paule Marshall's Portrayal of Immigrant Identity Themes." In *The Immigrant Experience in North American Literature: Carving Out a Niche.* Edited by Katherine B. Payant and Toby Rose. Westport, Conn.: Greenwood Press, 1999. Pp. 109–121.

Storhoff, Gary. "'Yesterday Comes Like Today': Communiitas in Paule Marshall's *The Chosen Place, The Timeless People.*" *MELUS* 23, no. 2:49–64 (summer 1998).

Washington, Elsie B. "Paule Marshall: Merging Our Culture." *Essence,* October 1991, p. 48.

Willis, Susan. "Describing Arcs of Recovery: Paule Marshall's Relationship to Afro-American Culture." In *Specifying: Black Women Writing the American Experience.* Madison: University of Wisconsin Press, 1987. Pp. 53–82.

INTERVIEWS

Bone, Robert. "Merle Kinbona Was Part Saint, Part Revolutionary, Part Obeah-Woman." *New York Times Book Review,* November 30, 1969, pp. 4, 54.

Bröck, Sabine. "'Talk as a Form of Action': An Interview with Paule Marshall, September, 1982." In *History and Tradition in Afro-American Culture.* Edited by Gunter H. Lenz. Frankfurt: Verlag, 1984. Pp. 194–206.

Chevigny, Bell Gale. "Review of *The Chosen Place, The Timeless People.*" *The Village Voice,* October 8, 1970, pp. 6, 30–31.

Christol, Helene. "Paule Marshall's Bajan Women in *Brown Girl, Brownstones.*" In *Women and War: The Changing Status of American Women from the 1930s to the 1950s.* Edited by Maria Diedrich and Dorothea Fischer-Hornung. New York: Berg, 1990. Pp. 141–153.

Dance, Daryl Cumber. "An Interview with Paule Marshall." *Southern Review* 28, no. 1:1–20 (January 1992).

DeVeaux, Alexis. "Paule Marshall—In Celebration of Our Triumph." *Essence,* May 1979, pp. 70–71, 96–98, 123–135.

Elam, Angela. "To Be in the World: In Interview with Paule Marshall." *New Letters* 62, no. 4:96–105 (1996).

Marshall, Paule, and Maryse Conde. "Return of the Native Daughter: An Interview with Paule Marshall and Maryse Conde." Translated by John Williams. *SAGE: A Scholarly Journal on Black Women* 3, no. 2:52–53 (fall 1986).

Ogundipe-Leslie, Omolara. "Recreating Ourselves All Over the World: Interview with Paule Marshall." *Matatu* 3, no. 6:25–38 (1989).

Pettis, Joyce. "A MELUS Interview: Paule Marshall." *MELUS* 17, no. 4:117–130 (winter 1991).

Washington, Mary Helen. "A Talk with Mary Helen Washington." In *Writing Lives: Conversations between Women Writers.* Edited by Mary Chamberlain. London: Virago, 1988. Pp. 161–167.

Williams, John. "Return of a Native Daughter: An Interview with Paule Marshall and Maryse Conde." *SAGE: A Scholarly Journal on Black Women* 3, no. 2:52–53 (1986).

—*DANA CAIRNS WATSON*

Terry Southern

1924–1995

*T*HE PHOTOGRAPHIC COLLAGE of counterculture icons that forms the cover of the Beatles' *Sgt. Peppers Lonely Hearts Club Band* album (1967) is a kind of shrine to cultural rebels and iconoclasts. Near the upper left, between cutouts of Lenny Bruce and W. C. Fields, is a man wearing dark sunglasses who would not have been recognized by most Beatles fans but was, nonetheless, a key figure in the shaping of the 1960s. That man was Terry Southern. A noted satiric novelist in the early part of his career, Southern achieved international celebrity as co-screenwriter (with Stanley Kubrick) of *Dr. Strangelove; or, How I Learned to Stop Worrying and Love the Bomb* (1964), the notorious black comedy that mocked the psychotic rationality of the nuclear arms race. Throughout the rest of the decade Southern was an extremely hot property in Hollywood. Among other projects Southern wrote *Barbarella* (1967), Roger Vadim's droll science-fiction sex farce that remains a masterpiece of camp. He later collaborated with Dennis Hopper and Peter Fonda to create *Easy Rider* (1969), the surprise hit that decisively turned mainstream Hollywood toward the youth market—and launched the New American Cinema, a golden era of innovative filmmaking that lasted well into the 1970s.

Although many of Terry Southern's contemporaries went on to enjoy lasting post-1960s fame and wealth, Southern found himself bedeviled by nagging tax problems, alcoholism, and the collapse of the counterculture he helped create, which rendered his later work unfashionable and unmarketable. After a sad, protracted decline, Southern died in near total obscurity in 1995. As fate would have it, a few years after his death, interest in Southern began to revive and his reputation as a brilliant comic writer and satiric genius seemed on its way to being restored to its former luster. More than a great humorist, Terry Southern was, perhaps more than anyone else, the very embodiment of the rebellious exuberance of the 1960s.

EARLY YEARS

Terry Southern was born on May 1, 1924, in Alvarado, Texas, a small town near Dallas, to Terrence Marion Southern and Helen Southern. His father was a druggist, a farmer, and, unfortunately, an alcoholic whose fortunes went into serious decline during the years of the Great Depression. Nonetheless Southern's boyhood seems to have been a happy one. As he told his biographer, Lee Hill, "Growing up in Texas [was] probably a lot like growing up in Alberta or Saskatchewan—ideal—from a certain Huck Finn point of view. Lots of hunting and fishing, lots of baseball and football, and only a handful of grown-ups." An avid reader from early on, Southern was nine years old when he discovered Edgar Allan Poe's "The Narrative of A. Gordon Pym," a grisly tale of cannibalism at sea which Southern later described as "an extraordinary turn-on for a young western lout." Suddenly passionate about "weirdo" literature, young Terry took to rewriting Poe's story to make it even more lurid and grotesque. In an interview with Paul Krassner in *Impolite Interviews* (1999), Southern recalls showing his version to a friend, who was appalled. "'God-damn, you must be crazy,' he said. I think that's when we began to drift apart—I mean, Texas and me."

Southern graduated from high school in June 1941. After attending North Texas Agricultural College for a year, he transferred to Southern Methodist University in Dallas in fall 1942. Although he could have sat out World War II with a college deferment, Southern was bored with college, anxious to see the wider world, and avid to become a writer. He enlisted in the army in March 1943. Shipped to the European theater of operations in October, Southern's regiment was initially stationed in England. After D day (June 6, 1944), Southern and his comrades were sent to the Continent. Though he was in the thick of the fight during the Battle of the Bulge in the winter of 1944–1945, Southern emerged from the war unhurt and was granted an honorable discharge from the service in August 1945. In Europe for two and a half years, Southern spent most of his leave time in London. In marked contrast to the racist, intellectually impoverished culture of Texas, England was literate, urbane, and socially sophisticated. A confirmed anglophile, Southern adopted what Lee Hill describes as "a persona that simultaneously embraced and mocked a certain English way of looking at the world. It was the attitude of an independently wealthy Oxford don without the snobbishness or affectation."

Southern returned to Texas after leaving the army, but he had seen too much of other worlds to last long in his home state. Still intent on pursuing a writing career he resumed his quest for a bachelor's degree by enrolling at the University of Chicago, under the GI Bill, in the fall of 1946. He soon transferred to Northwestern University, from which he graduated in 1948 with a B.A. in English.

PARIS

In September 1948 Southern made a more dramatic and decisive career move. Joining a wave of American war veteran expatriates, he relocated to Paris, ostensibly to begin further studies in literature at the Sorbonne's Faculté des Lettres but equally important was his desire to soak up the great city's cultural ambience. In a 1989 interview with Mike Golden, editor of *Smoke Signals,* he recalled, "Oh it was a terrific scene. Because the cafes were such great places to hang out, they were so open, you could smoke hash at the tables, if you were fairly discreet. There was the expatriot [*sic*] crowd, which was more or less comprised of interesting people, creatively inclined." In a matter of months the callow young Texan was well on his way to becoming an urbane, jazz-loving bohemian existentialist. He also met and befriended other aspiring artists and writers: the saxophone player Allen Eager; the future filmmaker Aram Avakian; the Canadian novelist Mordecai Richler; the then obscure and destitute future Nobel Prize–winner James Baldwin; the Scottish avant-garde writer-editor (and heroin addict) Alexander Trocchi; the fledgling *Paris Review* editors Peter Matthiessen, George Plimpton, and H. L. "Doc" Humes. But Southern's deepest bond was with Mason Hoffenberg, the brash scion of a wealthy New York family who was on the verge of developing what would prove to be a lifelong heroin habit. Of similarly irreverent sensibilities, Southern and Hoffenberg quickly became close friends and, later, literary collaborators.

During his four years in Paris Southern first began publishing fiction. He broke into print with "The Automatic Gate," a story about an unctuous Métro ticket collector that appeared in the June 1951 issue of *New-Story,* a short-lived Paris literary journal founded by Whit Burnett. In the November 1951 issue of the same journal, Southern placed "The Butcher," another character study of a working-class Parisian.

A signal event in Southern's development as a writer was his discovery of the English novelist Henry Green (the pseudonym of Henry Vincent Yorke, 1905–1973). A practitioner of Social

Realism in the 1930s, Green went on to develop a cunningly droll, detached narrative voice conveying stories of great emotional depth and perceptual refinement that shaded toward subtle surrealism and black comedy. After reading an adulatory article about Green in the *Partisan Review,* Southern devoured Green's novels, struck up a correspondence, and forged a lasting friendship with the older writer. Captivated by Green's inventive style and tragicomic view of life, Southern rapidly moved away from literary naturalism toward his true métier: deadpan surrealist satire. Southern's stylistic maturation was manifest in "The Accident," a story appearing in the first issue of the *Paris Review* (spring 1953), which was actually a couple of chapters from a longer work-in-progress that would become Southern's first novel, *Flash and Filigree* (1958).

GREENWICH VILLAGE

Southern returned to the United States in spring 1953 and settled in New York City, where he split the rent on a Greenwich Village apartment with two of his Paris buddies, Aram Avakian and Pud Gadiot. In the early 1950s Greenwich Village was every bit as vibrant as Paris. Indeed, in the interview with Mike Golden, Southern noted, "The Village and St. Germain des Pres [Paris] were sort of interchangeable." Aspiring young artists, theater people, jazz musicians, and writers flocked to the Manhattan enclave, intent on living creative lives outside the pall of an increasingly conformist 1950s America mired in consumerism, anticommunist paranoia, and mindless status seeking. Because he was deeply immersed in a self-consciously oppositional culture, Southern's estrangement from the American mainstream grew more pronounced. His alienation—leavened by a lively wit and a healthy sense of the absurd—found expression in his short stories and his novel in progress, *Flash and Filigree.*

Having been published abroad—with more stories pending in the *Paris Review*—Southern wasted no time in attempting to establish himself as a writer in his homeland. He sent new fiction to a wide swath of journals—high-, low-, and middlebrow—but only got back a sheaf of rejection slips. After Southern signed on with the Curtis Brown Agency, his agents began placing some of his stories, among them the surrealistic "The Sun and the Still-born Stars," in *Harper's Bazaar,* along with a more naturalistic story about street punks called "The Panthers." Over the next couple of years, Southern eked out a living, relying on the generosity of his roommate Pud Gadiot, checks from his parents, publishing fees for his short stories, and occasional editorial work. Lee Hill notes that Southern took pride in *not* taking odd jobs.

In fall 1955, at a party thrown by his friend the photographer Robert Frank, Southern met Carol Kauffman, a tall, attractive graduate student from Philadelphia. The two quickly fell in love and within a couple of months were living together in the Village. Sometime in spring 1956 Southern proposed marriage, and Carol readily accepted. They were wed on July 14 at Tupper Lake, in the heart of Adirondack Park, upstate New York.

Southern planned to return to Europe with Carol but lack of money was a hindrance. That problem was solved when Southern's friend Alexander Trocchi arrived in New York via Paris in 1956. At loose ends himself, Trocchi managed to land a job as the pilot of a barge hauling huge boulders down the Hudson River, from a Poughkeepsie quarry to an ocean-jetty being built at Far Rockaway, in Queens. Trocchi got Southern and other friends jobs with the barge company. In his interview with Mike Golden, Southern described the job as "one of those classic writer's jobs, like hotel clerk, night watchman, fire-tower guy, etcetera, with practically no duties." More than an odd job, the three-day barge excursions up and down the Hudson became, according to Southern, great social events:

> Nelson Algren came a couple of times, David Solomon and Seymour Krim, Christopher Logue and Jimmy Baldwin. And of course Mason [Hoffenberg] would come along quite often. I remember once, after a great hash[ish] rave-up, Jimmy just sort of collapsed over the side and Mason had to pull him back aboard, after extracting some sort of weird promise. In jest, of course. So life on the barge was not without interest.

After a summer "working" on the barge, Southern had managed to complete the manuscript of his first novel, *Flash and Filigree,* and save enough money from his wages to fund his long-anticipated return to Europe. In October 1956, while his book began to make the rounds of various publishers, Southern and his wife made the two-week journey across the Atlantic on a Scandinavian freighter.

FLASH AND FILIGREE

Though written in Paris and New York, *Flash and Filigree* focuses on a third great city: Los Angeles. In choosing Los Angeles as the setting for what was essentially a satiric novel about America, Southern was acknowledging that California's sprawling metropolis—with its eternally balmy weather, decentralized layout, lack of a sense of history, materialistic decadence, closed social caste system, and cultural blandness—epitomized the spiritual vacuity of corporate-era America. Southern's choice of milieu was, perhaps, also a tribute to another great American satirist, Nathanael West, who prophesied that Los Angeles would serve as the likely site for a coming national apocalypse in his masterwork, *Day of the Locust* (1939).

As his structuring device, Southern uses the cinematic technique of cross-cutting, that is, making narrative shifts back and forth between two parallel lines of action that occur simultaneously. Yet neither thread constitutes a plot in the classic sense of the term. The novel is too episodic for such narrative coherence, which would, at any rate, go against Southern's larger design: to present a world that keeps slipping from comfortable ordinariness into sudden, inexplicable bouts of chaos and madness. These unexpected turns toward the bizarre are made all the more unsettling as they are offset by a narrator who retains, in true Henry Green fashion, a sublime equanimity and deadpan narrative voice throughout.

What could be termed the "Flash" sections of the book center on Dr. Frederick Eichner, the "world's foremost dermatologist" and an avid sports-car enthusiast who revels in excessive speed (hence "Flash"). In the episode published in the *Paris Review,* Dr. Eichner is racing his "souped-up" Delahaye 235 over twisting canyon roads north of Los Angeles when he tries to beat a traffic light at ninety-five miles per hour. The resulting accident involves a fatality, though Eichner himself is unhurt. Brought to trial, Eichner struggles to clear his name with the help of Martin Frost, the kind of seedy, alcoholic private detective familiar to readers of noir fiction.

The bane of Dr. Eichner's life is one Felix Treevly, a mysterious young man of many guises who seems to be involved in an elaborate conspiracy against the doctor. Treevly also wants to deflower Barbara "Babs" Mintner, a nurse who works at Eichner's clinic. Young and beautiful, the virginal Babs ("Filigree" to Eichner's "Flash") is amusingly oblivious to the tremendous sexual magnetism she exerts on the men—and some of the women—around her. Treevly, in his persona as a love-struck university student named Ralph Edwards, pursues Babs with single-minded intensity and craftiness. Edwards' ardent attentions eventually culminate in a protracted, amorous wrestling match in his convertible at a drive-in movie theater. Willing and unwilling by turns, the frightened but aroused Babs finally succumbs to Ralph's exertions in a long, beautifully crafted scene full of furtive eroticism and wry humor.

Though certainly funny and entertaining, *Flash and Filigree* is not merely a picaresque romp. In the course of relating Treevly's intrigues involving Fred Eichner and Babs Mintner, Southern satirizes various American institutions, social mores, and common personality types. Treevly himself is the epitome of the sly, protean Confidence Man first anatomized by Herman Melville a century earlier. Dr. Eichner and his legal troubles afford a jaundiced view of expensive clinics, arrogant doctors, credulous juries, incompetent law enforcement, and the like. Babs's emotional immaturity and sexual innocence serve to lampoon the repressive, puritanical character of American culture in the 1950s.

With *Flash and Filigree,* Southern established a voice and a perspective that would guide all his future artistic endeavors. In an article on Southern for the *Dictionary of Literary Biography,* Jerry McAninch notes that *Flash and Filigree* exhibits "certain keynotes of style, theme, and character type which recur in other Southern novels . . . the disjointed narrative, the parallel plot, and perhaps most importantly, the sexual ingénue."

GENEVA

Terry and Carol Southern arrived in Paris near the end of October 1956. After a six-weeks' stay with Mason Hoffenberg, the Southerns moved on to Geneva, Switzerland, where Carol, the main breadwinner, had a job lined up teaching nursery school at UNESCO (the United Nations Educational, Scientific, and Cultural Organization). Despite limited resources, the couple spent much of their spare time touring Europe and socializing. They visited Mason Hoffenberg, Allen Ginsberg, and William Burroughs in Paris and Mordecai Richler and Henry

Green in London. In December 1956 Southern traveled to Paris to meet with Maurice Girodias, the founder and editor of Olympia Press. According to Lee Hill, after returning to Geneva with a contract for a "dirty book" that would pay a modest advance of one thousand dollars, Southern came up with a brief outline for *Candy* (1958), a quasi-pornographic satire of liberal do-gooders loosely based on Voltaire's *Candide:*

> A sensitive, progressive-school humanist who comes from Wisconsin to New York's lower East Side to be an art student, social worker, etc., and to find (unlike her father) "beauty in mean places." She has an especially romantic idea about "minorities" and of course gets raped by Negroes, robbed by Jews, knocked up by Puerto-Ricans, etc.— though her feeling of being needed sustains her for quite a while, through a devouring gauntlet of freaks, faggots, psychiatrists and aesthetic cults.

In March 1957 the London-based publishing house Andre Deutsch agreed to publish *Flash and Filigree* (which appeared a year later, in March 1958). On the strength of an outline, Deutsch also contracted with Southern for another novel that would become *The Magic Christian* (1959). Ensconced in peaceful surroundings conducive to writing and with his literary career finally flourishing, Southern worked on the two novels simultaneously and also returned, with renewed enthusiasm, to short fiction. All was not idyllic, however. Initially excited by the idea behind *Candy,* Southern grew bored with the writing and progress nearly ground to a halt. He asked Mason Hoffenberg to help him finish the novel. Hoffenberg obliged. Even then "it dragged on," Southern later told his interviewer Mike Golden, "because a lot of times we were in different places. He would be in the south of France, and I would be in Paris, then it might be the other way around. So we'd be mailing each other the stuff . . . so it took awhile." Though relatively short at about 67,000 words, the manuscript was not completed until summer 1958, a year and a half after Southern submitted his outline to Girodias.

CANDY

Candy Christian is the quintessential Terry Southern heroine: young, beautiful, and excruciatingly naive and vulnerable in matters of sex—in short, the perfect male fantasy. As Jerry McAninch puts it, Candy is

> an updated female Candide with a touch of DeSade's Justine and a bow to John Bunyan's hero [who] cheerfully insists on sacrificing herself to the masses of lecherous males who parade through the novel . . . She is the American Dream, the ideal girl-next-door, all witless innocence and virginal submission, all body and no brains.

The novel begins with Candy encountering the insatiable, and often twisted, male libido in the person of her college philosophy instructor, Professor Mephesto—Southern's satirical stereotype of the pompous, lecherous academic. Mephesto takes her at her word when she declares in a paper titled "Contemporary Human Love" that "to give of oneself fully—is not merely a duty prescribed by an outmoded superstition, it is a beautiful and thrilling privilege." Inviting her to his office, Mephesto flatters, wheedles, and pleads until Candy overcomes her fears and agrees to give herself to him "fully." Unbeknownst to Candy, one of Mephesto's male lovers (also a student) has spied on their liaison. Aroused, he proceeds to engage Mephesto in a bizarre ritual: "The two of them [danced] about the clothes-strewn room, stark naked, flailing each other wildly with wet hand towels, moaning and sobbing, their bodies reddened and welted." Rather than outrage or disgust at this spectacle, Candy feels guilt over initially denying Mephesto's pleadings, thinking that "her terrible selfishness" has driven him "in his frustration, to . . . goodness knows what." Thus Southern establishes Candy's improbable but amusing character as a deluded altruist in matters of sex: a trope that allows him to write pornography and social satire in equal measure.

In the wake of her encounter with Professor Mephesto, Candy decides to "give herself" to Emmanuel, the family's Mexican gardener. Unfortunately, her father enters her room in the middle of the tryst and is horror-stricken. In the ensuing melee the gardener embeds his trowel in Mr. Christian's cranium, causing what amounts to a frontal lobotomy. While her father recuperates in the hospital, Candy stays with her uncle, Jack, and his wife, Livia, a frigid but otherwise sex-obsessed alcoholic. Sex-starved Uncle Jack importunes Candy in her father's hospital room. In a variation on the episode with the gardener, Jack and Candy are caught flagrante delicto by a "heavily built" nurse and the three end up thrashing around on Mr. Christian's sickbed until it collapses and spills all four to the floor.

The "ignominious situation" in the hospital room leads to a series of equally absurd and lurid episodes that lampoon the medical profession, particularly psychiatrists and gynecologists. After Candy generously accommodates a messenger boy, she is drugged and fondled by Dr. Dunlap, the hospital director. Candy later witnesses Livia's humiliation at the hands of the onanistic Dr. Krankeit, and is even attacked by his mother (who is masquerading as a cleaning woman). Overwhelmed by the insanity at the hospital, Candy decides to go to New York City, where she hopes to "lose the old Candy in the nameless city streets."

On the streets of Greenwich Village, Candy meets an oversexed hunchback with Tourette's syndrome. Feeling sorry for him because of his deformity, she invites the man to her apartment, where she wines and dines him. He responds by demanding sex. Candy refuses at first but then relents, thinking she has hurt the man's feelings and is, at any rate, morally obliged to accommodate someone so cursed by nature. In the most outlandish and outré scene in a novel replete with them, Candy demands the man's despised feature as an instrument of her sexual pleasure: "'Your *hump,* your *hump'"* cried the girl, 'GIVE ME YOUR HUMP!'"

In the book's closing chapters Candy is groped in a restaurant lavatory, picked up on vice charges, molested by one of her arresting officers, and then rescued by Pete Uspy, a member of a religious cult called "The Crackers." She joins the cult and soon becomes a protégé of its leader, Grindle, whose idea of spiritual counseling consists of a few banal maxims and frequent and vigorous bouts of sex. In the end, Candy ventures to Lhasa, Tibet, in quest of the highest level of enlightenment— only to be ravished in a ruined temple by a "holy man" who turns out to be her demented father.

A spoof of academia, medicine, male lust, modern religious cults, and a host of other things, *Candy* is also, arguably, a satire of its own audience, or at least a segment of that audience. So argued critic Albert Goldman in a contemporary review: "Taken not as a book but as an act in the current cultural situation, *Candy* is a perfect Put On of that liberal, intellectual audience of readers and critics who are forever trying to understand and explain everything, and who seem constitutionally incapable of enjoying fantasy or humor without indulging in the cant of 'redeeming social value.'" Aiming high and low, *Candy* also spoofs the culture's bottom feeders by satirizing pornography. In its grotesque exaggeration of smut's already excessive clichés—absurdly casual, frequent, and arduous sexual acrobatics; bizarre practices and preferences; obsessive voyeurism—*Candy* points up the silliness inherent in pornography, a discourse doomed to forever repeat itself because its purview is necessarily limited and utterly predictable.

Maurice Girodias published *Candy* in October 1958 under the joint pseudonym Maxwell Kenton. According to Lee Hill, Southern had already used the alias with David Burnett, with whom he had written "some short detective stuff." He resurrected the name when Mason Hoffenberg had what Southern later described as "an attack of conscience." Southern told Mike Golden, "We took the name Maxwell Kenton so [Hoffenberg's] mother would be spared anguish at her Mah-Jong parties." Pseudonym notwithstanding, the Paris vice squad banned the book as obscene. Girodias, ever crafty, simply changed the title to *Lollipop* and reissued the novel two months later. An underground hit among the Paris cognoscenti, *Candy* was smuggled through U.S. customs. A few copies circulated around New York City in the years preceding the novel's official American publication in 1964. By then American pop culture was on Southern's wavelength; *Candy* was a hit, staying on the best-seller list for the better part of a year.

THE MAGIC CHRISTIAN

Still living in Geneva, Southern completed his third novel, *The Magic Christian,* in the early part of 1959, a few months after the initial publication of *Candy.* In classic Terry Southern fashion, *The Magic Christian* is a highly episodic black comedy that features bizarre characters and events. Uncharacteristically, though, the novel contains no sex. Instead, Southern focuses entirely on his odd protagonist, a fifty-three-year-old American billionaire named Guy Grand, a "grand guy." Intent on "making it hot for people," Grand devises demonic, hilarious pranks and practical jokes that are designed to point up the venality of his fellow citizens or the decadence of American culture, and sometimes both. His first great guerrilla-theater project is to have a large, heated concrete vat constructed in downtown Chicago, fill it with excrement, drop in ten thousand one-hundred-dollar bills, and make a sign that says "FREE $ HERE" on the side of the vat. The ensuing "commotion" provokes "the wrath of the public press against him . . . earning him the label, 'Eccentric' and again towards the end, 'Crackpot.'"

Guy Grand's stunts are of two types: small-scale capers that prove everyone has a price and large-scale operations aimed at subverting and disrupting cultural institutions and sacred cows such as newspapers, dog shows, the movies, cosmetics, boxing matches, television soap operas, the automobile industry, big-game hunting, and cruise ships. These interventions are partly for his personal amusement and partly to war against the bread-and-circus civilization of modern corporate capitalism, which he appears to detest.

Grand's large-scale escapades are expensive, risky, and involve considerable social fallout. To lay siege to American journalism, Grand buys a Boston newspaper and starts inserting foreign-language words in the midst of news items. As the paper's circulation plummets, Grand redesigns the paper, eliminating comics, editorials, feature stories, reviews, and advertising in favor of presenting "only the factual news in a straightforward manner." Paid circulation ceases altogether but Grand continues to have thousands of copies distributed throughout the city, causing a major refuse problem, widespread unrest, and, eventually, a full-scale riot in Lexington Square, carefully orchestrated by Grand. The National Guard has to be called up and martial law imposed to restore order. A media outcry and official investigations follow and Guy Grand has to pay out two million dollars in bribes "to keep clear" of the consequences.

Another Grand target is the pretentious elitism epitomized by dog shows. Buying a controlling interest in "the three largest kennel clubs on the eastern seaboard," Grand puts himself in a position to wreak havoc on an elegant Madison Square Garden dog show. In the midst of the festivities Grand introduces a big cat ("some kind of terrible black panther or dyed jaguar—hungry he was too, and cross as a pickle"). Before the day is out, the ravenous feline has "not only brought chaos into the formal proceedings, but [has] actually destroyed about half the 'Best of Breed.'"

Aiming at mainstream popular culture, Guy Grand buys a large Kansas City movie theater and begins to tinker with the films it shows. A packed house anticipates "a smart new musical" but gets a "cheap foreign film" instead. Forty-five minutes into the intolerably boring foreign film, Grand stops the projector and apologizes to the audience over the public address system. The relieved moviegoers anxiously await the film they came to see, only to be subjected once again to the foreign film, this time run upside down. Refunds are offered to the irate customers but Grand also sabotages the refunding process by constantly phoning the cashier's office. On other evenings Grand arranges to have alarming footage inserted into the films being shown. A formerly innocuous scene between Greer Garson and Walter Pidgeon in *Mrs. Miniver* is interrupted by an inexplicable and ominous close-up of a knife. A brief shot quietly inserted into a scene from the Oscar-winning *Best Years of Our Lives* purports to show the veteran who lost his hands in the war (played by real war hero Harold Russell) groping, with his metal hooks, under his fiancé's skirt.

Equally outrageous Guy Grand shenanigans include purchasing a cosmetics company only to adulterate products with delayed-action stench-bombs; paying the contender for a championship boxing title to act "in the most flamboyantly homosexual manner possible"; bribing actors in a popular television soap opera to depart from the script and denounce the show, on air, as "slobbering pomp and drivel"; manufacturing a convertible that is "longer and wider than the largest Greyhound bus in operation"; turning up at a big-game hunting expedition in the Congo with a seventy-five-millimeter howitzer. Grand's "last major project" is the building and sailing of a cruise ship (the SS *Magic Christian*) for the moneyed elite, only to subject his wealthy clientele to all manner of absurdity, terror, and humiliation on the ship's maiden voyage. As one might gather from the foregoing synopsis, *The Magic Christian* is episodic, sometimes—but not always—hilarious, deeply cynical, and extremely wide-ranging and ambitious in the scope of its satire. It is, in short, a highly entertaining novel—and Southern's best.

EAST CANAAN, CONNECTICUT

Andre Deutsch published *The Magic Christian* in England in spring 1959 to somewhat tepid reviews. At about the same time, Terry and Carol Southern decided to return to the United States, having resided in Geneva for two and a half years. After a series of sometimes awkward stints as houseguests of friends in the New York area, the Southerns bought a weathered farmhouse on twenty-seven acres of land in East Canaan, Connecticut, mostly with money from Carol's mother's inheritance. Southern wrote book reviews and occasional essays for the *Nation* and other New York magazines to bring in some sorely needed revenue. He also resumed work on "The Hipsters," a quasi-autobiographical novel-in-progress he had started in Geneva (which was never finished). Interruptions were constant, as the Southerns often had friends stay with them at the farmhouse and they made frequent trips to New York City, 120 miles south, to delve into the art and jazz scenes, hobnob with old friends, or cultivate literary contacts. It was at this time that Southern coined the wry and slightly cynical term "the Quality Lit Game" to refer to, in John Marquand's words, "the *New York Review of Books* crowd" but also, as Lee Hill puts it, "to express his ambivalence toward the somewhat

unholy blurring of commerce, careerism, and politics with lofty literary aspirations."

Having landed a job as an editor at Frederick Fell, Southern's old friend Alexander Trocchi enlisted Southern and Richard Seaver as coeditors on an anthology of avant-garde writing with the working title "Beyond the Beat." In the midst of the project, however, Trocchi had to flee the country for England, one step ahead of narcotics agents. Finished by Southern and Seaver and eventually published as *Writers in Revolt* (1963), the book contained selections by Marquis De Sade, Charles Baudelaire, Antonin Artaud, Louis Ferdinand Céline, Edward Dahlberg, Samuel Beckett, Henry Miller, Jean-Paul Sartre, Jean Genet, Allen Ginsberg, Hubert Selby Jr., and others. Though long out of print, *Writers in Revolt* remains a definitive compendium of modern underground writing.

DR. STRANGELOVE

The period from winter 1960 to fall 1962 was, in terms of financial instability, on a par with Southern's bachelor days in Greenwich Village circa 1953 through 1956. What had been an era of relative solvency ended on or about December 29, 1960, when Carol gave birth to a son, Nile. She stopped working to take care of the baby, making Terry the breadwinner—a dubious proposition at best. Now chronically and sometimes desperately short of cash, Southern supported his family on the meager proceeds from his short fiction, reviews, articles, and occasional editorial work. All of that began to change, however, when Southern got wind of the fact that filmmaker Stanley Kubrick had obtained a copy of *The Magic Christian* from Peter Sellers and had liked the book. Knowing that Kubrick would be receptive to him, Southern peddled the idea of a profile to several magazines. *Esquire* took him up on it, and the two met for a series of interviews in New York in summer 1962. As Southern later recalled,

"Somehow or other we [got] into this rather heavy rap—about *death*, and *infinity*, and the origin of *time*—you know the sort of thing. We never got through the interview, but the point is we met a few times, had a few laughs, and some groovy rap." A few months later, on November 2, Southern received a telegram from London. It was from Kubrick, offering two thousand dollars a month for three months to help work on the script for his new film. In dire need of paying work, Southern accepted the offer, half aware that it would drastically change the direction of his life.

Stanley Kubrick, just thirty-four years old in 1962, had already made such noted films as *The Killing, Paths of Glory, Spartacus,* and *Lolita.* A highly organized perfectionist known for his obsessive attention to detail, Kubrick was regarded as one of Hollywood's most talented and promising young directors. Kubrick's forthcoming film was to be an adaptation of the British novel *Two Hours to Doom,* a cold war suspense thriller by Peter Bryant (pseudonym for Peter George), a former Royal Air Force lieutenant turned mystery writer who was also active in the nuclear disarmament movement. The book (titled *Red Alert* in its U.S. edition) presents the ultimate nightmare scenario: a U.S. Air Force general goes insane, fakes a nuclear war alert at his Strategic Air Command base in Sonora, New Mexico, and orders the bombers under his command to attack the Soviet Union— drastic action allowed under an emergency protocol. As the planes speed toward their targets, American and Soviet leaders frantically try to avert nuclear Armageddon—and just barely succeed.

Fascinated by the technological and geopolitical intricacies of the nuclear arms race, Kubrick was, at the same time, horrified by the mad rationality of it all. *Two Hours to Doom* was the perfect vehicle for him but early efforts at a screenplay, cowritten with Peter George, rendered unsatisfactory results. Serious in tone and full of arcane technical detail, George's novel matter-of-factly depicted events that boggled the mind. It finally dawned on Kubrick that so surreal a scenario would have to be treated as black comedy to tacitly acknowledge its inherent absurdity. In an interview for *Films and Filming* (June 1963), Kubrick stated that in trying to "imagine the scenes fully one had to keep leaving things out of it which were either absurd or paradoxical, in order to keep it from being funny, and these things seemed to be very real." He concluded that "the perfect tone to adopt for the film would be what I now call nightmare comedy." Kubrick's biographer, John Baxter, argues that the change in tone was equally a matter of pragmatism. With "half a dozen other nuclear or post-nuclear dramas . . . either in preparation or . . . already circulating," Kubrick needed to make his movie distinctive.

Kubrick and George retained the novel's plot structure and extensive technical paraphernalia but overlaid that with comic dialogue and silly character names, such as General "Buck" Schmuck, Admiral Percy Buldike, Lt. "Binky" Ballmuff, Capt. "Ace" Angst, and so forth. Kubrick was closer to what he wanted but not quite there. The revised script still contained some nagging defects: prolix dialogue, a sometimes too obvious straining for laughs, or simply unaccountable weirdness. It was at this point that Kubrick called in Southern. Coincidentally, Kubrick's telegraph inviting Southern to London was sent only days after the resolution of the Cuban missile crisis: the moment the two superpowers came within a hair's breadth of thermonuclear war.

As soon as Southern arrived, Peter George bowed out of the film project. A chronically depressed alcoholic, George had to be hospitalized for bleeding ulcers, and he committed suicide in 1966. If Kubrick's collaboration with George had been less than he had hoped for, his writing partnership with Southern proved to be stellar. Kindred spirits in their iconoclasm, Southern and Kubrick quickly developed a symbiotic working relationship that would result in a markedly improved script. In his interview with Mike Golden, Southern described their routine with fondness:

> Working with Stanley was terrific. It was ideal, although the circumstances may seem peculiar—in the back seat of a big car. The film was being shot at Shepperton [Studios], outside London, in the winter. So he would pick me up at 4:30 in the morning and we would make this hour-long trip to the studio. It was in a big Bentley or a Rolls [Royce], so the passenger part was something like a railway compartment, with folding-out writing desks and good lighting. It would be pitch-black outside and really cold, and we would be in this cozy-rosey compartment, in a creative groove, working on the scene to be shot that day.

Mike Golden asked Southern whether they were writing the shot or rewriting it. Southern replied, "Well, let's say [we were] trying to improve it. Kubrick would say 'Now what's the most outrageous thing this guy (a character in the scene) would say at this point?' and hopefully I would come up with something like 'If you try any preversion [*sic*] in there, I'll blow your head off.'"

The script developed by Kubrick and Peter George included a cumbersome framing device in which a "weird, hydra-headed furry" extraterrestrial named Nardac Blefescu introduces the story and comments on it at the end. Kubrick wisely chose to drop the framing segments, which would have given the picture the smarmy aura of a cheap 1950s science fiction movie. Another major change was the elimination of a massive pie-fight in the War Room during the film's final scene. According to Southern, the pie-fight was supposed to exemplify the internecine rivalry among the various branches of the U.S. military. As such it needed to be edgy, even vicious, but all the pie throwing proved to be too much fun for the partici-

pants, who were caught on film laughing gleefully. As Southern pointed out to Mike Golden, "It was like a comedy scene, when everything else in the film had been played straight." Though Kubrick went to a great deal of trouble to set up and shoot the pie-fight, his decision to delete it was fortuitous. To end the film with slapstick would have ruined the deadpan absurdist tone that had been so carefully cultivated up to that point.

Judicious scene trimming helped but, in the final analysis, it was really Southern's zany wit, linguistic inventiveness, and perfect comic pitch that turned the lumbering, unfunny Kubrick-George script into the satiric masterpiece *Dr. Strangelove; or, How I Learned to Stop Worrying and Love the Bomb* (1964). This is patently obvious when one compares the Kubrick-George version to Southern's at almost any juncture. A particularly dramatic example of Southern's skillful revision is manifest in one of the film's funniest and most famous scenes: President Merkin Muffley's emergency phone call to the Russian premier. From the Kubrick-George script:

> Hello? ... Yes ... Uh-huh ...certainly I understand ... Oh someone tried it on you once before ... Look, Belch, I'll tell you why I called ... Hello ... Hello ... Can you hear me? ... Say, could they turn the music down a little? ... Oh, well, could they stop playing? ... Oh, good, I thought we lost the connection there for a minute ... yes, I hear you very clearly ... Well, look ... (clears throat) You know how we've always talked about the possibility of something going wrong? ... With the H-bomb ... uh-huh ... that's right ... Well, it happened ... Hello? ... Can you still hear me? ...What? ... Not missiles—planes ... that's right ... B-90's ... That's right ... Thirty-four of them ... In about an hour and a half ... uh-huh ... Uh-huh ... Uh-huh ... Well, how do you think I feel about it? ... I know that ... Uh-huh ... Uh-huh ... Well, why do you think I'm calling you?

Southern's version of the same passage:

Hello? Uh, hello? Hello, Dmitri? Listen, I can't hear too well, do you suppose you could turn the music down just a little? Oh, that's much better. Yes. Fine, I can hear you now, Dmitri. Clear and plain and coming through fine. I'm coming through fine too, eh? Good, then. Well then, as you say we're both coming through fine. Good. Well, it's good that you're fine, and—and I'm fine. I agree with you. It's great to be fine. (Laughs) Now then, Dmitri, you know how we've always talked about the possibility of something going wrong with the bomb. The *BOMB,* Dmitri. The *hydrogen* bomb. Well now, what happened is, uh, one of our base commanders, he had a sort of, well, he went a little *funny* in the head. You know. Just a little ... funny. And uh, he went and did a silly thing. Well, I'll tell you what he did, he ordered his planes ... to attack your country. Well, let me *finish,* Dmitri. Let me finish, Dmitri. Well, listen, how do you think I feel about it? Can you imagine how I feel about it, Dmitri? Why do you think I'm calling you? Just to say hello? *Of course* I like to speak to you. *Of course* I like to say hello. Not now, but any time, Dmitri. I'm just calling up to tell you something terrible has happened. It's a friendly call. Of course it's a friendly call. Listen, if it wasn't friendly ... you probably wouldn't have even got it ...

Southern's rendition is vastly superior to the Kubrick-George version not only in terms of pacing and language but also because it manages to make Muffley and Premier Kissof (Belch in the earlier version) into three-dimensional, quirky characters with a prior history. In Southern's hands, the Soviet premier—who is a cipher in the earlier version—comes alive as a comically petulant and emotionally vulnerable child to President Muffley's unctuous school-teacher persona. What makes the scene both surreal and hilarious, of course, is the juxtaposition of puerile banalities with the terrifying magnitude of the situation, with the fate of the Earth hanging in the balance.

The figure of Dr. Strangelove—the sinister former Nazi (with an unruly bionic arm) who is the president's key policy advisor on nuclear war—does not appear in George's novel or in the Kubrick-George script. It is not clear whether Kubrick or Southern invented him but his addition to the script turned out to be a stroke of comic genius. Played with maniacal verve by Peter Sellers (who also played President Muffley and Royal Air Force captain Lionel Mandrake), Dr. Strangelove comes to embody the demented logic of the cold war in the way he obsesses over technical means with no thought as to the gruesome end results. In his own peculiar way, Strangelove is just as mad as General Jack D. Ripper (played by Sterling Hayden), the paranoid SAC commander who launches the unauthorized attack Equally crazy is General "Buck" Turgidson (played by George C. Scott), head of the Strategic Air Command, who advises an all-out attack in support of Ripper's rogue initiative. The only sane person in the War Room is the bald, bespectacled, and mild-mannered President Muffley, who functions as the straight man to his asinine cohorts.

Peter George's didactic novel ends optimistically, with nuclear war averted and American and Soviet leaders sobered as to the dire implications of the arms race. Kubrick, always distrustful of the supposed beneficence of modern technology and cynical about human nature, gave the film an apocalyptic ending that remained unchanged throughout the George and Southern collaborations. In the end, one of the American bombers reaches its target and drops a hydrogen bomb, which triggers a secret Soviet doomsday device designed to lay waste to the entire planet. During the film's closing seconds Vera Lynn sings "We'll Meet Again" on the soundtrack as a series of nuclear explosions spell the end of life on Earth.

After fifteen weeks of shooting, principal photography on *Dr. Strangelove* was wrapped up in early April 1963 and postproduction was completed that fall. The film opened in January 1964 and proved to be a sensation, despite critical controversy over the propriety of mocking the nation's civilian and military elites, especially in the wake of President Kennedy's assassination. At the time of the film's release, Southern and Hoffenberg had just signed a deal with Putnam for an American edition of *Candy.* Furthermore, on the strength of his work on *Dr. Strangelove,* Southern was approached by Hollywood producers John Calley and Martin Ransohoff to work on *The Loved One,* an adaptation of Evelyn Waugh's 1948 spoof of the funeral industry. Lee Hill identifies January 1964 as "the flash point for [Southern's] increasing celebrity."

THE LOVED ONE

In spring 1964 Southern and his family moved out to Hollywood, where he started work on *The Loved One* (1965) with coscreenwriter Christopher Isherwood. Basking in the twin glories of *Dr. Strangelove* and *Candy,* Southern shed the last vestiges of his life as a struggling author of "Quality Lit" for that of celebrity screenwriter with unlimited access to all the elements of a sybaritic lifestyle: plenty of money, alcohol, drugs, and beautiful young women. Predictably, Southern's eight-year marriage began to falter, especially after Carol returned to their Connecticut home with Nile that fall. Southern was supposed to return as well, but he had met a young dancer named Gail Gerber and the two had fallen in love. Eventually Carol took Nile and left the East Canaan house. The marriage was essentially over by the end of 1964 but its demise was not made official by divorce until 1972. Gerber stayed with Southern until the end of his life, but they never married.

Increasingly muddled in his personal life, Southern helped bring an interesting muddle to the big screen. If *Dr. Strangelove* pushed the envelope of what was possible in cinematic black comedy, *The Loved One* burst the bubble altogether. Easily one of the weirdest, most incongruous films of the 1960s or any era, *The Loved One* lived up to its tagline—"The motion picture with something to offend everyone!"—by lampooning the funeral business, Hollywood studios, corporate America, the military, the space race, prudery, homosexuality, cult gurus, gluttony, "lonely-hearts" columns, and many other aspects of American culture.

The main plot, loosely adapted from Evelyn Waugh's novel by director Tony Richardson together with Isherwood and Southern, concerns a young Englishman named Dennis Barlow (played by the gap-toothed comic actor Robert Morse) who comes to Hollywood to seek work under the sponsorship of his uncle, set designer Sir Francis Hinsely (Sir John Gielgud). Shortly after Barlow's arrival, however, Sir Francis is fired from his studio job and subsequently hangs himself. While arranging his uncle's interment at Whispering Glades, an outsized funeral theme park (exteriors shot at the Harold Lloyd Estate), Barlow meets Aimée Thanatogenous (Greek for "child of death"; played by Anjanette Comer), a chaste funeral cosmetician, and is instantly smitten. Barlow's subsequent efforts to win Miss Thanatogenous are not only hampered by her inherent modesty but also by the strict rules of the Whispering Glades owner, the "Blessed Reverend" Wilbur Glenworthy (Jonathan Winters), which forbid staff fraternization with clientele. Another stumbling block is the jealous rivalry of Mr. Joyboy (Rod Steiger), a fey, mother-fixated embalmer. If that were not enough, Barlow is embarrassed by his employment at The Happier Hunting Grounds, a mere pet cemetery. Unable to choose between Mr. Joyboy and Barlow, Aimée seeks the advice of Guru Brahmin—in reality, a gruff, alcoholic newspaper columnist named Mr. Slump, who has just been fired. The bitter, inebriated Slump counsels her to commit suicide. She obliges, by embalming herself.

Such is, more or less, the substance of Waugh's novel. In *The Log Book of "The Loved One,"* a commemorative tie-in edition published at the time of the film's release, Southern admitted that he and his writing cohorts got carried away and expanded Waugh's original narrative to elephantine proportions. The first rough cut of the film was almost five hours long and required massive editing. The film historian Gene D. Phillips notes in *The Cinema of Tony Richardson: Essays and Interviews* (1999) that "in the course of all these revisions, Waugh's original story got mislaid, just as he feared it would." While the love triangle plot at the heart of the novel shrank, Southern and his coscreenwriters concocted a bizarre subplot in which the Reverend Mr. Glenworthy teams up with the space program to launch corpses into orbit so as to relieve congestion at Whispering Glades. In the end, both plot strands are tied together when Barlow surreptitiously arranges to have Aimée's corpse blasted into space in the place of a deceased war hero. (In Waugh's novel Barlow cremates Aimée in the Happier Hunting Grounds incinerator.)

The final result of so much writing, tinkering, reshuffling, and poetic license was a sprawling, episodic mess of a film that did not please critics or charm the moviegoing public. The consensus was that Tony Richardson had lost control of his material. Gene D. Phillips observes that, despite some zany moments, "*The Loved One* takes far too many liberties with the Waugh original to retain much of its flavor." Evelyn Waugh hated the film and asked to be disassociated from it. Almost as if in protest, he died two weeks after *The Loved One* premiered in London in spring 1966.

THE CINCINNATI KID

Immediately after *The Loved One* was completed, Southern was hired by the producer Martin Ransohoff to help refine and improve the script of *The Cincinnati Kid* (1965), a suspense film that would do for stud poker what Robert Rossen's *The Hustler* (1961) had done for pool. Based on Richard Jessup's 1963 novel of the same name, *The Cincinnati Kid* starred Steve McQueen in the title role, as a young card sharp come to depression-era New Orleans to take on "The Man," that is, Lancey Howard (Edward G. Robinson), aging master of the game. The stakes are high: a sizable fortune and confirmed status as the country's top player.

The project proved to be a something of a headache for Ransohoff. Sam Peckinpah, the film's original director, was fired after shooting unauthorized nude scenes. A relatively inexperienced Norman Jewison was brought in to replace Peckinpah a week into principal photography. The script was bothersome as well. Jessup's novel was relatively short and straightforward and needed embellishment to give it more depth and texture but script development proved complicated and costly. Before Southern was brought in, Paddy Chayefsky wrote a script, then George Good, then Ring Lardner Jr. Along the line, several plot complications were added to heighten dramatic tension. One invention had the Kid confronting a moral dilemma when he discovers that the game is rigged against his chief opponent, Lancey Howard. Also added was a romantic subplot in which the Kid has an affair with his friend's wife, Melba (Ann-Margret), which jeopardizes his relationship with his girlfriend, Christian (Tuesday Weld). A good film but by no means a great one, *The Cincinnati Kid* was a hit at the box office when it was released in October 1965. Southern shared screenwriting credit with Ring Lardner Jr.

CASINO ROYALE

In early 1966 Peter Sellers contacted Southern through his agent, Gareth Wigan, and asked Southern to write some dialogue for him. The film Sellers was working on was *Casino Royale* (1967), a big-budget James Bond spoof that was the brainchild of Charles K. Feldman, a prominent Hollywood agent and producer of such classics as *Red River, The Glass Menagerie, A Streetcar Named Desire, The Seven Year Itch,* and *Walk on the Wild Side.* Feldman owned the rights to *Casino Royale,* the only Ian Fleming property *not* owned by Albert R. "Cubby" Broccoli and Harry Saltzman. Having just produced Woody Allen's hit sex comedy *What's New, Pussycat?* (1965), Feldman hoped to repeat his success with *Casino Royale.* In adapting Fleming's novel to the screen, Feldman took what was essentially a grim and serious spy thriller and turned it into a boisterous farce. Worried, perhaps, that the public would not buy such an irreverent take on their beloved James Bond, Feldman hoped to cover his bets by throwing excessive amounts of money and talent at the project. In addition to Sellers, the all-star cast included David Niven, Woody Allen, Ursula Andress, Charles Boyer, William Holden, John Huston, Deborah Kerr, and Orson Welles. Inevitably, assembling so many major stars for one picture produced ego clashes. Allen and Sellers quickly came to loathe each other, as did Sellers and Welles. Temperamental and volatile, Sellers would disappear from the set for days at a time, bringing production to a grinding halt. Feldman himself sabotaged the film by constantly meddling with every aspect of the project. He fired Joseph McGrath, his original director, and later rehired him, after hiring and firing Val Guest, Ken Hughes, Robert Parrish, and John Huston. Feldman went through writers with equal abandon. Wolf Mankowitz, John Law, and Michael Savers ultimately received screenwriting credit but Woody Allen, Val Guest, Ben Hecht, Joseph Heller, Billy Wilder, Peter Sellers, and Southern also worked on the script.

After a full year in production, *Casino Royale* was released in Britain in late January 1967.

The final result of so much creative overkill was an unfunny, sprawling mess even more disjointed and silly than *The Loved One.* Flogged by critics and disavowed by James Bond purists, *Casino Royale* was something of an embarrassment to those officially associated with it but Southern emerged unscathed; like most of the writers on the project, he received no screen credit. Lee Hill reports that Southern did receive twenty-five thousand dollars compensation, plus free transatlantic air fare, first-class lodging in London, and a generous per diem.

BARBARELLA

Southern's next major assignment was to polish the film script of *Barbarella, Queen of the Galaxy,* a spoof of the science-fiction-fantasy genre. An international film project (filmed in Rome with financing from France, Italy, and the United States) produced by Paramount's Dino De Laurentiis, directed by Roger Vadim and starring Vadim's wife, Jane Fonda, *Barbarella* was based on a popular French comic strip of the same name, created by Jean-Claude Forest. Vittorio Bonicelli, Claude Brulé, Brian Degas, and Jean-Claude Forest wrote the original screenplay in French. The British screenwriter Tudor Gates translated the script into English, and director Vadim and writer Clement Biddle Wood worked on rewrites until Southern was hired on in April 1967 while the film was being shot. Though it is difficult to know what Southern's specific contributions were to the final script, the film's voluptuous but naive heroine, its gentle mockery of genre conventions, and its lighthearted comic tone are very much in keeping with Southern's sensibilities. Characterized by Roger Vadim as "a kind of sexual Alice in Wonderland of the future," *Barbarella* follows the forty-first-century adventures of the scantily clad title character (played by Jane Fonda) as she travels to the distant planet of Lytheon in an effort to find and thwart Duran Duran (Milo O'Shea), an evil scientist who threatens the universal peace. But the plot is incidental to the real purpose of the film, which is to display Fonda as provocatively as possible while slyly mocking her character's sexual innocence. Dressed out in Federico Fellini–inspired costumes and garish futuristic sets, *Barbarella* aspires to be nothing more than a motion-picture comic book—campy, silly, and prurient throughout.

EASY RIDER

In fall 1967, while work on *Barbarella* was winding down, Southern was approached by Peter Fonda and Dennis Hopper with a proposal for a modern Western that would feature its two protagonists on motorcycles instead of horses. Southern was taken with the idea and the three began a series of marathon story conferences in New York City in late November. What ultimately emerged was a story that involved two stunt riders, Wyatt, known by the moniker "Captain America" (played by Fonda), and Billy (Hopper), who buy cocaine in Mexico and sell it to a dealer in Los Angeles. After Wyatt stashes the profits in the teardrop gas tank of his bike, the two proceed east, across the country's southern tier, toward Key West, where they hope to buy a boat and live the good life. Along the way, they encounter various contradictory embodiments of contemporary America: a rancher and his family, a hippie commune, southern rednecks, and, most notably, George Hanson (Jack Nicholson, in his breakthrough role), an alcoholic lawyer with progressive tendencies. Hanson joins the pair but is later murdered by rednecks. Wyatt and Billy make it to New Orleans in time for Mardi Gras but the festivities turn into a nightmare after they meet two prostitutes and decide to take LSD in a New Orleans cemetery. Chastened by the somber experiences they have had along the way, Wyatt

and Billy resume their journey to Key West— only to encounter armed rednecks in a pickup truck who shoot them dead. So much for their version of the American dream.

Fonda and Hopper verbalized the story but Southern actually *wrote* most of the script, invented the Hanson character, and came up with the title (which is a slang term for the boyfriend of a prostitute who lives off her earnings). Southern and Fonda finished the script in spring 1968, but Hopper and Fonda cut out much of Southern's dialogue during the film's shooting phase, which was completed by June. *Easy Rider's* downbeat, nihilistic perspective on America was in perfect keeping with a major sea change in the zeitgeist of the counterculture, a change precipitated by the assassinations of Martin Luther King Jr. and Bobby Kennedy and the disastrously violent Chicago Democratic Convention that summer (which Southern attended with Jean Genet and William S. Burroughs, on assignment for *Esquire* magazine). When the film was released in summer 1969, it struck a deep chord with disillusioned American youth and became a runaway hit that grossed more than nineteen million dollars at the box office—fifty-six times what it cost to make. As principal screenwriter, Southern should have been made wealthy but he got next to nothing because he waived his usual fee for scale wages to accommodate Fonda and Hopper's slim production budget. Though a profit-sharing deal was talked about, it was never put in place. To add insult to financial injury, Fonda and Hopper insisted on sharing screenwriting credit with Southern and proceeded, forever after, to minimize Southern's contributions to the film.

AFTER THE DELUGE

The late 1960s was one of the busiest periods of Southern's career as a writer. In addition to his work on *Easy Rider*, Southern wrote a screen adaptation of his own novel, *The Magic Christian,* for a 1970 Joseph McGrath film starring Peter Sellers and Ringo Starr. At the same time Southern adapted John Barth's first novel, *End of the Road* (1958), for a low-budget film directed by his friend Aram Avakian and starring Stacey Keach and James Earl Jones. Produced by Southern, Stephen Kesten, and Max Raab, the 1970 film *End of the Road* is a harrowing study of a man succumbing to madness, but it was largely ignored by critics and the public. Meanwhile, Southern also completed *Blue Movie,* a novel about the making of a high-quality pornographic film—an idea he and Kubrick had pondered during their *Dr. Strangelove* days. Published in 1970, *Blue Movie* was generally lambasted by critics.

As the 1960s ended and the counterculture it spawned gave way to a resurgent military-industrial hegemony marked by the old priorities—neopuritanism, law and order, accumulation of capital—Terry Southern fell on hard times. The Internal Revenue Service hounded him for back taxes, his particular brand of humor and satire fell out of vogue, and he could no longer get projects funded. He retreated to the old farmhouse in East Canaan with Gail Gerber, taught screenwriting at Columbia University, and only occasionally surfaced in other venues. He wrote captions for several books of photographs (two on the Rolling Stones, one on Virgin Records); created the script for *The Electric Lady* (1980), an inconsequential soft-core pornography film; and joined his friend Harry Nilsson in cowriting *The Telephone* (1988), a Whoopi Goldberg comedy that garnered terrible reviews. Southern's last hurrah was *Texas Summer* (1991), a novel that harks back to his boyhood in depression-era Texas. After a life of creativity, travel, hedonism, and celebrity worthy of one of his film scripts, Terry Southern had come full circle. He died from respiratory disease on October 29, 1995. He was seventy-one years old.

Selected Bibliography

WORKS OF TERRY SOUTHERN

NOVELS

Candy. (With Mason Hoffenberg under the joint pseudonym Maxwell Kenton) Paris: Olympia Press, 1958.

Flash and Filigree. London: Andre Deutsch, 1958.

The Magic Christian. London: Andre Deutsch, 1959.

Blue Movie. New York: New World Publishing, 1970.

Texas Summer. New York: Arcade/Little, Brown, 1991.

SCREENPLAYS

Dr. Strangelove; or, How I Learned to Stop Worrying and Love the Bomb. (With Stanley Kubrick.) Produced and directed by Stanley Kubrick. Columbia Pictures, 1964.

The Cincinnati Kid. (With Ring Lardner Jr.) Produced by Martin Ransohoff, directed by Norman Jewison. MGM, 1965.

The Loved One. (With Christopher Isherwood.) Produced by Haskell Wexler, directed by Tony Richardson. MGM, 1965.

Barbarella, Queen of the Galaxy. (With Vittori Bonicelli, Claude Brulé, Brian Degas, Jean-Claude Forest, Tudor Gates, Roger Vadim, and Clement Biddle Wood.) Produced by Dino De Laurentiis, directed by Roger Vadim. Paramount Pictures, 1968.

Easy Rider. (With Peter Fonda and Dennis Hopper.) Produced by Peter Fonda, directed by Dennis Hopper. Columbia Pictures, 1969.

End of the Road. (With Dennis McGuire and Aram Avakian.) Produced by Southern, Stephen Kesten, and Max Raab, directed by Aram Avakian. Allied Artists, 1970.

SHORT STORIES AND JOURNALISM

Red Dirt Marijuana and Other Tastes. New York: New World Publishing, 1967.

Now Dig This! The Unpeakable Writings of Terry Southern, 1950–1995. Edited by Nile Southern and Josh Alan Friedman. New York: Grove Press, 2001.

NONFICTION

Writers in Revolt. Edited with Richard Seaver and Alexander Trocchi. New York: Frederick Fell, 1963.

The Log Book of "The Loved One." Photographs by William Claxton. New York: Random House, 1965.

The Rolling Stones on Tour: A Log Book. Photographs by Annie Leibowitz. Paris and London: Dragon's Dream, 1978.

The Early Stones: Legendary Photographs of a Band in the Making, 1963–1973. (With Perry Richardson) Photographs by Michael Cooper. New York: Hyperion, 1992.

Virgin: A History of Virgin Records. (With Perry Anderson) London: A Publishing Company, 1995.

SPOKEN WORD RECORDING

Give Me Your Hump: The Unspeakable Terry Southern Record. Koch Records, 2001.

CRITICAL AND BIOGRAPHICAL STUDIES

Golden, Mike. "'Now Dig This': The Terry Southern Interview." *Smoke Signals* (http://www.carminestreet.com/smoke_signals.html#terry.southern).

Hill, Lee. *A Grand Guy: The Art and Life of Terry Southern.* New York: HarperCollins, 2001.

McAninch, Jerry. "Terry Southern." In *Dictionary of Literary Biography.* Vol. 2, *American Novelists since World War II.* Detroit: Gale, 1978. Pp. 452–455.

Murray, D. M. "Candy Christian as a Pop-Art Daisy Miller." *Journal of Popular Culture* 5:340–348 (1971).

Silva, Edward T. "From Candide to Candy: Love's Labor Lost." *Journal of Popular Culture* 8:783–791 (1974).

Southern, Nile. "Grand Dad Terry: Growing up with Terry Southern." *Gadflyonline* (http://www.gadfly.org/7-23-01/FTR-SOUTHERN.html).

FILM BASED ON A WORK OF TERRY SOUTHERN

The Magic Christian. Produced by Denis O'Dell, directed by Joseph McGrath. Commonwealth United Entertainment, 1969.

—ROBERT NIEMI

William Stafford

1914–1993

For WILLIAM STAFFORD, the process of writing was the product. It would be difficult to find a more prolific American twentieth-century poet. His habit of writing daily—usually beginning at about four or five in the morning—garnered him close to 5,000 individually published poems and sixty-seven books of verse and prose. The fact that his first book was not published until he was forty-six years old makes this accomplishment all the more significant. His commitment to process also is evidenced in his journal entries and essays on writing, the workshop, and pedagogy. The critic Peter Stitt, in *On William Stafford,* writes that "William Stafford's conception of his poetry is really not any larger than the scope of the individual poem, as seen—reductively, the critic has to feel—from inside the creative process." When panning through Stafford's body of work, one sees remarkable similarities over a forty-year span. But when one zooms in on particular poems, which is the recommended practice, one sees subtle modulations and intricacies rather than global transformations in Stafford's writing.

At the heart of Stafford's poetry is an anticipated nostalgia and active engagement with that past through written art. "Art is a touch-and-go affair," Stafford says in one journal entry. He goes on:

> Some things, when you learn how, you're not doing them anymore. For they are a gift; you can't demand them. You have no right, just the privilege, and it may be taken away or awarded all over again. [Søren] Kierkegaard tells how a head of lettuce, to have that succulent heart, requires time, leisure. He compares this to the meditation time,

the dwelling in the inner life, that real human living requires.

The notion of acquiring and realizing one's soul, in Stafford's vision, is achieved most profoundly and resonantly through the everyday discipline of looking inward. This, in turn, provides him a view of the precise mystery that is the world. His poems—primarily hovering around the length of a sonnet with the compressed meditative and imagistic sweep of a haiku or tanka—investigate and illustrate the struggles and rewards of this universally introspective project.

Because Stafford's poems strive to approach rather than to arrive, the reader also must be attentive and open. For Stafford, epiphany begets epiphany begets epiphany; there is no end to this process, only edge after edge of possibility. Or, as he says in "An Introduction to Some Poems" (from *Someday, Maybe,* 1973), "The authentic is a line from one thing / along to the next." Despite this open-ended approach to writing, his vision has a clear direction. Back of it, his technique and lexicon are as fluid, musical, and agile as they are colloquial, plain, and simple. His evenness in tone has drawn comparisons to Randall Jarrell and William Carlos Williams. As Ralph J. Mills notes in "Like Talk," Stafford himself comments that Thomas Hardy was his "most congenial poetry landmark." One could say that Stafford's most resilient attribute is the seeming absence of poetic tricks. In presenting him with the National Book Award in 1963 for his second book, *Traveling through the Dark* (1962), the judges wrote, "Stafford's poems are clean, direct, and whole. They are both tough and gentle; their music knows also the value of silence." This is indeed true, for a consistent understatement and a benevolent authority are the prime movers in generating the resonance underneath Stafford's poems.

Part of this authority is founded in a firm moral vision. While his poems do not adhere to one strand of faith, there is an inherent goodness that wants to exist in Stafford's world: the anonymous acts of charity afforded by nature, the magnanimous gestures of strangers and weather, the humble perfection of animals. All of these elements are heard in Stafford's daily attempts to capture natural speech while still maintaining their integrity as "local things." In this way, Stafford carries on the discursive tradition of speaking to and for the middle classes as seen in the work of William Wordsworth and Robert Frost, among others. The poet James Dickey, in *On William Stafford,* writes that Stafford's "natural speech is a gentle, mystical, half-mocking and highly personal daydreaming about the landscape of the western United States." Stephen Stepanchev, in *American Poetry Since 1945: A Critical Survey,* comments that Stafford is a kind of "Western Robert Frost, forever amazed by the spaces of America, inner and outer. . . . Sometimes he sees ironic reversals in the old struggle between man and nature and makes wry comment. . . . Out of such awareness comes . . . a sharp appraisal of one's surroundings and a self-reliance in tune with nature—reminiscent of [Ralph Waldo] Emerson." Still, Stafford is no blind idealist. While he may want to believe in a benign will of the universe, he does not close his eyes to the harsher and crueler events in the worlds of nature and modern daily living. In this way, Stafford aligns himself with Wallace Stevens, Robinson Jeffers, and Czeslaw Milosz, among others.

Whatever emotional hues they may project, all things, for Stafford, are first words. Certain words serve as points on a compass that point him, and us, as he says in his poem "Vocation"

(from *Traveling in the Dark*), toward "what the world is trying is to be." The critic Judith Kitchen notices this aspect of Stafford's poetry, saying, "It is possible to view William Stafford's work, more than the work of most other poets, as if it had been written all at once. . . . It is difficult to tell poems that were first printed in *West of Your City* [his first book, published in 1960] from poems that appeared over twenty-five years later in *An Oregon Message.*" Among Stafford's linguistic touchstones are "home," "snow," "Father," "listen," "swerve," "world," and "river." As one eases through his oeuvre, these words accrue significance. Sometimes they serve as symbols for larger concepts and ideas; at other times they are as they may appear in the world of physical experience. "Home" can be the self or the poet. "Snow" is at times the page. Complicit in metaphor are the poem, all art, and all created things. While "Father" is frequently the speaker/poet's father, at other times he is the speaker/poet himself. "Listen" and "swerve" not only are involuntary and practiced acts of the speaker/poet, they also serve as instructions for himself, his students, and his ostensible readers. "World" for Stafford is a place whose clarity often is shrouded by a gauzy light; perhaps it is closest to the imagination, the soul, the mind, or the sublimely realized self. Whichever, for Stafford it is mysteriously and undeniably there. For "river" Stafford brings his own story to the trope. As Stafford wrote in *You Must Revise Your Life* (1986),

My life in writing, or my life as a writer, comes to me as two parts, like two rivers that blend. One part is easy to tell: the times, the places, events, people. The other part is mysterious; it is my thoughts, the flow of my inner life, the reveries and impulses that never get known—perhaps even to me. . . .

My writings are current manifestations of that blending.

He elaborates on this idea as he recounts an adolescent memory—what Stafford called a "dream vision"—along the banks of the Cimarron River. It was, he says:

> . . . one experience too strange and fervent to become a story.
>
> It was like an Indian vision-quest. I was in Liberal High School, and one autumn afternoon on a weekend I got on my bike with a camping pack (the sleeping bag was probably a blanket and safety pins) and rode ten or twelve miles to the Cimarron River northeast of town. I hid my bike and climbed into the breaks above the river. It is all open country, miles of red-brown brush and grass. A few cottonwoods and willows lined the river far down—maybe a mile—from me. On that still, serene day I stayed and watched. How slow and majestic the day was, and the sunset. No person anywhere, nothing, just space, the solid earth, gradually a star, the stars. Quail sounds, a coyote yapping.
>
> In the middle of the night I woke and saw a long, lighted passenger train slowly pulling along across the far horizon. No sound. Steady stars. The morning was dim, sure, an imperceptible brightening of sky with yellow, gray, orange, and then the powerful sun. That encounter with the size and serenity of the earth and its neighbors in the sky has never left me. The earth was my home; I would never feel lost while it held me.

The quiet strength and calm certitude found in Stafford's work seem to stem from this experience. Which is to say that he has traveled through self-examination—all of its attendant doubt, despair, joy, and faith—and arrived at some "crescendo of knowing," as he puts it in "Representing Far Places."

Stafford's poems, for all of their gentle nuggets of wisdom and generosity, contain a streak of moral rebellion. In his own quiet manner, he was particularly critical of the U.S. government and military. With the onset of World War II, his moral convictions were tested, and Stafford registered as a conscientious objector. Kitchen quotes from a passage he wrote in 1985 in *Down in My Heart*: "Back then—and now, one group stays apart from the usual ways of facing war.

They exist now—and they did then—in all countries. Those who refuse the steps along that way are a small group, and their small role is a footnote in the big histories." Still, Stafford steers clear of ever sounding bitter, elitist, and didactic in his poems. He avoids preaching and explicit political posturing by focusing on the singular elements and inhabitants affected by militaristic violence and political turmoil, voicing his stance in the language of poetry, which he calls, in *You Must Revise Your Life,* speaking without mistakes, "'lucky talk.' A Poem is a lucky piece of talk." He chooses to stay alert to the "maintenance or repair work of my integrity," which he performed every morning composing poems. His strongest poems not only arrive at dramatization of a consciousness; they also illuminate the conception of a singular, yet universal reality.

LIFE AND CAREER

William Edgar Stafford, born January 17, 1914, in Hutchinson, Kansas, was the eldest of three children born to Earl Ingersoll, a businessman, and Ruby Nina Mayher Stafford, a homemaker. Despite growing up during the Great Depression, Stafford seems to have lived a happy childhood, spending the lion's share of his youth in the countryside and working to help the family make ends meet. Early jobs for Stafford included farming, tending sugar beet fields, delivering newspapers (which at one point served as the family's only source of income), and working as an electrician's assistant. To find and keep work, the family moved frequently throughout the state of Kansas, including stops in Hutchinson, Wichita, Liberal, Garden City, El Dorado, and Lawrence.

One constant in the Stafford home was books. "And in the center of town," Stafford writes in *You Must Revise Your Life,* "was a library, another kind of edge, out there forever, to explore. . . . This territory of the book looms so much in our lives that it seems natural that we would write, engaging in the other half of the transaction." The other constant was church, most likely situated next to the libraries in many of the towns the Staffords called home. Stafford learned the values of justice, individuality, and tolerance in these communities. His father served as an ethical and moral role model, while his mother provided him with a more personal response to living; it was her voice, Stafford said, that he heard most in his poems. "In later life," Stafford recalls in the same volume, "other people, other writers, would talk to me about rebellion, about resentments against parents. My parents didn't fit the patterns I heard about. . . . And they never pretended that I wouldn't have my own life, my own way of living. They stood to one side and watched." Here we can see the beginnings of Stafford's poetic project: an individual's intimate response to the shared experiences of the human condition.

After high school Stafford attended El Dorado and Garden City junior colleges and earned a bachelor's degree from the University of Kansas in 1937. It was at the University of Kansas that Stafford began to take his writing seriously, primarily composing stories centered on his family's travels through Kansas. In his brief essay "Sometimes, Reading" (from *Crossing Unmarked Snow: Further Views on the Writer's Vocation,* 1998), Stafford recalls a definitive moment in his development as a writer:

> That one time, reading, it was in the browsing room at the University of Kansas, just before World War II. I happened to reach for a text, *The Birth of Tragedy.* An hour later when I looked up—a changed world, deeper but full of wonder and excitement, not to be trusted, but infinitely ready for revelation. Why hadn't my professors told me about this new hemisphere? They had cheated me. Or didn't they know about it?
>
> Sure, I had read before, the family evenings, the library at Liberal during high school; my world

was full of books, Kipling . . . Willa Cather . . . Edgar Lee Masters. . . . But this—this Nietzsche, these blazes of outrageous but tantalizing discovery: "Every word is a prejudice"; "The best way through the mountains is from peak to peak, but it takes long legs"; "The right eye shouldn't trust the left." . . . A new expanse became mine, wild, reckless (so reckless it could be conservative too), a rampage of gusto: Galileo . . . Pascal . . . Kirkegaard . . . George Eliot . . . Tolstoy, Gandhi, Saint Teresa . . . Goethe . . . Wittgenstein. . . . The spaciousness of it all I link to that evening in the browsing room.

The sources of independent thinking that play a significant role in the molding of Stafford the poet as well as Stafford the teacher are evident in this documented memory.

His most formative years would come with the onset of World War II. Stafford registered as a conscientious objector during the United States's involvement. From 1941 to 1945, he lived in camps in Arkansas, California, and Illinois, working on forestry and soil-conservation projects as well as fighting fires. Because the American public largely supported World War II, Stafford's choice was an unpopular, yet courageous one. "My four years," Stafford writes in his *Writing the World,* "of 'alternative service under civilian direction' turned my life sharply into that independent channel of the second river—a course hereafter distinguished from any unexamined life, from the way it might have been in any of my hometowns." The long hours of physical labor in the camps were exhausting, so Stafford and his fellow conscientious objectors set aside time in the early morning to read and write. This was a habit Stafford carried with him for the rest of his life. "That dawn time," he wrote in *You Must Revise Your Life,* "is precious: the world is quiet; no one will interrupt; you are rested and ready."

In a camp in Santa Barbara, California, he met Dorothy Hope Frantz, a teacher and the daughter of a minister. A year later, on April 6, 1944, they married. The war not yet over,

Stafford remained in the camp while Frantz taught in nearby public schools. Just after their first anniversary, the Nazi regime fell in Europe, and the bombings of Nagasaki and Hiroshima followed that August. World War II officially ended, and Stafford's tenure in the camps concluded a few months later. He and his wife established a home in southern California. Later in 1945 Stafford received his master's degree from the University of Kansas. "My habit of early morning writing," Stafford later wrote in *You Must Revise Your Life,* "stayed and became confirmed through many moves and jobs in the next few years." These jobs included teaching in southern California public schools and for the Church World Service, a relief agency located in the San Francisco area.

Stafford published his first works in the late 1940s. A few of his early poems appeared in *Poetry.* His first book, *Down in My Heart,* published by Brethren Publishing House in 1947, is Stafford's nonfiction account of his experiences in the conscientious objector camps. An earlier version of the manuscript served as his thesis at the University of Kansas. In describing the book, Jeff Gundy writes:

> *Down in My Heart* takes us deep into the challenges and conundrums of peace-making, revealing both Stafford's particular philosophy of nonviolence in its formative stages and his debts to historic peace-church philosophies and strategies.
>
> . . . Unlike many first works, it is not an introspective bildungsroman; the narrative includes lightly fictionalized versions of Stafford's own encounters, but the narrator serves mainly as observer, only occasionally as participant. The narrative more often focuses on group experience and its significance than on merely personal feelings, and the overall design is to present, as the introduction says, "a series of incidents, purposely planned to give the texture of *our* lives."

Down in My Heart introduces us to Stafford's independent, sometimes austere, and ultimately hopeful persona.

In 1948 Stafford accepted a full-time teaching position at Lewis and Clark College in Portland, Oregon. The Staffords—he and Frantz eventually had four children—would call Oregon home (with periodic excursions) for the rest of their lives. That landscape, along with his childhood Kansas, serves as the groundswell for the majority of his poems. "One excursion," Stafford writes in *You Must Revise Your Life,* "made a big difference." In 1950 he enrolled in the Iowa Writers' Workshop. "Those years (1950–1952) marked my first sustained relation to other writers. . . . These two years remain the principal reference point I have for the literary life as lived by others." His primary instructors were Paul Engle, Walter Clark, and Verlin Cassell. Other visiting writers included Robert Penn Warren, Randall Jarrell, Reed Whittemore, and Karl Shapiro. "I enjoyed Engle's free and easy manner," Stafford continued, "coming in with an armload of manuscripts and quipping as he came. I followed Clark around to listen to his sociability and his stories." Classmates included Donald Justice, W. D. Snodgrass, and Philip Levine. Stafford, however, stood apart from them, by choice and by experience. When he left Iowa, Stafford was thirty-eight, married, and had two children. His peers were much younger and were still developing their writing habits. Their shared experience of living through World War II set Stafford apart from them even further. (Many of Stafford's contemporaries served in the armed forces during World War II, including Richard Hugo and Randall Jarrell.) Furthermore, his peers did not have the experiences Stafford had as a conscientious objector. His writing habits, formed in the camps, were fully developed. His vision and voice largely had taken shape. Judith Kitchen concludes that for Stafford "the courses and workshops at Iowa did have some effect; they served almost as a foil for the development of his own idiosyncratic attitudes toward the teaching of writing."

In 1955 Stafford earned his Ph.D. from the University of Iowa and taught in the English Department at Manchester College in Indiana. In 1956 he revisited San Jose, California, teaching literature at San Jose State College (now San Jose State University) and writing for one year, and then returned to Lewis and Clark College in 1957, which served as his primary employer until his retirement from teaching in 1980. He was awarded the Union League Civic and Arts Poetry Prize from *Poetry* magazine in 1959. In 1960, eight years after leaving Iowa, Talisman Press published his first book of poems, *West of Your City.* Stafford, then forty-six, had been publishing poems and teaching for nearly fifteen years. Many critics point to this as the foundation for the consistent maturity in Stafford's work. His second book, *Traveling through the Dark,* was published by Harper and Row in 1962 and won the National Book Award for 1963. The book's recognition solidified Stafford's place in contemporary American poetry. He began giving readings across the United States and teaching at various universities and colleges on leaves of absence from Lewis and Clark.

In 1964 he was given the Shelley Memorial Award from the Poetry Society of America, and in 1966 he was granted a Guggenheim Fellowship. In 1970 he was named consultant in poetry for the Library of Congress, and in 1972 he traveled extensively to such countries as Pakistan, India, Iran, Egypt, and Thailand with the United States Information Agency. In the late 1960s and early 1970s, as the United States's involvement in the Vietnam War and the subsequent unrest in America escalated, Stafford—by now known for his pacifist leanings and practices—was invited to give readings at college campuses. A reluctant spokesperson but a sober, intelligent, and compassionate witness, Stafford read during this time at the campuses of Kent State, the University of California at Berkeley, and the University of Wisconsin at Madison,

among others. The often hostile antiwar demonstrations Stafford encountered there made him uncomfortable, further testing and validating his independent current. "Both sides," Stafford writes of this time, "spread out leaving pacifists where they usually were, alone."

He published eight more books with Harper and Row/HarperCollins. This would be an admirable amount of poetry for any poet whose publishing career spanned more than fifty years. These were books Stafford published with *one* publisher, however, and they constitute only one-eighth of his body of work. In recognition of his considerable contribution to American letters, he was awarded the Western States Book Awards Lifetime Achievement in Poetry in 1992, a year before his death. In their jurors' citation (given in full in Andrews' *On William Stafford*), the judges—William Kittredge, Marvin Bell, Denise Chavez, and Naomi Shihab Nye—wrote:

As an international representative of poets, William Stafford's gentle attentions have encouraged free expression, while his intellectual jujitsu has caused many impulsive thinkers to reconsider. . . . Meanwhile, his poems—observant, engaged, resonant, and just plain irresistible—bear witness to both the care and disregard around us, naming the places, catching the shine of the ordinary, pulling the rug out from under vanity and pretension, giving fresh credit to the selfless and decent, acknowledging the inevitable, nudging us toward observant lives and peaceful interactions. His way of writing and of offering his work stands in silent rebuke to all that is loud, strident, assertive, and shallow. Yet close readers of Stafford's poetry know that there is a wildness at its center, by turns as gentle or tough as an undomesticated animal in an indifferent wilderness. He, of course, presents his poems and himself as if they should be taken for granted. We would like to say on this occasion that we do not.

Six major critical books on Stafford's poetry as well as book reviews and essays nearing the thousands by fellow writers, critics, and scholars—including Judith Kitchen, Tom Andrews, Peter Stitt, Sanford Pinsker, Richard Hugo, Margaret Atwood, James Dickey, Charles Simic, Fred Chappell, Robert Creeley, Louis Simpson, Richard Howard, and Henry Taylor—complete the Stafford bibliography, which continues to expand. In his last poem, "Are You Mr. William Stafford?" (from *The Way It Is: New and Selected Poems,* 1998), written the day he died, Stafford has one last quest. The poem is about acceptance, which Stafford practiced and received much of his life:

You can't tell when strange things with meaning
will happen. I'm [still] here writing it down
just the way it was. "You don't have to
prove anything," my mother said. "Just be ready
for what God sends." I listened and put my hand
out in the sun again. It was all easy.

Well, it was yesterday. And the sun came,
Why
It came.

WEST OF YOUR CITY

The poems in *West of Your City* are direct and personal and introduce us to the Stafford we hear and recognize through his entire writing career. In his first book of verse Stafford speaks truthfully about intimate details that sometimes lead to full-fledged disclosure. Critics dubbed this trend "confessionalism," with Robert Lowell's *Life Studies* (1959), Sylvia Plath's *Colossus* (1962), and Anne Sexton's *To Bedlam and Part Way Back* (1960) becoming the definitive texts of this period. Stafford's poems stand apart from the others, primarily because the closeness of the voice engages itself in subjects that are not private. Perhaps what aligns them with these and other poems of that time is their tentative but distinctive break from formal poetic conventions. Many poems in *West of Your City* hover around blank verse and slant rhyme.

The idea of home, its loss through the baptism of experience, and its slow recovery through acts of memory and writing are the book's concerns. Judith Kitchen writes that "home becomes the theme for this book, and the loss of home becomes its obsession." *West of Your City* examines the personal experiences of the speaker/poet as they mesh with the lives of others. Reviewing the book, the poet Robert Creeley comments, in *On William Stafford,* that "Stafford familiarizes his reality, makes it often subject to a 'we,' generalizing in that way the personal insight."

One way in which he achieves this intimate universality is by addressing his assumed audience directly. The first line in the poem "Midwest" contains the second-person possessive adjective found in the book's title:

West of your city into the fern
sympathy, sympathy rolls the train
all through the night on a lateral line
where the shape of game fish tapers down
from a reach where cougar paws touch water.

Stafford cultivates the ambiguity of direct address—he addresses his readers and, by extension, himself—by surrounding the mysterious "your" with sensory-specific but nonsingular details. Stafford places us in an archetypal nature, where each item keeps its integrity and gives an aura of something luminous.

"At the Bomb Testing Site" contains Stafford's characteristic understatement. Sympathetic and vigilant, the speaker of this poem—positioned on soon-to-be ground zero sand in Nevada or New Mexico—never takes his eye and mind off the lizard, despite the harsh and brutal immediacy of their surroundings. This is a tactic Stafford employs in many of his poems, though the landscapes are not always this catastrophic. In this poem, his vision is fixed upon humankind's inhumanity to humankind and to nature:

At noon in the desert a panting lizard
waited for history, its elbows tense,

watching the curve of a particular road
as if something might happen.

It was looking at something farther off
than people could see, an important scene
acted in stone for little selves
at the flute end of consequences.

There was just a continent without much on it
under a sky that never cared less.
Ready for a change, the elbows waited.
The hands gripped hard on the desert.

While the "elbows" and "hands" immediately may seem to belong to the lizard, the singular universality that informs much of Stafford's work sets in motion an ambiguity that implies the speaker's features as well. Nature "couldn't care less" about the impending test blast, but the lizard and invisible speaker wait in a history where something could happen. Stafford carefully chooses the lizard, an animal whose survival historically has been predicated on adaptation, as the understated protagonist of the poem. The lizard anticipates the atomic rehearsal; indeed, the mitigating circumstances the poem's title implies suggest a kind of survival for those who witness it, feel it, and recall it in their own fashion. As in many of Stafford's poems, beneath the pressure of reality, there is hope in anticipating, witnessing, and telling of the event.

Other poems offer glimpses of the devotion, courage, and conviction in Stafford's vision, particularly as they apply to family, including "The Move to California," "A Visit Home," and "Circle of Breath." Still others are rooted in nature and the potential for spiritual renewal within it. "Outside," "The Well Rising," and "Bi-Focal" illustrate such transcendence, as the speaker concludes in "Bi-Focal":

So, the world happens twice—
once what we see it as;
second it legends itself
deep, the way it is.

The double vision of his consciousness that Stafford began to witness along the banks of the Cimarron River as an adolescent starts to surface in these and other poems. In *West of Your City,* Stafford begins his lifelong practice of saying the everyday and the singular in one breath.

TRAVELING THROUGH THE DARK

Traveling through the Dark solidified Stafford's reputation. In his compressed, yet fluidly conversational way, Stafford explores inhabitants and ideas lurking within and behind landscapes. In these new poems, he also begins to address other concerns and obsessions that we see here for the first, but not for the last time: the nature of thought and acquiring wisdom, the ever shrinking distance between generations, and the role of poetry and teaching in his life.

The book's title poem is perhaps Stafford's most widely read. The title itself, implying a journey, carries equal amounts of hope, fear, and lament. Simple in form (four quatrains and an ending couplet, slant end-rhyme) and voice (conversational, void of ornament), "Traveling through the Dark" is, like many of Stafford's poems, readily accessible. It is precisely this immediate access that allows its complexities to surface. The strategies Stafford employs in this poem are those he uses in many of his poems; the way in which we read it might serve us well in reading the rest of his poems. Frequently anthologized, it is perhaps Stafford's most important poem:

Traveling through the dark I found a deer
dead on the edge of the Wilson River road.
It is usually best to roll them into the canyon:
that road is narrow; to swerve might make more
   dead.

By glow of the tail-light I stumbled back of the
   car

and stood by the heap, a doe, a recent killing;
she had stiffened already, almost cold.
I dragged her off; she was large in the belly.

My fingers touching her side brought me the
    reason—
her side was warm; her fawn lay there waiting,
alive, still, never to be born.
Beside that mountain road I hesitated.

The car aimed ahead its lowered parking lights;
under the hood purred the steady engine.
I stood in the glare of the warm exhaust turning
    red;
around our group I could hear the wilderness
    listen.

I thought hard for us all—my only swerving—,
then pushed her over the edge into the river.

In these typically quiet eighteen lines, Stafford lays bare that moment in which one's conscience is ultimately tested and one's worldview is forever branded by experience. There is no right solution to the situation into which the speaker has traveled; by extension, the speaker cannot commit any moral infraction, that is, unless he chooses not to act. Paradox permeates and supports the poem. In Judith Kitchen's comprehensive reading of this poem, she notes Stafford's contradictory impulses, concluding that the poem "shows a man aware of what his action (or his poem) did not do, as well as what it did."

The poem's story begins in a hopeful enough vein, with the speaker finding a deer. But the initial word of the second line, "dead," introduces us to the first emotional modulation. This sets in motion the poem's appositive strategy. In this case it is an enjambment suspending the knowledge of the deer's fate. Through much of the poem small epiphanies hover on the horizon and are never fully realized. This is Stafford's anticipatory pacing at its most suggestive. Stafford then supplies a name for the river and its road. Placed in a particular landscape, we,

too, become part of the poem's contradictory, yet inclusive project. The third line contains a statement of casual wisdom and acknowledges that coming across roadkill, even that as mutually damaging as deer, is a common occurrence. This line also speaks to duty; the speaker, loyal to the earth, takes on the responsibility of clearing the road to avoid making "more dead."

The second stanza introduces us to the particulars of the car, the instrument that killed the deer, the same instrument that affords the speaker the luxury of quicker travel. Modern technology gives Stafford the poles from which he generates much of his ironic posture. The second line in this stanza reinforces Stafford's careful pacing, referring to the deer as "the heap," then "a doe," and finally "a recent killing." This rapid succession of an evolving catalogue shows the speaker coming to terms with this circumstance alongside the reader. In other words, there is no moral agenda to the poem. Stafford is relating an experience as sincerely as he can. Almost covertly, he tucks in a last detail in this stanza that further complicates the experience of the poem: "she was large in the belly."

The killed deer, we learn, is pregnant, but Stafford wastes no time in telling us directly what he already has implied. His trust in understatement gives him the ability to move into more philosophical concerns: "My fingers touching her side brought me the reason—," a reason that he never states in the poem. We, like him, are almost left guessing what that reason could be. This enigmatic reason is the poem's moral center because we learn in the next line that the deer's side "was warm." Apart from the speaker and the car, the fawn in its killed parent is the only other thing living in the poem. Aware of this irony—the car (not necessarily the speaker's car, but a car nevertheless) and fawn as the two blind witnesses to the killing—Stafford places himself at the center. Of the three, the speaker is the only one possessing an ability to think rationally and, by extension, morally. The speaker's logic tells him that the fawn is, paradoxically enough, "alive, still, never to be born" and that "Beside that mountain road I hesitated." Here the stanza ends, and here is one of the longer pauses in contemporary American poetry. A defining moment is about to surface, or, as Kitchen puts it: "The thought that precedes that action is the subject of this poem, just as it was the triggering impulse for the poem in the first place."

The fourth stanza begins with the car gazing, just as its owner seems to gaze, with its lowered parking lights aiming into the night forest and its engine idling. The third line contains a characteristic ambiguity found in many of Stafford's poems: "I stood in the glare of the warm exhaust turning red." Is it the exhaust turning red by the taillight's glare, or is it the speaker himself turning red—literally by the same glare and emotionally by the inescapable grief to which he, unexpectedly, has borne witness? Certainly, the intent of the poem savors both equally. And what Stafford calls "our group"—the whole world—waits and listens for what might come next.

Solidifying the poem's understated strategy, Stafford yields to its denouement with only a couplet, implying at once that the resolution is as simple, clear, and unavoidable as it is excruciating, lamentable, and mysteriously, yet undoubtedly right. He mitigates his decision by offering an aside, set off by dashes, "—my only swerving—," as if to chastise himself for nearly veering off his moral course. This aside is crucial in understanding Stafford's body of work. He is a poet who signs himself over to what John Keats termed "negative capability" or what Stafford himself called "being willingly fallible." Only after one investigates every side of a situation can one sincerely decide what is right, and that singular rightness is predicated on one's experiences. Because Stafford acknowledges the mere possibility of alternative endings, he widens the scope of the poem. We almost can hear Stafford ask, "well, what would you have done?" and we have the distinct impression that Stafford would have listened intently and seriously considered the many responses. Inclusive and contradictory, "Traveling through the Dark" is a vivid illustration of what transpires when the pressure of reality distills in the individual and justifies, in such cases, the need for solipsistic and humanitarian thinking simultaneously.

Countering this self-confrontation are poems that contain Stafford's surprising turns of phrasing and generous empathy. In "Thinking for Berky" the speaker assumes the levelheaded thinking that the poem's title character, for reasons beyond her control, apparently never acquired. As in "Traveling through the Dark," an automobile triggers the poem; this time it is the siren of police or ambulance. Lying in bed, the speaker has

> . . . joined the ambulance or the patrol
> screaming toward some drama, the kind of end
> that Berky must have some day, if she isn't dead.

Berky, we learn through the speaker's recollection of her life, is someone whose earliest experiences were damaging beyond repair. The speaker uses himself as a foil for Berky's hardships: "Windiest nights, Berky, I have thought for you, / and no matter how lucky I've been I've been I've touched wood." Luck, the good and the bad, resides under the surface of things for Stafford. Out of luck comes responsibility, and Stafford speculates on Berky's fate: "There are things not solved in our town though tomorrow came: / there are things are things time passing can never make come true." The subtle shift in tenses—"came" to "come"—sheds light on Stafford's view of time; it is not linear. The million intricate moves justice requires are eerily and satisfyingly enigmatic. Does Berky stand a chance in the world and against herself? As in "Traveling through the Dark," Stafford raises more questions than can be answered. Witnessing is the matter for Stafford, not answers.

Other poems draw on landscape, family, teaching, and writing. "Lake Chelan" shows Stafford at his understated best, with its straightforward imagery; simple, yet lush diction; elegant rhythms; and subtle alliteration. "Parentage" portrays the speaker's father as an overwhelmed hero; conversely, the speaker expresses a desire to be "as afraid as the teeth are big" and "as dumb as the wise are wrong": "I'd just as soon be pushed by events to where I belong." "On Quitting a Little College" possesses Stafford's calm conversational tone, even in stressful situations. "Lit Instructor"—with its penultimate line "well, Right has a long and intricate name"—speaks to his approaches to teaching. "Representing Far Places" is reminiscent of Walt Whitman in its acceptance of contradiction, as its concluding couplet says: "It is all right to be simply the way you have to be, / among contradictory ridges in some crescendo of knowing." This poem and others in *Traveling through the Dark* seem to speak to the other poems whose clarity is shrouded in the immediacy of experience. This is Stafford's way—to listen to himself and those around him, to bear witness to what he experiences, and to carry out his duty as a writer, which is, as he says in his *ars poetica* "Vocation," "to find what the world is trying to be."

THE RESCUED YEAR, ALLEGIANCES, AND SOMEDAY, MAYBE

The poems in Stafford's next three books published by Harper and Row progress in his trademark deceptively simple manner and voice. Time allows us to examine how these poems function alongside those that precede and follow them. This is a strategy Stafford seemed to employ as well. *The Rescued Year* (1966) contains poems first published in *West of Your City,* including "At the Bomb Testing Site,"

"Vacation," "One Home," "Listening," "Bi-Focal," and "The Move to California." Placing them next to newer poems in this collection offers a richer, more complicated view on familiar and pervading themes.

The new poems explore grandeur contained in the mundane. Stafford finds this most predominantly in rural landscapes, and he approaches these landscapes through careful observation of the particulars within these scenes. These meditations sometimes approach a truth; more frequently, however, doubt surfaces. Back of doubt is fear, and it is the prevalence of fear that separates *The Rescued Year* from his earlier work. Stanley Moss concludes, in *On William Stafford,* "In the course of this volume, Stafford moves from half-innocence to experience to loneliness." Such is the case in "The Epitaph Ending in And," which approaches prophecy. Its vision is post-apocalyptic, yet infinitesimal:

> In the last storm, when hawks
> blast upward and a dove is
> driven into the grass, its broken wings
> a delicate design, the air between
> wracked thin where it stretched before,
> a clear spring bent close too often
> (that Earth should ever have such wings
> burnt on in blind color!), this will be
> good as an epitaph:
>
> Doves did not know where to fly, and

The ending never comes, which is precisely the point. Ninety percent of the poem is prologue to the epitaph itself, which is as heartbreaking a line as one will find in Stafford. As it does at the end of "Traveling through the Dark," the conclusion comes in a voice that is sure, steady, and quiet. Replete with dolor, "The Epitaph Ending in And" also contains embedded signs of hope: enjambments clue us in to a subconscious optimism ("a dove is" and "this will be"), verbs and adverbs reach toward an apex ("blast upward" and "stretched before"), and nouns and adjectives recall a fragile purity ("delicate design" and "clear spring"). Even punctuation (the exclamation point in the ante-penultimate line), a crucial component to a poem of one sentence, shows a speaker astonished. Unlike his other poems that are rooted in place, this poem is at once otherworldly and firmly situated in what we could call our real world. Only no one is there, and the last word—"and"— begs for continuance, for someone to complete the epitaph and thereby join the speaker, nullifying, however provisionally, the unwanted solitude.

This solitude, however, does not still Stafford. Rather, he moves with tentative steps, which reinforce the care in which he takes his steps as a poet. Slant rhyme and a loose blank verse once more are the primary vehicles. "Doubt on the Great Divide" is one such poem that employs these techniques:

> Better to stand in the dark of things and crash,
> hark yourself, blink in the day, eat bitter bush
> and look out over the world. A steadfast wire
> shaking off birds into paralyzed air
> crosses the country; in the sound of noon you
> stand
> while tethers whisper out and come to their end.
>
> Mountains that thundered promises now say
> something small—
> wire in the wind, and snow beginning to fall.

Beginning with an acceptance of the dark, it shifts quickly into something distasteful and, by the third line, into a wide gaze "over the world." What is there for Stafford is the particular, a telephone wire: that ten-thousand-volt perch for birds. The air seems constricted with paralysis, and the sound of noon is nothing more than the sound of the speaker listening to that shudder of surprise in their wings. Instead of stretching on forever, as it might have done in *West of Your City,* this landscape contains finite elements, namely, the tether's whispers. The concluding couplet, in contrast to what its words say,

implies something larger: the once wide landscape is shrinking under the pressure of modernity and can manage only a few small phrases, the last of which are just "beginning to fall."

The book's title poem, in contrast, is as expansive and hopeful as we have seen Stafford. The poem resides in familial memory, recalling a year spent near the Colorado border when his sister "gracefully / grew up." The library looms luminously with books waiting to be read and, next to it, the havens of school and church. The father is the predominant character of the poem, the person who propels the act of memory into an act of recovery:

> In all his ways I hold that rescued year—
> comes that smoke like love into the broken
> coal, that forms to chunks again and lies
> in the earth again in its dim folds, and comes a
> sound,
> then shapes to make a whistle fade,
> and in the quiet I hold no need, no hurry:
> any day the dust will move, maybe settle;
> the train that left will roll back into our station,
> the name carved on the platform unfill with rain,
> and the sound that followed the couplings back
> will ripple forward and hold the train.

The entropic progression found in the elements—fire to earth to smoke to dust—is the same progression that evolves in the mind via memory, via the poetic act. The assertions are calm and nostalgic in the truest sense, aching for what was once his. What is rescued, finally, in these poems is the speaker's connection to the landscape, the world of the poem and the poem of the world that always has held a home for him.

Allegiances (1970), with rural landscapes and family as its abiding subjects, complements Stafford's earlier books. "Vacation Trip" reflects on "Vacation" (from *West of Your City*). "Father's Voice" works in concert with "Circle of Breath," "Listening," and "The Farm on the Great Plains" (from *West of Your City*); "Elegy," "Parentage," and "Fall Journey" (from *Travel-*

ing through the Dark); and "My Father: October 1942" and "The Rescued Year" (from *The Rescued Year*). These poems, however, set themselves apart from their predecessors in that they reside in memory more explicitly, and the poems that transpire in the present tense are often explicitly acts of the imagination. They are darker poems, as he says in "A Gesture toward an Unfound Renaissance," that "look back through the door that always closes." In this way the locales and people in the poems take on a presence rather than the stark nearness in, for example, "At the Bomb Testing Site" or "Traveling through the Dark."

If the vision is more blurred in this volume, as critics and reviewers have noted, then it is a vision filtered with a gauzy, near luminous haze. The poems are shorter, as well, but they still possess the nonchalance and torque readers of Stafford have come to expect. Stafford is able to pack more into a smaller space by listening more intently to his triggering subjects of poems, as well as to himself, as he speaks them. Take, for instance, "With Kit, Age 7, at the Beach:"

We would climb the highest dune,
from there to gaze and come down:
the ocean was performing;
we contributed our climb.

Waves leapfrogged and came
straight out of the storm.
What should our gaze mean?
Kit waited for me to decide.

Standing on such a hill,
what would you tell your child?
That was an absolute vista.
Those waves raced far, and cold.

"How far could you swim, Daddy,
in such a storm?"
"As far as was needed," I said,
and as I talked, I swam.

There is no spiritual moment here. This poem anticipates a parent's greatest fear: outliving his or her child. The first three stanzas progressively set the stage for the speaker's response to his son's question that comes in the fourth.

The poem begins serenely enough, perched on the highest dune to watch the ocean. There is no fear in these opening lines; there is only communion. This is soon overtaken by awe as the father and child gaze into something they both seem to feel but do not have the words to clarify. Still, we get that sense there is something specific in mind, because anticipation builds into that distinctly vague expectation: mortality. On such matters, the speaker waits to speak while his son waits for him to decide. This new ineffable exchange produces the enigmatic "absolute vista," which is so powerful, distant, and hostile that Stafford's only recourse is to paternal instinct. And if the father's response is expected, the line that follows it is not: "and as I talked, I swam." Without it, this is a lesser poem. It surprises for many reasons. These three iambs, on the surface, speak to nothing extraordinary, if one knows how to swim. The understatement does not contain the composure we have come to expect from Stafford. Rather, it is the result of a lack of oxygen, real and imagined. This is as close to panicking as Stafford comes; the thought of losing his son to the storming ocean, to nature—that place in which he thought he would never feel abandoned—has frozen him, almost. Conversely, his imagination is charged, and this poem also almost never ends, as the speaker places himself in the ocean's throe, swimming for the rest of his foreseeable life to save his son's. Certainly, the poet is also acutely aware of the irony in this imagined scene: should he die while saving his son, his son also will die. If the vision is blurred in these poems, one now sees why. Stafford holds up this poem, and this collection, as illustrations of moments when clarity yields uncertainty.

This almost mute bewilderment carries over into *Someday, Maybe*. The poet and critic Laurence Lieberman writes in *On William Stafford* that in this collection "Stafford celebrates the common bonds—the mediating site—between the earth and the single frail human vessel, astonished to find that any one of us in the depths of 'our stillness' can *contain* such magnitude of subterranean currents." The tentative title is suggestive of a stubborn will acting against exactness. Stafford opens the collection with "An Introduction to Some Poems" and says,

> Look: no one ever promised for sure
> that we would sing. We have decided
> to moan.

The voice is agitated, more so than ever. Published in 1973, *Someday, Maybe* reflects the environment in which the poems were written. The United States by then was entrenched in the war in Vietnam, and at home the truth and severity of the Watergate political scandal, which brought about President Richard Nixon's resignation, were beginning to surface in the news. "Thirteenth and Pennsylvania" is an act of contrition. Set at an intersection three blocks from the White House, Stafford confesses his sins and, by extension, speaks on Nixon's behalf to "your thousands, people," to "absolve this man." "New Letters from Thomas Jefferson" depicts the elder statesman as lost in and fearful of the present state of the union, and the speaker characteristically backpedals into nature; nature, however, is a place where "particles were signaling" that which cannot be seen.

Searching for clarity and serenity, Stafford turns to animals and Native American myth and legend to reconnect with those who live as one with the land. Many poems assume the identity of an animal. "Existences" takes the point of view of a creature that is wolflike, half-wild and half-tame. The speaker has a master, whom it licks and then bites. It envies the chorus of leaves that speaks for it. Living in caves, it is touched "by grace of shadows." When anyone

approaches, it becomes "a track in the dust." The center of this poem is escape, and in the background is an awareness of a dominating presence. The poem addresses Stafford's concern for the nation and his desire to retreat to nature; the caveat to keep moving suggests that relief is far off.

Many poems directly address intimate and historical figures. In an interview titled "A Witness for Poetry" (in *You Must Revise Your Life*), Stafford discusses his concern for communication and preservation through the act of witnessing in the medium of poetry:

> Ideally, every letter should have the trancelike, forward unfolding into the subject matter that a poem should have. I think poems are pieces of talk, savored and sustained. I would call them "lucky talk." A poem is a lucky piece of talk. Letters are usually addressed to someone we are sympathetic with. It can be direct. It appeals to many common experiences, usually. I think a poem is like that.

"Report to Crazy Horse" is one such poem with a large scope; it offers the poet's own story in an abridged, yet archetypal fashion and quickly moves into larger and more immediate concerns:

> All the Sioux were defeated. Our clan
> got poor, but a few got richer.
> They fought two wars. I did not
> take part. No one remembers your vision
> or even your real name. Now
> the children go to town and like
> loud music. I married a Christian.

The genocide of the Native Americans is alluded to, as is the Great Depression and Stafford's time as a conscientious objector. The students, as Stafford sees them, are not concerned with such matters; rather, they prefer the city to the countryside, Jimi Hendrix to Friedrich Nietzsche. In this way Stafford grieves innocence lost. The second stanza clarifies the poet's vision at this point in his career:

In our schools we are learning
to take aim when we talk, and we have
found out our enemies. They shift when
words do; they even change and hide
in every person. A teacher here says
hurt or scorned people are places
where real enemies hide. He says
we should not hurt or scorn anyone,
but help them. And I will tell you
in a brave way, the way Crazy Horse
talked: that teacher is right.

The implication here is that those lessons go unheeded once the students grow up, graduate, enter the draft, and go out into the world. Evidence of this can be found in the Native Americans' plight, victims of genocide in the early nineteenth century as well as in the country's present involvement in Vietnam. The possibility for cruelty exists in each of us, Stafford suggests, and he holds these historical facts as proof. The shifting enemy—sometimes ourselves, sometimes language itself—seems to be below and above all radar. Stafford turns to the teacher's veracity for wisdom, if not comfort.

The next two stanzas move into the present and portray a Western town in slow but steady decline. Stafford does so in a direct voice, talking not only to the Native American warrior/leader but also to his readers, who likewise are the subjects of this poem:

I will tell you a strange thing:
at the rodeo, close to the grandstand,
I saw a farm lady scared by a blown
piece of paper; and at that place
horses and policemen were no longer
frightening, but suffering faces were,
and the hunched-over backs of the old.

Crazy Horse, tell me if I am right:
these are the things we thought we were
doing something about.

This town is forlorn, defeated, and so fragile that scraps of trash frighten some of them. And

what troubles Stafford's speaker the most is the apparent fact that these problems are frequently addressed, never resolved, and always repeated.

In the next stanza the speaker offers another internal conflict, his abiding patriotism, even in the face of these facts:

                    . . . now I salute
the white man's flag. But when I salute
I hold my hand alertly on the heartbeat
and remember all of us and how we depend
on a steady pulse together.

When this speaker salutes, recites, and sings his allegiances, he has thought them through and concludes that

        . . . All of our promises,
our generous sayings to each other, our
honorable intentions—those I affirm
when I salute. . . .

The stress surely falls on "salute." This is a religious moment for the speaker, feeling as though he were

                . . . joining a religious
colony at prayer in the gray dawn
in the deep aisles of a church.

The final two stanzas serve as warning and imagistic validation of "the way it is now, and it is our way, / the way we were trying to find." The chokecherry trees, the clay in the soil, and the Musselshell rocks are all proof of his active witnessing to what good still exists and that we might reclaim them someday, maybe.

STORIES THAT COULD BE TRUE

After publishing poems for nearly thirty years, Stafford released *Stories That Could Be True* (1977), a volume of new and selected poems. Serious readers of Stafford's poetry now had a unified collection of poems from which to gauge the depth and breadth of his vision and craft. The reviewer William H. Pritchard noted in *On William Stafford,* however, that one "should not (I found out, going through the collected volume) read too many poems at the same sitting, else they blur into one another." He continues to praise Stafford's calm and consistent tone, concluding that "the attractiveness of his poetry importantly depends upon it."

In *Stories That Could Be True* the reader is able easily to identify the threads that run through Stafford's well-known poems: memory, nature, family, and religion. More important, one can see how Stafford views these themes and obsessions not as separate items but as one unified way of living. In the new poems Stafford returns from these largely nostalgic poems and locates himself in the present tense. A new poem that comes from the collection's title is one firmly rooted in the present, with all of its uncertainties, doubts, and possibilities. "A Story That Could Be True" plays with the possibility of being removed from one's history:

> If you were exchanged in the cradle and
> your real mother died
> without ever telling the story
> then no one knows your name,
> and somewhere in the world
> your father is lost and needs you
> but you are far away.

Exploring the concept of family, Stafford exiles his speaker from those who might help him find his identity. Stafford plays off the expectation that his readers have come to know these parents from earlier poems. Once again, the speaker is (as the title of the book's opening section indicates) learning to live in the world. The poem's tone shifts slightly from the hypothetical vein to a more immediate one, and the speaker finds himself slightly more self-aware as he observes the passersby on any street corner in every city. This is precisely Stafford's method: creating an experience in poetry that

mirrors his quest for self-knowledge and wisdom as well as an acceptance of it. The speaker's situation seems grim, if not heartbreaking, as we learn that the speaker's father "can never find / how true you are, how ready." The loss, even before their relationship begins, is final. Waiting for some kind of history to happen as he travels through this dark and cold world void of history, he asks himself the question we also might be asking, not only of the speaker but also of ourselves: "Who are you really, wanderer?" With no one but himself to reply, Stafford surprisingly advances into the affirmative, couching fate as a possibility: "'Maybe I'm a king.'" Stafford addresses this kind of acceptance with place, despite one's past, in a 1978 interview with Charles Digregorio (from *You Must Revise Your Life*):

> I don't think it is hard to get a feeling for Oregon even if you weren't born and raised here. I don't feel any particular connection with a certain part of the country. It's just that wherever one lives, the arts are immediate experiences; you converge with your locale. I don't think the locale is crucial, but it is crucial that wherever you are, you converge with it. . . .
>
> I think my poetry would be different if I were somewhere else, but it is mostly because of the people, not the land.

"Ask Me" is a poem that posits a weighty question:

> . . . ask me
> mistakes I have made. Ask me whether
> what I have done is my life. . . .

At its foundation, what makes "Ask Me" so characteristically Stafford is the tentative tone with which he begins the poem, "Some time when the river is ice." From this slippery slope, he carries on a discussion in two arenas at once: internally (through self-interrogation) and with the assumed reader (through direct address). As Judith Kitchen points out, Stafford's questions—

declaratively phrased in a hypothetical future—
we, too, begin to wonder what else a life could
be. The second stanza supplies a portrait of
Stafford with which we are familiar:

> I will listen to what you say.
> You and I can turn and look
> at the silent river and wait. We know
> the current is there, hidden; and there
> are comings and goings from miles away
> that hold the stillness exactly before us.
> What the river says, that is what I say.

Because the current has been frozen, so has the
speaker. Whatever current exists is no longer
visible and must be taken on faith. Stafford
embodies this stillness-in-motion paradox, letting that speak for him. There is no answer to
the questions he poses in the first stanza. Rather,
"Ask Me" hovers—as do many of these poems,
particularly in their new configuration—toward
acceptance; the subtexts of an ars poetica flow
just beneath the surface of the words, inaudible
but nevertheless articulate.

A GLASS FACE IN THE RAIN, AN OREGON MESSAGE, AND PASSWORDS

The poems in *A Glass Face in the Rain: New
Poems* (1982) mark Stafford's return to his abiding subjects: family, writing, and landscape.
Each section of the book contains a poem about
writing set off in italic type. This is the first
time readers see Stafford consciously arranging
these metapoems. "After Arguing against the
Contention That Art Must Come from Discontent," "A Course in Creative Writing," and "Fiction" further illustrate how Stafford's approach
to writing and teaching are one and the same.
"If I Could Be Like Wallace Stevens" is as
much an homage to the poet as it is a self-
portrait, and it offers another glimpse into
Stafford's approach to writing, concluding:

> My pride would be to find out; I'd
> bow to see, play the fool,

> ask, beg, retreat like a wave—
> but somewhere deep I'd hold the pearl,
> never tell. "Mr. Charley,"
> I'd say, "talk some more. Boast again."
> And I'd play the banjo and sing.

Other poems show Stafford giving a more
concentrated focus on his own mortality as well
as the mortality of those he loves. For Stafford,
contemplating endings implies the consideration
of beginnings, as in "How It Began." By the
end of the poem, the puppies the speaker has
found transcend their easy sentimentality and
cuteness and become the symbol of how Stafford
once lived in the world, "happy and blind."
Implicit in this nostalgia is the loss of youth
and innocence. "Tuned in Late One Night,"
located in the more immediate present, is aware
of the loss implied in "How It Began." The
speaker of this poem tries to reconnect with
what is now distant through radio waves that,
quite literally, stretch across the universe. The
speaker—in this vast solitude, craving a com-
forting connection—wants an

> expression pure as all the space
> around me: I want to tell what is. . . .

> Remember?"

Dwelling on the past reaffirms Stafford's moral
stance and place in the world:

> But some of us knew even then it was better
> to lose if that was the way our chosen
> side came out, in truth, at the end.

These lines seem culled from a lifetime of
practice and could speak directly to Stafford's
experience as a conscientious objector. The
poem's final stanza works as a kind of vita nova,
and Stafford once more gives us glimpses of
that ineffable desire to create:

> Now I am fading, with this ambition:
> to read with my brights full on,

to write on a clear glass typewriter,
to listen with sympathy,
to speak like a child.

An Oregon Message (1987) is full of poems that ask the reader to step in to the imaginative process with him. Stafford does this to widen the circle of recovering the past, because the past, childhood, can be reinhabited only this way. By bringing the past into the present, Stafford's poems—residing on the page—become a perpetual present that chronicles the now fluid past. "First Grade" is a lighter poem that for all its humor touches on those defining moments of identity we encounter in elementary school:

In the play Amy didn't want to be
anybody; so she managed the curtain.
Sharon wanted to be Amy. But Sam
wouldn't let anybody be anybody else—
he said it was wrong. "All right," Steve said,
"I'll be me, but I don't like it."
So Amy was Amy, and we didn't have the play.
And Sharon cried.

The pressures of insecurity, the seemingly petty squabbles brought about by peer pressure—these are things, Stafford is saying, that we carry for the rest of our lives, things that find their way into the public and private realms with equal force. The poem is also a commentary on a life led in the arts. Stafford chooses a play in which to set the poem and asks his readers to consider the very poem in front of them as a kind of play as well. Playful, humorous, and ultimately serious, "First Grade" is a fable of sorts, whose moral could be what Stafford has been advocating all along: self-acceptance. Or, as he concluded in an interview with Clinton Larson, "The Poet as Religious Moralist" (from *You Must Revise Your Life*):

We should all reach out for insight and company, even while maintaining whatever we do see in a special way. I think there might be a danger for artists in any group that might feel itself under the necessity of *competing*—in art there is no competing, I say.

. . . I feel so easy about the prevalence that I do not have to try to maintain what is like breathing. I don't forget to breathe, and I don't forget to genuflect, in my thought, toward the whole tide of my living values.

In "Thinking about Being Called Simple by a Critic," Stafford cultivates this playful vein and aligns himself with William Carlos Williams. The plums of Williams's poem "This Is Just to Say" are now in Stafford's refrigerator, and Stafford finds solace in thinking of how Williams, too, was criticized for being laconic and uninteresting at times. Stafford concludes:

. . . In the dark with the truth
I began the sentence of my life
and found it so simple there was no way
back into qualifying my thoughts
with irony or anything like that.
I went to the fridge and opened it—
sure enough the light was on.
I reached in and got the plums.

The collection's strongest poems, however, are those that work in an elegiac mode. "1940" is classic Stafford:

It is August. Your father is walking you
to the train for camp and then the War
and on out of his life, but you don't know.

Little lights along the path glow under their hoods
and your shoes go brown, brown in the brightness
till the next interval, when they disappear in the
    shadow.

You know they are down there, by the crunch of
    stone
and a rustle when they touch a fern. Somewhere
    above,
cicadas arch their gauze of sound all over town.

Shivers of summer wind follow across the park
and then turn back. You walk on toward
September, the depot, the dark, the light, the dark.

At once an elegy for his father and for his own childhood, this poem places the past in the present with the brief opening sentence. The poem's complexities and richness surface as this immediate context is coupled with the speaker's acknowledgment of ignorance: "but you don't know." This is yet another example of Stafford's strategy—simple diction conveying complex perceptions. "1940" is representative of Stafford's best work in that it shows the poet's return to a specific place and time in both subject and technique. Slant rhyme and elastic iambs contain the past—a time before World War II, incarceration in conscientious objector camps, and the death of his father—in a malleable fashion. As a result, both the poet and the reader approach the poem with defenses down and are willing to suspend whatever disbelief and fear they have. The repetition of "the dark" in the last line—in addition to completing the rhyme scheme—subtly echoes Stafford's early classic poem "Traveling through the Dark" and also quietly emphasizes his increasing awareness of his approaching death.

This awareness reintroduces the thread of fear to Stafford's larger canvas in *Passwords* (1991). Judith Kitchen charts the forms of fear in the book, and her findings reveal this:

> "Scarier," "afraid," "never afraid," "scared," "brave," "fears," "shivers," "afraid even now,"— the words occur in that order, leading inevitably to one of the later poems and the phrase "if you survive." This hints at a temporal urgency in *Passwords*; its "moment" (or time sense) contains an instance of personal loss and the various fears that surround such a loss. If Stafford seemed to come to terms with death in his two previous books (*A Glass Face in the Rain* and *An Oregon Message*), *Passwords* demonstrates otherwise. Stafford's oldest son, Bret, had recently died.

In this way, the fears expressed in *Allegiances*, published more than twenty years earlier, have surfaced as a reality and are dealt with in the section "Elegies." In a poem-by-poem sequence, Stafford moves through the grieving process. Many of the poems use second-person and third-person plural pronouns, usually hinting at or quietly including his wife and surviving children. "For a Lost Child," "Consolations," "Security," "Long Distance," "Your Life," and "Yes" address the process of mourning and, by extension, the process of healing through writing. While few of these poems cast an optimistic light on learning how to live in the world, many of them show Stafford coming to terms with loss.

The poems in *Password*'s concluding section, "Vita," are intensely private, yet accessible. They seem autobiographical; it is difficult to differentiate the speaker of the poems from Stafford, the man we may have come to know through his extensive writings, appearances, interviews, and classroom sessions. Stafford may have dismissed such delineations as not crucial to grasping the purpose of the poems. In Christopher Buckley and Christopher Merrill's study, Stafford is quoted as writing, "I thrive on such a sequence; my poems live by touching these particular (but *emblematic*) parts of my (implied at least) own life." "In Camp" seems to speak directly of his experiences in the conscientious objector camps during World War II. Despite the less-than-desirable conditions detailed in the first two stanzas, the poem concludes: "In camps like that, if I should go again, / I'd still study the gospel and play the accordion." "Life Work," as Kitchen points out, works as a coda to "Traveling through the Dark." She says that "whereas in the earlier poem the speaker had to confront the harsh reality of animal life and death before traveling on, in 'Life Work' he is more closely identified with the physical self and, by extension, with death." The form of "Life Work"—three quatrains and a closing couplet, suggestive slant rhymes that coalesce the line's ending words—also resembles that of "Traveling through the Dark":

Even now in my hands the feel of the shovel
  comes back,
the shock of gravel or sand. Sun-scorch on my
  shoulders
bears down. The boss is walking around barking.
All the cement mixers rattle and jolt.

That day the trench we are digging goes deeper
and deeper, over my head; then the earth heaves
in one giant coffin gulp. They keep
digging and pulling and haul me out still
  breathing.

The sky, right there, was a precious cobalt dome
so near it pressed on my face. Beside me my hands
lay twitching and begging at the end of my arms.
Nothing is far anymore, after that trench, the
  stones. . . .

Oh near, and blessing again and again: my breath.
And the sky, and steady against my back, the
  earth.

Stasis, not motion, moves the speaker through
this poem. The speaker is acutely aware of his
body, pressed as it is between earth and sky.
Pulled from a kind of grave, his life's work, he
is granted breath again, which is close by and
blessed. "Vita," the collection's last poem, is as
clear as it is enigmatic:

God guided my hand
and it wrote,
"Forget my name."

World, please note—
a life went by, just
a life, no claims,

a stutter in the millions
of stars that pass,
a voice that lulled—

a glance
and a world
and a hand.

In each stanza, the speaker disappears a little
more, until all that remains is a trinity Stafford

would call holy: an observation, a reality, and
the process of writing. For all the complexities
at work in his poetry, Stafford concludes his last
collection with a single gesture that clarifies
and justifies his many intricate moves.

Selected Bibliography

WORKS OF WILLIAM STAFFORD

POETRY
West of Your City. Los Gatos, Calif.: Talisman Press, 1960.

Traveling through the Dark. New York: Harper & Row, 1962.

The Rescued Year. New York: Harper & Row, 1966.

Allegiances. New York: Harper & Row, 1970.

Poems for Tennessee. With Robert Bly and William Matthews. Martin: Tennessee Poetry Press, 1971.

Someday, Maybe. New York: Harper & Row, 1973.

The Earth. Port Townsend, Wash.: Graywolf Press, 1974.

Stories That Could Be True: New and Collected Poems. New York: Harper & Row, 1977; London: Harper & Row, 1980.

Things That Happen Where There Aren't Any People. Brockport, N.Y.: BOA Editions, 1980.

A Glass Face in the Rain: New Poems. New York: Harper & Row, 1982; London: Harper & Row, 1985.

Segues: A Correspondence in Poetry. With Marvin Bell. Boston: David R. Godine, 1983.

Smoke's Way: Poems from Limited Editions. Port Townsend, Wash.: Graywolf Press, 1983.

An Oregon Message. New York: Perennial Library, 1987.

Writing the World. Baltimore, Md.: Alembic Press, 1988.

Passwords. New York: HarperPerennial, 1991.

The Animal That Drank Up Sound. Illustrated by Debra Frasier. San Diego: Harcourt, Brace, Jovanovich, 1992. (A children's book.)

The Darkness around Us Is Deep: Selected Poems of William Stafford. Edited and with an introduction by Robert Bly. New York: HarperPerennial, 1993.

The Way It Is: New and Selected Poems. Introduction by Naomi Shihab Nye. Saint Paul, Minn.: Graywolf Press, 1998.

PROSE

Down in My Heart. Elgin, Ill.: Brethren Publishing House, 1947; Columbia, S.C.: Bench Press, 1985; Corvallis, Ore.: Oregon State University Press, 1998.

Writing the Australian Crawl: Views on the Writer's Vocation. Ann Arbor: University of Michigan Press, 1978.

You Must Revise Your Life. Ann Arbor: University of Michigan Press, 1986.

Journal excerpt. In *Seneca Review,* Special Issue, *Taking Note: From Poets' Notebooks* 21, no. 2: 226–230 (1991). (Contains excerpts from the notebooks of thirty-two contemporary poets.)

"Ave Atque Vale: The Welcome and Farewell of Life." In *What Will Suffice: Contemporary American Poets on the Art of Poetry.* Edited by Christopher Buckley and Christopher Merrill. Salt Lake City: Gibbs-Smith, 1995. P. 146. (Prose comment to the poem "The Old Writers' Welcome to the New.")

Crossing Unmarked Snow: Further Views on the Writer's Vocation. Edited by Paul Merchant and Vincent Wixon. Ann Arbor: University of Michigan Press, 1998.

CRITICAL AND BIOGRAPHICAL STUDIES

Andrews, Tom. "'Knowing': Glimpses into Something Ever Larger." *Field* 41:38–40 (fall 1989). (Reprinted in *On William Stafford: The Worth of Local Things.* Edited by Tom Andrews. Ann Arbor: University of Michigan Press, 1993.)

———, ed. *On William Stafford: The Worth of Local Things.* Ann Arbor: University of Michigan Press, 1993.

Barnes, Dick. "The Absence of the Artist." *Field* 28:27–34 (spring 1983).

Carpenter, David A. *William Stafford.* Boise State University Western Writers Series, no. 72. Boise, Idaho: Boise State University Press, 1986.

Gundy, Jeff. "Without Heroes, Without Villains: Identity and Community in *Down in My Heart.*" In *On William Stafford: The Worth of Local Things.* Edited by Tom Andrews. Ann Arbor: University of Michigan Press, 1993.

Haines, John. "A Comment on William Stafford's 'A Way of Writing' in *Field* 2." *Field* 3:64–66 (fall 1970). (Reprinted in *On William Stafford* [1993].)

Holden, Jonathan. *The Mark to Turn: A Reading of William Stafford's Poetry.* Lawrence: University Press of Kansas, 1976.

Howard, Ben. "Together and Apart." *Poetry* 160, no. 1:34–44 (April 1992). (Review of *Passwords.*) (Reprinted in *On William Stafford* [1993].)

Hugo, Richard. "The Third Time the World Happens: A Dialogue on Writing between Richard Hugo and William Stafford." *Northwest Review* 13:26–47 (spring 1973).

Jackson, Richard. *Acts of Mind: Conversations with Contemporary Poets.* Tuscaloosa: University of Alabama Press, 1983. Pp. 126–131.

Kitchen, Judith. *Writing the World: Understanding William Stafford.* Corvallis: Oregon State University Press, 1999.

Lensing, George S., and Ronald Moran. "William Stafford." In their *Four Poets and the Emotive Imagination: Robert Bly, James Wright, Louis Simpson, and William Stafford.* Baton Rouge: Louisiana State University Press, 1976. Pp. 177–216.

Lieberman, Laurence. *Unassigned Frequencies: American Poetry in Review, 1964–77.* Urbana: University of Illinois Press, 1977.

Miller, Tom P. "'In Dear Detail, By Ideal Light': The Poetry of William Stafford." *Southwest Review* 56, no. 4:341–345 (autumn 1971).

Mills, Ralph J. "Like Talk." In *On William Stafford: The Worth of Local Things.* Edited by Tom Andrews. Ann Arbor: University of Michigan Press, 1993.

Nathan, Leonard. "One Vote." *New England Review and Bread Loaf Quarterly* 5, no. 5:521–524 (1983). (Reprinted in *On William Stafford* [1993].)

Pinsker, Sanford. "William Stafford: 'The Real Things We Live By.'" In his *Three Pacific Northwest Poets: William Stafford, Richard Hugo, David Wagoner.* Boston: Twayne, 1987. Pp. 7–55.

Simic, Charles. "At the Bomb Testing Site." *Field* 41:8–10 (fall 1989). (Reprinted in *On William Stafford* [1993].)

Stepanchev, Stephen. *American Poetry since 1945: A Critical Survey*. New York: Harper & Row, 1965.

Stitt, Peter. "William Stafford's Wilderness Quest" and "Interview with William Stafford." In his *The World's Hieroglyphic Beauty: Five American Poets*. Athens: University of Georgia Press, 1985. Pp. 57–106.

—*ALEXANDER LONG*

Richard Yates

1926–1992

STUDENTS OR CASUAL readers of the works of Richard Yates would do well to know beforehand what sort of world they are about to enter. Stephen Amidon gives us a very good introduction to that world in the first paragraph of his review in the *Atlantic Monthly* of Yates's collected stories:

> Richard Yates just might have been the saddest writer America has produced. Solitude and sorrow pervade his fiction, marking it so deeply that his reluctant suburbanites, demobilized GIs, corporate drones, and dreamy women, seem to be unwittingly engaged in the pursuit of unhappiness. Moments of joy or communion are as brief and bittersweet for them as day trips from a convalescent ward. Set in the era when American triumphalism was achieving its self-congratulatory summit, Yates's work consistently reminds the reader of the depths awaiting those unable to make the climb.

Although this may not sound very inviting, we are drawn to Yates's work the same way we are drawn to take a quick glimpse of ourselves in the glass of a shop window while walking down a sidewalk. We may not like everything we see, but we cannot deny the honesty of the reflection. Yates holds up a looking glass that penetrates into the very depths of our hearts and souls, and we are in turn fascinated and horrified by what we see.

THE JOURNEY TO *REVOLUTIONARY ROAD*

Richard Walden Yates was born on February 3, 1926, in Yonkers, New York. His father, Vincent Matthew Yates, known as "Mike," was a salesman for the Mazda lamp division of General Electric. His mother, Ruth Mauer Yates, who had attended art school in her home state of Ohio, was an aspiring sculptor. The couple had one other child, Yates's older sister Ruth, who was born in 1922. In 1929 the union of the pragmatic father and the artistic mother ended in divorce. The children lived with their mother but they saw their father often and depended upon him financially for the rest of his life.

Yates grew up in a household where sacrifices were made to further his mother's largely unsuccessful artistic career. He and his sister were moved from apartment to apartment throughout the New York City area with the breezy assurances from their mother that something would happen soon to erase their poverty. Throughout her life, Ruth Mauer Yates believed that public recognition and the acclaim and monetary rewards that went with it were imminent. This self-indulgent, self-deluding woman bred in her son disdain for irresponsible, pretentious artistic posers: those who believe that their dream is indeed reality. Although he resented her maternal shortcomings, Yates held a deep admiration for her devotion to her art.

Yates's mother was also a social climber. She believed that if she mingled with the right people they would find her fascinating and her sculptures desirable. When Yates finished grammar school, his mother insisted that he enroll in a New England prep school where he could possibly become friendly with the children of wealthy art lovers. His parents fought over the idea; his father was dismayed by what he saw as an unnecessary drain on his earnings. Mrs. Yates, however, prevailed. She persuaded the officials at the Avon Old Farms School in Avon, Connecticut, to allow her son to enter on reduced tuition. His father agreed to pay the reduced fee and, in 1941, Yates became a student there. In 1942, at the age of fifty-two, Vincent Matthew Yates died. Even with the sudden loss of her major source of income, Yates's mother managed to keep Yates at Avon until his graduation in 1944. Yates's memories of his days at Avon and the impact of his father's death are poignantly recalled in his novel *A Good School* (1978).

After graduation, Yates was drafted into the army. He was shipped to Europe, where he engaged in military actions in Belgium and France. When the war ended in 1946, Yates returned to New York and looked for work to support himself and his mother. His experience as editor of his prep school's newspaper helped him get a job rewriting copy for the United Press. After nearly three years of living with his increasingly eccentric and needy mother, Yates married Sheila Bryant in 1948. The following year, Yates took a job as publicity writer for the Remington Rand Corporation, a manufacturer of business machines.

Yates had developed lung problems (pleurisy) while fighting in the Battle of the Bulge and was treated for tuberculosis in 1950. After spending almost two years in veterans' hospitals, Yates was given an army disability pension that enabled him to travel to England and France with his wife and their newborn daughter, Sharon. The illness had taken a severe toll on his lungs, and he remained a semi-invalid for the rest of his life. The family left America in 1951 and took up residence with Sheila's English aunt in London. After two years, however, the discord that often arises in such living arrangements forced Sheila to return to America with their child. Yates stayed behind, living alone in London, Antibes, and Cannes.

Yates began writing short stories in his early teens. In an interview for *Contemporary Au-*thors, Yates said, "I've been writing since I was fourteen or fifteen years old. Mostly, I think, because there was so little else I could do and be praised for. I wasn't a good student in school. I wasn't an athlete. I think some kids gravitate toward the occupation that pleases most other people." In 1948 he read the book that gave serious direction to his writing, as he commented in the *New York Times Book Review:*

No single book made me decide to be a writer; that decision came as a consequence of boyhood and had little to do with books at all. But it was F. Scott Fitzgerald's *The Great Gatsby,* which I read for the first time at 22, that persuaded me to quit fooling around and get to work. The purity of that novel, the grace and the swiftly gathering power of it, showed me what a high, fine thing writing could be—and suggested too, as if in whispers, how much it might cost.

It is not known when Yates first read Gustave Flaubert's *Madame Bovary,* another masterpiece of tragic realism, but that novel also had a profound and lifelong influence on him and his worldview. As in the works of Flaubert and Fitzgerald, Yates's stories and novels reveal characters whose only crime is that they are genuinely human. In his 1972 interview for the literary journal *Ploughshares,* Yates said, "I much prefer the kind of story where the reader is left wondering who's to blame until it begins to dawn on him (the reader) that he himself must bear some of the responsibility because he's human and therefore infinitely fallible."

Like Flaubert and Fitzgerald, Yates does not require the presence of an evil villain to bring about the tragic downfall of his characters. It is in their very nature, in their sheer humanness, their inability to be anything other than what they are, that their inescapable tragedy lies. Remarkably, only one of Yates's characters, April Wheeler in *Revolutionary Road* (1961), chooses to leave her horrific circumstances behind by committing suicide. All the others manage to grope blindly through their lives, trying to do their best no matter how often they fall short of their goal. Yet Yates is consistently nonjudgmental with his characters. He is quite aware that we are all potential failures, and, in his way, he shows great compassion for the human condition.

In 1953 Yates returned to his wife and daughter, who were then living with Sheila's mother and brother in the fashionable town of Redding, Connecticut. Yates once again found himself living in a difficult household. Indeed, Sheila's mother and brother were the models for the self-deluding Mrs. Givings and her seriously unstable son, John, in *Revolutionary Road.* Yates also continued working for Remington Rand, but now on a freelance basis, going into New York occasionally to drop off and pick up assignments. In the midst of all this grim domestic drudgery two things happened that changed Yates's life forever: his short story "Jody Rolled the Bones" was published in the *Atlantic Monthly* magazine, and he met the man who was to be the greatest champion of his writing, Seymour Lawrence.

Educated at Harvard, Lawrence first became interested in publishing while serving as editor and publisher of that university's literary journal, *Wake,* from 1945 to 1953. After graduation, Lawrence found work in Boston as special assistant to the editor at the *Atlantic Monthly.* It was in this position that he first saw Yates's work. He recalled his first encounter with the author's work in "Richard Yates: A Requiem," an article published in *Poets and Writers Magazine,* in 1993:

> I was Dick Yates' friend and publisher for forty years, dating back to the publication of his story "Jody Rolled the Bones" in the February 1953 issue of the *Atlantic Monthly,* where I worked as a junior editor. . . . [The story] won First Prize as the most notable *Atlantic* "First" of the year. . . . Dick and I soon became drinking pals. We would often meet for lunch or dinner at the Harvard Club in New York. . . . On one of those boozy nights,

sometime in 1953, I encouraged him to write a novel but he didn't get started on it until 1955.

Five years later, after several false starts, he delivered the final manuscript of what would become a contemporary classic, *Revolutionary Road.*

REVOLUTIONARY ROAD

Revolutionary Road is a novel about marital disintegration and moral failure as well as a novel about fear and madness and the inability of big dreams to expand and liberate narrow minds, hearts, and souls. Frank and April Wheeler, a married couple in their late twenties, live the 1950s version of the good life in a new suburban Connecticut development: Revolutionary Hill Estates. As an adolescent, Frank, the youngest of three sons born to Earl Wheeler and his unnamed wife, dreams of riding the rails to the West Coast. His desire to get away from home is fulfilled when the U.S. Army "had taken him at eighteen, had thrust him into the final spring offensive of the war in Germany and given him a confused but exhilarating tour of Europe for another year before it set him free." When he returns to America Frank enrolls in Columbia College, and all those who meet him agree that he is a young man of great promise: "an intense, nicotine-stained, Jean-Paul Sartre sort of man" who only needs time and freedom to find himself and his true calling. He knows that he will eventually settle for good in Europe, which he claims is the only place worth living, and he wears his disdain for America and all things American as easily as he wears the uniform of the young intellectual: an aged tweed jacket and worn-out khakis. The only thing missing in his life is a "first-rate girl." Soon after college ends, Frank begins to have doubts about his brilliant future. He works at odd jobs—longshoreman, night cashier in a cafeteria—menial work that he knows is beneath him but necessary to make ends meet while he thinks things out. Then he meets April Johnson, an "exceptionally first-rate girl." Soon she is sharing his apartment, a love nest of makeshift furniture, packing crate bookcases, and posters of France. A quick trip to city hall makes them Mr. and Mrs. Franklin H. Wheeler. Their days are spent at boring, meaningless jobs, but their nights are filled with animated discussions of art and literature and "the shortcomings of other people's personalities." The shortcomings of the couple's own personalities quickly become evident. Their tiny apartment is soon bursting with the emotional baggage they both own. Frank's father considers his son a disgrace, calling him an "ungrateful, spiteful, foul-mouthed weakling, boozing his way through Greenwich Village." April's parents, a mysterious, careless, and wealthy couple who were married at sea and divorced within a year, had abandoned her soon after her birth, leaving her to be raised by a series of aunts. Her father committed suicide and her mother died in an alcoholic treatment center while April was still a child.

As a result of their pasts, Frank and April are filled with neuroses and complexes. They are haunted by feelings of self-doubt and insecurity, yet they imagine themselves to be superior people who deserve the best life has to offer. Frank has a violent temper that finds expression in fits of shouting and physical destruction. April counters this with her passive-aggressive nature, threatening to leave at one moment and quickly reconciling the next. Both regret their periodic outbursts and, after each one, they lick their wounds and hold firmly to the belief that something will happen to make it all better. Add to this their penchant for consuming great quantities of alcohol, and one sees disaster looming.

"And one big thing went wrong right away. According to their plan, which called for an eventual family of four, her first pregnancy came seven years too soon." April clearly does not want to have the baby, and Frank is terrified and outraged to learn that she plans to induce a miscarriage. His fury is not so much a result of her decision; he really does not want a child in his life right now either, but he is angry that she made the decision without consulting him. He insists on having control of the situation and he gets it by forbidding April to terminate her pregnancy. April agrees to give birth and, from that point, they begin a steady descent into the conventional mediocrity of suburban smugness that they so despise.

But all of this is merely prologue; the novel truly begins in 1955, when the Wheeler's first child, Jennifer, is six years old and her brother, Michael, is four. The family has moved from their bohemian apartment on the western edge of Greenwich Village to a respectable home in suburban Connecticut, on Revolutionary Road. Frank has taken a decent position at Knox Business Machines, where his father had worked for decades with little advancement, and April stays home with the children. Outwardly, their life is indistinguishable from that of their neighbors and best friends, Shep and Milly Campbell. Both men take the train to boring, unfulfilling jobs, and both women fill their hours raising their children and doing housework. The monotony is broken briefly when they and others in the same situation decide to form a community theater group, the Laurel Players.

Yates brilliantly has them choose *The Petrified Forest* as the group's first (and last) production. The play, written by Robert Sherwood, tells the story of a young woman, Gabrielle, who lives in her father's roadside gas station/café in the Arizona desert. She longs to leave her dismal life and flee to France, as her mother had done years earlier. April, who has graduated from a drama academy, plays Gabrielle. The other players lack her formal training and on opening night that lack is painfully obvious. The performance is a disaster.

Frank watches the play from the last row of the theater, and as he drives April home after the performance, she makes it clear that she is disappointed and sad and just wants to be left alone. Frank will have none of that: he wants her to feel better immediately, to get over it; he wants things to be like they were in the "old days." April begs him to stop talking and, when he pulls the car off of the highway and moves closer to put his arm around her shoulders, she bolts from the car and runs away. Enraged, he pursues her. They begin shouting insults and accusations at one another, and at one point, Frank pulls his arm back to hit her, but he brings his fist down four times on the roof of the car instead. For the moment, their anger is spent and they climb back to the car and continue home.

Frank and April spend the remainder of the weekend being coldly cordial to one another, and on Monday Frank goes to work at the "dullest job you could possibly imagine," hung over, bewildered, and feeling sorry for himself. He decides that this will be the day he will make a long-held fantasy become real: that of seducing a rather dim receptionist named Maureen Grube. After plying her with drinks at lunch, the deed is finally done in her apartment.

When Frank returns home in the evening, feeling on top of the world and very much in control, he is met in the carport by an April who is immeasurably different from the one he left that morning. She is wearing a black cocktail dress, ballet slippers, and a little white apron. It is Frank's thirtieth birthday and April surprises him with a family party. She also surprises him with a bold plan for their future: after much thought and practical preparation, she has decided that they should leave the suburbs behind and start a new life in Europe. She explains to an incredulous Frank that she blames all their troubles on their decision to have their first child, Jennifer, six years ago.

That's how we both got committed to this enormous delusion—because that's what it is, an enormous, obscene delusion—this idea that people have to resign from real life and "settle down" when they have families. It's the great sentimental lie of the suburbs, and I've been making you subscribe to it all this time.

April truly believes that Frank is destined for something greater than the Knox Company. Living in Europe, perhaps Paris, with her as the breadwinner, will give him the time to find that "something," whatever it may be.

Initially, Frank is overjoyed. This is an old dream come true: a chance to perhaps capitalize on the promise he showed while attending Columbia, a chance to escape the quicksand of the American suburbs. "Economic circumstances might force you to live in this environment, but the important thing was to keep from being contaminated. The important thing, always, was to remember who you were."

"There now began a time of such joyous derangement, of such exultant carelessness, that Frank Wheeler could never afterwards remember how long it lasted." At the office he is charming to Maureen Grube but he makes it clear that there can be no further involvement. In an unusual burst of responsible behavior, he tackles a long overdue assignment: the rewriting of a promotional handout that will be distributed at an electronics convention in Toledo. The piece, "Speaking of Production Control," brings Frank favorable notice from Bart Pollock, a Knox Company executive, who offers Frank a promotion and a raise. When he tells this news to April, he is dismayed that, instead of being pleased and proud of him, she questions why he did not tell Pollock of their plan to leave the country.

Frank is clearly a more careful and conservative man than he is willing to admit. Although he seems to take pleasure and some pride in announcing to friends and neighbors the decision to move to Europe, he is reluctant to strike the match that will burn the bridge between himself and the Knox Company. Over a multi-drink lunch with Pollock, Frank finally says that he will be leaving the company in the fall. Pollock assumes that another company has lured Frank away and he pulls out all the stops in an effort to keep Frank at Knox. In a final, desperate, act of sentimentality, Pollock tells Frank, "I believe it'd be a fine memorial and tribute to your dad." It is all Frank can do to keep from crying.

Frank is terrified of the unknown, of not being in control of his fate. His old self-doubts have been haunting him since April announced her plan. He is not as certain as he once was that he really is much more than just another middle-class office worker with a wife, kids, and a mortgage. In addition, he is not so sure he likes the idea of being wholly dependent upon April, in Europe or anywhere else. (The contemporary reader of this novel must keep in mind that in 1955 in America it was very unusual for a married woman with children to have a job; and it was considered shameful for a wife to go to work to support an able-bodied husband.)

Frank feels torn in two: the safety and surety of the very life he has professed to despise has become more attractive than anything Europe could offer. It becomes vitally important to him to find a way out of April's plan. Ironically, it is April herself who provides Frank with the way out he craves. She is pregnant again.

Initially April sinks into despair at the hopelessness of their situation. She declares that her carelessness has ruined the plans she has for him. Frank comforts her with words of encouragement: this is only a postponement, everything will be fine, they can go to Europe another time. "He gave up trying to control his face, which now hung aching with joy over her shoulder as he pressed and stroked her with both hands. . . . The pressure was off; life had come mercifully back to normal." While Frank is washing up for dinner, he rehearses possible arguments to convince April that staying put and having this child would be best for everyone. But, as he looks in the linen closet for a towel, he finds hidden in the folds of some sheets a rubber syringe; the instrument April has bought to induce a miscarriage. He confronts her in the kitchen and there is a short contest of wills.

Frank realizes that threatening and bullying will not work and he begins a campaign to change April's mind. It begins like a courtship: Frank is on his best behavior, taking her on long drives to expensive countryside restaurants and out for evenings in New York. Yates describes Frank's actions in both military and public relations terms: "His main tactical problem, in this initial phase of the campaign, was to find ways of making his position attractive, as well as commendable." Frank is only mildly successful; April has begun to waiver slightly, but he worries about what she might do while he is not at home. There is just a small window of opportunity available to April wherein she may perform the abortion on herself with relative safety. Frank is desperate and as a last resort, he begins to make her doubt her own sanity. He receives help for this tactic from an unexpected source: the realtor, Mrs. Givings, her husband, and their grown son, John, who is institutionalized in the state hospital for the mentally deranged.

John Givings is the antithesis of Frank: Where Frank is finicky about his clothing and grooming, John has a careless disregard for his appearance; while Frank takes great pains in mentally rehearsing almost everything he says, John speaks his mind freely without thought of the impression he is making. The Givings have been allowed by John's doctor to take their son for monthly visits to the Wheeler's home. It is hoped that time spent with "sensitive, congenial people of his own age" will lead to John being allowed to have home visits with his mother and father. April, weakened by Frank's pseudo-Freudian pronouncements regarding her desire to abort her pregnancy, is so unnerved by the erratic behavior John exhibits on his second visit to their home that she agrees she may indeed need psychiatric help.

Frank acts quickly to consolidate what he perceives as his victory over April's will. He tells friends and colleagues that the plans for Europe are off, for now. He accepts Bart Pollock's offer of a new position and a raise and, in a moment of supreme egoistic stupidity, rekindles his affair with Maureen Grube.

The date by which April might have safely induced a miscarriage passes, and the Wheelers begin their descent into suburban normalcy. One night, in an attempt to fight off boredom, the Wheelers and the Campbells decide to revisit on of their old haunt, Vito's Log Cabin: a sleazy dive that features dancing to the Steve Kovick Quartet every Friday and Saturday night. After numerous rounds of drinks, Milly Campbell gets sick and the foursome leaves to go home. Shep Campbell's car, however, is blocked in the parking lot and, after some drunken discussion, it is decided that Frank will drive Milly home and Shep and April will follow later. Back in Vito's, April and Shep begin a mutual seduction that climaxes in the backseat of Shep's car.

April has reached her breaking point. There follows another horrific visit from the Givings and a violent argument with Frank. The morning after the argument, however, she is up early, smiling shyly, and preparing a perfect breakfast for the two of them. She sends Frank off to his office with a kiss and goes about her housework. Yates draws this scene masterfully. The reader has a strong sense that something is about to jump out and say "Boo!" The tension is almost unbearable. April takes a wastebasket out to the incinerator on the hill behind the house. She sits there for a moment listening to children's voices that come to her from somewhere beyond the hill; she thinks they may be the voices of her own children, who are staying with the Campbell's. She recalls a heartbreaking memory from her childhood and returns home. There she writes a note for Frank: "Dear Frank,

Whatever happens please don't blame yourself." She then props the number for the hospital on the telephone and sterilizes the rubber syringe.

At two that afternoon, Milly calls Shep at his office to tell him that an ambulance has just left the Wheeler's driveway. Shep locates Frank and takes him to the hospital, where they learn that April has died on the operating table. The doctors could not stop the bleeding. Yates leaves unanswered the question of what April may have hoped to accomplish by performing the abortion on herself. Was she hoping to make the new life in Europe a possibility again? Was she simply so overcome by sadness and disappointment that she knew that her action would result in her death? Yates gives us a little insight into April's state of mind in part of a conversation that takes place between April and Shep at Vito's. Shep had asked her about her early days in New York:

"You still felt that life was passing you by?"

"Sort of. I still had this idea that there was a whole world of marvelous golden people somewhere, as far ahead of me as the seniors at Rye when I was in sixth grade; people who knew everything instinctively, who made their lives work out the way they wanted without even trying, who never had to make the best of a bad job because it never occurred to them to do anything less than perfectly the first time. Sort of heroic super-people, all of them beautiful and witty and calm and kind, and I always imagined that when I did find them I'd suddenly know that I belonged among them, that I was one of them, that I'd been meant to be one of them all along, and everything in the meantime had been a mistake; and they'd know it too. I'd be like the ugly duckling among the swans. . . . It's a thing I wouldn't wish on anybody. It's the most stupid, ruinous kind of self-deception there is, and it gets you into nothing but trouble."

In the aftermath, the Wheeler children are sent to live with Frank's older brother's family. Frank moves back to the city, where he exists as a "walking, talking, smiling, lifeless man," and the tragedy becomes nothing more than an interesting story for Milly to tell over drinks to the new owners of the house on Revolutionary Road.

Critical reaction to *Revolutionary Road* was, for the most part, favorable. In his review for *Commentary,* Theodore Solotaroff wrote,

> What makes the book as good as it is, is mainly Yates's ability to tell the truth—both about the little, summary moments of work and marriage today and—though less clearly—about the social issues which the behavior and fate of the Wheelers represent. Passage after passage has the simple, unmistakable ring of authenticity.

However, Orville Prescott wrote in a *New York Times* review, "Whether the mentally ill Wheelers deserve the five years of labor Mr. Yates lavished upon them is another question." That "five years of labor" and the birth of another daughter, Monica, was more than the Yates's marriage could bear, which ended in divorce in 1959.

Yates had taught creative writing at the New School for Social Research from 1959 through 1962 and at Columbia University from 1960 through 1962, but the publication and reception of *Revolutionary Road* opened many more academic doors to him. For the rest of his life, Yates was able to supplement his writing income by accepting teaching positions at universities. Yates's good fortune continued into 1962, when *Revolutionary Road* was nominated for the National Book Award. In that year he also received a Guggenheim Fellowship, and his second book, a collection of short stories, was published.

ELEVEN KINDS OF LONELINESS

Yates's first story in this collection, "Dr. Jack-o'-Lantern," relates a few days in the life of a foster child, Vincent "Vinny" Sabella. Vincent has spent most of his life in an orphanage but is now being raised by foster parents. On his first day of fourth grade in his new suburban school, Vincent is clearly a misfit. His ragged clothes and "street kid" speech and mannerisms set him apart from his classmates who live in homes with yards and who have caring parents, siblings, pets, and friends. His situation has filled his young and attractive teacher, Miss Price, with a sense of mission. She calls upon her class to do all that they can to make the new boy feel at home.

The first order of business this school day is the telling of "reports." Nancy Parker is chosen, and she stands before the class and relates her past weekend activities. On Friday, her brother had come home and taken the whole family for a drive in his new Pontiac. They drove to White Plains and had dinner in a restaurant and were going to see a horror movie, *Dr. Jekyll and Mr. Hyde,* but it was decided that Nancy was too young. She concludes her report with details of the rest of her weekend, creating a picture of an orderly, secure, well-to-do, educated, and loving household. Warren Berg is next to give his report. He and his best friend, Bill Stringer, rode their bikes into White Plains and saw *Dr. Jekyll and Mr. Hyde.* Warren regales his classmates with graphic descriptions of Dr. Jekyll's transformation. His weekend ended with his dad helping him and Bill rig up a rubber tire swing that will transport them over a ravine and back again. He is clearly proud of the fact that he can accomplish something that involves some risk of injury.

Vincent struggles through his first week. He stands apart from his classmates at recess; when they go to their homes for lunch, he is left alone in the classroom with his paper bag. Additionally, Miss Price's well-meant attempts to help Vincent fit in have resulted in his being seen as the teacher's pet. He wants desperately to just be "one of the guys."

The following Monday, Vincent's hand is the first one up when Miss Price asks if any student would like to give a report of their weekend. He stands before the class and gives a sensational account. "I sore that pitcha. Doctor Jack-o'-Lantern and Mr. Hide." He continues, "And then on Sunday my mudda and fodda come out to see me in this car they got. This Buick. My fodda siz, 'Vinny, wanna go for a little ride?' I siz, 'Sure, where yiz goin'?'" The rest of his story includes a high-speed police chase, his father getting shot in the shoulder, and Vincent driving him to the hospital. Yates writes, "By this time the few members of the class who could bear to look at him were doing so with heads on one side and mouths partly open, the way you look at a broken arm or a circus freak." At lunch, Miss Price suggests to Vincent that it would have been much better if he had told the class about the shopping trip he took with his foster mother to buy his obviously new windbreaker.

Vincent rushes to the bathroom and vomits up his pimento cheese sandwich. He steps outside into an alleyway and begins to chalk all the dirty words he can think of on a blank concrete wall. He is about to start his fifth word when he is discovered by some of his classmates. Miss Price is made aware of Vincent's misbehavior and tells him to stay after school. "While the room was clearing out she sat at her desk, closed her eyes and massaged the frail bridge of her nose with thumb and forefinger, sorting out half-remembered fragments of a book she had once read on the subject of seriously disturbed children." Vincent is made to wash the words from the wall and then endure a dose of Miss Price's pseudo-psychological platitudes. Outside, Warren and Bill are waiting to hear what happened. Vincent earns their admiration with a tale of being punished severely with a ruler by Miss Price. However, his story bursts like a soap bubble when a very friendly Miss Price catches up with them on the sidewalk and is especially nice to Vincent. The boys are furious with Vincent and begin to

shove him back and forth. "Ruler, my eye!" "Jeez, you lie about everything, don'tcha, Sabella?" "Why don'tcha run on home with Miss Price, Doctor Jack-o'-Lantern?"

Vincent's frustration is overwhelming. He had nearly crossed the gap that divided him from his peers. It was as if he had taken a turn on Warren and Bill's tire swing, flying far over the ravine only to be met with the force of Miss Price, who returned him to where he had started. He exacts a cruel revenge on her by returning to the concrete wall and drawing a vulgar picture of a nude woman. After standing back and admiring his work, he prints beneath it "Miss Price."

The other stories in this collection present the same sort of class division, misunderstanding, and miscommunication. "The Best of Everything" tells of a somewhat sophisticated office girl who is on the brink of marrying an insensitive oaf. In "Jody Rolled the Bones," the soldiers under the command of Sergeant Reece lose all sense of personal discipline and corporate achievement when a less demanding officer replaces Reece. A wife who has visited her husband every Sunday for four years in the tuberculosis ward of a veterans' hospital realizes, in "No Pain Whatsoever," that she lives a life of neither a wife nor a widow. The young man in "A Glutton for Punishment" is a chronic, compulsive failure who tries desperately to keep his wife from knowing that he has just lost yet another job. Leon Sobel is a former sheet metal worker with literary pretensions in "A Wrestler with Sharks." "Fun with a Stranger" explores the strange, defensive loyalty students have for their unpromising and disappointing teacher, Miss Snell. "The B.A.R. Man" is a pathetic and cruel veteran of World War II whose only sense of accomplishment is tied to the training he received in firing the Browning Automatic Rifle (BAR), training and discipline that he is unable or unwilling to incorporate into his life in postwar New York.

"A Really Good Jazz Piano" is the only story in this collection set in Europe. Two well-to-do recent Yale graduates, Ken Platt and Carson Wyler, are spending a summer in France. Ken "discovers" an African American pianist in Cannes who plays "a really good jazz piano" and convinces Carson to come down from Paris and evaluate his find. Despite their posturing as sophisticated men of the world, they reveal themselves to be nothing more than racist clods. "Out with the Old" is another story of life within a veterans' hospital tuberculosis ward. The accepted roles and routines of these semi-invalid men are upset by visits home during the Christmas holiday.

Perhaps the most ambitious story in the collection is "Builders." Whereas the previous ten stories had been written in the early 1950s while Yates was in Europe, "Builders" was written in 1961. Yates, referring to the writing of his second novel, *A Special Providence* (1969), said in his 1972 interview with DeWitt Henry and Geoffrey Clark for *Ploughshares,* "I thought I'd try a direct autobiographical blowout, and see if I could make decent fiction out of that. So as a sort of experimental warm-up, I wrote the story called 'Builders,' which was almost pure personal history, with a protagonist named Robert Prentice, who was clearly and nakedly myself."

Prentice dreams of living the life of a Hemingway-type writer but sells himself and his talent short by answering an ad that reads, "Unusual free-lance opportunity for talented writer. Must have imagination." The placer of the ad, taxi driver Bernie Silver, wants someone who can ghostwrite a romanticized version of Silver's daily life. Silver imagines himself as a dispenser of wisdom, a compassionate friend, and an agent of positive change to those who are fortunate enough to ride in his cab. His overbearing self-importance even allows him to lecture Prentice on how to hone his craft:

Do you see where writing a story is building something too? Like building a house? I mean a house has got to have a roof, but you're going to be in trouble if you build your roof first, right? Before you build your roof you have got to build your walls. Before you build your walls you got to lay your foundation—and I mean all the way down the line. Before you lay your foundation you got to bulldoze and dig yourself the right kind of hole in the ground. Am I right?

But, most important of all, there must be a source of illumination:

"Where are the windows?" he demanded, spreading his hands. "That's the question. Where does the light come in? Because do you see what I mean about the light coming in, Bob? I mean the—the *philosophy* of your story; the *truth* of it; the—"

Prentice agrees to expand upon Silver's plot summaries. Silver is pleased with Prentice's work and the two men begin encouraging each other's delusions of greatness. Soon, however, there are arguments over money. Silver is quick to promise but slow to pay. As Silver becomes more demanding and his story ideas more ludicrous, Prentice realizes that his dream of "building my life on the pattern of Ernest Hemingway's" is as far-fetched as Silver's sappy scenarios. The two dissolve their partnership and Silver decides that his ideas would be better presented in comic strip form. Years later Prentice recalls Silver's question about the windows:

Bernie, old friend, forgive me, but I haven't got the answer to that one. I'm not even sure if there are *any* windows in this particular house. Maybe the light is just going to have to come in a best it can, through whatever chinks and cracks have been left in the builder's faulty craftsmanship, and if that's the case you can be sure that nobody feels worse about it than I do. God knows, Bernie, God knows there certainly ought to be a window around here somewhere, for all of us.

Near the end of this unabashedly autobiographical long story, Prentice/Yates gives us some insight into his own journey as a writer; casting off his early model, adopting another and finally finding his own voice. "With Hemingway safely abandoned, I had moved on to a F. Scott Fitzgerald phase; then, the best of all, I had begun to find what seemed to give every indication of being my own style." Yates's indebtedness to Fitzgerald is the subject of a later story, "Saying Goodbye to Sally."

A PERIOD OF EXPLORATION

It would be seven years before Yates published another book. During that time, based on the critical reception of *Revolutionary Road* and *Eleven Kinds of Loneliness,* Yates was offered several writing and teaching jobs. In 1962 producer, director John Frankenheimer, who was completing work on one of his finest films, *The Manchurian Candidate,* asked Yates to write the screenplay for William Styron's *Lie Down in Darkness.* Disregarding the hard lessons learned by other writers who had been lured to Hollywood, his idol F. Scott Fitzgerald among them, Yates accepted Frankenheimer's offer and moved to Los Angeles. The screenplay was finished in 1963 but was never filmed. Yates said in the *Ploughshares* interview,

> The movie was never produced because it fell apart in the casting—they couldn't get Natalie Wood for the lead—but the screenplay was accepted, and everybody seemed to like it, including Styron himself. And it was fascinating work, trying to turn verbal images into visual images for the screen—I greatly enjoyed doing it. But I kept finding out that there were things Styron had done with his pencil that couldn't possibly have been accomplished with a camera—subtleties that would inevitably have been lost in the translation. If the picture had been made it would have been a competent movie, I think, but it wouldn't have been anywhere near as rich or as rewarding as the book.

Ploughshares Books published the screenplay in 1985.

A curious anomaly occurred in 1963 when Yates, the chronicler of human hopelessness and failure, took a job writing speeches for a champion of human potential, Attorney General Robert F. Kennedy. William Styron had recommended Yates for the position and for eight months, Yates wrote "everything that came out of his [RFK's] mouth," according to Elizabeth Venant of the *Los Angeles Times.* Yates gave up the job in November after Robert's brother, President John F. Kennedy, was assassinated in Dallas, Texas.

A job editing a collection of short stories, *Stories for the Sixties* (1963), plus a grant from the National Institute of Arts and Letters provided Yates some solvency in early 1964. In the fall of that year, Yates was offered a teaching position at the University of Iowa's prestigious Iowa Writers' Workshop. Although the salary was low (less than a thousand dollars a month) the workload was light and allowed Yates ample time to pursue his writing. Indeed, the job description asked for little more than occasional teaching, some fiction writing, and acting as a role model for his students. To supplement his teaching income, Yates continued to write screenplays. The only one filmed was *The Bridge at Remagen,* which he wrote in collaboration with William Roberts and Roger Hirson. The movie tells the story of a group of American soldiers who are ordered to capture an important bridge on the Rhine River during the last few months of World War II. It was released in 1969 and starred George Segal and Robert Vaughn.

Yates's health, both physical and mental, was chronically precarious after his bout with tuberculosis. His condition was not helped by the fact that he was a heavy smoker and a very heavy drinker. His abuses caught up with him in August of 1965 and he was required to be hospitalized in the Neuropsychiatric Institute at the University of California in Los Angeles for three months. There are several hints throughout Yates's admittedly autobiographical fiction that there may have been several such hospitalizations. Mental illness and alcoholism play increasingly important parts in Yates's work from this period onward.

In November of 1965 Yates was able to return to his duties at the University of Iowa, write screenplays for Columbia Pictures, and work on his second novel. In 1966 Yates was given a National Endowment for the Arts Award and the following year he received a Rockefeller grant. This period of stability was further solidified in 1968, when Yates married his second wife, Martha Speer. The following year *A Special Providence* was published.

A SPECIAL PROVIDENCE

The rather lengthy prologue to *A Special Providence* presents eighteen-year-old Private Robert Prentice, who is travelling from his army base in Virginia to New York City. He is spending his weekend pass visiting his mother before being shipped out to the war in Europe. His mother, Alice, lives in a seedy apartment, works in a lens-grinding shop, drinks too much, and believes strongly in her and her son's "special providence." She divorced Robert's father, George, when Robert was three and she was thirty-eight, and went to Paris with her little boy to "become an artist of distinction—a sculptor." On her return to America six months later, she pushed George to his economic limit with her ever increasing demands for more alimony and child support. George argued passionately that she should learn to live within her means but this line of reasoning produced hysterical outbursts from Alice and George cowered in acquiescence. Finally the strain of working harder to produce more money was too much for George; he dropped dead in his office during Robert's second year in a "good New England

prep school." Mother and son managed to adjust to the sudden loss of income, but Alice became more self-deluding in her sense of artistic uniqueness and Robert, who has left school temporarily to take a job at an automobile-parts warehouse, begins to imagine himself as "the hero of some inspiring movie about the struggles of the poor."

Part one begins at an Army training camp. Prentice tries hard to fit in. His penchant for looking at life as a series of cinematic stock images is evident in his selection of a role model for proper soldierly behavior: John Quint, a pipe smoking intellectual. Hearing Quint raise a question during an Army indoctrination session, Prentice realizes,

> He knew what he wanted in the Army now. The hell with this childish nonsense of being "liked" or "disliked," of being "accepted" or not. All he wanted now, beyond a certain competence, was to be as intelligent and articulate as Quint, as independent as Quint, as aloof from the Army's indignities as Quint. He very nearly wanted to be Quint.

Quint becomes a reluctant mentor to Prentice but soon realizes the boy is a hopeless incompetent: "Damn it, Prentice, if you had made the formation this morning you would've heard the announcement. Now I've got to explain everything to you, as usual." Despite Quint's frustrations with Prentice, the two men become friends. While fighting together in the Battle of the Bulge, Quint and Prentice develop serious cases of pneumonia. Surprisingly, Quint asks Prentice for advice, "I mean I think we both ought to go to Agate and tell him we're sick. Tell him we can't make it, and go back to the aid station. Right now. Doesn't that sound sensible." Yates continues:

> It was an oddly dramatic moment—exactly like a moment in the movies when the music stops dead on the soundtrack while the hero makes up his mind—and it didn't take Prentice long to decide what his answer would be. It didn't even matter

that it had to come out in his absurd falsetto. "No," he said. "I don't want to."

Uncharacteristically, Quint does not attack Prentice's Hollywood bravado. He puts his pipe in his mouth and stares down at his overshoes. It is clear that Quint will not leave the front and seek the medical attention he knows he desperately needs. Later, after Prentice's and Quint's platoons have separated, Prentice's illness causes him to pass out into a "silent, spinning darkness; and soon there was a dream in which his mother appeared, saying 'Just rest, now, Bobby. Just rest.'"

In part two, Yates expands what we have already learned of Prentice's childhood in the prologue. It is a long, heart-wrenching story of a boy's total devotion to his seriously delusional mother. We are shown clearly how Robert Prentice became the man he is and what produced his skewed sense of self.

Prentice awakes at the beginning of part three to find himself in an Army hospital far from the front lines. After five weeks there, his pneumonia is cured and he returns to his platoon where he learns of Quint's death. Prentice, of course, blames himself. He tries writing to Quint's family but quickly abandons the effort. True to his sense of high drama, Prentice decides that "The only way he could ever make amends was with action, not words—with whatever action might still be possible on the dangerous land beyond this river—and he put himself to sleep with daydreams of heroic combat and rescue and self-sacrifice." As the war ends, however, "He had proved nothing, he had made no viable gesture of atonement, and he knew now that he probably never will. If he could talk with Quint's ghost now he could only say: 'I'm sorry; there's nothing more I can do.'" However, as he takes a Russian girl out for a dalliance in a field of grass, he is happy to be nineteen and alive.

The epilogue brings us back to New York City, where Alice is anxiously awaiting the return of her son. Dining with her friend, Na-talie, she can hardly contain her excitement as she relates how her life will change once her Bobby is home. She imagines that her son will insist that she quit her job. He will be the breadwinner and provide her the security and freedom to produce enough good pieces of sculpture to have a solo exhibition. This marvelous bubble of make-believe is burst, however, when she receives a letter from Prentice. In it he tells her that he is not coming home; he intends to live in England and perhaps go to school there. He has enclosed some money orders and wishes her good luck.

A PRODUCTIVE DECADE

The critics and the book buying public ignored *A Special Providence*. It won no awards and was never reprinted. Yates himself admitted to the novel's weakness in his *Ploughshares* interview: "I suspect that's why *A Special Providence* is a weak book—one of the reasons, anyway. It's not properly formed; I never did achieve enough fictional distance on the character of Robert Prentice." Later in that interview he confesses:

> What happened after those two books [*Revolutionary Road* and *Eleven Kinds of Loneliness*] was my own fault and nobody else's. If I had followed them up with another good novel a few years later, and then another a few years after that, and so on, I might very well have begun to build the kind of reputation some successful writers enjoy. Instead I tinkered and brooded and fussed for more than seven years over the book that finally became *A Special Providence,* and it was a failure in my own judgment as well as that of almost everyone else, and was generally ignored.

It would be six years before his next novel, *Disturbing the Peace* (1975), was published. During those years depression, alcoholism, and frequent breakdowns increasingly plagued Yates. He was denied tenure at the University of Iowa in 1971, and his marriage to Martha ended in divorce in 1975. The custody of their daughter, Gina, was awarded to Martha. In spite of all this personal turmoil, the period between 1975 and 1985 proved to be Yates's most productive decade. His old friend, Seymour Lawrence, now owner of his own publishing house, contracted to pay Yates $1,500 per month. Relieved of his teaching duties and somewhat stable financially, Yates managed to publish three novels within three years: *Disturbing the Peace* (1975), *The Easter Parade* (1976), and *A Good School* (1978). Although all three were well received and helped to restore his reputation, they were burdened with the same flaw he himself found in *A Special Providence*: the lack of fictional distance between the author and his character.

Disturbing the Peace is a journey into madness. John Wilder, during an alcoholic binge, has threatened to kill his wife and children. He is committed to Bellevue for psychiatric evaluation. After agreeing to attend Alcoholics Anonymous meetings, Wilder is released and tries to rebuild his life. True to the Yatesean formula, however, he fails miserably. He skips his AA meetings, his marriage falls apart, and he takes up with a much younger woman, Pamela Hendricks, whose friends encourage Wilder to make a movie of his Bellevue experience. Pamela's father provides the money necessary for her to take Wilder to Hollywood in hopes of finding a movie studio that would be interested in his story. Chester Pratt, Pamela's former lover, is hired by a Hollywood producer to write the screenplay of Wilder's story. He is everything Wilder/Yates aspires to: a successful novelist, witty, urbane, in touch with himself and his times, a man for whom AA has produced the desired results. After a series of increasingly horrific breakdowns, Wilder is permanently confined in a mental institution.

Perhaps hoping to provide the necessary "fictional distance," Yates presents a female protagonist, Emily Grimes, in *The Easter Parade*. Yates tells us in the first line of the novel what we can expect, "Neither of the Grimes sisters would have a happy life, and looking back it always seemed that the trouble began with their parent's divorce." The following 229 pages chronicle their unhappiness and hopelessness over four decades. In the *Atlantic Monthly*, James Atlas wrote,

> In *The Easter Parade* and *Disturbing the Peace*, Yates gives such savage portraits of his characters' inadequacies that one no longer cares about them; having nervous breakdowns, sopping up gin, they seem beyond salvaging. The novelist, like the tyrant, has complete authority over his subjects, and must rule with at least occasional benevolence or risk revolt. It isn't enough to claim accuracy, to reproduce an alcoholic's haggard speech or a failed artist's delusions of fame; there must be some tempering sense of grace or pity.

Compared to his previous work, Yates's next novel, *A Good School*, is a breath of fresh air. The protagonist, Bill Grove, manages to suffer the indignities of being the out-of-place new boy at a struggling New England prep school and, in the end, emerges strong and hopeful. The "tempering sense of grace or pity" that Atlas sought is evident from the very beginning. Indeed, what Yates has written here is nothing less than a heartfelt appreciation of and gratitude for the struggles his father must have endured to provide him with an above average education.

Bill Grove's family is the familiar Yatesean autobiographical model. His father, Mike, who has a beautiful tenor voice and is often asked to sing "Danny Boy," works for the Mazda Light Division of the General Electric Company. His mother, divorced from Mike and living with their son and daughter in a Greenwich Village apartment, "became a sculptor who longed to have rich people admire her work and accept her into their lives." On the advice of someone she met at a society wedding, Bill's mother investigates the possibility of sending the fifteen-year-old to Dorset Academy. Bill's father agrees to pay the costs: "It isn't hard to guess how my father must have felt about all this. The notion of an expensive boarding school must have struck him as preposterous, and the cost of it must surely have put him into debt. But he was very agreeable about it to me." The gentleness of this passage is in sharp contrast to the hysteria encountered in the same scene as written nine years earlier in *A Special Providence*.

Dorset Academy, founded by an eccentric millionaire, Abigail Church Hooper, has a reputation for accepting troubled or difficult boys. Bill struggles to fit in socially but realizes that the only way he will receive respect and recognition is by doing what he does best, writing. He wins an essay-writing contest whose prize is appointment to the editorial board of the school newspaper, the Dorset *Chronicle*. His pride is evident when his father comes to Dorset for a visit: "When they'd walked enough for his father to see most of the architecture, Grove took him up to the *Chronicle* office—it was all he had to be proud of—and showed him that." The father and son part tenderly. Soon thereafter his classmates notice that Bill is absent from school and it is announced that he is away attending his father's funeral.

World War II and financial troubles soon devastate the peace of Dorset Academy. Teachers and students enlist for military duty and Mrs. Hooper decides to close the bankrupt school. It will be leased by the army to use as a recovery facility for blinded veterans. Bill, now editor in chief of the *Chronicle*, writes a brilliant piece for the paper's last issue welcoming the men who will be housed in the dormitories during their rehabilitation.

In the afterword, as in the foreword, Bill Grove speaks directly to the reader. He recounts what became of some of his teachers and classmates after the closing of Dorset. But it is the memory of his father that he wants to share.

My father has been often on my mind lately, perhaps because in four more years I will be as old as he was when he died. My mother is long dead too, now and so is my sister—she died young—but it is my father who haunts me most.

He wishes he had the opportunity to thank his father for making his life at Dorset possible and convince him that it was worth the effort.

It saw me through the worst of my adolescence, as few other schools would have done, and it taught me the rudiments of my trade. I learned to write by working on the Dorset *Chronicle,* making terrible mistakes in print that hardly anybody ever noticed. Couldn't that be called a lucky apprenticeship? And is there no further good to be said of the school, or of my time in it? Or of me?

I will probably always ask my father such questions in the privacy of my heart, seeking his love as I failed and failed to seek it when it mattered; but all that—as he used to suggest on being pressed to sing "Danny Boy," taking a backward step, making a little negative wave of the hand, smiling and frowning at the same time—all that is in the past.

As was the case with Yates's previous work, *A Good School* was virtually ignored by the general reading public but elicited warm praise from the critics. Jerome Klinkowitz, in his book, *The New American Novel of Manners,* wrote: "If writing were baseball, this would be Richard Yates's perfect game."

DECLINE AND DEATH

In 1976 Yates's apartment in New York City caught fire, and he was seriously burned. After spending a month in bed recovering, Yates moved to Boston. In his essay "A Salute to Mister Yates," published in *Broken Vessels* in 1991, writer and longtime friend, Andre Dubus, described Yates's apartment:

For several years in the seventies and eighties, Dick lived in an apartment on Beacon Street in

Boston. It is a street with trees and good old brick buildings. He lived on the second floor, in two rooms. The front room was where he wrote and slept. A door at the far end of it, behind his desk, opened to the kitchen; and adjacent to that was the room I never saw him enter. I suppose his youngest daughter, Gina, slept there when she came to visit. Gina's paintings and drawings hung in the first room, above the bed against one wall, and his desk facing another. . . . It was, I believed—and still do—a place that should have been left intact when Dick moved, a place young writers should be able to go to, and sit in, and ask themselves whether or not their commitment to writing had enough heart to live, thirty years later, as Dick did: with time his only luxury, and absolute honesty one of his few rewards.

During his ten years in Boston, Yates supported himself with awards, grants and brief teaching jobs. In 1975 he had received a grant from the National Institute of Arts and Letters, followed in 1976 by a Rosenthal Foundation award. Yates received the National Magazine Award for his short story "Oh, Joseph, I'm So Tired" in 1978, and in 1984 he was awarded $25,000 by the National Endowment for the Arts. Although he was turned down for a teaching position at Amherst College in 1976, he did manage to teach briefly at Boston College in 1982 and Emerson College in 1984. Despite this, Yates's financial problems were reaching a critical stage. Yates began borrowing money from his publisher against future book sales. His book sales, however, barely amounted to enough to cover past advances. Critics politely applauded his second collection of short stories, *Liars in Love* (1981), but his last two novels, *Young Hearts Crying* (1984) and *Cold Springs Harbor* (1986), were considered failures. Indeed, one of Yates's closest friends, Anatole Broyard, wrote a scathing review of *Young Hearts Crying* for the *New York Times Book Review* entitled "Two-Fisted Self Pity." All three books make use of familiar Yates material, but they never achieve the craftsmanship of his earliest novel nor do they fulfill the promise of maturity exhibited in *A Good School.*

Yates left Boston in 1986 and moved to California at the invitation of his former student, David Milch. Milch, a successful producer, offered Yates a job writing pilot scripts for television. For three years Yates lived in an apartment in Los Angeles with his daughter, Monica, writing scripts that never made it to production and teaching briefly at the University of Southern California.

Yates accepted a one-year teaching position at the University of Alabama and moved to Tuscaloosa in 1990. At this time his health, never very good, had deteriorated to the point that he was required to use an oxygen tank to help him breathe. Nevertheless, he began work on a new novel, *Uncertain Times,* based on his eight months as Robert Kennedy's speechwriter. By 1991 he was so weak he could write for little more than an hour a day. He had completed nearly half of the book when he was admitted to the Veteran's Administration hospital in Birmingham, Alabama, for minor surgery to repair a hernia. It was too much for his weakened condition, and he died on November 7, 1992, shortly after the surgery was performed. The cause of death was listed as emphysema.

A RESURGENCE OF INTEREST

At the time of his death, most of Yates's work was out of print. The chance of it ever being reprinted was greatly diminished when Yates's strongest supporter, Seymour Lawrence, died in 1994. Stewart O'Nan, in a 1999 *Boston Review* article entitled "The Lost World of Richard Yates: How the Great Writer of the Age of Anxiety Disappeared from Print" wrote:

> For now, writers will have to keep the novels and stories of Richard Yates alive, rescuing copies from used book stores and passing them along to students and fellow writers just as they've passed

along James Salter's *A Sport and a Pastime,* Marilynne Robinson's *Housekeeping,* and William Maxwell's *Time Will Darken It* for years. We shouldn't have to do it, but we will, gladly. Perhaps in the future, if we're lucky, someone will do it for us.

In 2001 someone did. Henry Holt and Company published *The Collected Stories of Richard Yates.* The volume, with an introduction by Richard Russo, contains all the stories found in *Eleven Kinds of Loneliness* and *Liars in Love* plus nine uncollected stories. Of these, "Evening on the Cote d'Azur" and "Thieves" were published in *Ploughshares* in 1974 and 1976. The other seven make their first appearance in this volume. Additionally, St. Martin's Press has begun publishing Yates's novels in its Picador USA trade paperback editions. As of December 2001 they had released *The Easter Parade* and *A Good School.* Perhaps these new editions will help fulfill the wish Yates expressed to Dubus in "A Salute to Mister Yates." The two were comparing the amount of money each had received from Guggenheim Fellowships, and Dubus was questioning how Yates could survive in Boston on so little. Dubus finally understands what drives Yates and asks him:

> "If they gave you a *hund*red thousand you wouldn't buy a damned thing, would you? You'd live in the same place and write every day and you wouldn't change a *thing,* would you?"
>
> "I don't want money," [Yates] said. "I just want readers."

Selected Bibliography

WORKS OF RICHARD YATES

NOVELS

Revolutionary Road. Boston: Atlantic–Little, Brown, 1962. Reissued in 2000 by Vintage Press.

A Special Providence. New York: Knopf, 1969.

Disturbing the Peace. New York: Seymour Lawrence–Delacorte, 1975.

The Easter Parade. New York: Seymour Lawrence–Delacorte, 1976. Reissued in 2001 by Picador USA.

A Good School. New York: Seymour Lawrence–Delacorte, 1978. Reissued in 2001 by Picador USA.

Young Hearts Crying. New York: Seymour Lawrence–Delacorte, 1984.

Cold Springs Harbor. New York: Seymour Lawrence–Delacorte, 1986.

SHORT STORIES

Eleven Kinds of Loneliness. Boston: Atlantic–Little, Brown, 1962. (Contains "Doctor Jack-o-Lantern," "The Best of Everything," "Jody Rolled the Bones," "No Pain Whatsoever," "A Glutton for Punishment," "A Wrestler with Sharks," "Fun with a Stranger," "The B.A.R. Man," "A Really Good Jazz Piano," "Out With the Old," "Builders.")

Liars in Love. New York: Seymour Lawrence–Delacorte, 1981. (Contains "Oh, Joseph, I'm So Tired," "A Natural Girl," "Trying Out for the Race," "Liars in Love," "A Compassionate Leave," "Regards at Home," "Saying Goodbye to Sally.")

The Collected Stories of Richard Yates. New York: Henry Holt, 2001. (Contains all the stories in *Eleven Kinds of Loneliness* and *Liars in Love* plus "The Canal," "A Clinical Romance," "Bells in the Morning," "Evening on the Cote d'Azur," "Thieves," "A Private Possession," "The Comptroller and the Wild Wind," "A Last Fling, Like," "A Convalescent Ego.")

OTHER WORKS

Stories for the Sixties, edited and with an introduction by Richard Yates. New York: Bantam, 1963.

William Styron's "Lie Down in Darkness." Screenplay. Watertown, Mass.: Ploughshares Books, 1985.

The Bridge at Remagen. Screenplay by Richard Yates, William Roberts, and Roger Hirson. Directed by John Guillermin. United Artists, 1969.

UNCOLLECTED FICTION AND ESSAYS

"Lament for a Tenor." *Cosmopolitan* 136:50–57 (February 1954).

"The End of the Great Depression." *Transatlantic Review* 11:76–83 (winter 1962).

"Appreciation." *December* 23, no. 1:41–44 (1981).

"Some Very Good Masters." *New York Times Book Review,* April 19, 1981, p. 3.

"R.V. Cassill's Clem Anderson." *Ploughshares* 14:189–196 (1988).

"Uncertain Times" (portion of the unfinished novel). *Open City* 3:35–71 (1995).

CRITICAL AND BIOGRAPHICAL STUDIES

Amidon, Stephen. "A Harrowing Mirror of Loneliness." *Atlantic Monthly* 288, no. 1:154–156 (July/August 2001).

Atlas, James. "A Sure Narrative Voice." *Atlantic Monthly* 248, no. 5:84–86 (November 1981).

Broyard, Anatole. "Two-Fisted Self Pity." *New York Times Book Review,* October 28, 1984, p. 3.

Castronovo, David, and Steven Goldleaf. *Richard Yates.* New York: Twayne Publishers, 1996.

Dubus, Andre. "A Salute to Mister Yates." In his *Broken Vessels.* Boston: Godine, 1991. Pp. 93–96.

———. "Good-bye to Richard Yates." In his *Meditations from a Movable Chair.* New York: Knopf, 1998. Pp. 83–84.

Klinkowitz, Jerome. "Richard Yates: The Wedding of Language and Incident." In his *The New American Novel of Manners: The Fiction of Richard Yates, Dan Wakefield, and Thomas McGuane.* Athens, Ga.: the University of Georgia Press, 1986. Pp. 14–59.

Lawrence, Seymour. "Richard Yates: A Requiem," *Poets and Writers Magazine* 21, no. 5:12–17 (September/October 1993).

O'Nan, Stewart. "The Lost World of Richard Yates: How the Great Writer of the Age of Anxiety Disappeared from Print," *Boston Review* 24, no. 5:39–48 (October/November 1999).

Prescott, Orville. "Books of the Times," *New York Times,* March 10, 1961, p. 25.

Ross, Jean W. *Contemporary Authors,* New Revision Series. Vol. 10. Detroit: Gale, 1983. Pp. 534–536.

Solotaroff, Theodore. "The Wages of Maturity," *Commentary* 32, no. 1:89–92 (July 1961).

Venant, Elizabeth. "A Fresh Twist in the Road: For Richard Yates, A Specialist in Grim Irony, Late Fame's a Wicked Return," *Los Angeles Times,* July 9, 1989, p. 1.

INTERVIEWS

DeWitt, Henry, and Geoffrey Clark. "An Interview with Richard Yates." *Ploughshares* 1, no. 3:65–78 (1972).

"The Books That Made Writers." *New York Times Book Review,* November 25, 1979, pp. 7, 80, 82, 84.

—CHARLES R. BAKER

Index

Index

Arabic numbers printed in bold-face type refer to extended treatment of a subject.

IV, 241–242, 243, 253
"Ballad of Carmilhan, The" (Longfellow), **II,** 505
"ballad of chocolate Mabbie, the" (Brooks), **Supp. IV, Part 1,** 15
"Ballad of Dead Ladies, The" (Villon), **Retro. Supp. I,** 286
"Ballad of East and West" (Kipling), **Supp. IX,** 246
"Ballad of Jesse Neighbours, The" (Humphrey), **Supp. IX,** 100
"Ballad of Jesus of Nazareth, A" (Masters), **Supp. I, Part 2,** 459
"Ballad of John Cable and Three Gentlemen" (Merwin), **Supp. III, Part 1,** 342
"Ballad of Nat Turner, The" (Hayden), **Supp. II, Part 1,** 378
"Ballad of Pearl May Lee, The" (Brooks), **Supp. III, Part 1,** 74, 75
"Ballad of Remembrance, A" (Hayden), **Supp. II, Part 1,** 368, 372, 373
Ballad of Remembrance, A (Hayden), **Supp. II, Part 1,** 367
"Ballad of Ruby, The" (Sarton), **Supp. VIII,** 259–260
"Ballad of Sue Ellen Westerfield, The" (Hayden), **Supp. II, Part 1,** 364
"Ballad of the Brown Girl, The" (Cullen), **Supp. IV, Part 1,** 168
Ballad of the Brown Girl, The (Cullen), **Supp. IV, Part 1,** 167, 168, 169–170, 173
"Ballad of the Children of the Czar, The" (Schwartz), **Supp. II, Part 2,** 649
"Ballad of the Girl Whose Name Is Mud" (Hughes), **Retro. Supp. I,** 205
"Ballad of the Goodly Fere," **III,** 458
"Ballad of the Harp-Weaver" (Millay), **III,** 135
"Ballad of the Sad Cafe, The" (McCullers), **II,** 586, 587, 588, 592, 595, 596–600, 604, 605, 606
"Ballad of the Sixties" (Sarton), **Supp. VIII,** 259
"Ballad of Trees and the Master, A" (Lanier), **Supp. I, Part 1,** 370
"Ballad of William Sycamore, The" (Benét), **Supp. XI,** 44, 47
"Ballade" (MacLeish), **III,** 4
"Ballade at Thirty-Five" (Parker), **Supp. IX,** 192
"Ballade for the Duke of Orléans" (Wilbur), **Supp. III, Part 2,** 556
"Ballade of Broken Flutes, The" (Robinson), **III,** 505
"Ballade of Meaty Inversions" (White),

Supp. I, Part 2, 676
Ballads and Other Poems (Longfellow), **II,** 489; **III,** 412, 422
Ballads for Sale (Lowell), **II,** 527
"Ballads of Lenin" (Hughes), **Supp. I, Part 1,** 331
Ballantine's Reader's Circle, **Supp. XI,** 186
Ballantyne, Sheila, **Supp. V,** 70
Ballard, Josephine, *see* McMurtry, Josephine
"Ballet in Numbers for Mary Ellen, A" (Karr), **Supp. XI,** 241
"Ballet of a Buffoon, The" (Sexton), **Supp. II, Part 2,** 693
"Ballet of the Fifth Year, The" (Schwartz), **Supp. II, Part 2,** 650
Ballew, Leighton M., **I,** 95
Balliett, Carl, Jr., **IV,** 376
"Balloon Hoax, The" (Poe), **III,** 413, 420
Ballou, Robert O., **II,** 365
Balo (Toomer), **Supp. III, Part 2,** 484
Balsan, Consuelo, **IV,** 313–314
Balthus, **Supp. IV, Part 2,** 623
Baltimore, Lord, **I,** 132
Baltimore Afro-American (newspaper), **Supp. I, Part 1,** 326, 331
Baltimore Evening Sun (newspaper), **III,** 104, 105, 106, 110, 116
Baltimore Herald (newspaper), **III,** 102
Baltimore Saturday Visitor (newspaper), **III,** 411
Baltimore Sun (newspaper), **III,** 102, 103, 104, 105, 110; **Supp. I, Part 1,** 365; **Supp. XI,** 209
Balzac, Honoré de, **I,** 103, 123, 339, 376, 474, 485, 499, 509, 518; **II,** 307, 322, 324, 328, 336, 337; **III,** 61, 174, 184, 320, 382; **IV,** 192; **Retro. Supp. I,** 91, 217, 218, 235; **Supp. I, Part 2,** 647
Bambara, Toni Cade, **Supp. XI,** 1–23
Banana Bottom (McKay), **Supp. X,** 132, **139–140**
Bancal, Jean, **Supp. I, Part 2,** 514
Bancroft, George, **I,** 544; **Supp. I, Part 2,** 479
Band of Angels (Warren), **IV,** 245, 254–255
Banderas, Antonio, **Supp. VIII,** 74
Banfield, Raffaello de, **IV,** 400
Bang the Drum Slowly (Harris), **II,** 424–425
Banjo: A Story without a Plot (McKay), **Supp. X,** 132, **138–139**
"Banjo Song, A" (Dunbar), **Supp. II, Part 1,** 197
"Bank of England Restriction, The" (Adams), **I,** 4

Bankhead, Tallulah, **IV,** 357; **Supp. IV, Part 2,** 574
Banks, Russell, **Supp. V, 1–19,** 227; **Supp. IX,** 153; **Supp. X,** 85; **Supp. XI,** 178
Bannon, Barbara, **Supp. XI,** 228
Banta, Martha, **II,** 292
"Banyan" (Swenson), **Supp. IV, Part 2,** 651, 652
Baptism, The (Baraka), **Supp. II, Part 1,** 40, 41–42, 43
Baptism of Desire (Erdrich), **Supp. IV, Part 1,** 259
"Bar at the Andover Inn, The" (Matthews), **Supp. IX,** 168
"B.A.R. Man, The" (Yates), **Supp. XI,** 341
Barabtarlo, Gennady, **Retro. Supp. I,** 278
Baraka, Imamu Amiri (LeRoi Jones), **Retro. Supp. I,** 411; **Supp. I, Part 1,** 63; **Supp. II, Part 1, 29–63,** 247, 250; **Supp. III, Part 1,** 83; **Supp. IV, Part 1,** 169, 244, 369; **Supp. VIII,** 295, 329, 330, 332; **Supp. X,** 324, 328
"Barbados" (Marshall), **Supp. XI,** 281
"Barbara Frietchie" (Whittier), **Supp. I, Part 2,** 695–696
Barbarella (film), **Supp. XI,** 293, **307–308**
"Barbarian Status of Women, The" (Veblen), **Supp. I, Part 2,** 636–637
Barbarous Coast, The (Macdonald), **Supp. IV, Part 2,** 472, 474
Barbary Shore (Mailer), **III,** 27, 28, 30–31, 33, 35, 36, 40, 44
Barber, David, **Supp. IV, Part 2,** 550
Barber, Rowland, **Supp. IV, Part 2,** 581
Barber, Samuel, **Supp. IV, Part 1,** 84
"Barclay of Ury" (Whittier), **Supp. I, Part 2,** 693
Bard of Savagery, The: Thorstein Veblen and Modern Social Theory (Diggins), **Supp. I, Part 2,** 650
"Bare Hills, The" (Winters), **Supp. II, Part 2,** 790
Bare Hills, The (Winters), **Supp. II, Part 2,** 786, 788
"Barefoot Boy, The" (Whittier), **Supp. I, Part 2,** 691, 699–700
Barefoot in the Park (Simon), **Supp. IV, Part 2,** 575, 578–579, 586, 590
Barely and Widely (Zukofsky), **Supp. III, Part 2,** 627, 628, 635
Barfield, Owen, **III,** 274, 279
"Bargain Lost, The" (Poe), **III,** 411
Barishnikov, Mikhail, **Supp. VIII,** 22
Barker, Clive, **Supp. V,** 142

Boulanger, Nadia, **Supp. IV, Part 1,** 81

"Boulot and Boulette" (Chopin), **Supp. I, Part 1,** 211

Boulton, Agnes, **III,** 403, 407

Bound East for Cardiff (O'Neill), **III,** 388

"Bouquet, The" (Stevens), **IV,** 90

"Bouquet of Roses in Sunlight" (Stevens), **IV,** 93

Bourdin, Henri L., **Supp. I, Part 1,** 251

Bourgeois Poet, The (Shapiro), **Supp. II, Part 2,** 701, 703, 704, 713, 714–716

Bourget, James, **IV,** 319

Bourget, Paul, **II,** 325, 338; **IV,** 311, 315; **Retro. Supp. I,** 224, 359, 373

Bourjaily, Vance, **III,** 43; **IV,** 118; **Supp. IX,** 260

Bourke-White, Margaret, **I,** 290, 293–295, 297, 311

Bourne, Charles Rogers, **I,** 215

Bourne, Mrs. Charles Rogers, **I,** 215

Bourne, Randolph, **I, 214–238,** 243, 245, 246–247, 251, 259; **Supp. I, Part 2,** 524

Boutroux, Emile, **II,** 365

Bowditch, Nathaniel, **Supp. I, Part 2,** 482

Bowen, Barbara, **Supp. IX,** 311

Bowen, Croswell, **III,** 407

Bowen, Elizabeth, **Retro. Supp. I,** 351; **Supp. IV, Part 1,** 299; **Supp. VIII,** 65, 165, 251, 265; **Supp. IX,** 128

Bowen, Francis, **Supp. I, Part 2,** 413

Bowen, Louise de Koven, **Supp. I, Part 1,** 5

Bowen, Merlin, **III,** 97

Bowen, Michael, **Supp. VIII,** 73

Bowers, Claude G., **II,** 317

Bowers, John, **Supp. XI,** 217–218

"Bowl of Blood, The" (Jeffers), **Supp. II, Part 2,** 434

Bowles, Jane (Jane Auer), **II,** 586; **Supp. IV, Part 1,** 89, 92

Bowles, Paul, **I,** 211; **II,** 586; **Supp. II, Part 1,** 17; **Supp. IV, Part 1,** 79–99

Bowles, Samuel, **I,** 454, 457; **Retro. Supp. I,** 30, 32, 33

"Bowls" (Moore), **III,** 196

Bowman, James, **I,** 193

"Bows to Drouth" (Snyder), **Supp. VIII,** 303

Box and Quotations from Chairman Mao Tse-tung (Albee), **I,** 89–91, 94

Box, Edgar (pseudonym), *see* Vidal, Gore

Box Garden, The (Shields), **Supp. VII,** 314–315, 320

"Box Seat" (Toomer), **Supp. III, Part 2,** 484; **Supp. IX,** 316, 318

Boy, A (Ashbery), **Supp. III, Part 1,** 5

"Boy in France, A" (Salinger), **III,** 552–553

"Boy Riding Forward Backward" (Francis), **Supp. IX,** 82

"Boy Who Wrestled with Angels, The" (Hoffman), **Supp. X,** 90

Boyce, Horace, **II,** 136

Boyd, Blanche, **Supp. I, Part 2,** 578

Boyd, Brian, **Retro. Supp. I,** 270, 275

Boyd, Ernest Augustus, **III,** 121

Boyd, James, **I,** 119

Boyd, Janet L., **Supp. X,** 229

Boyd, Nancy (pseudonym), *see* Millay, Edna St. Vincent

Boyd, Thomas, **I,** 99; **IV,** 427

Boyer, Charles, **Supp. XI,** 307

Boyesen, H. H., **II,** 289

"Boyhood" (Farrell), **II,** 28

Boyle, Kay, **III,** 289; **IV,** 404

Boyle, T. C. (Thomas Coraghessan), **Supp. VIII, 1–17**

Boyle, Thomas John. *See* Boyle, T. C.

Boynton, H. W., **Supp. IX,** 7

Boynton, Henry W., **I,** 357

Boynton, Percy H., **II,** 533; **III,** 72

Boynton, Percy Holmes, **Supp. I, Part 2,** 415

"Boys and Girls" (Cisneros), **Supp. VII,** 59–60

Boy's Froissart, The (Lanier), **Supp. I, Part 1,** 361

Boy's King Arthur, The (Lanier), **Supp. I, Part 1,** 361

Boy's Mabinogion, The (Lanier), **Supp. I, Part 1,** 361

Boys of '76, The (Coffin), **III,** 577

"Boys of '29, The" (Holmes), **Supp. I, Part 1,** 308

Boy's Percy, The (Lanier), **Supp. I, Part 1,** 361

Boy's Town (Howells), **I,** 418

Boy's Will, A (Frost), **II,** 152, 153, 155–156, 159, 164, 166; **Retro. Supp. I,** 124, 127, 128, 131

Bozrah (biblical person), **IV,** 152

"Brace, The" (Bausch), **Supp. VII,** 48

Bracebridge Hall, or, The Humorists (Irving), **I,** 339, 341; **II,** 308–309, 313

Bracher, Frederick, **I,** 378, 380; **Supp. I, Part 1,** 185, 198

Brackenridge, Hugh Henry, **Supp. I, Part 1,** 124, 127, 145; **Supp. II, Part 1,** 65

Brackett, Leigh, **Supp. IV, Part 1,** 130

Bradbury, David L., **Supp. I, Part 2,** 402

Bradbury, John M., **I,** 142, 288–289; **II,** 221; **III,** 502; **IV,** 130, 135, 142, 258

Bradbury, Malcolm, **Supp. VIII,** 124

Bradbury, Ray, **Supp. I, Part 2,** 621–622; **Supp. IV, Part 1,** 101–118

Braddon, Mary E., **Supp. I, Part 1,** 35, 36

Bradfield, Scott, **Supp. VIII,** 88

Bradford, Gamaliel, **I,** 248, 250

Bradford, Roark, **Retro. Supp. I,** 80

Bradford, William, **Supp. I, Part 1,** 110, 112, **Part 2,** 486, 494

Bradlee, Ben, **Supp. V,** 201

Bradley, Bill, **Supp. VIII,** 47

Bradley, F. H., **Retro. Supp. I,** 57, 58

Bradley, Francis Herbert, **I,** 59, 567–568, 572, 573

Bradley, William A., **Supp. I, Part 1,** 173

Bradstreet, Anne, **I,** 178–179, 180, 181, 182, 184; **III,** 505; **Retro. Supp. I,** 40; **Supp. I, Part 1, 98–123, Part 2,** 300, 484, 485, 496, 546, 705; **Supp. V,** 113, 117–118

Bradstreet, Elizabeth, **Supp. I, Part 1,** 108, 122

Bradstreet, Mrs. Simon, *see* Bradstreet, Anne

Bradstreet, Simon, **I,** 178; **Supp. I, Part 1,** 103, 110, 116

Brady, Alice, **III,** 399

Brady, Charles, **Supp. I, Part 2,** 626

Brady, Charles A., **III,** 72

"Bragdowdy and the Busybody, The" (Thurber), **Supp. I, Part 2,** 617

"Brahma" (Emerson), **II,** 19, 20

"Brahmin Dons Homespun, A" (Blair), **Supp. I, Part 2,** 426

Brahms, Johannes, **III,** 118, 448

"Brain and Brawn, Broadway in Review" (Gilder), **Supp. I, Part 2,** 627

"Brain and the Mind, The" (James), **II,** 346

"Brain Damage" (D. Barthelme), **Supp. IV, Part 1,** 44

Braithewaite, W. S., **Retro. Supp. I,** 131

Braithwaite, William Stanley, **Supp. IX,** 309

Bramer, Monte, **Supp. X,** 152

Brancaccio, Patrick, **Supp. I, Part 1,** 148

Branch, Edgar M., **II,** 52; **IV,** 213

Branch Will Not Break, The (Wright), **Supp. III, Part 2,** 596, 598–601; **Supp. IV, Part 1,** 60; **Supp. IX,** 159

Brancusi, Constantin, **III,** 201; **Retro.**

Supp. I, Part 1, 200

Chicago Tribune (newspaper), **II,** 417; **Supp. I, Part 2,** 490, 606; **Supp. IV, Part 1,** 205, **Part 2,** 570; **Supp. V,** 239, 282; **Supp. VIII,** 80; **Supp. X,** 11, 15

Chicago Tribune Book World (publication), **Supp. IV, Part 1,** 208

"Chicano/Borderlands Literature and Poetry" (Ríos), **Supp. IV, Part 2,** 537, 538, 542, 545

Chick, Nancy, **Supp. IV, Part 1,** 1

"Chickamauga" (Bierce), **I,** 201

"Chickamauga" (Wolfe), **IV,** 460

"Chickamauga" (Wright), **Supp. V,** 334

Chickamauga (Wright), **Supp. V,** 333, 343–344

"Chiefly about War Matters" (Hawthorne), **II,** 227; **Retro. Supp. I,** 165

"Child" (Plath), **Supp. I, Part 2,** 544

"Child, The" (Ríos), **Supp. IV, Part 2,** 543

"Child by Tiger, The" (Wolfe), **IV,** 451

"Child Is Born, A" (Benét), **Supp. XI,** 46

"Child Is the Meaning of This Life, The" (Schwartz), **Supp. II, Part 2,** 659–660

"Child Margaret" (Sandburg), **III,** 584

"Child of Courts, The" (Jarrell), **II,** 378, 379, 381

Child of God (McCarthy), **Supp. VIII, 177–178**

"CHILD OF THE THIRTIES" (Baraka), **Supp. II, Part 1,** 60

"Child on Top of a Greenhouse" (Roethke), **III,** 531

Child Savers, The: The Invention of Delinquency (Platt), **Supp. I, Part 1,** 27

"Childhood" (Wilder), **IV,** 375

"Childhood" (Wright), **Supp. V,** 341

Childhood, A: The Biography of a Place (Crews), **Supp. XI,** 102–103, 245

"Childhood Sketch" (Wright), **Supp. III, Part 2,** 589

"Childhood, When You Are in It . . ." (Kenyon), **Supp. VII,** 160, 170

"Childless Woman" (Plath), **Supp. I, Part 2,** 544

"Childlessness" (Merrill), **Supp. III, Part 1,** 323

Children (Gurney), **Supp. V,** 95, 96

"Children" (Stowe), **Supp. I, Part 2,** 587

Children, The (Wharton), **IV,** 321, 326; **Retro. Supp. I,** 381

Children and Others (Cozzens), **I,** 374

Children is All (Purdy), **Supp. VII,** 277, 278, 282

"Children of Adam" (Whitman), **IV,** 342; **Retro. Supp. I,** 403, 405

Children of Light (Stone), **Supp. V,** 304–306

Children of Light and the Children of Darkness, The (Niebuhr), **III,** 292, 306, 310

Children of the Frost (London), **II,** 469, 483

Children of the Market Place (Masters), **Supp. I, Part 2,** 471

"Children on Their Birthdays" (Capote), **Supp. III, Part 1,** 114, 115

"Children Selecting Books in a Library" (Jarrell), **II,** 371

"Children, the Sandbar, That Summer" (Rukeyser), **Supp. VI,** 274

Children's Hour, The (Hellman), **Supp. I, Part 1,** 276–277, 281, 286, 297

"Children's Rhymes" (Hughes), **Supp. I, Part 1,** 340

Childress, Mark, **Supp. X,** 89

Child's Garden of Verses, A (Stevenson), **Supp. IV, Part 1,** 298, 314

"Child's Reminiscence, A" (Whitman), **IV,** 344

Childwold (Oates), **Supp. II, Part 2,** 519–520

Chill, The (Macdonald), **Supp. IV, Part 2,** 473

Chills and Fever (Ransom), **III,** 490, 491–492, 493

Chilly Scenes of Winter (Beattie), **Supp. V,** 21, 22, 23, 24, 26, 27

"Chimes for Yahya" (Merrill), **Supp. III, Part 1,** 329

Chin, Frank, **Supp. V,** 164, 172

"China" (Johnson), **Supp. VI, 193–194**

China Men (Kingston), **Supp. V,** 157, 158, 159, 160, 161, 164–169; **Supp. X,** 292

China Trace (Wright), **Supp. V,** 332, 340, 341, 342;

"Chinaman's Hat," **Supp. V,** 169

Chinese Classics (Legge), **III,** 472

Chinese Materia Medica (Smith), **III,** 572

"Chinese Nightingale, The" (Lindsay), **Supp. I, Part 2,** 392–393, 394

Chinese Nightingale and Other Poems, The (Lindsay), **Supp. I, Part 2,** 392

Chinese Siamese Cat, The (Tan), **Supp. X,** 289

"Chinoiseries" (Lowell), **II,** 524–525

Chirico, Giorgio de, **Supp. III, Part 1,** 14

"Chiron" (Winters), **Supp. II, Part 2,** 801

Chodorov, Jerome, **IV,** 274

"Choice, The" (Karr), **Supp. XI,** 251

"Choice of Profession, A" (Malamud), **Supp. I, Part 2,** 437

Chomei, Kamo No, **IV,** 170, 171, 184

Chomsky, Noam, **Supp. IV, Part 2,** 679

Choosing not Choosing (Cameron), **Retro. Supp. I,** 43

Chopin, Felix, **Supp. I, Part 1,** 202

Chopin, Frédéric, **Supp. I, Part 1,** 363

Chopin, Jean, **Supp. I, Part 1,** 206

Chopin, Kate, **II,** 276; **Retro. Supp. I,** 10, 215; **Supp. I, Part 1, 200–226; Supp. V,** 304; **Supp. X,** 227

Chopin, Mrs. Oscar, *see* Chopin, Kate

Chopin, Oscar, **Supp. I, Part 1,** 206–207

"Choral: The Pink Church" (Williams), **Retro. Supp. I,** 428

"Chord" (Merwin), **Supp. III, Part 1,** 356

Choruses from Iphigenia in Aulis (Doolittle, trans.), **Supp. I, Part 1,** 257, 268, 269

"Chosen Blindness" (Karr), **Supp. XI,** 251

Chosen Country (Dos Passos), **I,** 475, 490–491

Chosen Place, The Timeless People, The (Marshall), **Supp. XI,** 275, 276, **282–284**

Chosön (Lowell), **II,** 513

Choukri, Mohamed, **Supp. IV, Part 1,** 92

Chovteau, Mane Thérèse, **Supp. I, Part 1,** 205

Chrisman, Robert, **Supp. IV, Part 1,** 1

"Christ for Sale" (Lowell), **II,** 538

"Christ's Passion" (Karr), **Supp. XI,** 251

Christabel (Coleridge), **Supp. IV, Part 2,** 465

Christian Century (publication), **III,** 297; **Supp. VIII,** 124, 125

Christian Dictionary, A (Wilson), **IV,** 153

"Christian in World Crisis, The" (Merton), **Supp. VIII,** 203

"Christian Minister, The" (Emerson), **II,** 10

Christian Philosopher, The (Mather), **Supp. II, Part 2,** 463–464

Christian Realism and Practical Problems (Niebuhr), **III,** 292, 308

Christian Register (publication), **I,** 471–472

"Christian Roommates, The" (Updike),

Newton, Isaac, **I,** 132, 557; **II,** 6, 103, 348–349; **III,** 428; **IV,** 18, 149

"New-Wave Format, A" (Mason), **Supp. VIII,** 141, 143, 147

New-York Review and Atheneum Magazine (Bryant and Anderson, eds.), **Supp. I, Part 1,** 156

"Next in Line, The" (Bradbury), **Supp. IV, Part 1,** 102

Next Room of the Dream, The (Nemerov), **III** 269, 275, 278, 279–280, 284

"'Next to Reading Matter'" (Henry), **Supp. II, Part 1,** 399

Next-to-Last Things: New Poems and Essays (Kunitz), **Supp. III, Part 1,** 257–259, 261, 262, 265, 266, 268

Nexus (Miller), **III,** 170, 187, 188, 189

Niagara movement, **Supp. II, Part 1,** 168, 172, 176, 177, 180

Niatum, Duane, **Supp. IV, Part 1,** 331, **Part 2,** 505

Nice Jewish Boy, The (Roth), **Supp. III, Part 2,** 412

Nicholas II, Tsar, **Supp. I, Part 2,** 447

Nichols, Charles, **Retro. Supp. I,** 194

Nichols, Lewis, **Supp. I, Part 1,** 199

Nichols, Luther, **Supp. X,** 265

Nichols, Mike, **Supp. IV, Part 1,** 234, **Part 2,** 577

Nicholson, Colin, **Supp. VIII,** 129

Nicholson, Jack, **Supp. V,** 26 ; **Supp. VIII,** 45; **Supp. XI,** 308

Nick Adams Stories, The (Hemingway), **II,** 258; **Retro. Supp. I,** 174

"Nick and the Candlestick" (Plath), **Supp. I, Part 2,** 544

Nickel Mountain: A Pastoral Novel (Gardner), **Supp. VI,** 63, 64, 68, **69**

Nicoll, Allardyce, **III,** 400, 408

Nicoloff, Philip, **II,** 7, 23

Niebuhr, Elisabeth, **II,** 584

Niebuhr, Gustav, **III,** 292

Niebuhr, H. Richard, **I,** 494, 566

Niebuhr, Lydia, **III,** 292

Niebuhr, Reinhold, **III, 290–313; Supp. I, Part 2,** 654

Niedecker, Lorine, **Supp. III, Part 2,** 616, 623

Nielsen, Ed, **Supp. IX,** 254

Nielson, Dorothy, **Supp. I, Part 2,** 659

Nietzsche, Friedrich Wilhelm, **I,** 227, 283, 383, 389, 396, 397, 402, 509; **II,** 7, 20, 27, 42, 90, 145, 262, 462, 463, 577, 583, 585; **III,** 102–103, 113, 156, 176; **IV,** 286, 491; **Supp. I, Part 1,** 254, 299, 320, **Part 2,** 646; **Supp. IV, Part 1,** 104, 105–106, 107, 110, 284, **Part 2,** 519; **Supp. V,** 277, 280; **Supp. VIII,** 11,

181, 189; **Supp. X,** 48

Nietzscheanism, **I,** 54, 104, 383, 388, 506–507, 532; **II,** 47, 478, 480–481; **III,** 602

Niflis, N. Michael, **Supp. IV, Part 1,** 175

Nigger Heaven (Van Vechten), **Supp. II, Part 2,** 739, 744–746

Nigger of the "Narcissus," The (Conrad), **II,** 91; **Retro. Supp. I,** 106

"NIGGY THE HO" (Baraka), **Supp. II, Part 1,** 54

"Night above the Avenue" (Merwin), **Supp. III, Part 1,** 355

"Night among the Horses, A" (Barnes), **Supp. III, Part 1,** 33–34, 39, 44

Night at the Movies, A, or, You Must Remember This: Fictions (Coover), **Supp. V,** 50–51

"Night at the Opera, A" (Matthews), **Supp. IX,** 167

Night Dance (Price), **Supp. VI,** 264

"Night Dances, The" (Plath), **Supp. I, Part 2,** 544

"Night, Death, Mississippi" (Hayden), **Supp. II, Part 1,** 369

"Night Dream, The" (MacLeish), **III,** 15

"Night Ferry" (Doty), **Supp. XI,** 124

Night in Acadie, A (Chopin), **Supp. I, Part 1,** 200, 219, 220, 224

"Night in June, A" (Williams), **Retro. Supp. I,** 424

"Night in New Arabia, A" (Henry), **Supp. II, Part 1,** 402

Night in Question, The: Stories (Wolff), **Supp. VII,** 342–344

"Night Journey" (Roethke), **Supp. III, Part 1,** 260

Night Light (Justice), **Supp. VII,** 126–127

'Night, Mother (Norman), **Supp. VIII,** 141

Night Music (Odets), **Supp. II, Part 2,** 541, 543, 544

"Night of First Snow" (Bly), **Supp. IV, Part 1,** 71

Night of January 16th (Rand), **Supp. IV, Part 2,** 527

"Night of the Iguana, The" (Williams), **IV,** 384

Night of the Iguana, The (Williams), **IV,** 382, 383, 384, 385, 386, 387, 388, 391, 392, 393, 394, 395, 397, 398

Night Rider (Warren), **IV,** 243, 246–247

"Night Shift" (Plath), **Supp. I, Part 2,** 538

"Night Sketches: Beneath an Umbrella" (Hawthorne), **II,** 235–237, 238, 239, 242

Night Thoughts (Young), **III,** 415

Night Traveler, The (Oliver), **Supp. VII,** 233

"Night Watch, The" (Wright), **Supp. V,** 339

"Night We All Had Grippe, The" (Jackson), **Supp. IX,** 118

"Night-Blooming Cereus, The" (Hayden), **Supp. II, Part 1,** 367

Night-Blooming Cereus, The (Hayden), **Supp. II, Part 1,** 367, 373

Night-Born, The (London), **II,** 467

"Nightbreak" (Rich), **Supp. I, Part 2,** 556

"Nightmare" (Kumin), **Supp. IV, Part 2,** 442

"Nightmare" poems (Benét), **Supp. XI,** 46, 58

"Nightmare Factory, The" (Kumin), **Supp. IV, Part 2,** 445, 453

Nightmare Factory, The (Kumin), **Supp. IV, Part 2,** 444–447, 451

Nights (Doolittle), **Supp. I, Part 1,** 270, 271

Nights and Days (Merrill), **Supp. III, Part 1,** 319, 320, 322–325

"Nights and Days" (Rich), **Supp. I, Part 2,** 574

"Night-Side" (Oates), **Supp. II, Part 2,** 523

Night-Side (Oates), **Supp. II, Part 2,** 522

"Night-Sweat" (Lowell), **II,** 554

"Night-Talk" (Ellison), **Supp. II, Part 1,** 248

Nightwood (Barnes), **Supp. III, Part 1,** 31, 32, 35–37, 39–43

Nigro, August, **IV,** 119

Nihilism, **I,** 104, 124, 126, 128, 130, 163; **III,** 277, 613; **IV,** 4, 484, 485, 491, 492, 494

"Nihilist as Hero, The" (Lowell), **II,** 554

Nikolai Gogol (Nabokov), **Retro. Supp. I,** 266

Niles, Thomas, **Retro. Supp. I,** 35

Niles, Thomas, Jr., **Supp. I, Part 1,** 39

Nilsson, Christine, **Supp. I, Part 1,** 355

Nilsson, Harry, **Supp. XI,** 309

Nimitz, Chester, **Supp. I, Part 2,** 491

"Nimram" (Gardner), **Supp. VI,** 73

Nims, John Frederick, **III,** 527

Nin, Anaïs, **III,** 182, 184, 190, 192; **Supp. III, Part 1,** 43; **Supp. IV, Part 2,** 680; **Supp. X,** 181–200

"9" (Oliver), **Supp. VII,** 244

3

"Winter in Dunbarton" (Lowell), **II,** 547

Winter in the Blood (Welch), **Supp. IV, Part 2,** 562

Winter Insomnia (Carver), **Supp. III, Part 1,** 138

"Winter Landscape" (Berryman), **I,** 174; **Retro. Supp. I,** 430

Winter Lightning (Nemerov), **III,** 269

Winter of Our Discontent, The (Steinbeck), **IV,** 52, 65–66, 68

"Winter on Earth" (Toomer), **Supp. III, Part 2,** 486

"Winter Piece, A" (Bryant), **Supp. I, Part 1,** 150, 155

"Winter Rains, Cataluña" (Levine), **Supp. V,** 182

"Winter Remembered" (Ransom), **III,** 492–493

"Winter Scenes" (Bryant), *see* "Winter Piece, A"

"Winter Sleep" (Wylie), **Supp. I, Part 2,** 711, 729

Winter Stars (Levis), **Supp. XI,** 259, **266–268**

"Winter Stars" (Levis), **Supp. XI,** 267–268

"Winter Swan" (Bogan), **Supp. III, Part 1,** 52

Winter Trees (Plath), **Supp. I, Part 2,** 526, 539, 541

"Winter Weather Advisory" (Ashbery), **Supp. III, Part 1,** 26

"Winter Words" (Levine), **Supp. V,** 192

Winternitz, Mary, *see* Cheever, Mrs. John (Mary Winternitz)

Winterrowd, Prudence, **I,** 217, 224

Winters, Jonathan, **Supp. XI,** 305

Winters, Yvor, **I,** 59, 63, 70, 386, 393, 397, 398, 402, 404, 471, 473; **II,** 246; **III,** 194, 217, 432, 498, 502, 526, 550; **IV,** 96, 153, 425; **Supp. I, Part 1,** 268, 275; **Supp. II, Part 2,** 416, 666, 785–816; **Supp. IV, Part 2,** 480; **Supp. V,** 180, 191–192

Winterset (Anderson), **III,** 159

Winther, Sophus Keith, **III,** 408

Winthrop, John, **Supp. I, Part 1,** 99, 100, 101, 102, 105, **Part 2,** 484, 485

Winthrop Covenant, The (Auchincloss), **Supp. IV, Part 1,** 23

Wirt, William, **I,** 232

Wirth, Louis, **IV,** 475

Wisconsin Library Bulletin (journal), **Retro. Supp. I,** 141

"Wisdom Cometh with the Years" (Cullen), **Supp. IV, Part 1,** 166

Wisdom of the Desert, The: Sayings from the Desert Fathers of the

Fourth Century (Merton), **Supp. VIII,** 201

Wisdom of the Heart, The (Miller), **III,** 178, 184

Wise Blood (O'Connor), **III,** 337, 338, 339–343, 344, 345, 346, 350, 354, 356, 357

Wise Men, The (Price), **Supp. VI,** 254

"Wiser Than a God" (Chopin), **Supp. I, Part 1,** 208

"Wish for a Young Wife" (Roethke), **III,** 548

Wismer, Helen Muriel, *see* Thurber, Mrs. James (Helen Muriel Wismer)

Wisse, Ruth R., **I,** 166

Wister, Owen, **I,** 62

"Witch Burning" (Plath), **Supp. I, Part 2,** 539

"Witch Doctor" (Hayden), **Supp. II, Part 1,** 368, 380

"Witch of Coös, The" (Frost), **II,** 154–155; **Retro. Supp. I,** 135

"Witch of Owl Mountain Springs, The: An Account of Her Remarkable Powers" (Taylor), **Supp. V,** 328

"Witch of Wenham, The" (Whittier), **Supp. I, Part 2,** 694, 696

"Witchbird" (Bambara), **Supp. XI,** 11

"Witchcraft in Bullet Park" (Gardner), **Supp. I, Part 1,** 198

Witchcraft of Salem Village, The (Jackson), **Supp. IX,** 121

Witches of Eastwick, The (Updike), **Retro. Supp. I,** 330, 331

Witching Hour, The (Rice), **Supp. VII,** 299–300

"With a Little Help from My Friends" (Kushner), **Supp. IX,** 131

"With Che at Kitty Hawk" (Banks), **Supp. V,** 6

"With Che at the Plaza" (Banks), **Supp. V,** 7

"With Che in New Hampshire" (Banks), **Supp. V,** 6

With Eyes at the Back of Our Heads (Levertov), **Supp. III, Part 1,** 276–277

With Her in Ourland (Gilman), **Supp. XI,** 208–209

"With Kit, Age 7, at the Beach" (Stafford), **Supp. XI,** 323

"With Mercy for the Greedy" (Sexton), **Supp. II, Part 2,** 680

With Shuddering Fall (Oates), **Supp. II, Part 2,** 504–506

"With the Dog at Sunrise" (Kenyon), **Supp. VII,** 170

With the Empress Dowager of China (Carl), **III,** 475

With the Old Breed: At Peleliu and

Okinawa (Sledge), **Supp. V,** 249–250

"Withered Skins of Berries" (Toomer), **Supp. III, Part 2,** 485; **Supp. IX,** 320

Witherington, Paul, **I,** 96; **Supp. I, Part 1,** 148

Witherspoon, John, **Supp. I, Part 2,** 504

Without a Hero (Boyle), **Supp. VIII,** 16

Without Stopping (Bowles), **Supp. IV, Part 1,** 79, 81, 85, 90, 91, 92

"Without Tradition and within Reason: Judge Horton and Atticus Finch in Court" (Johnson), **Supp. VIII,** 127

"Witness" (Dubus), **Supp. VII,** 89

"Witness" (Clampitt), **Supp. IX,** 42–43, 45, 46

"Witness, The" (Porter), **III,** 443–444

"Witness for Poetry, A" (Stafford), **Supp. XI,** 324

Witness to the Times! (McGrath), **Supp. X,** 118

Witness Tree, A (Frost), **II,** 155; **Retro. Supp. I,** 122, 137, 139

"Witnessing My Father's Will" (Karr), **Supp. XI,** 241

Wit's End: Days and Nights of the Algonquin Round Table (Gaines), **Supp. IX,** 190

Wits Recreations (Mennes and Smith), **II,** 111

Witt, Grace, **III,** 49

Witt, Shirley Hill, **Supp. IV, Part 2,** 505

Wittgenstein, Ludwig, **Retro. Supp. I,** 53; **Supp. III, Part 2,** 626–627; **Supp. X,** 304

Wittliff, William, **Supp. V,** 227

"Witty War, A" (Simpson), **Supp. IX,** 268

"Wives and Mistresses" (Hardwick), **Supp. III, Part 1,** 211–212

Wizard of Oz (Baum), **Supp. IV, Part 1,** 113

Wizard of Oz, The (film), **Supp. X,** 172, 214

Wodehouse, P. G., **Supp. IX,** 195

Woiwode, Larry, **Supp. VIII,** 151

Wojahn, David, **Supp. IX,** 161, 292, 293

Wolcott, James, **Supp. IX,** 259

Wolf, Christa, **Supp. IV, Part 1,** 310, 314

Wolf, William John, **III,** 313

Wolf: A False Memoir (Harrison), **Supp. VIII,** 40, **41–42,** 45

Wolf Willow: A History, a Story, and a Memory of the Last Plains Frontier

A Complete Listing of Authors in
American Writers

Irving, John   Supplement VI
Irving, Washington   Volume 2
Jackson, Shirley   Supplement IX
James, Henry   Volume 2
James, Henry   Retrospective Supplement I
James, William   Volume 2
Jarrell, Randall   Volume 2
Jeffers, Robinson   Supplement II
Jewett, Sarah Orne   Volume 2
Johnson, Charles   Supplement VI
Jones, James   Supplement XI
Jong, Erica   Supplement V
Justice, Donald   Supplement VII
Karr, Mary   Supplement XI
Kazin, Alfred   Supplement VIII
Kennedy, William   Supplement VII
Kenyon, Jane   Supplement VII
Kerouac, Jack   Supplement III
Kincaid, Jamaica   Supplement VII
King, Stephen   Supplement V
Kingsolver, Barbara   Supplement VII
Kingston, Maxine Hong   Supplement V
Kinnell, Galway   Supplement III
Kosinski, Jerzy   Supplement VII
Kumin, Maxine   Supplement IV
Kunitz, Stanley   Supplement III
Kushner, Tony   Supplement IX
LaBastille, Anne   Supplement X
Lanier, Sidney   Supplement I
Lardner, Ring   Volume 2
Lee, Harper   Supplement VIII
Levertov, Denise   Supplement III
Levine, Philip   Supplement V
Levis, Larry   Supplement XI
Lewis, Sinclair   Volume 2
Lindsay, Vachel   Supplement I
London, Jack   Volume 2
Longfellow, Henry Wadsworth   Volume 2
Lowell, Amy   Volume 2
Lowell, James Russell   Supplement I
Lowell, Robert   Volume 2
McCarthy, Cormac   Supplement VIII
McCarthy, Mary   Volume 2
McCullers, Carson   Volume 2

Macdonald, Ross   Supplement IV
McGrath, Thomas   Supplement X
McKay, Claude   Supplement X
MacLeish, Archibald   Volume 3
McMurty, Larry   Supplement V
McPhee, John   Supplement III
Mailer, Norman   Volume 3
Malamud, Bernard   Supplement I
Marquand, John P.   Volume 3
Marshall, Paule   Supplement XI
Mason, Bobbie Ann   Supplement VIII
Masters, Edgar Lee   Supplement I
Mather, Cotton   Supplement II
Matthews, William   Supplement IX
Matthiessen, Peter   Supplement V
Maxwell, William   Supplement VIII
Melville, Herman   Volume 3
Melville, Herman   Retrospective Supplement
    I
Mencken, H. L.   Volume 3
Merrill, James   Supplement III
Merton, Thomas   Supplement VIII
Merwin, W. S.   Supplement III
Millay, Edna St. Vincent   Volume 3
Miller, Arthur   Volume 3
Miller, Henry   Volume 3
Minot, Susan   Supplement VI
Momaday, N. Scott   Supplement IV
Monette, Paul   Supplement X
Moore, Lorrie   Supplement X
Moore, Marianne   Volume 3
Morison, Samuel Eliot   Supplement I
Morris, Wright   Volume 3
Morrison, Toni   Supplement III
Muir, John   Supplement IX
Mumford, Lewis   Supplement III
Nabokov, Vladimir   Volume 3
Nabokov, Vladimir   Retrospective Supplement
    I
Naylor, Gloria   Supplement VIII
Nemerov, Howard   Volume 3
Niebuhr, Reinhold   Volume 3
Nin, Anaïs   Supplement X
Norris, Frank   Volume 3

Veblen, Thorstein   Supplement I
Vidal, Gore   Supplement IV
Vonnegut, Kurt   Supplement II
Wagoner, David   Supplement IX
Walker, Alice   Supplement III
Wallace, David Foster   Supplement X
Warren, Robert Penn   Volume 4
Welty, Eudora   Volume 4
Welty, Eudora   Retrospective Supplement I
West, Nathanael   Volume 4
Wharton, Edith   Volume 4
Wharton, Edith   Retrospective Supplement I
White, E. B.   Supplement I
Whitman, Walt   Volume 4
Whitman, Walt   Retrospective Supplement I
Whittier, John Greenleaf   Supplement I
Wilbur, Richard   Supplement III
Wideman, John Edgar   Supplement X

Wilder, Thornton   Volume 4
Williams, Tennessee   Volume 4
Williams, William Carlos   Volume 4
Williams, William Carlos   Retrospective Supplement I
Wilson, August   Supplement VIII
Wilson, Edmund   Volume 4
Winters, Yvor   Supplement II
Wolfe, Thomas   Volume 4
Wolfe, Tom   Supplement III
Wolff, Tobias   Supplement VII
Wright, Charles   Supplement V
Wright, James   Supplement III
Wright, Richard   Volume 4
Wylie, Elinor   Supplement I
Yates, Richard   Supplement XI
Zukofsky, Louis   Supplement III

BELMONT UNIVERSITY LIBRARY